Lecture Notes in Computer Science 5339

Commenced Publication in 1973
Founding and Former Series Editors:
Gerhard Goos, Juris Hartmanis, and Jan van Leeuwen

Editorial Board

David Hutchison
  Lancaster University, UK
Takeo Kanade
  Carnegie Mellon University, Pittsburgh, PA, USA
Josef Kittler
  University of Surrey, Guildford, UK
Jon M. Kleinberg
  Cornell University, Ithaca, NY, USA
Alfred Kobsa
  University of California, Irvine, CA, USA
Friedemann Mattern
  ETH Zurich, Switzerland
John C. Mitchell
  Stanford University, CA, USA
Moni Naor
  Weizmann Institute of Science, Rehovot, Israel
Oscar Nierstrasz
  University of Bern, Switzerland
C. Pandu Rangan
  Indian Institute of Technology, Madras, India
Bernhard Steffen
  University of Dortmund, Germany
Madhu Sudan
  Massachusetts Institute of Technology, MA, USA
Demetri Terzopoulos
  University of California, Los Angeles, CA, USA
Doug Tygar
  University of California, Berkeley, CA, USA
Gerhard Weikum
  Max-Planck Institute of Computer Science, Saarbruecken, Germany

Matthew K. Franklin   Lucas Chi Kwong Hui
Duncan S. Wong (Eds.)

Cryptology and Network Security

7th International Conference, CANS 2008
Hong-Kong, China, December 2-4, 2008
Proceedings

Volume Editors

Matthew K. Franklin
University of California
Department of Computer Science
Davis, CA, USA
E-mail: franklin@cs.ucdavis.edu

Lucas Chi Kwong Hui
The University of Hong Kong
Department of Computer Science
Hong Kong, China
E-mail: hui@cs.hku.hk

Duncan S. Wong
City University of Hong Kong
Department of Computer Science
Hong Kong, China
E-mail: duncan@cityu.edu.hk

Library of Congress Control Number: 2008939862

CR Subject Classification (1998): E.3, D.4.6, F.2.1, C.2, J.1, K.4.4, K.6.5

LNCS Sublibrary: SL 4 – Security and Cryptology

ISSN   0302-9743
ISBN-10   3-540-89640-6 Springer Berlin Heidelberg New York
ISBN-13   978-3-540-89640-1 Springer Berlin Heidelberg New York

This work is subject to copyright. All rights are reserved, whether the whole or part of the material is concerned, specifically the rights of translation, reprinting, re-use of illustrations, recitation, broadcasting, reproduction on microfilms or in any other way, and storage in data banks. Duplication of this publication or parts thereof is permitted only under the provisions of the German Copyright Law of September 9, 1965, in its current version, and permission for use must always be obtained from Springer. Violations are liable to prosecution under the German Copyright Law.

Springer is a part of Springer Science+Business Media

springer.com

© Springer-Verlag Berlin Heidelberg 2008
Printed in Germany

Typesetting: Camera-ready by author, data conversion by Scientific Publishing Services, Chennai, India
Printed on acid-free paper   SPIN: 12577507   06/3180   5 4 3 2 1 0

Preface

The seventh international conference on Cryptology and Network Security (CANS 2008) was held at HKU Town Center, Hong Kong, China, during December 2–4, 2008. The conference was organized by the Department of Computer Science, the University of Hong Kong, and was fully supported by the Center for Information Security and Cryptography at the University of Hong Kong, the Cyberport Institute of Hong Kong at the University of Hong Kong and the Department of Computer Science at the City University of Hong Kong.

The goal of CANS is to promote research on all aspects of network security, as well as to build a bridge between research on cryptography and network security. Previous CANS conferences have been held in Taipei, Taiwan (2001), San Francisco, USA (2002), Miami, USA (2003), Xiamen, China (2005), Suzhou, China (2006), and Singapore (2007). The conference proceedings of recent years were published by Springer in the *Lecture Notes in Computer Science* series.

The Program Committee received 73 submissions, and accepted 27 papers for presentation. The final versions of the accepted papers, which the authors finalized on the basis of comments from the reviewers, were included in the proceedings. The reviewing process took nine weeks; each paper was carefully evaluated by at least three members from the Program Committee. The individual reviewing phase was followed by a Web-based discussion. Based on the comments and scores given by reviewers, the final decisions on acceptance were made. We appreciate the hard work of the members of the Program Committee and the external referees who gave many hours of their valuable time.

In addition to the contributed papers, there were two invited talks. One was given by Juan Garay and the other one was by Xiaoyun Wang.

We would like to thank all the people involved in organizing this conference. In particular, we would like to thank the Organizing Committee members, colleagues and our student helpers for their time and effort. Finally, we would like to thank all the authors who submitted papers to the conference.

December 2008

Matthew K. Franklin
Lucas Chi Kwong Hui
Duncan S. Wong

Organization

CANS 2008 was organized by the Department of Computer Science, The University of Hong Kong, China, and held during December 2–4, 2008.

General Chair

Lucas C.K. Hui   The University of Hong Kong, China

Program Co-chairs

Matt Franklin   UC Davis, USA
Duncan S. Wong   City University of Hong Kong, China

Steering Committee

Yvo Desmedt   University College London, UK
Matt Franklin   UC Davis, USA
Yi Mu   University of Wollongong, Australia
David Pointcheval   CNRS and ENS, France
Huaxiong Wang   Nanyang Technological University, Singapore

Organizing Committee

K.P. Chow   The University of Hong Kong, China
Bruce Cheung   The University of Hong Kong, China
Lucas C.K. Hui   The University of Hong Kong, China
Raymond Szeto   The University of Hong Kong, China

Program Committee

Michel Abdalla   École Normale Supérieure, France
Joonsang Baek   I2R, Singapore
Feng Bao   I2R, Singapore
Hao Chen   East China Normal University, China
Liqun Chen   HP Bristol Labs, UK
Mike Burmester   Florida State University, USA
Ed Dawson   QUT, Australia
Robert Deng   SMU, Singapore
Dengguo Feng   Chinese Academy of Sciences, China
Eiichiro Fujisaki   NTT Labs, Japan

Jun Furukawa   NEC, Japan
David Galindo   University of Malaga, Spain
Aline Gouget   Gemalto, France
Aggelos Kiayias   University of Connecticut, USA
Eike Kiltz   CWI, The Netherlands
Kwangjo Kim   Info. and Comm. University, Korea
Dong Hoon Lee   Korea University, Korea
Arjen Lenstra   EPFL, Switzerland
Benoit Libert   UCL, Belgium
Javier Lopez   University of Malaga, Spain
Mitsuru Matsui   Mitsubishi Electric, Japan
Yi Mu   University of Wollongong, Australia
Jörn Müller-Quade   Universität Karlsruhe, Germany
Tatsuaki Okamoto   NTT Labs, Japan
Giuseppe Persiano   Università di Salerno, Italy
Josef Pieprzyk   Macquarie University, Australia
C. Pandu Rangan   IIT, India
Berry Schoenmakers   TU Eindhoven, The Netherlands
Willy Susilo   University of Wollongong, Australia
Tsuyoshi Takagi   Future University - Hakodate, Japan
Guilin Wang   University of Birmingham, UK
Huaxiong Wang   NTU, Singapore
Xiaoyun Wang   Tsinghua/Shandong University, China
Yiqun Lisa Yin   Independent Consultant, USA
Fangguo Zhang   Sun Yat-sen University, China
Yunlei Zhao   Fudan University, China
Jianying Zhou   I2R, Singapore

External Reviewers

Man Ho Au   Flavio Garcia   Paul Morrissey
Shaoying Cai   Qiong Huang   Kyosuke Osaka
David Cash   Xinyi Huang   Arpita Patra
Julien Cathalo   Vincenzo Iovino   Wen-Feng Qi
Kyu Young Choi   Bum Han Kim   Yi Qian
Ashish Choudary   Jangseong Kim   Chun Ruan
Ji Young Chun   Daniel Kraschewski   German Saez
Andrew Clark   Hwaseong Lee   Jason Smith
Blandine Debraize   Ji-Seon Lee   Xiao Tan
Cécile Delerablée   Jiguo Li   Ivan Visconti
Nico Döttling   Jin Li   Sree Vivek
Sharmila devi selvi   Tieyan Li   Baodian Wei
Oriol Farras   Xibin Lin   Jian Weng
Clemente Galdi   Jospeh K. Liu   Wei Wu
Debin Gao   George Mohay   Xiaokang Xiong

Guomin Yang			Jeong Jae Yu			Tsz Hon Yuen
Yanjiang Yang		Yong Yu				Yao-Dong Zhao
Chan Yeob Yeun

Supporting Institutions

Center for Information Security and Cryptography (CISC), The University of Hong Kong, China
The Cyberport Institute of Hong Kong, The University of Hong Kong, China
Department of Computer Science, City University of Hong Kong, China

Table of Contents

Cryptosystems

Chosen-Ciphertext Secure Proxy Re-encryption without Pairings   1
  Robert H. Deng, Jian Weng, Shengli Liu, and Kefei Chen

Hybrid Damgård Is CCA1-Secure under the DDH Assumption   18
  Yvo Desmedt, Helger Lipmaa, and Duong Hieu Phan

Efficient Dynamic Broadcast Encryption and Its Extension to
Authenticated Dynamic Broadcast Encryption   31
  *Masafumi Kusakawa, Harunaga Hiwatari, Tomoyuki Asano, and
  Seiichi Matsuda*

Cryptanalysis of Short Exponent RSA with Primes Sharing Least
Significant Bits   49
  *Hung-Min Sun, Mu-En Wu, Ron Steinfeld, Jian Guo, and
  Huaxiong Wang*

Signatures

Efficient and Short Certificateless Signature   64
  Raylin Tso, Xun Yi, and Xinyi Huang

Sanitizable Signatures Revisited   80
  Tsz Hon Yuen, Willy Susilo, Joseph K. Liu, and Yi Mu

An Efficient On-Line/Off-Line Signature Scheme without Random
Oracles   98
  Marc Joye

On the Security of Online/Offline Signatures and Multisignatures from
ACISP'06   108
  Fagen Li, Masaaki Shirase, and Tsuyoshi Takagi

Identification, Authentication and Key Management

A Killer Application for Pairings: Authenticated Key Establishment in
Underwater Wireless Sensor Networks   120
  David Galindo, Rodrigo Roman, and Javier Lopez

Anonymous and Transparent Gateway-Based Password-Authenticated
Key Exchange   133
  Michel Abdalla, Malika Izabachène, and David Pointcheval

Cryptanalysis of EC-RAC, a RFID Identification Protocol 149
    Julien Bringer, Hervé Chabanne, and Thomas Icart

Cryptographic Algorithms and Protocols

Counting Method for Multi-party Computation over Non-abelian
Groups 162
    Youming Qiao and Christophe Tartary

Keyword Field-Free Conjunctive Keyword Searches on Encrypted Data
and Extension for Dynamic Groups 178
    Peishun Wang, Huaxiong Wang, and Josef Pieprzyk

Analysis and Design of Multiple Threshold Changeable Secret Sharing
Schemes 196
    Tiancheng Lou and Christophe Tartary

Black-Box Constructions for Fully-Simulatable Oblivious Transfer
Protocols 214
    Huafei Zhu

Skew Frobenius Map and Efficient Scalar Multiplication for
Pairing–Based Cryptography 226
    Yumi Sakemi, Yasuyuki Nogami, Katsuyuki Okeya,
    Hidehiro Kato, and Yoshitaka Morikawa

Stream Ciphers and Block Ciphers

Cryptanalysis of MV3 Stream Cipher 240
    Mohammad Ali Orumiehchi, S. Fahimeh Mohebbipoor, and
    Hossein Ghodosi

3D: A Three-Dimensional Block Cipher 252
    Jorge Nakahara Jr.

Cryptographic Foundations

Construction of Resilient Functions with Multiple Cryptographic
Criteria 268
    Chao Li, Shaojing Fu, and Bing Sun

Enumeration of Homogeneous Rotation Symmetric Functions over F_p . . . 278
    Shaojing Fu, Chao Li, and Bing Sun

Unconditionally Reliable Message Transmission in Directed
Hypergraphs 285
    Kannan Srinathan, Arpita Patra, Ashish Choudhary, and
    C. Pandu Rangan

Applications and Implementations

An Open Framework for Remote Electronic Elections 304
    Yu Zhang

Conditional Payments for Computing Markets 317
    Bogdan Carbunar and Mahesh Tripunitara

High-Speed Search System for PGP Passphrases 332
    Koichi Shimizu, Daisuke Suzuki, and Toyohiro Tsurumaru

Workload Characterization of a Lightweight SSL Implementation
Resistant to Side-Channel Attacks 349
    Manuel Koschuch, Johann Großschädl, Udo Payer,
    Matthias Hudler, and Michael Krüger

Security in Ad Hoc Networks and Wireless Sensor Networks

Authenticated Directed Diffusion 366
    Eric K. Wang, Lucas C.K. Hui, and S.M. Yiu

A New Message Recognition Protocol for Ad Hoc Pervasive
Networks 378
    Atefeh Mashatan and Douglas R. Stinson

Author Index 395

Chosen-Ciphertext Secure Proxy Re-encryption without Pairings

Robert H. Deng[1], Jian Weng[1,2], Shengli Liu[3], and Kefei Chen[3]

[1] School of Information Systems
Singapore Management University, Singapore 178902
[2] Department of Computer Science
Jinan University, Guangzhou 510632, P.R. China
[3] Dept. of Computer Science and Engineering
Shanghai Jiao Tong University, Shanghai 200240, P.R. China
robertdeng@smu.edu.sg, cryptjweng@gmail.com, {slliu,kfchen}@sjtu.edu.cn

Abstract. In a proxy re-encryption system, a semi-trusted proxy can convert a ciphertext originally intended for Alice into a ciphertext intended for Bob, without learning the underlying plaintext. Proxy re-encryption has found many practical applications, such as encrypted email forwarding, secure distributed file systems, and outsourced filtering of encrypted spam. In ACM CCS'07, Canetti and Hohenberger presented a proxy re-encryption scheme with chosen-ciphertext security, and left an important open problem to construct a chosen-ciphertext secure proxy re-encryption scheme without pairings. In this paper, we solve this open problem by proposing a new proxy re-encryption scheme without resort to bilinear pairings. Based on the computational Diffie-Hellman (CDH) problem, the chosen-ciphertext security of the proposed scheme is proved in the random oracle model.

Keywords: Proxy re-encryption, bilinear pairing, chosen-ciphertext security.

1 Introduction

1.1 Background

Imagine that one day you are going on vacation and will be inconvenient to read your email. You wish to have the mail server forward all of your encrypted email to your colleague Bob, who can then read the email by only using his own secret key. A naive way is to have the mail server store your secret key and act as follows: when an email encrypted for you arrives, the mail server decrypts it using the stored secret key and re-encrypts the plaintext using Bob's public key. However, such a solution is highly undesirable, especially in the case that the email server is untrustworthy, since the email server learns both the plaintext and your secret key.

Proxy re-encryption (PRE), introduced by Blaze, Bleumer and Strauss [4], is a novel solution to the above situation. In a PRE system, a proxy is given a re-encryption key $rk_{i,j}$ so that it can convert a ciphertext under public key pk_i into a ciphertext of the same message under a different public key pk_j. The proxy, however, learns nothing about the messages under either key. Now, as to the aforementioned situation, you can have the mail server act as a proxy, and give him the proxy re-encryption key instead of your secret key. Then he can translate your encrypted emails into those encrypted under Bob's public key, without learning the content of the emails. Proxy re-encryptions have found many other practical applications, such as distributed file systems, outsourced filtering of encrypted spam, and access control over network storage [1,2,22].

Blaze, Bleumer and Strauss [4] categorized two types of PRE schemes. If the re-encryption key $rk_{i,j}$ allows the proxy to convert ciphertexts under pk_i into ciphertexts under pk_j and *vice versa*, then the scheme is called *bidirectional*. If $rk_{i,j}$ allows the proxy to convert only from pk_i to pk_j, then the scheme is called *unidirectional*. Blaze et al. [4] proposed the first bidirectional PRE scheme in 1998. In 2005, Ateniese et al. [1,2] presented a unidirectional PRE scheme based on bilinear pairings. Both of these schemes are only secure against chosen-plaintext attack (CPA). However, applications often require security against chosen-ciphertext attacks (CCA).

To fill this gap, Canetti and Hohenberger [11] presented an elegant construction of CCA-secure bidirectional PRE scheme. Later, Libert and Vergnaud [21] presented a unidirectional PRE scheme with CCA security. Both of these constructions rely on bilinear pairings. In spite of the recent advances in implementation technique, the pairing computation is still considered as a very expensive operation compared with standard operations such as modular exponentiation in finite fields [8]. It would be desirable for cryptosystems to be constructed without relying on pairings, especially in computation-limited settings. In view of this, Canetti and Hohenberger [11] left an important open problem in ACM CCS'07, i.e., how to construct a CCA-secure proxy re-encryption scheme without pairings.

1.2 Our Contributions

In this paper, we circumvent several obstacles to construct a proxy re-encryption scheme without pairings. Based on the CDH problem, we prove the chosen-ciphertext security for our proposed scheme in the random oracle model. As a result, we solve the aforementioned open problem left by Canetti and Hohenberger [11] in ACM CCS'07. Compared with existing CCA-secure proxy re-encryption schemes, our scheme is much more efficient due to the following facts: (i) our scheme does not use the costly bilinear pairing which is used in existing CCA-secure proxy re-encryption schemes; (ii) the computational cost and the ciphertext length in our proxy re-encryption scheme decrease with re-encryption, whereas those in existing CCA-secure proxy re-encryption schemes remain unchanged or even increase with re-encryption.

1.3 Related Works

Boneh, Goh and Matsuo [7] described a hybrid proxy re-encryption system based on the ElGamal-type public key encryption system [14] and Boneh-Boyen's identity-based encryption system [3]. Green and Ateniese [16] considered proxy re-encryption in identity-based scenarios: based on Boneh and Franklin's identity-based encryption system [6], they presented the first CPA and CCA-secure identity-based proxy re-encryption (IB-PRE) schemes in the random oracle model. Later, Chu and Tzeng [12] presented the constructions of CPA and CCA-secure IB-PRE schemes without random oracles.

Another kind of cryptosystems related to proxy re-encryption is the *proxy encryption* cryptosystem introduced by Mambo and Okamoto [23]. In a proxy encryption scheme [18,13], a delegator Alice allows a delegatee Bob to decrypt ciphertexts intended for her with the help of a proxy: an encryption for Alice is first partially decrypted by the proxy, and then fully decrypted by Bob. However, this approach requires that Bob obtain and store an additional secret for each delegation. In contrast, the delegatee in proxy re-encryption systems only needs to store his own decryption key.

Proxy re-encryption should not be confused with the universal re-encryption [17], in which the ciphertexts are re-randomized instead of the underlying public key being changed.

1.4 Outline

The rest of the paper is organized as follows. Section 2 reviews the definition and security notions for PRE systems. In Section 3, we first give an intuition for our construction, and then propose a bidirectional PRE scheme without pairings. A comparison between our scheme and other existing PRE schemes is also given in this section. In Section 4, we first review some complexity assumptions, and then prove the chosen-ciphertext security for our scheme. Finally, Section 5 lists open research problems and concludes this paper.

2 Definition and Security Notions of Proxy Re-encryptions

Throughout this section, we concentrate on the bidirectional proxy re-encryptions. For unidirectional proxy re-encryptions, please refer to [21,1,2].

2.1 Definition

Formally, a bidirectional PRE scheme consists of the following five algorithms [11]:

KeyGen(1^κ): The key generation algorithm takes as input a security parameter 1^κ. It generates a public key pk and the corresponding secret key sk.

ReKeyGen(sk_i, sk_j): The re-encryption key generation algorithm takes as input two secret keys sk_i and sk_j. It outputs a re-encryption key $rk_{i \leftrightarrow j}$.

Encrypt(pk, m): The encryption algorithm takes as input a public key pk and a message $m \in \mathcal{M}$. It outputs a ciphertext C under pk. Here $\mathcal{M}$ denotes the message space.

ReEncrypt$(rk_{i \leftrightarrow j}, C_i)$: The re-encryption algorithm takes as input a re-encryption key $rk_{i \leftrightarrow j}$ and a ciphertext C_i under public key pk_i. It outputs a ciphertext C_j under public key pk_j.

Decrypt(sk, C): The decryption algorithm takes as input a secret key sk and a cipertext C. It outputs a message $m \in \mathcal{M}$ or the error symbol $\perp$.

Roughly speaking, the correctness requires that, for all $m \in \mathcal{M}$ and all $(pk, sk) \leftarrow$ KeyGen(1^κ), it holds that Decrypt$(sk, $Encrypt$(pk, m)) = m$. Besides, for all $(pk_i, sk_i) \leftarrow$ KeyGen(1^κ) and $(pk_j, sk_j) \leftarrow$ KeyGen(1^κ), it holds that Decrypt $(sk_j,$ ReEncrypt(ReKeyGen$(sk_i, sk_j),$ Encrypt$(pk_i, m))) = m$.

Remark. A proxy re-encryption scheme is said to be *multi-hop*, if a ciphertext can be consecutively re-encrypted, i.e., it can be re-encrypted from pk_1 to pk_2 and then to pk_3 and so on. In contrast, a proxy re-encryption scheme is said to be *single-hop*, if a re-encrypted ciphertext can not be further re-encrypted. In this paper, we concentrate on single-hop proxy re-encryption schemes. Besides, for consistency and easy explanation, we adopt a term as used in [21]: the original ciphertext is called *second-level ciphertext*, while the re-encrypted ciphertext is called *first-level ciphertext*.

2.2 Security Notions

In this subsection, we review the security notions for PRE systems [11]. Concretely, the chosen-ciphertext security for a PRE scheme Π can be defined via the following game between an adversary $\mathcal{A}$ and a challenger $\mathcal{C}$:

Phase 1. $\mathcal{A}$ adaptively issues queries $q_1, \cdots, q_m$ where query q_i is one of the following:

- *Uncorrupted key generation query* $\langle i \rangle$: $\mathcal{C}$ first runs algorithm KeyGen to obtain a public/secret key pair (pk_i, sk_i), and then sends pk_i to $\mathcal{A}$.
- *Corrupted key generation query* $\langle j \rangle$: $\mathcal{C}$ first runs algorithm KeyGen to obtain a public/secret key pair (pk_j, sk_j), and then gives (pk_j, sk_j) to $\mathcal{A}$.
- *Re-encryption key generation query* $\langle pk_i, pk_j \rangle$: $\mathcal{C}$ first runs algorithm ReKeyGen(sk_i, sk_j) to generate a re-encryption key $rk_{i \leftrightarrow j}$, and then returns $rk_{i \leftrightarrow j}$ to $\mathcal{A}$. Here sk_i and sk_j are secret keys with respect to pk_i and pk_j respectively. It is required that pk_i and pk_j were generated beforehand by algorithm KeyGen. As argued in [11], we require that either both pk_i and pk_j are corrupted, or alternately both are uncorrupted.
- *Re-encryption query* $\langle pk_i, pk_j, C_i \rangle$: $\mathcal{C}$ responds with the resulting ciphertext $C_j =$ ReEncrypt(ReKeyGen$(sk_i, sk_j), C_i)$, where sk_i and sk_j are secret keys with respect to pk_i and pk_j respectively. It is required that pk_i and pk_j were generated beforehand by KeyGen.
- *Decryption query* $\langle pk, C \rangle$: Challenger $\mathcal{C}$ returns the result of Decrypt (sk, C) to $\mathcal{A}$, where sk is the secret key with respect to pk. It is required that pk was generated beforehand by KeyGen.

Challenge. Once $\mathcal{A}$ decides that Phase 1 is over, it outputs a target public key pk^* and two equal-length plaintexts $m_0, m_1 \in \mathcal{M}$ on which it wishes to be challenged. Here it is required that $\mathcal{A}$ did not previously corrupt the secret key corresponding to pk^*. Challenger $\mathcal{C}$ flips a random coin $\delta \in \{0, 1\}$, and sets the challenge ciphertext to be $C^* = \mathsf{Encrypt}(pk^*, m_\delta)$, which is sent to $\mathcal{A}$.

Phase 2. $\mathcal{A}$ issues additional queries $q_{m+1}, \cdots, q_{max}$ where each of the queries is one of the following:

- *Uncorrupted key generation query* $\langle i \rangle$: $\mathcal{C}$ responds as in Phase 1.
- *Corrupted key generation query* $\langle j \rangle$: $\mathcal{C}$ responds as in Phase 1. Here it is required that $pk_j \neq pk^*$. Besides, if $\mathcal{A}$ has obtained a *derivative*[1] (pk', C') of (pk^*, C^*), it is required that $pk_j \neq pk'$.
- *Re-encryption key generation query* $\langle pk_i, pk_j \rangle$: Challenger $\mathcal{C}$ responds as in Phase 1.
- *Re-encryption query* $\langle pk_i, pk_j, C_i \rangle$: Here it is required that pk_i and pk_j were generated beforehand by algorithm KeyGen. If (pk_i, C_i) is a derivative of (pk^*, C^*) and the secret key with respect to pk_j has been corrupted, then $\mathcal{C}$ responds with the error symbol $\bot$. Otherwise, $\mathcal{C}$ responds as in Phase 1.
- *Decryption query* $\langle pk, C \rangle$: Here it is required that pk was generated beforehand by algorithm KeyGen. If (pk, C) is a derivative of (pk^*, C^*) or pk was not generated beforehand by KeyGen, then $\mathcal{C}$ responds with the error symbol $\bot$. Else, $\mathcal{C}$ responds as in Phase 1.

Guess. Finally, $\mathcal{A}$ outputs a guess $\delta' \in \{0, 1\}$.

We refer to adversary $\mathcal{A}$ as an IND-PRE-CCA adversary, and we define his advantage in attacking scheme Π as

$$\mathrm{Adv}_{\Pi, \mathcal{A}}^{\text{IND-PRE-CCA}} = \left| \Pr[\delta' = \delta] - \frac{1}{2} \right|,$$

where the probability is taken over the random coins consumed by the challenger and the adversary. Note that the chosen plaintext security for a PRE scheme can be similarly defined as the above game except that the adversary is not allowed to issue any decryption queries.

---

[1] Derivative of (pk^*, C^*) is inductively defined in [11] as below:

1. (pk^*, C^*) is a derivative of itself;
2. If (pk, C) is a derivative of (pk^*, C^*) and (pk', C') is a derivative of (pk, C), then (pk', C') is a derivative of (pk^*, C^*).
3. If $\mathcal{A}$ has issued a re-encryption query $\langle pk, pk', C \rangle$ and obtained the resulting re-encryption ciphertext C', then (pk', C') is a derivative of (pk, C).
4. If $\mathcal{A}$ has issued a re-encryption key generation query $\langle pk, pk' \rangle$ or $\langle pk', pk \rangle$, and $\mathsf{Decrypt}(sk', C') \in \{m_0, m_1\}$ (here sk' is the secret key with respect to pk'), then (pk', C') is a derivative of (pk, C).

Definition 1. *A PRE scheme Π is said to be $(t, q_u, q_c, q_{rk}, q_{re}, q_d, \epsilon)$-IND-PRE-CCA secure, if for any t-time IND-PRE-CCA adversary $\mathcal{A}$ who makes at most q_u uncorrupted key generation queries, at most q_c corrupted key generation queries, at most q_{rk} re-encryption key generation queries, at most q_{re} re-encryption queries and at most q_d decryption queries, we have $Adv_{\Pi,\mathcal{A}}^{IND\text{-}PRE\text{-}CCA} \leq \epsilon$.*

3 Proposed Proxy Re-encryption Scheme

In this section, we will describe the main idea of our PRE scheme, and then propose the concrete construction. A comparison between our scheme and other PRE schemes is also given in this section.

Before going on, we explain some notations used in the rest of this paper: For a prime q, let $\mathbb{Z}_q$ denote the set $\{0, 1, 2, \cdots, q-1\}$, and $\mathbb{Z}_q^*$ denote $\mathbb{Z}_q \backslash \{0\}$. For a finite set S, $x \xleftarrow{\$} S$ means choosing an element x from S with a uniform distribution.

3.1 Main Idea

The idea behind our construction begins with the CCA-secure "hashed" ElGamal encryption scheme [14,9,15] given in Figure 1. It is important to note that, in the ciphertext component $F = H_2(pk^r) \oplus (m\|\omega)$, the public key pk is embedded in the hash function H_2 and masked by $(m\|\omega)$. This frustrates the proxy to re-encrypt the ciphertext, and hence this original scheme can not be directly used for our PRE scheme. To circumvent this obstacle, we slightly modify the scheme as shown in Figure 2 (see the bolded parts). Now, the ciphertext component F does not involve the public key, and the ciphertext component $E = pk^r = g^{xr}$ can be successfully re-encrypted into another ciphertext component $E' = E^{\frac{y}{x}} = g^{yr}$ (under the public key $pk' = g^y$) using the re-encryption key $rk_{x \leftrightarrow y} = \frac{y}{x}$.

Indeed, the modified scheme can achieve the chosen-ciphertext security as a traditional public key encryption. However, it does not satisfy the chosen-ciphertext security for proxy re-encryptions. To explain more clearly, let's take the following attack as an example:

Suppose $\mathcal{A}$ is given a challenged ciphertext under a target public key $pk^* = g^x$, say $C^* = (E^*, F^*) = (g^{xr^*}, H_2(g^{r^*}) \oplus (m_\delta \| \omega^*))$. Then adversary $\mathcal{A}$ can win the IND-PRE-CCA game as follows: He first picks $z \xleftarrow{\$} \{0,1\}^{l_0+l_1}$, and modifies the challenged ciphertext to get a new, although invalid, ciphertext

Setup(1^κ):	Encrypt(pk, m):	Decrypt($(E,F), sk$):
$x \xleftarrow{\$} \mathbb{Z}_q^*; pk = g^x; sk = x$	$\omega \xleftarrow{\$} \{0,1\}^{l_1}; r = H_1(m, \omega)$	$m\|\omega = F \oplus H_2(E^{sk})$
Return (pk, sk)	$E = g^r; F = H_2(pk^r) \oplus (m\|\omega)$	If $E = g^{H_1(m,\omega)}$ return m
	Return $C = (E, F)$	Else return $\bot$

Note: H_1 and H_2 are hash functions such that $H_1 : \{0,1\}^{l_0} \times \{0,1\}^{l_1} \to \mathbb{Z}_q^*, H_2 : \mathbb{G} \to \{0,1\}^{l_0+l_1}$. The massage space is $\mathcal{M} = \{0,1\}^{l_0}$.

Fig. 1. CCA-secure "hashed" ElGamal encryption scheme

Setup(1^κ):	Encrypt(pk, m):	Decrypt($(E, F), sk$):
$x \xleftarrow{\$} \mathbb{Z}_q^*; pk = g^x; sk = x$	$\omega \xleftarrow{\$} \{0,1\}^{l_1}; r = H_1(m, \omega)$	$m\|\omega = F \oplus H_2(E^{\frac{1}{sk}})$
Return (pk, sk)	$E = \boldsymbol{pk^r}; F = H_2(\boldsymbol{g^r}) \oplus (m\|\omega)$	If $E = g^{H_1(m,\omega)}$ return m
	Return $C = (E, F)$	Else return $\bot$

Fig. 2. Modified CCA-secure "hashed" ElGamal encryption scheme

$C' = (E', F') = (E^*, F^* \oplus z) = (g^{xr^*}, H_2(g^{r^*}) \oplus (m_\delta\|\omega^*) \oplus z)$. Next, he issues a corrupted key generation query to obtain a public/secret key pair $(pk', sk') = (g^y, y)$, and then issues a re-encryption query to obtain a re-encrypt ciphertext, say $C'' = (E'', F'') = (g^{yr^*}, H_2(g^{r^*}) \oplus (m_\delta\|\omega^*) \oplus z)$, under the public key $pk' = g^y$. Finally, using the secret key $sk' = y$, $\mathcal{A}$ can recover $(m_\delta\|\omega^*)$ as $(m_\delta\|\omega^*) = F'' \oplus H_2((E'')^{\frac{1}{y}}) \oplus z$, and eventually obtain the bit δ. Note that according to the constraints described in the IND-PRE-CCA game, it is legal for $\mathcal{A}$ to issue the above queries. As a consequence, he wins the IND-PRE-CCA game.

The above attack succeeds due to the fact that, the validity of second-level ciphertexts can only be checked by the decryptor, not any other parties including the proxy. So, to achieve the IND-PRE-CCA security for a PRE scheme, the proxy must be able to check the validity of second-level ciphertexts. Furthermore, since a PRE scheme requires the proxy to re-encrypt ciphertexts *without* seeing the plaintexts, the validity of second-level ciphertexts must be publicly verifiable. It is worth noting that, it is not an easy job to construct a CCA-secure PRE scheme with public verifiability and yet without pairings (e.g., all existing CCA-secure PRE schemes achieve the public verifiability relying on bilinear pairings).

In this paper, we achieve this goal by resorting to the Schnorr signature scheme [24], which is given in Figure 3. Note that it is non-trivial to incorporate the Schnorr signature scheme into the modified ElGamal encryption scheme to obtain a secure PRE scheme. One may think that, it can be done by choosing a signing/verification key pair (vk_s, sk_s), signing the ciphertext C to obtain a signature σ, and publishing (vk_s, C, σ) as the final ciphertext. Unfortunately, this does not work, since the adversary can still harmfully maul the above ciphertext. Namely, he can choose another signing/verification key pair to sign the ciphertext component C, and then obtain another valid ciphertext. The problem lies in the *loose* integration between the ciphertext component C and the signature σ.

We here briefly explain how to *tightly* integrate the Schnorr signature scheme with the modified ElGamal encryption scheme to obtain our PRE scheme. To do so, we first slightly modify the Schnorr signature scheme as shown in Figure 4 (see

Setup(1^κ):	Sign(sk, m):	Verify($pk, (c, s), m$):
$x \xleftarrow{\$} \mathbb{Z}_q^*; pk = g^x; sk = x$	$u \xleftarrow{\$} \mathbb{Z}_q^*; D = g^u$	$D_v = g^s pk^{-e}; e_v = H(m, D_v)$
Return (pk, sk)	$e = H(m, D); s = (u + sk \cdot e) \mod q$	If $e = e_v$ return 1
	Return $\sigma = (e, s)$	Else return 0

Note: H is a hash function such that $H : \{0,1\}^* \to \mathbb{Z}_q^*$.

Fig. 3. Schnorr signature scheme

Setup(1^κ):	Sign(sk, m):	Verify($pk, (D, s), m$):
$x \xleftarrow{\$} \mathbb{Z}_q^*; pk = g^x; sk = x$ Return (pk, sk)	$u \xleftarrow{\$} \mathbb{Z}_q^*; D = g^u$ $e = H(m, D); s = (u + sk \cdot e) \mod q$ Return $\boldsymbol{\sigma = (D, s)}$	If $\boldsymbol{g^s = D \cdot pk^{H(m,D)}}$ return 1 Else return 0

Fig. 4. Modified Schnorr signature scheme

the bolded parts). Next, given the ciphertext components $(E, F) = (pk^r, H_2(g^r) \oplus (m\|\omega))$, to tightly integrate (E, F) with the Schnorr signature, we generate the Schnorr signature as follows: Viewing F as the message to be signed, and $(E, r) = (pk^r, r)$ as the verification/signing key pair (here the base pk in pk^r is similarly viewed as the base g in g^x), we pick $u \xleftarrow{\$} \mathbb{Z}_q^*$ and output the signature as $(D, s) = (pk^u, u + rH_3(D, E, F))$. The final ciphertext is (D, E, F, s). We here also briefly explain the re-encryption algorithm: Suppose the proxy wants to re-encrypt a ciphertext $C = (D, E, F, s)$ under public key $pk = g^x$ to another one under public key $pk' = g^y$. The proxy first checks $pk^s \stackrel{?}{=} D \cdot E^{H_3(D,E,F)}$ to ensure the validity of the ciphertext, and then outputs $C' = (E', F) = (E^{\frac{y}{x}}, F)$ as the re-encrypted ciphertext (here $\frac{y}{x}$ is the re-encryption key).

Roughly speaking, the intuition why our PRE scheme can ensure the IND-PRE-CCA security comes from the following facts: on the one hand, the first-level ciphertext is in fact a ciphertext of the modified CCA-secure ElGamal encryption scheme, and hence it is impossible for the adversary to gain any advantage through malicious manipulating the first-level ciphertext; on the other hand, the validity of the second-level ciphertext can be verified by the proxy and further by the decryptor, and thus it is also impossible for the adversary to gain any advantage through malicious manipulating the second-level ciphertext. In Section 4, we will give a formal security proof for our PRE scheme.

3.2 Construction

We now present the detailed construction of our PRE scheme. Here let's first describe some system-wide parameters. Let p and q be two big primes such that $q|p-1$ and the bit-length of q is κ. Let g be a generator of group $\mathbb{G}$, which is a subgroup of $\mathbb{Z}_p^*$ with order q. Besides, let H_1, H_2 and H_3 be cryptographic hash functions such that $H_1 : \{0, 1\}^{l_0} \times \{0, 1\}^{l_1} \to \mathbb{Z}_q^*, H_2 : \mathbb{G} \to \{0, 1\}^{l_0+l_1}$ and $H_3 : \{0, 1\}^* \to \mathbb{Z}_q^*$. Here l_0 and l_1 are security parameters, and the message space is $\{0, 1\}^{l_0}$. The proposed PRE system consists of the following algorithms:

KeyGen(1^κ): Given a security parameter 1^κ, this key generation algorithm picks a random $x \xleftarrow{\$} \mathbb{Z}_q^*$, and then sets $pk = g^x$ and $sk = x$.

ReKeyGen(sk_i, sk_j): On input two secret keys $sk_i = x_i$ and $sk_j = x_j$, this algorithm outputs the bidirectional re-encryption key $rk_{i \leftrightarrow j} = x_j/x_i \mod q$.

Encrypt(pk, m): On input a public key pk and a plaintext $m \in \{0, 1\}^{l_0}$, this algorithm works as below:

1. Pick $u \xleftarrow{\$} \mathbb{Z}_q^*, \omega \xleftarrow{\$} \{0,1\}^{l_1}$, and compute $r = H_1(m, \omega)$.
2. Compute $D = pk^u, E = pk^r, F = H_2(g^r) \oplus (m\|\omega), s = u + r \cdot H_3(D, E, F)$ mod q.
3. Output the ciphertext $C = (D, E, F, s)$.

ReEncrypt$(rk_{i \leftrightarrow j}, C_i, pk_j)$: On input a re-encryption key $rk_{i \leftrightarrow j}$, a second-level ciphertext C_i under public key pk_i, this algorithm re-encrypt this ciphertext under public key pk_j as follows:
1. Parse C_i as $C_i = (D, E, F, s)$.
2. Check whether $pk_i^s = D \cdot E^{H_3(D,E,F)}$ holds. If not, output $\bot$.
3. Otherwise, compute $E' = E^{rk_{i \leftrightarrow j}} = g^{(r \cdot x_i)x_j/x_i} = g^{r \cdot x_j}$, and output the first-level ciphertext $C_j = (E', F)$.

Decrypt(C, sk): On input a secret key $sk = x$ and ciphertext C, this algorithm works according to two cases:
- C is a second-level ciphertext $C = (D, E, F, s)$: If $(g^x)^s = D \cdot E^{H_3(D,E,F)}$ does not hold, output $\bot$, else compute $m\|\omega = F \oplus H_2(E^{\frac{1}{x}})$, and return m if $E = (g^x)^{H_1(m,\omega)}$ holds and $\bot$ otherwise.
- C is a first-level ciphertext $C = (E', F)$: Compute $m\|\omega = F \oplus H_2(E'^{\frac{1}{x}})$. If $E' = (g^x)^{H_1(m,\omega)}$ holds return m; otherwise return $\bot$.

3.3 Comparison

In this subsection, we provide a comparison of our scheme with other existing PRE schemes. To conduct a fair comparison, we choose Canetti and Hohenberger's PRE schemes [11], which are also bidirectional and achieve chosen-ciphertext security. Two PRE schemes are presented in [11], including one secure in the random oracle model (refereed to as CH Scheme I) and another one secure in the standard model (refereed to as CH Scheme II). Table 1 gives a comparison between our scheme and these two schemes. The comparison results indicate that our scheme is much more efficient than the other two schemes. For example, the encryption in CH Scheme I needs 4 exponentiations, 1 pairing and 1 one-time signature signing, while the encryption in our scheme involves only 3 exponentiations. It's worth pointing out that, the computational cost and the ciphertext size in our scheme *decrease* with re-encryption, while those in CH Schemes I and II remain unchanged. Note that the computational cost and the ciphertext in some schemes such as [1,2,12,21] *increase* with re-encryption. Although the ciphertext in our scheme involves less group elements than that in CH Schemes I and II, we do not claim that our ciphertext is shorter than theirs, since their schemes are implemented in the bilinear group which enables short representation of a group element. However, the pairings in bilinear group in turn add heavy computational overhead to their schemes. The security of our scheme relies on the CDH assumption, which is weaker than the decisional bilinear Diffie-Hellman (DBDH) assumption used in CH Schemes I and II. Both our scheme and CH Scheme I are provably secure in the random oracle model, while CH Scheme II can be proved without random oracles. We leave an open problem to construct a CCA-secure PRE scheme relying on neither pairing nor random oracle model.

Table 1. Efficiency Comparison between Canetti-Hohenberger PRE Schemes and Our Scheme[3]

Schemes		CH Scheme I	CH Scheme II	Our Scheme
Comput. Cost	Encrypt	$1t_p + 4t_e + 1t_s$	$1t_p + 3t_e + 1t_{me} + 1t_s$	$3t_e$
	Re-Encrypt	$4t_p + 1t_e + 1t_v$	$4t_p + 2t_e + 1t_v$	$3t_e$
	Decrypt 2nd-level CiphTxt	$5t_p + 1t_e + 1t_v$	$5t_p + 2t_e + 1t_v$	$4t_e$
	Decrypt 1st-level CiphTxt	$5t_p + 1t_e + 1t_v$	$5t_p + 2t_e + 1t_v$	$2t_e$
CiphTxt Length	2nd-level CiphTxt	$1|pk_s|+3|\mathbb{G}_e|+1|\mathbb{G}_T|+1|\sigma_s|$	$1|pk_s|+3|\mathbb{G}_e|+1|\mathbb{G}_T|+1|\sigma_s|$	$3|\mathbb{G}|+1|\mathbb{Z}_q|$
	1st-level CiphTxt	$1|pk_s|+3|\mathbb{G}_e|+1|\mathbb{G}_T|+1|\sigma_s|$	$1|pk_s|+3|\mathbb{G}_e|+1|\mathbb{G}_T|+1|\sigma_s|$	$2|\mathbb{G}|$
Without Random Oracles?		×	✓	×
Underlying Assumptions		DBDH	DBDH	CDH

Note: t_p, t_e and t_{me} represent the computational cost of a bilinear pairing, an exponentiation and a multi-exponentiation respectively, while t_s and t_v represent the computational cost of a one-time signature signing and verification respectively. $|\mathbb{G}|, |\mathbb{Z}_q|, |\mathbb{G}_e|$ and $|\mathbb{G}_T|$ denote the bit-length of an element in groups $\mathbb{G}, \mathbb{Z}_q, \mathbb{G}_e$ and $\mathbb{G}_T$ respectively. Here $\mathbb{G}$ and $\mathbb{Z}_q$ denote the groups used in our scheme, while $\mathbb{G}_e$ and $\mathbb{G}_T$ are the bilinear groups used in CH scheme I and II, i.e., the bilinear pairing is $e: \mathbb{G}_e \times \mathbb{G}_e \rightarrow \mathbb{G}_T$. Finally, $|pk_s|$ and $|\sigma_s|$ denote the bit length of the one-time signatures public key and a one-time signature respectively.

4 Security Analysis

In this section, we prove the IND-PRE-CCA security for our scheme in the random oracle model. Before presenting the security analysis, we first review some related complexity assumptions.

4.1 Complexity Assumptions

Definition 2. *Let $\mathbb{G}$ be a cyclic multiplicative group with prime order q. The computational Diffie-Hellman (CDH) problem in group $\mathbb{G}$ is, given a tuple $(g, g^a, g^b) \in \mathbb{G}^3$ with unknown $a, b \xleftarrow{\$} \mathbb{Z}_q^*$, to compute g^{ab}.*

Definition 3. *For a polynomial-time adversary $\mathcal{B}$, we define his advantage in solving the CDH problem in group $\mathbb{G}$ as*

$$Adv_{\mathcal{B}}^{CDH} \triangleq Pr\left[\mathcal{B}(g, g^a, g^b) = g^{ab}\right],$$

where the probability is taken over the randomly choices of a, b and the random bits consumed by $\mathcal{B}$. We say that the (t, ϵ)-CDH assumption holds in group $\mathbb{G}$ if no t-time adversary $\mathcal{B}$ has advantage at least ϵ in solving the CDH problem in group $\mathbb{G}$.

Bao et al. [5] introduced a variant of the CDH problem named divisible computation Diffie-Hellman (DCDH) problem. The DCDH problem in group $\mathbb{G}$ is,

---

[3] In Table 1, we neglect some operations such as hash function evaluation, modular multiplication and XOR, since the computational cost of these operations is far less than that of exponentiations or pairings. Note that, using the technique in [10,19,20], both the re-encryption and decryption in CH scheme I and II can further save two pairings, at the cost of several exponentiation operations.

given $(g, g^{\frac{1}{a}}, g^b) \in \mathbb{G}^3$ with unknown $a, b \xleftarrow{\$} \mathbb{Z}_q^*$, to compute g^{ab}. In [5], Bao et al. presented the relation between CDH problem and DCDH problem in the following lemma:

Lemma 1. *The DCDH problem in group $\mathbb{G}$ is equivalent to the CDH problem in the same group.*

4.2 Security Proof

In this subsection, we present the security proof for our scheme.

Theorem 1. *Our PRE scheme is IND-PRE-CCA secure in the random oracle model, assuming the CDH assumption holds in group $\mathbb{G}$ and the Schnorr signature is existential unforgeable against chosen message attack (EUF-CMA). Concretely, if there exists a $(t, q_{H_1}, q_{H_2}, q_{H_3}, q_u, q_c, q_{rk}, q_{re}, q_d, \epsilon)$-IND-PRE-CCA adversary $\mathcal{A}$ against our scheme, then, for any $0 < \nu < \epsilon$, there exists*

- *either an algorithm $\mathcal{B}$ which can solve the (t', ϵ')-CDH problem in group $\mathbb{G}$ with*

$$t' \leq t + (q_{H_1} + q_{H_2} + q_{H_3} + q_u + q_c + q_{rk} + q_{re} + q_d)\mathcal{O}(1)$$
$$+ (q_u + q_c + 3q_{re} + 2q_{H_1}q_d)t_e,$$
$$\epsilon' \geq \frac{1}{q_{H_2}}\left(2(\epsilon - \nu) - \frac{q_{H_1}(1+q_d)}{2^{l_0+l_1}} - \frac{q_{re}+q_d}{q}\right),$$

   where t_e denotes the running time of an exponentiation in group $\mathbb{G}$.
- *or an attacker who breaks the EUF-CMA security of the Schnorr signature with advantage ν within time t'.*

Proof. Without loss of generality, we assume that the Schnorr signature is (t', ν)-EUF-CMA secure for some probability $0 < \nu < \epsilon$. Since the CDH problem is equivalent to the DCDH problem, for convenience, we here prove this theorem under the DCDH problem. Suppose there exists a t-time adversary $\mathcal{A}$ who can break the IND-PRE-CCA security of the proposed PRE scheme with advantage $\epsilon - \nu$. Then we show how to construct an algorithm $\mathcal{B}$ which can solve the (t', ϵ')-DCDH problem in group $\mathbb{G}$.

Suppose $\mathcal{B}$ is given as input an DCDH challenge tuple $(g, g^{\frac{1}{a}}, g^b)$ with unknown $a, b \xleftarrow{\$} \mathbb{Z}_p^*$. Algorithm $\mathcal{B}$'s goal is to output g^{ab}. Algorithm $\mathcal{B}$ acts as the challenger and plays the IND-PRE-CCA game with adversary $\mathcal{A}$ in the following way.

Hash Oracle Queries. At any time adversary $\mathcal{A}$ can issue the random oracle queries H_1, H_2 and H_3. Algorithm $\mathcal{B}$ maintains three hash lists $H_1^{\text{list}}, H_2^{\text{list}}$ and H_3^{list} which are initially empty, and responds as below:

- H_1 *queries*: On receipt of an H_1 queries on (m, ω), if this query has appeared on the H_1^{list} in a tuple (m, ω, r), return the predefined value r as the result of the query. Otherwise, choose $r \xleftarrow{\$} \mathbb{Z}_q^*$, add the tuple (m, ω, r) to the list H_1^{list} and respond with $H_1(m, \omega) = r$.

- H_2 *queries*: On receipt of an H_2 query $R \in \mathbb{G}$, if this query has appeared on the H_2^{list} in a tuple (R, β), return the predefined value β as the result of the query. Otherwise, choose $\beta \xleftarrow{\$} \{0,1\}^{l_0+l_1}$, add the tuple (R, β) to the list H_2^{list} and respond with $H_2(R) = \beta$.
- H_3 *queries*: On receipt of an H_3 query (D, E, F), if this query has appeared on the H_3^{list} in a tuple (D, E, F, γ), return the predefined value γ as the result of the query. Otherwise, choose $\gamma \xleftarrow{\$} \mathbb{Z}_q^*$, add the tuple (D, E, F, γ) to the list H_3^{list} and respond with $H_3(D, E, F) = \gamma$.

Phase 1. In this phase, adversary $\mathcal{A}$ issues a series of queries as in the definition of the IND-PRE-CCA game. $\mathcal{B}$ maintains a list K^{list} which is initially empty, and answers these queries for $\mathcal{A}$ as follows:

- *Uncorrupted key generation query* $\langle i \rangle$. Algorithm $\mathcal{B}$ first picks $x_i \xleftarrow{\$} \mathbb{Z}_q^*$ and defines $pk_i = \left(g^{1/a}\right)^{x_i}$, $c_i = 0$. Next, it adds the tuple (pk_i, x_i, c_i) to K^{list} and returns pk_i to adversary $\mathcal{A}$. Here the bit c_i is used to denote whether the secret key with respect to pk_i is corrupted, i.e., $c_i = 0$ indicates uncorrupted and $c_i = 1$ means corrupted.
- *Corrupted key generation query* $\langle j \rangle$. Algorithm $\mathcal{B}$ first picks $x_j \xleftarrow{\$} \mathbb{Z}_q^*$ and defines $pk_j = g^{x_j}$, $c_j = 1$. Next, it adds the tuple (pk_j, x_j, c_j) to K^{list} and returns (pk_j, x_j) to adversary $\mathcal{A}$.
- *Re-encryption key generation query* $\langle pk_i, pk_j \rangle$: Recall that according to the definition of IND-PRE-CCA game, it is required that pk_i and pk_j were generated beforehand, and either both of them are corrupted or alternately both are uncorrupted. Algorithm $\mathcal{B}$ first recovers tuples (pk_i, x_i, c_i) and (pk_j, x_j, c_j) from K^{list}, and then returns the re-encryption key x_j/x_i to $\mathcal{A}$.
- *Re-encryption query* $\langle pk_i, pk_j, C_i (= (D, E, F, s)) \rangle$: If $pk_i^s \neq D \cdot E^{H_3(D,E,F)}$, then output $\perp$. Otherwise, algorithm $\mathcal{B}$ responds to this query as follows:
    1. Recover tuples (pk_i, x_i, c_i) and (pk_j, x_j, c_j) from K^{list} (recall that according to the definition of IND-PRE-CCA game, K^{list} should contain these two tuples).
    2. If $c_i = c_j$, compute $E' = E^{x_j/x_i}$ and return (E', F) as the first-level ciphertext to $\mathcal{A}$.
    3. Else, search whether there exists a tuple $(m, \omega, r) \in H_1^{\text{list}}$ such that $pk_i^r = E$. If yes, compute $E' = pk_j^r$ and return (E', F) as the first-level ciphertext to $\mathcal{A}$; otherwise return $\perp$.
- *Decryption query* $\langle pk, C \rangle$: Recall that according to the definition of IND-PRE-CCA game, K^{list} should contain a tuple (pk, x, c) with respect to the public key pk. Algorithm $\mathcal{B}$ responds to this query as follows:
    1. If $c = 1$ (which means that the public key is corrupted and the corresponding secret key is x), algorithm $\mathcal{B}$ runs $\mathsf{Decrypt}(C, x)$ and returns the result to $\mathcal{A}$.

2. Otherwise, parse C as $C = (D, E, F, s)$ (in the case of a second-level ciphertext) or $C = (E, F)$ (in the case of a first-level ciphertext). If $C = (D, E, F, s)$ and $pk^s \neq D \cdot E^{H_3(D,E,F)}$, return $\perp$ to $\mathcal{A}$ indicating that C is an invalid ciphertext.
3. Search lists H_1^{list} and H_2^{list} to see whether there exist $(m, \omega, r) \in H_1^{\text{list}}$ and $(R, \beta) \in H_2^{\text{list}}$ such that

$$pk^r = E, \beta \oplus (m\|\omega) = F \text{ and } R = g^r.$$

If yes, return m to $\mathcal{A}$. Otherwise, return $\perp$.

Challenge. When $\mathcal{A}$ decides that Phase 1 is over, it outputs a target public key pk^* and two equal-length messages $m_0, m_1 \in \{0,1\}^{l_0}$. Algorithm $\mathcal{B}$ responds as follows:

1. Recover tuple (pk^*, x^*, c^*) from H_1^{list}. Recall that according to the constraints described in IND-PRE-CCA game, H_1^{list} should contain this tuple, and c^* is equal to 0 (indicating that $pk^* = g^{\frac{x^*}{a}}$).
2. Pick $e^*, s^* \xleftarrow{\$} \mathbb{Z}_q^*$, and compute $D^* = \left(g^b\right)^{-e^* x^*} \left(g^{\frac{1}{a}}\right)^{x^* s^*}$ and $E^* = \left(g^b\right)^{x^*}$.
3. Pick $F^* \xleftarrow{\$} \{0,1\}^{l_0+l_1}$ and define $H_3(D^*, E^*, F^*) = e^*$.
4. Pick $\delta \xleftarrow{\$} \{0,1\}, \omega^* \xleftarrow{\$} \{0,1\}^{l_1}$, and implicitly define $H_2(g^{ab}) = (m_\delta\|\omega^*) \oplus F^*$ and $H_1(m_\delta, \omega^*) = ab$ (Note that algorithm $\mathcal{B}$ does not know ab and g^{ab}).
5. Return $C^* = (D^*, E^*, F^*, s^*)$ as the challenged ciphertext to adversary $\mathcal{A}$.

Note that by the construction given above, by letting $u^* \triangleq s^* - abe^*$ and $r^* \triangleq ab$, we can see that the challenged ciphertext C^* has the same distribution as the real one, since H_2 acts as a random oracle, and

$$D^* = \left(g^b\right)^{-e^* x^*} \left(g^{\frac{1}{a}}\right)^{x^* s^*} = \left(g^{\frac{x^*}{a}}\right)^{s^* - abe^*} = (pk^*)^{s^* - abe^*} = (pk^*)^{u^*},$$

$$E^* = \left(g^b\right)^{x^*} = \left(g^{\frac{x^*}{a}}\right)^{ab} = (pk^*)^{ab} = (pk^*)^{r^*},$$

$$F^* = H_2(g^{ab}) \oplus (m_\delta\|\omega^*) = H_2(g^{r^*}) \oplus (m_\delta\|\omega^*),$$

$$s^* = (s^* - abe^*) + abe^* = u^* + ab \cdot H_3(D^*, E^*, F^*) = u^* + r^* \cdot H_3(D^*, E^*, F^*).$$

Phase 2. Adversary $\mathcal{A}$ continues to issue the rest of queries as in Phase 1, with the restrictions described in the IND-PRE-CCA game. Algorithm $\mathcal{B}$ responds to these queries for $\mathcal{A}$ as in Phase 1.

Guess. Eventually, adversary $\mathcal{A}$ returns a guess $\delta' \in \{0,1\}$ to $\mathcal{B}$. Algorithm $\mathcal{B}$ randomly picks a tuple (R, β) from the list H_2^{list} and outputs R as the solution to the given DCDH instance.

Analysis. Now let's analyze the simulation. The main idea of the analysis is borrowed from [8]. We first evaluate the simulations of the random oracles. From the construction of H_3, it is clear that the simulation of H_3 is perfect. As long as adversary $\mathcal{A}$ does not query (m_δ, ω^*) to H_1 nor g^{ab} to H_2, where δ and ω^* are chosen by $\mathcal{B}$ in the Challenge phase, the simulations of H_1 and H_2 are perfect. By AskH_1^* we denote the event that (m_δ, ω^*) has been queried to H_1. Also, by AskH_2^* we denote the event that g^{ab} has been queried to H_2.

As argued before, the challenged ciphertext provided for $\mathcal{A}$ is identically distributed as the real one from the construction. From the description of the simulation, it can be seen that the responses to $\mathcal{A}$'s re-encryption key queries are also perfect.

Next, we analyze the simulation of the re-encryption oracle. The responses to adversary $\mathcal{A}$'s re-encryption queries are perfect, unless $\mathcal{A}$ can submit valid second-level ciphertexts without querying hash function H_1(denote this event by ReEncErr). However, since H_1 acts as a random oracle and adversary $\mathcal{A}$ issues at most q_{re} re-encryption queries, we have

$$\Pr[\mathsf{ReEncErr}] \leq \frac{q_{re}}{q}.$$

Now, we evaluate the simulation of the decryption oracle. The simulation of the decryption oracle is perfect, with the exception that simulation errors may occur in rejecting some valid ciphertext. Fortunately, these errors are not significant as shown below: Suppose that (pk, C), where $C = (D, E, F, y)$ or $C = (E, F)$, has been issued as a *valid* ciphertext. Even C is valid, there is a possibility that C can be produced without querying g^r to H_2, where $r = H_1(m, \omega)$. Let Valid be an event that C is valid, and let AskH_2 and AskH_1 respectively be events that g^r has been queried to H_2 and (m, ω) has been queried to H_1 with respect to $(E, F) = (pk^r, H_2(g^r) \oplus (m \| \omega))$, where $r = H_1(m, \omega)$. We then have

$$\begin{aligned}\Pr[\mathsf{Valid}|\neg\mathsf{AskH}_2] &= \Pr[\mathsf{Valid} \wedge \mathsf{AskH}_1|\neg\mathsf{AskH}_2] + \Pr[\mathsf{Valid} \wedge \neg\mathsf{AskH}_1|\neg\mathsf{AskH}_2] \\ &\leq \Pr[\mathsf{AskH}_1|\neg\mathsf{AskH}_2] + \Pr[\mathsf{Valid}|\neg\mathsf{AskH}_1 \wedge \neg\mathsf{AskH}_2] \\ &\leq \frac{q_{H_1}}{2^{l_0+l_1}} + \frac{1}{q}.\end{aligned}$$

Let DecErr be the event that $\mathsf{Valid}|\neg\mathsf{AskH}_2$ happens during the entire simulation. Then, since q_d decryption oracles are issued, we have

$$\Pr[\mathsf{DecErr}] \leq \frac{q_{H_1} q_d}{2^{l_0+l_1}} + \frac{q_d}{q}.$$

Now let Good denote the event $\mathsf{AskH}_2^* \vee (\mathsf{AskH}_1^* | \neg \mathsf{AskH}_2^*) \vee \mathsf{ReEncErr} \vee \mathsf{DecErr}$. If event Good does not happen, it is clear that adversary $\mathcal{A}$ can not gain any advantage in guessing δ due to the randomness of the output of the random oracle H_2. Namely, we have $\Pr[\delta = \delta' | \neg \mathsf{Good}] = \frac{1}{2}$. Hence, by splitting $\Pr[\delta' = \delta]$, we have

$$\Pr[\delta' = \delta] = \Pr[\delta' = \delta | \neg\mathsf{Good}]\Pr[\neg\mathsf{Good}] + \Pr[\delta' = \delta | \mathsf{Good}]\Pr[\mathsf{Good}]$$
$$\leq \frac{1}{2}\Pr[\neg\mathsf{Good}] + \Pr[\mathsf{Good}]$$
$$= \frac{1}{2}(1 - \Pr[\mathsf{Good}]) + \Pr[\mathsf{Good}]$$
$$= \frac{1}{2} + \frac{1}{2}\Pr[\mathsf{Good}]$$

and

$$\Pr[\delta' = \delta] \geq \Pr[\delta' = \delta | \neg\mathsf{Good}]\Pr[\neg\mathsf{Good}] = \frac{1}{2}(1 - \Pr[\mathsf{Good}]) = \frac{1}{2} - \frac{1}{2}\Pr[\mathsf{Good}].$$

Then we have
$$\left|\Pr[\delta' = \delta] - \frac{1}{2}\right| \leq \frac{1}{2}\Pr[\mathsf{Good}].$$

By definition of the advantage $(\epsilon - \nu)$ for the IND-PRE-CCA adversary, we then have

$$\epsilon - \nu = \left|\Pr[\delta' = \delta] - \frac{1}{2}\right|$$
$$\leq \frac{1}{2}\Pr[\mathsf{Good}] = \frac{1}{2}\left(\Pr[\mathsf{AskH}_2^* \vee (\mathsf{AskH}_1^* | \neg\mathsf{AskH}_2^*) \vee \mathsf{ReEncErr} \vee \mathsf{DecErr}]\right)$$
$$\leq \frac{1}{2}\left(\Pr[\mathsf{AskH}_2^*] + \Pr[\mathsf{AskH}_1^* | \neg\mathsf{AskH}_2^*] + \Pr[\mathsf{ReEncErr}] + \Pr[\mathsf{DecErr}]\right).$$

Since $\Pr[\mathsf{ReEncErr}] \leq \frac{q_{re}}{q}$, $\Pr[\mathsf{DecErr}] \leq \frac{q_{H_1}q_d}{2^{l_0+l_1}} + \frac{q_d}{q}$ and $\Pr[\mathsf{AskH}_1^* | \neg\mathsf{AskH}_2^*] \leq \frac{q_{H_1}}{2^{l_0+l_1}}$, we obtain

$$\Pr[\mathsf{AskH}_2^*] \geq 2(\epsilon - \nu) - \Pr[\mathsf{AskH}_1^* | \neg\mathsf{AskH}_2^*] - \Pr[\mathsf{DecErr}] - \Pr[\mathsf{ReEncErr}]$$
$$\geq 2(\epsilon - \nu) - \frac{q_{H_1}}{2^{l_0+l_1}} - \frac{q_{re}}{q} - \frac{q_{H_1}q_d}{2^{l_0+l_1}} + \frac{q_d}{q}$$
$$= 2(\epsilon - \nu) - \frac{q_{H_1}(1 + q_d)}{2^{l_0+l_1}} - \frac{q_{re} + q_d}{q}.$$

Meanwhile, if event AskH_2^* happens, algorithm $\mathcal{B}$ will be able to solve the DCDH instance, and consequently, we obtain

$$\epsilon' \geq \frac{1}{q_{H_2}}\left(2(\epsilon - \nu) - \frac{q_{H_1}(1 + q_d)}{2^{l_0+l_1}} - \frac{q_{re} + q_d}{q}\right).$$

From the description of the simulation, the running time of algorithm $\mathcal{B}$ can be bounded by

$$t' \leq t + (q_{H_1} + q_{H_2} + q_{H_3} + q_u + q_c + q_{rk} + q_{re} + q_d)\mathcal{O}(1) + (q_u + q_c + 3q_{re} + 2q_{H_1}q_d)t_e$$

This completes the proof of Theorem 1.

5 Conclusions

We presented a new bidirectional proxy re-encryption scheme, and proved its security under the computational Diffie-Hellman problem. Our proposed scheme does not rely on the costly bilinear pairings, and hence is very efficient. As a result, we solved the open problem left by Canetti and Hohenberger in ACM CCS'07.

We left some open problems in this area, such as designing (1) bidirectional /unidirectional CCA-secure proxy re-encryption scheme without pairings in the *standard model* and (2) bidirectional/unidirectional CCA-secure proxy re-encryption scheme with *multi-hop* and without pairings.

Acknowledgements

This work is supported by the Office of Research, Singapore Management University. It is also partially supported by the National Science Foundation of China under Grant Nos. 90704004 and 60673077.

References

1. Ateniese, G., Fu, K., Green, M., Hohenberger, S.: Improved Proxy Re-encryption Schemes with Applications to Secure Distributed Storage. In: Proc. of NDSS 2005, pp. 29–43 (2005)
2. Ateniese, G., Fu, K., Green, M., Hohenberger, S.: Improved Proxy Re-encryption Schemes with Applications to Secure Distributed Storage. ACM Transactions on Information and System Security (TISSEC) 9(1), 1–30 (2006)
3. Boneh, D., Boyen, X.: Efficient Selective-ID Secure Identity Based Encryption Without Random Oracles. In: Cachin, C., Camenisch, J.L. (eds.) EUROCRYPT 2004. LNCS, vol. 3027, pp. 223–238. Springer, Heidelberg (2004)
4. Blaze, M., Bleumer, G., Strauss, M.: Divertible Protocols and Atomic Proxy Cryptography. In: Nyberg, K. (ed.) EUROCRYPT 1998. LNCS, vol. 1403, pp. 127–144. Springer, Heidelberg (1998)
5. Bao, F., Deng, R.H., Zhu, H.: Variations of Diffie-Hellman Problem. In: Qing, S., Gollmann, D., Zhou, J. (eds.) ICICS 2003. LNCS, vol. 2836, pp. 301–312. Springer, Heidelberg (2003)
6. Boneh, D., Franklin, M.: Identity based encryption from the Weil pairing. In: Kilian, J. (ed.) CRYPTO 2001. LNCS, vol. 2139, pp. 213–229. Springer, Heidelberg (2001)
7. Boneh, D., Goh, E.-J., Matsuo, T.: Proposal for P1363.3 Proxy Re-encryption, http://grouper.ieee.org/groups/1363/IBC/submissions/ NTTDataProposal-for-P1363.3-2006-09-01.pdf
8. Baek, J., Safavi-Naini, R., Susilo, W.: Certificateless Public Key Encryption without Pairing. In: Zhou, J., López, J., Deng, R.H., Bao, F. (eds.) ISC 2005. LNCS, vol. 3650, pp. 134–148. Springer, Heidelberg (2005)
9. Baek, J., Safavi-Naini, R., Susilo, W.: Certificatless Public Key Encryption without Pairing. In: Zhou, J., López, J., Deng, R.H., Bao, F. (eds.) ISC 2005. LNCS, vol. 3650, pp. 134–148. Springer, Heidelberg (2005)

10. Canetti, R., Goldwasser, S.: An Efficient Threshold Public Key Cryptosystem Secure against Adaptive Chosen Ciphertext Attack. In: Stern, J. (ed.) EUROCRYPT 1999. LNCS, vol. 1592, pp. 90–106. Springer, Heidelberg (1999)
11. Caneti, R., Hohenberger, S.: Chosen-Ciphertext Secure Proxy Re-Encryption. In: Proceeding of ACM CCS 2007 (2007)
12. Chu, C., Tzeng, W.: Identity-Based Proxy Re-Encryption without Random Oracles. In: Garay, J.A., Lenstra, A.K., Mambo, M., Peralta, R. (eds.) ISC 2007. LNCS, vol. 4779, pp. 189–202. Springer, Heidelberg (2007)
13. Dodis, Y., Ivan, A.-A.: Proxy Cryptography Revisited. In: Proc. of NDSS 2003 (2003)
14. ElGamal, T.: A Public Key Cryptosystem and a Signature Scheme Based on Discrete Logarithms. In: Blakely, G.R., Chaum, D. (eds.) CRYPTO 1984. LNCS, vol. 196, pp. 10–18. Springer, Heidelberg (1985)
15. Fujisaki, E., Okamoto, T.: Secure Integration of Asymmetric and Symmetric Encryption Schemes. In: Wiener, M. (ed.) CRYPTO 1999. LNCS, vol. 1666, pp. 537–554. Springer, Heidelberg (1999)
16. Green, M., Ateniese, G.: Identity-Based Proxy Re-Encryption. In: Katz, J., Yung, M. (eds.) ACNS 2007. LNCS, vol. 4521, pp. 288–306. Springer, Heidelberg (2007)
17. Golle, P., Jakobsson, M., Juels, A., Syverson, P.F.: Universal Re-Encryption for Mixnets. In: Okamoto, T. (ed.) CT-RSA 2004. LNCS, vol. 2964, pp. 163–178. Springer, Heidelberg (2004)
18. Jakobsson, M.: On Quorum Controlled Asymmetric Proxy Re-encryption. In: Imai, H., Zheng, Y. (eds.) PKC 1999. LNCS, vol. 1560, pp. 112–121. Springer, Heidelberg (1999)
19. Kiltz, E., Galindo, D.: Direct Chosen-Ciphertext Secure Identity-Based Key Encapsulation without Random Oracles. Cryptology ePrint Archive, Report 2006/034 (2006), http://eprint.iacr.org/
20. Kiltz, E.: Chosen-Ciphertext Secure Identity-Based Encryption in the Standard Model with Short Ciphertexts. Cryptology ePrint Archive, Report 2006/122 (2006), http://eprint.iacr.org/
21. Libert, B., Vergnaud, D.: Unidirectional Chosen-Ciphertext Secure Proxy Reencryption. In: Cramer, R. (ed.) PKC 2008. LNCS, vol. 4939, pp. 360–379. Springer, Heidelberg (2008)
22. Matsuo, T.: Proxy Re-Encryption Systems for Identity-Based Encryption. In: Takagi, T., Okamoto, T., Okamoto, E., Okamoto, T. (eds.) Pairing 2007. LNCS, vol. 4575, pp. 247–267. Springer, Heidelberg (2007)
23. Mambo, M., Okamoto, E.: Proxy Cryptosystems: Delegation of the Power to Decrypt Ciphertexts. IEICE Trans. Fund. Electronics Communications and Computer Science E80-A(1), 54–63 (1997)
24. Schnorr, C.P.: Efficient Identifications and Signatures for Smart Cards. In: Brassard, G. (ed.) CRYPTO 1989. LNCS, vol. 435, pp. 239–251. Springer, Heidelberg (1990)

Hybrid Damgård Is CCA1-Secure under the DDH Assumption

Yvo Desmedt[1], Helger Lipmaa[2], and Duong Hieu Phan[3]

[1] University College London, UK
[2] Cybernetica AS, Estonia
[3] University of Paris 8, France

Abstract. In 1991, Damgård proposed a simple public-key cryptosystem that he proved CCA1-secure under the Diffie-Hellman Knowledge assumption. Only in 2006, Gjøsteen proved its CCA1-security under a more standard but still new and strong assumption. The known CCA2-secure public-key cryptosystems are considerably more complicated. We propose a hybrid variant of Damgård's public-key cryptosystem and show that it is CCA1-secure if the used symmetric cryptosystem is CPA-secure, the used MAC is unforgeable, the used key-derivation function is secure, and the underlying group is a DDH group. The new cryptosystem is the most efficient known CCA1-secure hybrid cryptosystem based on standard assumptions.

Keywords: CCA1-security, Damgård's cryptosystem, DDH, hybrid cryptosystems.

1 Introduction

CCA2-security in the standard model is currently the strongest widely accepted security requirement for public-key cryptosystems. The first practical CCA2-secure cryptosystem was proposed by Cramer and Shoup [CS98]. In their scheme, the plaintext is a group element. However, in practice one really needs a hybrid cryptosystem where the plaintext can be an arbitrarily long bitstring. The first related hybrid cryptosystem was proposed by Shoup in [Sho00]. In [KD04], Kurosawa and Desmedt proposed another hybrid cryptosystem that, taking account the comments of Gennaro and Shoup [GS04], is up to now the most efficient published hybrid CCA2-secure cryptosystem that is based on the Decisional Diffie-Hellman (DDH) assumption.

Existing CPA-secure cryptosystems like Elgamal [Elg85] are considerably simpler. CPA-security is however a very weak security notion. In this paper we concentrate on an intermediate security notion, CCA1-security (or "non-adaptive CCA-security"). Recall that already in 1991, Damgård [Dam91] proposed a simple CCA1-secure cryptosystem, although with the security proof relying on the non-standard Diffie-Hellman Knowledge assumption [Dam91, BP04]. In 2006, Gjøsteen proved that a generalization of Damgård's cryptosystem is CCA1-secure under a strong conventional assumption [Gjø06]. Recently, Lipmaa [Lip08] gave a considerably simpler proof of Gjøsteen's result.

Table 1. Comparison between a few discrete-logarithm based hybrid cryptosystems. Here, x is the bit length of group element representations and $|m|$ is the length of symmetrically encrypted plaintext. In encryption/decryption, e means one exponentiation, s — one symmetric-key IND-CCA secure encryption/decryption of $|m|$-bit string (this may also consist of an IND-CPA secure encryption/decryption together with a MAC on the ciphertext), t — one computation of a target collision-resistant hash function, u — one computation of a universal one-way hash function. Non-cryptographic operations, e.g., of key-derivation functions, are not included to the computation cost. If the assumption is not well-established, a link to the paper(s) defining the assumption is given.

Name	Security	Assumption	Encrypt.	Decrypt.	|Ciphertext|	|pk|
Hybrid						
This paper	CCA1	DDH	$3e+s$	$2e+s$	$2x+|m|+|t|$	x
[HK07, Sect. 4.2]	CCA2	DDH	$4e+t+s$	$2e+t+s$	$2x+|m|+|t|$	$3x$+hash
[KD04, GS04]	CCA2	DDH	$4e+t+s$	$2e+t+s$	$2x+|m|+|t|$	$2x$+hash
[ABR01]	CCA2	[ABR01]	$2e+s$	$1e+s$	$x+|m|+|t|$	x
[Sho00]	CCA2	DDH	$5e+s$	$3e+s$	$3x+|m|+|t|$	$4x$+hash
Non-hybrid						
[CS04]	CCA2	DDH	$5e+u$	$3e+u$	$4x$	$5x$+hash
Lite [CS04]	CCA1	DDH	$4e$	$3e$	$4x$	$4x$
[Dam91]	CCA1	[Gjø06, Lip08]	$3e$	$2e$	$3x$	$2x$
[Elg85]	CPA	DDH	$2e$	e	$2x$	x

We propose a Damgård-based hybrid cryptosystem that we call "Hybrid Damgård". This scheme can also be seen as a simplification of the Kurosawa-Desmedt cryptosystem [KD04]. We prove that Hybrid Damgård is CCA1-secure if the used symmetric cryptosystem is semantically secure, the used MAC is unforgeable, the used key-derivation function is secure, and the underlying group is a DDH group. Hybrid Damgård is currently the most efficient CCA1-secure hybrid cryptosystem that is based on the DDH assumption. It is essentially as efficient as Damgård's original CCA1-secure cryptosystem, requiring the encrypter and the decrypter to additionally evaluate only some secret-key or non-cryptographic operations. See Tbl. 1 for a comparison. In addition, Hybrid Damgård is a hashless cryptosystem.

In the security proof, we use a standard game hopping technique, similar to the one in [KD04, GS04]. Also our proof is only slightly more complex than that given by Gjøsteen, the additional complexity is only due to use of additional symmetric primitives.

Recent Work. Essentially the same cryptosystem was very recently discussed in [DP08] and [KPSY08]. In [DP08], the authors proved CCA2-security of the Hybrid Damgård cryptosystem under a strong knowledge assumption (corresponding to KA3 of [BP04]). One can extract a CCA1-security proof from it under a somewhat weaker knowledge assumption (corresponding to KA2 of [BP04]). In a yet unpublished eprint [KPSY08], the authors proved that the Hybrid Damgård is CCA2-secure under the DDH assumption; however, the used hash function and symmetric cryptosystem have to satisfy stronger assumptions. They also briefly mention that it is CCA1-secure under the same assumptions we use.

Notation. For a set A, let $U(A)$ denote the uniform distribution on it.

2 Preliminaries

Let $|B| < |A|$. A function kdf $: A \to B$ is *key derivation function*, KDF, if the distributions kdf$(U(A))$ and $U(B)$ are computationally indistinguishable. If $|A| < |B|$, then KDF is a pseudorandom generator. Otherwise, KDF may be a non-cryptographic function.

Decisional Diffie-Hellman Assumption
Definition 1. *Let $\mathbb{G}$ be a group of order q with a generator g. A DDH distinguisher Alice has success* AdvDDH$_{\mathbb{G},g}$(Alice), *defined as*

$$\left| \begin{array}{l} \Pr[x, y \leftarrow \mathbb{Z}_q : A(\mathbb{G}, q, g, g^x, g^y, g^{xy}) = 1] - \\ \Pr[x, y \leftarrow \mathbb{Z}_q, z \leftarrow \mathbb{Z}_q \setminus \{xy\} : A(\mathbb{G}, q, g, g^x, g^y, g^z) = 1] \end{array} \right|$$

in attacking DDH group $\mathbb{G}$, where the probability is taken over the choice of random variables and over the random coin tosses of Alice. We say that $\mathbb{G}$ is a (τ, ε)-DDH group if AdvDDH$_{\mathbb{G},g}$(Alice) $\leq \varepsilon$ *for any τ-time adversary Alice and for any generator g.*

Usually, one takes $z \leftarrow \mathbb{Z}_q$. The difference between Alice's success in these two variants of the DDH game is clearly upper bounded by $1/q$, see e.g. [CS04, Lem. 1]. We later use a variation where also x is fixed (i.e., g^x is a subindex of AdvDDH), but this variation is equally powerful because of the random self-reducibility of DDH. Moreover, because of the random self-reducibility of DDH, the choice of g is not important.

We say that (g_1, g_2, g_3, g_4) is a *DDH tuple* if $(g_3, g_4) = (g_1, g_2)^r$ for some $r \in \mathbb{Z}_q$.

Public-Key Cryptosystems. Let pub $=$ (pub.gen, pub.enc, pub.dec) be a public-key cryptosystem for a fixed security parameter λ. In particular, pub.gen(1^λ) returns a new secret/public key pair (sk, pk), pub.enc(pk; $m;r$) encrypts the message m by using randomizer r, and pub.dec(sk; C) decrypts a ciphertext C such that pub.dec(sk; pub.enc(pk; $m; \cdot$)) $= m$; the result of pub.dec may be a special symbol $\bot$.

Consider the next *CCA2 game* between the adversary Alice and the challenger:

Setup. The challenger runs pub.gen(1^λ) to obtain a random instance of a secret and public key pair (sk, pk). It gives the public key pk to Alice.
Query phase 1. Alice adaptively issues decryption queries C. The challenger responds with pub.dec(sk; C).
Challenge phase. Alice outputs two (equal length) messages $\hat{m}_0, \hat{m}_1$. The challenger picks a random $b_{Alice} \leftarrow \{0, 1\}$ and sets $\hat{C} \leftarrow$ pub.enc(pk; $\hat{m}_{b_{Alice}}, \hat{r}$) for random $\hat{r}$. It gives $\hat{C}$ to Alice.
Query phase 2. Alice continues to issue decryption queries C as in phase 1, but with the added constraint that $C \neq \hat{C}$. The challenger responds each time with pub.dec(sk; C).

Guess. Alice outputs her guess $b'_{Alice} \in \{0,1\}$ for b_{Alice} and wins the game if $b_{Alice} = b'_{Alice}$.

Definition 2 (CPA/CCA1/CCA2 Security of Public-Key Cryptosystems). *A CCA2 adversary Alice has success* $\mathsf{AdvCCA2}_{\mathsf{pub}}(Alice) := |2\Pr[b_{Alice} = b'_{Alice}] - 1|$ *in attacking* pub*, where the probability is taken over the choice of b_{Alice} and over the random coin tosses of Alice. We say that* pub *is* $(\tau, \gamma_1, \gamma_2, \mu, \varepsilon)$-*CCA2-secure if* $\mathsf{AdvCCA2}_{\mathsf{pub}}(Alice) \le \varepsilon$ *for any τ-time adversary Alice that makes up to γ_i queries in phase* $i \in \{1,2\}$, *with the total queried message length being up to μ bits.* pub *is* $(\tau, \gamma, \mu, \varepsilon)$-*CCA1-secure if it is* $(\tau, \gamma, 0, \mu, \varepsilon)$-*CCA2-secure.* pub *is* (τ, ε)-*CPA-secure if it is* $(\tau, 0, 0, 0, \varepsilon)$-*CCA2-secure. The values* $\mathsf{AdvCPA}^{\mathsf{pub}}$ *and* $\mathsf{AdvCCA1}^{\mathsf{pub}}$ *are defined accordingly.*

Damgård Cryptosystem [Dam91]

Setup: On input the security parameter λ, return a λ-bit prime q, a group $\mathbb{G}$ of order q, and its randomly chosen generator $g \in \mathbb{G}$.

Key setup pub.gen: Generate $(\alpha, \beta) \leftarrow \mathbb{Z}_q^2$. Set sk $\leftarrow (\alpha, \beta)$ and pk $\leftarrow (c \leftarrow g^\alpha, d \leftarrow g^\beta)$.

Encryption pub.enc: Given a message $m \in \mathbb{G}$, do the following. First, set $r \leftarrow \mathbb{Z}_q$ and then $u_1 \leftarrow g^r$, $u_2 \leftarrow c^r$, $e \leftarrow m \cdot d^r$. The ciphertext is (u_1, u_2, e).

Decryption pub.dec: Given a ciphertext (u_1, u_2, e), do the following. If $u_2 \ne u_1^\alpha$ then output $m \leftarrow \bot$. Otherwise, compute $m \leftarrow e/u_1^\beta$ and return m.

Descriptions of some other known public-key cryptosystems are given in Appendix.

Symmetric Cryptosystems. Let sym = (sym.gen, sym.enc, sym.dec) be a symmetric cryptosystem for a fixed security parameter λ. In particular, sym.gen(1^λ) returns a new secret key sk, sym.enc(sk; m; r) encrypts the message m by using randomizer r, and sym.dec(sk; C) decrypts a ciphertext C such that sym.dec(sk; sym.enc(sk; m; r)) = m.

CPA/CCA1/CCA2-security of symmetric cryptosystems is defined similarly as in the case of public-key cryptosystems. Consider the next *CCA2 game* between the adversary Alice and the challenger:

Setup. The challenger runs pub.gen(1^λ) to obtain a random instance of a secret key sk

Query phase 1. Alice adaptively issues encryption queries m, where the challenger responds with sym.enc(sk; m, r) for random r, and decryption queries C, where the challenger responds with sym.dec(sk; C).

Challenge phase. Alice outputs two (equal length) messages $\hat{m}_0, \hat{m}_1$. The challenger picks a random $b_{Alice} \leftarrow \{0,1\}$ and sets $\hat{C} \leftarrow$ sym.enc(sk; $\hat{m}_{b_{Alice}}, \hat{r}$) for random $\hat{r}$. It gives $\hat{C}$ to Alice.

Query phase 2. Alice continues to issue encryption queries m and decryption queries C as in phase 1, but with the added constraint that $C \ne \hat{C}$. The challenger as in phase 1.

Guess. Alice outputs her guess $b'_{Alice} \in \{0,1\}$ for b_{Alice} and wins the game if $b_{Alice} = b'_{Alice}$.

Definition 3 (CPA/CCA1/CCA2 Security of Symmetric Cryptosystems). *A CCA2 adversary Alice has success* $\mathsf{AdvCCA2_{sym}}(\mathcal{A}lice) := |2\Pr[b_{\mathcal{A}lice} = b'_{\mathcal{A}lice}] - 1|$ *in attacking* sym, *where the probability is taken over the choice of* $b_{\mathcal{A}lice}$ *and over the random coin tosses of Alice. We say that* pub *is* $(\tau, \gamma_1, \gamma_2, \mu, \varepsilon)$-CCA2-*secure if* $\mathsf{AdvCCA2_{pub}}(\mathcal{A}lice) \leq \varepsilon$ *for any* τ-*time adversary Alice that makes up to* γ_i *queries in phase* $i \in \{1, 2\}$, *with the total queried message length being up to* μ *bits.* sym *is* $(\tau, \gamma, \mu, \varepsilon)$-CCA1-*secure if it is* $(\tau, \gamma, 0, \mu, \varepsilon)$-CCA2-*secure.* sym *is* (τ, ε)-CPA-*secure if it is* $(\tau, 0, 0, 0, \varepsilon)$-CCA2-*secure. The values* $\mathsf{AdvCPA^{sym}}$ *and* $\mathsf{AdvCCA1^{sym}}$ *are defined accordingly.*

MAC. A MAC mac = (mac.tag, mac.ver), on key κ and message e produces a tag t = mac.tag($\kappa; e$). A MAC is *unforgeable* if for random κ, after obtaining t' ← mac.tag($\kappa; e'$) for (at most one) adversarially chosen e', it is hard to compute a forgery, i.e., a pair (e, t) such that $e \neq e'$ but mac.ver($\kappa; e, t$) = ⊤.

A standard way of constructing a CCA2-secure symmetric cryptosystem is to encrypt a message m by using a CPA-secure cryptosystem, $e \leftarrow$ sym.enc($K; m, r$) and then returning e together with a tag t ← mac.tag($\kappa; e$). Here, (K, κ) is a pair of independent random keys.

3 Hybrid Damgård Cryptosystem

We now propose a new cryptosystem, *Hybrid Damgård*, an hybrid variant of the Damgård cryptosystem that uses some ideas from the Kurosawa-Desmedt cryptosystem as exposed by [GS04].

Setup: On input the security parameter λ, return a λ-bit prime q, a group $\mathbb{G}$ of order q, and its two randomly chosen different generators $g_1, g_2 \in \mathbb{G}$. Choose a CPA-secure symmetric cryptosystem sym = (sym.gen, sym.enc, sym.dec), an unforgeable MAC mac = (mac.tag, mac.ver), and a KDF kdf from $\mathbb{G}$ to the set of keys of (sym, mac).

Key setup pub.gen: Generate $(\alpha_1, \alpha_2) \leftarrow \mathbb{Z}_q^2$. Set sk ← (α_1, α_2) and pk ← $(c \leftarrow g_1^{\alpha_1} g_2^{\alpha_2})$.

Encryption pub.enc: Given a message $m \in \{0, 1\}^*$, do the following. First, generate $r \leftarrow \mathbb{Z}_q$, and randomizer ρ for sym, and then

$$u_1 \leftarrow g_1^r, \quad u_2 \leftarrow g_2^r, \quad (K, \kappa) \leftarrow \mathsf{kdf}(c^r),$$
$$e \leftarrow \mathsf{sym.enc}(K; m, \rho), \quad \mathsf{t} \leftarrow \mathsf{mac.tag}(\kappa; e).$$

The ciphertext is $(u_1, u_2, e, \mathsf{t})$.

Decryption pub.dec: Given a ciphertext $(u_1, u_2, e, \mathsf{t})$, do the following. Compute $(K, \kappa) \leftarrow \mathsf{kdf}(u_1^{\alpha_1} u_2^{\alpha_2})$. If mac.ver($\kappa; e, \mathsf{t}$) = ⊥ then return $m \leftarrow$ ⊥ else return $m \leftarrow$ sym.dec($K; e$).

Theorem 1. *Fix a group* $\mathbb{G}$, *a symmetric cryptosystem* sym = (sym.gen, sym.enc, sym.dec), *a MAC* mac = (mac.tag, mac.ver), *and a hash function* kdf *from* $\mathbb{G}$ *to the set of keys for* (sym, mac). *Then the Hybrid Damgård cryptosystem* pub *is CCA1-secure if (1) the DDH assumption holds, (2)* kdf *is a KDF, (3)* sym *is CPA-secure, and (4)* mac *is unforgeable.*

Proof. Use the next sequence of game hops. Assume that Alice is a $(\tau, \gamma, \mu, \varepsilon)$ CCA1-adversary for pub. In every game **Game**$_i$ we modify the CCA1 game so that there Alice has advantage $\Pr[X_i]$, where for every i, $|\Pr[X_{i+1}] - \Pr[X_i]|$ is negligible. Moreover, $|\Pr[X_{i+1}] - \Pr[X_i]|$ is estimated by defining an event F_{i+1} such that events $X_i \wedge \neg F_{i+1}$ iff $X_{i+1} \wedge \neg F_{i+1}$. Then clearly $|\Pr[X_{i+1}] - \Pr[X_i]| \leq \Pr[F_{i+1}]$ [CS98]. The full proof is slightly more complicated since the games build up a tree instead of a chain. All games are fairly standard. Details follow.

Game$_0$

This is the original CCA1 game. Alice gets a random public key $\mathsf{pk} = (c)$, makes a number of decryption queries $(u_1, u_2, e, \mathsf{t})$, receives a challenge ciphertext $(\hat{u}_1, \hat{u}_2, \hat{e}, \hat{\mathsf{t}})$, makes some more decryption queries $(u_1, u_2, e, \mathsf{t})$, and then makes a guess. In this game, Alice has success $\Pr[X_0] = \varepsilon$. To simplify further analysis, we assume that the challenger has created the values $(\hat{u}_1, \hat{u}_2, \hat{K}, \hat{\kappa})$ before the phase-1 queries.

Game$_1$

Here we redefine the internal way of computing the key during the decryption queries and the challenge ciphertext creation. Namely, we let $(K, \kappa) \leftarrow \mathsf{kdf}(u_1^{\alpha_1} u_2^{\alpha_2})$. This does not change the ciphertexts, and thus also in **Game**$_1$, Alice has success $\Pr[X_1] = \varepsilon$.

Game$_2$

In this game, the challenge ciphertext is created by choosing $(\hat{u}_1, \hat{u}_2) \leftarrow (g_1^{\hat{r}_1}, g_2^{\hat{r}_2})$ for random $\hat{r}_1 \neq \hat{r}_2$. Assume that in **Game**$_2$, Alice has success probability $\Pr[X_2]$. We now construct a DDH adversary Bob with advantage related to $|\Pr[X_1] - \Pr[X_2]|$. Bob gets (g_1, q, g_2) as an input, where g_1 generates a group $\mathbb{G}$ of order q and a $g_2 \leftarrow \mathbb{G} \backslash \{g_1\}$. Bob and Alice choose appropriate $(\mathsf{sym}, \mathsf{mac}, \mathsf{kdf})$. He then runs Alice step-by-step.

- Bob asks for his challenge $(\hat{u}_1, \hat{u}_2) \in \mathbb{G}^2$. He generates random $\alpha_1, \alpha_2 \leftarrow \mathbb{Z}_q$, sets $\mathsf{sk} \leftarrow (\alpha_1, \alpha_2)$ and $\mathsf{pk} \leftarrow (c \leftarrow g_1^{\alpha_1} g_2^{\alpha_2})$. He sends pk to Alice.
- When Alice makes a phase-1 decryption query with a purported ciphertext $(u_1, u_2, e, \mathsf{t})$, Bob returns m according to the decryption formula: $(K, \kappa) \leftarrow \mathsf{kdf}(u_1^{\alpha_1} u_2^{\alpha_2})$. If $\mathsf{mac.ver}(\kappa; e, \mathsf{t}) = \bot$ then $m \leftarrow \bot$ else $m \leftarrow \mathsf{sym.dec}(K; e)$.
- When Alice submits her message pair (m_0, m_1), Bob sets $b_{\mathcal{A}lice} \leftarrow \{0, 1\}$, and sends $(\hat{u}_1, \hat{u}_2, \hat{e}, \hat{\mathsf{t}})$ as the challenge ciphertext to Alice, where $\hat{e} \leftarrow \mathsf{sym.enc}(\hat{K}; m_{b_{\mathcal{A}lice}}, \hat{\rho})$, for uniform randomizer $\hat{\rho}$, and $\hat{\mathsf{t}} \leftarrow \mathsf{mac.tag}(\hat{\kappa}; \hat{e})$ for $(\hat{K}, \hat{\kappa}) \leftarrow \mathsf{kdf}(\hat{u}_1^{\alpha_1} \hat{u}_2^{\alpha_2})$.
- Finally, Alice replies with a guess $b'_{\mathcal{A}lice}$. Bob outputs $b'_{\mathcal{B}ob} \leftarrow 1$ if $b'_{\mathcal{A}lice} = b_{\mathcal{A}lice}$, and $b'_{\mathcal{B}ob} \leftarrow 2$ otherwise.

Let $b_{\mathcal{B}ob} = 1$ if $(g_1, g_2, \hat{u}_1, \hat{u}_2)$ is a random DDH tuple, and $b_{\mathcal{B}ob} = 2$ if it is a random non-DDH tuple, and assume that $\Pr[b_{\mathcal{B}ob} = 1] = 1/2$. In particular if $b_{\mathcal{B}ob} = 2$ then $\hat{u}_1 \leftarrow g_1^{\hat{r}_1}, \hat{u}_2 \leftarrow g_2^{\hat{r}_2}$ for random $\hat{r}_1 \neq \hat{r}_2$.

If $b_{\mathcal{B}ob} = 1$ then all steps are emulated perfectly for **Game**$_1$. Thus, $\Pr[b'_{\mathcal{A}lice} = b_{\mathcal{A}lice} | b_{\mathcal{B}ob} = 1] = \Pr[X_1]$. If $b_{\mathcal{B}ob} = 2$ then all steps are emulated perfectly for **Game**$_2$ and thus $\Pr[b'_{\mathcal{A}lice} = b_{\mathcal{A}lice} | b_{\mathcal{B}ob} = 2] = \Pr[X_2]$.

Thus, $\Pr[b'_{\mathcal{B}ob} = b_{\mathcal{B}ob}] = \frac{1}{2}\Pr[b'_{\mathcal{B}ob} = 1|b_{\mathcal{B}ob} = 1] + \frac{1}{2}\Pr[b'_{\mathcal{B}ob} = 2|b_{\mathcal{B}ob} = 2] = \frac{1}{2}\Pr[b'_{\mathcal{A}lice} = b_{\mathcal{A}lice}|b_{\mathcal{B}ob} = 1] + \frac{1}{2} - \frac{1}{2}\Pr[b'_{\mathcal{A}lice} = b_{\mathcal{A}lice}|b_{\mathcal{B}ob} = 2] = \frac{1}{2} + \frac{1}{2}(\Pr[X_1] - \Pr[X_2])$, and $|\Pr[X_1] - \Pr[X_2]| = |2\Pr[b'_{\mathcal{B}ob} = b_{\mathcal{B}ob}] - 1|$ is the advantage of $\mathcal{B}$ob distinguishing random DDH tuples and random non-DDH tuples of form $\{(g_1, g_2, \hat{u}_1, \hat{u}_2) : (g_1, g_2, \hat{u}_1) \leftarrow \mathbb{G}^3, \hat{u}_2 \leftarrow \mathbb{G} \setminus \{\hat{u}_1\}\}$. Thus,

$$|\Pr[X_1] - \Pr[X_2]| \leq \varepsilon_{\mathsf{ddh}} ,$$

where $\varepsilon_{\mathsf{ddh}}$ is the probability of breaking the DDH assumption, given resources comparable to the resources of the adversary.

Game$_3$

First, recall that $(\hat{u}_1, \hat{u}_2)$ is computed before the phase-1. Now, we let the decryption oracle to reject all ciphertexts (u_1, u_2) such that $(u_1, u_2) \neq (\hat{u}_1, \hat{u}_2)$ and (g_1, g_2, u_1, u_2) is not a DDH tuple. Here, F_3 is the event that such a ciphertext would have been accepted in **Game$_2$**. Clearly, $\Pr[F_3] \leq \gamma_1 \cdot \Pr[F'_3]$, where F'_3 is the event that such a ciphertext would have been accepted in a randomly chosen phase-1 query of **Game$_2$**, and γ_1 is again the number of queries in phase-1. We defer the computation of $\Pr[F'_3]$ to later games where it is substantially easier to do.

Complete description of **Game$_3$** is given in Fig. 1 (here we can explicitly use the value of w since we are done with a DDH reduction that had to compute w; the upcoming DDH reduction in **Game$_4$** computes something different). It also points out differences between **Game$_3$** and **Game$_4$**.

Game$_4$

In this game we change six lines as specified in Fig. 1. Let $\mathcal{A}$lice be an adversary in **Game$_4$** again. Because of the change on line **D05**, other changes are only decorative and do not change $\mathcal{A}$lice's view. Thus, let F'_4 be the event that during a randomly chosen phase-1 query of **Game$_3$**, the line **D08** is executed.

Consider a concrete phase-1 decryption query. Then

$$\log_{g_1} c = \alpha_1 + w\alpha_2 , \qquad (1)$$
$$\log_{g_1} v = r_1\alpha_1 + r_2 w\alpha_2 . \qquad (2)$$

Equations (1) and (2) are linearly independent and thus v can take on any value from $\mathbb{G}$, and thus is uniformly distributed over $\mathbb{G}$. Thus,

$$\Pr[F'_4] = \Pr[F'_3] .$$

Now we do a fork in the hopping. Games **Game$_5$** and **Game$_6$** bound $\Pr[X_4]$. Game **Game$'_5$** bounds $\Pr[F'_4]$.

Game$_5$

Game$_5$ is the same as **Game$_4$**, except that here we compute $(\hat{K}, \hat{\kappa}) \leftarrow$ "random keys". Because in **Game$_4$**, $\hat{v}$ is completely random, and is not used anywhere, except once as an input to kdf, then it is easy to see that

$$|\Pr[X_5] - \Pr[X_4]| \leq \varepsilon_{\mathsf{kdf}} ,$$

Setup. Fix $\mathbb{G}$, q, two random different generators $g_1, g_2 \in \mathbb{G}$ where $g_2 = g_1^w$ for a random $w \leftarrow \mathbb{Z}_q \setminus \{1\}$, sym, mac and kdf. The challenger does the following.
- **S01** $\alpha_1, \alpha_2 \leftarrow \mathbb{Z}_q$ $\underline{\underline{\alpha \leftarrow \mathbb{Z}_q}}$
- **S02** $\mathsf{sk} \leftarrow (\alpha_1, \alpha_2)$ $\underline{\underline{\mathsf{sk} \leftarrow \alpha}}$
- **S03** $\mathsf{pk} \leftarrow \underline{(c \leftarrow g_1^{\alpha_1} g_2^{\alpha_2})}$ $\underline{\underline{\mathsf{pk} \leftarrow (c \leftarrow g_1^{\alpha})}}$
- **S04** Send the public key pk to $\mathcal{A}$lice
- **S05** $\hat{r}_1 \leftarrow \mathbb{Z}_q, \hat{r}_2 \leftarrow \mathbb{Z}_q \setminus \{\hat{r}_1\}$
- **S06** $\hat{u}_1 \leftarrow g_1^{\hat{r}_1}, \hat{u}_2 \leftarrow g_2^{\hat{r}_2}$
- **S07** $\underline{\hat{v} \leftarrow \hat{u}_1^{\alpha_1} \hat{u}_2^{\alpha_2}}$ $\underline{\underline{\hat{v} \leftarrow \mathbb{G}}}$
- **S08** $(\hat{K}, \hat{\kappa}) \leftarrow \mathsf{kdf}(\hat{v})$

Query phase 1. $\mathcal{A}$lice adaptively issues decryption queries $(u_1, u_2, e, \mathsf{t})$. The challenger does the following.
- **D01** If $(u_1, u_2) = (\hat{u}_1, \hat{u}_2)$ then
- **D02**   If $\mathsf{mac.ver}(\hat{\kappa}; e, \mathsf{t}) = \bot$ then return $\bot$
- **D03**   Return $\mathsf{sym.dec}(\hat{K}; e)$
- **D04** else if $u_1^w \neq u_2$ then
- **D05** $\underline{v \leftarrow u_1^{\alpha_1} u_2^{\alpha_2}}$ $\underline{\underline{v \leftarrow \mathbb{G}}}$
- **D06** $(K, \kappa) \leftarrow \mathsf{kdf}(v)$
- **D07**   If $\mathsf{mac.ver}(\kappa; e, \mathsf{t}) = \bot$ then return $\bot$
- **D08**   Return $\bot$. // Event F_3: Difference between $\underline{\mathbf{Game}_2}/\underline{\mathbf{Game}_3}$
- **D09** else
- **D10** $\underline{v \leftarrow u_1^{\alpha_1} u_2^{\alpha_2}}$ $\underline{\underline{v \leftarrow u_1^{\alpha}}}$
- **D11** $(K, \kappa) \leftarrow \mathsf{kdf}(v)$
- **D12**   If $\mathsf{mac.ver}(\kappa; e, \mathsf{t}) = \bot$ then return $\bot$
- **D13**   Return $\mathsf{sym.dec}(K; e)$

Challenge phase. $\mathcal{A}$lice outputs two (equal length) messages $\hat{m}_0, \hat{m}_1$. The challenger picks a random $b_{\mathcal{A}\text{lice}} \leftarrow \{0, 1\}$. The challenger sets $\hat{e} \leftarrow \mathsf{sym.enc}(K; \hat{m}_{b_{\mathcal{A}\text{lice}}}, \hat{\rho})$, for uniform randomizer $\hat{\rho}$, and $\hat{\mathsf{t}} \leftarrow \mathsf{mac.tag}(\hat{\kappa}; \hat{e})$. It gives $\hat{C} \leftarrow (\hat{u}_1, \hat{u}_2, \hat{e}, \hat{\mathsf{t}})$ to $\mathcal{A}$lice.

Guess. $\mathcal{A}$lice outputs its guess $b'_{\mathcal{A}\text{lice}} \in \{0, 1\}$ for $b_{\mathcal{A}\text{lice}}$ and wins the game if $b_{\mathcal{A}\text{lice}} = b'_{\mathcal{A}\text{lice}}$.

Fig. 1. Games $\underline{\mathbf{Game}_3}$ and $\underline{\mathbf{Game}_4}$. Two games differ only in a few lines. In those lines, the part that is only executed in $\underline{\mathbf{Game}_3}$ has been underlined, while the part that is only executed in $\underline{\mathbf{Game}_4}$ has been underwaved.

where $\varepsilon_{\mathsf{kdf}}$ is the probability of distinguishing the output of kdf from completely random keys, using resources similar to the resources of the given adversary.

$\underline{\mathbf{Game}_6}$

$\underline{\mathbf{Game}_6}$ is the same as $\underline{\mathbf{Game}_5}$, except that we change the line **D03** to "return $\bot$". Let F_6 be the event that line **D03** is ever executed in $\underline{\mathbf{Game}_6}$ in any decryption request. If F_6 occurs then $\mathcal{A}$lice has broken the MAC keyed by $\hat{\kappa}$ (which in $\underline{\mathbf{Game}_6}$ is truly random). Thus, $\Pr[F_6] \leq \gamma \varepsilon_{\mathsf{mac}}$, where $\varepsilon_{\mathsf{mac}}$ is the advantage with which one can break the MAC using resources similar to those of $\mathcal{A}$lice. Then, clearly,

$$|\Pr[X_6] - \Pr[X_5]| \leq \Pr[F_6] \leq \gamma \varepsilon_{\mathsf{mac}} \ .$$

Observe that $\hat{K}$ is completely random and thus used for no other purpose than to encrypt $m_{b_{\mathcal{A}\text{lice}}}$. It is thus easy to see that

$$|\Pr[X_6] - 1/2| \leq \varepsilon_{\text{enc}} ,$$

where ε_{enc} is the probability of breaking the semantic security of sym, using resources comparable to the resources of the adversary.

Game$_{5'}$

Game$_{5'}$ is the same as **Game$_4$**, except that we change the line **D06** to $(K, \kappa) \leftarrow$ "random keys". Let $F'_{5'}$ be the event that line **D08** is executed in a randomly chosen decryption query of phase-1 in **Game$_{5'}$**. Because in **Game$_{5'}$**, in line **D05**, the value of v is completely random and not used anywhere, except once as an input to kdf, then it is easy to see that

$$|\Pr[F'_{5'}] - \Pr[F'_4]| \leq \varepsilon'_{\text{kdf}} ,$$

where $\varepsilon'_{\text{kdf}}$ is the advantage with which one can distinguish the output of kdf from a random key pair, using resources similar to those of the given adversary.

Now, in **Game$_{5'}$**, the key κ used in line **D07** is completely random. From this, it easily follows that

$$\Pr[F'_{5'}] \leq \varepsilon'_{\text{mac}} ,$$

where $\varepsilon'_{\text{kdf}}$ is the probability of breaking mac, using resources similar to those of the given adversary.

Completing The Proof

We have

$$\Pr[F_3] \leq \gamma_1 \Pr[F'_3] = \gamma_1 \Pr[F'_4] \leq \gamma_1 (\Pr[F'_{5'}] + \varepsilon'_{\text{kdf}}) \leq \gamma_1 (\varepsilon'_{\text{mac}} + \varepsilon'_{\text{kdf}}) .$$

Finally,

$$|\Pr[X_0] - 1/2| \leq \varepsilon_{\text{ddh}} + \varepsilon_{\text{kdf}} + \varepsilon_{\text{enc}} + \gamma_1 (\varepsilon_{\text{mac}} + \varepsilon'_{\text{mac}} + \varepsilon'_{\text{kdf}}) . \quad (3)$$

□

4 Why We Cannot Prove CCA2-Security

We will now briefly show why this proof technique cannot show that Hybrid Damgård is CCA2-secure in the standard model and "standard" assumptions from KDF, MAC and secret-key cryptosystem. Consider any phase-2 decryption query in **Game$_4$**. Let $\hat{v} := \hat{u}_1^{\alpha_1} \hat{u}_2^{\alpha_2}$. Then from $\mathcal{A}$lice's point of view, during a query of phase-2, (α_1, α_2) is a random point satisfying two linearly independent equations, Eq. (1) and the equation

$$\log_{g_1} \hat{v} = \hat{r}_1 \alpha_1 + \hat{r}_2 w \alpha_2 . \quad (4)$$

During an arbitrary query of phase-2, suppose that Alice queries an invalid ciphertext $(u_1, u_2, e, \mathsf{t})$ to the decryption oracle where $u_1 = g_1^{r_1}$ and $u_2 = g_2^{r_2}$ with $r_1 \neq r_2$. Thus also Eq. (2) holds. Now, Eq. (1), (2) and (4) are *not* linearly independent and thus we cannot claim as in the previous papers that the value v is uniform and random.

More precisely, to distinguish v from random, Alice participates in the next game. She first sees tuple

$$(g_1, g_2, c \leftarrow g_1^{\alpha_1} g_2^{\alpha_2}; \hat{u}_1 \leftarrow g_1^{\hat{r}_1}, \hat{u}_2 \leftarrow g_2^{\hat{r}_2}, \hat{v} \leftarrow g_1^{\hat{r}_1 \alpha_1} g_2^{\hat{r}_2 \alpha_2})$$

for randomly chosen $\alpha_1, \alpha_2, \hat{r}_1 \neq \hat{r}_2$. Second, she sends to challenger a tuple

$$u_1 \leftarrow g_1^{r_1}, u_2 \leftarrow g_2^{r_2} ,$$

for $r_1 \neq r_2$. Third, she gets back a value v such that either $v = u_1^{\alpha_1} u_2^{\alpha_2} = g_1^{r_1 \alpha_1} g_2^{r_2 \alpha_2}$ (if $b_{Alice} = 1$), or $v \leftarrow \mathbb{G}$ (if $b_{Alice} = 0$).

Clearly, we can assume that Alice knows the values r_1, r_2. Note that her task is equivalent to deciding whether $v/c^{r_1} = g_2^{(r_2-r_1)\alpha_2} = u_2^{r_2-r_1}$ or whether $v = c^{r_1} u_2^{r_2-r_1}$, which she can do trivially. Therefore, v is not pseudorandom.

Recently, [KPSY08] have given a CCA2-security proof of the Hybrid Damgård under a stronger assumption on the hash function.

Acknowledgments. Part of this work was done while the second and the third author were working at University College London. Yvo Desmedt is the BT Chair of Information Security and funded by EPSRC EP/C538285/1. Helger Lipmaa was supported by Estonian Science Foundation, grant #6848, European Union through the European Regional Development Fund and the 6th Framework Programme project AEOLUS (FP6-IST-15964).

References

[ABR01] Abdalla, M., Bellare, M., Rogaway, P.: The Oracle Diffie-Hellman Assumptions And An Analysis of DHIES. In: Naccache, D. (ed.) CT-RSA 2001. LNCS, vol. 2020, pp. 143–158. Springer, Heidelberg (2001)

[BP04]   Bellare, M., Palacio, A.: Towards Plaintext-Aware Public-Key Encryption Without Random Oracles. In: Lee, P.J. (ed.) ASIACRYPT 2004. LNCS, vol. 3329, pp. 48–62. Springer, Heidelberg (2004)

[CS98]   Cramer, R., Shoup, V.: A Practical Public Key Cryptosystem Provably Secure against Adaptive Chosen Ciphertext Attack. In: Krawczyk, H. (ed.) CRYPTO 1998. LNCS, vol. 1462, pp. 13–25. Springer, Heidelberg (1998)

[CS04]   Cramer, R., Shoup, V.: Design And Analysis of Practical Public-Key Encryption Schemes Secure against Adaptive Chosen Ciphertext Attack. SIAM Journal of Computing 33(1), 167–226 (2004)

[Dam91] Damgård, I.: Towards Practical Public Key Systems Secure against Chosen Ciphertext Attacks. In: Feigenbaum, J. (ed.) CRYPTO 1991. LNCS, vol. 576, pp. 445–456. Springer, Heidelberg (1992)

[DP08]   Desmedt, Y., Phan, D.H.: A CCA Secure Hybrid Damgård's ElGamal Encryption. In: Bao, F., Chen, K. (eds.) ProvSec 2008. LNCS, vol. 5324. Springer, Heidelberg (2008)

[Elg85]   Elgamal, T.: A Public Key Cryptosystem And A Signature Scheme Based on Discrete Logarithms. IEEE Transactions on Information Theory 31(4), 469–472 (1985)
[Gjø06]   Gjøsteen, K.: A New Security Proof for Damgård's ElGamal. In: Pointcheval, D. (ed.) CT-RSA 2006. LNCS, vol. 3860, pp. 150–158. Springer, Heidelberg (2006)
[GS04]   Gennaro, R., Shoup, V.: A Note on An Encryption Scheme of Kurosawa And Desmedt. Technical Report 2004/194, International Association for Cryptologic Research (August 10, 2004) (last revision May 18, 2005),
http://eprint.iacr.org/2004/194
[HK07]   Hofheinz, D., Kiltz, E.: Secure Hybrid Encryption from Weakened Key Encapsulation. In: Menezes, A. (ed.) CRYPTO 2007. LNCS, vol. 4622, pp. 553–571. Springer, Heidelberg (2007)
[KD04]   Kurosawa, K., Desmedt, Y.: A New Paradigm of Hybrid Encryption Scheme. In: Franklin, M.K. (ed.) CRYPTO 2004. LNCS, vol. 3152, pp. 426–442. Springer, Heidelberg (2004)
[KPSY08]   Kiltz, E., Pietrzak, K., Stam, M., Yung, M.: A New Randomness Extraction Paradigm for Hybrid Encryption. Technical Report 2008/304, International Association for Cryptologic Research (October 2008),
http://eprint.iacr.org/2008/304
[Lip08]   Lipmaa, H.: On CCA1-Security of Elgamal And Damgård Cryptosystems. Technical Report 2008/234, International Association for Cryptologic Research (October 2008), http://eprint.iacr.org/2008/234
[Sho00]   Shoup, V.: Using Hash Functions as A Hedge against Chosen Ciphertext Attack. In: Preneel, B. (ed.) EUROCRYPT 2000. LNCS, vol. 1807, pp. 275–288. Springer, Heidelberg (2000)

A Some Known Public-Key Cryptosystems

Cramer-Shoup Cryptosystem from [CS98]

Setup: On input the security parameter λ, return a λ-bit prime q, a group $\mathbb{G}$ of order q, and a universal one-way family $\mathcal{UOWHF}$ of hash functions.

Key Setup pub.gen: Let $(g_1, g_2) \in \mathbb{G}^2$ be two random generators, let $(\alpha_1, \alpha_2, \beta_1, \beta_2, \gamma) \leftarrow \mathbb{Z}_q^5$. Compute $c \leftarrow g_1^{\alpha_1} g_2^{\alpha_2}$, $d \leftarrow g_1^{\beta_1} g_2^{\beta_2}$, $h \leftarrow g_1^{\gamma}$. Choose uowhf $\leftarrow \mathcal{UOWHF}$. The public key is pk $\leftarrow (g_1, g_2, c, d, h, \text{uowhf})$, the private key is sk $\leftarrow (\alpha_1, \alpha_2, \beta_1, \beta_2, \gamma)$.

Encryption pub.enc: Given a message $m \in \mathbb{G}$, do the following. First, set $r \leftarrow \mathbb{Z}_q$ and then $u_1 \leftarrow g_1^r$, $u_2 \leftarrow g_2^r$, $e \leftarrow m \cdot h^r$, $v \leftarrow (cd^{\text{uowhf}(u_1, u_2, e)})^r$. The ciphertext is (u_1, u_2, e, v).

Decryption pub.dec: Given a ciphertext (u_1, u_2, e, v), do the following. Set $k \leftarrow \text{uowhf}(u_1, u_2, e)$. If $u_1^{\alpha_1 + \beta_1 k} u_2^{\alpha_1 + \beta_1 k} \neq v$ then output $m \leftarrow \bot$. Otherwise, compute $m \leftarrow e/u_1^{\gamma}$ and return m.

Cramer-Shoup Lite Cryptosystem from [CS98, Sect. 5.4]

Setup: On input the security parameter λ, return a λ-bit prime q, a group $\mathbb{G}$ of order q.

Key Setup pub.gen: Let $(g_1, g_2) \in \mathbb{G}^2$ be two random generators, let $(\alpha_1, \alpha_2, \gamma) \leftarrow \mathbb{Z}_q^3$. Compute $c \leftarrow g_1^{\alpha_1} g_2^{\alpha_2}$, $h \leftarrow g_1^{\gamma}$. The public key is pk $\leftarrow (g_1, g_2, c, h)$, the private key is sk $\leftarrow (\alpha_1, \alpha_2, \gamma)$.

Encryption pub.enc: Given a message $m \in \mathbb{G}$, do the following. First, set $r \leftarrow \mathbb{Z}_q$ and then $u_1 \leftarrow g_1^r$, $u_2 \leftarrow g_2^r$, $e \leftarrow m \cdot h^r$, $v \leftarrow c^r$. The ciphertext is (u_1, u_2, e, v).

Decryption pub.dec: Given a ciphertext (u_1, u_2, e, v), do the following. If $u_1^{\alpha_1} u_2^{\alpha_1} \neq v$ then output $m \leftarrow \bot$. Otherwise, compute $m \leftarrow e/u_1^\gamma$ and return m.

Shoup Hybrid Cryptosystem from [Sho00]

Setup: On input the security parameter λ, return a λ-bit prime q, a group $\mathbb{G}$ of order q, and a universal one-way family $\mathcal{UOWHF}$ of hash functions.

Key Setup pub.gen: Generate a random generator $g_1 \leftarrow \mathbb{G}$, and $(w, \alpha, \beta, \gamma) \leftarrow \mathbb{Z}_q^4$. Compute $g_2 \leftarrow g_1^w$, $c \leftarrow g_1^\alpha$, $d \leftarrow g_1^\beta$, $h \leftarrow g_1^\gamma$. Choose uowhf $\leftarrow \mathcal{UOWHF}$. The public key is pk $\leftarrow (g_1, g_2, c, d, h, \text{uowhf})$, the private key is sk $\leftarrow (w, \alpha, \beta, \gamma)$.

Encryption pub.enc: Given a message $m \in \{0,1\}^*$, do the following. First, set $r \leftarrow \mathbb{Z}_q$ and then $u_1 \leftarrow g_1^r$, $u_2 \leftarrow g_2^r$, $(K, \kappa) \leftarrow \text{kdf}(h^r)$, $e \leftarrow \text{sym.enc}(K; m, \rho)$ for uniform randomizer ρ, $\text{t} \leftarrow \text{mac.tag}(\kappa; e)$, $v \leftarrow (cd^{\text{uowhf}(u_1, u_2)})^r$. The ciphertext is $(u_1, u_2, v, e, \text{t})$.

Decryption pub.dec: Given a ciphertext $(u_1, u_2, v, e, \text{t})$, do the following. Set $k \leftarrow \text{uowhf}(u_1, u_2)$, $(K, \kappa) \leftarrow \text{kdf}(u_1^\gamma)$. If $\text{mac.ver}(\kappa; e, \text{t}) = \bot$ or $u_1^{\alpha + \beta k} \neq v$ or $u_2 \neq u_1^w$ then output $m \leftarrow \bot$. Otherwise, compute $m \leftarrow \text{sym.dec}(K; e)$ and return m.

DHIES Cryptosystem from [ABR01]. The DHIES cryptosystem is very simple but relies on a nonstandard assumption that was called "oracle-DDH" in [ABR01]. Briefly, it is assumed that one cannot distinguish tuples $(g^u, g^v, \mathsf{h}(g^{uv}))$ and (g^u, g^v, r) for random group elements $u, v \leftarrow \mathbb{Z}_q$ and a random string r, even if given access to an oracle that on any input $x \neq g^u$ computes $\mathsf{h}(x^v)$.

Setup: On input the security parameter λ, return a λ-bit prime q, a group $\mathbb{G}$ of order q, and its randomly chosen generator $g \in \mathbb{G}$. Choose a CPA-secure symmetric cryptosystem sym = (sym.gen, sym.enc, sym.dec), a secure MAC mac = (mac.tag, mac.ver), and a hash function family $\mathcal{H}$ from $\mathbb{G}^2$ to the set of keys of sym and mac.

Key Setup pub.gen: Choose a hash function $\mathsf{h} \leftarrow \mathcal{H}$. Generate $\alpha \leftarrow \mathbb{Z}_q$. Set sk $\leftarrow \alpha$ and pk $\leftarrow (c \leftarrow g^\alpha, \mathsf{h})$.

Encryption pub.enc: Given a message $m \in \{0,1\}^*$, do the following. First, set $r \leftarrow \mathbb{Z}_q$ and then $u \leftarrow g^r$, $(K, \kappa) \leftarrow \mathsf{h}(c^r)$, $e \leftarrow \text{sym.enc}(K; m, \rho)$ for uniform randomizer ρ, $\text{t} \leftarrow \text{mac.tag}(\kappa; e)$. The ciphertext is (u, e, t).

Decryption pub.dec: Given a ciphertext (u, e, t), do the following. Compute $(K, \kappa) \leftarrow \mathsf{h}(u^\alpha)$. If $\text{mac.ver}(\kappa; e, \text{t}) = \bot$ then return $m \leftarrow \bot$ else return $m \leftarrow \text{sym.dec}(K; e)$.

Kurosawa-Desmedt Hybrid Cryptosystem from [KD04]. We give a description due to [GS04] that differs from the original description from [KD04] in two aspects. It replaces the original (information-theoretically) rejection-secure CCA2-secure sym of [KD04] with a CPA-secure sym and a (computationally) secure mac = (mac.tag, mac.ver). It also allows to use a computationally secure KDF.

Setup: On input the security parameter λ, return a λ-bit prime q, a group $\mathbb{G}$ of order q, and its two randomly chosen different generators $g_1, g_2 \in \mathbb{G}$. Choose a CPA-secure symmetric cryptosystem sym = (sym.gen, sym.enc, sym.dec), a secure MAC mac = (mac.tag, mac.ver), a KDF kdf from $\mathbb{G}$ to the set of keys of (sym, mac), and a target-collision-resistant function family $\mathcal{TCR} : \mathbb{G}^2 \to \mathbb{Z}_q$.

Key Setup pub.gen: Choose a hash function tcr $\leftarrow \mathcal{TCR}$. Generate $(\alpha_1, \alpha_2, \beta_1, \beta_2) \leftarrow \mathbb{Z}_q^4$. Set sk $\leftarrow (\alpha_1, \alpha_2, \beta_1, \beta_2)$ and pk $\leftarrow (c \leftarrow g_1^{\alpha_1} g_2^{\alpha_2}, d \leftarrow g_1^{\beta_1} g_2^{\beta_2}, \text{tcr})$.

Encryption pub.enc: Given a message $m \in \{0,1\}^*$, do the following. First, set $r \leftarrow \mathbb{Z}_q$ and then $u_1 \leftarrow g_1^r$, $u_2 \leftarrow g_2^r$, $(K, \kappa) \leftarrow \text{kdf}\left((cd^{\text{tcr}(u_1, u_2)})^r\right)$, $e \leftarrow \text{sym.enc}(K; m, \rho)$ for uniform randomizer ρ, t $\leftarrow \text{mac.tag}(\kappa; e)$. The ciphertext is (u_1, u_2, e, t).

Decryption pub.dec: Given a ciphertext (u_1, u_2, e, t), do the following. Compute $k \leftarrow \text{tcr}(u_1, u_2)$, $(K, \kappa) \leftarrow \text{kdf}(u_1^{\alpha_1 + \beta_1 k} u_2^{\alpha_2 + \beta_2 k})$. If mac.ver$(\kappa; e, \text{t}) = \bot$ then return $m \leftarrow \bot$ else return $m \leftarrow \text{sym.dec}(K; e)$.

Hofheinz-Kiltz DDH-Based Cryptosystem. In [HK07, Sect. 4.2], the authors proposed the next DDH-based cryptosystem.

Setup: On input the security parameter λ, return a λ-bit prime q, a group $\mathbb{G}$ of order q, and its randomly chosen generator $g \in \mathbb{G}$. Choose a CCA2-secure symmetric cryptosystem sym = (sym.gen, sym.enc, sym.dec), a KDF kdf from $\mathbb{G}$ to the set of keys of (sym, mac), and a target-collision-resistant function family $\mathcal{TCR} : \mathbb{G} \to \mathbb{Z}_q$.

Key Setup pub.gen: Choose a hash function tcr $\leftarrow \mathcal{TCR}$. Generate $(\alpha_1, \alpha_2, \beta) \leftarrow \mathbb{Z}_q^3$. Set sk $\leftarrow (\alpha_1, \alpha_2, \beta)$ and pk $\leftarrow (c \leftarrow g^{\alpha_1}, d \leftarrow g^{\alpha_2}, h \leftarrow g^\beta, \text{tcr})$.

Encryption pub.enc: Given a message $m \in \{0,1\}^*$, do the following. First, set $r \leftarrow \mathbb{Z}_q$ and then $u_1 \leftarrow g^r$, $u_2 \leftarrow (c^{\text{tcr}(u_1)} \cdot d)^r$, $K \leftarrow \text{kdf}(h^r)$, $e \leftarrow \text{sym.enc}(K; m, \rho)$ for uniform randomizer ρ. The ciphertext is (u_1, u_2, e).

Decryption pub.dec: Given a ciphertext (u_1, u_2, e), do the following. If $u_1 \notin \mathbb{G}$ or $u_1^{\alpha_1 \cdot \text{tcr}(u_1) + \alpha_2} \neq u_2$ then return $\bot$. Compute $K \leftarrow \text{kdf}(u_1^\beta)$. Return $m \leftarrow \text{sym.dec}(K; e)$, possibly $m = \bot$.

Efficient Dynamic Broadcast Encryption and Its Extension to Authenticated Dynamic Broadcast Encryption

Masafumi Kusakawa, Harunaga Hiwatari, Tomoyuki Asano, and Seiichi Matsuda

Sony Corporation. 5-1-12 Kitashinagawa, Shinagawa-ku, Tokyo, 141-0001, Japan
{Masafumi.Kusakawa,Harunaga.Hiwatari,Tomoyuki.Asano,
SeiichiA.Matsuda}@jp.sony.com

Abstract. We propose two public-key broadcast encryption schemes. Our **Scheme1** is a variant of the dynamic broadcast encryption scheme proposed by Delerablée et al. [9]. The computational cost and the encryption (public) key size are more efficient than the original scheme. We observe that by using a decryption key in the original scheme, we can encrypt a message more efficiently without a part of an encryption key. In order to let any user receive this benefit, we introduce a "dummy key" which is similar to a decryption key. **Scheme2** is an extension of **Scheme1** to achieve an authenticated dynamic broadcast encryption scheme that enables receivers to verify the producer of broadcasted content. In **Scheme2**, we adopt the signature scheme proposed by Barreto et al. [3]. To our knowledge, **Scheme2** is the first scheme that achieves provable security for broadcast encryption and signature with common parameters and keys.

1 Introduction

Background. Broadcast encryption (BE), introduced by Berkovits [4] and Fiat and Naor [11] independently, is a technology which allows a sender to broadcast a content efficiently and securely to unrevoked users. In a BE system, an authority generates decryption keys for each user, and distributes them beforehand via secure channel. The sender encrypts a content with a session key and broadcasts it with a header containing information that allows unrevoked users to decrypt the session key. An unrevoked user decrypts the header with her/his decryption key and the ciphertext with the obtained session key.

BE schemes can be roughly classified into two types. One is symmetric-key setting [1,2,11,16] in which the sender and each user need to share secret keys in advance. The other is public-key setting [7,8,9,10,17,19] in which the sender can broadcast a content by using only public information. We call this type "public-key BE". The schemes classified into the former have a restriction that only a trusted party such as an authority can be a sender, however, the computational cost is small. These schemes are suitable for a content delivery system using physical media such as DVDs. On the other hand, public-key BE schemes have a disadvantage that the computational cost is large, however any entity can be a sender. Therefore, they are considered to be suitable for the situation where it is difficult for a sender and receivers to share secret keys in advance. In this paper, we focus on public-key BE schemes.

For evaluation of these schemes, there are important criteria: encryption key (ek) size, decryption key (dk) size, header (hdr) size, encryption cost, and decryption cost. The ek and dk size are the size of information that each device needs to possess in the memory for encryption and decryption, respectively. The hdr size affects the size of physical media or bandwidth of network. The encryption and decryption cost are the computational cost for each device to compute a header and session key, respectively.

Related Work. Boneh, Gentry, and Waters proposed a bilinear map based scheme (BGW05) [7]. This is the first scheme to achieve constant hdr size regardless of the number of revoked users and fully collusion resistant that means the scheme is secure against a collusion of all users. In this scheme, ek, dk, and hdr size for total users n are $O(n)$, $O(n)$,[1] and $O(1)$, respectively. The encryption and decryption cost depend on the number of unrevoked users.

Delerablée, Paillier, and Pointcheval proposed another fully collusion resistant scheme (DPP07) [9], where users can join the system after the setup phase. They call it a dynamic broadcast encryption scheme. Its ek, dk, and hdr size are $O(n)$, $O(1)$, and $O(r)$, and the encryption and decryption cost are $O(r^2)$ and $O(r)$, respectively, where r denotes the number of revoked users.

Sakai and Furukawa proposed an identity based broadcast encryption scheme (SF07) [19], where a sender does not have to know uniquely assigned values for each user, while ek, dk, and hdr size are the same as BGW05. Delerablée proposed a similar scheme (D07) [8] in which ek, dk, and hdr size are respectively $O(m), O(m)$, and $O(\lceil n/m \rceil)$ where m is the system parameter.

In public-key BE, any sender can broadcast a content without being identified. Let us consider the case where a content is software or firmware used to update some devices. In such a case, it is important for recipients to verify that the content is generated by a specified entity and unchanged in transit, in order to avoid malicious software which may act harmfully to the recipient or device.

We can use an independent signature scheme to assure the integrity and the authenticity of contents. However, it requires the user devices to prepare another memory space for the verification key and parameters. Hence, it is preferred that a scheme realizes both functions of a public-key BE and a signature with common parameters and keys. Kanazawa, Ohkawa, Doi, Okamoto, and Okamoto proposed a scheme (KODOO07) which realizes these properties with common parameters and keys [13]. In this scheme, they applied Schnorr's signature scheme [20] to BGW05 by adding n elements to the encryption key. However, its security analysis is heuristic and insufficient.

---

[1] In BGW05, since each receiver needs to possess a part of the encryption key for decryption, dk size becomes $O(n)$.

Table 1. Comparison of public-key BE schemes for ek, dk, and hdr size

	ek size			dk size ($\mathbb{G}_1, \mathbb{G}_2$)		hdr size	authenticated
	$\mathbb{G}_1, \mathbb{G}_2$	$\mathbb{G}_T$	$\mathbb{Z}_p^*$	secret	public[a]	$\mathbb{G}_1, \mathbb{G}_2, \mathbb{Z}_p^*$	BE?
BGW05 (Special case)	$2n+1$	0	0	1	$2n$	2	no
BGW05 (General case)	$2\sqrt{n}$	0	0	1	$2\sqrt{n}-2$	2	no
KODOO07 [13][b]	$3n+1$	0	0	1	$3n$	4	yes
DPP07 [9]	$n+2$	$n+1$	n	1	2	$2r+2$	no
SF07 [19]	$2n+2$	0	0	1	n	2	no
D07 ($m=n$) [8]	$n+2$	1	0	1	n	2	no
Scheme1 (Ours)	$n+4$	0	$n+1$	1	2	$2r+2$	no
Scheme2 (Ours)	$n+2$	0	n	1	2	$2r+5$	yes

[a] "Public" means the necessary information for decryption although it does not have to be kept in a secret manner.
[b] The security proof of this scheme is not sufficient.

Note that Mu, Susilo, Lin, and Ruan proposed an authenticated broadcast encryption scheme [15] and Li, Xin, and Hu proposed a scheme which they called "Identity-based broadcast signcryption"[14]. In these schemes however, any sender needs to share a secret key with each user. Therefore, we do not consider that they are included in public-key BE schemes.

Our Contribution. In this paper, we improve DPP07 and propose two schemes. Our Scheme1 reduces ek size and encryption cost, and Scheme2 is an authenticated public-key BE scheme with common parameters and keys based on Scheme1. We show the comparison of previously proposed public-key BE schemes and ours in Table 1.

Let $e : \mathbb{G}_1 \times \mathbb{G}_2 \to \mathbb{G}_T$ be a bilinear map. The bit size of elements in $\mathbb{G}_T$ is usually larger than $\mathbb{G}_1$ and $\mathbb{G}_2$. In DPP07, the published encryption key ek contains n elements over $\mathbb{G}_T$. On the other hand, Scheme1 uses the sender's decryption key instead of these elements and hence we can remove them. It also reduces the computational cost over $\mathbb{G}_T$ from $O(r^2)$ to $O(1)$. However, this applies only senders who have a decryption key. For senders who do not have a decryption key, we publish a dummy decryption key. It enables an arbitrary entity to take the above benefit. Consequently, Scheme1 reduces ek size and encryption cost compared with DPP07.

In Scheme2, we apply the signature scheme proposed by Barreto, Libert, McCullagh, and Quisquater [3] to Scheme1. It realizes the authenticated public-key BE scheme with common parameters and keys for both functions of confidentiality and authenticity.

The message confidentiality of our schemes is based on the general Diffie-Hellman exponent (GDDHE) problem [6] introduced by Boneh, Boyen, and Goh, in the generic model. The signature unforgeability of Scheme2 is proved by using $(t+1, n)$-strong Diffie-Hellman (SDH) problem, which is a generalization of q-SDH problem [5]. We consider that Scheme2 is the first scheme that achieves provably secure authenticated dynamic broadcast encryption.

2 Efficient Dynamic Broadcast Encryption (DBE)

In this section, we briefly review properties of bilinear maps at first, then we propose an efficient dynamic broadcast encryption scheme (Scheme1), where we adapt two modifications to DPP07. As a result, we can reduce encryption cost and eliminate n elements of the encryption key (ek). The first trick changes the way to compute an intermediate value over $\mathbb{G}_T$ which is used to derive a session key in encryption algorithm. In DPP07, it is computed by using Aggregate algorithm [9] over $\mathbb{G}_T$ using $V_i \in \mathbb{G}_T$ $(i = 1, \ldots, n)$ in ek. In Scheme1 however, it is computed by using the decryption key of the sender. It makes the V_is unnecessary in Scheme1, and also makes computational cost over $\mathbb{G}_T$ constant regardless of the number of revoked users.

Since the above modification requires a decryption key for encryption, only senders possessing a decryption key can obtain the benefit. For senders without possessing a decryption key, we introduce the second modification by publishing a dummy decryption key (we call it merely "dummy key"). This enables anyone to compute the intermediate value over $\mathbb{G}_T$ without V_is, and consequently, we can remove them from the encryption key.

2.1 Bilinear Maps

Let $\mathbb{G}_1, \mathbb{G}_2$, and $\mathbb{G}_T$ be cyclic groups of prime order p, we follow the notation of bilinear map [7,9]. Here, $\mathbb{G}_1$ and $\mathbb{G}_2$ are additive groups, and $\mathbb{G}_T$ is a multiplicative group. Let $G \in \mathbb{G}_1$ and $H \in \mathbb{G}_2$ be the generators. For all $P \in \mathbb{G}_1$ and $Q \in \mathbb{G}_2$, a bilinear map is a map $e : \mathbb{G}_1 \times \mathbb{G}_2 \to \mathbb{G}_T$ with the following properties, (1) BilinearityFFor all $a, b \in \mathbb{Z}_p$, we have $e(aP, bQ) = e(P, Q)^{ab}$ and (2) Non-degeneracyF$e(G, H) \neq 1$.

2.2 Definition of Dynamic Broadcast Encryption

We follow the definition of DBE given by Delerablée et al. [9]. There is a key generation center (KGC) as an authority. It creates and publishes a system parameter params and an initial encryption key ek using Setup algorithm. It keeps mk secret, and publishes params and ek. Note that all of the following algorithms use params and we omit the notation about it for simplicity. The KGC executes Join algorithm when a user i joins the system. It sends a decryption key dk_i to the user via secure channel and replaces ek by the updated one. In order to broadcast a content M, a sender encrypts M with the session key K obtained with Encrypt algorithem to generate a ciphertext C and broadcasts (hdr, C). To obtain M, an unrevoked user j decrypts C with K derived by Decrypt alogrithm.

Setup(λ): Takes as input a security parameter λ, this algorithm outputs a master key mk, a set of system parameters params, and an encryption key ek.

Join(i, ek, mk): Takes as input a user counter i, the encryption key ek, and the master key mk. This algorithm outputs a decryption key dk_i for the user i and an updated encryption key ek.

Encrypt(ek, $\mathcal{R}$): Takes as input the encryption key ek and a set of uniquely assigned values for revoked users $\mathcal{R} = \{u_{\mathcal{R}_1}, \ldots, u_{\mathcal{R}_r}\}$ where r is the number of revoked users. This algorithm outputs a header hdr and a session key $K \in \mathcal{KS}$, where $\mathcal{KS}$ denotes the space of session keys.

Decrypt(hdr, dk_j): Takes as input a header hdr and the decryption key dk_j. This algorithm outputs the session key K if the user j is not revoked, otherwise a symbol $\perp$.

2.3 Scheme1

Our Scheme1 is an improvement of a DBE scheme which we call DPP07 proposed by Delerablée et al. [9]. It consists of four algorithms, {Setup, Join, Encrypt, Decrypt} as described below. Note that, Aggregate and Decrypt algorithms (including Aggregate' algorithm) are the same as in DPP07. It should be also noted that {Join, Encrypt, Decrypt} algorithms use params generated by Setup algorithm and we omit the notation about it for simplicity.

Setup(λ): Takes as input a security parameter λ, this algorithm chooses a λ-bit prime p, selects cyclic groups $(\mathbb{G}_1, \mathbb{G}_2, \mathbb{G}_T)$ of order p and a bilinear map $e : \mathbb{G}_1 \times \mathbb{G}_2 \to \mathbb{G}_T$, and sets a set of system parameters params $= (p, \mathbb{G}_1, \mathbb{G}_2, \mathbb{G}_T, e)$. It also selects two random generators $G \in \mathbb{G}_1, H \in \mathbb{G}_2$ and a secret value $\gamma \in_R \mathbb{Z}_p^*$. The master key is $\mathsf{mk} = (\gamma, G)$. $W = \gamma G \in \mathbb{G}_1$ is computed using the master key. Next, it chooses an unique value $u_0 \in_R \mathbb{Z}_p^* \setminus \{-\gamma\}$ for a dummy user and computes a dummy key $\mathsf{dk}_0 = \left(u_0, A_0 = \frac{1}{\gamma + u_0} G \in \mathbb{G}_1, H_0 = \frac{1}{\gamma + u_0} H \in \mathbb{G}_2\right)$. Finally, it initializes encryption key $\mathsf{ek} = (W, H, H_0, u_0, A_0)$. The algorithm outputs (params, mk, ek).

Join(i, ek, mk): Takes as input a user counter i, the encryption key ek, and the master key mk, this algorithm chooses an unique value $u_i \in_R \mathbb{Z}_p^* \setminus \{-\gamma\}$ for user i, computes $A_i = \frac{u_i}{\gamma + u_i} G \in \mathbb{G}_1, B_i = \frac{1}{\gamma + u_i} H_0 \in \mathbb{G}_2$, and sets user i's decryption key $\mathsf{dk}_i = (u_i, A_i, B_i)$. Then it updates the encryption key as $\mathsf{ek} = \mathsf{ek} \cup \{(u_i, B_i)\}$, and outputs the updated ek and dk_i. Note that user i does not have to keep (u_i, B_i) in a secret manner.

Encrypt(ek, $\mathcal{R}$): Takes as input the encryption key ek and the set of uniquely assigned values for revoked users $\mathcal{R} = \{u_{\mathcal{R}_1}, \ldots, u_{\mathcal{R}_r}\}$, the algorithm chooses $k \in_R \mathbb{Z}_p^*$. We define $h_0(\gamma) = \gamma + u_0$, $h_l(\gamma) = \prod_{i=1}^{l}(\gamma + u_{\mathcal{R}_i})$, $P_0 = H_0 \in \mathbb{G}_2$, and $P_l = \frac{1}{h_l(\gamma)} H_0 \in \mathbb{G}_2$ for $l = 1, \ldots, r$ at first.
- If $r = 0$, the algorithm computes $K' = e(A_0, H) \in \mathbb{G}_T$.
- Otherwise, it computes $P_l(l = 1, \ldots, r)$ using Aggregate algorithm [9] which we describe below. Then, the Encrypt algorithm derives $\gamma P_r = P_{r-1} - u_{\mathcal{R}_r} P_r \in \mathbb{G}_2$ and $K' = e(A_0, \gamma P_r + u_0 P_r) = e(G, H_0)^{\frac{1}{h_r(\gamma)}} \in \mathbb{G}_T$. After that, it also computes the session key $K = (K')^k \in \mathbb{G}_T$ and sets a header as $\mathsf{hdr} = (kW, kP_r, (u_{\mathcal{R}_1}, P_1), \ldots, (u_{\mathcal{R}_r}, P_r))$. The output of this algorithm is (hdr, K).

Aggregate$((u_{\mathcal{R}_1}, B_{\mathcal{R}_1}), \ldots, (u_{\mathcal{R}_r}, B_{\mathcal{R}_r}))$ [9]: Let $P_{0,l} = B_{\mathcal{R}_l}(l = 1, \ldots r)$. For all (j, l) such that $j = 1, \ldots, r-1$ and $l = j+1, \ldots, r$, this algorithm computes $P_{j,l} = \frac{1}{u_j - u_l}(P_{j-1,j} - P_{j-1,l}) \in \mathbb{G}_2$, and outputs $P_r = P_{r-1,r}$.

Decrypt$(\mathsf{hdr}, \mathsf{dk}_j)$ [9]: If the header hdr contains the unique value u_j assigned for user j then the algorithm outputs $\bot$ and terminates the procedure.
 - If $r = 0$, the algorithm sets $B_{j,\mathcal{R}} = B_j \in \mathbb{G}_2$.
 - Otherwise, it executes Aggregate' algorithm [9] which we describe below as $B_{j,\mathcal{R}} \leftarrow$ Aggregate'$(u_j, B_j, (u_{\mathcal{R}_1}, P_1), \ldots, (u_{\mathcal{R}_r}, P_r)) = \frac{1}{h_r(\gamma)} B_j = \frac{1}{(\gamma + u_j) h_r(\gamma)} H_0 \in \mathbb{G}_2$.

The algorithm computes the session key $K = e(kW, B_{j,\mathcal{R}}) \cdot e(A_j, kP_r) \in \mathbb{G}_T$ and outputs it.

Aggregate'$(u_j, B_j, (u_{\mathcal{R}_1}, P_1), \ldots, (u_{\mathcal{R}_r}, P_r))$[9]: At first, the algorithm initializes $tmp = B_j$. For $i = 1$ to r, it computes $tmp = \frac{1}{u_j - u_{\mathcal{R}_i}}(P_i - tmp) \in \mathbb{G}_2$ and increments i. Finally it outputs tmp as $B_{j,\mathcal{R}}$.

Correctness. In Scheme1, the output of Encrypt algorithm, namely the session key K, is the same as DPP07. Decrypt algorithm (including Aggregate' algorithm) is also the same. Hence the correctness of K holds as well as DPP07.

Relationship Between DPP07 *and* Scheme1. We describe the differences of algorithms between DPP07 and Scheme1.

Setup: In Scheme1 the algorithm generates a dummy key $\mathsf{dk}_0 = (u_0, A_0, B_0 = H_0)$ and publishes it, while in DPP07 does not. Due to the dummy key, an arbitrary entity can compute a session key K efficiently without n elements V_i ($i = 1, \ldots, n$) in the encryption key. However, publishing dk_0 enables any entity to decrypt an arbitrary header even if she/he does not have a decryption key. To avoid this, the dummy user corresponding to dk_0 is always revoked by the long-term revocation [9] mechanism, namely introducing $H_0 = \frac{1}{\gamma + u_0} H$ instead of H itself.

Join: In DPP07, the encryption key ek contains $V_i \in \mathbb{G}_T$ ($i = 1, \ldots, n$), and V_is corresponding to the revoked users are used for computing the session key K in Encrypt algorithm. On the other hand, our modification to Encrypt algorithm makes these elements unnecessary in Scheme1, and hence the total size of ek becomes smaller than DPP07 by an additive factor of n.

Encrypt: The main difference is the way to generate K'. In DPP07, the algorithm computes $P_l(l = 1, \ldots, r)$ by executing Aggregate algorithm [9] over $\mathbb{G}_2$, then computes $K' = e(G, H)^{\frac{1}{h_r(\gamma)}}$ by executing the same algorithm over $\mathbb{G}_T$ with the revoked user's V_i. It requires a sender to compute $O(r^2)$ calculation over $\mathbb{G}_2$ for P_ls and $O(r^2)$ calculation over $\mathbb{G}_T$ for K'.

In Scheme1, the algorithm also executes Aggregate algorithm to compute $P_l(l = 1, \ldots, r)$ and its computational cost over $\mathbb{G}_2$ is the same as DPP07. However, it derives γP_r from P_r and P_{r-1}, and computes $K' = e(A_0, \gamma P_r + u_0 P_r)$ by using γP_r and A_0 contained in dk_0. The cost to derive K' becomes one time execution of the bilinear map e and two additions and multiplications over $\mathbb{G}_2$, respectively. Hence we reduce $O(r^2)$ computation over $\mathbb{G}_T$ to constant overhead regardless of the number of revoked users r.

2.4 Security Analysis

In this section, we define the security model for a DBE scheme and a problem which is included in the GDDHE framework [6], then we show the difficulty to solve it. Finally we give a reduction from the security of Scheme1 to the problem.

Security Model. We define chosen ciphertext security of a DBE scheme against a static adversary.

Definition 1. *The chosen ciphertext security against a static adversary of a DBE scheme is defined using the following game between adversary $\mathcal{A}$ and challenger $\mathcal{B}$. In the following game, t, n, and q_D denote the number of decryption keys that the adversary $\mathcal{A}$ can obtain, the number of total users, and the number of decryption queries, respectively. For any probabilistic polynomial time adversary $\mathcal{A}$, if it wins the following game at most negligible advantage, we say that the DBE scheme is (t, n, q_D)-IND-DBE-s-CCA secure (where 's' stands for 'static').*

Setup Phase: *The challenger $\mathcal{B}$ executes Setup algorithm in order to generate a system parameter* params, *an encryption key* ek, *and a master key* mk. *Then, it provides* params *and* ek *to the adversary $\mathcal{A}$.*

Join Phase: *$\mathcal{B}$ initializes $i = 0$, $j = t$, and $\mathcal{S}^* = \phi$ (ϕ denotes empty set) where i, j, and $\mathcal{S}^*$ are a counter for corrupt users and uncorrupt users, and a set of uniquely assigned values for corrupt users, respectively. $\mathcal{A}$ issues the join queries $JQ_l \in \{\text{'corrupt'}, \text{'uncorrupt'}\}$ ($l = 1, \ldots, n$). $\mathcal{A}$ must issue 'corrupt' queries exactly t times. If the received query is 'corrupt', then $\mathcal{B}$ assigns an unique value u_i for corrupt user i, sets $\mathcal{S}^* = \mathcal{S}^* \cup \{u_i\}$, increments i, returns dk_i, and updates ek. If the received query is 'uncorrupt', $\mathcal{B}$ assigns an unique value u_j for the uncorrupt user j, generates the public information B_j for the user j, returns (u_j, B_j), and updates ek.*

Query Phase 1: *$\mathcal{A}$ adaptively issues decryption queries $DQ_\varpi = (\mathsf{hdr}, u_l)$ ($\varpi = 1, \ldots, z$) where u_l and hdr denote an unique value assigned for user l and an arbitrary header hdr, respectively. $\mathcal{B}$ returns the output of $\mathsf{Decrypt}(\mathsf{hdr}, \mathsf{dk}_l)$.*

Challenge Phase: *$\mathcal{B}$ generates $(\mathsf{hdr}^*, K^*) \leftarrow \mathsf{Encrypt}(\mathsf{ek}, \mathcal{S}^*)$. Then, $\mathcal{B}$ selects $b \in_R \{0, 1\}$, sets $K_b = K^*$ and $K_{1-b} \in_R \mathcal{KS}$ where $\mathcal{KS}$ denotes the space of session keys. Finally, $\mathcal{B}$ provides $(\mathsf{hdr}^*, K_0, K_1)$ to $\mathcal{A}$.*

Query Phase 2: *$\mathcal{A}$ adaptively issues decryption queries $DQ_\varpi (\varpi = z+1, \ldots, q_D)$ as in query phase 1, but with the constraint that $\mathsf{hdr} \neq \mathsf{hdr}^*$. $\mathcal{B}$ responds as in query phase 1.*

Guess Phase: *Finally, $\mathcal{A}$ outputs $b' \in \{0, 1\}$.*

If $b' = b$, then $\mathcal{A}$ wins the game. We denote the advantage of $\mathcal{A}$ in the game as

$$\mathsf{Adv}^{\mathsf{ind}}_{\mathsf{DBE}}(t, n, q_D, \mathcal{A}) = |\Pr[b' = 1 | b = 1] - \Pr[b' = 1 | b = 0]|.$$

IND-DBE-s-CPA. In analogy with [7,8], we define chosen plaintext security against a static adversary by prohibiting to issue decryption queries.

Definition 2. *If* $\mathsf{Adv}^{\mathsf{ind}}_{\mathsf{DBE}}(t,n,0,\mathcal{A})$ *is negligible for any probabilistic polynomial time algorithm* $\mathcal{A}$, *we say the* DBE *scheme is* (t,n)-IND-DBE-s-CPA *secure.*

GDDHE Problem. Delerablée et al. [9] defined an instance of the GDDHE problem by using the GDDHE framework [6]. We call this (t,n)-GDDHE$_{\mathsf{DPP07}}$ problem where t and n are the total number of colluders and users, respectively. They proved the hardness of (t,n)-GDDHE$_{\mathsf{DPP07}}$ problem in the generic model, and showed that the security of DPP07 is based on this problem. In **Scheme1**, we slightly change encryption key, and it makes a slight difference between problems where each scheme is based on. We define (t,n)-GDDHE$_{\mathsf{Ours}}$ problem as follows.

Definition 3. *For random and distinct values* $x_i, x_j (0 \leq i \leq t-1, t \leq j \leq n) \in \mathbb{Z}_p^*$, *we define* $f(X)$ *and* $g(X)$ *as follows,*

$$f(X) = \prod_{i=0}^{t-1}(X + x_i) = (X + x_0)\cdots(X + x_{t-1}),$$
$$g(X) = \prod_{j=t}^{n-1}(X + x_j) = (X + x_t)\cdots(X + x_{n-1}).$$

Let G *and* H *be generators of cyclic groups* $\mathbb{G}_1$ *and* $\mathbb{G}_2$, *respectively.* (t,n)-GDDHE$_{\mathsf{Ours}}$ *problem is defined as follows. For a random value* $\alpha \in_R \mathbb{Z}_p^*$, *given*

$$\begin{pmatrix} G, \alpha G, \alpha^2 G, \ldots, \alpha^{t-1}G, \; \alpha f(\alpha)G, \; k\alpha f(\alpha)G, \\ H, \alpha H, \alpha^2 H, \ldots, \alpha^n H, \qquad\qquad kg(\alpha)H, \; v \end{pmatrix},$$

decide whether $v = e(G,H)^{kf(\alpha)g(\alpha)} \in \mathbb{G}_T$ *or a random value over* $\mathbb{G}_T$.

Note that the instance $e(G,H)^{f^2(\alpha)g(\alpha)} \in \mathbb{G}_T$ is included in (t,n)-GDDHE$_{\mathsf{DPP07}}$ problem, while not in (t,n)-GDDHE$_{\mathsf{Ours}}$ problem. This is the all of the difference between them, and we can have the following corollary for their relationship.

Corollary 1. *Let* t *and* n *denote attack parameters. Let an algorithm* $\mathcal{A}^P$ *solve a problem* P *with advantage* $\mathsf{Adv}^P(t,n,\mathcal{A}^P)$ *and let the advantage* $\mathsf{Adv}^P(t,n)$ *be* $\max_{\mathcal{A}^P} \mathsf{Adv}^P(t,n,\mathcal{A}^P)$. *Then we have*

$$\mathsf{Adv}^{\mathsf{GDDHE}_{\mathsf{Ours}}}(t,n) \leq \mathsf{Adv}^{\mathsf{GDDHE}_{\mathsf{DPP07}}}(t,n).$$

Note that Delerablée et al. showed the difficulty of (t,n)-GDDHE$_{\mathsf{DPP07}}$ problem in the generic model [9, Corollary 1].

Reduction to (t,n)-GDDHE$_{\mathsf{Ours}}$ Problem. We show that the security of **Scheme1** is based on the hardness to solve (t,n)-GDDHE$_{\mathsf{Ours}}$ problem. For simplicity, we use t and n as the number of colluders and total users, respectively. However, it should be noted that these numbers include one dummy user in **Scheme1**. It means that the security reduction to (t,n)-GDDHE$_{\mathsf{DPP07}}$ problem shows that DPP07 is (t,n)-IND-DBE-s-CPA secure, while in **Scheme1**, the reduction to (t,n)-GDDHE$_{\mathsf{Ours}}$ problem shows $(t-1,n-1)$-IND-DBE-s-CPA security.

Table 2. Comparison of computational cost in Encrypt algorithm

	over $\mathbb{G}_2$		the bilinear map	over $\mathbb{G}_T$		
	Addition	Multiplication		Multiplication	Exponentiation	Inversion
DPP07	$\frac{r(r-1)}{2}$	$\frac{r(r-1)}{2}+2$	0	$\frac{r(r-1)}{2}$	$\frac{r(r-1)}{2}+1$	$\frac{r(r-1)}{2}$
Scheme1	$\frac{r(r-1)}{2}+2$	$\frac{r(r-1)}{2}+4$	1	0	1	0

Theorem 1. *For arbitrary (t,n) that satisfies $0 < t \leq n$,*

$$\mathsf{Adv}^{\mathsf{ind}}_{\mathsf{Scheme1}}(t-1, n-1) \leq 2\mathsf{Adv}^{\mathsf{GDDHE_{Ours}}}(t,n),$$

where $\mathsf{Adv}^{\mathsf{ind}}_{\mathsf{Scheme1}}(t-1, n-1) = \max_{\mathcal{A}} \mathsf{Adv}^{\mathsf{ind}}_{\mathsf{Scheme1}}(t-1, n-1, 0, \mathcal{A})$ *for any probabilistic polynomial time adversary $\mathcal{A}$.*

The proof is almost the same as the one of DPP07 [9], and we omit it due to the lack of space. The differences from DPP07 are: one response for a '*corrupt*' join query contains the dummy key while other $t-1$ responses contain a user's private key, and $V, V_i \in \mathbb{G}_T$ ($i=1,\ldots,n$) are not used. Therefore, it is clear that Scheme1 satisfies $(t-1, n-1)$-IND-DBE-s-CPA security.

Chosen Ciphertext Security. Delerablée et al. [9] note if a DBE scheme is IND-DBE-s-CPA secure, then it can be IND-DBE-s-CCA secure by using Fujisaki-Okamoto transform [12] with small cost. It can also be applied to Scheme1.

2.5 Efficiency

We compare the efficiency between DPP07 and Scheme1. In both schemes, dk and hdr size, and decryption cost are the same. Therefore, we focus on the encryption cost and ek size.

Encryption Cost. The difference between these schemes is the way to compute K' in Encrypt algorithm. Therefore, we compare only computational cost for K' as shown in Table 2, where we observe that the algorithm in Scheme1 requires only constant additional computations compared with DPP07, namely one computation of the bilinear map, and two additions and scalar multiplications over $\mathbb{G}_2$. On the other hand, multiplications, exponentiations, and inversions over $\mathbb{G}_T$ are reduced by $r(r-1)/2$, respectively. This means that the computational cost over $\mathbb{G}_T$ was reduced from $O(r^2)$ to $O(1)$. Note that the recent result [21] for bilinear map computations shows that the computational cost of a bilinear map is comparable with a scalar multiplication on an elliptic curve.

Encryption (Public) Key Size. ek in DPP07 consists of label $\mathsf{lab}_i = (u_i \in \mathbb{Z}_p^*, B_i \in \mathbb{G}_2, V_i \in \mathbb{G}_T)$ for $i = 1, \ldots, n$ in addition to $W \in \mathbb{G}_1, H \in \mathbb{G}_2$ and $V \in \mathbb{G}_T$, and hence $3n+3$ elements in total. On the other hand, ek in Scheme1 consists of $(u_i \in \mathbb{Z}_p^*, B_i \in \mathbb{G}_2)$ for each user i in addition to $u_0 \in \mathbb{Z}_p^*, W, A_0 \in \mathbb{G}_1$ and $H, H_0 \in \mathbb{G}_2$, so $2n+5$ elements in total, and it is smaller than DPP07 if $n > 2$. This is since our modification to Encrypt algorithm makes V_is unnecessary.

Note that, the above comparison only considers the number of elements included in ek. When we consider the bit size given in [5], the sizes of an element in $\mathbb{G}_1$, $\mathbb{G}_2$ and $\mathbb{G}_T$ become 318-bit, 318-bit, and 953-bit, respectively. In this case, the bit size of ek in DPP07 becomes $318(n+2)+953(n+1)+159n = 1430n+1589$, while in Scheme1 becomes $318(n+4) + 159(n+1) = 477n + 1431$. This shows that ek size of Scheme1 is smaller than DPP07 for any n.

3 Authenticated Dynamic Broadcast Encryption (ADBE)

In this section, we propose an authenticated dynamic broadcast encryption scheme (Scheme2), which realizes not only efficient dynamic broadcast encryption but also secure signature using common parameters and decryption (signing) key. The decryption key is used both to sign and verify a signature. We construct Scheme2 by applying the signature scheme due to Barret et al. [3] to Scheme1.

3.1 Definition of Authenticated Dynamic Broadcast Encryption

An ADBE scheme provides a valid signature for a plaintext M generated with a decryption key of DBE. The signature can be verified by any unrevoked user. We define each algorithm used in an ADBE scheme. Since Setup and Join algorithms are the same as DBE, we omit the explanation of them. A sender broadcasts (hdr, C, sig_i) generated by Encrypt/Sign algorithm, with which an unrevoked user verifies the authenticity and obtains M with Decrypt/Verify algorithm.

Encrypt/Sign(ek, $\mathcal{R}$, M, dk_i): Takes as input an encryption key ek, a set of uniquely assigned values for revoked users $\mathcal{R} = \{u_{\mathcal{R}_1}, \ldots, u_{\mathcal{R}_r}\}$, a plaintext $M \in \mathcal{MS}$, and a decryption key dk_i of user i, where $\mathcal{MS}$ denotes the message space. This algorithm outputs a header hdr, a ciphertext $C \in \mathcal{CS}$ which is an encryption of M with a session key K, and a signature sig_i, where $\mathcal{CS}$ denotes the ciphertext space.

Decrypt/Verify(hdr, dk_j, C, sig_i): Takes as input a header hdr, a decryption key dk_j of user j, a ciphertext C, and a signature sig_i. If j is unrevoked and sig_i is a valid signature, then this algorithm outputs the unique value u_i assigned for user i and the result of decryption with the session key K. Otherwise, it outputs $\perp$.

3.2 Scheme2

Scheme2 consists of four algorithms, {Setup, Join, Encrypt/Sign, Decrypt/Verify} as described below. Note that Join, Aggregate, and Aggregate' algorithms are the same as in Scheme1, and we omit the description of them.

Setup(λ): Takes as input a security parameter λ, this algorithm chooses a λ-bit prime p, selects cyclic groups $(\mathbb{G}_1, \mathbb{G}_2, \mathbb{G}_T)$ of order p and a bilinear map $e : \mathbb{G}_1 \times \mathbb{G}_2 \to \mathbb{G}_T$. It also chooses two cryptographic hash functions

$\mathcal{H}_1 : \{0,1\}^y \times \mathbb{G}_T^2 \to \mathbb{Z}_p^*$ and $\mathcal{H}_2 : \mathbb{G}_T \to \{0,1\}^y$ where we define the message space $\mathcal{MS}$, the session key space $\mathcal{KS}$, and the ciphertext space $\mathcal{CS}$ as y-bit binary space, respectively, in accordance with [3]. Then it sets a set of system parameters params $= (p, \mathbb{G}_1, \mathbb{G}_2, \mathbb{G}_T, e, \mathcal{H}_1, \mathcal{H}_2)$. Next, it selects two random generators $G \in \mathbb{G}_1, H \in \mathbb{G}_2$ and a secret value $\gamma \in_R \mathbb{Z}_p^*$. The master key is mk $= (\gamma, G)$. It computes $W = \gamma G \in \mathbb{G}_1$ with mk. Finally it sets an initial encryption key as ek $= (W, H)$. The algorithm outputs params, mk, and ek.

Encrypt/Sign(ek, $\mathcal{R}, M, \mathrm{dk}_i$): Takes as input an encryption key ek, the set of uniquely assigned values for revoked users $\mathcal{R} = \{u_{\mathcal{R}_1}, \ldots, u_{\mathcal{R}_r}\}$ where r denotes the number of revoked users, a plaintext M, and a decryption key dk_i of user i, this algorithm chooses $k \in_R \mathbb{Z}_p^*$. We use the definition of $h_l(\gamma)$ given in Sect. 2.3 and also define $P'_0 = H \in \mathbb{G}_2$ and $P'_l = \frac{1}{h_l(\gamma)} H \in \mathbb{G}_2$ for $l = 1, \ldots, r$.
 - If $r = 0$, this algorithm treats user i as a revoked user. It sets $r = 1$, $u_{\mathcal{R}_1} = u_i$, and $P'_1 = B_i \in \mathbb{G}_2$, and computes $K' = e(\frac{1}{u_i} A_i, H) \in \mathbb{G}_T$.
 - Otherwise, it computes $P'_l (l=1,\ldots,r)$ using Aggregate algorithm, $\gamma P'_r = P'_{r-1} - u_{\mathcal{R}_r} P'_r \in \mathbb{G}_2$, and $K' = e(\frac{1}{u_i} A_i, \gamma P'_r + u_i P'_r) \in \mathbb{G}_T$.

Then the algorithm derives the temporary key $TK = (K')^k \in \mathbb{G}_T$ and the session key $K = \mathcal{H}_2(TK) \in \{0,1\}^y$, and sets the header as hdr $= (kW, kP'_r, (u_{\mathcal{R}_1}, P'_1), \ldots, (u_{\mathcal{R}_r}, P'_r))$. It also encrypts M to the ciphertext C with K as $C = M \oplus K \in \{0,1\}^y$. Next, it chooses $\rho \in_R \mathbb{Z}_p^*$ and computes $\delta_i = (K')^\rho \in \mathbb{G}_T$, $h_i = \mathcal{H}_1(C, TK, \delta_i)$, and $\sigma_i = \frac{\rho - h_i}{u_i} A_i \in \mathbb{G}_1$. In the case of $\rho = h_i$, it chooses another ρ and computes δ_i, h_i, and σ_i once again. It also constructs the signature $\mathrm{sig}_i = (u_i, h_i, \sigma_i)$, and outputs hdr, sig_i, and C.

Decrypt/Verify(hdr, $\mathrm{dk}_j, C, \mathrm{sig}_i$): If there is the unique value u_j assigned for user j in the broadcasted header hdr, then the algorithm outputs $\perp$ and terminates the procedure. Otherwise, it executes Aggregate$'$ algorithm as $B_{j,\mathcal{R}} \leftarrow$ Aggregate$'(u_j, B_j, (u_{\mathcal{R}_1}, P'_1), \ldots, (u_{\mathcal{R}_r}, P'_r)) = \frac{1}{(\gamma + u_j) h_r(\gamma)} H \in \mathbb{G}_2$, and computes the temporary key as $TK = e(kW, B_{j,\mathcal{R}}) \cdot e(A_j, kP'_r) \in \mathbb{G}_T$. To verify the signature sig_i, it sets $\gamma P'_r = P'_{r-1} - u_{\mathcal{R}_r} P'_r \in \mathbb{G}_2$ and computes $K' = e(\frac{1}{u_j} A_j, \gamma P'_r + u_j P'_r) \in \mathbb{G}_T$ and $\delta_j = e(\sigma_i, \gamma P'_r + u_i P'_r) \cdot (K')^{h_i} \in \mathbb{G}_T$. If $h_i \neq \mathcal{H}_1(C, TK, \delta_j)$, then it outputs $\perp$ meaning that the signature is invalid. Otherwise, it computes the session key $K = \mathcal{H}_2(TK) \in \{0,1\}^y$, obtains the plaintext M from the ciphertext C with K as $M = C \oplus K \in \{0,1\}^y$, and outputs (u_i, M).

Correctness. The correctness of the temporary key TK is the same as the session key K in Scheme1. Decrypt/Verify algorithm computes $\gamma P'_r = P'_{r-1} - \frac{u_{\mathcal{R}_r}}{\gamma + u_{\mathcal{R}_r}} P'_{r-1} = \frac{\gamma}{\gamma + u_{\mathcal{R}_r}} P'_{r-1} \in \mathbb{G}_2$ and $K' = e\left(\frac{1}{u_j} A_j, \gamma P'_r + u_j P'_r\right) = e(G, H)^{\frac{1}{h_r(\gamma)}} \in \mathbb{G}_T$. If (hdr, C, sig_i) $\leftarrow$ Encrypt/Sign(ek, $\mathcal{R}, M, \mathrm{dk}_i$), the value of δ_j becomes

$$\delta_j = e(\sigma_i, \gamma P'_r + u_i P'_r) \cdot (K')^{h_i} = e\left(\frac{\rho - h_i}{\gamma + u_i} G, \frac{\gamma + u_i}{h_r(\gamma)} H\right) \cdot e(G, H)^{\frac{h_i}{h_r(\gamma)}} = (K')^\rho = \delta_i.$$

Consequently, the verification equation $h_i = \mathcal{H}_1(C, TK, \delta_j)$ is satisfied.

3.3 Security Analysis

Scheme2 achieves both functions of dynamic broadcast encryption and signature, where a user's decryption key is used to encrypt and decrypt the header, to sign and verify a signature. Hence we need to consider not only message confidentiality but also signature unforgeability.

Message Confidentiality. We define IND-ADBE-s-CCA and IND-ADBE-s-CPA security for an ADBE scheme.

Definition 4. *The chosen ciphertext security against a static adversary for an ADBE scheme is defined using the following game between adversary $\mathcal{A}$ and challenger $\mathcal{B}$. In the following game, t, n, q_{ES}, and q_{DV} denote the number of decryption keys that the adversary $\mathcal{A}$ can obtain, the number of total users, the number of encrypt/sign queries, and the number of decrypt/verify queries, respectively. For any probabilistic polynomial time adversary $\mathcal{A}$, if it wins the following game at most negligible advantage $\mathsf{Adv}^{\mathsf{ind}}_{\mathsf{ADBE}}(t, n, q_{ES}, q_{DV}, \mathcal{A})$, we say that the ADBE scheme is (t, n, q_{ES}, q_{DV})-IND-ADBE-s-CCA secure.*

In the following game, the definition of Setup and Join phases are the same as the game for DBE in Sect. 2.4.

Query Phase 1: *The adversary $\mathcal{A}$ adaptively issues encrypt/sign queries ESQ_ω ($\omega = 1, \ldots, z$) and decrypt/verify queries DVQ_ϖ ($\varpi = 1, \ldots, z'$),*
- **Encrypt/Sign query:** *$\mathcal{A}$ issues an arbitrary plaintext $M \in \mathcal{MS}$, the set of uniquely assigned values for revoked users $\mathcal{R} = \{u_{\mathcal{R}_1}, \ldots, u_{\mathcal{R}_{r'}}\}$ which $\mathcal{A}$ chooses arbitrarily, and a unique value u_l of an arbitrary signer l as $ESQ_\omega = (M, \mathcal{R}, u_l)$. $\mathcal{B}$ returns $(\mathsf{hdr}, C, \mathsf{sig}_l) \leftarrow \mathsf{Encrypt/Sign}\,(\mathsf{ek}, \mathcal{R}, M, \mathsf{dk}_l)$.*
- **Decrypt/Verify query:** *$\mathcal{A}$ issues a unique value u_j of an arbitrary user j, an arbitrary header hdr, a ciphertext C, and a signature sig_l as $DVQ_\varpi = (\mathsf{hdr}, C, \mathsf{sig}_l)$. $\mathcal{B}$ returns the output of $\mathsf{Decrypt/Verify}(\mathsf{hdr}, \mathsf{dk}_j, C, \mathsf{sig}_l)$.*

Challenge Phase: *$\mathcal{A}$ arbitrarily chooses a signer l^* and two plaintexts $M_0, M_1 \in \mathcal{MS}$, then sends M_0, M_1 and l^*'s unique value u_{l^*} to $\mathcal{B}$. $\mathcal{B}$ chooses $b \in_R \{0, 1\}$ and returns $(\mathsf{hdr}^*, C^*, \mathsf{sig}_{l^*}) \leftarrow \mathsf{Encrypt/Sign}(\mathsf{ek}, \mathcal{S}^*, M_b, \mathsf{dk}_{l^*})$.*

Query Phase 2: *$\mathcal{A}$ adaptively issues encrypt/sign queries $ESQ_\omega (\omega = z + 1, \ldots, q_{ES})$ and decrypt/verify queries $DVQ_\varpi (\varpi = z' + 1, \ldots, q_{DV})$ as in query phase 1, but with the constraint that $(\mathsf{hdr}, C, \mathsf{sig}_l) \neq (\mathsf{hdr}^*, C^*, \mathsf{sig}_{l^*})$ in decrypt/verify queries. $\mathcal{B}$ responds as in query phase 1 for each query.*

Guess Phase: *Finally, $\mathcal{A}$ outputs $b' \in \{0, 1\}$.*

If $b' = b$, then $\mathcal{A}$ wins the game. We denote the advantage of $\mathcal{A}$ in the game as

$$\mathsf{Adv}^{\mathsf{ind}}_{\mathsf{ADBE}}(t, n, q_{ES}, q_{DV}, \mathcal{A}) = |\Pr[b' = 1 | b = 1] - \Pr[b' = 1 | b = 0]|.$$

IND-ADBE-s-CPA. In analogy with [7,8], we define chosen plaintext security against a static adversary by prohibiting to issue decrypt/verify queries.

Definition 5. *If $\mathsf{Adv}^{\mathsf{ind}}_{\mathsf{ADBE}}(t, n, q_{ES}, 0, \mathcal{A})$ is negligible for any probabilistic polynomial time algorithm $\mathcal{A}$, we say the ADBE scheme is (t, n, q_{ES})-IND-ADBE-s-CPA secure.*

Reduction to (t, n)-GDDHE$_{\text{Ours}}$ Problem. The message confidentiality of Scheme2 is based on the hardness to solve (t, n)-GDDHE$_{\text{Ours}}$ problem as well as Scheme1.

Theorem 2. *Let $\mathcal{H}_1$ be a random oracle. We assume that if a value v is uniformly distributed over $\mathbb{G}_T$, $\mathcal{H}_2(v)$ is uniformly distributed over $\mathcal{KS}$. For arbitrary (t, n) that satisfies $0 < t \leq n$,*

$$\frac{1}{2}\left(1 - \frac{(q_{H_1} + q_{ES})q_{ES}}{p}\right) \mathsf{Adv}^{\mathsf{ind}}_{\mathsf{Scheme2}}(t, n, q_{ES}) \leq \mathsf{Adv}^{\mathsf{GDDHE_{Ours}}}(t, n)$$

where $\mathsf{Adv}^{\mathsf{ind}}_{\mathsf{Scheme2}}(t, n, q_{ES}) = \max_{\mathcal{A}} \mathsf{Adv}^{\mathsf{ind}}_{\mathsf{Scheme2}}(t, n, q_{ES}, 0, \mathcal{A})$ for any probabilistic polynomial time adversary $\mathcal{A}$ and q_{H_1} denotes the number of $\mathcal{H}_1$ queries.

Proof. Let t and n be the number of colluders and total users, respectively. We assume that there is an adversary $\mathcal{A}$ who breaks message confidentiality of Scheme2 with (t, n) as attack parameters. We construct a reduction algorithm $\mathcal{B}$ which solves (t, n)-GDDHE$_{\text{Ours}}$ problem as follows.

At first, for any $x_i, x_j \in \mathbb{Z}_p^*$ such that satisfy $(\alpha + x_i)|f(\alpha)$ and $(\alpha + x_j)|g(\alpha)$, respectively, we define $f_i(\alpha) = \frac{1}{\alpha + x_i}f(\alpha) = \sum_{z=0}^{t-1} c_z \alpha^z$ and $g_j(\alpha) = \frac{1}{\alpha + x_j}g(\alpha) = \sum_{z=0}^{n-t-1} d_z \alpha^z$. Note that $c_0, \ldots, c_{t-1}$ and $d_0, \ldots, d_{n-t-1}$ can be computed from $x_0, \ldots, x_{t-1}$ and $x_t, \ldots, x_{n-1}$, respectively. Since $\deg(f_i(\alpha)) = t - 1$ and $\deg(g_j(\alpha)) = n - t - 1$, we can also compute $f_i(\alpha)G \in \mathbb{G}_1$ and $g_j(\alpha)H \in \mathbb{G}_2$ by using the instance of (t, n)-GDDHE$_{\text{Ours}}$ problem. In the same manner, we can compute a polynomial $\frac{1}{h(\alpha)}f(\alpha)g(\alpha)H \in \mathbb{G}_2$ if $h(\alpha)$ satisfies $h(\alpha)|f(\alpha)g(\alpha)$.

Setup Phase. The challenger $\mathcal{B}$ generates each value as follows. Let $W' = \alpha f(\alpha)G \in \mathbb{G}_1$, and $\mathcal{B}$ computes $H' = f(\alpha)g(\alpha)H \in \mathbb{G}_2$ from $x_0, \ldots, x_{n-1}$, $H, \alpha H, \ldots, \alpha^n H$. Note that if we regard $\gamma = \alpha \in \mathbb{Z}_p^*$ and $G' = f(\alpha)G \in \mathbb{G}_1$, then we have $W' = \gamma G'$. $\mathcal{B}$ gives params $= (p, \mathbb{G}_1, \mathbb{G}_2, \mathbb{G}_T, e, \mathcal{H}_1, \mathcal{H}_2)$ and ek $= (W', H')$ to the adversary $\mathcal{A}$.

$\mathcal{H}_1$ Queries. We treat $\mathcal{H}_1$ as a random oracle. $\mathcal{A}$ issues $\mathcal{H}_1$ queries with (C, TK, δ_l) at most q_{H_1} times. Upon receiving a query from $\mathcal{A}$, if there exists (C, TK, δ_l) in the list L_1, $\mathcal{B}$ returns the corresponding answer h. Otherwise, $\mathcal{B}$ selects $h \in_R \mathbb{Z}_p^*$, adds (C, TK, δ_l, h) to L_1, and returns h.

Join Phase. $\mathcal{B}$ initializes $i = 0$, $j = t$, and $\mathcal{S}^* = \phi$. $\mathcal{A}$ issues the join queries $JQ_l \in \{\text{'corrupt'}, \text{'uncorrupt'}\}$ $(l = 1, \ldots, n)$. If the received query is *'corrupt'*, then $\mathcal{B}$ sets $u_l = x_i \in \mathbb{Z}_p^*$, $\mathcal{S}^* = \mathcal{S}^* \cup \{u_l\}$, $A_l = x_i f_i(\alpha)G \in \mathbb{G}_1$, and $B_l = f_i(\alpha)g(\alpha)H \in \mathbb{G}_2$ for the corrupt user i. $\mathcal{B}$ returns $\mathsf{dk}_l = (u_l, A_l, B_l)$, updates ek as ek $=$ ek $\cup \{(u_l, B_l)\}$, and increments i. Otherwise, $\mathcal{B}$ sets $u_l = x_j \in \mathbb{Z}_p^*$, $B_l = f(\alpha)g_j(\alpha)H \in \mathbb{G}_2$ for the uncorrupt user j, returns (u_l, B_l), updates ek as ek $=$ ek $\cup \{(u_l, B_l)\}$, and increments j. Note that the set of uniquely assigned values for corrupt users becomes $\mathcal{S}^* = \{u_{S_1^*}, \ldots, u_{S_t^*}\} = \{x_0, \ldots, x_{t-1}\}$ at the end of this phase.

Query Phase. $\mathcal{A}$ adaptively issues encrypt/sign queries $ESQ_\omega = (M, \mathcal{R}, u_l)(\omega = 1, \ldots, q_{ES})$ where $M \in \mathcal{MS}$, $\mathcal{R} = \{u_{\mathcal{R}_1}, \ldots, u_{\mathcal{R}_{r'}}\}$. If $\mathcal{R} = \phi$, then $\mathcal{B}$ sets $\mathcal{R} = \{u_{\mathcal{R}_1} = u_l\}$. $\mathcal{B}$ computes $P'_m = \frac{1}{h_m(\alpha)} H' = \frac{f(\alpha)g(\alpha)}{h_m(\alpha)} H = \sum_{\omega=0}^{n-m} z_\omega \alpha^\omega H \in \mathbb{G}_2$ for $m = 1, \ldots, r'$ using $x_0, \ldots, x_{n-1}$ and $H, \alpha H, \ldots, \alpha^n H$. Then, $\mathcal{B}$ chooses $k' \in_R \mathbb{Z}_p^*$, and constructs a header $\mathsf{hdr} = (k'W', k'P'_{r'}, (u_{\mathcal{R}_1}, P'_1), \ldots, (u_{\mathcal{R}_{r'}}, P'_{r'}))$. Next, $\mathcal{B}$ computes $u_{\mathcal{R}_{r'}} P'_{r'}$, $\alpha P'_{r'} = P'_{r'-1} - \frac{u_{\mathcal{R}_{r'}}}{\alpha + u_{\mathcal{R}'_r}} P'_{r'-1}$, and

$$K' = e\left(\frac{1}{\alpha + u_{\mathcal{S}_i^*}} G', \alpha P'_{r'} + u_{\mathcal{S}_i^*} P'_{r'}\right) = e(G', H')^{\frac{1}{h_{r'}(\alpha)}} \in \mathbb{G}_T$$

by using $\frac{u_{\mathcal{S}_i^*}}{\alpha + u_{\mathcal{S}_i^*}} G' = x_i f_i(\alpha) G$ of an arbitrary corrupt user $\mathcal{S}_i^*$. $\mathcal{B}$ also computes $TK = (K')^{k'} \in \mathbb{G}_T$ and $K = \mathcal{H}_2(TK)$. Then $\mathcal{B}$ encrypts M with K as $C = M \oplus K \in \{0,1\}^y$. Subsequently, $\mathcal{B}$ generates a signature sig_l. In the case of $u_l \in \{u_{\mathcal{S}_1^*}, \ldots, u_{\mathcal{S}_t^*}\}$, $\mathcal{B}$ already has dk_l for any corrupt user l and it is easy to execute remaining procedure of Encrypt/Sign algorithm. Otherwise $\mathcal{B}$ selects $\sigma_l \in_R \mathbb{G}_1$ and $h_l \in_R \mathbb{Z}_p^*$ and constructs $\delta_l = e(\sigma_l, \alpha P'_{r'} + u_l P'_{r'}) \cdot (K')^{h_l} \in \mathbb{G}_T$. If there already exists (C, TK, δ_l) computed above in the list L_1, $\mathcal{B}$ aborts this game. Otherwise $\mathcal{B}$ adds (C, TK, δ_l, h_l) to the list L_1. Finally $\mathcal{B}$ constructs $\mathsf{sig}_l = (u_l, h_l, \sigma_l)$ and returns $(\mathsf{hdr}, C, \mathsf{sig}_l)$.

Challenge Phase. $\mathcal{A}$ issues $M_0, M_1 \in \mathcal{MS}$ and the unique value u_l of a signer l to $\mathcal{B}$. $\mathcal{B}$ selects $b \in_R \{0,1\}$ and generates $(\mathsf{hdr}^*, C^*, \mathsf{sig}_l^*)$ as follows. $\mathcal{B}$ computes $P_i (i = 1, \ldots, t) \in \mathbb{G}_2$ with $\mathcal{S}^* = \{u_{\mathcal{S}_1^*}, \ldots, u_{\mathcal{S}_t^*}\}$ as the set of uniquely assigned values for corrupt users, and constructs $\mathsf{hdr}^* = (kW', \frac{k}{f(\alpha)} H', (u_{\mathcal{S}_1^*}, P'_1), \ldots, (u_{\mathcal{S}_t^*}, P'_t))$. $\mathcal{B}$ also computes K' in the same manner as encrypt/sign phase and sets $TK^* = v$. Then $\mathcal{B}$ sets $K^* = \mathcal{H}_2(TK^*)$ and encrypts M_b with K^* as $C^* = M_b \oplus K^* \in \{0,1\}^y$. Subsequently, $\mathcal{B}$ generates the signature sig_l^*. $\mathcal{B}$ selects $\sigma_l^* \in_R \mathbb{G}_1$ and $h_l^* \in_R \mathbb{Z}_p^*$, and constructs $\delta_l^* = e(\sigma_l^*, \alpha P'_t + u_l P'_t) \cdot (K')^{h_l^*} \in \mathbb{G}_T$. If there already exists (C^*, TK^*, δ_l^*) computed above in the list L_1, $\mathcal{B}$ aborts this game. Otherwise, $\mathcal{B}$ adds $(C^*, TK^*, \delta_l^*, h_l^*)$ to L_1. Finally, $\mathcal{B}$ constructs $\mathsf{sig}_l = (u_l, h_l^*, \sigma_l^*)$ and returns $(\mathsf{hdr}^*, C^*, \mathsf{sig}_l^*)$.

Guess Phase. For b' returned from $\mathcal{A}$, $\mathcal{B}$ outputs real if $b' = b$, otherwise outputs rand. $\mathsf{Adv}^{\mathsf{GDDHE}_{\mathsf{Ours}}}(t, n, \mathcal{B})$ can be transformed as follows,

$$\mathsf{Adv}^{\mathsf{GDDHE}_{\mathsf{Ours}}}(t, n, \mathcal{B}) = \frac{1}{2}\left(1 - \frac{(q_{H_1} + q_{ES})q_{ES}}{p}\right) \mathsf{Adv}^{\mathsf{ind}}_{\mathsf{Scheme2}}(t, n, q_{ES}, \mathcal{A}).$$

□

Signature Unforgeability. We define EUF-ADBE-s-CMA security for an ADBE scheme.

Definition 6. *The existential unforgeability against a static chosen message adversary for any ADBE scheme is defined using the following game between adversary $\mathcal{A}$ and challenger $\mathcal{B}$. In the following game, t, n, q_{ES}, and q_{DV} denote the* number of decryption keys that the adversary $\mathcal{A}$ can obtain, the number of total users, the number of encrypt/sign queries, and the number of decrypt/verify queries, respectively. For any probabilistic polynomial time adversary $\mathcal{A}$, if it wins the following game at most negligible advantage, we say that the ADBE scheme is (t, n, q_{ES}, q_{DV})-EUF-ADBE-s-CMA secure.

The following game consists of four phases, Setup, Join, Query, and Output. The definition of Setup and Join phases are the same as the game in Definition 4. Query phase is the same as Query phase 1 of the game in Definition 4 expect for the total number of encrypt/sign and decrypt/verify queries.

Query Phase: The adversary $\mathcal{A}$ adaptively issues encrypt/sign queries ESQ_ω ($\omega = 1, \ldots, q_{ES}$) and decrypt/verify queries DVQ_ϖ ($\varpi = 1, \ldots, q_{DV}$).
Output Phase: $\mathcal{A}$ outputs (hdr*, C^*, sig$_{j^*}$) where $u_{j^*} \notin \mathcal{S}^*$.

The adversary $\mathcal{A}$ wins the game if the output of Decrypt/Verify(hdr*, dk$_l$, C^*, sig$_{j^*}$) where $u_l \notin \mathcal{S}^*$ is not $\bot$. We denote the advantage of $\mathcal{A}$ in the game by Adv$_{\mathsf{ADBE}}^{\mathsf{euf}}$ $(t, n, q_{ES}, q_{DV}, \mathcal{A})$.

$(t, n, q_{ES}, 0)$-*EUF-ADBE-s-CMA.* In analogy with IND-ADBE-s-CPA security, we consider $(t, n, q_{ES}, 0)$-EUF-ADBE-s-CMA security against a static adversary for an ADBE scheme by prohibiting to issue decrypt/verify queries.

$(t + 1, n)$-SDH Problem. The signature unforgeability of Scheme2 is based on the difficulty to solve $(t+1, n)$-SDH problem. At first, we define (t, n)-SDH problem as follows.

Definition 7. *Let G and H be generators of cyclic group $\mathbb{G}_1$ and $\mathbb{G}_2$, respectively. (t,n)-SDH problem is defined as follows. For a random value $\alpha \in_R \mathbb{Z}_p^*$, given*
$$(G, \alpha G, \alpha^2 G, \ldots, \alpha^t G, H, \alpha H, \alpha^2 H, \ldots, \alpha^n H),$$
compute $\frac{1}{\alpha+w} G \in \mathbb{G}_1$ for an arbitrary value $w \in \mathbb{Z}_p^* \setminus \{-\alpha\}$.

Boneh et al. proved the hardness to solve q-SDH problem in the generic model [5, Theorem 12]. By using this proof, the hardness to solve $(t+1, n)$-SDH problem can be also proven in the generic model with some changes. In the proof of Theorem 12 [5], three lists L_1, L_2, and L_T are used to simulate group operations over $\mathbb{G}_1, \mathbb{G}_2$, and $\mathbb{G}_T$, respectively. We change the initial numbers of their elements as $\tau_1 = t+2$, $\tau_2 = n+1$, and $\tau_T = 0$. The simulation is the same except for the above change and the degrees of polynomial $F_{1,i}, F_{2,i}$, and $F_{T,i}$ included in the list L_1, L_2 and L_T, respectively. When the simulation is finished, the degrees of $F_{1,i}, F_{2,i}$ are at most n, and the degree of $F_{T,i}$ is at most $2n$ because we need to consider homomorphism and its inverse queries. Consequently, by the applying above values to Theorem 12 [5], we have the following corollary.

Corollary 2. *For any probabilistic algorithm $\mathcal{A}$ that totalizes at most q queries to the oracles performing group operations in $\mathbb{G}_1, \mathbb{G}_2$, and $\mathbb{G}_T$ and evaluations of the bilinear map e,*

$$\mathsf{Adv}^{\mathsf{SDH}}(t+1, n, \mathcal{A}) \leq \frac{(q+n+t+3)^2 \cdot n}{p-1},$$

where $\mathsf{Adv}^{\mathsf{SDH}}(t+1, n, \mathcal{A})$ is the advantage of probabilistic polynomial time adversary $\mathcal{A}$ to solve $(t+1, n)$-SDH problem.

Theorem 3. *Let $\mathcal{H}_1$ be a random oracle. We assume that if a value v is uniformly distributed over $\mathbb{G}_T$, $\mathcal{H}_2(v)$ is uniformly distributed over $\mathcal{KS}$. If there is a forger $\mathcal{A}$ which has running time t_1 and advantage $\mathsf{Adv}^{\mathsf{euf}}_{\mathsf{Scheme2}}(t, n, q_{ES}, 0, \mathcal{A}) \geq 10(q_{ES}+1)(q_{ES}+q_{H_1})/2^\lambda$, then $(t+1, n)$-SDH problem can be solved within expected time*

$$t_1' \leq 120686 q_{H_1} \frac{t_1 + O(n^2 q_{ES})\tau_{\mathbb{G}_{1,2},mul} + O(q_{ES})\tau_p}{\mathsf{Adv}^{\mathsf{euf}}_{\mathsf{Scheme2}}(t, n, q_{ES}, 0, \mathcal{A})} + O(n^2)\tau_{\mathbb{G}_{1,2},mul},$$

where q_{H_1} denotes the number of $\mathcal{H}_1$ queries.

Proof. We use the same definitions for $f_i(\alpha)$ and $g_j(\alpha)$ defined in the proof of message confidentiality.

Setup Phase. $\mathcal{B}$ chooses $w_0, \ldots, w_{n-1} \in_R \mathbb{Z}_p^*$ and computes $c_0, \ldots, c_t \in \mathbb{Z}_p$ and $d_0, \ldots, d_{n-t} \in \mathbb{Z}_p$ that satisfies $f(\alpha) = (\alpha + w_0) \cdots (\alpha + w_{t-1}) = \sum_{i=0}^{t} c_i \alpha^i$ and $g(\alpha) = (\alpha + w_t) \cdots (\alpha + w_{n-1}) = \sum_{j=0}^{n-t} d_j \alpha^j$. Note that, in the proofs of theorem 1 and 2, $f(\alpha)$ and $g(\alpha)$ are fixed by the instance of (t, n)-$\mathsf{GDDHE}_{\mathsf{Ours}}$ problem. In this proof however, $\mathcal{B}$ can compute $f(\alpha)G$ and $g(\alpha)H$ by using random values $w_0, \ldots, w_{n-1} \in_R \mathbb{Z}_p^*$ and the instance of $(t+1, n)$-SDH problem.

$\mathcal{B}$ also computes $W' = \alpha f(\alpha)G = \sum_{i=0}^{t} c_i \alpha^{i+1} G \in \mathbb{G}_1$ and $H' = f(\alpha)g(\alpha)H \in \mathbb{G}_2$. Note that, if we regard $\gamma = \alpha \in \mathbb{Z}_p^*$ and $G' = f(\alpha)G \in \mathbb{G}_1$, then we have $W' = \gamma G'$. $\mathcal{B}$ gives $\mathsf{params} = (p, \mathbb{G}_1, \mathbb{G}_2, \mathbb{G}_T, e, \mathcal{H}_1, \mathcal{H}_2)$ and $\mathsf{ek} = (W', H')$ to $\mathcal{A}$. We regard $\mathcal{H}_1$ as a random oracle, and queries to $\mathcal{H}_1$ are treated as the same as in the proof of Theorem 2. Join and Query phases are also the same except for replacing x_i and x_j with w_i and w_j.

Output Phase. Under the above settings, we can apply the Forking Lemma [18]. This lemma shows that $\mathcal{B}$ can construct a Turing machine $\mathcal{A}'$ which generates two valid signatures such that the messages and the commitments are the same while hashed values and signatures are different, by using the forger $\mathcal{A}$ against Scheme2 as a subroutine. $\mathcal{B}$ executes $\mathcal{A}'$ and obtains two output $(\mathsf{hdr}^*, C^*, \mathsf{sig}_{j^*})$ and $(\mathsf{hdr}^*, C^*, \mathsf{sig}'_{j^*})$ where $\mathsf{sig}_{j^*} = (w, h, \sigma_{j^*})$ and $\mathsf{sig}'_{j^*} = (w, h', \sigma'_{j^*})$ for the same w that satisfies $w \notin \{w_i | i = 0, \ldots, t-1\}$. So we have, $e\left(\sigma_{j^*}, \frac{\alpha+w}{h_{r'}(\alpha)}H'\right) \cdot e\left(G', \frac{1}{h_{r'}(\alpha)}H'\right)^h = e\left(\sigma'_{j^*}, \frac{\alpha+w}{h_{r'}(\alpha)}H'\right) \cdot e\left(G', \frac{1}{h_{r'}(\alpha)}H'\right)^{h'} \in \mathbb{G}_T$. From this equation, $\mathcal{B}$ can compute $\frac{1}{\alpha+w}f(\alpha)G = \frac{\sigma_{j^*}-\sigma'_{j^*}}{h'-h} \in \mathbb{G}_T$. $\mathcal{B}$ derives $\frac{1}{\alpha+w}G \in \mathbb{G}_1$

from $\frac{1}{\alpha+w}f(\alpha)G$ by using the same calculation with [3,5], namely, $\mathcal{B}$ computes $\beta_{-1}, \beta_0, \ldots, \beta_t \in \mathbb{Z}_p^*$ that satisfies $f(\alpha)/(\alpha+w) = \beta_{-1}/(\alpha+w) + \sum_{i=0}^{t-1}\beta_i\alpha^i$, then it derives $\frac{1}{\alpha+w}G \in \mathbb{G}_1$ as $\frac{1}{\alpha+w}G = \frac{1}{\beta_{-1}}\left(\frac{1}{\alpha+w}f(\alpha)G - \sum_{i=0}^{t-1}\beta_i\alpha^i G\right)$. Note that $(w, \frac{1}{\alpha+w}G)$ is the correct answer to the given $(t+1,n)$-SDH problem.

From all discussions described above, if $\mathcal{A}$ can forge a signature in time t_1 and with advantage $\mathsf{Adv}^{\mathsf{euf}}_{\mathsf{Scheme2}}(t, n, q_{ES}, 0, \mathcal{A}) \geq 10(q_{ES}+1)(q_{ES}+q_{H_1})/2^\lambda$, then $\mathcal{B}$ can solve $(t+1, n)$-SDH problem in expected time

$$t_1' \leq 120686 q_{H_1} \frac{t_1 + O(n^2 q_{ES})\tau_{\mathbb{G}_{1,2},mul} + O(q_{ES})\tau_p}{\mathsf{Adv}^{\mathsf{euf}}_{\mathsf{Scheme2}}(t,n,q_{ES},0,\mathcal{A})} + O(n^2)\tau_{\mathbb{G}_{1,2},mul}.$$

□

4 Conclusion

In this paper, we proposed two efficient dynamic public-key broadcast encryption schemes. Our Scheme1 reduces public key size and the encryption cost by modifying DPP07. Scheme2 achieves broadcast encryption and signature with the same parameters and keys. The message confidentiality of our schemes are based on the hardness to solve GDDHE problem in the standard model (Scheme1) and in the random oracle model (Scheme2). We also showed that the signature unforgeability of Scheme2 is based on the hardness to solve $(t+1,n)$-SDH problem in the random oracle model. Consequently, Scheme1 realizes an efficient dynamic broadcast encryption and Scheme2 is the first one which gives security proof for authenticated dynamic broadcast encryption with common parameters and keys, simultaneously.

References

1. Asano, T.: A revocation scheme with minimal storage at receivers. In: Zheng, Y. (ed.) ASIACRYPT 2002. LNCS, vol. 2501, pp. 433–450. Springer, Heidelberg (2002)
2. Attrapadung, N., Imai, H.: Graph-decomposition-based frameworks for subset-cover broadcast encryption and efficient instantiations. In: Roy, B. (ed.) ASIACRYPT 2005. LNCS, vol. 3788, pp. 100–120. Springer, Heidelberg (2005)
3. Barreto, P.S.L.M., Libert, B., McCullagh, N., Quisquater, J.-J.: Efficient and provably-secure identity-based signatures and signcryption from bilinear maps. In: Roy, B. (ed.) ASIACRYPT 2005. LNCS, vol. 3788, pp. 515–532. Springer, Heidelberg (2005)
4. Berkovits, S.: How to broadcast a secret. In: Davies, D.W. (ed.) EUROCRYPT 1991. LNCS, vol. 547, pp. 535–541. Springer, Heidelberg (1991)
5. Boneh, D., Boyen, X.: Short signatures without random oracles and the sdh assumption in bilinear groups. J. Cryptology 21(2), 149–177 (2008)
6. Boneh, D., Boyen, X., Goh, E.-J.: Hierarchical identity based encryption with constant size ciphertext. In: Cramer, R. (ed.) EUROCRYPT 2005. LNCS, vol. 3494, pp. 440–456. Springer, Heidelberg (2005)

7. Boneh, D., Gentry, C., Waters, B.: Collusion resistant broadcast encryption with short ciphertexts and private keys. In: Shoup, V. (ed.) CRYPTO 2005. LNCS, vol. 3621, pp. 258–275. Springer, Heidelberg (2005)
8. Delerablée, C.: Identity-based broadcast encryption with constant size ciphertexts and private keys. In: Kurosawa, K. (ed.) ASIACRYPT 2007. LNCS, vol. 4833, pp. 200–215. Springer, Heidelberg (2007)
9. Delerablée, C., Paillier, P., Pointcheval, D.: Fully collusion secure dynamic broadcast encryption with constant-size ciphertexts or decryption keys. In: Takagi, T., Okamoto, T., Okamoto, E., Okamoto, T. (eds.) Pairing 2007. LNCS, vol. 4575, pp. 39–59. Springer, Heidelberg (2007)
10. Dodis, Y., Fazio, N.: Public key broadcast encryption for stateless receivers. In: Feigenbaum, J. (ed.) DRM 2002. LNCS, vol. 2696, pp. 61–80. Springer, Heidelberg (2003)
11. Fiat, A., Naor, M.: Broadcast encryption. In: Stinson, D.R. (ed.) CRYPTO 1993. LNCS, vol. 773, pp. 480–491. Springer, Heidelberg (1994)
12. Fujisaki, E., Okamoto, T.: Secure integration of asymmetric and symmetric encryption schemes. In: Wiener, M. (ed.) CRYPTO 1999. LNCS, vol. 1666, pp. 537–554. Springer, Heidelberg (1999)
13. Kanazawa, F., Ohkawa, N., Doi, H., Okamoto, T., Okamoto, E.: Improvement of broadcast encryption with sender authentication and its security. 2007-csec-37, IPSJ SIG Technical Report (2007)
14. Li, F., Xin, X., Hu, Y.: Indentity-based broadcast signcryption. Computer Standards and Interfaces 30(1–2), 89–94 (2008)
15. Mu, Y., Susilo, W., Lin, Y.-X., Ruan, C.: Identity-based authenticated broadcast encryption and distributed authenticated encryption. In: Maher, M.J. (ed.) ASIAN 2004. LNCS, vol. 3321, pp. 169–181. Springer, Heidelberg (2004)
16. Naor, D., Naor, M., Lotspiech, J.: Revocation and tracing schemes for stateless receivers. In: Kilian, J. (ed.) CRYPTO 2001. LNCS, vol. 2139, pp. 41–62. Springer, Heidelberg (2001)
17. Naor, M., Pinkas, B.: Efficient trace and revoke schemes. In: Frankel, Y. (ed.) FC 2000. LNCS, vol. 1962, pp. 1–20. Springer, Heidelberg (2001)
18. Pointcheval, D., Stern, J.: Security arguments for digital signatures and blind signatures. J. Cryptology 13(3), 361–396 (2000)
19. Sakai, R., Furukawa, J.: Identity-based broadcast encryption. Cryptology ePrint Archive, Report 2007/217 (2007), http://eprint.iacr.org/
20. Schnorr, C.P.: Efficient signature generation by smart cards. J. Cryptology 4(3), 161–174 (1991)
21. Scott, M., Costigan, N., Abdulwahab, W.: Implementing cryptographic pairings on smartcards. In: Goubin, L., Matsui, M. (eds.) CHES 2006. LNCS, vol. 4249, pp. 134–147. Springer, Heidelberg (2006)

Cryptanalysis of Short Exponent RSA with Primes Sharing Least Significant Bits

Hung-Min Sun[1], Mu-En Wu[1], Ron Steinfeld[3],
Jian Guo[2], and Huaxiong Wang[2,3]

[1] Department of Computer Science,
National Tsing Hua University, Taiwan
hmsun@cs.nthu.edu.tw, mn@is.cs.nthu.edu.tw
[2] School of Physical & Mathematical Sciences,
Nanyang Technological University, Singapore
{guojian,hxwang}@ntu.edu.sg
[3] Centre for Advanced Computing - Algorithms and Cryptography,
Department of Computing, Macquarie University, Australia
rons@ics.mq.edu.au

Abstract. LSBS-RSA denotes an RSA system with modulus primes, p and q, sharing a large number of least significant bits. In *ISC 2007*, Zhao and Qi analyzed the security of short exponent LSBS-RSA. They claimed that short exponent LSBS-RSA is much more vulnerable to the lattice attack than the standard RSA. In this paper, we further raise the security boundary of the Zhao-Qi attack by considering another polynomial. Our improvemet supports the result of analogue Fermat factoring on LSBS-RSA, which claims that p and q cannot share more than $\frac{n}{4}$ least significant bits, where n is the bit-length of pq. In conclusion, it is a trade-off between the number of sharing bits and the security level in LSBS-RSA. One should be more careful when using LSBS-RSA with short exponents.

Keywords: RSA, least significant bits (LSBs), LSBS-RSA, short exponent attack, lattice reduction technique, the Boneh-Durfee attack.

1 Introduction

Since 1978, RSA [20] is the most popular cryptosystem in the world. Its security is based on the hardness of factoring problem. Generally we apply 1024-bit RSA modulus to achieve the goal of factoring-infeasible, but such large modulus also causes the inefficiency in encryption and decryption of RSA. Consequently, many practical issues have been considered when implementing RSA such as how to reduce the encryption time (or signature-verification time), how to reduce the decryption time (or signature-generation time) [16], [17], etc.. One of the most common methods to reduce the decryption time is using a short private exponent d. However, in 1990 Wiener [25] showed that choosing too small private exponent is insecure when using RSA system. Indeed, instances of RSA with $d < N^{0.25}$

can be efficiently broken by the continued fraction attack, which is also called the Wiener attack. The boundary of the Wiener attack had been extended by Boneh and Durfee [3] in 1998. They took advantage of lattice reduction technique and showed that instance of RSA with $d < N^{0.292}$ should be considered insecure. Although their method is heuristic, the experiments demonstrate the effectiveness of the attack.

LSBS-RSA denotes an RSA system with modulus primes sharing a large number of least significant bits. This RSA variant was suggested to improve the computational efficiency of server-aided signature generation [6], [22]. Steinfeld and Zheng analyzed the security of LSBS-RSA under the partial key exposure attacks in [21], and [22]. Sun et. al. [19] further improved this result by using the property of LSBS-RSA. Their results show that LSBS-RSA with small public exponent is inherently resistant to the partial key exposure attacks. This gives an advantage of using small exponent LSBS-RSA in applications. However, it does not imply that LSBS-RSA is secure against all the small exponent attacks. Zhao and Qi [26] showed that LSBS-RSA is much more vulnerable than the standard RSA against the attack by using lattice reduction technique. Here we call the Zhao-Qi attack throughout this paper. Let α be the parameter such that $|p - q| = r \cdot 2^{(\frac{1}{2}-\alpha)n}$ for some odd integer r. The Zhao-Qi attack shows that LSBS-RSA is insecure under the condition

$$\beta < \tfrac{1}{6}\alpha + \tfrac{13}{12} - \tfrac{1}{3}\sqrt{\alpha^2 + (6\gamma + 1)\alpha + \tfrac{12\gamma+1}{4}},$$

where β and γ satisfy $d = N^\beta$ and $e = N^\gamma$, respectively. For example, if p and q share $0.2n$ least significant bits and $e \approx N$ (i.e., $\gamma = 1$, $\alpha = 0.3$), then LSBS-RSA will be insecure when $d < N^{0.335}$.

In this paper, we give a revised version of the Zhao-Qi attack to further raise the security boundary. Also, we provide a new method by considering another polynomial to attacking LSBS-RSA, which conducts to a better result compared with the Zhao-Qi attack. Our result shows that LSBS-RSA is insecure under the condition

$$\beta < \tfrac{2}{3}\alpha + \tfrac{5}{6} - \tfrac{4}{3}\sqrt{\alpha^2 + (\tfrac{3}{2}\gamma - \tfrac{1}{2})\alpha - \tfrac{6\gamma-1}{16}}.$$

Take the case $e \approx N$ for example, if the modulus primes share the $0.2n$ least significant bits (i.e., $\gamma = 1$, $\alpha = 0.3$), LSBS-RSA will be insecure if $d < N^{0.662}$, which is much higher than Zhao and Qi's boundary. Moreover, compared with the Boneh-Durfee attack [3], [4] and de Weger's attack on RSA with small prime difference [24], our result yields an improvement when primes sharing a large number of least significant bits.

The remainder of this paper is organized as follows. In Section 2, we briefly review LSBS-RSA, lattice reduction technique, and the Zhao-Qi attack. In Section 3, we revise the Zhao-Qi attack to raise the security boundary. Section 4 shows the proposed method to analyze the security boundary of short exponent LSBS-RSA. Further discussions are shown in Section 5. Finally, we conclude this paper and give some open problems in Section 6.

2 Preliminaries

2.1 LSBS-RSA and the Notation: α, β, and γ

An RSA system with modulus primes sharing a large number of least significant bits is called LSBS-RSA. Denote an LSBS-RSA modulus $N = pq$ as the product of two large primes p and q, with p & q share the $(\frac{1}{2} - \alpha)n$ least significant bits, where $q < p < 2q$, and n is the bit-length of N. We may write $|p - q| = r \cdot 2^{(\frac{1}{2}-\alpha)n}$ for some integer r of αn bits and it is obvious that $\alpha \leq \frac{1}{2}$. In the following table we define the notation α, β, and γ used in the paper.

α: α is the parameter such that $|p - q| = r \cdot 2^{(\frac{1}{2}-\alpha)n}$ for some odd integer r
β: β is the parameter such that $d = N^\beta$.
γ: γ is the parameter such that $e = N^\gamma$.

In addition, we define the function "LSB$(\cdot)$". Given an integer x of m bits, whose binary representation is

$$(x)_2 = (x_m, x_{m-1}, ...x_j, ..., x_i, ..., x_2, x_1)_2,$$

where $x_i = 0$ or 1 for $i = 1, ..., m$. Then, x_m should be 1, which is called the most significant bit of x. x_1 could be 0 or 1, which is called the least significant bit of x. Denote "LSB$_{i^-j}(x)$" as the i-th to j-th least significant bits of $(x)_2$, where $i < j$. That is,

$$\text{LSB}_{i^-j}(x) = (x_j, ..., x_i)_2.$$

And denote "LSB$_i(x)$" as the i-th least significant bit of $(x)_2$. That is,

$$\text{LSB}_i(x) = x_i.$$

The following lemma shows the exposed portion of the modulus primes if p and q share a number of least significant bits.

Lemma 1. *Let $N = pq$ denote an n-bit modulus in LSBS-RSA, where $LSB_{1^-m}(p) = LSB_{1^-m}(q)$. There exists an algorithm to compute the $LSB_{1^-2m}(p+q)$, $LSB_{1^-m}(p)$, and $LSB_{1^-m}(q)$ in time polynomial in n.*

Proof. Let $p = p_H \cdot 2^m + l$ and $q = q_H \cdot 2^m + l$. Thus, l is a solution to the modular quadratic congruence $x^2 \equiv N \pmod{2^m}$, and it can be computed at most for 4 candidates in time polynomial in n (see Lemma 1 in [22] for more detail). Consider the identity

$$\left(\tfrac{p+q}{2}\right)^2 = \left(\tfrac{p-q}{2}\right)^2 + N.$$

Replacing p and q by $p_H \cdot 2^m + l$ and $q_H \cdot 2^m + l$, respectively, conducts to

$$\text{LSB}_{1^-2m-2}\left(l \cdot (p_H + q_H) \cdot 2^m + l^2\right) = \text{LSB}_{1^-2m-2}(N).$$

Note that l is an odd integer. Thus, $l^{-1} \pmod{2^{2m-2}}$ exists and we denote it as l^{-1} for short. We have

$$\text{LSB}_{1\tilde{}2m-2}((p_H + q_H) \cdot 2^m) = \text{LSB}_{1\tilde{}2m-2}\left(l^{-1} \cdot (N - l^2)\right), \tag{1}$$

which implies

$$\text{LSB}_{1\tilde{}2m-1}\left(\tfrac{p+q}{2}\right) = \text{LSB}_{1\tilde{}2m-1}((p_H + q_H)\,2^{m-1} + l)$$
$$= \text{LSB}_{1\tilde{}m}(p_H + q_H) \parallel \text{LSB}_m\left((p_H + q_H)\,2^{m-1} + l\right) \parallel \text{LSB}_{1\tilde{}m-1}(l), \tag{2}$$

where "$\parallel$" denotes the symbol for concatenation. Combining (1) and (2) we can compute $\text{LSB}_{1\tilde{}2m-1}\left(\tfrac{p+q}{2}\right)$. Thus, we have

$$\text{LSB}_{1\tilde{}2m}(p + q) = \text{LSB}_{1\tilde{}2m-1}\left(\tfrac{p+q}{2}\right) \parallel 0,$$

which completes the proof.

The following corollary is the key point we used in the paper to improve the Zhao-Qi attack.

Corollary 1. *Let $N = pq$ denote an n-bit modulus of LSBS-RSA, where p and q share the $(\tfrac{1}{2} - \alpha)n$ least significant bits, i.e., $\text{LSB}_{1\tilde{}(\tfrac{1}{2}-\alpha)n}(p) = \text{LSB}_{1\tilde{}(\tfrac{1}{2}-\alpha)n}(q)$. Then, $\text{LSB}_{1\tilde{}(\tfrac{1}{2}-\alpha)n}(p+q)$, $\text{LSB}_{1\tilde{}(\tfrac{1}{2}-\alpha)n}(p)$, and $\text{LSB}_{1\tilde{}(\tfrac{1}{2}-\alpha)n}(q)$, are known to the attacker.*

Proof. The proof is quite easy. We just replace m in Lemma 1 by $(\tfrac{1}{2} - \alpha)n$.

Note that we should set $\alpha > \tfrac{1}{4}$. In case of $\alpha \leq \tfrac{1}{4}$, which means that p and q share the $\tfrac{n}{4}$ least significant bits at least, the modulus N can be factored in time polynomial in n (see Corollary 1 in [22]). This result is analogue to the result of Fermat's factoring method, which factors N immediately if p and q share the $\tfrac{n}{4}$ most significant bits at least. We call the factoring attack when $\alpha \leq \tfrac{1}{4}$ as "Analogue Fermat factoring" in the paper.

2.2 Lattice Attack

A vector space L is called a lattice if L is spanned by ω linearly independent vectors, denoted as $\mathbf{u}_1, \mathbf{u}_2, ..., \mathbf{u}_\omega \in \mathbb{Z}^n$, over $\mathbb{Z}$. That is,

$$L = \left\{ \sum_{i=1}^{\omega} a_i \mathbf{u}_i \mid \text{where } a_i \in \mathbb{Z} \text{ and } \mathbf{u}_i \in \mathbb{Z}^n \text{ for } i = 1, ..., \omega \right\}.$$

$\mathbf{u}_1, \mathbf{u}_2, ..., \mathbf{u}_\omega$ are also called the basis of lattice L. We say that L is full rank if $\omega = n$. The determinant of a full rank lattice L, denoted as $\det(L)$, is equal to the determinant of the n by n matrix whose rows are $\mathbf{u}_1, \mathbf{u}_2, ..., \mathbf{u}_\omega$. Next we show the result of the output of the LLL algorithm, which produces a new basis of lattice L with the following properties.

Lemma 2. *[15] Suppose that L is a lattice with basis $\{\mathbf{u}_1, \mathbf{u}_2, ..., \mathbf{u}_\omega\}$. Given the input $\{\mathbf{u}_1, \mathbf{u}_2, ..., \mathbf{u}_\omega\}$, LLL algorithm can produce a new basis $\{\mathbf{b}_1, \mathbf{b}_2, ..., \mathbf{b}_\omega\}$ satisfying:*

1. $\|\mathbf{b}_i^*\|^2 \leq 2 \|\mathbf{b}_{i+1}^*\|^2$ for $i = 1, ..., \omega - 1$.
2. If $\mathbf{b}_i = \mathbf{b}_i^* + \sum_{j=1}^{i-1} \mu_{i,j} \mathbf{b}_j^*$, then $|\mu_j| \leq \frac{1}{2}$ for all j and $i = 1, ..., \omega$.

We call $\{\mathbf{b}_1, \mathbf{b}_2, ..., \mathbf{b}_\omega\}$ an LLL-reduced basis of L. Here, we just mention one of the properties of LLL-reduced basis that will be used in the paper.

Theorem 1. *Let $\{\mathbf{b}_1, \mathbf{b}_2, ..., \mathbf{b}_\omega\}$ be an LLL-reduced basis of L. Then,*

$$\|\mathbf{b}_1\| \leq 2^{\frac{\omega}{2}} \det(L)^{\frac{1}{\omega}}, \text{ and } \|\mathbf{b}_2\| \leq 2^{\frac{\omega}{2}} \det(L)^{\frac{1}{\omega-1}}.$$

Coppersmith [7] took the advantage of LLL algorithm to find the small roots of a modular equation. Suppose that the norm of a polynomial $h(x, y) = \sum_{i,j} a_{i,j} x^i y^j$ is defined as $\|h(x, y)\|^2 = \sum_{i,j} a_{i,j}^2$. Howgrave-Graham [13] followed Coppersmith's method to show the following lemma, which is a powerful tool in the cryptanalysis of RSA systems.

Lemma 3. *(Howgrave-Graham) Let $h(x, y) \in \mathbb{Z}[x, y]$ be a bivariate polynomial which is a sum of at most ω monomials. Suppose that*

1. $h(x_0, y_0) = 0 \pmod{e^m}$, where $m \in \mathbb{N}$
2. $\|h(xX, yY)\| < \frac{e^m}{\sqrt{\omega}}$, where $|x_0| < X$, $|y_0| < Y$.

Then $h(x_0, y_0) = 0$ holds over the integers.

The proof of Lemma 3 can be found in earlier citations, such as [7], [3], [4], [8], [9].

In the heuristic variant of the lattice attacks (with bivariate\trivariate modular polynomials) that we consider in this paper, we hope that we get two algebraically independent polynomials from the lattice. Given a modular polynomial $f(x, y) = 0 \pmod{e}$ with ω monomials. We may construct a set of polynomials with the same root as $f(x, y) = 0 \pmod{e}$, and regard these polynomials as a basis of the lattice L by representing their coefficients as the vectors with ω components. Then, applying the LLL algorithm to produce the first two shortest vectors in LLL basis, denoted as $f_1(x, y)$ and $f_2(x, y)$, whose norms are smaller than $2^{\frac{\omega}{2}} \det(L)^{\frac{1}{\omega}}$ and $2^{\frac{\omega}{2}} \det(L)^{\frac{1}{\omega-1}}$, respectively. Thus, according to Lemma 3, if we set $2^{\frac{\omega}{2}} \det(L)^{\frac{1}{\omega}} < \frac{e^m}{\sqrt{\omega}}$, then the root of $f_1(x, y) \pmod{e}$ and $f_2(x, y) \pmod{e}$ also hold over $\mathbb{Z}$. We then take their resultant with respect to one of the variables to eliminate it and get a univariate equation and solve for the root in the other variable. It is a well-known technique called the lattice attack. Zhao and Qi [26] used this technique to attack short exponent LSBS-RSA. Next, we briefly describe their attack.

2.3 The Zhao-Qi Attack

Assume that an LSBS-RSA modulus $N = pq$ satisfies $p - q = r \cdot 2^{(\frac{1}{2}-\alpha)n}$, where r is an odd integer. Then,

$$p + q = (p - q) + 2q = r \cdot 2^{(\frac{1}{2}-\alpha)n} + 2q. \tag{3}$$

Applying (3) to RSA equation yields

$$ed = k\left[(N+1) - 2q - r \cdot 2^{(\frac{1}{2}-\alpha)n}\right] + 1.$$

Consider the polynomial

$$f(x, y, z) = x(A - 2y - az) + 1, \tag{4}$$

where $A = N + 1$, and $a = 2^{(\frac{1}{2}-\alpha)n}$. Then $(x_0, y_0, z_0) = (k, q, r)$ is a root of $f(x, y, z) \pmod{e}$. Define $X = N^{\gamma+\beta-1}$, $Y = N^{\frac{1}{2}}$, and $Z = N^\alpha$, then we have $|x_0| < X$, $|y_0| < Y$, and $|z_0| < Z$, respectively.

Note that $f(x, y, z)$ can be further reduced by multiplying $(-a)^{-1} \pmod{e}$ to eliminate the coefficient of xz. Thus, we transform the equation (4) to

$$F(x, y, z) = A'x + B'xy + xz + C' \pmod{e}.$$

In order to construct the lattice, Zhao and Qi considered the polynomials

$$\begin{aligned}
g_{l,i,b}(x, y, z) &:= e^{m-l} x^i y^b F^l(x, y, z), \text{ for } l = 0, ..., m-1; i = 1, ..., m-l;\\
b &= 0, 1; h'_{j,l}(x, y, z) := e^{m-l}(az)^j F^l(x, y, z), \text{ for } l = 0, ..., m \text{ and } j = 0, ..., t;\\
h''_{j,l}(x, y, z) &:= e^{m-l} y^j F^l(x, y, z), \text{ for } l = 0, ..., m \text{ and } j = 1, ..., t;
\end{aligned} \tag{5}$$

where m and t are two parameters in $\mathbb{N}$. It can be observed that $(x_0, y_0, z_0) = (k, q, r)$ is a root of $g_{l,i,b}(x, y, z)$, $h'_{j,l}(x, y, z)$, and $h''_{j,l}(x, y, z)$ modulo e^m.

Zhao and Qi solved the modular equation (4) by using the lattice reduction technique shown above. According to their calculation, the sufficient condition to find (x_0, y_0, z_0) is

$$\beta < \tfrac{1}{6}\alpha + \tfrac{13}{12} - \tfrac{1}{3}\sqrt{\alpha^2 + (6\gamma + 1)\alpha + \tfrac{12\gamma+1}{4}}. \tag{6}$$

This gives the security boundary of the Zhao-Qi attack. In the next section we revise the Zhao-Qi attack to further raise the above security boundary.

3 The Zhao-Qi Attack Revised

In this section we point out that the boundary of the Zhao-Qi attack can be further raised by using Corollary 1. Note that, in LSBS-RSA, according to Corollary 1, $\text{LSB}_{1-(\frac{1}{2}-\alpha)n}(p)$ can be computed efficiently in polynomial time in n. We may denote $q = \widetilde{q} \cdot 2^{(\frac{1}{2}-\alpha)n} + q_0$ and replace y by $y \cdot 2^{(\frac{1}{2}-\alpha)n} + q_0$ in (4). Then, (4) is transformed to

$$f'(x, y, z) = x\left[(A - 2q_0) - 2ay - az)\right] + 1,$$

where $A = N + 1$, and $a = 2^{(\frac{1}{2}-\alpha)n}$. Then $(x_0, y_0, z_0) = (k, \widetilde{q}, r)$ is a root of $f'(x, y, z) \pmod{e}$. Note that the size of the root y_0 is reduced when compared with that of $f(x, y, z)$. In fact, since the sizes of $\widetilde{q}$ and r are about αn bits, we may further simplify $f'(x, y, z)$ to

$$f''(x, y) = x\left[(A - 2q_0) - ay)\right] + 1 \pmod{e}, \tag{7}$$

with the root $(k, 2\widetilde{q}+r) \pmod{e}$. The problem of solving (7) is similar to the *Small Inverse Problem* introduced in 1999 by Boneh and Durfee [3], [4]. However, we do not deal with this polynomial here, instead of considering another polynomial which will yield a better boundary. We show the detail in the next section.

4 Proposed Attack

According to Corollary 1, $\text{LSB}_{1-(1-2\alpha)n}(p+q)$ is known to attackers in an LSBS-RSA system. In this section we take this advantage to further extend the boundary of the revised Zhao-Qi attack. Denote

$$p + q = \overline{\phi} \cdot 2^{(1-2\alpha)n} + \phi_0,$$

where $\phi_0 = \text{LSB}_{1-(1-2\alpha)n}(p+q)$, and $\overline{\phi}$ is an unknown number of $(2\alpha - \frac{1}{2})n$ bits. Thus, the RSA equation can be derived to

$$ed = k\left[(N + 1 - \phi_0) - \left(\overline{\phi} \cdot 2^{(1-2\alpha)n}\right)\right] + 1.$$

Consider the modular equation

$$f^*(x, y) = x(B - by) + 1 \pmod{e}, \tag{8}$$

where $B = N + 1 - \phi_0$, $b = a^2 = 2^{(1-2\alpha)n}$, then $(x_0, y_0) = (k, \overline{\phi})$ is a root of $f(x, y) \pmod{e}$. Define $X = N^{\gamma+\beta-1}$, $Y = N^{2\alpha-\frac{1}{2}}$, we have $|x_0| < X$, and $|y_0| < Y$. Note that the form of the modular equation (8) is the same as the form in (7). In particular, the upper bound Y in (8) is much smaller than that in (7). This is the reason why we use the polynomial (8) instead of using (7) to attack short exponent LSBS-RSA, because the boundary derived from (8) will be better than the boundary derived from (7). However, this is not enough. We further simplify the equation (8) by multiplying $(-b)^{-1} \pmod{e}$ (note that this inverse exists since b is a power of 2 while e is odd). The advantage is that the coefficient of the leading monomial xy is 1 and hence we remove the powers of b from the determinant of the lattice and allow larger β while satisfying the determinant inequality.

Consequently, we get the alternative polynomial having $(x_0, y_0) = (k, \overline{\phi})$ as a zero root modulo e, that is

$$f(x, y) = xy + B'x + C' \pmod{e}, \tag{9}$$

where $B' = B(-b)^{-1} \pmod{e}$ and $C' = (-b)^{-1} \pmod{e}$. We construct the lattice by considering the polynomials

$$g_{i,l}(x, y) := x^i f^l(x, y) e^{m-l} \pmod{e^m}, \text{ for } l = 0, ..., m; \ i = 0, ..., m-l;$$
$$h_{j,l}(x, y) := y^j f^l(x, y) e^{m-l} \pmod{e^m}, \text{ for } l = 0, ..., m \text{ and } j = 1, ..., t.$$

Take the case $m = 3$, $t = 1$, for example. The coefficient matrix for this case is $M =$

ijl	1	x	xy	x^2	x^2y	x^2y^2	x^3	x^3y	x^3y^2	x^3y^3	xy^2	x^2y^3	x^3y^4
000	e^3												
100	xe^3	e^3X											
001	fe^2	-	-	e^2XY									
200	x^2e^3			e^3X^2									
101	xfe^2	-			e^2X^2Y								
002	f^2e	-	-	-	-	eX^2Y^2							
300	x^3e^3						e^3X^3						
201	x^2fe^2			-				e^2X^3Y					
102	xf^2e	-		-	-				eX^3Y^2				
003	f^3	-	-	-	-	-	-	-	-	X^3Y^3			
010	ye^3										e^3Y		
011	yfe^2		-								-	e^2XY^2	
012	yf^2e		-		-						-	-	eX^2Y^3
013	yf^3		-		-	-		-	-	-	-	-	X^3Y^4

Let M_x and M_y denote the matrices with the coefficient vectors of $g_{i,l}(x, y)$ and $h_{j,l}(x, y)$, respectively. We have

$$\det(M_x) = e^{\frac{m(m+1)(m+2)}{3}} \cdot X^{\frac{m(m+1)(m+2)}{3}} \cdot Y^{\frac{m(m+1)(m+2)}{6}}$$
$$\det(M_y) = e^{\frac{tm(m+1)}{2}} \cdot X^{\frac{tm(m+1)}{2}} \cdot Y^{\frac{t(m+1)(m+t+1)}{2}}. \tag{10}$$

Applying $X = e^{\frac{\gamma+\beta-1}{\gamma}}$, and $Y = e^{\frac{2\alpha-1/2}{\gamma}}$ to (10) yields

$$\det(M_x) = e^{\frac{m(m+1)(m+2)}{3} + \left(\frac{\gamma+\beta-1}{\gamma} \cdot \frac{m(m+1)(m+2)}{3}\right) + \left(\frac{2\alpha-1/2}{\gamma} \cdot \frac{m(m+1)(m+2)}{6}\right)}$$

$$= e^{\frac{m(m+1)(m+2)}{3} \cdot \left(2 + \frac{\alpha+\beta-5/4}{\gamma}\right)}$$

$$\det(M_y) = e^{\frac{tm(m+1)}{2} + \left(\frac{\gamma+\beta-1}{\gamma} \cdot \frac{tm(m+1)}{2}\right) + \left(\frac{2\alpha-1/2}{\gamma} \cdot \frac{t(m+1)(m+t+1)}{2}\right)}$$

$$= e^{\frac{tm(m+1)}{2} \cdot \left(2 + \frac{\beta-1}{\gamma}\right) + \left(\frac{2\alpha-1/2}{\gamma} \cdot \frac{t(m+1)(m+t+1)}{2}\right)}.$$

Note that if we only consider the x-shift, i.e., $g_{i,l}(x, y)$, to satisfy the requirement in Lemma 3 we have to set $\det(M_x) < e^{m\omega_x}$, where $\omega_x = \frac{(m+1)(m+2)}{2}$ is the dimension of M_x. Thus, we have

$$\frac{m(m+1)(m+2)}{3} \cdot \left(2 + \frac{\alpha+\beta-5/4}{\gamma}\right) < m \cdot \frac{(m+1)(m+2)}{2}. \tag{11}$$

Simplifying (11) yields
$$\alpha + \beta < \tfrac{5}{4} - \tfrac{\gamma}{2}. \tag{12}$$

Note that for the usual case ($\alpha = \tfrac{1}{2}$, $\gamma = 1$), we may attack RSA when $\beta < \tfrac{1}{4}$, which achieves the same boundary as the Wiener attack [25].

Moreover, we further include the y-shift, i.e., $h_{j,l}(x,y)$, to our attack. By setting $\det(M) = \det(M_x) \cdot \det(M_y) < e^{m\omega}$, where $\omega = \frac{(m+1)(m+2)}{2} + t(m+1)$ is the dimension of M, we have

$$\frac{m(m+1)(m+2)}{3} \cdot \left(2 + \frac{\alpha+\beta-5/4}{\gamma}\right) + \frac{tm(m+1)}{2} \cdot \left(2 + \frac{\beta-1}{\gamma}\right) + \left(\frac{2\alpha-1/2}{\gamma} \cdot \frac{t(m+1)(m+t+1)}{2}\right)$$
$$< \frac{m(m+1)(m+2)}{2} + tm(m+1),$$

which leads to

$$\frac{m(m+2)}{3} \cdot \left(\frac{1}{2} + \frac{\alpha+\beta-5/4}{\gamma}\right) + \frac{tm}{2} \cdot \frac{\beta-1}{\gamma} + \left(\frac{2\alpha-1/2}{\gamma} \cdot \frac{t(m+t+1)}{2}\right) < 0, \tag{13}$$

After simplifying the left hand side of (13) as a quadratic polynomial with variable t we get

$$\left[\frac{2\alpha-1/2}{\gamma}\right] \cdot t^2 + \left[m\frac{\beta-1}{\gamma} + (m+1)\frac{2\alpha-1/2}{\gamma}\right] \cdot t + \left[\frac{2m(m+2)}{3}(\tfrac{1}{2} + \frac{\alpha+\beta-5/4}{\gamma})\right] < 0. \tag{14}$$

Note that the left hand side of (14) would be minimized at

$$t = \frac{-\left[m\frac{\beta-1}{\gamma} + (m+1)\frac{2\alpha-1/2}{\gamma}\right]}{2\left[\frac{2\alpha-1/2}{\gamma}\right]} = \frac{-[m(\beta-1)+(m+1)(2\alpha-1/2)]}{4\alpha-1} = \frac{(\tfrac{3}{2}-2\alpha-\beta)m - 2\alpha+\tfrac{1}{2}}{4\alpha-1}. \tag{15}$$

Plugging (15) in (14) yields

$$\left[\frac{2\alpha-1/2}{2\gamma}\right] \cdot \left(\frac{(\tfrac{3}{2}-2\alpha-\beta)m - 2\alpha+\tfrac{1}{2}}{4\alpha-1}\right)^2 + \left[m\frac{\beta-1}{2\gamma} + (m+1)\frac{2\alpha-1/2}{2\gamma}\right] \cdot \frac{(\tfrac{3}{2}-2\alpha-\beta)m - 2\alpha+\tfrac{1}{2}}{4\alpha-1}$$
$$+ \left[\frac{2m(m+2)}{3}(\tfrac{1}{2} + \frac{\alpha+\beta-5/4}{\gamma})\right] < 0. \tag{16}$$

Multiplying (16) by 2γ yields

$$(2\alpha - \tfrac{1}{2}) \cdot \left(\frac{(\tfrac{3}{2}-2\alpha-\beta)m - 2\alpha+\tfrac{1}{2}}{4\alpha-1}\right)^2 + \left[m(\beta-1) + (m+1)(2\alpha-\tfrac{1}{2})\right] \cdot \frac{(\tfrac{3}{2}-2\alpha-\beta)m - 2\alpha+\tfrac{1}{2}}{4\alpha-1}$$
$$+ \frac{2m(m+2)}{3}(\tfrac{\gamma}{2} + \alpha + \beta - \tfrac{5}{4}) < 0.$$

After simplifying the first term and the second term we have

$$\frac{1}{2(4\alpha-1)} \cdot \left((\tfrac{3}{2} - 2\alpha - \beta)m - 2\alpha + \tfrac{1}{2}\right)^2 - \frac{1}{4\alpha-1} \cdot \left((\tfrac{3}{2} - 2\alpha - \beta)m - 2\alpha + \tfrac{1}{2}\right)^2$$
$$+ \left[\frac{2m(m+2)}{3}(\tfrac{\gamma}{2} + \alpha + \beta - \tfrac{5}{4})\right] < 0.$$

Combining the first term and the second term we get

$$\tfrac{-1}{2(4\alpha-1)} \cdot \left(\left((\tfrac{3}{2}-2\alpha-\beta)m - 2\alpha + \tfrac{1}{2}\right)^2 + \left[\tfrac{2m(m+2)}{3}(\tfrac{\gamma}{2}+\alpha+\beta-\tfrac{5}{4})\right]\right) < 0$$

which is simplified to

$$\tfrac{2m(m+2)}{3}(\tfrac{\gamma}{2}+\alpha+\beta-\tfrac{5}{4}) \cdot 2(4\alpha-1)) < \left((\tfrac{3}{2}-2\alpha-\beta)m - 2\alpha + \tfrac{1}{2}\right)^2.$$

Thus, we get the inequality

$$(2\gamma + 4\alpha + 4\beta - 5)(4\alpha - 1) < \frac{3\left((\tfrac{3}{2}-2\alpha-\beta)m-2\alpha+\tfrac{1}{2}\right)^2}{m(m+2)} = \frac{3\left((\tfrac{3}{2}-2\alpha-\beta)-\tfrac{2\alpha}{m}+\tfrac{1}{2m}\right)^2}{1+\tfrac{2}{m}}. \tag{17}$$

As m goes to infinity, (17) becomes

$$(2\gamma + 4\alpha + 4\beta - 5)(4\alpha - 1) < 3\left(\tfrac{3}{2} - 2\alpha - \beta\right)^2. \tag{18}$$

We give more discussions in the next section.

5 Further Discussions

5.1 The Summary of Our Attack

In conclusion, the boundary that our attack can succeed is

$$\beta < \tfrac{2}{3}\alpha + \tfrac{5}{6} - \tfrac{4}{3}\sqrt{\alpha^2 + (\tfrac{3}{2}\gamma - \tfrac{1}{2})\alpha - \tfrac{6\gamma-1}{16}},$$

where $\tfrac{1}{4} \leq \alpha \leq \tfrac{1}{2}$. For the case $\gamma = 1$, we have the boundary

$$\beta < \tfrac{2}{3}\alpha + \tfrac{5}{6} - \tfrac{4}{3}\sqrt{\alpha^2 + \alpha - \tfrac{5}{16}}. \tag{19}$$

The curve of (19) is shown in Fig 1. We also show the other attacks, which includes the Wiener attack, Boneh-Durfee attack, and the Analogue Fermat factoring. As can be seen in Fig 1, if p and q share the $\tfrac{n}{4}$ least significant bits at least, i.e., $\alpha \leq 0.25$, the Analogue Fermat factoring can factor N efficiently. The Wiener attack and the Boneh-Durfee attack (short for B-D attack) work in the case $\beta < \tfrac{1}{4}$ and $\beta < 0.284$, respectively. We should point out in B-D attack [3], [4], Boneh and Durfee use the geometrically progressive matrices to eliminate the larger terms in the coefficient matrix, and thus the upper bound is further extended from $d < N^{0.284}$ to $d < N^{0.292}$. This technique can also be applied to our method but we do not discuss it here.

5.2 Experiments

We have performed the experiments on a server containing Intel processors of 2.4 GHz Core 2 Quad, with 2 GB Memory. The lattice basis reductions are done using Shoup's NTL [14]. We have to mention that, like the Boneh-Durfee attack,

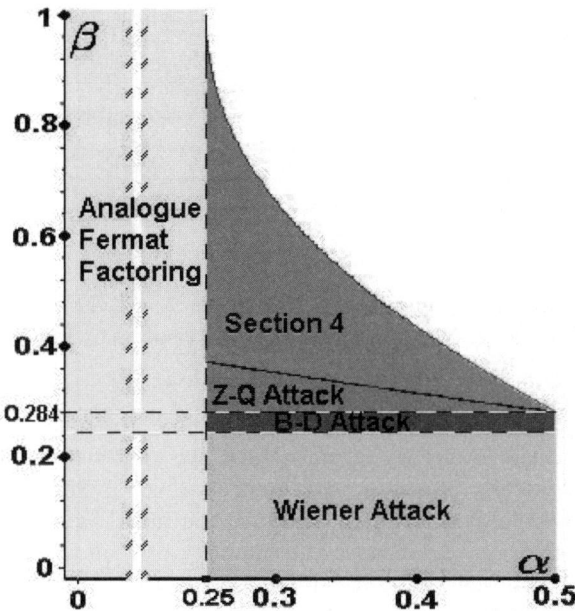

Fig. 1. Insecure Region of α and β for which LSBS-RSA with $\gamma = 1$

our attack is also heuristic since the resultant computations may fail even with low probability. Also, we just experimented for the samples on LSBS-RSA with short private exponent, and $e \approx N$ (*i.e.*, $\gamma \approx 1$). Note that the size of 1024 bits, or 2048 bits for the modulus are often used in the current computational environment. However, we just experimented for the size of 128 bits for the reason of simplicity. The experimental results are shown in the following.

n	α	d	β	m	t	Rank of Lattice	Running Time	Advantage over Z-Q Attack
128 bits	0.275	90 bits	0.704	5	12	93	36 sec	43 bits
128 bits	0.300	77 bits	0.607	5	7	63	9.5 sec	31 bits
128 bits	0.350	61 bits	0.478	5	3	39	3.0 sec	17 bits
128 bits	0.425	45 bits	0.350	5	2	33	0.7 sec	5 bits

The entries for β in the table are the tested values for which the attacks succeeded. As can be seen in the last column of the table, our attacks achieved the higher boundary than the one of the Zhao-Qi attack. In addition, we have to point out that considering LSBS-RSA with $\gamma < 1$ (*i.e.*, $e \ll N$) and $\beta < 1$ (*i.e.*, $d \ll N$) is not practical. Up to now there is no research about designing LSBS-RSA with short private and public exponents simultaneously. The most related work for designing short private and public exponents RSA was proposed by Sun *et. al.*[16], [17], but the modulus primes in their key-generation schemes cannot be determined as desired. Hence, it seems meaningless to cryptanalyze

Table 1. The upper bound or lower bound of β for which our attack can succeed in LSBS-RSA

$\gamma = \log_N(e)$	$\gamma = 1.0$	$\gamma = 0.9$	$\gamma = 0.86$	$\gamma = 0.8$	$\gamma = 0.7$	$\gamma = 0.6$	$\gamma = 0.55$
$\alpha = 0.5$	0.284	0.323	0.339	0.364	0.407	0.452	0.476
$\alpha = 0.4$	0.437	0.468	0.480	0.500	0.534	0.571	0.590
$\alpha = 0.3$	0.662	0.681	0.688	0.700	0.721	0.743	0.754
$\alpha = 0.25$	1	1	1	1	1	1	1

the security of short exponent LSBS-RSA with $\gamma < 1$. Even so, in Table 1 we still summarize the largest β for which the proposed attack can succeed.

5.3 Further Improvement

To further extend the boundary of our attack, we may focus on the approximation to $p + q$. Generally, $p + q$ is estimated as $2\lceil\sqrt{N}\rceil$. Sun, Wu, & Chen [18] proposed a method, called *EPF*, to estimate the most significant bits of $p + q$. With this technique, we may reduce the quantity of Y in (8) and this may conduct to a better boundary of LSBS-RSA for security. More precisely, suppose that $p + q$ is estimated as ϕ_E, with the error $|(p+q) - \phi_E| < 2^m$, where $m < \frac{n}{2}$, then the RSA equation can be represented as

$$ed = x\left[(N+1) - (\phi_E + y)\right] + 1,$$

where $x_0 = k$, and $y_0 < 2^m$ are two unknown numbers. The above equation gives us a motivation to combine de Weger's result [24] with our attack. Next, we briefly describe it.

5.4 LSBS-RSA with Small Prime Difference

Recall that $p - q = r \cdot 2^{(\frac{1}{2}-\alpha)n}$, for some integer r. In general, the quantity of r is about $2^{\alpha n}$. Here we consider the case that bit-length of r is much smaller than αn. This means p and q share a number of the most significant bits. The cryptanalysis of this RSA modulus had been analyzed by de Weger [24]. We suppose that p and q share the α_M most significant bits, which implies $p - q < 2^{\frac{n}{2}-\alpha_M}$, and share the α_L least significant bits, which implies $p - q = r_L \cdot 2^{\alpha_L}$ for some integer r_L. Thus, $p - q$ can be represented as

$$p - q = r_L \cdot 2^{\alpha_L}, \text{ where } r_L < 2^{\frac{n}{2}-(\alpha_M+\alpha_L)}.$$

And then, $p + q$ can be computed from the identity:

$$(p+q)^2 = (p-q)^2 + 4N = r_L^2 \cdot 2^{2\alpha_L} + 4N.$$

Using the representation of $p + q$ above may yield a better boundary for the lattice attack on this kind of RSA variant. However, we do not show the detail here but leave it in the full version.

6 Conclusion and Future Work

In this paper, we give a revised version of the Zhao-Qi attack to further raise the security boundary of LSBS-RSA. In addition, we also propose a method by considering another polynomial to attacking LSBS-RSA, which conducts to a better result compared with the Zhao-Qi attack. Our result shows that LSBS-RSA is getting more vulnerable as smaller exponents or more number of primes sharing bits.

An interesting question is how to design an LSBS-RSA with short public and private exponents simultaneously. Note that in Sun *et. al.*'s schemes [16], [17], we cannot choose modulus primes randomly in order to produce desired public and private exponents. Up to now it is still an open problem to design such scheme to achieve balanced short exponents RSA with prime sharing a large number of least (or most) significant bits. Conversely, the cryptanalysis of such RSA variant, if it exists, is worth to research as well.

Although LSBS-RSA is beneficial to the computational efficiency in several applications, such as server-aided signature generation [6], we have to indicate using LSBS-RSA also raises the risk in the security [21], [22], [24], [26]. We believe it is a trade-off between the efficiency and the security level, and thus one should be more careful in using such RSA variants.

Acknowledgment

The work was supported in part by the National Science Council, Taiwan, under Contract No. NSC 96-2628-E-007-025-MY3, the Singapore National Research Foundation under Research Grant NRF-CRP2-2007-03, the Singapore Ministry of Education under Research Grant T206B2204 and the Australian Research Council under ARC Discovery Project DP0665035. Ron Steinfeld's work was supported by a Macquarie University Research Fellowship.

References

1. Boneh, D., Durfee, G., Frankel, Y.: An Attacks on RSA Given a Small Fraction of the Private Key Bits. In: Ohta, K., Pei, D. (eds.) ASIACRYPT 1998. LNCS, vol. 1514, pp. 25–34. Springer, Heidelberg (1998)
2. Boneh, D., Durfee, G., Frankel, Y.: Exposing an RSA Private Key Given a Small Fraction of its Bits, Full version of the work from Asiacrypt 1998 (1998), http://crypto.stanford.edu/~dabo/abstracts/bits_of_d.html
3. Boneh, D., Durfee, G.: Cryptanalysis of RSA with private key d less than $N^{0.292}$. In: Stern, J. (ed.) EUROCRYPT 1999. LNCS, vol. 1592, pp. 1–11. Springer, Heidelberg (1999)
4. Boneh, D., Durfee, G.: Cryptanalysis of RSA with private key d less than $N^{0.292}$. IEEE Transactions on Information Theory 46(4), 1339–1349 (2000)
5. Blömer, J., May, A.: New Partial Key Exposure Attacks on RSA. In: Boneh, D. (ed.) CRYPTO 2003. LNCS, vol. 2729, pp. 27–43. Springer, Heidelberg (2003)

6. Bellare, M., Rogaway, P.: The exact security of digital signatures: How to sign with RSA and Rabin. In: Maurer, U.M. (ed.) EUROCRYPT 1996. LNCS, vol. 1070, pp. 399–416. Springer, Heidelberg (1996)
7. Coppersmith, D.: Finding a Small Root of a Bivariate Integer Equation; Factoring with High Bits Known. In: Maurer, U.M. (ed.) EUROCRYPT 1996. LNCS, vol. 1070, pp. 178–189. Springer, Heidelberg (1996)
8. Coron, J.-S.: Finding Small Roots of Bivariate Integer Polynomial Equations Revisited. In: Cachin, C., Camenisch, J.L. (eds.) EUROCRYPT 2004. LNCS, vol. 3027, pp. 492–505. Springer, Heidelberg (2004)
9. Coron, J.-S.: Finding Small Roots of Bivariate Integer Polynomial Equations: A Direct Approach. In: Menezes, A. (ed.) CRYPTO 2007. LNCS, vol. 4622, pp. 379–394. Springer, Heidelberg (2007)
10. Durfee, G., Nguyen, P.Q.: Cryptanalysis of the RSA Schemes with Short Secret Exponent form Asiacrypt 1999. In: Okamoto, T. (ed.) ASIACRYPT 2000. LNCS, vol. 1976, pp. 1–11. Springer, Heidelberg (2000)
11. Ernst, M., Jochemsz, E., May, A., de Weger, B.: Partial Key Exposure Attacks on RSA up to Full Size Exponents. In: Cramer, R. (ed.) EUROCRYPT 2005. LNCS, vol. 3494, pp. 371–386. Springer, Heidelberg (2005)
12. Hastad, J.: Solving simultaneous modular equations of low degree. SIAM J. of Computing 17, 336–341 (1988)
13. Howgrave-Graham, N.: Finding small roots of univariate modular equations revisited. In: Darnell, M.J. (ed.) Cryptography and Coding 1997. LNCS, vol. 1355, pp. 131–142. Springer, Heidelberg (1997)
14. Shoup, V.: NTL: A Library for doing Number Theory, http://shoup.net/ntl
15. Lenstra, A., Lenstra, H., Lovasz, L.: Factoring Polynomials with Rational Coefficients. Mathematiche Annalen 261, 515–534
16. Sun, H.-M., Yang, W.-C., Laih, C.-S.: On the design of RSA with short secret exponent. In: Lam, K.-Y., Okamoto, E., Xing, C. (eds.) ASIACRYPT 1999. LNCS, vol. 1716, pp. 150–164. Springer, Heidelberg (1999)
17. Sun, H.-M., Yang, C.-T.: RSA with balanced short exponents and its application to entity authentication. In: Vaudenay, S. (ed.) PKC 2005. LNCS, vol. 3386, pp. 199–215. Springer, Heidelberg (2005)
18. Sun, H.-M., Wu, M.-E., Chen, Y.-H.: Estimating the Prime Factors of an RSA Modulus and an Extension of the Wiener Attack. In: Katz, J., et al. (eds.) ACNS 2007. LNCS, vol. 4521, pp. 116–128. Springer, Heidelberg (2007)
19. Sun, H.-M., Wu, M.-E., Wang, H., Guo, J.: On the Improvement of the BDF Attack on LSBS-RSA. In: Mu, Y., Susilo, W., Seberry, J. (eds.) ACISP 2008. LNCS, vol. 5107, pp. 84–97. Springer, Heidelberg (2008)
20. Rivest, R., Shamir, A., Aldeman, L.: A Method for Obtaining Digital Signatures and Public-Key Cryptosystems. Communications of the ACM 21(2), 120–126 (1978)
21. Steinfeld, R., Zheng, Y.: An Advantage of Low-Exponent RSA with Modulus Primes Sharing Least Significant Bits. In: Naccache, D. (ed.) CT-RSA 2001. LNCS, vol. 2020, pp. 52–62. Springer, Heidelberg (2001)
22. Steinfeld, R., Zheng, Y.: On the Security of RSA with Primes Sharing Least-Significant Bits. Appl. Algebra Eng. Commun. Comput. 15(3-4), 179–200 (2004)
23. Verheul, E.R., van Tilborg, H.C.A.: Cryptanalysis of less short RSA secret exponents. Appl. Algebra Eng. Commun.

24. de Weger, B.: Cryptanalysis of RSA with small prime difference. Applicable Algebra in Engineering, Communication and Computing 13, 17–28 (2002)
25. Wiener, M.J.: Cryptanalysis of short RSA secret exponents. IEEE Trans. Information Theory 36(3), 553–559 (1990)
26. Zhao, Y.-D., Qi, W.-F.: Small Private-Exponent Attack on RSA with Primes Sharing Bits. In: Garay, J., et al. (eds.) ISC 2007. LNCS, vol. 4779, pp. 221–229. Springer, Heidelberg (2007)

Efficient and Short Certificateless Signature

Raylin Tso[1,*], Xun Yi[2], and Xinyi Huang[3,**]

[1] Department of Computer Science, National Chengchi University, Taiwan
raylin@cs.nccu.edu.tw
[2] School of Computer Science and Mathematics, Victoria University, Australia
Xun.Yi@vu.edu.au
[3] Centre for Computer and Information Security Research,
School of Computer Science and Software Engineering,
University of Wollongong, Australia
xh068@uow.edu.au

Abstract. A certificateless signature (CLS) scheme with short signature size is proposed in this paper. Our scheme is as efficient as BLS short signature scheme in both communication and computation, and therefore turns out to be more efficient than other CLS schemes proposed so far. We provide a rigorous security proof of our scheme in the random oracle model. The security of our scheme is based on the k-CAA hard problem and a new discovered hard problem, namely, modified k-CAA problem. Our scheme can be applied to systems where signatures are typed in by human or systems with low-bandwidth channels and/or low-computation power, such as PDAs or cell phones.

Keywords: Bilinear pairing, certificateless signature, random oracle, short signature.

1 Introduction

Nowadays, the main difficulty in developing secure systems based on public key cryptography is the deployment and management of infrastructures to support the authenticity of cryptographic keys. The general approach to solve this problem is to use a Public Key Infrastructure (PKI) in which a trusted authority, called Certification Authority (CA), issues certificates to bind users and their public keys. However, the PKI is costly to use as it involves certificate revocation, storage, distribution, and verification.

In order to overcome the above mentioned problem, identity-based (ID-based) cryptography was firstly introduced by Shamir [19] in 1984. In an ID-based cryptosystem, one can use its unique identifier (e.g., names or e-mail addresses) as the public key. The user's identifier is publicly known and thus does not need certificates to prove its authenticity. Consequently, the problems associated with

---

* Supported by National Science Council of Taiwan (NSC 97-2218-E-004-002).
** Supported by the National Natural Science Foundation of China (No. 60673070) and the Natural Science Foundation of Jiangsu Province (No. BK2006217).

certificates can be eliminated. However, ID-based cryptosystems have an inherent key escrow issue as a third party "Private Key Generator" (PKG) generates the private keys for all users in the system. Therefore, the PKG must be fully trusted in ID-based cryptosystems.

Certificateless cryptography, firstly introduced by Al-Riyami and Paterson [2] in 2003, intends to solve the key escrow issue inherent in ID-based cryptography, and meanwhile to eliminate the use of certificates as in the conventional PKI. In a certificateless cryptosystem, private keys of users are generated by not only the PKG but also users themselves. In other words, PKG only issues a partial private key to each user while the user independently generates its additional public/secret key pair. Consequently, the PKG is unable to obtain secret keys of users. The cryptographic operations in certificateless system can be performed successfully only when both the partial private key and the secret key are known. In this way, the key escrow problem can be overcome. Following Al-Riyami and Paterson's pioneering work [2], many certificateless schemes have been proposed in recent years, such as [1,10,12,15,16,21,22,23,25] and etc..

1.1 Motivations

In the definition of the security model for certificateless signature (CLS) schemes, some papers (e.g., [1,14,15,17]) assume that the adversary should be allowed to obtain signatures signed with false public keys chosen by the adversary. But, in real world, the signatures that a "realistic" adversary can obtain are generated by a signer using the partial private key and the secret key corresponding to its original public key. Therefore, the adversary defined in those security models seems to enjoy more power than it could have in the real world. This assumption provides a higher security for the schemes on one hand but also limits the efficiency of the schemes on the other hand. This is because CLS schemes with a high security level usually sacrifice some efficiency in computation and/or communication and may not be practical for systems with low-bandwidth channels and/or low-computation power, such as PDAs or cell phones.

Except for the scheme proposed by Huang *et al.* [15], no secure CLS scheme has a short size of signature, although many short signatures in traditional PKI have been proposed [8,9,24]. As mentioned in [6], there are several important practical reasons for the desirableness of short signatures. For example, battery life is the major limitation on wireless devices such as PDAs, cell phones, RFID chips and sensors. Communicating even one bit of data uses significantly more power than executing one 32-bit instruction [3]. Reducing the number of bits to communicate saves power and is important to increase battery life. Also, in many settings, communication is not reliable, and thus the number of bits one has to communicate should be kept as few as possible. This inspired us to propose a more efficient certificateless short signature scheme.

1.2 Our Contributions

In this paper, on the basis of BLS short signature scheme [9], an efficient certificateless signature scheme with short signature size is proposed. Our scheme is as efficient as BLS short signature scheme (which is the traditional PKI model) in both communication and computation, and turns out to be more efficient than other CLS schemes proposed so far. This is achieved at the cost of stronger complexity assumptions.

In addition, as mentioned in [15], the security model defined in some CLS schemes (e.g., [16,21]) assume that, when an adversary queries the oracle **Public-Key-Replace** to replace a real public key with a false public key chosen by itself, the adversary is required to provide both the false public key and the corresponding secret value as the input. This is unreasonable since an adversary may pick a random public key for which the corresponding secret value is unknown even for himself. In other words, this definition may not cover the case in which an adversary may successfully forge a new signature with a false public key without knowing the corresponding secret value (to the false public key). Our definition for CLS scheme does not have such a problem and an adversary is not required to provide a secret value corresponding to a false public key as the input to the oracle **Public-Key-Replace**.

Based on the k-CAA problem, we define a new hard problem named "modified k-CAA problem". Assuming the hardness of these problems, we provide a rigorous security proof for our scheme in the random orale model .

The rest of this paper is organized as follows. In Section 2, we give some preliminaries (including the new discovered hardness assumption) which will be required throughout this paper. Section 3 is the presentation of our certificateless short signature scheme and in Section 4, we give the security proofs for our new scheme. Section 5 gives the performance comparison of our scheme with other schemes and the conclusion is given in Section 6.

2 Preliminaries

Before presenting our results, we first briefly review the notion of certificateless signature and its security definition. We will also review the definition for groups equipped with a bilinear map, and precisely state the hardness assumptions.

2.1 Certificateless Signatures

Following the definition in [2], a certificateless signature scheme is specified by seven randomized algorithms: **Setup, Partial-Private-Key-Extract, Set-Secret-Value, Set-Private-Key, Set-Public-Key, Sign** and **Verify**.

Setup. This algorithm takes as input a security parameter 1^k and returns the system parameters *params* and the master secret key *msk*. Usually, this algorithm is run by the KGC. We assume throughout that *params* are publicly and authentically available, but that only the KGC knows *msk*.

Partial-Private-Key-Extract. This algorithm takes the system parameter *params*, the master secret key *msk* and an identity *ID* as input. It returns a partial private key D_{ID}. Usually, this algorithm is run by the KGC and its output is transported to the identity *ID* over a confidential and authentic channel.

Set-Secret-Value. This algorithm takes as input the system parameter *params* and an identity *ID* as input and outputs a secret value x_{ID}. This algorithm is run by the identity *ID* for itself.

Set-Private-Key. This algorithm takes the system parameter *params*, a partial private key D_{ID} and a secret value x_{ID} of an identity *ID* as input. The value x_{ID} is used to transform D_{ID} into the (full) private key SK_{ID}. The algorithm returns SK_{ID}. This algorithm is run by the identity *ID* for itself.

Set-Public-Key. This algorithm takes the system parameter *params*, an identity *ID* and the identity's private key PK_{ID} as input. It outputs the public key PK_{ID} for the identity *ID*.

Sign. This algorithm takes the system parameter *params*, an identity *ID*, the private key SK_{ID} of *ID* and a message *M* as input. It outputs a certificateless signature σ.

Verify. This algorithm takes the system parameter *params*, an identity *ID*, the identity's public key PK_{ID} and a message/signature pair (M, σ) as input. It output *true* if the signature is correct, or *false* otherwise.

2.2 Security Model

In this section, we discuss the definition of the security for a certificateless signature scheme.

For certificateless cryptosystems, the widely accepted notion of security was defined by Al-Riyami and Paterson in [2]. According to their definitions as well as the definitions in [25], there are two types of adversary with different capabilities:

Type I Adversary: This type of adversary $\mathcal{A}_I$ models a dishonest user who does not have access to the master key *msk* but has the ability to replace the public key of any entity with a value of his choice.

Type II Adversary: This type of adversary $\mathcal{A}_{II}$ models a malicious KGC who has access to the master key *msk* but *cannot perform public keys replacement*[1].

Generally, there are five oracles which can be accessed by the adversaries according to the game specifications which will be given later.

1. **Create-User:** On input an identity $ID \in \{0,1\}^*$, if *ID* has already been created, nothing is to be carried out. Otherwise, the oracle runs the algorithms **Private-Key-Extract, Set-Secret-Value, Set-Public-Key** to obtain the partial private key D_{ID}, secret value x_{ID} and public key PK_{ID}. In this case, *ID* is said to be created. In both cases, PK_{ID} is returned.

2. **Public-Key-Replace:**[2] On input an identity *ID* and a user public key PK'_{ID}, the original user public key of *ID* is replaced with PK'_{ID} if *ID* has been created. Otherwise, no action will be taken.

---
[1] It is important that in certificateless cryptosystems, KGC must be semi-trusted and cannot perform the public key replacement. This is because that any adversary who knows the master key can impersonate anyone if he is allowed to replace the public key of the entity.

[2] Different from the security model defined in [16,21], in this oracle, an adversary is not required to provide the secret value x'_{ID} which is used to generated the public key PK'_{ID}.

3. **Secret-Value-Extract:** On input an identity, it returns the corresponding user secret key x_{ID} if ID has been created. Otherwise, returns a symbol $\bot$. Note that x_{ID} is the secret value associated with the original public key PK_{ID}. This oracle does not output the secret value associated with the replaced public key PK'_{ID}.
4. **Partial-private-Key-Extract:** On input an identity ID, it returns the partial private key D_{ID} if ID has been created. Otherwise, returns a symbol $\bot$.
5. **Sign:** On input an identity ID and a message $m \in \{0,1\}^*$, the signing oracle proceeds in one of the both cases below.
    - If ID has not been created, returns $\bot$.
    - If ID has been created, returns a valid signature σ such that $true \leftarrow$ Veify(m, σ, ID, PK_{ID}). Here PK_{ID} is the public key returned from the oracle **Create-User**.

The standard notion of security for a signature scheme is called existential unforgeability against adaptive chosen message attack defined by Goldwasser, Micali and Revist [11]. To define the existential unforgeability of a certificateless signature against Type I adversary $\mathcal{A}_I$ and Type II adversary $\mathcal{A}_{II}$, we define two games, one for $\mathcal{A}_I$ and the other for $\mathcal{A}_{II}$.

Game 1: This game is executed between a challenger $\mathcal{C}$ and an adaptive chosen message and chosen identity adversary $\mathcal{A}_I$.

Setup. The challenger $\mathcal{C}$ runs the algorithm **Setup** of the certificateless signature scheme to obtain both the public parameter $params$ and the master secret key msk. The adversary $\mathcal{A}_I$ is given $params$ but the master secret key msk is kept by the challenger.

Queries. $\mathcal{A}_I$ adaptively access all the oracles defined in Section 2.2 in a polynomial number of times.

Forgery. Eventually, $\mathcal{A}_I$ outputs a forgery $(ID^*, PK_{ID^*}, m^*, \sigma^*)$ and wins the game if the following conditions hold true:
1. $true \leftarrow$ Verify$(params, ID^*, PK_{ID^*}, m^*, \sigma^*)$.
2. (ID^*, m^*) has never been submitted to the oracle **Sign**.
3. ID^* has never been submitted to the oracle **Partial-Private-Key-Extract** and **Secret-Value-Extract**.

Definition 1. Define $Adv_{\mathcal{A}_I}$ to be the probability that a Type I adaptively chosen message and chosen identity adversary $\mathcal{A}_I$ wins in the above game, taken over the coin tosses made by $\mathcal{A}_I$ and the challenger. We say a certificateless signature scheme is secure against Type I attack, if, for all probabilistic polynomial-time (PPT) adversary $\mathcal{A}_I$, the success probability $Adv_{\mathcal{A}_I}$ is negligible.

Game 2: This game is executed between a challenger $\mathcal{C}$ and an adaptive chosen message and chosen identity adversary $\mathcal{A}_{II}$.

Setup. The challenger $\mathcal{C}$ runs the algorithm **Setup** of the certificateless signature scheme to obtain both the public parameter $params$ and the master secret key msk. The adversary $\mathcal{A}_{II}$ is given both $params$ and msk.

Queries. $\mathcal{A}_{II}$ adaptively access all the oracles defined in Section 2.2 in a polynomial number of times.

Forgery. Eventually, $\mathcal{A}_{II}$ outputs a forgery $(ID^*, PK_{ID^*}, m^*, \sigma^*)$ and wins the game if the following conditions hold true:

1. $true \leftarrow \text{Verify}(params, ID^*, PK_{ID^*}, m^*, \sigma^*)$.
2. (ID^*, m^*) has never been queried to the oracle **Sign**.
3. ID^* has never been submitted to the oracle **Secret-Value-Extract**.

Definition 2. Define $Adv_{\mathcal{A}_{II}}$ to be the probability that a Type II adaptively chosen message and chosen identity adversary $\mathcal{A}_{II}$ wins in the above game, taken over the coin tosses made by $\mathcal{A}_{II}$ and the challenger. We say a certificateless signature scheme is secure against Type II attack, if, for all probabilistic polynomial-time (PPT) adversary $\mathcal{A}_{II}$, the success probability $Adv_{\mathcal{A}_{II}}$ is negligible.

Definition 3. A certificateless signature scheme is existentially unforgeable against adaptive chosen message and chosen identity attack if it is secure against both Type I and Type II attacks defined above.

2.3 Bilinear Groups and Complexity Assumptions

Let $\mathbb{G}_1, \mathbb{G}_2$ be two multiplicative cyclic groups of order p for some large prime p. Our scheme makes use of the *bilinear* map $\hat{e} : \mathbb{G}_1 \times \mathbb{G}_1 \to \mathbb{G}_2$ between these two groups. The bilinear map should be satisfied with the following properties:

1. **Bilinear:** A map $\hat{e} : \mathbb{G}_1 \times \mathbb{G}_1 \to \mathbb{G}_2$ is bilinear if $\hat{e}(g^a, h^b) = \hat{e}(g, h)^{ab}$ for all $g, h \in \mathbb{G}_1$ and $a, b \in \mathbb{Z}_p^*$.
2. **Non-degenerate:** The map does not send all pairs in $\mathbb{G}_1 \times \mathbb{G}_1$ to the identity in $\mathbb{G}_2$. Observe that since $\mathbb{G}_1, \mathbb{G}_2$ are groups of prime order, this implies that if g is a generator of $\mathbb{G}_1$, then $\hat{e}(g, g)$ is a generator of $\mathbb{G}_2$.
3. **Computable:** There is an efficient algorithm to compute $\hat{e}(g, h)$ for any $g, h \in \mathbb{G}_1$.

A bilinear map satisfying the three properties above is said to be an *admissible* bilinear map. We can make this map using the Weil pairing or the Tate pairing [4,5,9]

Next, we describe the complexity assumptions which are required for the security proof of our scheme.

We first introduce a problem given by Mitsunari et al. [18] which is called k-CAA (Collusion Attack Algorithm with k traitors) problem and then give a modified problem.

Definition 4. k-**CAA Problem** [18]
For $x, h_1, \cdots, h_k \in \mathbb{Z}_p^*$, and a generator g of $\mathbb{G}_1$. Given g, g^x and k pairs $(h_1, g^{(x+h_1)^{-1}}), \cdots, (h_k, g^{(x+h_k)^{-1}})$, output a new pair $(h^*, g^{(x+h^*)^{-1}})$ for some $h^* \notin \{h_1, \cdots, h_k\}$.

The k-CAA problem is believed to be hard. Mitsunari et al. firstly introduced this problem and gave a traitor tracing scheme [18] based on this problem. Although their application to tracing traitors is proved by Tô et al. [20] to be insecure, the k-CCA problem still remains to be hard without broken. Zhang et al. [24] recently gave a secure and efficient signature scheme based on the same problem.

In addition to the k-CAA problem, the security of our scheme also bases on a modified version of the original k-CAA problem. We call it as the Modified k-CAA Problem which is defined as follows:

Definition 5. Modified k-CAA Problem
For randomly picked $x, a, b, h_1, \cdots, h_k \in \mathbb{Z}_p^*$, and a generator g of $\mathbb{G}_1$. Let $g_1 = g^{ab} \neq g$. Given g, g^x, g^a, g^b, g^{bx} and k pairs $(h_1, g_1^{(x+h_1)^{-1}}), \cdots, (h_k, g_1^{(x+h_k)^{-1}})$, output either a new pair $(h^*, g_1^{(x+h^*)^{-1}})$ for some $h^* \notin \{h_1, \cdots, h_k\}$ or g_1.

Note that in the above definition, g_1 is not given to the problem. If we define $g_1 = g$ in the input, then g^a, g^b and g^{bx} are useless and can be ignored. In this case, the problem is to find a new pair $(h^*, g^{(x+h^*)^{-1}})$ for some $h^* \notin \{h_1, \cdots, h_k\}$.

3 The Proposed Certificateless Short Signature Scheme

In this section, we will describe our certificateless short signature scheme. It consists of the following algorithms:

Setup: Let $(\mathbb{G}_1, \mathbb{G}_2)$ be bilinear groups of some prime order $p \geq 2^k$, k be the security parameter of the scheme. $\hat{e} : \mathbb{G}_1 \times \mathbb{G}_1 \to \mathbb{G}_2$ is an admissible bilinear pairing. Let $H_0 : \{0,1\}^* \to \mathbb{G}_1^*$, $H_1 : \{0,1\}^* \to \mathbb{Z}_p^*$ be two secure cryptographic hash functions. KGC chooses a random number $s \in \mathbb{Z}_p^*$ and an arbitrary generator $g \in \mathbb{G}_1$. It sets $P_{pub} = g^s$, publishes $params = \{\mathbb{G}_1, \mathbb{G}_2, g, \hat{e}, H_0, H_1, P_{pub}\}$ and keeps the master secret key $msk = s$ secretly.

Partial-Private-Key-Extract: Given an entity's identity $ID \in \{0,1\}^*$, KGC sets $Q_{ID} = H_0(ID)$ and computes the entity's partial private key $D_{ID} = Q_{ID}^s$. KGC transmits D_{ID} to ID over a confidential and authentic channel.

Set-Secret-Value: The entity ID chooses a random number $x_{ID} \in \mathbb{Z}_p^*$.

Set-Private-Key: The entity ID sets his private key as $SK_{ID} = (D_{ID}, x_{ID})$.

Set-Public-Key: Given x_{ID}, the entity ID computes the public key $PK_{ID} = (PK_1, PK_2) = (g^{x_{ID}}, Q_{ID}^{x_{ID}})$.

Sign: To sign a message $m \in \{0,1\}^*$, the entity ID first sets $h = H_1(m||ID||PK_{ID})$ and then computes the signature $\sigma = D_{ID}^{(x_{ID}+h)^{-1}}$.

Verify: Given a pair (m, σ) and ID's public key $PK_{ID} = (g^{x_{ID}}, Q_{ID}^{x_{ID}})$, any verifier first checks the equation $\hat{e}(PK_1, Q_{ID}) = \hat{e}(PK_2, g)$. If it holds, then computes $h = H_1(m||ID||PK_{ID})$ and checks the equation

$$\hat{e}(\sigma, PK_1 \cdot g^h) \stackrel{?}{=} \hat{e}(H_0(ID), P_{pub}).$$

If the equality holds, outputs $true$, otherwise, outputs $false$.

Correctness: If σ is a valid signature on m, then the correctness holds since

$$\hat{e}(\sigma, PK_1 \cdot g^h)$$
$$= \hat{e}(D_{ID}^{(x_{ID}+h)^{-1}}, g^{x_{ID}} \cdot g^h) = \hat{e}(H_0(ID)^{s(x_{ID}+h)^{-1}}, g^{x_{ID}+h})$$
$$= \hat{e}(H_0(ID), g)^{s(x_{ID}+h)^{-1}(x_{ID}+h)} = \hat{e}(H_0(ID), g)^s$$
$$= \hat{e}(H_0(ID), g^s) = \hat{e}(H_0(ID), P_{pub}).$$

4 Security Proofs

Theorem 1. Unforgeability against Type I Adversary: If there exists a Type I adaptively chosen message and chosen ID adversary $\mathcal{A}_I$ who can ask at most q_C **Create-User** queries, q_{KEx} **Partial-Private-Key-Extract** queries, q_{VEx} **Secret-Value-Extract** queries and q_S **sign** queries, respectively, and can break the proposed scheme in polynomial time with success probability ε, then there exists an algorithm $\mathcal{F}$ which, using $\mathcal{A}_I$ as a black box, can solve the modified k-CAA problem [Definition 5] (where $k \geq q_S$ and is in proportion to the number of the H_1-hash queries) with probability $Adv_{\mathcal{F}}^{mk-CAA} \geq (1 - \frac{1}{q_C})^{q_{PKEx}+q_{VEx}} (1 - \frac{1}{q_S+1})^{q_S} \frac{1}{q_C(q_S+1)} \varepsilon$.

Proof: If there exists an adversary $\mathcal{A}_I$ who can break the unforgeability of the proposed scheme via Type I attack, then, we can construct another adversary $\mathcal{F}$ such that $\mathcal{F}$ can use $\mathcal{A}_I$ as a black-box and solve the modified k-CAA problem.

Let g be a generator of $\mathbb{G}_1$, x, a, b be three random numbers of $\mathbb{Z}_p^*$ and $g_1 = g^{ab} \in \mathbb{G}_1$. Let $h_1, \cdots, h_k \in \mathbb{Z}_p^*$ be k random numbers. $\mathcal{F}$ is given the challenge $\{g, g^x, g^a, g^b, g^{bx}, (h_1, g_1^{(x+h_1)^{-1}}), \cdots, (h_k, g_1^{(x+h_k)^{-1}})\}$. The purpose of $\mathcal{F}$ is either to find a new pair $(h^*, g_1^{(x+h^*)^{-1}})$ for some $h^* \notin \{h_1, \cdots, h_k\}$ or to find g_1, which are the solutions to the modified k-CAA problem.

Setup: In order to solve the problem, $\mathcal{F}$ utilizes $\mathcal{A}_I$ as a black-box. To get the black-box $\mathcal{A}_I$ run properly, $\mathcal{F}$ will simulate the environments of the proposed scheme and the oracles which $\mathcal{A}_I$ can access. In this proof, we regard the hash functions H_0, H_1 as random oracles. $\mathcal{F}$ starts by picking an admissible bilinear pairing $\hat{e} : \mathbb{G}_1 \times \mathbb{G}_1 \to \mathbb{G}_2$, and sets $P_{pub} = g^a$. $\mathcal{F}$ then sends $params = (\mathbb{G}_1, \mathbb{G}_2, \hat{e}, g, P_{pub})$ to $\mathcal{A}_I$ and allows $\mathcal{A}_I$ to run.

Due to the ideal randomness of the H_1-hash, we may assume that $\mathcal{A}_I$ is well-behaved in the sense that it always requests a H_1-hash of $m||ID||PK_{ID}$ before it requests a signature for m signed by ID's public key PK_{ID}. In addition, it always requests a H_1-hash of $m^*||ID^*||PK_{ID^*}$ that it outputs as its forgery. It is trivial to modify any adversary-algorithm $\mathcal{A}_I$ to have this property.

Query: At any time, $\mathcal{A}_I$ is allowed to access the following oracles in a polynomial number of times. These oracles are all simulated by $\mathcal{F}$.

1. **Create-User:** $\mathcal{A}_I$ can query this oracle by given an identity ID_i. In response to these queries, $\mathcal{F}$ first chooses a random number $t \in \{1, \cdots, q_C\}$.

(1) If $i \neq t$, $\mathcal{F}$ chooses $d_i, x_i \in_R \mathbb{Z}_p^*$ and sets $H_0(ID_i) = g^{d_i}$, $PK_{ID_i} = (PK_{(ID_i,1)}, PK_{(ID_i,2)}) = (g^{x_i}, g^{d_i x_i})$. In this case, the corresponding partial private key of the entity ID_i is $D_{ID_i} = H_0(ID_i)^a = g^{ad_i} = P_{pub}^{d_i}$ and the secret value is $x_{ID_i} = x_i$.
(2) If $i = t$, $\mathcal{F}$ sets $H_0(ID_t) = g^b$ and $PK_{ID_t} = (PK_{(ID_t,1)}, PK_{(ID_t,2)}) = (g^x, g^{bx})$. In this case, $\mathcal{F}$ will set $D_{ID_t} = x_{ID_t} = \perp$ which means that it cannot compute the secret value and the partial private key of ID_t.
In both cases, returns $H_0(ID_i)$ and PK_{ID_i}.

2. **Partial-Private-Key-Extract:** At any time, $\mathcal{A}_I$ can query the oracle by given an identity ID_i. $\mathcal{F}$ outputs a symbol $\perp$ if ID_i has not been created. If ID_i has been created and $i \neq t$, $\mathcal{F}$ returns $D_{ID_i} = g^{ad_i}$. Otherwise, $\mathcal{F}$ returns $failure$ and terminates the simulation.

3. **Public-Key-Replace:** $\mathcal{A}_I$ can request to replace public key PK_{ID_i} of an entity ID_i with new public key PK'_{ID_i} chosen by $\mathcal{A}_I$ itself. $\mathcal{F}$ replaces the original public key PK_{ID_i} with PK'_{ID_i} if ID_i has been created. Otherwise, outputs $\perp$. Here, to replace a public key, the secret value corresponding to the new public key is not required.

4. **Secret-Value-Extract:** Given ID_i chosen by $\mathcal{A}_I$, outputs $\perp$ if ID_i has not been created. If ID_i has been created and $i \neq t$, $\mathcal{F}$ returns x_{ID_i} to $\mathcal{A}_I$. Otherwise, $i = t$ and $\mathcal{F}$ reports $failure$ and terminates the simulation.

5. **H_1 Queries:** $\mathcal{A}_I$ can query the random oracle H_1 at any time on an input $\omega_i = (m_l \| ID_j \| PK_{ID_k})$. For i-th H_1 query asked by $\mathcal{A}_I$ on input ω_i, $\mathcal{F}$ first checks if $ID_j = ID_t$ and $PK_{ID_k} = PK_{ID_t}$ or not. Here PK_{ID_t} is the original public key.
   - If $ID_j = ID_t$ and $PK_{ID_k} = PK_{ID_t}$, then $\mathcal{F}$ first flips a biased coin which outputs a value $c_i = 1$ with probability ζ, and $c_i = 0$ with probability $1 - \zeta$ (the value of ζ will be optimized later).
     (1) If $c_i = 1$, $\mathcal{F}$ picks a random value $h'_i \in \mathbb{Z}_p^*$ where $h'_i \notin \{h_1, \cdots, h_k\}$ and responds h'_i to $\mathcal{A}_I$ as the value of $H_1(\omega_i)$.
     (2) If $c_i = 0$, $\mathcal{F}$ returns a value $h''_i \in_R \{h_1, \cdots, h_k\}$ as the output of $H_1(\omega_i)$ where h''_i must be a fresh value which means that it has not been assigned as an output of H_1 queries before.
   - Otherwise, $\mathcal{F}$ picks and responds with a random value $\mu_i \in \mathbb{Z}_p^*$.
   In either cases, $\mathcal{F}$ records (ω_i, h'_i, c_i), (ω_i, h''_i, c_i) or (ω_i, μ_i) to a H_1-$List$ which is initially empty.

6. **Sign:** For each sign query on an input (m_l, ID_j), output $\perp$ if ID_j has not been created. For any input (m_l, ID_j) with ID_j which has already been created, since we assume that $\mathcal{A}_I$ is well-behaved, we know that $\mathcal{A}_I$ has already queried the random oracle H_1 on the input $\omega_i = (m_l \| ID_j \| PK_{ID_j})$.
   - If $ID_j \neq ID_t$, $\mathcal{F}$ uses the private key (x_{ID_j}, D_{ID_j}) of ID_j and $\mu_i = H_1(\omega_i)$ on the H_1-$List$ to generate the valid signature σ_i for the message m_l and the identity ID_j.
   - If $ID_j = ID_t$, then, $\mathcal{F}$ first checks the H_1-$List$.
     (1) If $c_i = 1$, $\mathcal{F}$ reports $failure$ and terminates the simulation.
     (2) Otherwise, $c_i = 0$ and $h''_i = H_1(m_l \| ID_t \| PK_{ID_t})$ is on the H_1-$List$. For easy of description, we assume $h''_i = h_i \in \{h_1, \cdots, h_k\}$.

$\mathcal{F}$ then returns $\sigma_i = g_1^{(x+h_i)^{-1}}$. Note that

$$\hat{e}(\sigma_i, PK_{(ID_t,1)} \cdot g^{h_i}) = \hat{e}(g_1^{(x+h_i)^{-1}}, g^x \cdot g^{h_i}) = \hat{e}(g_1, g)$$
$$= \hat{e}(g^{ab}, g) = \hat{e}(g^b, g^a) = \hat{e}(H_0(ID_t), P_{pub}).$$

Therefore, σ_i is a valid signature on m_l and ID_t.

Forgery: After all the queries, $\mathcal{A}_I$ outputs a forgery $(ID^*, PK_{ID^*} = (PK_{(ID^*,1)}, PK_{(ID^*,2)}), m^*, \sigma^*)$ and wins the game.

If σ^* is a valid forgery, then $h^* = H_1(m^*||ID^*||PK_{ID^*})$ which is on the H_1-List, and $\hat{e}(\sigma^*, PK_{(ID^*,1)} \cdot g^{h^*}) = \hat{e}(H_0(ID^*), P_{pub})$ where $PK_{ID^*} = g^{x^*}$ may be a new public key replaced by $\mathcal{A}_I$ or the original public key generated by the oracle **Create-User**. In addition, $\hat{e}(PK_{(ID^*,1)}, Q_{ID^*}) = \hat{e}(PK_{(ID^*,2)}, g)$ if $\mathcal{A}_I$ wins the game. If $ID^* \neq ID_t$, then $\mathcal{F}$ outputs $failure$ and terminates the simulation. Otherwise, $ID^* = ID_t$ and $\mathcal{F}$ will check the H_1-List.

(1) If $c^* = 0$, $\mathcal{F}$ outputs $failure$ and terminates the simulation.
(2) Otherwise, $c^* = 1$ and $h^* \notin \{h_1, \cdots, h_k\}$. If $(PK_{(ID^*,1)}, PK_{(ID^*,2)}) = (PK_{(ID_t,1)}, PK_{(ID_t,2)})$ is the original public key generated by the oracle, then, $\mathcal{F}$ outputs a new pair $(h^*, \sigma^*) = (h^*, g_1^{(x+h^*)^{-1}})$ which will be the solution to the modified k-CAA problem. If $(PK_{(ID^*,1)}, PK_{(ID^*,2)})$ is a new public key replaced by $\mathcal{A}_I$, then, using the knowledge of exponent assumption introduced in [7,13], $\mathcal{F}$ can either extract x^* if $(PK_{(ID^*,1)}, PK_{(ID^*,2)}) = (g^*, g^{bx^*})$ is generated from (g, g^b) or extract r if $(PK_{(ID^*,1)}, PK_{(ID^*,2)}) = ((g^x)^r, (g^{bx})^r)$ is generated from (g^x, g^{bx}). Consequently, $g_1 = (\sigma^*)^{(x^*+h^*)}$ can be computed if x^* extracted or a new pair $(h', g_1^{(x+h')^{-1}}) = (h^*/r, (\sigma^*)^r)$ can be found if r extracted, which is also the solution to the modified K-CAA problem.

It remains to compute the probability that $\mathcal{F}$ solves the modified k-CAA problem. Actually, $\mathcal{F}$ succeeds if:

Λ_1 : $\mathcal{F}$ does not abort during the simulation.
Λ_1 : σ^* is a valid forgery on (ID^*, PK_{ID^*}, m^*).
Λ_1 : $ID^* = ID_t$ and $c^* = 1$.

The advantage of $\mathcal{F}$ is $Adv_{\mathcal{F}}^{BCk-CAA} = Pr[\Lambda_1 \wedge \Lambda_2 \wedge \Lambda_3] = Pr[\Lambda_1] \cdot Pr[\Lambda_2|\Lambda_1] \cdot Pr[\Lambda_3|\Lambda_1 \wedge \Lambda_2]$. If Λ_1 happens, then:

- $\mathcal{F}$ does not output $failure$ during the simulation of the oracle **Partial-Private-Key-Extract**. This happens with probability $(1 - \frac{1}{q_C})^{q_{PKEx}}$.
- $\mathcal{F}$ does not output $failure$ during the simulation of the oracle **Secret-Value-Extract**. This happens with probability $(1 - \frac{1}{q_C})^{q_{VEx}}$.
- $\mathcal{F}$ does not output $failure$ during the simulation of **sign** oracle. This happens with probability $(1 - \frac{1}{q_C}\zeta)^{q_S} \geq (1 - \zeta)^{q_S}$.

Consequently, $Pr[\Lambda_1] \geq (1 - \frac{1}{q_C})^{q_{PKEx}+q_{VEx}}(1 - \zeta)^{q_S}$. In addition, $Pr[\Lambda_2|\Lambda_1] = \varepsilon$ and $Pr[\Lambda_3|\Lambda_1 \wedge \Lambda_2] = \frac{\zeta}{q_C}$. Therefore, $Adv_{\mathcal{F}}^{BCk-CAA} \geq (1 - \frac{1}{q_C})^{q_{PKEx}+q_{VEx}}$

Table 1. Performance Evaluation

	Type	PK-Size (bits)	Sig-Length (bits)	Sign	Verify
Ours	CLS	$2\|G_1\|$ (≈ 320)	$\|G_1\|$ (≈ 160)	$1E_{G_1}$	$1\hat{e} + 1E_{G_1}$
BLS [9]	No	$\|G_1\|$ (≈ 160)	$\|G_1\|$ (≈ 160)	$1E_{G_1}$	$1\hat{e} + 1E_{G_1}$
Scheme I [15]	CLS	$\|G_1\|$ (≈ 160)	$\|G_1\|$ (≈ 160)	$1E_{G_1}$	$2\hat{e}$
ZWXF [25]	CLS	$\|G_1\|$ (≈ 160)	$2\|G_1\|$ (≈ 320)	$3E_{G_1}$	$3\hat{e}$
HSMZ [16]	CLS	$2\|G_1\|$ (≈ 320)	$\|G_1\|+1\|q\|$ (≈ 320)	$2E_{G_1} + 1E_{G_2}$	$1\hat{e} + 1E_{G_2}$
AP03 [2]	CLS	$2\|G_1\|$ (≈ 320)	$\|G_1\|+1\|q\|$ (≈ 320)	$2E_{G_1} + 1E_{G_2}$	$1\hat{e} + 1E_{G_2}$
eCLS [10]	CLS	$\|G_1\|$ (≈ 160)	$2\|G_1\|$ (≈ 320)	$2E_{G_1}$	$2\hat{e} + 1E_{G_1}$
Scheme II [15]	CLS	$\|G_1\|$ (≈ 160)	$\|G_1\|+2\|p\|$ (≈ 480)	$3E_{G_1} + 1E_{G_2}$	$1\hat{e} + 3E_{G_1} + 1E_{G_2}$
oCLS [10]	CLS	$\|G_1\|$ (≈ 160)	$\|G_1\|+\|G_2\|$ (≈ 1184)	$2E_{G_1}$	$1\hat{e} + 1E_{G_2}$

$(1-\zeta)^{q_S}\frac{\zeta}{q_C}\varepsilon$. The function $\zeta(1-\zeta)^{q_S}$ is maximized at $\zeta = \frac{1}{q_S+1}$. Therefore,

$$Adv_{\mathcal{F}}^{BCk-CAA} \geq (1-\frac{1}{q_C})^{q_{PKEx}+q_{VEx}}(1-\frac{1}{q_S+1})^{q_S}\frac{1}{q_C(q_S+1)}\varepsilon.$$

This ends the proof. □

Theorem 2. Unforgeability against Type II Adversary: If there exists a Type II adaptively chosen message and chosen ID adversary $\mathcal{A}_{II}$ who can ask at most q_C **Create-User** queries, q_{VEx} **Secret-Value-Extract** queries and q_S **Sign** queries, respectively, and can break the proposed scheme in polynomial time with success probability ε, then there exists an algorithm $\mathcal{F}$ which, using $\mathcal{A}_{II}$ as a black box, can solve the k-CAA problem [Definition 4] (where $k \geq q_S$ and is in proportion to the number of the H_1-hash queries) with probability $Adv_{\mathcal{F}}^{k_C AA} \geq (1-\frac{1}{q_C})^{q_{VEx}}(1-\frac{1}{q_S+1})^{q_S}\frac{1}{q_C(q_S+1)}\varepsilon.$

Proof: The proof is similar to that of proving Theorem 1 with a little modification. See Appendix for details. □

Theorem 1 is proved in a relatively weaker model than the normal one. That is, we do not allow the adversary to obtain valid signatures according to the replaced public key.

As mentioned in Section 1, this model is also acceptable as the signatures that a "realistic" adversary can obtain are usually generated by a signer under its original public key. Therefore, this modification is reasonable and Huang et al.'s first scheme with short signature size [15] is also analyzed in this weak model.

5 Performance Comparison

In this section, we compare our certificateless short signature scheme with other existing CLS schemes and BLS short signature scheme [9] from the aspect of communication cost and computation cost in signature signing and verification, respectively.

In the comparison, the operations such as $\hat{e}(g,g)$, $\hat{e}(PK_1, Q_{ID}) = \hat{e}(PK_2, g)$ or $\hat{e}(H_0(ID), P_{pub})$ are pre-computable or only need to be computed once. Therefore, these computations are neglected in the comparison. In Table 1, certificateless signature schemes are marked with "CLS". Other schemes are marked with"No". We denote by $\hat{e}$ a computation of the pairing, E_{G_1} an exponentiation in $\mathbb{G}_1$, and E_{G_2} an exponentiation in $\mathbb{G}_2$. Usually, pairing operations cost much more than other computations. One $\hat{e}$ operation is about 10 times more expensive than one $E_{(.)}$ operation.

We can see in Table 1 that our scheme is as efficient as BLS short signature [9] but our scheme is certificateless whereas BLS scheme is not. This means there is no need to verify a certificate in our scheme while using BLS scheme, a verifier needs to verify the certificate in order to confirm the correctness of the public key, as in the conventional Public key Infrastructure (PKI), which is generally considered to be costly to use and manage. From this point of view, our scheme is superior than BLS short signature scheme.

Among all certificateless signature schemes, Huang et al.'s first scheme in [15] is the only signature scheme providing short signature-length (about 160 bits) as ours. However, our scheme is more efficient than their scheme in the verification phase. To the best of our knowledge, our scheme is the most efficient CLS scheme in the aspects of both communication and computation costs.

6 Conclusion

In this paper, we proposed a certificateless signature scheme which is as efficient as BLS short signature. We also defined a new hard problem "modified k-CAA problem" based on the k-CAA problem. The security of the proposed scheme is proved in the random oracle model under the hardness of k-CAA problem and modified k-CAA problem.

References

1. Au, M.H., Chen, J., Liu, J.K., Mu, Y., Wong, D.S., Yang, G.: Malicious KGC attacks in certificateless cryptography. In: Proceedings of ASIACCS 2007, pp. 302–311 (2007)
2. Al-Riyami, S.S., Paterson, K.G.: Certificateless public key cryptography. In: Laih, C.-S. (ed.) ASIACRYPT 2003. LNCS, vol. 2894, pp. 452–473. Springer, Heidelberg (2003)
3. Barr, K., Asanovic, K.: Energy aware lossless data compression. In: Proceedings of the ACM Conference on Mobile Systems, Applications, and Services (MobiSys) (2003)
4. Barreto, P.S.L.M., Kim, H.Y., Lynn, B., Scott, M.: Efficient algorithm for pairing-based cryptosystems. In: Yung, M. (ed.) CRYPTO 2002. LNCS, vol. 2442, pp. 354–369. Springer, Heidelberg (2002)
5. Barreto, P.S.L.M., Lynn, B., Scott, M.: On the selection of pairing-friendly groups. In: Matsui, M., Zuccherato, R.J. (eds.) SAC 2003. LNCS, vol. 3006, pp. 17–25. Springer, Heidelberg (2004)

6. Bellare, M., Neven, G.: Multi-signatures in the plain public-key model and a general forking lemma. In: Proceedings of the 13th ACM Confetence on Computer and Communication Security, pp. 390–398 (2006)
7. Bellare, M., Palacio, A.: The knowledge-of-exponent assumptions and 3-round zero-knowledge protocols. In: Franklin, M. (ed.) CRYPTO 2004. LNCS, vol. 3152, pp. 273–289. Springer, Heidelberg (2004)
8. Boneh, D., Boyen, X.: Short signatures withou rando oracles. In: Cachin, C., Camenisch, J.L. (eds.) EUROCRYPT 2004. LNCS, vol. 3027, pp. 56–73. Springer, Heidelberg (2004)
9. Boneh, D., Lynn, B., Shacham, H.: Short signatures from the weil pairing. In: Boyd, C. (ed.) ASIACRYPT 2001. LNCS, vol. 2248, pp. 514–533. Springer, Heidelberg (2001)
10. Choi, K.Y., Park, J.H., Hwang, J.Y., Lee, D.H.: Efficient certificateless signature schemes. In: Katz, J., Yung, M. (eds.) ACNS 2007. LNCS, vol. 4521, pp. 443–458. Springer, Heidelberg (2007)
11. Goldwasser, S., Micali, S., Rivest, R.L.: A digital signature scheme secure against adaptive chosen-message attacks. SIAM Journal of Computing 17(2), 281–308 (1988)
12. Gorantla, M.C., Saxena, A.: An efficient certificateless signature scheme. In: Hao, Y., Liu, J., Wang, Y.-P., Cheung, Y.-m., Yin, H., Jiao, L., Ma, J., Jiao, Y.-C. (eds.) CIS 2005. LNCS, vol. 3802(II), pp. 110–116. Springer, Heidelberg (2005)
13. Hada, S., Tanaka, T.: On the existence of 3-round zero-knowledge protocols. In: Krawczyk, H. (ed.) CRYPTO 1998. LNCS, vol. 1462, pp. 408–423. Springer, Heidelberg (1998)
14. Hu, B.C., Wong, D.S., Zhang, Z., Deng, X.: Certificatelss signature: a new security model and an improved generic construction. Designs, Codes and Cryptography 42(2), 109–126 (2007)
15. Huang, X., Mu, Y., Susilo, W., Wong, D.S., Wu, W.: Certificateless signature revisted. In: Pieprzyk, J., Ghodosi, H., Dawson, E. (eds.) ACISP 2007. LNCS, vol. 4586, pp. 308–322. Springer, Heidelberg (2007)
16. Huang, X., Susilo, W., Mu, Y., Zhang, F.: On the security of certificateless signature schemes from Asiacrypt 2003. In: Desmedt, Y.G., Wang, H., Mu, Y., Li, Y. (eds.) CANS 2005. LNCS, vol. 3810, pp. 13–25. Springer, Heidelberg (2005)
17. Liu, J.K., Au, M.H., Susilo, W.: Self-generated-certificate public key cryptography and certificateless signature/encryption scheme in the standard model. In: Proceedings of ASIACCS 2007, pp. 273–283 (2007)
18. Mitsunari, S., Sakai, R., Kasahara, M.: A new traitor tracing. Journal of IEICE Trans. Fundamentals E85-A(2), 481–484 (2002)
19. Shamir, A.: Identity-based cryptosystems and signature schemes. In: Blakely, G.R., Chaum, D. (eds.) CRYPTO 1984. LNCS, vol. 196, pp. 47–53. Springer, Heidelberg (1985)
20. Tô, V., Safavi-Naini, R., Zhang, F.: New traitor tracing schemes using bilinear map. In: Proceedings of 2003 DRM Workshop, pp. 67–76 (2003)
21. Yap, W.L., Heng, S.H., Goi, B.M.: An efficient certificteless signature. In: Zhou, X., Sokolsky, O., Yan, L., Jung, E.-S., Shao, Z., Mu, Y., Lee, D.C., Kim, D.Y., Jeong, Y.-S., Xu, C.-Z. (eds.) EUC Workshops 2006. LNCS, vol. 4097, pp. 322–331. Springer, Heidelberg (2006)
22. Yap, W.L., Chow, S.S.M., Heng, S.H., Goi, B.M.: Security Mediated Certificateless Signatures. In: Katz, J., Yung, M. (eds.) ACNS 2007. LNCS, vol. 4521, pp. 459–477. Springer, Heidelberg (2007)

23. Yum, D.H., Lee, P.J.: Generic construction of certificateless signature. In: Wang, H., Pieprzyk, J., Varadharajan, V. (eds.) ACISP 2004. LNCS, vol. 3108, pp. 200–211. Springer, Heidelberg (2004)
24. Zhang, F., Safavi-Naini, R., Susilo, W.: An efficient signature scheme from binilear pairings and its applications. In: Bao, F., Deng, R., Zhou, J. (eds.) PKC 2004. LNCS, vol. 2947, pp. 277–290. Springer, Heidelberg (2004)
25. Zhang, Z., Wong, D.S., Xu, J., Feng, D.: Certificateless public-key signature: security model and efficiet construction. In: Zhou, J., Yung, M., Bao, F. (eds.) ACNS 2006. LNCS, vol. 3989, pp. 293–308. Springer, Heidelberg (2006)

Appendix

Proof of Theorem 2

Proof: If there exists an adversary $\mathcal{A}_{II}$ who can break the unforgeability of the proposed scheme via Type II attack, then, we can construct another adversary $\mathcal{F}$ such that $\mathcal{F}$ can use $\mathcal{A}_{II}$ as a black-box and solve the k-CCA problem.

Let g be a generator of $\mathbb{G}_1$, and $x, h_1, \cdots, h_k \in \mathbb{Z}_p^*$ be $k+1$ random numbers. $\mathcal{F}$ is given the challenge $\{g, g^x, (h_1, g^{(x+h_1)^{-1}}), \cdots, (h_k, g^{(x+h_k)^{-1}})\}$. The purpose of $\mathcal{F}$ is to output a tuple $(h, g^{(x+h^*)^{-1}})$ for some $h^* \notin \{h_1, \cdots, h_k\}$, which is the solution to the k-CAA problem.

Setup: In order to solve the problem, $\mathcal{F}$ utilizes $\mathcal{A}_{II}$ as a black-box. To get the black-box $\mathcal{A}_{II}$ run properly, $\mathcal{F}$ will simulate the environments of the proposed scheme and the oracles which $\mathcal{A}_{II}$ can access. In this proof, we regard the hash functions H_0, H_1 as random oracles. $\mathcal{F}$ starts by picking an admissible bilinear pairing $\hat{e} : \mathbb{G}_1 \times \mathbb{G}_1 \to \mathbb{G}_2$, and sets $P_{pub} = g^s$, where s is randomly chosen from $\mathbb{Z}_p^*$. $\mathcal{F}$ then sends $params = (\mathbb{G}_1, \mathbb{G}_2, \hat{e}, g, P_{pub})$ together with the master secret key s to $\mathcal{A}_{II}$ and allows $\mathcal{A}_{II}$ to run.

Due to the ideal randomness of the H_1-hash, we may assume that $\mathcal{A}_{II}$ is well-behaved in the sense that it always requests a H_1-hash of $m||ID||PK_{ID}$ before it requests a signature for m signed by ID's public key PK_{ID}. In addition, it always requests a H_1-hash of $m^*||ID^*||PK_{ID^*}$ that it outputs as its forgery. It is trivial to modify any adversary-algorithm $\mathcal{A}_{II}$ to have this property.

Query: At any time, $\mathcal{A}_{II}$ is allowed to access the following oracles in a polynomial number of times. These oracles are all simulated by $\mathcal{F}$. Different from the proof for Type I adversary, there is no oracle **Partial-Private-Key-Extract**. This is because that $\mathcal{A}_{II}$ has already obtained the master secret key s so he can compute the partial private key (i.e., $D_{ID} = H_0(ID)^s$) of any entity using the master key s.

1. **Create-User:** $\mathcal{A}_{II}$ can query this oracle by given an identity ID_i. In response to these queries, $\mathcal{F}$ first chooses a random number $t \in \{1, \cdots, q_C\}$.
   (1) If $i \neq t$, $\mathcal{F}$ chooses $d_i, x_i \in_R \mathbb{Z}_p^*$ and computes $H_0(ID_i) = g^{d_i}$, $PK_{ID_i} = (PK_{(ID_i,1)}, PK_{(ID_i,2)}) = (g^{x_i}, g^{x_i d_i})$. In this case, the corresponding partial private key of the entity ID_i is $D_{ID_i} = g^{sd_i}$ and the secret value is $x_{ID_i} = x_i$.

(2) If $i = t$, $\mathcal{F}$ chooses $d_t \in_R \mathbb{Z}_p^*$ and computes $H_0(ID_t) = g^{d_t}$. However, $\mathcal{F}$ sets $PK_{ID_t} = (PK_{(ID_t,1)}, PK_{(ID_t,2)}) = (g^x, g^{xd_t})$. In this case, $\mathcal{F}$ will set $D_{ID_t} = g^{sd_t}$ and $x_{ID_t} = \bot$ which means that it cannot compute the secret value of ID_t.

In both cases, returns $H_0(ID_i)$ and PK_{ID_i}.

2. **Public-Key-Replace:** $\mathcal{A}_{II}$ can request to replace public key PK_{ID_i} of an entity ID_i with new public key PK'_{ID_i} chosen by $\mathcal{A}_{II}$ itself. $\mathcal{F}$ replaces the original public key PK_{ID_i} with PK'_{ID_i} if ID_i has been created. Otherwise, outputs $\bot$. Here, to replace a public key, the secret value corresponding to the new public key is not required.

3. **Secret-Value-Extract:** Given ID_i chosen by $\mathcal{A}_{II}$, outputs $\bot$ if ID_i has not been created. If ID_i has been created and $i \neq t$, $\mathcal{F}$ returns x_{ID_i} to $\mathcal{A}_{II}$. Otherwise, $i = t$ and $\mathcal{F}$ reports $failure$ and terminates the simulation.

4. **H_1 queries:** $\mathcal{A}_{II}$ can query the random oracle H_1 at any time on an input $\omega_i = (m_l \| ID_j \| PK_{ID_k})$. For i-th H_1 query asked by $\mathcal{A}_{II}$ on input ω_i, $\mathcal{F}$ first checks if $ID_j = ID_t$ and $PK_{ID_k} = PK_{ID_t}$ or not. Here PK_{ID_t} is the original public key.
   - If $ID_j = ID_t$ and $PK_{ID_k} = PK_{ID_t}$, then $\mathcal{F}$ first flips a biased coin which outputs a value $c_i = 1$ with probability ζ, and $c_i = 0$ with probability $1 - \zeta$ (the value of ζ will be optimized later).
     (1) If $c_i = 1$, $\mathcal{F}$ picks a random value $h'_i \in \mathbb{Z}_p^*$ where $h'_i \notin \{h_1, \cdots, h_k\}$ and responds h'_i to $\mathcal{A}_{II}$ as the value of $H_1(\omega_i)$.
     (2) If $c_i = 0$, $\mathcal{F}$ returns a value $h''_i \leftarrow_R \{h_1, \cdots, h_k\}$ as the output of $H_1(\omega_i)$ where h''_i must be a fresh value which means that it has not been assigned as an output of H_1 queries before.
   - Otherwise, $\mathcal{F}$ picks and responds with a random value $\mu_i \in \mathbb{Z}_p^*$.

   In either cases, $\mathcal{F}$ records (ω_i, h'_i, c_i), (ω_i, h''_i, c_i) or (ω_i, μ_i) to a H_1-$List$ which is initially empty.

5. **Sign:** For each sign query on an input (m_l, ID_j), output $\bot$ if ID_j has not been created. For any input (m_l, ID_j) with ID_j which has already been created, since we assume that $\mathcal{A}_{II}$ is well-behaved, we know that $\mathcal{A}_{II}$ has already queried the random oracle H_1 on the input $\omega_i = (m_l \| ID_j \| PK_{ID_j})$.
   - If $ID_j \neq ID_t$, $\mathcal{F}$ uses the private key (x_{ID_j}, D_{ID_j}) of ID_j and $\mu_i = H_1(\omega_i)$ on the H_1-$List$ to generate the valid signature σ_i for the message m_l and the identity ID_j.
   - If $ID_i = ID_t$, then, $\mathcal{F}$ first checks the H_1-$List$.
     (1) If $c_i = 1$, $\mathcal{F}$ reports $failure$ and terminates the simulation.
     (2) Otherwise, $c_i = 0$ and $h''_i = H_1(m_l \| ID_t \| PK_{ID_t})$ is on the H_1-$List$. For easy of description, we assume $h''_i = h_i \in \{h_1, \cdots, h_k\}$. $\mathcal{F}$ then returns $\sigma_i = g^{sd_t(x+h_i)^{-1}}$. Note that

$$\hat{e}(\sigma_i, PK_{(ID_t,1)} \cdot g^{h_i}) = \hat{e}(g^{sd_t(x+h_i)^{-1}}, g^x \cdot g^{h_i}) = \hat{e}(g^{sd_t}, g)$$
$$= \hat{e}(g,g)^{sd_t} = \hat{e}(g^{d_t}, g^s) = \hat{e}(H_0(ID_t), P_{pub}).$$

Therefore, σ_i is a valid signature on m_l and ID_t.

Forgery: After all the queries, $\mathcal{A}_{II}$ outputs a forgery $(ID^*, PK_{ID^*} = (PK_{(ID^*,1)}, PK_{(ID^*,2)}), m^*, \sigma^*)$ and wins the game.
If σ^* is a valid forgery, then $h^* = H_1(m^*||ID^*||PK_{ID^*})$ which is on the H_1-List, and

$$\hat{e}(\sigma^*, PK_{(ID^*,1)} \cdot g^{h^*}) = \hat{e}(H_0(ID^*), P_{pub})$$

where $PK_{(ID^*,1)} = g^{x_{ID^*}}$ must be the original public key generated by the oracle **Create-User**. If $ID^* \neq ID_t$, then $\mathcal{F}$ outputs $failure$ and terminates the simulation. Otherwise, $ID^* = ID_t$ and $\mathcal{F}$ will check the H_1-List.

(1) If $c^* = 0$, $\mathcal{F}$ outputs $failure$ and terminates the simulation.
(2) Otherwise, $c^* = 1$ and $h^* \notin \{h_1 \cdots, h_k\}$. $\mathcal{F}$ computes $\xi = (\sigma^*)^{(sd_t)^{-1}}$ and outputs the tuple $(h^*, \xi) = (h^*, g^{(x+h^*)^{-1}})$ which will be the solution to the k-CAA problem.

It remains to compute the probability that $\mathcal{F}$ solves the k-CAA problem. Actually, $\mathcal{F}$ succeeds if:

Λ_1 : $\mathcal{F}$ does not abort during the simulation.
Λ_2 : σ^* is a valid forgery on (ID^*, PK_{ID^*}, m^*).
Λ_3 : $ID^* = ID_t$ and $c^* = 1$.

The advantage of $\mathcal{F}$ is

$$Adv_{\mathcal{F}}^{k-CAA} = Pr[\Lambda_1 \wedge \Lambda_2 \wedge \Lambda_3] = Pr[\Lambda_1] \cdot Pr[\Lambda_2|\Lambda_1] \cdot Pr[\Lambda_3|\Lambda_1 \wedge \Lambda_2].$$

If Λ_1 happens, then

- $\mathcal{F}$ does not output $failure$ during the simulation of the oracle **Secret-Value-Extract**. This happens with probability $(1 - \frac{1}{q_C})^{q_{VEx}}$.
- $\mathcal{F}$ does not output $failure$ during the simulation of signing oracle. This happens with probability $(1 - \frac{1}{q_C}\zeta)^{q_S} \geq (1 - \zeta)^{q_S}$.

Consequently, $Pr[\Lambda_1] \geq (1 - \frac{1}{q_C})^{q_{VEx}}(1 - \zeta)^{q_S}$. In addition, $Pr[\Lambda_2|\Lambda_1] = \varepsilon$ and $Pr[\Lambda_3|\Lambda_1 \wedge \Lambda_2] = \frac{\zeta}{q_C}$. Therefore, $Adv_{\mathcal{F}}^{k-CAA} \geq (1 - \frac{1}{q_C})^{q_{VEx}}(1 - \zeta)^{q_S}\frac{\zeta}{q_C}\varepsilon$. The function $\zeta(1 - \zeta)^{q_S}$ is maximized at $\zeta = \frac{1}{q_S+1}$. Therefore,

$$Adv_{\mathcal{F}}^{k-CAA} \geq (1 - \frac{1}{q_C})^{q_{VEx}}(1 - \frac{1}{q_S+1})^{q_S}\frac{1}{q_C(q_S+1)}\varepsilon.$$

This ends the proof □

Sanitizable Signatures Revisited

Tsz Hon Yuen[1], Willy Susilo[1], Joseph K. Liu[2], and Yi Mu[1]

[1] Centre for Computer and Information Security Research,
School of Computer Science and Software Engineering,
University of Wollongong, Australia
{thy738,wsusilo,ymu}@uow.edu.au
[2] Cryptography and Security Department,
Institute for Infocomm Research, Singapore
ksliu@i2r.a-star.edu.sg

Abstract. A sanitizable signature scheme is a signature scheme which allows a sanitizer to hide parts of the original message after the message is signed, without interacting with the signer. There exists many security models, properties and constructions for sanitizable signatures, which are useful in different scenarios. The aim of this paper is twofold. Firstly, we summarize different properties in the literature and gives some generic conversions between them. We propose a security model to capture most of these properties. Secondly, we present the *first* concrete construction of sanitizable signatures which is proven secure in the standard model.

Keywords: sanitizable signatures, pairings, standard model.

1 Introduction

A digital signature prohibits any alteration of the original message once it is signed. It protects the signer against the message forgery. Nevertheless, it also prevents the message from being process further legitimately as well, which sometimes is actually desirable.

In a networking scenario where an application level firewall is employed, the firewall can examine the packets at the application level. A packet reaches the firewall and is passed to an application-specific proxy, which inspects the validity of the packet. For example, if a Web request (HTTP) comes in, the data payload containing the HTTP request will be passed to an HTTP-proxy process. When the data payload does not satisfy the condition setup in the application proxy, the packet will be dropped. The problem arises when the overall packets are actually authenticated by the sender. If the complete packets are delivered to the receiver, then the receiver can verify the authenticity of the packets by verifying the signature attached. Nonetheless, if part of the packets have been dropped, then these packets can no longer be authenticated unless the sender signs the "new" packets again. The application-proxy cannot sign on behalf of the signer since the application-proxy does not hold the sender's secret key. In this scenario, we require the "sanitized" packets to be authenticated, and therefore the application-proxy should be able to somehow obtain the correct signature on the sanitized packets. This is where sanitizable signature can come into play.

A more typical example of sanitizable signature includes the case when the government wants to release some *partial* information in an officially signed document, then unfortunately this partial information needs to be signed again. In this particular case, a government officer may want to delete some sensitive information such as personal information or national secrets. In order to avoid the process of having the message to be signed again (since the original signer may not be available at that time), a sanitizable signature can be used to sign the document; and the sensitive information is sanitized *prior to* the release of the signature.

The major goal of sanitizable signature is to protect the confidentiality of part of the document while ensuring the integrity of the document. This is called the "digital document sanitizing problem" in [20]. Similar solutions have been proposed earlier in [21] as "content extraction signature"; and in [15] as "redactable signature". Ateniese et al. [1] introduced the "sanitizable signature" which can change the signed document instead of hiding the signed document. Following these works, several authors [19,22,16,18,14,7] proposed various sanitizable signature schemes with different properties.

One of the major differences between the existing schemes is due to the information used to replace a sanitized message. The majority of these works uses a special character, ϕ, to represent a sanitized message. In contrast to this approach, Miyazaki et al. [18] directly removed the sanitized message and the verifier does not even notice that the original document has been sanitized. Several other works [1,16,14] replaced the sanitized message to construct a new message. In order to prevent forgery by the adversary, the sanitizer needs to use his secret key in the sanitizing process. Chang et al. [7] proposed a scheme which hides the number (length) of sanitized messages. Another distinct feature among these works is how to restrict the sanitization for part of the document. Some schemes can sanitize any part of the document. Some schemes can prohibit some part of the documents from being sanitized, and this decision can be made after the document is signed, performed by either the signer or anyone else. Furthermore, the designation of sanitizer is another difference between these schemes. Some schemes select the designated sanitizer a priori when signing. On the contrary, anyone can sanitize a message in many other schemes. Transparency is also considered as a new property in some schemes. If a verifier knows which part of the document is sanitized, then the scheme has no transparency. If he does not know whether the message is sanitized, then the scheme has weak transparency. If he also does not know whether the message can be sanitized, then the scheme has strong transparency.

Our Contribution. In this paper, our contribution is twofold. Firstly, we formalize the security model for sanitizable signatures to capture different properties of sanitizable signatures in the literature. We provide a generic conversion between some of the properties of sanitizable signatures. Secondly, we also provide a new concrete construction which is proven secure in the standard model, without resolving the security to underlying signature schemes. It is *the first* in the literature to achieve this security level. In the construction, we use the first efficient range proof in pairings. We also propose a new notions called "signature of one-time knowledge". These two findings may have independent interest in other cryptographic primitives.

2 Preliminaries

We now give a brief revision on the property of pairings and two candidate hard problems from pairings that will be used later. Let $\mathbb{G}_1, \mathbb{G}_2, \mathbb{G}_T$ be multiplicative groups of prime order p. Let g and $\bar{g}$ be the generators of $\mathbb{G}_1$ and $\mathbb{G}_2$ respectively.

Definition 1. *A map $\hat{e} : \mathbb{G}_1 \times \mathbb{G}_2 \to \mathbb{G}_T$ is called a bilinear pairing if, for all $g \in \mathbb{G}_1$, $\bar{g} \in \mathbb{G}_2$ and $a, b \in \mathbb{Z}_p$, we have $\hat{e}(g^a, \bar{g}^b) = \hat{e}(g, \bar{g})^{ab}$, and if g and $\bar{g}$ are generators of $\mathbb{G}_1$ and $\mathbb{G}_2$ respectively, then $\hat{e}(g, \bar{g})$ generates $\mathbb{G}_T$.*

Definition 2 (CDH). *The Computational Diffie-Hellman (CDH) problem is that, given $g, g^x, g^y \in \mathbb{G}_1$ for unknown $x, y \in \mathbb{Z}_p^*$, to compute g^{xy}.*

We say that the (ϵ, t)-CDH assumption holds in $\mathbb{G}_1$ if no t-time algorithm has the non-negligible probability ϵ in solving the CDH problem.

Definition 3 (XDH). *The external Diffie-Hellman (XDH) problem is that, given $g, g^x, g^y, g^z \in \mathbb{G}_1$ for unknown $x, y, z \in \mathbb{Z}_p^*$, to decide if $z = xy$.*

We say that the (ϵ, t)-XDH assumption holds in $\mathbb{G}_1$ if no t-time algorithm has the non-negligible probability over half ϵ in solving the XDH problem. Notice that the XDH assumption means that the DDH assumption holds in the group $\mathbb{G}_1$. A stronger version of the assumption (symmetric XDH, or SXDH) holds if DDH is also intractable in $\mathbb{G}_2$.

3 Sanitizable Signatures Security Models

In this section we review the security notions and models of sanitizable signatures. We extend the model introduced in [22].

3.1 Notation

In this section, we describe some terms for sanitizable signatures.

Document, Message and Flag. We denote a *document* M as a list of *messages* $m_1||m_2||\ldots||m_n$, where the length n is the number of messages. We denote that $||$ is the concatenation. We use a *flag* ϕ as the sanitized message. For two messages M^1 and M^2 having the same length, we say that M^1 is a *subdocument* of M^2 if $m_i^1 = m_i^2$ for all i where m_i^1 are not sanitized.

State. For a message M, let st_M be the states of m_i. A state can be either:
- sanitized,

- disclosed and sanitizing is allowed, or
- disclosed and sanitizing is prohibited.

st_M is constructed as $(st_\mathsf{M}^S, st_\mathsf{M}^A, st_\mathsf{M}^P)$, where st_M^S is a set of indices of sanitized messages; st_M^A is a set of indices of the messages that are "disclosed and sanitizing is allowed"; st_M^P is a set of indices of the messages that are "disclosed and sanitizing is prohibited".

3.2 Syntax

Sanitizable signatures consist of four algorithms:

KeyGen. On input the security parameter 1^k, it outputs a public key and a private key (pk, sk) and the system parameter param.

Sign. On input a document M, a secret key sk, a state st_M of the document and the system parameter param, it outputs a signature σ.

Sanitize. On input a signature σ, (a document M,) a state st_M of M, a new state of the sanitized document $st_{\mathsf{M}'}$ and the system parameter param, it outputs a sanitized document M′ and a new signature σ'. It may output $\perp$ if there exists $i \in st_{M'}^S$ is also in st_M^P.

Verify. On input a signature σ, a document M, a state st_M of M, a public key pk and the system parameter param, it outputs $\top$ for valid signature and $\perp$ otherwise.

3.3 Security Model

Correctness. We require that $\mathbf{Verify}(\sigma', \mathsf{M}', st_{\mathsf{M}'}, \mathsf{pk}, \mathsf{param}) = \top$ if:

- $(\mathsf{pk}, \mathsf{sk}, \mathsf{param}) \leftarrow \mathbf{KeyGen}(1^k)$,
- $\sigma \leftarrow \mathbf{Sign}(\mathsf{M}, \mathsf{sk}, st_\mathsf{M}, \mathsf{param})$,
- $(\mathsf{M}', st_{M'}, \sigma') \leftarrow \mathbf{Sanitize}(\sigma, st_\mathsf{M}, st_{\mathsf{M}'}, \mathsf{pk}, \mathsf{param})$.

Unforgeability. We have the following game for unforgeability.

1. The simulator $\mathcal{S}$ gives param and pk to the adversary $\mathcal{A}$.
2. $\mathcal{A}$ is allowed to query the signing oracle q_s times adaptively. During the j-th query, on input a document $\mathsf{M}^j = m_1^j || m_2^j || \ldots, m_n^j$ and the state st_{M^j}, the oracle returns the corresponding signature σ.
3. Finally $\mathcal{A}$ outputs a document M^*, a signature σ^* and a state st_{M^*}.

$\mathcal{A}$ wins if $\mathbf{Verify}(\sigma^*, \mathsf{M}^*, st_{\mathsf{M}^*}, \mathsf{pk}, \mathsf{param}) = \top$ and one of the following holds:

1. M^* is not a subdocument of any M^j for $1 \leq j \leq q_s$.
2. M^* is a subdocument of some M^j for $1 \leq j \leq q_s$ and some m_i^* are sanitized, where $i \in st_{\mathsf{M}^j}^P$.
3. M^* is a subdocument of some M^j for $1 \leq j \leq q_s$ and there exists some i such that $i \in st_{\mathsf{M}^j}^S \wedge i \notin st_{\mathsf{M}^*}^S$.

Definition 4. *A sanitizable signature scheme is (ϵ, t, q_s)-unforgeable if there is no t time adversary winning the above game with probability at least ϵ with at most q_s queries to the signing oracle.*

Indistinguishability. We have the following game for indistinguishability.

1. The simulator S gives param and pk to the adversary $\mathcal{A}$.
2. $\mathcal{A}$ is allowed to query the signing oracle q_s times adaptively. The oracle is the same as in the game for unforgeability.
3. $\mathcal{A}$ gives S two documents M^{0*}, M^{1*} and a state st_{M^*}. It is required that:
   - $m_i^{0*} = m_i^{1*}$ for all $i \notin st_{\mathsf{M}^*}^S$ and
   - $m_i^{0*} \neq m_i^{1*}$ for some $i \in st_{\mathsf{M}^*}^S$.

   S first checks if the documents satisfy the requirements. Then S randomly chooses a bit b and sends the signature σ^{b*} for the document M^{b*}.
4. Finally $\mathcal{A}$ outputs a bit b'.

$\mathcal{A}$ wins the game if $b = b'$. The advantage of $\mathcal{A}$ is $|\Pr[b = b'] - 1/2|$.

Definition 5. *A sanitizable signature scheme is (ϵ, t, q_s)-indistinguishable if there is no t time adversary winning the above game with advantage at least ϵ with at most q_s queries to the signing oracle.*

3.4 Various Properties and Their Implications in Security

We will discuss various properties of sanitizable signature schemes. We extend the discussion from [22] by adding more properties from various schemes. We then explain the impacts on the security model.

State Controllability. We consider three types of state controllability:

1. The sanitizer can sanitize any message he wants and the signer cannot restrict it. In the security model, there is no state st_{M}^P.
2. The signer can assign the states st_{M}^P or st_{M}^A to the non-sanitized message. However the states cannot be changed from st_{M}^A to st_{M}^P without the signer's secret key after the signature is generated. This property imposes a restriction on the **Sanitize** protocol. To reflect this in the security model, we add an extra condition for the adversary to win the unforgeability game: M^* is a subdocument of some M^j for $1 \leq j \leq q_s$ and there exists some i such that $i \in st_{\mathsf{M}^j}^A \wedge i \notin st_{\mathsf{M}^*}^P$.
3. The signer can assign the states st_{M}^P or st_{M}^A to the non-sanitized message. The states can be changed from st_{M}^A to st_{M}^P without the signer's secret key. The current model is for this type. It was proposed by [19] to prevent the *additional sanitizing attack*.

Sanitized Message. We consider four different types of *sanitized message*:

1. The sanitization of the message causes the shortening of the message. In the security model, the sanitized message ϕ is equal to a null string. The definition of a *subdocument* is changed as follows: M^1 is a subdocument of

M^2 if it can be obtained from M^2 by removing some non-empty messages in it. The security model includes an extra *invisibility* game [18], which can be included in our indistinguishability game by setting the challenge document (to form the challenge signature) as a subdocument of both M^{0*} and M^{1*}.
2. Each sanitized message is represented by a special character ϕ. Everyone can notice where the document is sanitized. The current model is for this type.
3. Each sanitized message is represented by a special character ϕ and consecutive ϕs can be combined into one. The length of the sanitized message is hidden. The definition of a *subdocument* is changed as follows: M^1 is a subdocument of M^2 if it can be obtained from M^2 by removing some non-empty messages in it and replacing it by a single ϕ. The security model in [7], which can be included in our indistinguishability game by setting the challenge document as a subdocument of both M^{0*} and M^{1*}.
4. Each sanitized message can be changed to any message chosen by the sanitizer. In the security model, the sanitized message ϕ is equal to a new message m'_i.[1]

Designated Sanitizer. We consider two types of designation of sanitizer.

1. The signer cannot choose who are the designated sanitizers when he signs the document. The current model is for this type. In some protocols, **Sign** also outputs a secret information SI[2] to the sanitizer. **Sanitize** will then have an additional input SI. In the security model, the signing oracle should also output SI.[3]
2. The signer has to designate the specific sanitizers. In the protocol, **KeyGen** will also generate the keys for sanitizers. **Sign** should also take the sanitizers' public keys as the input. **Sanitize** will have the sanitizer's secret key as an additional input.[4] For the unforgeability and indistinguishability game, the adversary is given the public and private keys of the sanitizers. It prevents the attack from dishonest sanitizers like the *Deletion-of-Last-Sanitizer Attack* in [14]. At the challenge phase of the indistinguishability game, the adversary also gives the public keys of the sanitizers to the simulator. The adversary may have the secret keys of the challenge sanitizers.[5]

Transparency. We consider three types of transparency.

1. No transparency. The verifier knows which part of the document is sanitized. The current model is for this type. The *sanitized message* must be either type 2 or type 3.

---

[1] Possible extension includes *enforcing the same modification of different messages*, and *limiting the number of modifications* [16].
[2] SI is firstly formalized in [22], but the idea is implicit in early papers.
[3] If several SI can combine together to form an aggregate SI, the scheme has the *binding subdocuments* function [18].
[4] It is optional for **Verify** to take the sanitizers' public keys as the input, e.g. in [13,14]. It will then have the property *sanitizer identification*.
[5] [14] has extensions called *dishonest sanitation identification* and *dishonest sanitizer identification*. However there is no formal model proposed in [14].

2. Weak transparency. The verifier does not know if the message is sanitized. The verifier only knows if the state is st_M^P or not. In the model the states st_M^S and st_M^A are combined into one state when it is sent to the verifier. The *sanitized message* must be either type 1 or type 4.
3. Strong transparency. The verifier does not know if the message can be sanitized. In the model the state information is not sent to the verifier. The *sanitized message* must be either type 1 or type 4.

3.5 Generic Conversion

As there are different properties of sanitizable signatures needed in different scenarios, we propose some generic conversions between different properties.

State Controllability. Type 2 and type 3 can be converted to type 1 by forbidding state st_M^P in the scheme.

Sanitized Message. Type 4 can be converted to type 2 by using a special character ϕ. Type 3 can be converted to type 2 by using special characters ϕ_1 and ϕ_2 alternatively.

Designated Sanitizer. Type 1 can be converted to type 2 by verifiablely encrypting the secret information to the designated sanitizer. Type 2 can be converted to type 1 by publishing a private and public key pairs and always designating to that public key.

4 Basic Building Blocks

4.1 Signatures of Knowledge

Camenisch and Stadler [6] introduced notions for various proofs of knowledge of discrete logarithms and proofs of the validity of statements about discrete logarithms. For example,

$$PK\{(\alpha) : y = g^\alpha\},$$

denotes a "zero knowledge proof of knowledge of α such that $y = g^\alpha$", where y and g are known by the verifier. There are many signature schemes obtained from such PK using the Fiat-Shamir heuristic [9]. These schemes are known as the signatures of knowledge (SoK) [8]. For example, a SoK for a message m can be represented as:

$$SoK\{(\alpha) : y = g^\alpha\}(m).$$

The SoK system is widely used in signature protocols like group signatures, ring signatures, etc. However, the security of many existing SoK protocols rely on the random oracle model [2], due to the use of the Fiat-Shamir heuristic.

4.2 One Time Signature in the Standard Model

Recently, Bellare and Shoup [3] introduced two-tier signatures which can be constructed from three-move identification protocols using Fiat-Shamir transform in the standard model. It requires that the canonical identification protocol has special soundness and the hash function is collision resistant. Bellare and Shoup [3] suggested that two-tier signatures can be used to construct one time signatures in the standard model.

Various standard signatures without random oracles are proposed [4,23,10]. However the structure of some schemes are difficult to use to construct signatures with special properties. Sometimes we need to use a proof of knowledge of the randomness used in those signatures. Notice that since the randomness is only used once, it suffices to use the proof of knowledge protocol with the one time signature in [3]. We introduce the notion "Signature of One-Time Knowledge" (SOTK) for such situation:

$$SOTK\{(\alpha) : y = g^\alpha\}(m).$$

An example will be given at the end of this section. Notice that the underlying proof of knowledge protocol must have the special soundness property. The use of SOTK is of independent interest to construct different types of signatures in the standard model.

4.3 Commitment for Pairings

Groth and Sahai [11] generalized several commitments over the pairings. We review the one based on the external Diffie-Hellman (XDH) assumption.

Let $\mathbb{G}_1$ be the group that the DDH problem is hard. By entry-wise multiplication we get an abelian group $\mathbb{G}_1^2$. Let $(g,h), (u,v)$ be two elements in $\mathbb{G}_1^2$. We commit to $\phi \in \mathbb{Z}_p$, by choosing $\rho \in \mathbb{Z}_p$ at random and setting $Y := (g,h)^\phi \cdot (u,v)^\rho = (g^\phi u^\rho, h^\phi v^\rho)$. When (g,h) and (u,v) are linearly independent this determine $\phi \in \mathbb{Z}_p$; but if $(g,h) = (u,v)^s$ for some $s \in \mathbb{Z}_p$, then we have a perfectly hiding Pedersen commitment to ϕ. Under the XDH assumption, we cannot tell if (g,h) and (u,v) are linearly independent or not.

We extend the above commitment scheme to allow simultaneous commitment to a tuple of integers. Let $K = ((g_1,h_1), \ldots, (g_n,h_n), (u,v))$ be elements in $\mathbb{G}_1^2$. We commit to $\phi_1, \ldots, \phi_n \in \mathbb{Z}_p^n$, by choosing $\rho \in \mathbb{Z}_p$ at random and setting the commitment:

$$C_K(\phi_1, \ldots, \phi_n; \rho) := \prod_{i=1}^n (g_i, h_i)^{\phi_i} \cdot (u,v)^\rho = (\prod_{i=1}^n g_i^{\phi_i} u^\rho, \prod_{i=1}^n h_i^{\phi_i} v^\rho).$$

It is straightforward to show that the security of this commitment scheme and the security of the Groth and Sahai's XDH commitment scheme [11] are equivalent, provided that the mutual discrete logarithms of g_i and h_i are not known.

4.4 Efficient Range Proof

Proving that a committed number x lies in some interval $[a, b]$ is useful in many protocols. Usually we prove that both $x - a$ and $b - x$ are non-negative. It can be done by either Boudot's method [5] or prove that the number can be written as the sum of four squares [17]. The first method works on the RSA group and therefore not useful in pairings group with order p. In [17], their method uses commitment schemes where the group order is not known by the arguer.

We propose the use of Groth and Sahai's XDH commitment scheme [11] with Lipmaa's sum of square method [17] to construct an efficient range proof for pairings group with order p. To prove that μ is non-negative, the arguer A represents $\mu = \omega_1^2 + \omega_2^2 + \omega_3^2 + \omega_4^2$, using the algorithm in [17]. Let $K = ((g,h),(u,v))$ be the public key. He performs a proof of knowledge $PK((\omega_1, \omega_2, \omega_3, \omega_4, \rho) : Y = C_K(\sum_{i=1}^{4} \omega_i^2; \rho))$. The algorithm is as follows:

1. For $i = 1, \ldots, 4$, A chooses random $r_{1,i} \in_R \mathbb{Z}_p$ such that $\sum_{i=1}^{4} r_{1,i} = \rho$. A chooses random $\phi_i, r_{2,i}, r_3 \in_R \mathbb{Z}_p$. A computes:

$$T_{1,i} = (g,h)^{\omega_i} \cdot (u,v)^{r_{1,i}}, \quad T_{2,i} = (g,h)^{\phi_i} \cdot (u,v)^{r_{2,i}}, \quad T_3 = \prod_{i=1}^{4} (T_{1,i})^{\phi_i} \cdot (u,v)^{r_3}.$$

The arguer A sends $(\{T_{1,i}, T_{2,i}\}_{i \in [4]}, T_3)$ to the verifier V.

2. V generates a random challenge $c \in \mathbb{Z}_p$ and sends it to A.
3. A sends $(\{z_{1,i}, z_{2,i}\}_{i \in [4]}, z_3)$ to V, where:

$$z_{1,i} = \phi_i + c\omega_i, \quad z_{2,i} = r_{2,i} + cr_{1,i}, \quad z_3 = r_3 + c\sum_{j=1}^{4}(1 - \omega_j)r_{1,j}.$$

4. V checks that for $i = 1, \ldots 4$

$$(g,h)^{z_{1,i}} \cdot (u,v)^{z_{2,i}} \cdot T_{1,i}^{-c} = T_{2,i}, \quad \left(\prod_{i=1}^{4} T_{1,i}^{z_{1,i}}\right) \cdot (u,v)^{z_3} \cdot Y^{-c} = T_3.$$

Theorem 1. *The above protocol is an honest-verifier statistical zero-knowledge (HVSZK) proof that $Y = C_K(\mu)$ and $\mu \geq 0$, if the XDH assumption holds.*

Proof. COMPLETENESS. It is straightforward and is omitted due to space limit. HVSZK. For $i = 1, \ldots, 4$, the simulator generates random $\tilde{T}_{1,i}$ from $\mathbb{G}_1^2$, random $\tilde{z}_{1,i}, \tilde{z}_{2,i}, \tilde{z}_3, \tilde{c}$ from $\mathbb{Z}_p$. He computes:

$$\tilde{T}_{2,i} = (g,h)^{\tilde{z}_{1,i}} \cdot (u,v)^{\tilde{z}_{2,i}} \cdot \tilde{T}_{1,i}^{-\tilde{c}}, \quad \tilde{T}_3 = \left(\prod_{i=1}^{4} \tilde{T}_{1,i}^{\tilde{z}_{1,i}}\right) \cdot (u,v)^{\tilde{z}_3} \cdot Y^{-\tilde{c}}.$$

Then the resulting view $(\{\tilde{T}_{1,i}, \tilde{T}_{2,i}\}_{i \in [4]}, \tilde{T}_3; \tilde{c}; \{\tilde{z}_{1,i}, \tilde{z}_{2,i}\}_{i \in [4]}, \tilde{z}_3)$ has a distribution which is statistically close to the real distribution.

SPECIAL SOUNDNESS. For two accepting transcripts $(\{T_{1,i}, T_{2,i}\}_{i\in[4]}, T_3; c; \{z_{1,i}, z_{2,i}\}_{i\in[4]}, z_3)$ and $(\{T_{1,i}, T_{2,i}\}_{i\in[4]}, T_3; c'; \{z'_{1,i}, z'_{2,i}\}_{i\in[4]}, z'_3)$, the special soundness defined in [3] required that $(c; \{z_{1,i}, z_{2,i}\}_{i\in[4]}, z_3) \neq (c'; \{z'_{1,i}, z'_{2,i}\}_{i\in[4]}, z'_3)$. Then we have for $i = 1, \ldots, 4$

$$(g,h)^{z_{1,i}-z'_{1,i}} \cdot (u,v)^{z_{2,i}-z'_{2,i}} = T_{1,i}^{c-c'}, \qquad \left(\prod_{i=1}^{4} T_{1,i}^{z_{1,i}-z'_{1,i}}\right) \cdot (u,v)^{z_3-z'_3} = Y^{c-c'}.$$

If $c \neq c'$, we have:

$$\left(\prod_{i=1}^{4}(g,h)^{\frac{(z_{1,i}-z'_{1,i})^2}{c-c'}} \cdot (u,v)^{\frac{(z_{1,i}-z'_{1,i})(z_{2,i}-z'_{2,i})}{c-c'}}\right) \cdot (u,v)^{z_3-z'_3} = Y^{c-c'}.$$

Then we can set $\tilde{\omega}_i = \frac{(z_{1,i}-z'_{1,i})}{c-c'}$ for $i \in [4]$ and $\tilde{\rho} = \frac{\sum_{i=1}^{4}(z_{1,i}-z'_{1,i})(z_{2,i}-z'_{2,i})}{(c-c')^2} + \frac{z_3-z'_3}{c-c'}$, such that $Y = C_K(\sum_{i=1}^{4}\tilde{\omega}_i^2; \tilde{\rho})$. If $c = c'$, we have:

$$(g,h)^{z_{1,i}-z'_{1,i}} = (u,v)^{z'_{2,i}-z_{2,i}} \quad \text{for } i \in [4], \qquad \left(\prod_{i=1}^{4} T_{1,i}^{z_{1,i}-z'_{1,i}}\right) = (u,v)^{z'_3-z_3}.$$

If for all $i \in [4]$, $z'_{2,i} = z_{2,i}$, then it implies $z_{1,i} = z'_{1,i}$ and hence $z'_3 = z_3$. This makes the two transcripts completely the same. Therefore if for some $i \in [4]$, $z'_{2,i} \neq z_{2,i}$ and hence $(g,h)^{\frac{z_{1,i}-z'_{1,i}}{z'_{2,i}-z_{2,i}}} = (u,v)$. However, it contradicts the indistinguishability of the linear independence of the commitment. We can construct an algorithm to solve the XDH problem. □

To the best of the authors' knowledge, this is the first efficient range proof for the pairings. This proof may be useful in other cryptographic primitives.

4.5 Examples with Proof of Range

We give the example for SOTK, which will be used in our sanitizable signature scheme. We want to prove the following relations:

$$PK\{(\mu, \rho) : (x = g^\mu u^\rho \vee x' = g^\mu u^\rho) \wedge 0 \leq \mu \leq w\}.$$

To perform the range proof with our commitment scheme, we have to compute:

$$PK\{(\mu, \rho) : (Y := (y_1, y_2) = (g,h)^\mu \cdot (u,v)^\rho \wedge \mu \geq 0)$$
$$\wedge \ (Z := (g,h)^w \cdot Y^{-1} = (g,h)^{w-\mu} \cdot (u,v)^{-\rho} \wedge w - \mu \geq 0)$$
$$\wedge \ (y_1 = x \vee y_1 = x')\}.$$

WLOG, assume $y_1 = x'$. The arguer A represents $\mu = \omega_1^2 + \omega_2^2 + \omega_3^2 + \omega_4^2$ and $w - \mu = \eta_1^2 + \eta_2^2 + \eta_3^2 + \eta_4^2$, using the algorithm in [17]. The algorithm is as follows.

1. For $i = 1, \ldots, 4$, the arguer A chooses random $r_{1,i}, t_{1,i}, s_{1,i} \in_R \mathbb{Z}_p$ such that $\sum_{i=1}^{4} r_{1,i} = \sum_{i=1}^{4} t_{1,i} = \rho$ and $\sum_{i=1}^{4} s_{1,i} = -\rho$. A chooses random $\phi_i, r_{2,i}, r_3$, $\delta_i, t_{2,i}, t_3, \varphi_i, s_{2,i}, s_3, c_1 \in_R \mathbb{Z}_p$. A sends $(\{R_{1,i}, R_{2,i}\}_{i \in [4]}, R_3, \{T_{1,i}, T_{2,i}\}_{i \in [4]}, T_3, \{S_{1,i}, S_{2,i}\}_{i \in [4]}, S_3)$ to the verifier V, where:

$$R_{1,i} = (g,h)^{\omega_i} \cdot (u,v)^{r_{1,i}} \cdot (x,1), \quad R_{2,i} = (g,h)^{\phi_i} \cdot (u,v)^{r_{2,i}} \cdot (x,1)^{-c_1},$$

$$R_3 = \prod_{i=1}^{4}(R_{1,i})^{\phi_i} \cdot (u,v)^{r_3} \cdot (x'^{c_1} x^{(\sum_{i=1}^{4}\omega_i - 1)c_1}, 1),$$

$$T_{1,i} = (g,h)^{\delta_i} \cdot (u,v)^{t_{1,i}}, \quad T_{2,i} = (g,h)^{\delta_i} \cdot (u,v)^{t_{2,i}},$$

$$T_3 = \prod_{i=1}^{4}(T_{1,i})^{\delta_i} \cdot (u,v)^{t_3}, \quad S_{1,i} = (g,h)^{\eta_i} \cdot (u,v)^{s_{1,i}},$$

$$S_{2,i} = (g,h)^{\varphi_i} \cdot (u,v)^{s_{2,i}}, \quad S_3 = \prod_{i=1}^{4}(S_{1,i})^{\varphi_i} \cdot (u,v)^{s_3}.$$

2. V generates a random challenge $c \in \mathbb{Z}_p$ and sends it to A.
3. A sends $(c_1, c_2, \{z_{1,i}, z_{2,i}, z_{4,i}, z_{5,i}, z_{7,i}, z_{8,i}\}_{i \in [4]}, z_3, z_6, z_9)$ to V, where:

$$c_2 = c \oplus c_1, \quad z_{1,i} = \phi_i + c_1 \omega_i,$$

$$z_{2,i} = r_{2,i} + c_1 r_{1,i}, \quad z_3 = r_3 + c_1 \sum_{j=1}^{4}(1 - \omega_j) r_{1,j},$$

$$z_{4,i} = \delta_i + c_2 \omega_i, \quad z_{5,i} = t_{2,i} + c_2 t_{1,i}, \quad z_6 = t_3 + c_2 \sum_{j=1}^{4}(1 - \omega_j) t_{1,j},$$

$$z_{7,i} = \varphi_i + c \eta_i, \quad z_{8,i} = s_{2,i} + c s_{1,i}, \quad z_9 = s_3 + c \sum_{j=1}^{4}(1 - \eta_j) s_{1,j}.$$

4. V checks that $c = c_1 \oplus c_2$ and for $i = 1, \ldots, 4$:

$$(g,h)^{z_{1,i}} \cdot (u,v)^{z_{2,i}} \cdot R_{1,i}^{-c_1} = R_{2,i}, \quad \left(\prod_{i=1}^{4} R_{1,i}^{z_{1,i}}\right) \cdot (u,v)^{z_3} \cdot (x, y_2)^{-c_1} = R_3,$$

$$(g,h)^{z_{4,i}} \cdot (u,v)^{z_{5,i}} \cdot T_{1,i}^{-c_2} = T_{2,i}, \quad \left(\prod_{i=1}^{4} T_{1,i}^{z_{4,i}}\right) \cdot (u,v)^{z_6} \cdot (x', y_2)^{-c_2} = T_3,$$

$$(g,h)^{z_{7,i}} \cdot (u,v)^{z_{8,i}} \cdot S_{1,i}^{-c} = S_{2,i}, \quad \left(\prod_{i=1}^{4} S_{1,i}^{z_{7,i}}\right) \cdot (u,v)^{z_9} \cdot Z^{-c} = S_3.$$

Lemma 1. *The above protocol is an honest-verifier statistical zero-knowledge (HVSZK) proof that $(x = g^{-\mu} u^\rho \vee x' = g^{-\mu} u^\rho) \wedge 0 \leq \mu \leq w$, if the XDH assumption holds.*

The proof is very similar to the range proof and is omitted due to the space limit. To turn the above proof of knowledge into SOTK, we use the conversion from [3]. The signature scheme

$$SOTK\{(\mu, \rho) : (x = g^\mu u^\rho \vee x' = g^\mu u^\rho) \wedge 0 \leq \mu \leq w\}(m),$$

is as follows:

KeyGen. Randomly pick $K \in \{0,1\}^k$. The public key is $(g, h, x, x', \{R_{1,i}, R_{2,i}, T_{1,i}, T_{2,i}, S_{1,i}, S_{2,i}\}_{i \in [4]}, R_3, T_3, S_3, K)$. The private key is $(\{\phi_i, r_{1,i}, r_{2,i}, \delta_i, t_{1,i}, t_{2,i}, \varphi_i, s_{1,i}, s_{2,i}\}_{i \in [4]}, r_3, t_3, s_3, c_1, \mu, \rho)$. It also chooses a collision resistant hash function.

Sign. To sign a message m, the signer computes $c = H(K, \{R_{1,i}, R_{2,i}, T_{1,i}, T_{2,i}, S_{1,i}, S_{2,i}\}_{i \in [4]}, R_3, T_3, S_3, m)$. The signature is $(c_1, c_2, \{z_{1,i}, z_{2,i}, z_{4,i}, z_{5,i}, z_{7,i}, z_{8,i}\}_{i \in [4]}, z_3, z_6, z_9)$.

Verify. Verify as step (4) in the proof of knowledge and check if $c = H(K, \{R_{1,i}, R_{2,i}, T_{1,i}, T_{2,i}, S_{1,i}, S_{2,i}\}_{i \in [4]}, R_3, T_3, S_3, m)$.

For the security of the above scheme, it follows from theorem 6.1 and theorem 5.1 of [3], we only have to prove the special soundness for the proof of knowledge protocol and assume the hash function is collision resistant. Therefore the above SOTK scheme is a secure one-time signature.

5 Sanitizable Signature Scheme

We present our sanitizable signature scheme. It is motivated by Waters identity-based encryption [23]. Our scheme consists of the following algorithms.

Key Generation. Let $\mathbb{G}_1, \mathbb{G}_2, \mathbb{G}_T$ be groups of prime order p. Given a pairing: $\hat{e} : \mathbb{G}_1 \times \mathbb{G}_2 \to \mathbb{G}_T$. Select $g, h_1, \ldots, h_n \in \mathbb{G}_1$ and $g_2, u', u_1, \ldots, u_n \in \mathbb{G}_2$ and $w \in \mathbb{Z}_p^*$. The system parameter is $\mathsf{param} = (\mathbb{G}_1, \mathbb{G}_2, \mathbb{G}_T, \hat{e}, g, p, g_2, u', w, u_1, \ldots, u_n, h_1, \ldots, h_n)$. The signer randomly picks a secret key sk as $\alpha \in \mathbb{Z}_p^*$ and his public key pk is computed as $g_1 = g^\alpha$.

Sign. To sign a n-bit document $M = m_1 m_2 \ldots m_n \in \{0,1\}^n$ with a state st_M of M, the signer randomly picks $r \in \mathbb{Z}_p^*$ and returns (σ_1, σ_2), where:

$$\sigma_1 = g_2^\alpha (u' \prod_{i=1}^n u_i^{m_i})^r, \qquad \sigma_2 = g^r.$$

Sanitize. Upon input a signature (σ_1, σ_2), a document $M = m_1 m_2 \ldots m_n$, an old state st_M and a new state $st_{M'}$, the sanitizer does the followings:

1. Check for all $i \in st_{M'}^S$ is also in st_M^A. If not, return $\perp$ and exit.
2. Check if $e(g, \sigma_1) = e(g_1, g_2) \cdot e(\sigma_2, u' \prod_{i=1}^n u_i^{m_i})$. If not, return $\perp$ and exit.
3. For all $i \in st_{M'}^S$, pick a random $r_i \in \mathbb{Z}_w^*$, $s_i \in \mathbb{Z}_p^*$ and then compute:

$$A_i = \sigma_2^{m_i} g^{r_i} h_i^{s_i}, \qquad \sigma_1' = \sigma_1 \prod_{i \in st_{M'}^S} u_i^{r_i}, \qquad \sigma_{3,i} = u_i^{s_i},$$

$$\sigma_{4,i} = SOTK\{(r_i, s_i) : (A_i = g^{r_i}h_i^{s_i} \vee A_i/\sigma_2 = g^{r_i}h_i^{s_i}) \wedge 1 \leq r_i \leq w\}(\sigma_1').$$

4. For $i \in st_{M'}^S$, change the sanitized bit $m_i = \phi$ to form a document M'. The sanitized signature is $(\sigma_1', \sigma_2, \{A_i, \sigma_{3,i}, \sigma_{4,i} | i \in st_{M'}^S\})$.

Verify. Upon receiving a signature $(\sigma_1', \sigma_2, \{A_i, \sigma_{3,i}, \sigma_{4,i} | i \in st_{M'}^S\})$ and a document $M = m_1 m_2 \ldots m_n \in \{\phi, 0, 1\}^n$, check if:

$$e(g, \sigma_1') \cdot \prod_{i|m_i=\phi} e(h_i, \sigma_{3,i}) = e(g_1, g_2) \cdot e(\sigma_2, u' \prod_{j|m_j \neq \phi} u_j^{m_j}) \cdot \prod_{i|m_i=\phi} e(A_i, u_i),$$

and $\sigma_{4,i}$ are valid SOTK. Return $\top$ if the above holds. Otherwise return $\bot$.

5.1 Security Result

We prove the security of our scheme under the model of state type 1, message type 2, sanitizer type 1 and transparency type 1, defined in section 3.4. The correctness of our scheme is obvious.

Theorem 2. *Our sanitizable signature scheme is (ϵ, t, q_s)-unforgeable if the (ϵ', t')-CDH assumption holds and the SOTK is a strong one-time signature, where:*

$$\epsilon \leq (8q_s^2(n+1)^2 w^2 + 2)\epsilon' + \frac{2}{p}, \qquad t = t' - O(q_s n\rho + q_s \tau),$$

and ρ and τ are the time for a multiplication and an exponentiation in $\mathbb{G}$, respectively.

Proof. Assume there is a (ϵ, t, q_s)-adversary $\mathcal{A}$ exists. We are going to construct another PPT $\mathcal{B}$ that makes use of $\mathcal{A}$ to solve the CDH problem with probability at least ϵ' and in time at most t'.

$\mathcal{B}$ is given a problem instance as follow: Given a group $\mathbb{G}$, a generator $g \in \mathbb{G}$, two elements $g^a, g^b \in \mathbb{G}$. It is asked to output another element $g^{ab} \in \mathbb{G}$. In order to use $\mathcal{A}$ to solve for the problem, $\mathcal{B}$ needs to simulates a challenger and the signing oracle for $\mathcal{A}$. $\mathcal{B}$ does it in the following way.

Setup. Let $l = 2q_s$. $\mathcal{B}$ randomly selects an integer k such that $0 \leq k \leq n$. Also assume that $l(n+1)w < p$, for the given values of q_s, w and n. It randomly selects the following integers:

- $x' \in_R \mathbb{Z}_l$; $y' \in_R \mathbb{Z}_p$.
- $\hat{x}_i \in_R \mathbb{Z}_l$, for $i = 1, \ldots, n$. Let $\hat{X} = \{\hat{x}_i\}$.
- $\hat{y}_i, \hat{z}_i \in_R \mathbb{Z}_p$, for $i = 1, \ldots, n$. Let $\hat{Y} = \{\hat{y}_i\}$.

We further define the following functions for binary string $\mathbf{m} = (m_1, m_2, \ldots, m_n)$, where $m_i \in \{0, 1\}$ for $i = 1, \ldots n$, as follow:

$$F(\mathbf{m}) = x' + \sum_{i=1}^n \hat{x}_i m_i - lk \qquad \text{and} \qquad J(\mathbf{m}) = y' + \sum_{i=1}^n \hat{y}_i m_i.$$

$\mathcal{B}$ constructs a set of public parameters as follow:

$$g_2 = g^b, \quad u' = g_2^{-lk+x'}g^{y'}, \quad u_i = g_2^{\hat{x}_i}g^{\hat{y}_i}, \quad h_i = u_i^{\hat{z}_i} \text{ for } 1 \leq i \leq n.$$

We have the following equation:

$$u'\prod_{i=1}^{n} u_i^{m_i} = g_2^{F(\mathbf{m})}g^{J(\mathbf{m})}.$$

All the above public parameters and public key $g_1 = g^a$ are passed to $\mathcal{A}$.

<u>Oracle Simulation.</u> $\mathcal{B}$ simulates the signing oracle as follow. Upon receiving a j-th query for a document $\mathbf{m}_j$, although $\mathcal{B}$ does not know the secret key, it can still construct the signature by assuming $F(\mathbf{m}_j) \neq 0 \bmod p$. It randomly chooses $r_j \in_R \mathbb{Z}_p$ and computes the signature as

$$\sigma_{1,j} = g_1^{-\frac{J(\mathbf{m}_j)}{F(\mathbf{m}_j)}}(g_2^{F(\mathbf{m}_j)}g^{J(\mathbf{m}_j)})^{r_j}, \quad \sigma_{2,j} = g_1^{-\frac{1}{F(\mathbf{m}_j)}}g^{r_j}.$$

By letting $\tilde{r}_j = r_j - \frac{a}{F(\mathbf{m}_j)}$, it can be verified that $\sigma_{1,j}$ is a valid signature, shown as follow:

$$\sigma_{1,j} = g_1^{-\frac{J(\mathbf{m}_j)}{F(\mathbf{m}_j)}}(g_2^{F(\mathbf{m}_j)}g^{J(\mathbf{m}_j)})^{r_j}$$
$$= g^{-\frac{aJ(\mathbf{m}_j)}{F(\mathbf{m}_j)}}(g_2^{F(\mathbf{m}_j)}g^{J(\mathbf{m}_j)})^{\frac{a}{F(\mathbf{m}_j)}}(g_2^{F(\mathbf{m}_j)}g^{J(\mathbf{m}_j)})^{-\frac{a}{F(\mathbf{m}_j)}}(g_2^{F(\mathbf{m}_j)}g^{J(\mathbf{m}_j)})^{r_j}$$
$$= g_2^a(g_2^{F(\mathbf{m}_j)}g^{J(\mathbf{m}_j)})^{\tilde{r}_j},$$
$$\sigma_{2,j} = g_1^{-\frac{1}{F(\mathbf{m}_j)}}g^{r_j} = g^{r_j - \frac{a}{F(\mathbf{m}_j)}} = g^{\tilde{r}_j}.$$

To the adversary, all signatures given by $\mathcal{B}$ are indistinguishable from the signatures generated by the true challenger.

If $F(\mathbf{m}_j) = 0 \bmod p$, since the above computation cannot be performed (division by 0), the simulator aborts. To make it simple, the simulator will abort if $F(\mathbf{m}_j) = 0 \bmod l$. The equivalence can be observed as follow. From the assumption $l(n+1)w < p$, it implies $0 \leq lk < p$ and $0 \leq x' + \sum_{i=1}^{n}\hat{x}_i m_i < p$ ($\because x' < l, \hat{x}_i < l$). We have $-p < F(\mathbf{m}_j) < p$ which implies if $F(\mathbf{m}_j) = 0 \bmod p$ then $F(\mathbf{m}_j) = 0 \bmod l$. Hence, $F(\mathbf{m}_j) \neq 0 \bmod l$ implies $F(\mathbf{m}_j) \neq 0 \bmod p$. Thus the former condition will be sufficient to ensure that a signature can be computed without aborting.

<u>Output Calculation.</u> If $\mathcal{B}$ does not abort, $\mathcal{A}$ will return a document $\mathbf{m}^* = m_1^* \ldots m_n^*$ with a forged signature σ^*. If σ^* is not a sanitized signature and $\mathcal{A}$ wins the game, it means $\mathcal{A}$ can forge the Waters' signature [23] and hence $\mathcal{B}$ can solve the CDH problem.

If σ^* is a sanitized signature with $\sigma^* = (\sigma_1, \sigma_2, \sigma_4, \{A_i, \sigma_{3,i} | i \in st_{M'}^S\})$. Let $\sigma_2^* = g^{r^*}$, $\sigma_{3,i}^* = u_i^{s_i^*}$ and $A_i^* = g^{r_i^*}h_i^{s_i^*}$. $\mathcal{B}$ aborts if $x' + \sum_{i|m_i^* \neq \phi}\hat{x}_i - lk \neq 0 \bmod l$ or $\sum_{j|m_j^* = \phi}\hat{x}_i r_i^* \neq 0 \bmod l$ (notice that the latter condition can only be checked at the end of the output calculation).

By the verification equation, we can rewrite:

$$\sigma_1^* = g_2^a g_2^{(x'+\sum_{i|m_i \neq \phi} \hat{x}_i - lk)r^*} g^{(y'+\sum_{i|m_i \neq \phi} \hat{y}_i)r^*} g_2^{\sum_{i|m_i=\phi} \hat{x}_i r_i^*} g^{\sum_{i|m_i=\phi} \hat{x}_i r_i^*}$$
$$= g_2^a g^{(y'+\sum_{i|m_i \neq \phi} \hat{y}_i)r^* + \sum_{i|m_i=\phi} \hat{x}_i r_i^*}.$$

Therefore $\mathcal{B}$ can compute and output

$$Z = \sigma_1^* \sigma_2^{*-y'-\sum_{i|m_i \neq \phi} \hat{y}_i} \prod_{i|m_i=\phi} (\sigma_{3,i}^{*\hat{z}_i} A_i^{*-1})^{\hat{x}_i} = g_2^a = g^{ab}$$

as the answer to the CDH problem.

<u>Probability Analysis.</u> For the simulation to complete without aborting, we define the events A_i, A_1^*, A_2^* such that the following conditions fulfilled:

$$A_i : F(\mathfrak{m}_j) \neq 0 \bmod l \quad \text{where } j = 1, \ldots, q_s,$$
$$A_1^* : x' + \sum_{i|m_i^* \neq \phi} \hat{x}_i - lk = 0 \bmod p,$$
$$A_2^* : \sum_{i|m_i^*=\phi} \hat{x}_i r_i^* = 0 \bmod p.$$

The probability of $\mathcal{B}$ not aborting is

$$\Pr[\text{not abort}] \geq \Pr\left[\left(\bigwedge_{i=1}^{q_s} A_i\right) \wedge A_1^* \wedge A_2^*\right].$$

For the output calculation, as $\hat{x}_i < l$ and $0 \leq r_i^* \leq w$ (by the range proof), we have $-p < \sum_{i|m_i^*=\phi} \hat{x}_i r_i^* < p$. Therefore $\sum_{i|m_i^*=\phi} \hat{x}_i r_i^* = 0 \bmod p$ implies $\sum_{i|m_i^*=\phi} \hat{x}_i r_i^* = 0 \bmod lw$.

$$\Pr[A_2^*] = \Pr[\sum_{i|m_i^*=\phi} \hat{x}_i r_i^* = 0 \bmod p \wedge \sum_{i|m_i^*=\phi} \hat{x}_i r_i^* = 0 \bmod lw]$$
$$= \Pr[\sum_{i|m_i^*=\phi} \hat{x}_i r_i^* = 0 \bmod lw]\Pr[\sum_{i|m_i^*=\phi} \hat{x}_i r_i^* = 0 \bmod p \mid \sum_{i|m_i^*=\phi} \hat{x}_i r_i^* = 0 \bmod lw]$$
$$= \frac{1}{l(n+1)w}.$$

Notice that $\hat{x}_i$ is hidden in u_i by the random element $\hat{y}_i$. The adversary cannot make $\mathcal{B}$ abort by a chance better than making $\mathcal{B}$ abort by randomly choosing r_i^* and m_i^*.

Similarly, we have $\Pr[A_1^*] = \frac{1}{l(n+1)w}$ since the adversary can at most make $\mathcal{B}$ abort by randomly choosing m_i^*. If the adversary randomly chooses m_1^* such that A_1^* happens, he still needs to randomly choose r_i^* to make $\Pr[A_2^*]$ not happening.

Notice that the event A_i is independent of the event A_1^* and A_2^*. Therefore

$$\Pr[\text{not abort}] \geq \Pr[A_1^* \wedge A_2^*] \Pr[\bigwedge_{i=1}^{q_s} A_i | A_1^* \wedge A_2^*]$$

$$\geq \frac{1}{(l(n+1)w)^2}(1 - \sum_{i=1}^{q_s} \Pr[\neg A_i | A_1^* \wedge A_2^*])$$

$$= \frac{1}{(l(n+1)w)^2}(1 - \frac{q_s}{l}).$$

Putting $l = 2q_s$, we have

$$\Pr[\text{not abort}] \geq \frac{1}{8q_s^2(n+1)^2 w^2}.$$

We have the probability bound by combining the result from SOTK (which is based on [3]).

<u>Time Analysis.</u> In the proof, $\mathcal{A}$ has to compute $O(n)$ multiplication and $O(1)$ exponentiation for every signing oracle query. □

Theorem 3. *Our sanitizable signature scheme is indistinguishable if the SOTK is zero-knowledge.*

Proof. (Sketch) In the signature, σ_2^* is computed by from a random number r only. σ_1^* only contains the information of the sanitized message, but not the original message. The sanitized message for both M^{0*} and M^{1*} are the same. The part $(A_i^*, \sigma_{3,i}^*)$ only contains the information for $m_i^* \in st_{M^{b*}}^A$, which is the same when $b = 0$ or 1. σ_4^* is computed from a zero knowledge proof SOTK. Therefore our scheme is indistinguishable in an information theoretic sense.

5.2 Comparison

The comparison of different sanitizable signature schemes are summarized in Table 1. Different types of state controllability, sanitized message, designated sanitizer and transparency are explained in Section 3.4. The security of some schemes rely on the security of the underlying signature, hash function or commitment scheme used. There is no security theorem for [16]. Chang et al. [7] must be used with other sanitizable signature scheme (with unordered documents). Therefore its properties and security may change depending on the underlying scheme used.

For efficiency, our signature has one $\mathbb{G}_1$ and one $\mathbb{G}_2$ elements when it is not sanitized. This is efficient even when compared to standard signature scheme, when we take 170-bit for pairings. Each time when it is sanitized, it will generates extra 55 $\mathbb{G}_1$, 1 $\mathbb{G}_2$ and 29 $\mathbb{Z}_p$ elements. It is inefficient when compared to other schemes. However our scheme is the first scheme proven secure in the standard model, without resolving to the underlying signature.

Table 1. Comparison of Sanitizable Signature Schemes (refer to Section 3.4 for the meaning of the number)

Scheme	State	Message	Sanitizer	Transparency	Security	Model
[21]	2	2	1	1	RSA	ROM
[15]	1	2	1	1	underlying signature	standard
[20]	1	2	1	1	underlying signature	standard
[1]	2	4	2	2	underlying signature and chameleon hash	standard
[19]	3	2	1	1	underlying signature and commitment	standard
[22]	3	2	1	1	co-GDH	ROM
[16]	2	4	2	3	-	-
[18]	3	1	1	2	CDH	ROM
[14]	1	4	1	1	co-GDH	ROM
[7]	1*	3	1*	1	strong RSA + ?	standard
[12]	3	2	1	1	underlying signature, commitment and pseudo-random generator	standard
this paper	1	2	1	1	CDH + XDH	standard

6 Conclusion

In this paper, we firstly reviewed the existing works on sanitizable signature schemes by summarizing different properties used by different authors in the literature. We note that these properties are useful in many different security applications, but they are not required to co-exist concurrently. Furthermore, we also provided some generic transformations among them. Then, we presented a security model to capture most of these properties.

We presented the first concrete construction of sanitizable signature scheme that is provably secure under the standard assumption without random oracle. We provided a security analysis based on the model that we devised earlier. We also provided a fair comparison of the performance of our scheme compared to the existing ones. Moreover, we propose a notion called "Signatures of One-Time Knowledge". We also construct a range proof in the pairings.

References

1. Ateniese, G., Chou, D.H., de Medeiros, B., Tsudik, G.: Sanitizable signatures. In: de Capitani di Vimercati, S., Syverson, P.F., Gollmann, D. (eds.) ESORICS 2005. LNCS, vol. 3679, pp. 159–177. Springer, Heidelberg (2005)
2. Bellare, M., Rogaway, P.: Random oracles are practical: A paradigm for designing efficient protocols. In: ACM CCS 1993, pp. 62–73. ACM Press, New York (1993)
3. Bellare, M., Shoup, S.: Two-tier signatures, strongly unforgeable signatures, and fiat-shamir without random oracles. In: Okamoto, T., Wang, X. (eds.) PKC 2007. LNCS, vol. 4450, pp. 201–216. Springer, Heidelberg (2007)
4. Boneh, D., Boyen, X.: Short signatures without random oracles. In: Cachin, C., Camenisch, J.L. (eds.) EUROCRYPT 2004. LNCS, vol. 3027, pp. 56–73. Springer, Heidelberg (2004)

5. Boudot, F.: Efficient proofs that a committed number lies in an interval. In: Preneel, B. (ed.) EUROCRYPT 2000. LNCS, vol. 1807, pp. 431–444. Springer, Heidelberg (2000)
6. Camenisch, J., Stadler, M.: Efficient group signature schemes for large groups (extended abstract). In: Kaliski Jr., B.S. (ed.) CRYPTO 1997. LNCS, vol. 1294, pp. 410–424. Springer, Heidelberg (1997)
7. Chang, E.-C., Lim, C.L., Xu, J.: Short sanitizable signatures for strings using random trees. Private Communication (2007)
8. Chase, M., Lysyanskaya, A.: On signatures of knowledge. In: Dwork, C. (ed.) CRYPTO 2006. LNCS, vol. 4117, pp. 78–96. Springer, Heidelberg (2006)
9. Fiat, A., Shamir, A.: How to prove yourself: Practical solutions to identification and signature problems. In: Odlyzko, A.M. (ed.) CRYPTO 1986. LNCS, vol. 263, pp. 186–194. Springer, Heidelberg (1987)
10. Gentry, C.: Practical identity-based encryption without random oracles. In: Vaudenay, S. (ed.) EUROCRYPT 2006. LNCS, vol. 4004, pp. 445–464. Springer, Heidelberg (2006)
11. Groth, J., Sahai, A.: Efficient non-interactive proof systems for bilinear groups. In: Smart, N.P. (ed.) EUROCRYPT 2008. LNCS, vol. 4965, pp. 415–432. Springer, Heidelberg (2008)
12. Haber, S., Hatano, Y., Honda, Y., Horne, W., Miyazaki, K., Sander, T., Tezoku, S., Yao, D.: Efficient signature schemes supporting redaction, pseudonymization, and data deidentification. In: ASIACCS 2008, pp. 353–362. ACM, New York (2008)
13. Izu, T., Kanaya, N., Takenaka, M., Yoshioka, T.: Piats: A partially sanitizable signature scheme. In: Qing, S., Mao, W., López, J., Wang, G. (eds.) ICICS 2005. LNCS, vol. 3783, pp. 72–83. Springer, Heidelberg (2005)
14. Izu, T., Kunihiro, N., Ohta, K., Takenaka, M., Yoshioka, T.: A sanitizable signature scheme with aggregation. In: Dawson, E., Wong, D.S. (eds.) ISPEC 2007. LNCS, vol. 4464, pp. 51–64. Springer, Heidelberg (2007)
15. Johnson, R., Molnar, D., Song, D.X., Wagner, D.: Homomorphic signature schemes. In: Preneel, B. (ed.) CT-RSA 2002. LNCS, vol. 2271, pp. 244–262. Springer, Heidelberg (2002)
16. Klonowski, M., Lauks, A.: Extended sanitizable signatures. In: Rhee, M.S., Lee, B. (eds.) ICISC 2006. LNCS, vol. 4296, pp. 343–355. Springer, Heidelberg (2006)
17. Lipmaa, H.: On diophantine complexity and statistical zero-knowledge arguments. In: Laih, C.-S. (ed.) ASIACRYPT 2003. LNCS, vol. 2894, pp. 398–415. Springer, Heidelberg (2003)
18. Miyazaki, K., Hanaoka, G., Imai, H.: Digitally signed document sanitizing scheme based on bilinear maps. In: ASIACCS 2006, pp. 343–354. ACM, New York (2006)
19. Miyazaki, K., Iwamura, M., Matsumoto, T., Sasaki, R., Yoshiura, H., Tezuka, S., Imai, H.: Digitally signed document sanitizing scheme with disclosure condition control. IEICE Transactions 88-A(1), 239–246 (2005)
20. Miyazaki, K., Susaki, S., Iwamura, M., Matsumoto, T., Sasaki, R., Yoshiura, H.: Digital documents sanitizing problem. IEICE Technical Report, ISEC2003-20, 61–67 (2003)
21. Steinfeld, R., Bull, L., Zheng, Y.: Content extraction signatures. In: Kim, K.-c. (ed.) ICISC 2001. LNCS, vol. 2288, pp. 285–304. Springer, Heidelberg (2002)
22. Suzuki, M., Isshiki, T., Tanaka, K.: Sanitizable signature with secret information. In: Symposium on Cryptography and Information Security, vol. 4A1-2 (2006)
23. Waters, B.: Efficient identity-based encryption without random oracles. In: Cramer, R. (ed.) EUROCRYPT 2005. LNCS, vol. 3494, pp. 114–127. Springer, Heidelberg (2005)

An Efficient On-Line/Off-Line Signature Scheme without Random Oracles

Marc Joye

Thomson R&D France
Technology Group, Corporate Research, Security Laboratory
1 avenue de Belle Fontaine, 35576 Cesson-Sévigné Cedex, France
marc.joye@thomson.net

Abstract. On-line/off-line signature schemes allow one to quickly compute a digital signature from a pre-computed coupon. One of the most efficient schemes to date is the GPS scheme, due to Girault, Poupard and Stern. Its security stands in the random oracle model. This paper presents a novel on-line/off-line signature featuring the same on-line efficiency (only a single *small* integer multiplication has to be computed) but without relying on random oracles.

Keywords: Cryptography, digital signature, on-line/off-line signing, standard model.

1 Introduction

Likewise handwritten signatures, digital signatures should feature important requirements making them compelling for a number of applications. Namely, in addition to be unforgeable, they should offer the properties of authenticity, integrity and non-repudiation of signed messages. The advent of public-key cryptographic techniques made possible to allow anyone to perform publicly the verification of signatures. Informally, in a digital signature scheme, each user possesses a pair of matching public key and private key. The private key is used to sign messages while the public key is used to verify signatures.

There exist numerous digital signature schemes, the security of which rely on various intractability assumptions (e.g., discrete logarithms or integer factorization). Several signature schemes are shown to be secure even against chosen-message attacks. Existential unforgeability against chosen-message attacks is the security notion classically retained for signature schemes. Basically, it requires that an adversary having access to a signing oracle returning the signature on messages of its choice is unable to produce a valid signature on a message not previously submitted to the signing oracle [17]. In this paper, we are interested in secure yet efficient signature schemes. By efficiency, we mean here that the signing process should be as fast as possible. This leads us to the paradigm of *on-line/off-line signatures* introduced by Even *et al.* [10] and later improved by Shamir and Tauman [24]. See also [7] for a unifying paradigm encompassing the two approaches.

In an on-line/off-line signature scheme, the signing process is subdivided into two phases. The first phase, performed off-line, is independent of the message to be signed. The second phase, performed on-line, takes on input a value precomputed in the off-line phase and a message and produces a signature. Only the on-line phase is required to be fast. Many applications can afford slower computations as long as they are not performed on-line. Examples include a server pre-computing values at idle time or a low-end smart card with pre-computed values stored in memory. In the latter case, the pre-computed values are sometimes referred to as 'use & throw coupons' [22]. See also [27] for applications in routing protocols.

The so-called GPS signature scheme [16] (see also [15,23]), obtained from the companion identification scheme using the Fiat-Shamir heuristic [11], is one of the most efficient on-line/off-line signature schemes. The on-line phase boils down to the computation of a *small* integer (i.e., non-modular) multiplication. However, being built via the Fiat-Shamir heuristic, the security of the GPS signature scheme stands in the random oracle model [2]. The random oracle model is an idealized model assuming that the output of a hash function behaves as a random generator. Although guaranteeing that the general design should not be flawed, a proof in the random oracle model cannot be considered as an absolute proof. In [5,6], Canetti *et al.* show that there exist signature schemes secure in the random oracle model but for which no secure implementations do exist.

Several efficient on-line/off-line signature schemes in the standard model (i.e., without random oracles) are known [24,3,21,8,28] but none of them features the very fast on-line-phase of the GPS signature scheme. This paper fills the gap and provides such a scheme. The proposed on-line/off-line signature scheme even outperforms the GPS signature scheme for short messages since no prior hashing is required. Moreover, combined with [14], it yields a very efficient identity-based on-line/off-line signature scheme. We note that the GPS signature scheme has been standardized by ISO/IEC in 2008 [20].

The rest of this paper is organized as follows. In the next section, we introduce some definitions. In Section 3, we present our on-line/off-line signature scheme. Then, in Section 4, we prove its security and analyze its performance. Finally, we conclude in Section 5.

2 Preliminaries

2.1 Signature Schemes

A *signature scheme* is a triplet, (Gen, Sign, Verify), of probabilistic polynomial-time algorithms satisfying:

1. *Key generation algorithm* Gen. On input security parameter k, algorithm Gen produces a pair (pk, sk) of matching public and private keys.
2. *Signing algorithm* Sign. Given a message m in a set $\mathcal{M}$ of messages and a pair of matching public and private keys (pk, sk), Sign produces a signature σ.

3. *Verification algorithm* Verify. Given a signature σ, a message $m \in \mathcal{M}$ and a public key pk, Verify checks whether σ is a valid signature on m with respect to pk.

As aforementioned, the classical notion for the security of signature schemes is existential unforgeability against chosen-message attacks (in short, EUF-CMA).

Definition 1. *A signature scheme* (Gen, Sign, Verify) *is said secure if the success probability*

$$\mathsf{Succ}^{\mathsf{EUF\text{-}CMA}}(\mathcal{A}) := \Pr\left[\begin{array}{l}(\mathsf{pk},\mathsf{sk}) \leftarrow \mathsf{Gen}(1^k), (m_*, \sigma_*) \leftarrow \mathcal{A}^{\mathsf{Sign}(\mathsf{sk};\cdot)}(\mathsf{pk}) : \\ \mathsf{Verify}(\mathsf{pk}; m_*, \sigma_*) = true\end{array}\right]$$

is negligible, for every probabilistic polynomial-time adversary $\mathcal{A}$ having access to signing oracle Sign(sk; ·)*, and returning a valid signature σ_* on a message m_* that was not submitted to the signing oracle.*

When the signing algorithm is probabilistic, a setting slightly more general than the single-occurrence chosen-message attack scenario can be considered [25]. The corresponding security notion is referred to as *strong unforgeability against chosen-message attacks* (sEUF-CMA).

Definition 2. *A signature scheme* (Gen, Sign, Verify) *is said [strongly] secure if the success probability*

$$\mathsf{Succ}^{\mathsf{sEUF\text{-}CMA}}(\mathcal{A}) := \Pr\left[\begin{array}{l}(\mathsf{pk},\mathsf{sk}) \leftarrow \mathsf{Gen}(1^k), (m_*, \sigma_*) \leftarrow \mathcal{A}^{\mathsf{Sign}(\mathsf{sk};\cdot)}(\mathsf{pk}) : \\ \mathsf{Verify}(\mathsf{pk}; m_*, \sigma_*) = true\end{array}\right]$$

is negligible, for every probabilistic polynomial-time adversary $\mathcal{A}$ having access to signing oracle Sign(sk; ·)*, and returning a valid signature σ_* on a message m_* where (m_*, σ_*) is different from all pairs (m_i, σ_i) of chosen messages m_i submitted to the signing oracle and corresponding signatures σ_i returned by the signing oracle.*

2.2 Intractability Assumptions

Typically, the security of a signature scheme is conditioned to some intractability assumptions. For the proposed scheme, we will rely on the strong RSA assumption [1,13] and the short exponent discrete logarithm assumption [26] (also used in the GPS signature scheme).

Definition 3. *The* strong RSA assumption (sRSA) *is that it is hard, on input a safe*[1] *RSA modulus N and a random element $s \in \mathbb{Z}_N^*$, to find a pair $(u, r) \in \mathbb{Z}_N \times \mathbb{Z}_{>1}$ satisfying $s \equiv u^r \pmod{N}$. More formally, the success probability of any probabilistic polynomial-time adversary $\mathcal{A}$:*

$$\Pr[N \leftarrow \mathsf{sRSA}(1^k), s \leftarrow \mathbb{Z}_N^*, (u,r) \leftarrow \mathcal{A}(N,s) : u^r \equiv s \pmod{N} \land r > 1]$$

is negligible.

---
[1] An RSA modulus $N = pq$ is said safe when prime $p = 2p' + 1$ and prime $q = 2q' + 1$ for some primes p' and q'.

Definition 4. *The* short exponent discrete logarithm assumption (sDL) *is that it is hard, on input a safe RSA modulus N, a random element $s \in \mathbb{Z}_N^*$ and $v = s^z \bmod N$ for a [small] integer z, to recover the value of z. More formally, the success probability of any probabilistic polynomial-time adversary $\mathcal{A}$:*

$$\Pr\bigl[(N,z) \leftarrow \mathsf{sDL}(1^k), s \leftarrow \mathbb{Z}_N^*, v \leftarrow s^z \bmod N, z' \leftarrow \mathcal{A}(N,s,v) : z' = z\bigr]$$

is negligible.

3 Proposed On-Line/Off-Line Signature Scheme

Let ℓ_N, ℓ_Z, ℓ_S, ℓ_E, ℓ_H and ℓ_K be six security parameters, satisfying

$$\ell_N \geq 2(\ell_E + 2), \quad b(\ell_E - 1) \geq \ell_K + 1, \quad \ell_N - 4 \geq \ell_K \geq \ell_Z + \ell_H + \ell_S \quad (1)$$

for an integer $b \geq 1$. (Typical values for the security parameters are discussed in §4.2.)

The message space is defined as $\mathcal{M} = \{0,1\}^{\ell_H}$, which can also be viewed as the set of integers in the range $[0, 2^{\ell_H} - 1]$.

Key Generation. Choose two random primes $p = 2p'+1$ and $q = 2q'+1$ where p' and q' are primes of equal length, so that $N = pq$ is of length exactly ℓ_N. Choose at random two quadratic residues g and x in $\mathbb{Z}_N^*$. Finally, for a random ℓ_Z-bit integer z, compute $h = g^{-z} \bmod N$.

The public key is $\mathsf{pk} = \{g, h, x, N\}$ and the private key is $\mathsf{sk} = \{p, q, z\}$.

Signing. Let $m \in \mathcal{M}$ denote the message being signed.

– [*Off-line phase*] Randomly pick an ℓ_K-bit integer t and an ℓ_E-bit prime e. Next compute

$$y = (x\, g^{-t})^d \bmod N \quad \text{where } d = e^{-b} \bmod p'q' \; . \quad (2)$$

– [*On-line phase*] From a triplet (t, y, e) computed off-line, evaluate

$$k = t + mz \; . \quad (3)$$

and return the signature $\sigma = (k, y, e)$.

Verification. Signature $\sigma = (k, y, e)$ on message $m \in \mathcal{M}$ is accepted iff

1. e is an odd ℓ_E-bit integer,
2. k is an ℓ_K-bit integer, and
3. $y^{e^b}\, g^k\, h^m \equiv x \pmod{N}$.

As for the Cramer-Shoup signature scheme [9] and its derivatives [29,4,12], there is no need to check the primality of e in the verification algorithm. Observe also that the use of a prime power in Eq. (2) as in [12,18] —rather than simply a prime— speeds up the off-line phase but also reduces the length of the resulting signatures. Moreover, the use of a small value for z as in [16] speeds up the on-line phase and reduces the length of the signatures; in contrast, the schemes in [8,28] require a multiplication by a full-size integer in the on-line phase.

We note there is no hash function involved in the signing process. Long messages can however be dealt with by first reducing their length to the appropriate range using a collision-resistant function $H : \{0,1\}^* \to \mathcal{M}$.

4 Analysis

In this section, we show that our signature scheme is strongly secure under the strong RSA assumption and the short exponent discrete logarithm assumption (see Section 2). We also analyze its performance.

4.1 Proof of Security

Assume that there exists a polynomial-time chosen-message attacker $\mathcal{A}$, allowed to make q_S queries to a signing oracle $\mathcal{O}^\Sigma$, that is able to produce a signature forgery. For $i \in \{1, \ldots, q_S\}$, we let m_i be the ith message queried to $\mathcal{O}^\Sigma$ and $\sigma_i = (k_i, y_i, e_i)$ the ith corresponding signature returned by $\mathcal{O}^\Sigma$. We let $\sigma_* = (k_*, y_*, e_*)$ denote the forgery returned by $\mathcal{A}$ on a message $m_* \in \mathcal{M}$ and $(m_*, \sigma_*) \neq (m_i, \sigma_i)$ for all $i \in \{1, \ldots, q_S\}$. We will show that the existence of attacker $\mathcal{A}$ contradicts a cryptographic assumption (namely, the strong RSA assumption or the short exponent discrete logarithm assumption), which proves the security of the scheme.

We distinguish 3 types of attackers.

Type Ia: $e_* = e_{\hat{\imath}}$ and $y_* \neq y_{\hat{\imath}}$, for some $\hat{\imath} \in \{1, \ldots, q_S\}$.

In this case, we show that $\mathcal{A}$ can be used to solve the (safe) RSA problem. That is, given a safe RSA modulus N, an ℓ_E-bit prime $r \in \mathbb{Z}^*_{\phi(N)}$ and a random element $s \in \mathbb{Z}^*_N$, we want to find u such that $u \equiv s^{1/r} \pmod{N}$.[2]

- We randomly pick $\hat{\imath} \in \{1, \ldots, q_S\}$. For all $i \in \{1, \ldots, q_S\}$, $i \neq \hat{\imath}$, we let e_i be a random ℓ_E-bit prime; we also set $e_{\hat{\imath}} = r$. We assume that for all $i \in \{1, \ldots, q_S\}$, $i \neq \hat{\imath}$, we have $e_i \neq r$, which occurs with overwhelming probability. We create the public key $\mathsf{pk} = \{g, h, x, N\}$ with

$$g = s^{2 \prod_{i \neq \hat{\imath}} e_i^b} \bmod N, \quad h = g^{-z} \bmod N, \quad x = w^{2 \prod_i e_i^b} g^{t_{\hat{\imath}}} \bmod N$$

where z is a random ℓ_Z-bit integer, w is a random element in $\mathbb{Z}^*_N$ and $t_{\hat{\imath}}$ is a random ℓ_K-bit integer.
- The signing oracle can be simulated as follows. On input a message $m_j \in \mathcal{M}$, $j \in \{1, \ldots, q_S\}$, we return

---
[2] Note that such an attacker also breaks the strong RSA assumption.

- $\sigma_{\hat{\imath}} = (k_{\hat{\imath}}, y_{\hat{\imath}}, e_{\hat{\imath}})$ if $j = \hat{\imath}$, with

$$k_{\hat{\imath}} = t_{\hat{\imath}} + m_{\hat{\imath}}\, z, \quad y_{\hat{\imath}} = w^{2\prod_{i \neq \hat{\imath}} e_i^b} \bmod N\,;$$

- $\sigma_j = (k_j, y_j, e_j)$ otherwise, with

$$k_j = t_j + m_j\, z, \quad y_j = w^{2\prod_{i \neq j} e_i^b}\, s^{2(t_{\hat{\imath}} - t_j)\prod_{i \neq j, \hat{\imath}} e_i^b} \bmod N$$

where t_j is a random ℓ_K-bit integer.

- Let $\sigma_* = (k_*, y_*, e_*)$ with $e_* = e_{\hat{\imath}} = r$ be the signature forgery on a message $m_* \in \mathcal{M}$, returned by $\mathcal{A}$. Letting $t_* = k_* - m_* z$ and $\nu = 2(t_{\hat{\imath}} - t_*)\prod_{i \neq \hat{\imath}} e_i^b$, we have

$$\left(\frac{y_*}{y_{\hat{\imath}}}\right)^{r^b} \equiv g^{k_{\hat{\imath}} - k_*}\, h^{m_{\hat{\imath}} - m_*} \equiv s^{\nu} \pmod{N}\,.$$

Moreover, we have $t_{\hat{\imath}} \neq t_*$ as otherwise we would have $(y_*/y_{\hat{\imath}})^{r^b} \equiv 1 \pmod{N}$ and thus $y_* = y_{\hat{\imath}}$ since $\gcd(r^b, 2p'q') = 1$, a contradiction. As a result, we have $\gcd(r^b, \nu) = \gcd(r^b, t_{\hat{\imath}} - t_*) = r^\rho$ for some $\rho \in \{0, \ldots, b-1\}$ since prime power $r^b > |t_{\hat{\imath}} - t_*|$. Hence, by the extended Euclidean algorithm, we can find integers α and β such that $\alpha\, r^b + \beta\, \nu = r^\rho$. This implies

$$s \equiv s^{\alpha\, r^{b-\rho} + \beta\, \frac{\nu}{r^\rho}} \equiv \left(s^\alpha \left(\frac{y_*}{y_{\hat{\imath}}}\right)^\beta\right)^{r^{b-\rho}} \pmod{N}\,.$$

Consequently, $u := \left(s^\alpha (y_*/y_{\hat{\imath}})^\beta\right)^{r^{b-\rho-1}} \bmod N$ solves the RSA problem: $u \equiv s^{1/r} \pmod{N}$. □

Type Ib: $e_* = e_{\hat{\imath}}$ and $y_* = y_{\hat{\imath}}$, for some $\hat{\imath} \in \{1, \ldots, q_S\}$.

In this case, we show that $\mathcal{A}$ can be used to solve the short exponent discrete logarithm problem. That is, given a safe RSA modulus N, a random element $s \in \mathbb{Z}_N^*$ and $v = s^z \bmod N$ for an ℓ_Z-bit integer z, we want to recover the value of z.

- For all $i \in \{1, \ldots, q_S\}$, we let e_i be a random ℓ_E-bit prime. We create the public key $\mathsf{pk} = \{g, h, x, N\}$ with

$$g = s^{2\prod_i e_i^b} \bmod N, \quad h = v^{-2\prod_i e_i^b} \bmod N, \quad x = w^{2\prod_i e_i^b} \bmod N$$

where w is a random element in $\mathbb{Z}_N^*$.

- On input message $m_j \in \mathcal{M}$, $j \in \{1, \ldots, q_S\}$, we simulate the signing oracle by choosing a random ℓ_K-bit integer k_j and returning $\sigma_j = (k_j, y_j, e_j)$ with

$$y_j = \left(s^{-k_j}\, v^{m_j}\, w\right)^{2\prod_{i \neq j} e_i^b} \bmod N\,.$$

- Let $\sigma_* = (k_*, y_*, e_*)$ with $y_* = y_{\hat{\imath}}$ and $e_* = e_{\hat{\imath}}$ be the signature forgery on a message $m_* \in \mathcal{M}$, returned by $\mathcal{A}$. As both σ_* and $\sigma_{\hat{\imath}}$ are valid signatures, we have $g^{k_*} h^{m_*} \equiv g^{k_{\hat{\imath}}} h^{m_{\hat{\imath}}} \pmod{N}$ and so

$$k_* - z\,m_* \equiv k_{\hat{\imath}} - z\,m_{\hat{\imath}} \pmod{p'q'}$$

noting that $h = g^{-z} \bmod N$. Given the definition ranges, the above relation does hold over the integers. Hence, we have $k_* - k_{\hat{\imath}} = z(m_* - m_{\hat{\imath}})$. Moreover, we have $m_* \neq m_{\hat{\imath}}$ as otherwise we would have $k_* = k_j$ and thus $(m_*, \sigma_*) = (m_{\hat{\imath}}, \sigma_{\hat{\imath}})$, a contradiction. Therefore, we get

$$z = \frac{k_* - k_{\hat{\imath}}}{m_* - m_{\hat{\imath}}} \;,$$

the discrete logarithm of v w.r.t. s. □

Type II: $e_* \neq e_i$ for all $i \in \{1, \ldots, q_S\}$.

In this case, we show that $\mathcal{A}$ can be used to solve the flexible RSA problem (a.k.a. strong RSA problem). That is, given a safe RSA modulus N and a random element $s \in \mathbb{Z}_N^*$, we want to find (u, r) such that $s \equiv u^r \pmod{N}$ and $r > 1$.

- For all $i \in \{1, \ldots, q_S\}$, we let e_i be a random ℓ_E-bit prime. We create the public key $\mathsf{pk} = \{g, h, x, N\}$ with

$$g = s^{2 \prod_i e_i^b} \bmod N, \quad h = g^{-z} \bmod N, \quad x = g^a \bmod N$$

  where z is a random ℓ_Z-bit integer and a is a random integer in $\{1, \ldots, N^2\}$.

- On input message $m_j \in \mathcal{M}$, $j \in \{1, \ldots, q_S\}$, we simulate the signing oracle by choosing a random ℓ_K-bit integer t_j and returning $\sigma_j = (k_j, y_j, e_j)$ with

$$y_j = \left(s^{2 \prod_{i \neq j} e_i^b}\right)^{a - t_j} \bmod N, \quad k_j = t_j + m_j\, z \;.$$

- Let $\sigma_* = (k_*, y_*, e_*)$ be the signature forgery on a message $m_* \in \mathcal{M}$, returned by $\mathcal{A}$. Letting $\nu = 2(a - k_* + z\,m_*) \prod_i e_i^b$, we have

$$y_*^{e_*^b} \equiv x\, g^{-k_*}\, h^{-m_*} \equiv s^\nu \pmod{N} \;.$$

Since e_* is an odd ℓ_E-bit integer and $e_* \neq e_i$ for all $i \in \{1, \ldots, q_S\}$, it follows that $\delta := \gcd(e_*^b, \nu) = \gcd(e_*^b, a - k_* + z\,m_*)$. Hence, by the extended Euclidean algorithm, we can find integers α and β such that $\alpha \frac{e_*^b}{\delta} + \beta \frac{\nu}{\delta} = 1$, which, noting that $\gcd(\delta, 2p'q') = 1$, implies

$$s \equiv s^{\alpha \frac{e_*^b}{\delta} + \beta \frac{\nu}{\delta}} \equiv s^{\alpha \frac{e_*^b}{\delta}} y_*^{\beta \frac{e_*^b}{\delta}} \equiv (s^\alpha y_*^\beta)^{\frac{e_*^b}{\delta}} \pmod{N} \;.$$

If we set $u := s^\alpha y_*^\beta \bmod N$ and $r := e_*^b/\delta$ then (u, r) is a solution to the flexible RSA problem, provided that $r \neq 1$. Since a is chosen in $\{1, \ldots, N^2\}$ and since attacker $\mathcal{A}$ knows at best the value of $a \bmod p'q'$ from x, the probability that $r = 1$, or equivalently, that $e_*^b \mid (a - k_* + z\,m_*)$ is negligible. □

4.2 Efficiency Analysis

The proposed signature scheme involves several parameters, namely ℓ_N, ℓ_Z, ℓ_S, ℓ_E, ℓ_H and ℓ_K. We discuss below how to choose those parameters in order to get an adequate security. Our analysis is based on [16].

The security of the proposed signature scheme relies on the strong RSA assumption and the short exponent discrete logarithm assumption. Although in principle easier than the factoring problem, the best known way to solve the strong RSA problem consists in factoring the modulus. Therefore, an RSA modulus of length at least 1536 bits, or equivalently $\ell_N \geq 1536$, should validate the strong RSA assumption. Likewise the most efficient methods for computing short exponent discrete logarithms are in the square root of the size of the exponent. Hence, choosing $\ell_Z \geq 160$ should prevent the recovery of secret parameter z. Parameter ℓ_S must be chosen so as $\ell_K \gg \ell_Z + \ell_H$ in order to guarantee the statistical zero-knowledge property; as in [16], we advise to set $\ell_S \geq 80$. Finally, the length for prime e, ℓ_E, in the signing algorithm is subject to the requirement that it should be very unlikely to generate twice the same prime. To avoid such birthday attacks, the bit-length of prime e must be (roughly) at least $\kappa + \log_2 q_S$ to offer a κ-bit security, where q_S is the maximum number of allowed signature queries [19]. As a result, assuming $q_S \approx 2^{30}$, setting $\ell_E \geq 128$ appears to be a safe choice. The remaining parameters (i.e., ℓ_K and ℓ_H) must be chosen so as to satisfy Eq. (1).

Typically, if we choose $\ell_N = 1536$, $\ell_Z = 160$, $\ell_S = 80$ and $\ell_E = 128$, Eq. (1) yields

$$127b - 1 \geq \ell_K \geq 240 + \ell_H \ .$$

Hence, assuming we are signing 256-bit messages (or longer messages using a standard hash function like SHA-256) —that is, $\ell_H = 256$, we can set $b = 4$ and $\ell_K = 496$. So, for 1536-bit RSA moduli, a signature will be of length 2160 bits. But the main advantage of the proposed scheme resides in the efficacy of the on-line phase (cf. Eq. (3)). It only requires a small integer multiplication for obtaining $k = t + m z$. Both m (or a hashed value thereof) and z are short values; namely, of 256 and 160 bits with the above exemplary values —hence for those values, the evaluation of k basically costs 640 single-precision integer multiplications on a low-end 8-bit processor with the basic schoolboy method.

5 Conclusion

This paper proposed an efficient on-line/off-line signature scheme. Advantageously, the proposed scheme features a very fast on-line phase: only a single small integer multiplication is required. We note that this is slightly faster than the GPS signature scheme, at least for short messages. This property is especially desired for time-constrained applications and for low-end devices that do not have much in the way computational resources. Furthermore and contrarily to the GPS signature scheme, the security proof stands in the standard model (i.e., without random oracles).

Acknowledgments

We thank the anonymous reviewers for useful comments.

References

1. Barić, N., Pfitzmann, B.: Collision-free accumulators and fail-stop signature schemes without trees. In: Fumy, W. (ed.) EUROCRYPT 1997. LNCS, vol. 1233, pp. 480–494. Springer, Heidelberg (1997)
2. Bellare, M., Rogaway, P.: Random oracles are practical: A paradigm for designing efficient protocols. In: 1st ACM Conference on Computer and Communications Security, pp. 62–73. ACM Press, New York (1993)
3. Boneh, D., Boyen, X.: Short signatures without random oracles and the SDH assumption in bilinear groups. Journal of Cryptology 21(2), 149–177 (2004); An extended abstract appears in Eurocrypt 2004
4. Camenisch, J., Lysyanskaya, A.: A signature scheme with efficient protocols. In: Cimato, S., Galdi, C., Persiano, G. (eds.) SCN 2002. LNCS, vol. 2576, pp. 268–289. Springer, Heidelberg (2003)
5. Canetti, R., Goldreich, O., Halevi, S.: The random oracle methodology, revisited. In: 30th Annual ACM Symposium on Theory of Computing (STOC 1998), pp. 209–217. ACM Press, New York (1998)
6. Canetti, R., Goldreich, O., Halevi, S.: On the random oracle methodology as applied to length-restricted signature schemes. In: Naor, M. (ed.) TCC 2004. LNCS, vol. 2951, pp. 40–57. Springer, Heidelberg (2004)
7. Catalano, D., Di Raimondo, M., Fiore, D., Gennaro, R.: Off-line/on-line signatures; theoretical aspects and experimental results. In: Cramer, R. (ed.) PKC 2008. LNCS, vol. 4939, pp. 101–120. Springer, Heidelberg (2008)
8. Chevallier-Mames, B., Joye, M.: A practical and tightly secure signature scheme without hash function. In: Abe, M. (ed.) CT-RSA 2007. LNCS, vol. 4377, pp. 339–356. Springer, Heidelberg (2006)
9. Cramer, R., Shoup, V.: Signature scheme based on the strong RSA assumption. ACM Transactions on Information and System Security 3(3), 161–185 (2000)
10. Even, S., Goldreich, O., Micali, S.: On-line/off-line digital signatures. Journal of Cryptology 9(1), 35–67 (1996); A preliminary version appears in Crypto 1989
11. Fiat, A., Shamir, A.: How to prove yourself: Practical solutions to identification and signature problems. In: Odlyzko, A.M. (ed.) CRYPTO 1986. LNCS, vol. 263, pp. 186–194. Springer, Heidelberg (1987)
12. Fischlin, M.: The Cramer-Shoup strong-RSA signature scheme revisited. In: Desmedt, Y. (ed.) PKC 2003. LNCS, vol. 2567, pp. 116–129. Springer, Heidelberg (2002)
13. Fujisaki, E., Okamoto, T.: Statistical zero-knowledge protocols to prove modular polynomial equations. In: Kaliski Jr., B. (ed.) CRYPTO 1997. LNCS, vol. 1294, pp. 16–30. Springer, Heidelberg (1997)
14. Galindo, D., Herranz, J., Kiltz, E.: On the generic construction of identity-based signatures with additional properties. In: Lai, X., Chen, K. (eds.) ASIACRYPT 2006. LNCS, vol. 4284, pp. 178–193. Springer, Heidelberg (2006)
15. Girault, M.: Self-certified signatures. In: Davies, D.W. (ed.) EUROCRYPT 1991. LNCS, vol. 547, pp. 490–497. Springer, Heidelberg (1991)
16. Girault, M., Poupard, G., Stern, J.: On the fly authentication and signature schemes based on groups of unknown order. Journal of Cryptology 19(4), 463–487 (2006)
17. Goldwasser, S., Micali, S., Rivest, R.: A digital signature scheme secure against adaptive chosen message attacks. SIAM Journal of Computing 17(2), 281–308 (1988)

18. Groth, J.: Cryptography in subgroups of $\mathbb{Z}_n^*$. In: Kilian, J. (ed.) TCC 2005. LNCS, vol. 3378, pp. 50–65. Springer, Heidelberg (2005)
19. Hofheinz, D., Kiltz, E.: Programmable hash functions and their applications. In: Wagner, D. (ed.) CRYPTO 2008. LNCS, vol. 5157, pp. 21–38. Springer, Heidelberg (2008)
20. ISO/IEC 14888-2. Information technology – Security techniques – Digital signatures with appendix – Part 2: Integer factorisation based mechanisms, 2nd edn., April 15 (2008)
21. Kurosawa, K., Schmidt-Samoa, K.: New online/offline signature schemes without random oracles. In: Yung, M., et al. (eds.) PKC 2006. LNCS, vol. 3958, pp. 330–346. Springer, Heidelberg (2006)
22. Naccache, D., M'Raïhi, D., Vaudenay, S., Raphaeli, D.: Can D.S.A. be improved? Complexity trade-offs with the digital signature standard. In: De Santis, A. (ed.) EUROCRYPT 1994. LNCS, vol. 950, pp. 77–85. Springer, Heidelberg (1995)
23. Poupard, G., Stern, J.: Security analysis of a practical "on the fly" authentication and signature generation. In: Nyberg, K. (ed.) EUROCRYPT 1998. LNCS, vol. 1403, pp. 422–436. Springer, Heidelberg (1998)
24. Shamir, A., Tauman, Y.: Improved online/offline signature schemes. In: Kilian, J. (ed.) CRYPTO 2001. LNCS, vol. 2139, pp. 355–367. Springer, Heidelberg (2001)
25. Stern, J., Pointcheval, D., Malone-Lee, J., Smart, N.P.: Flaws in applying proof methodologies to signature schemes. In: Yung, M. (ed.) CRYPTO 2002. LNCS, vol. 2442, pp. 93–110. Springer, Heidelberg (2002)
26. van Oorschot, P.C., Wiener, M.: On Diffie-Hellman key agreement with short exponents. In: Maurer, U. (ed.) EUROCRYPT 1996. LNCS, vol. 1070, pp. 332–343. Springer, Heidelberg (1996)
27. Xu, S., Mu, Y., Susilo, W.: Online/offline signatures and multisignatures for AODV and DSR routing security. In: Batten, L.M., Safavi-Naini, R. (eds.) ACISP 2006. LNCS, vol. 4058, pp. 99–110. Springer, Heidelberg (2006)
28. Yu, P., Tate, S.R.: Online/offline signature schemes for devices with limited computing capabilities. In: Malkin, T. (ed.) CT-RSA 2008. LNCS, vol. 4964, pp. 301–317. Springer, Heidelberg (2008)
29. Zhu, H.: New digital signature scheme attaining immunity against adaptive chosen message attack. Chinese Journal of Electronics 10(4), 484–486 (2001)

On the Security of Online/Offline Signatures and Multisignatures from ACISP'06

Fagen Li[1,2,3], Masaaki Shirase[1], and Tsuyoshi Takagi[1]

[1] School of Systems Information Science,
Future University-Hakodate, Hakodate 041-8655, Japan
[2] School of Computer Science and Engineering,
University of Electronic Science and Technology of China, Chengdu 610054, China
[3] State Key Laboratory of Information Security,
Graduate School of Chinese Academy of Sciences, Beijing 100049, China
fagenli@fun.ac.jp

Abstract. Efficient authentication in routing protocols is one of the most important problems for security of ad hoc networks. In ACISP'06, Xu, Mu, and Susilo proposed an identity-based online/offline signature scheme for authentication in the AODV protocol and then transformed this scheme to an identity-based multisignature scheme which is suitable for the DSR protocol. In this paper, we show that their schemes cannot achieve the claimed security by demonstrating a forgery attack. In this attack, an adversary can forge a valid signature on any messages. Therefore, their signature schemes cannot guarantee the security of AODV and DSR protocols. We also show that their generic construction of identity-based multisignature from identity-based online/offline signature is not secure.

Keywords: Mobile ad hoc networks, identity-based cryptography, Online/offline signature, multisignature, forgery attack.

1 Introduction

Mobile ad hoc networks (MANETs) have wireless links and work independently of fixed infrastructure. They are self-organizing and self-configuring. The wireless nodes operate both as communication end-points as well as routers, enabling multi-hop wireless communication. The wireless devices imply limited power resources and bandwidth. Network topology may change rapidly due to mobility, interference, physical obstacles on the path, and so forth [11]. MANET is very useful in instant consultation between mobile users in the battlefields, emergency, and disaster situations, and so on. However, the wireless and dynamic nature of MANETs leave them more vulnerable to security attacks than wired networks. How to solve the security problem in MANETs has been a active research field in recent years.

The concept of identity-based (ID-based) cryptography was first introduced by Shamir in 1984 [23]. The basic idea behind an ID-based cryptosystem is that users can choose arbitrary strings, for example their email addresses or other online identifiers, as their public keys. The corresponding private keys are created by binding the identity with a master private key of a trusted authority (called private key generator (PKG)). This eliminates much of the overhead associated with key management. Several practical ID-based signature schemes have been devised since 1984 [7,10] but a satisfying ID-based encryption scheme only appeared in 2001 [2]. It was devised by Boneh and Franklin and cleverly uses bilinear maps (the Weil or Tate pairing) over supersingular elliptic curves. ID-based cryptography is more suitable for MANETs than traditional PKI schemes since it does not need to authenticate public keys and to maintain a public key directory. Several security schemes for MANETs using ID-based cryptography have been proposed, such as key management schemes [4,13,16,17], authenticated broadcasting schemes [1], multi-domain MANETs [18], and routing protocols[5,20,21].

The notion of online/offline signature was introduced by Even, Goldreich, and Micali [6]. In such schemes, the signature generation procedure is divided into two phases. The first phase is performed offline (before the message to be signed is given) and the second phase is performed online (after the message to be signed is given). To achieve efficient performance, the costly computation is shifted to the offline part. Online/offline signature schemes are particularly useful in resource-constrained environment. An ID-based online/offline signature scheme was proposed by Xu, Mu, and Susilo in 2005 [24].

Itakura and Nakamura [14] introduced the first multisignature scheme in which multiple signers can cooperate to sign the same message and any verifier can verify the validity of the multisignature. In general, the size of the multisignature is independent of the number of the signers. The multisignature can be generated in parallel manner and serial manner. In 2006, Gangishetti et al. [9] proposed ID-based parallel and serial multisignature schemes using bilinear pairings.

In ACISP'06, Xu, Mu, and Susilo [25] proposed an ID-based online/offline signature scheme for authentication in the AODV protocol [22] and then transformed this scheme to an ID-based multi-signature scheme which is suitable for the DSR protocol [15]. However, in this paper, we show that their schemes cannot achieve the claimed security by demonstrating a forgery attack. In this attack, an adversary can forge a valid signature on any messages. Therefore, their signature schemes cannot guarantee the security of AODV and DSR protocols. We also show that their generic construction of ID-based multisignature from ID-based online/offline signature is not secure.

The rest of this paper is organized as follows. We introduce the bilinear pairings in Section 2. We show that the Xu-Mu-Susilo ID-based online/offline signature scheme is not secure in Section 3. We show that the Xu-Mu-Susilo ID-based multisignature scheme is not secure in Section 4. We show that the Xu-Mu-Susilo generic construction of ID-based multisignature from ID-based online/offline signature is not secure in Section 5. The application of ID-based multisignature to DSR protocol is described in Section 6. Finally, the conclusions are given in Section 7.

2 Preliminaries

In this section, we briefly describe the basic definition and properties of the bilinear pairings.

Let G_1 be a cyclic additive group generated by P, whose order is a prime q, and G_2 be a cyclic multiplicative group of the same order q. A bilinear pairing is a map $\hat{e}: G_1 \times G_1 \to G_2$ with the following properties:

1. Bilinearity: $\hat{e}(aP, bQ) = \hat{e}(P, Q)^{ab}$ for all $P, Q \in G_1$, $a, b \in Z_q$.
2. Non-degeneracy: There exists P and $Q \in G_1$ such that $\hat{e}(P, Q) \neq 1$.
3. Computability: There is an efficient algorithm to compute $\hat{e}(P, Q)$ for all $P, Q \in G_1$.

Some mathematical problems in G_1 is described as follows.

- Discrete Logarithm Problem (DLP): Given two group elements P and Q, to find an integer $x \in Z_q^*$, such that $Q = xP$ whenever such an integer exists.
- Computational Diffie-Hellman Problem (CDHP): Given P, aP, bP for $a, b \in Z_q^*$, to compute abP.
- Decision Diffie-Hellman Problem (DDHP): Given P, aP, bP, cP for $a, b, c \in Z_q^*$, to decide whether $c \equiv ab \bmod q$.

The CDHP and DLP are assumed to be intractable. When the DDHP is easy while the CDHP is still believed to be hard on the group G_1, we call G_1 a Gap Diffie-Hellman (GDH) group. Such groups can be found on supersingular elliptic curves or hyperelliptic curves over finite field, and the bilinear parings can be derived from the Weil or Tate pairing. We can refer to [2,3,12] for more details. The security of the Xu-Mu-Susilo schemes [25] rely on the hardness of the CDHP problem.

3 Security of ID-Based Online/Offline Signature Scheme

In this section, we briefly describe the security model of ID-based online/offline signature schemes. Then we review the Xu-Mu-Susilo ID-based online/offline signature scheme [25]. Finally, we show that their scheme is not secure.

3.1 Security Model

An ID-based online/offline signature scheme consists of the following five algorithms.

- Setup: is a probabilistic algorithm run by a PKG that takes as input a security parameter k to output system parameters *params* and a master key s that is kept secret.
- Extract: is a key generation algorithm run by the PKG that takes as input the system parameters *params*, the master key s and an identity ID, and returns the corresponding private key D_{ID}.

- OffSign: is a probabilistic algorithm that takes as input the system parameters *params* and a signature key D_{ID}, and outputs an offline signature S.
- OnSign: is a probabilistic algorithm that takes as input a message m and an offline signature S, and returns an online signature σ.
- Verify: is a deterministic algorithm that takes as input (ID, m, S, σ), and returns either accept or reject.

For the unforgeability, we consider the following game played between a challenger $\mathcal{A}$ and an adversary $\mathcal{F}$.

- Initial: The challenger $\mathcal{A}$ runs the Setup algorithm to generate the system parameters *params* and sends it to the adversary $\mathcal{F}$.
- Attack: The adversary $\mathcal{F}$ performs the following queries:
  - Key extraction query: $\mathcal{F}$ produces an identity ID and receives corresponding private key D_{ID}.
  - Offline signature query: $\mathcal{F}$ produces an identity ID, and receives an offline signature generated by offline signature oracle using the private key corresponding to ID.
  - Online signature query: $\mathcal{F}$ produces a message m, and receives an online signature generated by online signature oracle. The online signature is corresponding to the offline signature.
- Forgery: After performing a polynomial number of queries, $\mathcal{F}$ produces a triple $(ID^*, m^*, S^*, \sigma^*)$ made of an identity ID^*, whose private key was never asked in key extraction queries. Besides, the pair (ID^*, m^*) was never asked in online/offline signature queries. $\mathcal{F}$ wins if the Verify algorithm accepts the triple $(ID^*, m^*, S^*, \sigma^*)$.

The advantage of $\mathcal{F}$ is defined as the probability that it wins.

Definition 1. *An adversary $\mathcal{F}$ is said to be an (ϵ, t, q_e, q_s)-forger of an ID-based online/offline signature if $\mathcal{F}$ has advantage at least ϵ in the above game, runs in time at most t, and makes at most q_e and q_s key extraction and signature queries, respectively. A scheme is said to be (ϵ, t, q_e, q_s)-existentially unforgeable if no (ϵ, t, q_e, q_s)-forger exists.*

Remark: The security model is not reasonable since it require two signature oracles. We should combine the offline signature query and online signature query into one signature query.

3.2 The Xu-Mu-Susilo Scheme

The Xu-Mu-Susilo ID-based online/offline signature scheme consists of the following five algorithms.

- Setup: Given a security parameter k, the PKG chooses groups G_1 and G_2 of prime order q (with G_1 additive and G_2 multiplicative), a generator P of G_1, a bilinear map $\hat{e}: G_1 \times G_1 \to G_2$, and hash functions $H_0: \{0,1\}^* \to G_1$

and $H_1 : \{0,1\}^* \to Z_q^*$. The PKG chooses a master key $s \in Z_q^*$ randomly and computes $P_{pub} = sP$. The PKG publishes system parameters $\{G_1, G_2, q, \hat{e}, P, P_{pub}, H_0, H_1\}$ and keeps the master key s secret.
- Extract: Given an identity ID, the PKG computes $Q_{ID} = H_1(ID)$ and the private key $D_{ID} = sQ_{ID}$. Then the PKG sends the private key to its owner in a secure way.
- OffSign: The signer chooses $r, x \in Z_q^*$ randomly and computes the offline signature pair (S, R), where $S = D_{ID} - xP_{pub}$ and $R = rP$.
- OnSign: In order to sign a message m, the signer computes the online signature $\sigma = H_1(m)r + x$. The resulting signature is a triple (S, σ, R).
- Verify: An online/offline signature (S, σ, R) of a message m for identity ID is accepted if and only if the following equation holds:

$$\hat{e}(S + \sigma P_{pub}, P) = \hat{e}(Q_{ID} + H_1(m)R, P_{pub}).$$

3.3 Our Analysis

We show that the Xu-Mu-Susilo ID-based online/offline signature scheme is not secure in their model. An adversary can forge a valid signature on any messages. To forge a signature $(ID^*, m^*, S^*, \sigma^*, R^*)$, $\mathcal{F}$ first chooses another message m' and performs the online/offline signature queries under identity ID^*. When $\mathcal{F}$ receives the signature $(ID^*, m', S', \sigma', R')$, it performs the following steps.

1. Compute $\sigma^* = H_1(m^*)H_1(m')^{-1}\sigma'$.
2. Compute $S^* = H_1(m^*)H_1(m')^{-1}S'$.
3. Compute $R^* = H_1(m')^{-1}Q_{ID^*} + R' - H_1(m^*)^{-1}Q_{ID^*}$.

The following equations show that the signature $(ID^*, m^*, S^*, \sigma^*, R^*)$ is valid.

$$\hat{e}(S^* + \sigma^* P_{pub}, P)$$
$$= \hat{e}(H_1(m^*)H_1(m')^{-1}S' + H_1(m^*)H_1(m')^{-1}\sigma' P_{pub}, P)$$
$$= \hat{e}(S' + \sigma' P_{pub}, P)^{H_1(m^*)H_1(m')^{-1}}$$
$$= \hat{e}(Q_{ID^*} + H_1(m')R', P_{pub})^{H_1(m^*)H_1(m')^{-1}}$$
$$= \hat{e}(H_1(m^*)H_1(m')^{-1}Q_{ID^*} + H_1(m^*)R', P_{pub})$$
$$= \hat{e}(H_1(m^*)H_1(m')^{-1}Q_{ID^*} + H_1(m^*)R' - Q_{ID^*} + Q_{ID^*}, P_{pub})$$
$$= \hat{e}(H_1(m^*)H_1(m')^{-1}Q_{ID^*} + H_1(m^*)R' - H_1(m^*)H_1(m^*)^{-1}Q_{ID^*} + Q_{ID^*}, P_{pub})$$
$$= \hat{e}(H_1(m^*)(H_1(m')^{-1}Q_{ID^*} + R' - H_1(m^*)^{-1}Q_{ID^*}) + Q_{ID^*}, P_{pub})$$
$$= \hat{e}(H_1(m^*)R^* + Q_{ID^*}, P_{pub})$$
$$= \hat{e}(Q_{ID^*} + H_1(m^*)R^*, P_{pub})$$

Therefore, $\mathcal{F}$ forge a valid signature (S^*, σ^*, R^*) on message m^*. That is, the Xu-Mu-Susilo ID-based online/offline signature scheme is not existentially unforgeable.

4 Security of ID-Based Multisignature Scheme

In this section, we briefly describe the security model of ID-based multisignature scheme. Then we review the Xu-Mu-Susilo ID-based multisignature scheme [25]. Finally, we show that their scheme is not secure.

4.1 Security Model

Xu, Mu, and Susilo extended the definition of accountable subgroup multisignature (ASM) [19] to ID-based ASM. In [19], the ASM is any subgroup G_{sub} of a given group G of potential signers, who sign a message.

An ID-based multisignature scheme consists of the following four algorithms. Here we assume that the group G_{sub} consists of L signers.

- Setup: is a probabilistic algorithm run by a PKG that takes as input a security parameter k to output system parameters *params* and a master key s that is kept secret.
- KeyGen: is a key generation algorithm run by the PKG that takes as input the system parameters *params*, the master key s, a subgroup G_{sub}, and an identity ID, and returns the corresponding private key D_{ID}.
- Sign: is a probabilistic algorithm that takes as input a description of subgroup G_{sub}, the identity of each member in G_{sub}, a message m, and each signer's private key D_{ID_i}, and outputs a multisignature σ.
- Verify: is a deterministic algorithm that takes as input the description of subgroup G_{sub}, the identity of each member in G_{sub}, the message m, and the multisignature σ, and returns either accept or reject.

For the unforgeability, we consider the following game played between a challenger $\mathcal{A}$ and an adversary $\mathcal{F}$. Here $S \subseteq G$ is a subgroup of a given group G.

- Initial: The challenger $\mathcal{A}$ runs the Setup algorithm to generate the system parameters *params* and sends it to the adversary $\mathcal{F}$.
- Attack: The adversary $\mathcal{F}$ performs the following queries:
  - Key generation query: $\mathcal{F}$ produces an identity ID of the uncorrupted player in S and receives corresponding private key D_{ID} and its temporary signature commitment S for current signature session.
  - Signature query: $\mathcal{F}$ produces a message m, and receives a signature generated by signature oracle using the private key corresponding to ID.
- Forgery: After performing a polynomial number of queries, $\mathcal{F}$ produces a triple (m^*, σ^*, S^*) such that
  - σ^* is a valid signature on the message m by the subgroup S of players.
  - there exists an uncorrupted player $P^* \in S$ who has never been asked by $\mathcal{F}$ to execute the signature query on m^* and S^*.

  $\mathcal{F}$ wins if the Verify algorithm accepts the triple (m^*, σ^*, S^*).

The advantage of $\mathcal{F}$ is defined as the probability that it wins.

Definition 2. *An adversary $\mathcal{F}$ is said to be an (ϵ, t, q_e, q_s)-forger of an ID-based multisignature signature if $\mathcal{F}$ has advantage at least ϵ in the above game, runs in time at most t, and makes at most q_e and q_s key extraction and signature queries, respectively. A scheme is said to be (ϵ, t, q_e, q_s)-existentially unforgeable if no (ϵ, t, q_e, q_s)-forger exists.*

4.2 The Xu-Mu-Susilo Scheme

The Xu-Mu-Susilo ID-based multisignature scheme consists of the following four algorithms.

- Setup: Given a security parameter k, the PKG chooses groups G_1 and G_2 of prime order q (with G_1 additive and G_2 multiplicative), a generator P of G_1, a bilinear map $\hat{e} : G_1 \times G_1 \to G_2$, and hash functions $H_0 : \{0,1\}^* \to G_1$ and $H_1 : \{0,1\}^* \to Z_q^*$. The PKG chooses a master key $s \in Z_q^*$ randomly and computes $P_{pub} = sP$. The PKG publishes system parameters $\{G_1, G_2, q, \hat{e}, P, P_{pub}, H_0, H_1\}$ and keeps the master key s secret.
- KeyGen: For each player $P_i (1 \leq i \leq L)$ with identity ID_i in G, the PKG computes $Q_{ID_i} = H_1(ID_i)$ and the private key $D_{ID_i} = sQ_{ID_i}$. Then the PKG sends the private key to its owner in a secure way.
- Sign: Each player $P_i (1 \leq i \leq L)$ in G performs the following steps:

    1. Chooses $r_i, x_i \in Z_q^*$ randomly.
    2. Compute the signature commitment for the current session as $C_i = D_{ID_i} - x_i P_{pub}$, $R_i = r_i P$, and $U_i = x_i P$
    3. Broadcast (C_i, R_i, U_i) to all the players.

Suppose the players in a subgroup $S = \{P_1, P_2, \ldots, P_l\}$ want to jointly sign a message m. Upon receiving (C_j, R_j) from $P_j (1 \leq j \leq l, j \neq i)$, each $P_i (1 \leq i \leq l)$ performs the following steps:

1. Check if the following equation holds:

$$\hat{e}(C_j, P) = \hat{e}(Q_{ID_j} - U_j, P_{pub}).$$

2. Compute $\tilde{C} = \sum_{j=1}^{l} C_j$ and $\tilde{R} = \sum_{j=1}^{l} R_j$.
3. Compute the signature as
    (a) Each P_i computes the signature $\sigma_i = H_1(m)r_i + x_i$ and broadcasts to $P_j (1 \leq j \leq l, j \neq i)$.
    (b) Upon receiving all the σ_j, P_i computes $\tilde{\sigma} = \sum_{j=1}^{l} \sigma_j$.

The resulting multisignature for message m is $(\tilde{\sigma}, \tilde{C}, \tilde{R})$. To further reduce the signature size, we combine $\tilde{\sigma}$ and $\tilde{C}$ to obtain a new parameter $\tilde{V}$ by

$$\tilde{V} = \tilde{C} + \tilde{\sigma} P_{pub}.$$

The final signature is a pair $(\tilde{V}, \tilde{R})$.

- Verify: An multisignature signature $(\tilde{V}, \tilde{R})$ of a message m for subgroup S is accepted if and only if the following equation holds:

$$\hat{e}(\tilde{V}, P) = \hat{e}(\sum_{i=1}^{l} Q_{ID_i} + H_1(m)\tilde{R}, P_{pub}).$$

4.3 Our Analysis

We show that the Xu-Mu-Susilo ID-based multisignature scheme is not secure in their model. An adversary can forge a valid signature on any messages. To forge a signature $(\tilde{V}^*, \tilde{R}^*)$ of message m^* for subgroup S^*, $\mathcal{F}$ first chooses another message m' and performs the signature query under subgroup S^*. When $\mathcal{F}$ receives the signature $(\tilde{V}', \tilde{R}')$, it performs the following steps.

1. Compute $\tilde{V}^* = H_1(m^*)H_1(m')^{-1}\tilde{V}'$.
2. Compute $\tilde{R}^* = H_1(m')^{-1}\sum_{i=1}^{l} Q_{ID_i^*} + \tilde{R}' - H_1(m^*)^{-1}\sum_{i=1}^{l} Q_{ID_i^*}$.

The following equations show that the signature $(\tilde{V}^*, \tilde{R}^*)$ is valid.

$\hat{e}(\tilde{V}^*, P)$
$= \hat{e}(H_1(m^*)H_1(m')^{-1}\tilde{V}', P)$
$= \hat{e}(\tilde{V}', P)^{H_1(m^*)H_1(m')^{-1}}$
$= \hat{e}(\sum_{i=1}^{l} Q_{ID_i^*} + H_1(m')\tilde{R}', P_{pub})^{H_1(m^*)H_1(m')^{-1}}$
$= \hat{e}(H_1(m^*)H_1(m')^{-1}\sum_{i=1}^{l} Q_{ID_i^*} + H_1(m^*)\tilde{R}', P_{pub})$
$= \hat{e}(H_1(m^*)H_1(m')^{-1}\sum_{i=1}^{l} Q_{ID_i^*} + H_1(m^*)\tilde{R}' - \sum_{i=1}^{l} Q_{ID_i^*} + \sum_{i=1}^{l} Q_{ID_i^*}, P_{pub})$
$= \hat{e}(H_1(m^*)H_1(m')^{-1}\sum_{i=1}^{l} Q_{ID_i^*} + H_1(m^*)\tilde{R}' - H_1(m^*)H_1(m^*)^{-1}\sum_{i=1}^{l} Q_{ID_i^*}$
$+ \sum_{i=1}^{l} Q_{ID_i^*}, P_{pub})$
$= \hat{e}(H_1(m^*)(H_1(m')^{-1}\sum_{i=1}^{l} Q_{ID_i^*} + \tilde{R}' - H_1(m^*)^{-1}\sum_{i=1}^{l} Q_{ID_i^*}) + \sum_{i=1}^{l} Q_{ID_i^*}, P_{pub})$
$= \hat{e}(H_1(m^*)\tilde{R}^* + \sum_{i=1}^{l} Q_{ID_i^*}, P_{pub})$
$= \hat{e}(\sum_{i=1}^{l} Q_{ID_i^*} + H_1(m^*)\tilde{R}^*, P_{pub})$

Therefore, $\mathcal{F}$ forge a valid signature $(\tilde{V}^*, \tilde{R}^*)$ on message m^*. That is, the Xu-Mu-Susilo ID-based multisignature signature scheme is not existentially unforgeable.

5 Security of the Generic Construction

In this section, we review the Xu-Mu-Susilo generic construction of ID-based multisignature scheme based on the ID-based online/offline signature scheme [25]. Then we show that their construction is not secure.

5.1 The Xu-Mu-Susilo Generic Construction

We describe the generic construction in Figure 1. For simplicity, we call ID-based online/offline signature and ID-based multisignature IBOS and IBMS, respectively.

5.2 Our Analysis

We show that the Xu-Mu-Susilo generic construction [25] is not secure in their model. An adversary can forge a valid signature on any messages. To forge a signature (C^*, σ^*) of message m^* for subgroup $S^* = S_1^* \cup S_2^*$, $\mathcal{F}$ first performs

---

IBMS.Setup(1^k):

1. $(s, params) \leftarrow$ IBOS.Setup(1^k)

2. Output the master key s and the system parameters $params$

IBMS.KeyGen($G_{sub}, ID_i, s, params$):

1. $D_{ID_i} \leftarrow$ IBOS.Extract($ID_i, s, params$)

2. Output the private key D_{ID_i}

IBMS.Sign(m, G_{sub}, D_{ID_i}):

1. $C_i \leftarrow$ IBOS.OffSign($ID_i, D_{ID_i}, params$)

2. $\sigma_i \leftarrow$ IBOS.OnSign($m, C_i, ID_i, D_{ID_i}, params$)

3. $C \leftarrow \sum_{i \in G_{sub}} C_i$

4. $\sigma \leftarrow \sum_{i \in G_{sub}} \sigma_i$

5. Output the signature (C, σ)

IBMS.Verify(m, G_{sub}, C, σ):

1. Accept or Reject $\leftarrow$ IBOS.Verify(m, G_{sub}, C, σ)

2. Output Accept or Reject

Fig. 1. The Xu-Mu-Susilo generic construction

a signature query on m^* under subgroup S_1^* and obtains a signature (C_1^*, σ_1^*). Then $\mathcal{F}$ performs a signature query on m^* under subgroup S_2^* and obtains a signature (C_2^*, σ_2^*). Finally, $\mathcal{F}$ computes $C^* = C_1^* + C_2^*$ and $\sigma^* = \sigma_1^* + \sigma_2^*$. It is obvious that (C^*, σ^*) is a valid signature on the message m^* under subgroup S^*. Therefore, the Xu-Mu-Susilo generic construction is not secure. Note that the Xu-Mu-Susilo ID-based multisignature signature scheme described in Section 4 also suffer form this attack.

6 About the Application to the DSR Protocol

DSR [15] is an on-demand routing protocol that allows nodes to dynamically discover a source route to any destination in the network. It consists of two phases: route discovery and route maintenance. When a source node needs to dynamically find a new route to the destination node, it broadcasts a route request (RREQ) packet. When the neighbor nodes receive the RREQ, if it is just the destination of the route discovery or there is the route information in its route cache to the same destination node, it adds the route information in the route record of the RREQ and returns a route reply (RREP) packet to the initiate source node. When the initiator receives this RREP, it caches this route in its route cache for use in sending subsequent packets to this destination. Otherwise, if this node receiving the route request has seen another RREQ from the same initiator to the same destination, or if this node's own address is already listed in the route record in the route request, this node discards the request. Otherwise, this node appends its own address to the route record of the RREQ and relay the RREQ. The route maintenance mechanism monitors the status of source routes in use, detects link failures and repairs routes with broken links. Xu, Mu, and Susilo [25] showed how to apply their ID-based multisignature scheme to the DSR protocol. However, this paper have showed that their multisignature scheme is not secure. So, their application to DSR protocol is also not secure.

7 Conclusions

We have showed that the Xu-Mu-Susilo ID-based online/offline signature and multisignature schemes are not secure in their model. An adversary can forge a valid signature on any messages. Therefore, their signature schemes cannot guarantee the security of AODV and DSR protocols. In addition, their generic construction of ID-based multisignature scheme based on the ID-based online/offline signature scheme is also not secure. Note that Galindo, Herranz, and Kiltz proposed an generic construction of ID-based online/offline signature in [8].

Acknowledgements

We would like to thank the anonymous reviewers for their valuable comments and suggestions. This work is supported by the National Natural Science Foundation of China (60673075), the National High Technology Research and Development Program of China (2006AA01Z428), the State Key Laboratory of Information Security, and the Youth Science and Technology Foundation of UESTC. Fagen Li is supported by the JSPS postdoctoral fellowship for research in Japan.

References

1. Bohio, M., Miri, A.: An authenticated broadcasting scheme for wireless ad hoc network. In: 2nd Annual Conference on Communication Networks and Services Research-CNSR 2004, Fredericton, Canada, pp. 69–74 (2004)
2. Boneh, D., Franklin, M.: Identity-based encryption from the weil pairing. In: Kilian, J. (ed.) CRYPTO 2001. LNCS, vol. 2139, pp. 213–229. Springer, Heidelberg (2001)
3. Cha, J.C., Cheon, J.H.: An identity-based signature from gap Diffie-Hellman groups. In: Desmedt, Y.G. (ed.) PKC 2003. LNCS, vol. 2567, pp. 18–30. Springer, Heidelberg (2002)
4. Deng, H., Mukherjee, A., Agrawal, D.: Threshold and identity-based key management and authentication for wireless ad hoc networks. In: International Conference on Information Technology: Coding and Computing, Las Vegas, NV, USA, pp. 107–111 (2004)
5. Deng, H., Agrawal, D.P.: TIDS: threshold and identity-based security scheme for wireless ad hoc networks. Ad Hoc Networks 2(3), 291–307 (2004)
6. Even, S., Goldreich, O., Micali, S.: On-line/off-ine digital signatures. Journal of Cryptology 9(1), 35–67 (1996)
7. Fiat, A., Shamir, A.: How to prove yourself: practical solutions to identification and signature problems. In: Odlyzko, A.M. (ed.) CRYPTO 1986. LNCS, vol. 263, pp. 186–194. Springer, Heidelberg (1987)
8. Galindo, D., Herranz, J., Kiltz, E.: On the generic construction of identity-based signatures with additional properties. In: Lai, X., Chen, K. (eds.) ASIACRYPT 2006. LNCS, vol. 4284, pp. 178–193. Springer, Heidelberg (2006)
9. Gangishetti, R., Gorantla, M.C., Das, M.L., Saxena, A.: Identity based multisignatures. Informatica 17(2), 177–186 (2006)
10. Guillou, L., Quisquater, J.J.: A "Paradoxical" Identity-based signature scheme resulting from zero-knowledge. In: Goldwasser, S. (ed.) CRYPTO 1988. LNCS, vol. 403, pp. 216–231. Springer, Heidelberg (1990)
11. Hegland, A.M., Winjum, E., Mjolsnes, S.F., Rong, C., Kure, O., Spilling, P.: A survey of key management in ad hoc networks. IEEE Communications Surveys & Tutorials 8(3), 48–66 (2006)
12. Hess, F.: Efficient identity based signature schemes based on pairings. In: Nyberg, K., Heys, H.M. (eds.) SAC 2002. LNCS, vol. 2595, pp. 310–324. Springer, Heidelberg (2003)
13. Hoeper, K., Gong, G.: Key revocation for identity-based schemes in mobile ad hoc networks. In: Kunz, T., Ravi, S.S. (eds.) ADHOC-NOW 2006. LNCS, vol. 4104, pp. 224–237. Springer, Heidelberg (2006)
14. Itakura, K., Nakamura, K.: A public-key cryptosystem suitable for digital multisignatures. NEC Research and Development 71, 1–8 (1983)
15. Johnson, D.B., Maltz, D.A., Hu, Y.C.: The Dynamic source routing protocol for mobile ad hoc networks (DSR). IETF INTERNET DRAFT, MANET working group, draft-ietf-manet-dsr-10.txt (July 2004)

16. Khalili, A., Katz, J., Arbaugh, W.A.: Toward secure key distribution in truly ad hoc networks. In: 2003 Symposium on Applications and the Internet Workshops, Orlando, FL, USA, pp. 342–364 (2003)
17. Li, G., Han, W.: A new scheme for key management in ad hoc networks. In: Lorenz, P., Dini, P. (eds.) ICN 2005. LNCS, vol. 3421, pp. 242–249. Springer, Heidelberg (2005)
18. Li, F., Hu, Y., Zhang, C.: An identity-based signcryption scheme for multi-domain ad hoc networks. In: Katz, J., Yung, M. (eds.) ACNS 2007. LNCS, vol. 4521, pp. 373–384. Springer, Heidelberg (2007)
19. Micali, S., Ohta, K., Reyzin, L.: Accountable-subgroup multisignatures. In: 8th ACM Conference on Computer and Communications Security-CCS 2001, Philadelphia, USA, pp. 245–254 (2001)
20. Park, B.N., Myung, J., Lee, W.: ISSRP: a secure routing protocol using identity-based signcryption scheme in ad-hoc networks. In: Liew, K.-M., Shen, H., See, S., Cai, W. (eds.) PDCAT 2004. LNCS, vol. 3320, pp. 711–714. Springer, Heidelberg (2004)
21. Park, B.N., Lee, W.: ISMANET: a secure routing protocol using identity-based signcryption scheme for mobile ad-hoc networks. IEICE Transactions on Communications E88-B(6), 2548–2556 (2005)
22. Perkins, C.E., Royer, E.M., Das, S.R.: Ad hoc on-demand distance vector (AODV) routing. IETF INTERNET DRAFT, MANET working group, Draft-ietf-manet-aodv-13.txt (February 2003)
23. Shamir, A.: Identity-based cryptosystems and signature schemes. In: Blakely, G.R., Chaum, D. (eds.) CRYPTO 1984. LNCS, vol. 196, pp. 47–53. Springer, Heidelberg (1985)
24. Xu, S., Mu, Y., Susilo, W.: Efficient authentication scheme for routing in mobile ad hoc networks. In: Enokido, T., Yan, L., Xiao, B., Kim, D.Y., Dai, Y.-S., Yang, L.T. (eds.) EUC-WS 2005. LNCS, vol. 3823, pp. 854–863. Springer, Heidelberg (2005)
25. Xu, S., Mu, Y., Susilo, W.: Online/offline signatures and multisignatures for AODV and DSR routing security. In: Batten, L.M., Safavi-Naini, R. (eds.) ACISP 2006. LNCS, vol. 4058, pp. 99–110. Springer, Heidelberg (2006)

A Killer Application for Pairings: Authenticated Key Establishment in Underwater Wireless Sensor Networks

David Galindo[1,*], Rodrigo Roman[2], and Javier Lopez[2]

[1] University of Luxembourg
david.galindo@uni.lu
[2] Department of Computer Science, University of Malaga, Spain
{roman,jlm}@lcc.uma.es

Abstract. Wireless sensors are low power devices which are highly constrained in terms of computational capabilities, memory, and communication bandwidth. While battery life is their main limitation, they require considerable energy to communicate data. The latter is specially dramatic in underwater wireless sensor networks (UWSN), where the acoustic transmission mechanisms are less reliable and more energy-demanding. Saving in communication is thus the primary concern in underwater wireless sensors. With this constraint in mind, we argue that non-interactive identity-based key agreement built on pairings provides the best solution for key distribution in large UWSN when compared to the state of the art. At first glance this claim is surprising, since pairing computation is very demanding. Still, pairing-based non-interactive key establishment requires minimal communication and at the same time enjoys excellent properties when used for key distribution.

Keywords: identity-based key agreement, underwater wireless sensor networks, key distribution, pairings.

1 Introduction

Sensors are inexpensive, battery-powered devices which have limited resources. A wireless sensor node typically consists of a power unit, a sensing unit, a processing unit, a storage unit and a wireless transmitter and receiver. Security is one of the principal concerns while designing protocols and mechanisms for wireless sensor networks (WSN). They usually are not tamper-resistant due to cost constraints, and it is easy to physically access them in most scenarios because they must be located near the physical source of the events. Furthermore, any device can access the information exchange because the communication channel is public. It is easy the for an adversary to manipulate the sensor nodes and the communication channel of an unprotected network on its own benefit.

Security protocols require the existence of some security credentials (i.e. pairwise keys) between peers in order to encrypt, authenticate and provide integrity

---
* Work done while the author was with the University of Malaga.

to the information flow. Key distribution is not trivial in WSN because in most cases it is not possible to know in advance which nodes are going to be neighbors, that is, which nodes need to share a pairwise key.

It is well-known that from an efficiency point of view, symmetric key cryptography outperforms public (or asymmetric) key cryptography. Indeed, public key primitives are of the order of hundred of times more computationally intensive that their symmetric key counterparts. The development of an efficient key management system (KMS) for creating pairwise keys between neighbors is a hot research topic, with many complex symmetric key cryptography based frameworks [AR06]. The better performance of symmetric key primitives can be even more acute in resource-constrained devices, for which frequently battery life is the main limitation, so the less computationally expensive (and hence less energy consuming) operations the better. This is the reason why in areas like wireless sensor network security, using public key cryptography has been considered prohibitive from the very beginning.

Somewhat surprisingly, this common wisdom is being challenged. The main reason behind this is the fact that communicating data in these devices requires considerable power, in contrast to wired devices. Therefore, it can be the case that the energy saving of a computationally inexpensive primitive is nullified by the bigger amount of data it requires to be sent. This has already been shown by Großschädl, Szekely and Tillich in [GST07], where the energy cost of two standardized symmetric and asymmetric key exchange protocols has been evaluated. Specifically, the symmetric key protocol used in that study is a light-weight variant of authenticated Kerberos [KN93], while the asymmetric key protocol is an elliptic curve version of Menezes-Qu-Vanstone [MQV95, DE06] (ECMQV). The striking result is that in standard medium-size wireless sensor networks, ECMQV consumes less power than Kerberos, due to the fact that it requires 50% less bits to be exchanged.

We go one step further by considering an extreme case of wireless communication, namely, communication between underwater sensor nodes. Classical electromagnetic waves communication is not satisfactory in underwater environments due to the conducting nature of the medium, especially in the case of sea water. Instead, acoustic communication is the most widely used technique, due to the low signal reduction of sound in water [LZC08]. Acoustic communication presents severe limitations in bandwidth and requires a huge amount of energy. According to Morgansen [Hic08], current state of the art in practical scenarios is transmission of 640 bits (80 bytes) per second. We argue than in this extremely constrained environment, non-interactive identity-based key establishment (NIKE) protocols such as SOK [SOK01, DE06] provides the most efficient solution to the problem of key distribution in large UWSN. This can seem quite surprising, since at the time of this writing efficient identity-based key cryptography is tied to a computational number-theoretic primitive called bilinear pairing (cf. Chapter 5 in [BSS05]), which is a computationally intensive operation. In a wired system, identity-based key agreement would in general only be used for its specific functionalities, but not from a computational efficiency point of view. At first sight, one would preclude its use in WSN for a similar reason. However, the use of NIKE in UWSN achieves the lowest bandwidth while providing the best properties for key distribution from a global point of view.

The structure of this paper is as follows: In Section 2 we revise the concept of wireless sensor networks and the need of key management systems with certain properties. Later, in the same section, we introduce the special features of underwater sensor networks (UWSN). In Section 3, we will revise the behaviour of non-interactive identity-based key agreement protocols, and analyze their suitability to UWSN in comparison with other "traditional" asymmetric protocols. In Section 4, we evaluate whether symmetric key-based KMS are more useful in underwater environments than identity-based protocols. Finally, in Section 5 we conclude the paper.

2 Wireless Sensor Networks

Wireless sensor networks are a very useful tool for solving problems in scenarios that require the acquisition and processing of physical measurements. The principal elements of a sensor network are the sensor nodes and the base station. Sensor nodes (nodes) are wireless-enabled, battery-powered, highly constrained devices that collect the physical information from their environment using an array of sensors such as thermistors, photodiodes, and so on. The base station is a more powerful device that serves as an interface between the nodes and the user. It collects the information coming from sensor nodes, and also send control information issued by the user. There can be from dozens to thousands of sensor nodes on a deployment field, although there is usually only one or more base stations on the same field.

Security is one of the principal concerns while designing protocols and mechanisms for WSN. In fact, sensor networks are inherently insecure due to the features of their nodes and the communication channel. As a result, it is easy for an adversary to manipulate the sensor nodes and the communication channel of an unprotected network on its own benefit. There must be some protocols and security mechanisms that guarantee the resiliency of the network against any kind of external or internal threat. The foundation of these mechanisms and protocols are the security primitives, such as Symmetric Key Cryptography (SKC), Public Key Cryptography (PKC) and Hash functions. Using these primitives, it is possible to assure the confidentiality and integrity of the communication channel, while authenticating the peers involved in the information exchange.

Due to its energy efficiency and fast speed, Symmetric Cryptography becomes an interesting choice for securing the foundations of a sensor network. It can provide confidentiality to the information flow, and is also able to provide integrity. There are many optimal SKC algorithms implemented on sensor networks (such as Skipjack), that have small requirements in terms of memory usage and encryption speed (2600 bytes and $25\mu s$/byte for Skipjack, respectively [CS06]). Moreover, some sensor nodes have transceivers that implement the IEEE 802.15.4 standard, which include a hardware implementation of the AES-128 algorithm.

However, as aforementioned, it is necessary to have certain security credentials in order to open a secure channel between two peers. As a result, if a sensor network relies only on SKC, it is necessary to implement certain key management systems (KMS) that distribute the pairwise keys over the nodes of the network before or after its deployment. The underlying problem here is the typical key management shortcomings of symmetric-key algorithms. To have a glance at these shortcomings, let us introduce some metrics to evaluate key distribution solutions, in particular, those proposed in [CY05, AR06]:

- **Scalability**: Ability to support large networks.
- **Efficiency**: Storage, processing and communication limitations on sensor nodes must be considered:
  - **Storage**: Amount of memory required to store security credentials.
  - **Processing**: Amount of processor cycles required to establish a key.
  - **Communication**: Number of messages exchanged during a key generation process.
  - **Key connectivity**: Probability that two (or more) sensor nodes store the same key or keying material.
- **Resilience**: Resistance against node capture.
- **Extensibility**: Key distribution mechanisms must be also flexible against substantial increase in the size of the network after deployment.

Typical shortcomings of SKC-based key distribution solutions are associated to either scalability, key connectivity, resilience and extensibility properties, being the main advantage of these solutions a low processing time. Public Key Cryptography (PKC) is useful in this context. By using authenticated key exchange protocols, the process of negotiating pairwise keys between previously unknown peers can be greatly simplified, as it enjoys benefits in every single property in the above-mentioned metrics, except for processing time. However, as we shall see, in UWSN the processing time gets its relevance lowered, as bandwidth is by far the most relevant parameter. Thanks to this, a specialized PKC-based key establishment mechanism, namely, non-interactive identity-based key agreement, outperforms previous SKC-based key distribution solutions.

2.1 Underwater Wireless Sensor Networks

The cost of using the communication channel largely impacts the energy required to run any interactive protocol between sensor nodes. Most previous analysis were done considering a sensor node that uses the air as a transmission medium. This is the most common situation for a WSN, and most prototypes have been deployed on such conditions. However, there are many potential applications where sensor nodes must be deployed in a lake or in the sea, either for long-term aquatic monitoring (Marine biology, deep-sea archaeology, seismic predictions, pollution detection, oil/gas field monitoring) or short-term aquatic exploration (Underwater natural resource discovery, anti-submarine mission, loss treasure

Table 1. Analysis of the energy consumption of acoustic modems

	MICA2	MICAz	UWM2000	UWM4000
Working range	150 m	100 m	1500 m	4000 m
Throughput	19.2 kbit/s	250 kbit/s	9600 bit/s	4800 bit/s
Tx. consumption	81mW	52.2mW	4000 mW	7000 mW
Rx. consumption	30mW	59.1mW	800 mW	800 mW
μJ per bit (Tx)	4.12 μJ	0.204 μJ	416.66 μJ	1458.33 μJ
μJ per bit (Rx)	16.8 μJ	16.8 μJ	83.33 μJ	166.66 μJ

discovery) [Cui07]. These networks have received the generic name of Underwater Sensor Networks (UWSN) [APM05].

In these UWSN, it is unpractical to use radio frequency transceivers, because of the severe attenuation factor presented by water. In order to open a communication channel between sensors, it is necessary to use specific underwater acoustic modems. These modems have different features than RF transceivers: they are highly unreliable, their bandwidth is much more limited, and sending or receiving one bit of information carries a high energy penalty.

The differences between radio transceivers and acoustic modems in terms of the energy consumed by transmitting and receiving one single bit of data are highlighted in Table 1. It can be seen that the difference in consumption (J per bit) between acoustic modems and RF transceivers is not negligible. For the radio transceivers, we have considered the most popular sensor nodes platforms as of today, which are the MICA2 and the MICAz [Inc08]. The MICA2 transceivers use the 868/916 MHz ISM bands, while the MICAz transceivers use the IEEE 802.15.4 standard. For the acoustic modems, we have considered the UWM2000 and UWM4000 modems [Inc07], which are commonly used in research literature.

These results have been obtained using the information contained in the modem and mote datasheets, under the following assumptions: i) For the UWM2000 modem, we have used the mean of the transmission power indicated in its datasheet (2-8W). ii) For the transceivers used in the MICA2 and MICAz motes, we have considered the most expensive transmission mode, which is theoretically able to send a bit of data to the maximum working range.

3 Non-interactive Identity-Based Key Agreement

If one uses traditional PKC-based authenticated key agreement to build key distribution solutions, then one is forced to use certificates, since they are needed to establish a trusted link between a public key and the identity of its owner (in our case a sensor node) in order to prevent man-in-the-middle attacks. In a WSN, nodes are supposed to establish pairwise keys with nodes that belong to the same network, and forbidden to do so with nodes or devices outside the network. Therefore, in key establishment protocols like ECMQV, the nodes must at the beginning exchange their public keys and certificates. It is natural to assume these certificates take the form of a signature by the base station on the identity and public key of the node. In general, nodes public and secret keys are set up by the base station. Such a setting can be viewed as a key-escrowed system, that is, there exists a trusted party who computes the secret keys of the users. As a consequence, one is tempted to use different forms of key-escrowed public key paradigms like identity-based cryptography, even if they do not provide certain properties such as forward secrecy.

The concept of identity-based cryptography was proposed by Shamir in [Sha85], aimed at simplifying certificate management inherent to the deployment of public key cryptography. The idea is that an arbitrary string id uniquely identifying a user (such as an e-mail address or a telephone number) can serve as a public key for a cryptographic scheme. The user cannot compute the corresponding secret key anymore, but instead it must authenticate itself to a Key Generation Center from which it obtains the corresponding private key $sk[id]$ via a secret channel.

The interest of IBC for WSN is that when using IBC systems only the identity of the sensors must be exchanged, and thus neither public keys nor certificates need not be sent. This results in an energy saving for the point of view of the communication between sensors, which can be very considerable depending on the sensor's transmitter. Additionally, in WSN it is often the case that a single party (base station) sets up the network, and this base station can naturally play the role of the Key Generation Center in an IBC system. The base station embeds the secret key $sk[id]$ prior its use in the field, and no authentic nor secret channel is needed for key setup.

In this section we recall a non-interactive authenticated identity-based key establishment scheme. Due to the lack of any standardized identity-based key exchange protocol, we describe a non-interactive scheme due to Sakai, Ohgishi and Kasahara [SOK01, DE06], which is the first identity-based authenticated key agreement protocol proposed in the literature. Also, for comparison purposes, the elliptic curve version of the Menezes-Qu-Vanstone authenticated key exchange protocol [MQV95, LMQ+03], which is one of the most standardized key exchange protocol using public key cryptography, is described in Algorithm 3.2. Note that we provide an abridged version of both schemes which suffices for our purposes. Moreover, we consider that the involved nodes must exchange their credentials due to extensibility issues (preexisting nodes may not have the public credentials of new nodes) and memory issues (nodes may not be able to store the credentials of all the nodes of the network).

3.1 SOK - Sakai, Ohgishi and Kasahara

We start by defining the concept of bilinear map. Let $\mathbb{G} = \langle \mathbf{g} \rangle$ be a cyclic group of order q for prime $q > 3$. A map $e : \mathbb{G} \times \mathbb{G} \to \mathbb{G}_1$ to a group $\mathbb{G}_1$ is called a *bilinear* map, if it satisfies the following two properties:

Bilinearity: $e(\mathbf{g}^a, \mathbf{g}^b) = e(\mathbf{g}, \mathbf{g})^{ab}$ for all integers a, b
Distorted: $e(\mathbf{g}, \mathbf{g}) \neq 1$ in $\mathbb{G}_1$.

See [BF03, Ver04] for ways of constructing bilinear maps.

In the SOK protocol, a hash function $H : \{0,1\}^* \to \mathbb{G}$ is included in the domain parameters of the system, together with $\mathbf{g}^z$, where the master secret key z is only known to the base station. Node A's secret key is $sk_A = H(id_A)^z$, while node B's secret key is defined as $sk_B = H(id_B)^z$. Notice that A's identity is id_A and B's identity is id_B.

Algorithm 3.1 SOK non-interactive ID-based key derivation for entity A

Input: Bilinear map domain parameters $\mathbb{G}, \mathbb{G}_1, e, \mathbf{g}^z, n$, the identity id_B and the secret key sk_A

Output: A secret key K_{AB} shared with entity with identity id_B

1: $K_{AB} \leftarrow KDF\big(e(H(id_B), sk_A)\big)$

Entity B runs the same algorithm by simply swapping the values (id_B, sk_A) in Algorithm 3.1 with (id_A, sk_B) and finally obtains the same key K_{AB} thanks to the bilinearity of the pairing,

$$e(H(id_B), sk_A) = e(H(id_B), H(id_A)^z) = e(H(id_B), H(id_A))^z =$$
$$= e(H(id_A)^z, H(id_B)) = e(sk_B, H(id_A))$$

3.2 ECMQV - Elliptic Curve Menezes-Qu-Vanstone

In the following we define the notation and behaviour of ECMQV. KDF is a key derivation function, which can be implemented with SHA-160 for example. Node A's public key is $\mathrm{pk}_A = g^{x_A}$, where x_A is A's secret key. Similarly for node B. In the first stage, the nodes exchange and verify certificates vouching for the fact that pk_A and pk_B are public keys from nodes belonging to the network. In a second stage, they exchange their ephemeral keys $E_A = g^{y_A}$ and $E_B = g^{y_B}$, where y_A, y_B are taken at random from the finite field $\mathrm{GF}(p)$. We assume certificates are minimalist and take the form of ECDSA [X905] signatures (r_A, s_A) and (r_B, s_B) by the owner/manufacturer of the network on the messages $id_A \| \mathrm{pk}_A$ and $id_B \| \mathrm{pk}_B$ respectively, where $\|$ denotes concatenation.

Entity B runs the same algorithm by simply swapping the values $(x_A, y_A, \mathrm{pk}_B, E_A, E_B)$ in Algorithm 3.2 with $(x_B, y_B, \mathrm{pk}_A, E_A, E_B)$ and finally obtains the same key K_{AB} (cf. [LMQ+03]).

3.3 Bandwidth and Energy Consumption

As we can see, the SOK protocol only requires the identities id_A, id_B of the sensors involved to compute a pairwise authenticated and confidential key. On the other hand, the communication overhead of the ECMQV protocol is dominated on by the exchange of public keys, certificates and ephemeral keys. On the computational side, SOK has to perform one hash operation, which is roughly

Algorithm 3.2 ECMQV key derivation for entity A

Input: Elliptic curve domain parameters G, g, n, the secret keys x_A, y_A and the public elements $\text{pk}_A, \text{pk}_B, E_A, E_B$
Output: A secret key K_{AB} shared with entity with public key pk_B
1: $m \leftarrow \lceil \log_2(n) \rceil / 2 \quad \{m \text{ is the half bitlength of } n\}$
2: $u_A \leftarrow (u_x \bmod 2^m) + 2^m \quad \{u_x \text{ is the } x\text{-coordinate of } E_A\}$
3: $s_A \leftarrow (y_A + u_A x_A) \bmod n$
4: $v_A \leftarrow (v_x \bmod 2^m) + 2^m \quad \{v_x \text{ is the } x\text{-coordinate of } E_B\}$
5: $z_A \leftarrow s_A v_A \bmod n$
6: $K_{AB} \leftarrow KDF(E_B^{s_A} \cdot \text{pk}_B^{z_A} \bmod n)$

equivalent to 1 exponentiation in $\mathbb{G}$ 'exp$_\mathbb{G}$', plus 1 pairing computation. ECMQV has to verify an ECDSA signature (one multi-exponentiation 'mexp(2)'), and to run its protocol (one multi-exponentiation 'mexp(2)', one exponentiation 'exp', and two square roots 'sqrt' to obtain the y-coordinate from the x-coordinate). Consequently, the overall energy cost and transmission cost of ECMQV for one node amounts to:

$$2\text{mexp}(2) + 1\text{exp} + 2\text{sqrt}(+\text{trans. 1410 bits} + \text{recep. 1410 bits}) \qquad (1)$$

whereas the energy cost and transmission cost of SOK for one node amounts to:

$$1\text{exp}_\mathbb{G} + 1\text{pairing}(+\text{trans. 384 bits} + \text{recep. 384 bits}) \qquad (2)$$

considering that i) one packet containing nodes identities, protocol ID, message ID, checksum, and low-level headers and footers, amounts to a total of 384 bits, ii) public keys have 161 bits (160 bits + 1 compression bit), iii) each ECDSA certificate has 320 bits, and iv) each ephemeral key contributes with 161 bits.

The SOK protocol only needs to exchange 384 bits, whereas the ECMQV protocol must exchange 1410 bits. Therefore, the SOK protocol requires the lowest bandwidth to accomplish its task. In fact, due to the unreliable nature of the acoustic channel, it is much better to use a protocol that exchanges as few bits as possible. The main limitation of the SOK protocol is the pairing computation, as it is very energy consuming. The most efficient implementation we are aware of is to be found in [OSLD08], where it is reported that a pairing for an 80-bit security level (RSA-1024 equivalent) in the ATmega128L microcontroller [Cor07] (one of the most popular microcontrollers for sensor nodes, featuring a 8-bit/7.3828 processor, 128 KB flash memory and 4KB SRAM memory) takes about 5.45s processing time and has around 125mJ energy cost. This is a rather large figure, but if we compare this amount of energy to that needed to transmit data in the UWM2000 and UWM4000 underwater sensors, we obtain that computing a pairing takes the same amount of energy than transmitting 300 and 85 bits respectively! Thus, put into perspective, computing a pairing in UWSN cannot be considered prohibitive at all.

This assertion is backed up by the results shown in table 2, which uses the energy figures for elliptic curve computations and pairing computations

Table 2. Energy cost of authenticated key exchange (in mJ)

MICA2	Comp.	Comm.		MICAz	Comp.	Comm.	
ECMQV	107.26	7.95	*115.21*	ECMQV	107.26	0.61	*107.87*
SOK	309.39	2.16	311.55	SOK	309.39	0.166	309.55
UWM2000	Comp.	Comm.		**UWM4000**	Comp.	Comm.	
ECMQV	107.26	704.98	812.24	ECMQV	107.26	2291.23	2398.49
SOK	309.39	191.99	*501.38*	SOK	309.39	623.99	*933.38*

of [SOS+08] to calculate the energy consumption of a sensor node engaged in authenticated key exchange protocols in "normal" and underwater sensor networks, in terms of mJ. The results are not surprising, since the cost of sending one bit through an acoustic channel is much greater than sending one bit through a radio frequency channel, and the transmission cost on SOK is much smaller than the transmission cost of ECMQV.

4 NIKE and Symmetric Key-Based KMS

Although we have shown that non-interactive identity-based key agreement (NIKE) protocols like SOK are better than traditional asymmetric key establishment protocols (e.g. ECMQV) in underwater environments, it is also important to compare them with symmetric key-based KMS. The problem of creating a secure and efficient key management system for sensor networks based on Symmetric Cryptography has spanned three major frameworks: "Key-Pool" framework, Mathematical framework and Negotiation framework (see Figure 1). In the "Key-Pool" framework, every node stores a small subset of keys (known as "key chain") retrieved from a large set of precalculated key (known as "key pool"). Two nodes will share a pairwise key if they have a common key inside their "key chains". In the Mathematical framework, two nodes calculate a common

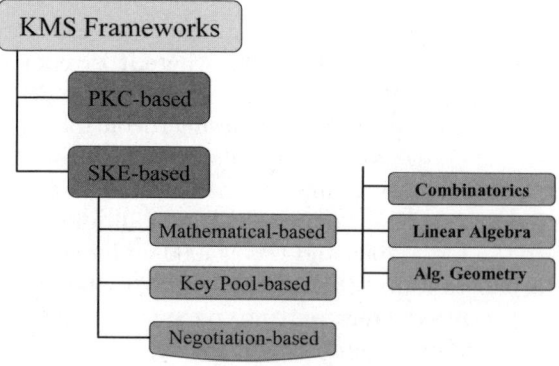

Fig. 1. KMS frameworks for WSN

pairwise key using mathematical concepts belonging to the fields of Linear Algebra, Combinatorics and Algebraic Geometry. Lastly, in the Negotiation framework, sensor nodes exchange information related to their pairwise keys just after the deployment of the network.

Most KMS belonging to any of the three major frameworks must exchange certain information (e.g. the indexes of the keys included inside a "key chain") in order to derive a pairwise key. Therefore, in terms of bandwidth and energy usage, they are not better than NIKE protocols for underwater environments. However, inside every framework there are some KMS that are optimized to minimize the communication overhead, even reducing the amount of information exchanged to only the ID of a node. Some "key pool" KMS reduce the communication overhead by linking the contents of the "key chains" to the IDs of the nodes [MHH05]. Also, in certain mathematical frameworks, the IDs of the nodes will be used as an input for a function that will return the pairwise key: Polynomial-based key predistribution KMS calculate $f(ID_i, ID_j) = f(ID_j, ID_i)$ (being f a bivariate polynomial) [LNL05], whereas Blom-based key predistribution KMS calculate $A(ID_i) \cdot G(ID_j) = A(ID_j) \cdot G(ID_i)$ (being A and G specially crafted matrices)) [DDH+05]. Finally, some negotiation KMS only need to broadcast small nonces that can be further combined into pairwise keys [LHKV04].

While all these optimized protocols could be used for underwater environments due to their low communication overhead, they have certain disadvantages that discourage their use in this particular environment. In "key pool"-related KMS, both their connectivity and their resilience is not good. As a result, there exists the possibility of two nodes not sharing a pairwise key, thus it is necessary to start expensive negotiations through the acoustic channel. Besides, if an adversary captures enough nodes of the network, it will obtain information of the pairwise keys shared by other nodes. The resilience of mathematical-based KMS is also deficient. This is not the only disadvantage of this framework: the scalability and the extensibility of the Blom scheme is unsatisfactory, and the security of both mathematical foundations (Blom schemes and bivariate polynomials) has not been formally demonstrated. About negotiation-based KMS, the security of the exchange of pairwise keys can usually be assured only just after the deployment of the network. Therefore, an adversary can eavesdrop the negotiation process of either new nodes that want to establish communication with old nodes or nodes that move from their original position and want to open a secure channel with their new neighbourhood.

In comparison with all these optimized symmetric key-based KMS, non-interactive identity-based key agreement protocols like SOK offers better scalability, key connectivity, extensibility, and network resilience. The amount of information that has to be stored inside the nodes is independent of the size of the network, thus there are no size restrictions. Also, all nodes can exchange their IDs at any given time, thus it is possible to open a secure connection between any pair of nodes and to add new nodes to the network. Moreover, if an adversary captures a sensor node, it will only obtain the information related to the node, thus he/she will be unable to eavesdrop any ongoing communication between other nodes. The primary downside of non-interactive identity-based key agreement is its energy consumption. However, the enhanced properties of this pairing-based key agreement (e.g. better extensibility) makes it a good candidate for real-life situations and scenarios. Besides, due to special requirements such as node mobility [Hic08], the batteries of underwater sensor nodes should have a higher capacity. As a result, the execution of few pairings during the lifetime of the network will not have a great influence in the node.

5 Conclusions

In this work we have focused on the fact that underwater wireless sensor networks consume a huge amount of energy in sending and receiving data. We have studied how identity-based cryptography can help to improve the energy cost of cryptographic key agreement between peers in UWSN. If previous work in the context of standard wireless sensor networks brought the novelty that the energy penalty of transmitting data made an asymmetric key agreement protocol energy-wise more efficient than a symmetric key protocol like Kerberos, our results bring the news that a computationally intensive primitive like non-interactive identity-based key agreement *outperforms* existing key distribution solutions in underwater wireless sensor networks. Future work includes implementing and evaluating identity-based key agreement in real underwater sensor nodes.

Acknowledgements

The authors wish to thank Prof. Gene Tsudik and Dr. Roberto Di Pietro for their useful input during the development of this paper.

This work has been partially supported by the ARES CONSOLIDER project (CSD2007-00004) and the CRISIS project (TIN2006-09242). The second author was funded by the Ministry of Education and Science of Spain under the "Programa Nacional de Formacion de Profesorado Universitario".

References

[APM05] Akyildiz, I., Pompili, D., Melodia, T.: Underwater acoustic sensor networks: Research challenges. Ad Hoc Networks Jounal (Elsevier) 3(3), 257–279 (2005)

[AR06] Alcaraz, C., Roman, R.: Applying key infrastructures for sensor networks in cip/ciip scenarios. In: López, J. (ed.) CRITIS 2006. LNCS, vol. 4347, pp. 166–178. Springer, Heidelberg (2006)

[BF03] Boneh, D., Franklin, M.: Identity-Based encryption from the Weil pairing. SIAM Journal of Computing 32(3), 586–615 (2003)

[BSS05] Blake, I.F., Seroussi, G., Smart, N.: Advances in Elliptic Curve Cryptography. London Mathematical Society Lecture Note Series, vol. 317. Cambridge University Press, Cambridge (2005)

[Cor07]   Atmel Corporation. Atmega128 product description (2007), http://www.atmel.com/dyn/products/product_card.asp?part_id=2018
[CS06]   Jun Choi, K., Song, J.-I.: Investigation of feasible cryptographic algorithms for wireless sensor network. In: Proceedings of the 8th International Conference on Advanced Communication Technology, ICACT 2006 (2006)
[Cui07]   Cui, J.-H.: Underwatersensor network lab — overview, achievements, plans (2007), http://uwsn.engr.uconn.edu
[CY05]   Camtepe, S.A., Yener, B.: Key distribution mechanisms for wireless sensor networks: a survey. Technical Report TR-05-07, College of William & Mary (March 2005)
[DDH+05]   Du, W., Deng, J., Han, Y.S., Varshney, P., Katz, J., Khalili, A.: A pairwise key pre-distribution scheme for wireless sensor networks. ACM Transactions on Information and System Security 8(2), 228–258 (2005)
[DE06]   Dupont, R., Enge, A.: Provably secure non-interactive key distribution based on pairings. Discrete Applied Mathematics 154(2), 270–276 (2006)
[GST07]   Großschädl, J., Szekely, A., Tillich, S.: The energy cost of cryptographic key establishment in wireless sensor networks. In: ASIACCS, pp. 380–382. ACM, New York (2007)
[Hic08]   Hickey, H.: Underwater communication: Robofish are the ultimate in ocean robots, keeping in touch without scientists' help (June 2008)
[Inc07]   LinkQuest Inc. Underwater acoustic modems (2007), http://www.link-quest.com/
[Inc08]   Crossbow Technology Inc. Wireless sensor nodes (2008), http://www.xbow.com/
[KN93]   Kohl, J.T., Neuman, B.C.: The Kerberos network authentication service (V5) (1993)
[LHKV04]   Charles Lai, B., Hwang, D.D., Pete Kim, S., Verbauwhede, I.: Reducing radio energy consumption of key management protocols for wireless sensor networks. In: Proceedings of the ACM/IEEE International Symposium on Low Power Electronics and Design (ISLPED 2004), pp. 351–356 (2004)
[LMQ+03]   Law, L., Menezes, A., Qu, M., Solinas, J., Vanstone, S.A.: An efficient protocol for authenticated key agreement. Des. Codes Cryptography 28(2), 119–134 (2003)
[LNL05]   Liu, D., Ning, P., Li, R.: Establishing pairwise keys in distributed sensor networks. ACM Transactions on Information and System Security 8(1), 41–77 (2005)
[LZC08]   Liu, L., Zhou, S., Cui, J.-H.: Prospects and problems of wireless communications for underwater sensor networks. Wireless Communications and Mobile Computing - Special Issue on Underwater Sensor Networks (to appear, 2008)
[MHH05]   Mehta, M., Huang, D., Harn, L.: Rink-rkp: A scheme for key predistribution and shared-key discovery in sensor networks. In: Proceedings of the 24th IEEE International Performance Computing and Communications Conference (IPCCC 2005), pp. 193–197 (2005)
[MQV95]   Menezes, A., Qu, M., Vanstone, S.: Some new key agreement protocols providing mutual implicit authentication. In: SecondWorkshop on Selected Areas in Cryptography (SAC 1995) (1995)
[OSLD08]   Oliveira, L.B., Scott, M., Lopez, J., Dahab, R.: Tinypbc: Pairings for authenticated identity-based non-interactive key distribution in sensor networks. In: 5th International Conference on Networked Sensing Systems (to appear, 2008), http://eprint.iacr.org/2007/482

[Sha85] Shamir, A.: Identity-based cryptosystems and signature schemes. In: Blakely, G.R., Chaum, D. (eds.) CRYPTO 1984. LNCS, vol. 196, pp. 47–53. Springer, Heidelberg (1985)

[SOK01] Sakai, R., Ohgishi, K., Kasahara, M.: Cryptosystems based on pairing over elliptic curve (in japanese). In: The 2001 Symposium on Cryptography and Information Security, Oiso, Japan (2001)

[SOS+08] Szczechowiak, P., Oliveira, L.B., Scott, M., Collier, M., Dahab, R.: Nanoecc: Testing the limits of elliptic curve cryptography in sensor networks. In: Verdone, R. (ed.) EWSN 2008. LNCS, vol. 4913, pp. 305–320. Springer, Heidelberg (2008)

[Ver04] Verheul, E.R.: Evidence that XTR is more secure than supersingular elliptic curve cryptosystems. J. Cryptology 17(4), 277–296 (2004)

[X905] Accredited Standards Committee X9. American national standard x9.62-2005, public key cryptography for the financial services industry, the elliptic curve digital signature algorithm (ecdsa) (2005)

Anonymous and Transparent Gateway-Based Password-Authenticated Key Exchange

Michel Abdalla, Malika Izabachène, and David Pointcheval

Ecole Normale Supérieure, CNRS, INRIA, France

Abstract. In Asiacrypt 2005, Abdalla *et al.* put forward the notion of gateway-based password-authenticated key exchange (GPAKE) protocol, which allows clients and gateways to establish a common session key with the help of an authentication server. In addition to the semantic security of the session key, their solution also provided additional security properties such as password protection with respect to malicious gateways and key privacy with respect to curious authentication servers. In this paper, we further pursue this line of research and present a new and stronger security model for GPAKE schemes, combining all above-mentioned security properties. In addition to allowing a security proof for all these security properties, the new security model has also other advantages over the previous one such as taking into account user corruptions. After describing the new security model, we then present a new variant of the GPAKE scheme of Abdalla *et al.* with similar efficiency. Like the original scheme, the new scheme is also *transparent* in that it does not differ significantly from a classical 2-PAKE scheme from the point of view of a client. Finally, we also show how to add client anonymity with respect to the server to the basic GPAKE scheme by using private information retrieval protocols.

1 Introduction

1.1 Motivation

To address practical scenarios in which the service provider is actually composed of two distinct entities, one being the direct interlocutor of the client and the other being a back-end server capable of checking the identity of the client, Abdalla *et al.* [1] put forward the notion of gateway-based authenticated key exchange. A gateway-based authenticated key exchange [1] is a three-party protocol, which provides a client C and a gateway G with a common session key with the help of an authentication server S, which authorizes or not the access for the client. Among the various means of authentication that can be considered, the most interesting one from a practical point of view is the password-based setting in which a simple human-memorizable secret, called a password, is used for authentication.

Due to the low entropy of passwords, gateway-based password-authenticated key exchange protocols may be subject to exhaustive search attacks, also known as *dictionary attacks* [7, 18, 21, 5, 10], in which the adversary tries to break the security of the scheme by trying all possible values for the password. In these attacks, which can be either online or off-line depending on whether the attacker needs to interact with the system in order to test whether a password guess is correct, the success probability of an attacker can be significantly high. Since online dictionary attacks cannot be avoided, the main goal of gateway-based authenticated key exchange protocols based on passwords is to show that off-line dictionary attacks are not possible. As in other password-based protocols, this is done by showing that, after k active attempts, the success probability of an adversary of impersonating one of parties or distinguishing a session key from a random key is at most $O(k/N)$, where N is the size of the dictionary and the hidden constant is preferably 1, and not much more than that as could be the case with partition attacks [9].

1.2 Related Work

Unfortunately, security against off-line dictionary attacks may not be sufficient since some of the parties involved in the protocol may be malicious. In particular, it may be possible for a malicious gateway to gain information about the values of user passwords and for the malicious authentication servers to learn the value of the session keys. To overcome this problem, Abdalla, Chevassut, Fouque, and Pointcheval [1] proposed a new setting for gateway-based systems, termed gateway-based password-authenticated key exchange (GPAKE), which protects both the session keys and the passwords. In their work, in addition to the usual notion of *semantic security* outlined above, two other security goals were considered: key privacy with respect to servers and password protection with respect to gateways. The former says that the session key should remain indistinguishable from random, even with respect to a honest-but-curious server that knows the passwords of all the users. The latter states that the gateway should not learn any information about the passwords of clients, from the authentication server.

1.3 Contributions

In this paper, we further investigate the line of research initiated by Abdalla *et al.* [1] on GPAKE schemes. In a first step, we provide in Section 2.2 a new and stronger security model which captures all of the above security notions in a single security game. The new model has several advantages over the previous one. First, the new model does not require a separate proof for each security property. Second, the new model also allows for corruptions of participants, thus dealing with the issue of forward secrecy. Third, in relation to the key privacy with respect to the server, the new security model also extends the class of sessions for which the session keys are private to the adversary, in particular allowing some sessions to remain fresh even after the corruption of a player.

After describing the new security model, we then present in Section 3 a new scheme based on the GPAKE scheme of Abdalla *et al.* [1]. Like the original scheme, our new GPAKE scheme does not require too much additional computational load for the client when compared to a classical 2-PAKE scheme. This is the so-called *transparency* property: from the client point of view, the scheme should not differ significantly from a classical 2-PAKE scheme between 2 parties. Though the security guarantees provided by the new scheme are stronger, the latter is only slightly less efficient than the original scheme proposed in [1]. The complexity assumptions used in the proof of security of the new scheme are also similar to those used by the original scheme in [1]. In both cases, the proof of security is in the random oracle model.

An additional feature considered in [1] was password privacy with respect to servers, in which users' passwords are kept secret even from servers. To achieve this goal, the responsibility for authenticating users was distributed among several servers using standard techniques in threshold-based cryptography. Such a technique can be applied to our new protocol too. In Section 4, we address a different and perhaps more crucial privacy concern: the possibility that servers can log connections and profile users. We would thus like to preserve the *anonymity* of the clients and ensure that the connections are unlinkable, in the same vein as [11]. Towards this goal, we show in Section 4 how to add client anonymity to the scheme in Section 3 by using Private Information Retrieval protocols (PIR) [15, 16]. The use of PIR is not new, but it shows a new feature of our GPAKE protocol: it can be efficiently interfaced with a PIR. Furthermore, this new feature can be used in conjunction to the previous password privacy with respect to the servers.

Finally, it is important to note that, since we designed our protocol with client anonymity in mind, it is not possible for a server to distinguish an honest authentication request by a client from an online impersonation attack by a malicious gateway. That is, the server cannot detect *online dictionary attacks*. As a result, clients' passwords should be renewed more often in the present scheme than in the case of standard 2-PAKE schemes. In cases where this is not possible, one should use instead a protocol without client anonymity and in which the server can detect online dictionary attacks.

2 Security Model

2.1 Notation

In the three-party-protocol, each participant will be denoted as $U \in \mathcal{U}$, which can be either a client, a gateway or the (authentication) server. In the password-based scenario, each client C holds a password $pw_C \in \mathcal{D}$, of small entropy and the server manages a database DB, with all the clients' passwords. Here, we suppose that there is only one (authentication) server.

We denote by $\mathcal{C}$ and $\mathcal{G}$ the sets of the clients and the gateways respectively and by S the server. We thus have $\mathcal{U} = \mathcal{C} \cup \mathcal{G} \cup \{S\}$. Since any party can be involved concurrently in several executions, several *instances* of a party can be activated: we denote by $\mathcal{I}$ the set of instances and by U_i^s the s-th instance of a participant U_i. When there is no ambiguity, we omit to precise the instance of the participant, for the sake of clarity in the writing. When C_i^s and G_j^t are engaged in a conversation to compute a common session key, in case of success, we denote the session key $sk_{i,j}^{s,t} = sk_{C_i^s} = sk_{G_j^t}$, and we say that C_i^s and G_j^t are *partners* in this session (see Definition 2).

Definition 1 (Gateway-based Authenticated Key-Exchange). *A gateway-based key-exchange protocol is specified by four polynomial-time algorithms P = (LL, CLIENT, GATEWAY, SERVER):*

- LL *specifies the initial distribution of the long-lived keys. It takes as input a security parameter k;*
- CLIENT *specifies how a client C behaves; It takes as input an instance C^s, a state s_C, the identity of the sender, and a message m. It outputs the message the client C should send as answer;*
- GATEWAY *specifies how a gateway G behaves; It takes as input an instance G^s, a state s_G, the identity of the sender, and a message m. It outputs the message the gateway G should send as answer;*
- SERVER *specifies how S behaves; It takes as input an instance S^s, a state s_S, the identity of the sender, and a message m. It outputs the message the server S should send as answer.*

In the definition above, the specific format of the input message m will depend on the specific protocol being analyzed. LL(k) is a probabilistic polynomial-time algorithm, which returns the long-lived keys for all the participants. In our particular case of password-based authentication for the client, and symmetric private and authenticated channels between the gateways and the server, they consist in:

- a password pw for each client (given to the server too);
- a symmetric key SecureChan–S–G for each gateway-server pair to provide a secure channel (with privacy, integrity and origin of the messages).

2.2 Security Model

In this section, we describe how an adversary will be allowed to interfere in the protocol. Our model *extends* the previous work on three-party and gateway-based key-exchange protocols [1, 2] by considering together the notions of:

- key privacy (semantic security of the session key) with respect to the server, and even under corrupted players (which includes forward-secrecy);
- client's password protection with respect to the gateway;
- client privacy (anonymity) with respect to the server.

The former extends the classical notion, and namely it includes the server in the adversary list. This also justifies the quite new latter notion of anonymity with respect to the server, that we do not trust, but just for authenticating a valid client, and authorizing the connection. As in [2], we do not trust the gateway, and thus the password must not be known to it.

We would like to emphasize that the stronger notion of semantic security that we study is of independent interest. It indeed extends usual security models for 2-party password-based key exchange protocols [5,10]: we consider a broader notion of freshness, which is crucial to define which sessions have to be protected or not. Usually, as soon as a user is corrupted, all the new sessions are not fresh. However, if the real users play the protocol, the session key may still be secure in practice, we will introduce that in our security model (this is definitely stronger than what can be achieved in the universal composability framework [12,13] as we see later).

Oracle Queries. As in [2], we adopt the Real-or-Random (RoR) security model, which means that the adversary interacts with the protocol via oracle queries (in any order it wants —concurrent executions—, and should not be able to distinguish truly random keys from the real keys. As it has been proved in [2], this model is stronger than the Find-then-Guess (FtG) security model, where the adversary only has to distinguish a random key from a real one, but in one session only. The oracle queries are the following ones:

- Execute(C_i^r, G_j^s, S^t): This query models passive attacks in which the adversary asks for an honest execution of the entire protocol. The adversary gets the whole transcript resulting from the communication between C_i^r, G_j^s and S^t.
- Send($U_i^r, U; m$): This query models an active attack, where the adversary chooses the message m it sends to the instance U_i^r, where $U_i \in \mathcal{C} \cup \mathcal{G} \cup \{S\}$ in the name of U. The adversary gets back the message U_i should produce upon receiving such a message m. If the message is invalid or if U_i^r is not in a waiting state, the query is ignored.

    Because of the private and authenticated channels between the gateways and the server, if the gateway G is not corrupted (the flag corrupt$_G$ is false), the recipient does not accept a message that has not really been sent by the legitimate sender.
- Reveal(U_j^s): if the session key for instance U_j^s has ever been defined, then the answer is the actual session key $sk_{U_j^s}$, otherwise, the answer is $\bot$.

Intuitively, the Execute-query models passive observations of transcripts and Send-queries model active attacks against some honest players. They can be combined in an attack game. Then, sessions obtained via Execute-queries are called "passive sessions", whereas sessions obtained via Send-queries are called "active sessions". Of course, Execute-queries can be simulated by a sequence of Send-queries, but such a sequence of Send-queries is counted as an "active session". In the password-based setting, our goal is to prove that the on-line dictionary attack is the best one: passive sessions do not leak any information about the password, an active session can help the adversary to test only one password.

The Reveal-query models a misuse of the established session key, and thus the leakage of information: session keys should not reveal any information about the password.

Semantic Security. One goal of our protocol is to ensure that the session keys established between C and G remain completely unknown to S and to any other party: *session key privacy*, also known as *semantic security*. Indeed, we want that the adversary could not get any relevant information on the fresh session keys (not obviously revealed, see the freshness notion below) from the above queries. To model the capability of the adversary to guess some information on the session key, we define an additional Test-query. for a random bit b as follows:

- Test(U_j^s): If no session key is defined for instance U_j^s or if instance U_j^s is not fresh (see notion of freshness below), then this query is answered by $\perp$. If this query has already been asked, then it outputs the same answer. Otherwise if $b = 1$, it outputs the real session key (from Reveal(U_j^s)), and if $b = 0$, it outputs a random one of same size. Finally, the flag test$_{U_j^s}$ becomes true.

Note that the answer of the oracle is independent of the number of queries the adversary asks. Indeed, the oracle always answers the same way: all the session keys obtained via Test-queries are either all real or all random, according to the bit b. Furthermore, as soon as the flag test$_{U_j^s}$ is set to true, no Reveal(U_j^s) can be asked.

Corruption. We say that a participant U is corrupted and we set corrupt$_U$ to true if one of the Corrupt-queries has been asked (it is initially set to false). Note that we consider weak corruptions only, where the long term secrets are revealed, but not the internal states.

- Corrupt(C_i): This query models corruption of the client in which the adversary learns the password of client C_i. We then set corrupt$_{C_i} \leftarrow$ true.
- Corrupt(G_j): This query models corruption of a gateway in which the adversary gets access (read/write) to the secure channel between the gateway G_j and the server. We then set corrupt$_{G_j} \leftarrow$ true.
- Corrupt(S): This query models corruption of the server S in which the adversary learns all the passwords stored into the server, i.e, pw_C for all the clients C, and gets access to the secure channels between the server and all the gateways (since we assumed a symmetric protection tool). We then set corrupt$_C \leftarrow$ true and corrupt$_G \leftarrow$ true for all the clients C and all the gateways G.

Partnering. We use the notion of partnering based on session identifiers (sid), as defined in [5]. In particular, the value of sid is taken to be the partial transcript of the communication between the client and the gateway before the session key has been accepted.

Definition 2. *Two instances C_i^s and G_j^t are said to be partners if and only if the following four conditions hold:*

1. *Both C_i^s and G_j^t have accepted;*
2. *Both C_i^s and G_j^t share the same sid;*
3. *The partner for C_i^s is G_j^t and vice-versa;*
4. *No instance other than C_i^s accepts with partner G_j^t and vice-versa.*

Freshness. The goal of the adversary in the Real-or-Random game is to guess the bit b used during Test-queries. However, this is clear that in some cases, the adversary trivially knows the actual session key. And, then, the Test-query answer would immediately lead to the bit b value, whereas the adversary did not really break the semantic security. For example, if the adversary asks a Reveal-query and a Test-query to the same session.

We thus need to restrict the use of the Test-queries: they must be asked to *fresh* sessions/instances only.

Informally, we say that an instance is not fresh, and fresh$_{U^s}$ is thus set to false, when the adversary could trivially distinguish a random session key from a real one, or when no key exists yet:

- if U has not accepted. Note that it will make no sense to consider this case since no session key has been defined: an instance that has not accepted is not fresh. Hence the initialization of the fresh-tags to false.
- if U has been asked a Reveal-query, any Test-query to U or its partner clearly reveal b. Such a Reveal-query thus flips the freshness status of the instance and its partner to false.

These two restrictions are classical, and in order to capture the forward-secrecy, a corruption that happens after the end of the protocol does not affect the freshness status. We consider this stronger forward-secrecy notion in this paper, contrarily to [1].

Moreover, in previous freshness definitions, as soon as a party was corrupted, the sessions initiated afterward were automatically not fresh (this is also the case in the UC security model, since a corrupted player is under the control of the adversary, and cannot play on its own). Here are some reasons for considering some sessions initiated after a corruption as not fresh:

- if C is corrupted, the adversary could trivially break the semantic security by playing the role of the gateway and the server, against the client: he chooses all gateway and server randomness to compute the common session key;
- if C is corrupted, then the adversary knows the client's password then he could play the role of the client, against the gateway;
- if G is corrupted, the adversary can play the role of the gateway, with both the server and the client.

However, even if everybody is corrupted but the adversary is passive during this session (an Execute-query or simple forwarding via Send-queries), there is no reason to mark this session as unfresh. In practice, even if the long term key of a player has been stolen, the latter can be sure for some session that it is talking with an honest player: it is useful to know that in such a case, the session key will be secret, hence the freshness of such a session.

Definition 3. *When a player U accepts (either C_i^s or G_j^t), if both this party and its partner are not corrupted; or, if all the messages received by this party were generated by an honest user (only oracle-generated-messages —see below— or a passive session —through an Execute-query); then fresh$_U \leftarrow$ true, else fresh$_U \leftarrow$*

false. Later, a Reveal-query can flip the status from true to false, as explained earlier.

Oracle-Generated Messages. When an instance U^s is asked a Send-query for a message m, so that m has been answered by a Send-query, then we say that this is an oracle-generated-message.

We write $\mathsf{OG}(U^s)$ when U^s receives an oracle-generated-message. More generally, we write $\mathsf{OG}(U^s, n)$, when the n-th flow (in the protocol) received by U^s, is an oracle-generated-message.

Definition 4. *We say that m is an oracle-generated-message if there exists an instance U_j^s, for $s \in \mathcal{I}$ and a participant $U_i \in \mathcal{U}$ such that $m = \mathsf{Send}(U_j^s, U_i; m')$ for some message m'.*

Due to the fact that we assume a secure channel, and thus authenticated, between the gateways and the server, all non-oracle-generated messages between the server and a non-corrupted gateway will be rejected with overwhelming probability, if we choose an appropriate symmetric encryption mechanism. Indeed, if the gateway is not corrupted no message can be correctly encrypted to and from it, when communicating with the server.

Secure Protocol. We consider an adversary $\mathcal{A}$, against a protocol P, which has access to Execute, Send, Reveal-queries, as defined above, as well as to Test-queries to *fresh instances* only. Let Succ be the event in which the adversary guesses correctly the bit b determining the behavior of the Test-query (whether it outputs the real session key or a random one). We define the AKE-advantage of the adversary $\mathcal{A}$ in breaking the semantic security of the protocol P by : $\mathsf{Adv}_P^{\mathsf{ake}}(\mathcal{A}) = 2 \cdot \Pr[\mathsf{Succ}] - 1$.

Definition 5. *We say that a password-authenticated key-exchange protocol P is secure if for every polynomial time adversary $\mathcal{A}$ that interacts actively with at most q instances,*

$$\mathsf{Adv}_P^{\mathsf{ake}}(\mathcal{A}) < \frac{c \cdot q}{N} + \mathsf{negl}(),$$

where N is the size of the dictionary where the passwords are uniformly drawn, and c is a small constant (ideally 1, but a larger constant may appear because of the proof details).

Note that the security notions of semantic security, key privacy with respect to the server, forward-secrecy, and password protection, as defined by [1] are implied by the above security definition. For the three first notions, this is clear since they are modeled by the Test-query. About the password-protection, if a corrupted gateway could learn some information about the password, then this information could be used by the adversary to perform a faster on-line dictionary attack.

3 Our New GPAKE Protocol

3.1 Description of Our Scheme

In this section, we describe our new GPAKE protocol, which is a slight variant of [1]. Let $(\mathbb{G}, g, q)$ be the description of a cyclic group $\mathbb{G}$ of order q generated by g. Let ℓ be the security parameter. We need several hash functions $\mathcal{G}$, $\mathcal{H}_1$, and $\mathcal{H}_2$:

$$\mathcal{G}: \mathcal{U}^2 \times \mathcal{D} \mapsto \mathbb{G}, \quad \mathcal{H}_1: \mathcal{U}^2 \times \mathbb{G}^3 \mapsto \{0,1\}^\ell, \quad \mathcal{H}_2: \mathcal{U}^2 \times \mathbb{G}^3 \mapsto \{0,1\}^\ell.$$

They will be modeled by random oracles in the security analysis. From each password $pw \in \mathcal{D}'$, we define $\text{PW} \stackrel{\text{def}}{=} \mathcal{G}(C, G, pw) \in \mathcal{D} \subset \mathbb{G}$, assumed to be the authentication means between the client C and the gateway G, with which the client wants to establish a secure channel (*transparency* means that the client does not need to know whether the gateway can compute everything by itself or needs some help from outside). The client knows pw, and the gateway will ask some help from the server who knows the PW's, since the storage limitation is not as strong for him. Such a random generation of the actual common secret PW (hence the use of a random oracle $\mathcal{G}$) is crucial for the PCDDH-assumption below. The new protocol still consists of four messages exchange between the client, the gateway and the server as in [1]. To achieve the stronger notion of freshness, which may include certain sessions with corrupted players, we need two additional zero-knowledge proofs of knowledge of the discrete logarithms of h and $\overline{Y}$ with respect to bases g and h (see Section 3.2). The complete description can be found in Figure 1, where NIZKPDL signatures of knowledge are described in the next section. Another difference with respect to the protocol of [1] is that, upon the reception of $X^\star$ and the client identity string C, the gateway just forwards these two elements to the server. Then, the gateway chooses the exponent y and computes $\overline{Y}$ and K at the same time. This allows us to introduce anonymity as we see later in Section 4.

3.2 Zero-Knowledge Proof of Knowledge of Discrete Logarithm

In our protocol, we need non-interactive zero-knowledge proofs of knowledge of discrete logarithms. This will actually be a signature of knowledge: we denote by $\text{NIZKPDL}(m; g, h)$ the signature of knowledge of the discrete logarithm of h in basis g on the message m. This is the Schnorr's signature [24, 25], proved secure in the random-oracle model [22, 23]. Granted the forking-lemma, when such a valid proof is generated by the adversary, extraction is possible, operating one rewind.

More precisely, let us describe the zero-knowledge proofs Π_1 and Π_2 used in our scheme, on the message $X^\star$. Let $\mathbb{G}$ be a cyclic group of order q generated by g. We use a non-interactive version of the Schnorr's proof system presented in [24, 25] to which we apply the Fiat-Shamir transformation [17] in the random-oracle model [6, 22, 23]:

- Public data: $h = g^s$, description of $(\mathbb{G}, g, q)$

Client C	Gateway G
$\mathcal{G}, \mathcal{H}_1, \mathcal{H}_2$	$\mathcal{G}, \mathcal{H}_1, \mathcal{H}_2$
$\text{PW} \stackrel{\text{def}}{=} \mathcal{G}(C, G, pw) \in \mathcal{D} \subset \mathbb{G}$	
$pw \in \mathcal{D}'$	

$$\text{accept} \leftarrow \text{false} \qquad\qquad \text{accept} \leftarrow \text{false}$$
$$x \stackrel{R}{\leftarrow} \mathbb{Z}_q, X \leftarrow g^x$$
$$X^\star \leftarrow X \times \text{PW} \quad \xrightarrow{\left(\begin{array}{c}\textbf{Flow 1}\\ C, X^\star\end{array}\right)} \quad \xrightarrow{\left(\begin{array}{c}\textbf{Flow 2}\\ C, G, X^\star\end{array}\right)}$$
$$\xleftarrow{\left(\begin{array}{c}\textbf{Flow 3}\\ \overline{X}, h, \Pi_1\end{array}\right)}$$
$$y \stackrel{R}{\leftarrow} \mathbb{Z}_q, \overline{Y} \leftarrow h^y$$
$$\Pi_2 \leftarrow \text{NIZKPDL}(X^\star; h, \overline{Y})$$
$$K \leftarrow \overline{X}^y$$
$$K \leftarrow \overline{Y}^x \xleftarrow{\left(\begin{array}{c}\textbf{Flow 4}\\ G, h, \overline{Y},\\ \text{AuthG},\\ \Pi_1, \Pi_2\end{array}\right)} \text{AuthG} \leftarrow \mathcal{H}_2(C, G, X^\star, \overline{Y}, K)$$
$$\text{AuthG}' \leftarrow \mathcal{H}_2(C, G, X^\star, \overline{Y}, K)$$
Π_1, Π_2 valid? $\wedge$ AuthG' $\stackrel{?}{=}$ AuthG
If no error/reject
$\quad sk \leftarrow \mathcal{H}_1(C, G, X^\star, \overline{Y}, K); \qquad\qquad sk \leftarrow \mathcal{H}_1(C, G, X^\star, \overline{Y}, K);$
$\quad \text{accept} \leftarrow \text{true} \qquad\qquad\qquad\qquad\qquad \text{accept} \leftarrow \text{true}$

The communication channel between the client and the gateway is not authenticated nor private

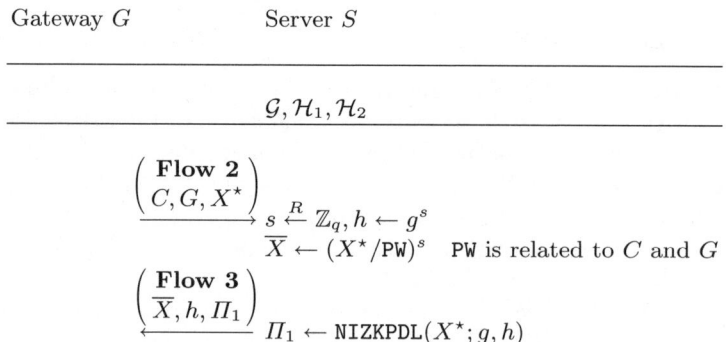

Gateway G	Server S
	$\mathcal{G}, \mathcal{H}_1, \mathcal{H}_2$

$$\xrightarrow{\left(\begin{array}{c}\textbf{Flow 2}\\ C, G, X^\star\end{array}\right)} \quad s \stackrel{R}{\leftarrow} \mathbb{Z}_q, h \leftarrow g^s$$
$$\overline{X} \leftarrow (X^\star/\text{PW})^s \quad \text{PW is related to } C \text{ and } G$$
$$\xleftarrow{\left(\begin{array}{c}\textbf{Flow 3}\\ \overline{X}, h, \Pi_1\end{array}\right)} \quad \Pi_1 \leftarrow \text{NIZKPDL}(X^\star; g, h)$$

The communication channel between the gateway and the server is secure (privacy, integrity and origin of the messages)

Fig. 1. Our new GPAKE

- Witness: the exponent s
- Proof of knowledge of the witness: the prover chooses a random exponent $\alpha \in \mathbb{Z}_q$ and sets $u = g^\alpha$. He computes $c = H(X^\star, g, h, u)$ and $v = \alpha - cs \mod q$. He then sends the proof (c, v) to the verifier.
- Verification of the proof: $c \stackrel{?}{=} H(X^\star, g, h, g^v h^c)$.

The forking lemma [22,23] shows that, in an execution in which a valid proof is generated, in polynomial time, it is possible to extract the witness, from one of the rewinds with a different random choice for the random oracle, but with any non-negligible (as small as required) probability.

Note however that during a rewind we have to make sure that no other extraction is needed, which would imply another rewind, and so. An exponential complexity could happen if several extractions are needed. But in our analysis, only one extraction is needed.

3.3 Computational Assumptions

For the security of our scheme, we need the following computational assumptions, which are either quite classical, or at least already used in the past [4]. The last one could be shown to hold in the generic-group model [26].

Computational-Diffie-Hellman Assumption. Let $(\mathbb{G}, g, q)$ be a represented group. The **CDH**-assumption states that given two elements $A = g^a$ and $B = g^b$, where a and b are drawn at random from $\mathbb{Z}_q$, it is hard to compute $C = A^b = B^a = g^{ab}$. More precisely, given the experiment,

$$\mathbf{Exp}^{\mathsf{cdh}}(\mathcal{A})$$
$$a, b \stackrel{R}{\leftarrow} \mathbb{Z}_q, A \leftarrow g^a, B \leftarrow g^b, C \leftarrow g^{ab}$$
$$C' \leftarrow \mathcal{A}(A, B)$$
$$\text{if } C = C', \text{output } 1, \text{else output } 0$$

the advantage of $\mathcal{A}$ in breaking the **CDH**-problem, defined by $\mathsf{Adv}^{\mathsf{cdh}}(\mathcal{A}) = \Pr[\mathbf{Exp}^{\mathsf{cdh}}(\mathcal{A}) = 1]$, in reasonable time, is negligible.

Decisional-Diffie-Hellman Assumption. The **DDH**-assumption states that the two distributions $(g, A = g^a, B = g^b, C = g^{ab})$ and $(g, A = g^a, B = g^b, C' = g^c)$, where a, b, c are drawn at random from $\mathbb{Z}_q$ are computationally indistinguishable. As previously done, we can define an experiment:

$$\mathbf{Exp}^{\mathsf{ddh}}_d(\mathcal{A})$$
$$a, b, c \stackrel{R}{\leftarrow} \mathbb{Z}_q, A \leftarrow g^a, B \leftarrow g^b$$
$$\text{if } d = 0, \text{set } C \leftarrow g^c, \text{else set } C \leftarrow g^{ab}$$
$$\text{output } d' \leftarrow \mathcal{A}(A, B, C)$$

The advantage of $\mathcal{A}$ in deciding the **DDH**-problem in reasonable time is negligible, where:

$$\mathsf{Adv}^{\mathsf{ddh}}(\mathcal{A}) = \left|\Pr[\mathbf{Exp}^{\mathsf{ddh}}_1(\mathcal{A}) = 1] - \Pr[\mathbf{Exp}^{\mathsf{ddh}}_0(\mathcal{A}) = 1]\right| = \mathsf{negl}().$$

Password-Based Chosen-Basis Diffie-Hellman Assumption. The following problem is a variant from [4]. Let $(\mathbb{G}, g, q)$ be a represented group. The following experiment, $\mathbf{Exp}_b^{\mathsf{pcddh}}(\mathcal{A}, \mathcal{D})$ defines how we simulate the interaction between the Password-based Chosen-basis Decisional Diffie-Hellman challenger, or PCDDH-challenger, and the adversary $\mathcal{A}$, where $\mathcal{D}$ is a dictionary of N random and independent elements in $\mathbb{G}$. In a find-stage, the adversary chooses a basis X. It then receives back PW, X' and Y, defined as follows:

$$\text{PW} \stackrel{R}{\leftarrow} \mathcal{D}, \quad s_0, s_1 \stackrel{R}{\leftarrow} \mathbb{Z}_q, \quad X' \leftarrow (X/\text{PW})^{s_b}, \quad Y \leftarrow g^{s_0}.$$

Then, the adversary has to guess the bit b:

$$\begin{array}{l}\mathbf{Exp}_b^{\mathsf{pcddh}}(\mathcal{A}, \mathcal{D}) \\ (X, s) \leftarrow \mathcal{A}(\texttt{find}, \mathcal{D}) \\ \text{PW} \stackrel{R}{\leftarrow} \mathcal{D}, s_0, s_1 \stackrel{R}{\leftarrow} \mathbb{Z}_q \\ X' \leftarrow (X/\text{PW})^{s_b}, Y \leftarrow g^{s_0} \\ \text{output } b' \leftarrow \mathcal{A}(\texttt{guess}, s, X', Y, \text{PW})\end{array}$$

The PCDDH-assumption states that the advantage of $\mathcal{A}$ in deciding the PCDDH-problem, with respect to the dictionary $\mathcal{D}$, in reasonable time, is essentially $1/N$:

$$\begin{aligned}\mathsf{Adv}_{\mathcal{D}}^{\mathsf{pcddh}}(\mathcal{A}) = & \ \Pr[\mathbf{Exp}_1^{\mathsf{pcddh}}(\mathcal{A}, \mathcal{D}) = 1] \\ & - \Pr[\mathbf{Exp}_0^{\mathsf{pcddh}}(\mathcal{A}, \mathcal{D}) = 1] \leq \tfrac{1}{N} + \mathsf{negl}().\end{aligned}$$

We insist on the fact that for the problem to be hard, the elements in the dictionary $\mathcal{D}$ must be independently drawn from $\mathbb{G}$. Namely, the relative discrete logarithms, of any quotient of any pair, in basis g must be hard to compute. Note that the computational variant, where the goal is to compute $X' = (X/\text{PW})^{s_0}$, given Y and PW, for a chosen X, with probability greater than $1/N$, holds under the CDH-assumption. Since the passwords are independent and random elements in $\mathcal{G}$, the adversary has to guess the password. Even without formal proof, such a decisional assumption seems reasonable under the DDH-one.

3.4 Security Result

Granted the PCDDH-assumption, one can prove the security of this protocol, in a strong sense, since the freshness notion is much more general than usual: it of course covers the forward-secrecy, by keeping a session as fresh even after a corruption of the parties. But even after corruptions, sessions where the adversary only forwards messages are also considered fresh. The security proof of our new GPAKE scheme can be found in the full version [3].

Theorem 1 (Security). *Let us consider protocol from Figure 1 over a group of prime order q, where $\mathcal{D}$ is a dictionary of size N. Let us consider an adversary $\mathcal{A}$ that is able to initiate concurrent executions of the protocol, and to corrupt any party (in a non-adaptive way, i.e. one cannot corrupt a player in the middle of a session, but before the session starts only). If $\mathcal{A}$ makes less than q_{send} sessions* with the parties, under the CDH, DDH, and PCDDH *assumptions, where* q_{send} *is the number of* Send-*queries of* $\mathcal{A}$*, we have,*

$$\text{Adv}^{\text{ake}}(\mathcal{A}) \leq \frac{12 q_{\text{send}}}{N} + \text{negl}().$$

One can note that Execute-queries have no impact in the above result. Information leaked during such session is indeed negligible.

4 Adding Client Anonymity

In many applications, anonymity is a crucial property to be satisfied, otherwise all the connections of the clients can be logged and then analyzed to profile the users.

For privacy reasons, a client may want to make his connections anonymous and unlinkable. One way is first to use different gateways. But the authentication server is unique, and thus one cannot use a different one for each connection. Whereas the server is the only party able to authorize, or not, the connection, we will try to hide the client identity to it.

To this aim, we can see the server as a virtual dynamic database: for each authorization request, the server builds the answers for all the possible clients, but the gateway gets the one related to the actual client: the gateway and the server can run a PIR protocol [15,16], so that the server does not learn anything about the client. Note that using an SPIR scheme [20] additionally provides privacy to the server, since the gateway will not learn more than the value it is interested in.

Recall that a PIR is a communication-efficient primitive which allows a user to retrieve a string in an n-string database without revealing anything about the index of the data the user is querying. An SPIR is a PIR, which satisfies the additional property of database privacy.

Several PIR have been proposed in the literature: with information-theoretic privacy for the user and/or the database, or with computational privacy only [14]. They may use one, or several duplicated databases [19]. Recently, [8] proposed an efficient SPIR scheme based on a new homomorphic public-key cryptosystem which reduces considerably the complexity of existing schemes.

The nice feature of our new GPAKE is the efficient implementation with any SPIR. Namely, any good SPIR scheme can be applied with our construction, and thus we do not need to choose, nor to describe, a specific scheme, but just to use the query of a "black-box" system. We will show that we can reduce considerably the size of the "virtual" database, which would have a practical impact, whatever actual PIR scheme we use.

With our construction, each client owns a password indexed by i, which index is the secret of the gateway. The server manages a database of size n, the number of clients, which contains all the passwords for each client.

A trivial way to introduce anonymity to the protocols (ours, and [1]) using an SPIR is to dynamically generate a database, for each session, as follows: upon reception of a Send-query, with input $X^\star$, the server computes the answers for each message $(C_i, G, X^\star)$, and thus for all the possible clients C_i, since it does not know which one is interacting with the gateway G: the dynamic database consists of all the blocks $B_i = (g^{s_i}, (X^\star/\texttt{PW}_i)^{s_i}, \Pi_i)$. Then, the gateway runs the SPIR protocol to get the correct B_i, while preserving the anonymity of the client. This transformation is quite generic, and one can note that the computational cost for the server for building the database is quite huge, essentially because of the multiple proofs Π_i.

We can easily improve efficiency in our case, by computing once (even pre-computing), and sending $h = g^s$ and Π_1, and then the dynamic database only consists of the n entries $B_i = (X^\star/\texttt{PW}_i)^s$. This considerably improves the computational cost, and the storage space.

5 Conclusion

In this paper, we first strengthen the security model for password-based authenticated key exchange: we applied it to the gateway-based setting, but it is also relevant in the classical two-party scenario. We then design a new gateway-based key exchange protocol: a practical application is the establishment of a secure channel between a client and an application server with the help of an authentication server. The application server does not learn anything about the authentication material, and the authentication server does not learn anything about the session key. We focus on the password-based authentication approach, which is a quite practical one. Eventually, we address anonymity: the server does not need to be aware of the actual client. It should just check whether the identity and the password match (are in the database). Our new protocol can be efficiently interfaced with any PIR protocol to achieve client-anonymity.

Acknowledgment

We would like to thank the anonymous referees for their fruitful comments. This work has been partially supported by the French ANR-SESUR-2007 PAMPA Project.

References

1. Abdalla, M., Chevassut, O., Fouque, P.-A., Pointcheval, D.: A simple threshold authenticated key exchange from short secrets. In: Roy, B.K. (ed.) ASIACRYPT 2005. LNCS, vol. 3788, pp. 566–584. Springer, Heidelberg (2005)
2. Abdalla, M., Fouque, P.-A., Pointcheval, D.: Password-based authenticated key exchange in the three-party setting. In: Vaudenay, S. (ed.) PKC 2005. LNCS, vol. 3386, pp. 65–84. Springer, Heidelberg (2005)

3. Abdalla, M., Izabachène, M., Pointcheval, D.: Anonymous and transparent gateway-based password-authenticated key exchange. In: Franklin, M.K., Hui, L.C.K., Wong, D.S. (eds.) Cryptology and Network Security, 7th International Conference, CANS 2008. LNCS. Springer, Heidelberg (2008), http://www.di.ens.fr/~pointche/pub.html
4. Abdalla, M., Pointcheval, D.: Interactive Diffie-Hellman assumptions with applications to password-based authentication. In: Patrick, A., Yung, M. (eds.) FC 2005. LNCS, vol. 3570, pp. 341–356. Springer, Heidelberg (2005)
5. Bellare, M., Pointcheval, D., Rogaway, P.: Authenticated key exchange secure against dictionary attacks. In: Preneel, B. (ed.) EUROCRYPT 2000. LNCS, vol. 1807, pp. 139–155. Springer, Heidelberg (2000)
6. Bellare, M., Rogaway, P.: Random oracles are practical: A paradigm for designing efficient protocols. In: Ashby, V. (ed.) ACM CCS 1993, pp. 62–73. ACM Press, New York (1993)
7. Bellovin, S.M., Merritt, M.: Encrypted key exchange: Password-based protocols secure against dictionary attacks. In: 1992 IEEE Symposium on Security and Privacy, pp. 72–84. IEEE Computer Society Press, Los Alamitos (1992)
8. Boneh, D., Goh, E.-J., Nissim, K.: Evaluating 2-DNF formulas on ciphertexts. In: Kilian, J. (ed.) TCC 2005. LNCS, vol. 3378, pp. 325–341. Springer, Heidelberg (2005)
9. Boyd, C., Montague, P., Nguyen, K.Q.: Elliptic curve based password authenticated key exchange protocols. In: Varadharajan, V., Mu, Y. (eds.) ACISP 2001. LNCS, vol. 2119, pp. 487–501. Springer, Heidelberg (2001)
10. Boyko, V., MacKenzie, P.D., Patel, S.: Provably secure password-authenticated key exchange using Diffie-Hellman. In: Preneel, B. (ed.) EUROCRYPT 2000. LNCS, vol. 1807, pp. 156–171. Springer, Heidelberg (2000)
11. Bringer, J., Chabanne, H., Pointcheval, D., Tang, Q.: Extended private information retrieval and its application in biometrics authentications. In: Bao, F., Ling, S., Okamoto, T., Wang, H., Xing, C. (eds.) CANS 2007. LNCS, vol. 4856, pp. 175–193. Springer, Heidelberg (2007)
12. Canetti, R.: Universally composable security: A new paradigm for cryptographic protocols. In: 42nd FOCS, pp. 136–145. IEEE Computer Society Press, Los Alamitos (2001)
13. Canetti, R., Halevi, S., Katz, J., Lindell, Y., MacKenzie, P.D.: Universally composable password-based key exchange. In: Cramer, R. (ed.) EUROCRYPT 2005. LNCS, vol. 3494, pp. 404–421. Springer, Heidelberg (2005)
14. Chor, B., Gilboa, N.: Computationally private information retrieval (extended abstract). In: STOC, pp. 304–313 (1997)
15. Chor, B., Goldreich, O., Kushilevitz, E., Sudan, M.: Private information retrieval. In: FOCS, pp. 41–50 (1995)
16. Chor, B., Kushilevitz, E., Goldreich, O., Sudan, M.: Private information retrieval. J. ACM 45(6), 965–981 (1998)
17. Fiat, A., Shamir, A.: How to prove yourself: Practical solutions to identification and signature problems. In: Odlyzko, A.M. (ed.) CRYPTO 1986. LNCS, vol. 263, pp. 186–194. Springer, Heidelberg (1987)
18. Jablon, D.P.: Extended password key exchange protocols immune to dictionary attacks. In: 6th IEEE International Workshops on Enabling Technologies: Infrastructure for Collaborative Enterprises (WETICE 1997), Cambridge, MA, USA, June 18–20, pp. 248–255. IEEE Computer Society, Los Alamitos (1997)

19. Kushilevitz, E., Ostrovsky, R.: Replication is NOT needed: SINGLE database, computationally-private information retrieval. In: 38th FOCS, pp. 364–373. IEEE Computer Society Press, Los Alamitos (1997)
20. Lincoln, L.: Symmetric Private Information Retrieval via Homomorphic Probabilistic Encryption. Ph.D thesis, Rochester Institute of Technology (2006), http://www.cs.rit.edu/7Elbl6598/thesis/Lincoln_full_Dobument.pdf
21. Lucks, S.: Open key exchange: How to defeat dictionary attacks without encrypting public keys. In: Workshop on Security Protocols, École Normale Supérieure (1997)
22. Pointcheval, D., Stern, J.: Security proofs for signature schemes. In: Maurer, U.M. (ed.) EUROCRYPT 1996. LNCS, vol. 1070, pp. 387–398. Springer, Heidelberg (1996)
23. Pointcheval, D., Stern, J.: Security arguments for digital signatures and blind signatures. Journal of Cryptology 13(3), 361–396 (2000)
24. Schnorr, C.-P.: Efficient identification and signatures for smart cards. In: Brassard, G. (ed.) CRYPTO 1989. LNCS, vol. 435, pp. 239–252. Springer, Heidelberg (1990)
25. Schnorr, C.-P.: Efficient signature generation by smart cards. Journal of Cryptology 4(3), 161–174 (1991)
26. Shoup, V.: Lower bounds for discrete logarithms and related problems. In: Fumy, W. (ed.) EUROCRYPT 1997. LNCS, vol. 1233, pp. 256–266. Springer, Heidelberg (1997)

Cryptanalysis of EC-RAC, a RFID Identification Protocol[*]

Julien Bringer[1], Hervé Chabanne[1], and Thomas Icart[1,2]

[1] Sagem Sécurité
[2] Université du Luxembourg
name.surname@sagem.com

Abstract. At RFID'08, Lee et al. have proposed a RFID scheme based on elliptic curve cryptography. This scheme, called Elliptic Curve Random Access Control (EC-RAC) has been conceived in order to be implemented on an efficient security processor designed for RFID tags. The aim of this scheme is to enable a fast, secure and private identification scheme. Security arguments are given to prove that RFID tags implementing this scheme are neither traceable nor cloneable.

We here show how tags can be tracked if one has eavesdropped the same tag twice and we show that a tag can be impersonated if it has been passively eavesdropped three times.

We propose a new scheme based on a modification of the Schnorr scheme as efficient as the initial scheme. We prove that this scheme is zero-knowledge, sound against active adversaries. Moreover, our proposal is private under the Decisional Diffie-Hellman assumption.

Keywords: Cryptanalysis, Privacy, Zero-Knowledge, Identification, RFID.

1 Introduction

Radio Frequency IDentification tags (RFID) are used in many contexts: access control, inventory, livestock management. Furthermore, such devices are expected to replace bar codes in the near future. RFID systems are constituted of tags and readers which can communicate together wirelessly. An identification scheme is used to identify devices. Many such schemes have been proposed so far, either based on symmetric cryptosystems [2,6,11,15,16,22] or asymmetric cryptosystems [14,3,8].

In a symmetric scheme, secret keys are shared between readers and tags. This implies that a reader contains all the key material of the system. However, this kind of scheme is in general not scalable: reader has to make as many computation as the number of RFID tags in the system. There exist some exceptions, for instance the work of Molnar et al. [15], the work of Avoine et al. [1] and the work of Bringer et al. [5]. Nevertheless, these schemes have a major drawback:

---

[*] This work has been partially founded by the ANR project T2TIT.

keys are shared between tags. As a consequence, the corruption of a tag leaks information on the other tags' key material.

In an asymmetric scheme, each device possesses its own secret – its private key – linked to a public value. Devices then prove their knowledge of their secrets. Asymmetric schemes can be designed to be scalable, but at a cost of many cryptographic computations. As a consequence, to be used on RFID tags, it is necessary to develop very efficient schemes which respect user's privacy.

1.1 Related Works

In [14], Lee *et al.* proposed an identification scheme. They also proposed a security model and proved the security (soundness and privacy) of the scheme in the model. As we show later, the scheme is not secure while the proofs in [14] are correct, this model has thus some weaknesses.

Among the few existing privacy models for identification devices – Juels and Weis [12], Burmester, van Le and de Medeiros [13] and Vaudenay [21] – we choose to work with Vaudenay's model as it is more general. A scheme proved private in this model is resistant against the tracking attacks, which is an important concern for RFID tags. Many schemes have been proved not private in this model in [17] and in [18].

In this paper, we present a new scheme, called Randomized Schnorr which is secure against active adversaries, private in Vaudenay's model and scalable. As in [14], all the readers in our scheme share the same private/public key pair and tags are aware of this public key. Readers (or Verifiers) are able to verify the authenticity of provers thanks to their private key while eavesdroppers cannot distinguish tags outputs.

Designated-Verifier Signature (DVS) schemes have been introduced in [10] and put forward the idea of a signer aware of the verifier's public key. As in [7], our scheme can be transformed into a signature scheme. Nevertheless, this is not the aim of the paper to determine whether the resulting signature schemes would be a DVS scheme.

1.2 Outlines

The paper is organized as follows: Section 2 describes the EC-RAC scheme and Section 3 its weaknesses. Section 4 deals with our security definition. Section 5 recalls the computational assumptions we use. Section 6 describes our proposal, its security and its privacy. Section 7 describes the differences between our proposal and EC-RAC in terms of performances, security and privacy. Section 8 concludes.

2 EC-RAC

Throughout this paper, $\mathbb{E}$ will denote an elliptic curve defined over a field $\mathbb{F}_p$ with p a prime integer. We assume $\mathbb{E}_p$, the group of points of the elliptic curve, has a prime order q. Let P be a generator of this group.

Cryptanalysis of EC-RAC, a RFID Identification Protocol

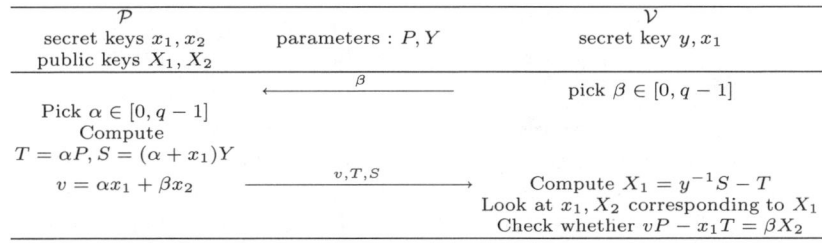

Fig. 1. The EC-RAC scheme

Each prover $\mathcal{P}$ has two private/public key pairs, namely $(x_1, X_1 = x_1 P)$ and $(x_2, X_2 = x_2 P)$ where x_1 and x_2 are random elements in $\mathbb{Z}_q$. The verifier $\mathcal{V}$ has also a pair $(y, Y = yP)$ and knows all the secret keys x_1 of all the tags. The protocol is described in Figure 1. It enables the verifier to retrieve X_1 and the tag to prove its knowledge of x_2.

Once the challenge β is received, a tag computes two scalar multiplications on the curve for T and S. They also compute some small algebraic operations to output v. In [14], RFID tags are able to compute such operations thanks to an efficient processor design.

2.1 Security Claims of [14]

In [14], many security propositions are proved in the generic group model. We recall here the two principal claims which ensure privacy and security against impersonation.

Firstly: eavesdroppers can neither track nor compute the public and secret values of a tag. To this aim, the values x_1, X_1, x_2, X_2 and y are proved to remain private for an eavesdropper in this model. These statements are correct, but we show that in fact it is possible to compute the value $x_1^{-1} P$ from two protocol transcripts of the same tag. Thus whenever someone can eavesdrop other communications from this tag, he can track it.

Secondly: it is proved that even with the verifier information which are x_1, X_1 and X_2, it is not possible to compute the tag secret value x_2. It is thus claimed that tags are uncloneable. Once more, it is not possible to compute these values, but we prove that when someone can eavesdrop the same tag three times, he has enough information to impersonate this tag as many times as wanted. This implies that it is not necessary to know neither x_1 nor x_2 to be successfully identified. These tags can thus be cloned without these values.

3 Attack on EC-RAC

3.1 The Tracking Attack

Assume an adversary has been able to eavesdrop a tag twice. He is in possession of two transcripts: β^i, v^i, T^i, S^i for $i \in \{1, 2\}$. Note that the following equations hold:

$$\beta^1 v^2 - \beta^2 v^1 = (\beta^1 \alpha^2 - \beta^2 \alpha^1)x_1 = \mu x_1 \quad (1)$$
$$\beta^1 T^2 - \beta^2 T^1 = (\beta^1 \alpha^2 - \beta^2 \alpha^1)P = \mu P \quad (2)$$

As a consequence, it is possible to get $x_1^{-1} P = (\mu x_1)^{-1} \mu P$.

Now if the adversary eavesdrops one new tag, he gets the values β^3, v^3, T^3, S^3. He uses one of the previously eavesdropped communication, say the first one, to compute $A = \beta^1 v^3 - \beta^3 v^1$ and $B = \beta^1 T^3 - \beta^3 T^1$. He then checks whether $A^{-1}B$ equals $x_1^{-1}P$. In case of equality, this means that it is the same tag, otherwise it is another one.

3.2 The Impersonating Attack

Assume an adversary has been able to eavesdrop a tag three times. He is in possession of three transcripts: β^i, v^i, T^i, S^i for $i \in \{1,2,3\}$. We have the following equalities:

$$\beta^1 v^2 - \beta^2 v^1 = (\beta^1 \alpha^2 - \beta^2 \alpha^1)x_1 = A \quad (3)$$
$$\beta^1 v^3 - \beta^3 v^1 = (\beta^1 \alpha^3 - \beta^3 \alpha^1)x_1 = B \quad (4)$$
$$B\beta^1 S^2 - B\beta^2 S^1 + A\beta^1 S^3 - A\beta^3 S^1 = (B\beta^1 - B\beta^2 + A\beta^1 - A\beta^3)x_1 Y \quad (5)$$

These equations determine a linear form:

$$(X, Y, Z) \mapsto B\beta^1 Y - B\beta^2 X + A\beta^1 Z - A\beta^3 X \quad (6)$$

The coefficients of this form are chosen to ensure that this form vanishes in the vector $(\alpha^1, \alpha^2, \alpha^3)$ and can be computed by an eavesdropper. As a consequence, if he applies this form to the vector (S^1, S^2, S^3), he computes $(B\beta^1 - B\beta^2 + A\beta^1 - A\beta^3)x_1 Y$. The value $B\beta^1 - B\beta^2 + A\beta^1 - A\beta^3$ vanishes if the vector $(1,1,1)$ is in the kernel of the form. This event has a probability $\frac{1}{p}$ to happen. For this reason, $B\beta^1 - B\beta^2 + A\beta^1 - A\beta^3$ is not equal to zero with an overwhelming probability and he can compute $x_1 Y$. This is another privacy leakage in the previous part, but computing this value also enables to impersonate tags.

To impersonate a tag eavesdropped three times, given a random value β, the adversary:

- computes $\lambda = \beta(\beta^1)^{-1}$,
- computes $T'_1 = \lambda T^1 = (\lambda \alpha^1) P$,
- computes $T'_2 = \lambda (S^1 - x_1 Y) + x_1 Y = (\lambda \alpha^1 + x_1) Y$,
- computes $v' = \lambda v^1 = \lambda \alpha^1 x_1 + \beta x_2$,
- and sends v', T'_1, T'_2.

These three values are the ones a legitimate tag would have computed for β and the random value $\alpha = \lambda \alpha^1$. As a remark, if the verifier has communicated with a tag, as he knows the secret value x_1 of the tag, he can directly impersonate the tag because he can compute $x_1 Y$.

These two attacks clearly contradict the security announcements of [14]. We do not manage to find a way to repair this scheme without using a hash function. In fact, if a tag proves his knowledge of a secret only by answering to one challenge, the answer needs to be a signature of the challenge. Furthermore, to respect privacy, this signature has to be a DVS privately verifiable. To the best of our knowledge, we are not aware of very efficient DVS schemes in term of space, computations and without hash computation. As a consequence, we prefer to use a three passes scheme such as a zero-knowledge scheme for these RFID tags.

4 Security Definitions

Following [21], we consider that provers are equipped with tags to identify themselves. Tags are transponders identified by a unique Serial Number (SN). Nevertheless, during the identification phase, a random virtual serial number (vSN) is used to address them, for instance as defined in the ISO/IEC 14443-3 standard [9].

4.1 Identification Protocol

An identification protocol is a succession of messages sent by a tag and a reader to each other. These messages form the protocol transcript. There exists a function VERIFY$_{KV_s}$ which determines whether a tag is identified by the verifier given a protocol transcript. KV_s is the secret key of the verifier.

We define the Setup algorithms of the model. They are built to ensure that even if verifier's secrets are revealed, the tags' secrets remain secret.

4.2 Setup Algorithms

- SETUPAUTHORITY$(1^k) \mapsto (KA_s, KA_p)$ outputs a private/public key pair of an authority.
- SETUPVERIFIER$_{KA_p}()$ generates a private/public key pair (KV_s, KV_p), possibly none. This pair can be used to protect communication between tags and verifiers.
- SETUPTAGSECRET$_{KA_p}$(SN) returns the parameters of the tag identified by SN. This algorithm outputs a couple (s, I) where s is the private key of the tag, $I = sP$ is its public key and identity.
- SETUPTAGSTATE$_{KV_p}$(SN, s, I) returns S: some data to initialize the internal memory of the tag.
- SETUPTAG$_{KV_p}$(SN) first uses SETUPTAGSECRET then SETUPTAGSTATE, and stores the pair $(I,$SN$)$ in a database.

4.3 Correctness

A scheme is correct if the identification of a tag created with the SETUPTAG$_{KV_p}$ algorithm succeeds except with a negligible probability.

4.4 Security against Impersonation

We give an informal definition of security against impersonation under active attacks. This definition has been formalized in [4]. We first describe a security game and then give the security definition.

Security Game: Assume there exist a system of tags which can be interrogated via the identification protocol. In a first phase, an adversary is allowed to communicate with all tags. In a second phase, the adversary can communicate with the verifier in order to impersonate one of the tags of the system.

Definition 1. *The scheme is **secure against active impersonation attacks** if adversaries cannot succeed at this game except with a negligible probability.*

For instance, EC-RAC is not secure in this model.

4.5 Privacy

To define privacy in Vaudenay's model, it is necessary to describe the capability of adversary.

Firstly, if an adversary does not have access to the result of the function VERIFY_{KV_s}, he is called **Narrow**. To prevent a tracking attack against a passive eavesdropper, it is sufficient to prove in the model that there exists no narrow adversary against the privacy of the scheme.

Secondly, differences exist between adversaries who are able to dump the RFID tags' internal state from adversaries who are not. An adversary who is able to corrupt a tag, to extract its secret and to reuse it, is a **Strong** adversary. If an adversary cannot corrupt a tag, he is a **Weak** adversary.

Finally, an adversary can be for instance narrow and weak. He then is called narrow-weak. For this reason, we here consider 4 kinds of adversaries[1]: weak, narrow-weak, strong, narrow-strong.

To prove privacy, as for the security, we need a game. In this game is defined an algorithm called a **Blinder**. Its name comes from the fact that it is an algorithm between tags and adversary which hides the formers from the latter. While the adversary tries to communicate to the tags, they are in fact communicating to the Blinder. Nevertheless the Blinder never knows which tag it is simulating, this is ensured by the model construction. For this reason, the Blinder cannot associate public values to some given tags. This is a consequence of the fact that the Blinder cannot interact with genuine tags.

Privacy Game: Assume there exist a system of tags which can be interrogated via the identification protocol. In one phase, adversaries can communicate with **legitimate** tags via the protocol. In another phase, adversaries can communicate with **simulated** tags through a Blinder.

Definition 2. *A scheme is private if there exists a Blinder such that no adversary has an advantage between the two phases except with a negligible probability.*

---

[1] In the original model, there are 8 kinds of adversary but we choose to simplify it for the sake of clarity of this paper.

This condition is a sufficient condition to prove the privacy of a scheme in Vaudenay's model. The complete Vaudenay's model is much more general: adversaries can use 7 oracles, they are 8 kinds of adversary, the blinder simulates 4 of the 7 oracles. Due to lack of space, we only recall in this paper a sufficient condition to prove privacy in the model.

As proved in [21], a private scheme in this model respects anonymity and untraceability. A scheme respects anonymity if no adversary is able to retrieve public information on the tag. A scheme is untraceable if an adversary cannot link tags thanks to their outputs. In this model, EC-RAC is not narrow-weak private, which is the lowest privacy level.

4.6 Zero-Knowledgeness

A **Zero-Knowledge** (ZK) scheme enables to prove the knowledge of a secret without revealing any information on this secret. **Honest-Verifier** ZK schemes do not reveal information on the secret to an honest verifier. An equivalent definition of Honest-Verifier ZK is that there exists a simulator which is able to **perfectly** simulate a prover only with the knowledge of public values and the knowledge of the next challenge of the verifier. A simulation is **perfect** when the distribution of simulated outputs is the same as the distribution of genuine outputs.

5 Computational Assumptions

The Discrete Logarithm (DL) problem can be defined as:

– Given P and aP in $\mathbb{E}_p$ with a randomly chosen in $[0, q-1]$,
– compute a.

The Computational Diffie-Hellman (CDH) problem can be defined as:

– Given P, aP and bP with a and b randomly chosen in $[0, q-1]$,
– compute abP.

Let us define the Decisional Diffie-Hellman (DDH) problem:

– Given P, aP, bP with a and b randomly chosen in $[0, q-1]$,
– given $cP = abP$ with probability $1/2$ and $cP = dP$ with probability $1/2$ with d randomly chosen in $[0, q-1]$,
– decide whether abP equals cP.

This last problem is used to prove that our scheme is private. The security of our scheme is ensured thanks to the One-More Discrete Logarithm (OMDL) assumption [4] (cf. Appendix A). Indeed, our proposal is a modification of the Schnorr scheme and it directly inherits its security properties as proved in section 6.3.

6 Our Proposal

The Schnorr scheme, described in [20] is an efficient ZK identification scheme. Its security is based on the hardness of the DL problem. This scheme is honest-verifier ZK. Nevertheless, there is an information leakage on the identity of the prover involved in such schemes (cf. Section 6.1 later).

We here describe the different setup algorithms of the presented schemes. The SETUPAUTHORITY(1^k) algorithm outputs a private/public key pair (KA_s, KA_p). KA_p defines a cyclic group $\mathbb{E}_p$ and a generator element P. This group is a group of points of an elliptic curve $\mathbb{E}$ on $\mathbb{F}_p$. In this group, the DDH problem is a hard problem. The order of the group is denoted q. The SETUPVERIFIER$_{KA_p}$ algorithm randomly chooses $v \leq q - 1$ and outputs (v, vP). This pair of keys is not used in the Schnorr scheme but we need it in our proposal. The SETUPTAGSECRET$_{KA_p}$(SN) algorithm randomly chooses $s \leq q - 1$ and outputs $(s, I = sP)$. The SETUPTAGSTATE$_{KV_p}$(SN,s,I) algorithm outputs the initial state of the tag linked to SN: (KA_p, vP, s). The SETUPTAG$_{KV_p}$(SN) algorithm uses the two last algorithms as explained in the model. As a consequence, we assume the verifier is aware of a list L of the form $\{..., (I, SN), ...\}$.

In the following scheme, a prover possessing a tag of state (KA_p, vP, s) wants to prove his knowledge of s while $I = g^s$ is in the list L. This list does not need to be secret.

6.1 The Original Schnorr Scheme

In a first step, the prover randomly chooses α in $[0, q-1]$. Then he computes $A = \alpha P$ and sends this value to the verifier. The verifier sends a challenge c randomly chosen in $[0, q-1]$. The prover responds with $y = \alpha + sc \mod q$. The verifier checks whether there exists $I \in L$ such that $yP - A = cI$. If this condition is verified, the prover is identified.

For the same reason, an eavesdropper who gets $\alpha P, c, y$ can thus determine the identity of the interrogated tag. This is an important privacy leakage.

6.2 Randomized Schnorr

The Randomized Schnorr scheme is described in Figure 2. The difference with the original Schnorr scheme is that the computation of $A_2 = \beta vP$ ensures that only the verifier can make the verification and computes the identity I. The scheme stays ZK because $\alpha + \beta$ 'hides' the secret as in the original Schnorr scheme. In fact, if v is given to an adversary, the scheme is equivalent to the Schnorr scheme. As v is only used to ensure privacy, the security and the zero-knowledgeness of the Randomized Schnorr are exactly the same as the ones of the Schnorr scheme. Nevertheless, thanks to the verifier secret key v, the scheme is now narrow-strong private because to identify a tag, it is necessary to be able to solve the DDH problem in basis vP.

From the verifier point of view, to determine the tag identity, it is only necessary to compute three scalar multiplications and then to make a table lookup in his list of identity. Therefore this scheme is perfectly scalable. Furthermore,

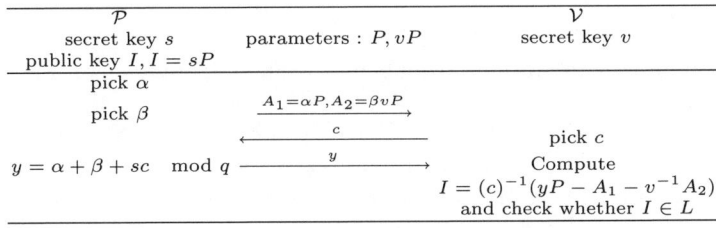

Fig. 2. Randomized Schnorr scheme

there is no need to keep this list secret, because even with the knowledge of tags' secrets, adversaries cannot identify tags.

6.3 Security: Correctness and Impersonation Resistance

Correctness: this scheme is clearly correct, as a legitimate tag succeeds with probability 1. **Impersonation Resistance**: the Randomized Schnorr scheme is a modification of the Schnorr scheme. For this reason, a relevant adversary against the former can be transformed into a relevant adversary against the latter. In [4], it is proved that there exists no active adversary against the Schnorr scheme under the OMDL assumtion. This implies that there exists no active adversary against the Randomized Schnorr Scheme.

Theorem 1. *Assume the Schnorr scheme is secure against active impersonation attacks, then Randomized Schnorr is secure against active impersonation attacks.*

Proof: Assume there exists an active adversary $\mathcal{A}^{RS}$ relevant against the Randomized Schnorr scheme. Given a system of tags $\mathcal{T}$ and a verifier executing the Schnorr scheme as identification protocol, we transform the tags' normal outputs to simulate tags' outputs in the Randomized Schnorr scheme. So doing, we convert $\mathcal{A}^{RS}$ into an adversary against Schnorr.

Before the first phase, we randomly choose a v and we compute vP. During the first phase, when $\mathcal{A}^{RS}$ interrogates a tag, this tag outputs A_1. We intercept this value, we randomly choose β, we compute $A_2 = \beta vP$, and we send A_1, A_2 to $\mathcal{A}^{RS}$. After the reception of c sent by $\mathcal{A}^{RS}$, the tag outputs y, we intercept this value to send $y + \beta \mod q$ to the adversary. Clearly, from $\mathcal{A}^{RS}$'s point of view, tags are using the Randomized Schnorr Scheme.

During the second phase, $\mathcal{A}^{RS}$ tries to impersonate a tag by interacting with the verifier. At each try, we intercept the communication. While $\mathcal{A}^{RS}$ sends A_1, A_2, we compute $A = A_1 + v^{-1}A_2$ and we send this value to the verifier. We only intercept the first message of the protocol.

As $\mathcal{A}^{RS}$ is able to impersonate tags against the Randomized Schnorr scheme then he is able to compute a couple A_1, A_2 to receive a challenge c and to compute y such that there exists an I verifying $I = c^{-1}(yP - (A_1 + v^{-1}A_2))$. For this reason, we are able to compute A, to receive c and to compute y such that there exists an I with $I = c^{-1}(yP - A)$. Using $\mathcal{A}^{RS}$, we are able to impersonate tag against the Schnorr scheme. □

6.4 Privacy

We here explain why the Randomized Schnorr scheme is narrow-strong private. A narrow-strong adversary is theoretically aware of the secret of all tags. Nevertheless, even with these secrets, this adversary cannot link tags' outputs and secrets under the DDH assumption for the Randomized Schnorr scheme. For this reason, in the privacy game, he cannot determine whether the system is simulated.

Theorem 2. *Assume the hardness of the DDH problem, then Randomized Schnorr is narrow-strong private.*

Proof: As explained, to prove the privacy, it is necessary to prove that we can simulate the tags outputs. In the following, we construct a simulation and we prove that an adversary cannot distinguish between this simulation and the outputs of genuine tags.

Transcripts of protocol instances between a legitimate device and any verifier is of the form $A_1 = \alpha P, A_2 = \beta vP, c, \alpha + \beta + sc$. A simulator outputs A_1, A_2, c, r_3. As the adversary is strong, we assume he is aware of all the secrets. To be relevant, an adversary $\mathcal{A}$ has to distinguish random instances A_1, A_2, c, r_3 from instances $A_1, A_2, c, \alpha + \beta + sc$. This is equivalent to consider $A_1, A_2, r_3' = r_3 - sc$ and $A_1, A_2, \alpha + \beta$. It is noticeable that r_3' is as random as r_3. In the following, we prove that distinguishing legitimate triplets and simulated triplets is harder than solving the DDH problem.

Given an instance $vP, \beta P, \gamma P$ of the DDH problem, we randomly choose r and we compute $A_1 = rP - \beta P$. The values $A_1, \gamma P, r$ are thus equivalent to a simulation of the protocol transcript. If $\gamma = \beta v$, we have $rvP = vA_1 + \gamma P$ thus $A_1, \gamma P, r$ comes from a valid transcript. Otherwise it is a random triplet because γ is random. For this reason, if there exists an adversary able to distinguish between simulated tags and genuine ones, he can solve the DDH problem. □

6.5 Zero-Knowledgeness

We here show how to simulate protocol transcript of the Randomized Schnorr Scheme. To prove the scheme is Honest Verifier Zero-Knowledge, we simulate transcripts of a tag of identity I, for a challenge c.

Theorem 3. *Randomized Schnorr is Honest-Verifier Zero-Knowledge.*

Proof: Given a c, we randomly choose $y \mod q$ and we compute $A = yP - cI$. We randomly choose β we compute $A_1 = A - \beta P$ and $A_2 = \beta(vP)$. We output A_1, A_2, c, y. This simulation is clearly perfect as $I = c^{-1}(yP - A_1 - v^{-1}A_2)$.

7 Comparison of Our Proposal with EC-RAC

We here summarize the differences between EC-RAC and our Randomized Schnorr in terms of security, privacy and computations. Table 1 gives the cost of the presented schemes. Furthermore, it sums up their privacy and their security. As in [14], this scheme should be implemented on elliptic curve over group of characteristic around 160 bits. The fourth and fifth column represents the number of scalar multiplication on the curve needed by a tag $\mathcal{T}$ and a verifier $\mathcal{V}$ during one identification session.

Table 1. Comparison of EC-RAC and Randomized Schnorr

Scheme	Security	Privacy	$\mathcal{T}$: Number of Multiplication	$\mathcal{V}$: Number of Multiplication
EC-RAC	Unsecure	Not private	2	4
Randomized Schnorr	Secure against Active Adversaries	Narrow-Strong Private	2	3

8 Conclusion

After a cryptanalysis of the EC-RAC scheme, we give an efficient identification scheme which can be implemented on special RFID tags where EC-RAC was intended to be implemented.

Our proposal, Randomized Schnorr, is secure against impersonation under active attacks. It respects owner's privacy even if the tags' secrets are revealed. It is Zero-Knowledge, this ensures that secrets cannot be computed even by the verifier. Randomized Schnorr is a very efficient and secure solution for RFID system which respects privacy.

Acknowledgments

The authors thank Jean-Sébastien Coron, Bruno Kindarji and the anonymous referees for their helpful comments.

References

1. Avoine, G., Buttyán, L., Holczer, T., Vajda, I.: Group-based private authentication. In: Proceedings of the International Workshop on Trust, Security, and Privacy for Ubiquitous Computing (TSPUC 2007). IEEE, Los Alamitos (2007)
2. Avoine, G., Dysli, E., Oechslin, P.: Reducing time complexity in RFID systems. In: Preneel, B., Tavares, S. (eds.) SAC 2005. LNCS, vol. 3897, pp. 291–306. Springer, Heidelberg (2006)
3. Batina, L., Mentens, N., Sakiyama, K., Preneel, B., Verbauwhede, I.: Low-cost elliptic curve cryptography for wireless sensor networks. In: Buttyán, L., Gligor, V.D., Westhoff, D. (eds.) ESAS 2006. LNCS, vol. 4357, pp. 6–17. Springer, Heidelberg (2006)
4. Bellare, M., Palacio, A.: GQ and Schnorr identification schemes: Proofs of security against impersonation under active and concurrent attacks. In: Yung, M. (ed.) CRYPTO 2002. LNCS, vol. 2442, pp. 162–177. Springer, Heidelberg (2002)
5. Bringer, J., Chabanne, H., Icart, T.: Improved privacy of the tree-based hash protocols using physically unclonable function. In: Ostrovsky, R., De Prisco, R., Visconti, I. (eds.) SCN 2008. LNCS, vol. 5229, pp. 77–91. Springer, Heidelberg (2008)

6. Feldhofer, M., Dominikus, S., Wolkerstorfer, J.: Strong authentication for RFID systems using the AES algorithm. In: Joye, M., Quisquater, J.-J. (eds.) CHES 2004. LNCS, vol. 3156, pp. 357–370. Springer, Heidelberg (2004)
7. Fiat, A., Shamir, A.: How to prove yourself: Practical solutions to identification and signature problems. In: Odlyzko, A.M. (ed.) CRYPTO 1986. LNCS, vol. 263, pp. 186–194. Springer, Heidelberg (1987)
8. Girault, M., Poupard, G., Stern, J.: On the fly authentication and signature schemes based on groups of unknown order. J. Cryptology 19(4), 463–487 (2006)
9. International Standards ISO/IEC. ISO 14443-3: Identification cards – Contactless Integrated Circuit(s) Cards – Proximity Cards. Part 3: Initialization and Anticollision. ISO (2001)
10. Jakobsson, M., Sako, K., Impagliazzo, R.: Designated verifier proofs and their applications. In: Maurer, U.M. (ed.) EUROCRYPT 1996. LNCS, vol. 1070, pp. 143–154. Springer, Heidelberg (1996)
11. Juels, A., Weis, S.A.: Authenticating pervasive devices with human protocols. In: Shoup, V. (ed.) CRYPTO 2005. LNCS, vol. 3621, pp. 293–308. Springer, Heidelberg (2005)
12. Juels, A., Weis, S.A.: Defining strong privacy for RFID. In: PERCOMW, pp. 342–347. IEEE Computer Society, Los Alamitos (2007)
13. Van Le, T., Burmester, M., de Medeiros, B.: Universally composable and forward-secure RFID authentication and authenticated key exchange. In: ASIACCS 2007, pp. 242–252. ACM, New York (2007)
14. Lee, Y.K., Batina, L., Verbauwhede, I.: EC-RAC (ECDLP based randomized access control): Provably secure RFID authentication protocol. In: RFID, pp. 97–104. IEEE, Los Alamitos (2008)
15. Molnar, D., Wagner, D.: Privacy and security in library RFID: issues, practices, and architectures. In: CCS, pp. 210–219. ACM, New York (2004)
16. Ohkubo, M., Suzuki, K., Kinoshita, S.: RFID privacy issues and technical challenges 48(9), 66–71 (2005)
17. Ouafi, K., Phan, R.C.-W.: Privacy of recent RFID authentication protocols. In: Chen, L., Mu, Y., Susilo, W. (eds.) ISPEC 2008. LNCS, vol. 4991, pp. 263–277. Springer, Heidelberg (2008)
18. Ouafi, K., Phan, R.C.-W.: Traceable privacy of recent provably-secure RFID protocols. In: Bellovin, S.M., Gennaro, R., Keromytis, A.D., Yung, M. (eds.) ACNS 2008. LNCS, vol. 5037, pp. 479–489. Springer, Heidelberg (2008)
19. Paillier, P., Vergnaud, D.: Discrete-log-based signatures may not be equivalent to discrete log. In: Roy, B. (ed.) ASIACRYPT 2005. LNCS, vol. 3788, pp. 1–20. Springer, Heidelberg (2005)
20. Schnorr, C.-P.: Efficient identification and signatures for smart cards. In: Brassard, G. (ed.) CRYPTO 1989. LNCS, vol. 435, pp. 239–252. Springer, Heidelberg (1990)
21. Vaudenay, S.: On privacy models for RFID. In: Kurosawa, K. (ed.) ASIACRYPT 2007. LNCS, vol. 4833, pp. 68–87. Springer, Heidelberg (2007)
22. Weis, S.A., Sarma, S.E., Rivest, R.L., Engels, D.W.: Security and privacy aspects of low-cost radio frequency identification systems. In: Security in Pervasive Computing, pp. 201–212. Springer, Heidelberg (2003)

A The One More Discrete Logarithm Assumption

The computational problem n-DL is defined as a natural extension of DL. A probabilistic algorithm $\mathcal{A}$ solving n-DL is given $n+1$ group elements $g_0, g_1, ..., g_n$ in G as well as a limited access to a discrete log oracle $\mathcal{O}_{DL}$. $\mathcal{A}$ is allowed to access $\mathcal{O}_{DL}$ at most n times, thus obtaining the discrete logarithm of n group elements of his choice with respect to a fixed base g. $\mathcal{A}$ must eventually output the $n+1$ discrete logs $k_0 = dl_g(g_0), ..., k_n = dl_g(g_n)$. The One-More Discrete Log assumption tells that no probabilistic algorithm can solve n-DL with non-negligible success probability over G for any integer $n+1$. It is easily seen that DL is contained as the special case DL =0-DL. This definition comes from [19].

Counting Method for Multi-party Computation over Non-abelian Groups

Youming Qiao[1] and Christophe Tartary[1,2]

[1] Institute for Theoretical Computer Science
Tsinghua University
Beijing, 100084
People's Republic of China
[2] Division of Mathematical Sciences
School of Physical and Mathematical Sciences
Nanyang Technological University
Singapore
jimmyqiao86@gmail.com,
ctartary@ntu.edu.sg

Abstract. In the Crypto'07 paper [5], Desmedt et al. studied the problem of achieving secure n-party computation over non-Abelian groups. The function to be computed is $f_G(x_1, \ldots, x_n) := x_1 \cdot \ldots \cdot x_n$ where each participant P_i holds an input x_i from the non-commutative group G. The settings of their study are the passive adversary model, information-theoretic security and black-box group operations over G.

They presented three results. The first one is that honest majority is needed to ensure security when computing f_G. Second, when the number of adversary $t \leq \lceil \frac{n}{2} \rceil - 1$, they reduced building such a secure protocol to a graph coloring problem and they showed that there exists a deterministic secure protocol computing f_G using exponential communication complexity. Finally, Desmedt et al. turned to analyze random coloring of a graph to show the existence of a probabilistic protocol with polynomial complexity when $t < n/\mu$, in which μ is a constant less than 2.948.

We call their analysis method of random coloring the *counting method* as it is based on the counting of the number of a specific type of random walks. This method is inspiring because, as far as we know, it is the first instance in which the theory of self-avoiding walk appears in multiparty computation.

In this paper, we first give an altered exposition of their proof. This modification will allow us to adapt this method to a different lattice and reduce the communication complexity by $1/3$, which is an important saving for practical implementations of the protocols. We also show the limitation of the counting method by presenting a lower bound for this technique. In particular, we will deduce that this approach would not achieve the optimal collusion resistance $\lceil \frac{n}{2} \rceil - 1$.

Keywords: Multiparty Computation, Passive Adversary, Non-Abelian Groups, Graph Coloring, Neighbor-Avoiding Walk, Random Walk.

1 Introduction

Multi-party computation allows multiple parties to cooperatively compute the value of a common function while keeping their own personal inputs secret. Since its introduction by Yao [17], it has become one of the major topics in cryptographic research, having applications in distributed voting, auctions, private information retrieval for instance [8]. The reader may be aware of a recent large-scale implementation of protocols for auction and benchmarks by Bogetoft et al. [2]. Many cryptographic primitives are based on mathematical structures being at least Abelian groups [13] as in [7, 10, 11, 12]. Similarly, numerous protocols for multiparty computation are designed over such structures [1, 3, 4]. However, the discovery of quantum algorithm to solve the factoring problem and the discrete logarithm problem [16] prevents many existing cryptographic schemes to be used on quantum computers. Since those machines seem to compute less efficiently over non-Abelian groups, designing cryptographic protocols over such mathematical structures becomes important.

The first multiparty computation protocol for non-Abelian group was designed by Desmedt et al. in [5]. They studied the existence of secure n-party protocols to compute the n-product function $f_G(x_1, \ldots, x_n) := x_1 \cdot \ldots \cdot x_n$ where each participant is given the private input x_i from some non-Abelian group G. They considered the passive (or semi-honest) adversary model [6] and information-theoretic security. They assumed that the parties were only allowed to perform black-box operations in the finite group G. This assumption means that the n parties can only perform three operations in $(G, \cdot)$: the group operation $((x, y) \mapsto x \cdot y)$, the group inversion $(x \mapsto x^{-1})$ and the uniformly random group sampling $(x \in_R G)$.

Their results are as follows: first, if the number of adversaries $t \geq \lceil \frac{n}{2} \rceil$ (dishonest majority) then it is impossible to construct a t-private protocol to compute f_G. Second, if $t < \lceil \frac{n}{2} \rceil$, they could reduce building a secure protocol to a graph coloring problem, and designed a deterministic t-private protocol computing f_G with exponential communication complexity of $O(n \binom{2t+1}{t}^2)$ group elements (when $t = O(n)$). Third, by using a probabilistic argument based on random coloring, they showed the existence of t-private protocols computing f_G with polynomial communication complexity of $O(n\,t^2)$ group elements when $t < \frac{n}{\mu}$, in which μ is a constant less than 2.948.

Since computationally bounded multi-party computation protocols for classical computers are often based on information theoretically secure ones, we believe that this result would show some insight on how to design computationally bounded multi-party computation algorithms relying on non-Abelian structures to be used over quantum machines.

In this paper, we further explore their analysis method of random graph coloring. We call this technique the *counting method* as it relies on counting the number of a specific type of random walks. This counting method is interesting for two reasons: not only it give us a cryptographic protocol for computing f_G due to the reductions presented by Desmedt et al., but to the best of our knowledge, it is also the first instance that applies the theory of self-avoiding walks to cryptography.

Our results are as follows: first, we give an alternative proof of the counting method from [5]. This modified demonstration will ensure that the protocol computing f_G remains secure when this method is applied to a different lattice as in Sect. 4. In this case, we will be able to reduce the communication complexity by $1/3$, which is an important saving for practical implementation of the protocol. However, the collusion resistance is not as good as the original case in [5]. Second, we give a lower bound on collusion resistance for the original case, showing that the counting method cannot give us the optimal collusion resistance $\lceil \frac{n}{2} \rceil - 1$.

In this article, we will first shortly recall the reduction proposed in [5] that relates the problem of designing a secure protocol computing f_G to a graph coloring problem. In Sect. 3, we show the outline of the counting approach, and construct a lower bound on the collusion resistance we can get from this method. In Sect. 4, we apply this method to square lattices which allows us to reduce the communication cost of the protocol by a third. Finally, we conclude our paper with remaining open questions about this method.

2 Reduction from Secure Computation to Graph Coloring

Since majority is required to ensure secure computation, we assume that $t < \lceil \frac{n}{2} \rceil$ in the remaining of the paper. In such a case, Desmedt et al. reduced the problem of designing protocol of securely computing the n-product function to the n-coloring for some specific graphs. In this section, we present these different reductions of their construction. First, we recall the definition of secure multi-party computation in the passive, computationally unbounded attack model, restricted to deterministic symmetric functionalities and perfect emulation as in [6].

We denote $[n]$ as the set of integers $\{1, \ldots, n\}$ and $\{0, 1\}^*$ as the set of all finite binary strings. $|A|$ denotes the cardinality of the set A.

Definition 1 ([6]). *We denote $f : (\{0, 1\}^*)^n \mapsto \{0, 1\}^*$ an n-input and single-output function. Let Π be an n-party protocol for computing f. We denote the n-party input sequence by $\mathbf{x} = (x_1, \ldots, x_n)$, the joint protocol view of parties in subset $I \subset [n]$ by $\mathbf{VIEW}_I^\Pi(\mathbf{x})$, and the protocol output by $\mathbf{OUT}^\Pi(\mathbf{x})$. For $0 < t < n$, we say that Π is a t-private protocol for computing f if there exists a probabilistic polynomial-time algorithm S, such that, for every $I \subset [n]$ with $|I| \leq t$ and every $\mathbf{x} \in (\{0, 1\}^*)^n$, the random variables*

$$\langle S(I, \mathbf{x}_I, f(\mathbf{x})), f(\mathbf{x}) \rangle \text{ and } \left\langle \mathbf{VIEW}_I^\Pi(\mathbf{x}), \mathbf{OUT}^\Pi(\mathbf{x}) \right\rangle$$

are identically distributed, where $\mathbf{x}_I$ denotes the projection of the n-ary sequence $\mathbf{x}$ on the coordinates in I.

In the remaining of this paper, we assume that party P_i has a personal input $x_i \in G$ (for $i \in [n]$) and the function to be computed is the n-product $f_G(x_1, \ldots, x_n) = x_1 \cdot \ldots \cdot x_n$.

In the first step of the reduction, Desmedt et al. proved that if one can construct a symmetric (strong) t-private protocol Π' to compute the shared 2-product function $g_G(x, y) = x \cdot y$ where the inputs x and y are distributed among the n parties, then, $(n-1)$ iterations of Π' would give us a t-private n-party protocol for f_G. Note that the output $g_G(x, y)$ of Π' is to be distributed amongst the n parties, too.

The second phase of reduction in [5] consists of constructing a t-private n-party shared 2-product Π' from a suitable coloring over particular planar directed graphs.

In that model, the colors stand for the n participants, each directed edge represents one group element sent from one party to another and the non-commutativity of G is reflected in the planar property of the graph.

Finally, Desmedt et al. showed that it was sufficient to color triangular lattices defined as in Definition 2 using a coloring following the requirements of Definition 4.

Definition 2. *The graph $G_{tri}(\ell', \ell)$ is an $\ell' \times \ell$ undirected grid such that:*

- *[horizontal edges] for $i \in [\ell']$ and for $j \in [\ell-1]$, there is an edge between nodes (i,j) and $(i, j+1)$,*
- *[vertical edges] for $i \in [\ell' - 1]$ and for $j \in [\ell]$, there is an edge between nodes (i,j) and $(i+1, j)$,*
- *[diagonal edges] for $i \in [\ell' - 1]$ and for $j \in \{2, \ldots, \ell\}$, there is an edge between nodes (i,j) and $(i+1, j-1)$.*

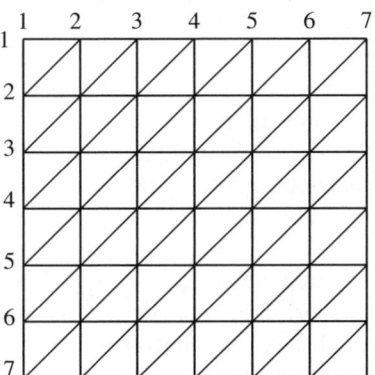

Fig. 1. The grid $G_{tri}(6, 6)$

The security requirement of the protocol is reflected in the following constraint for the coloring of $G_{tri}(\ell, \ell)$ (i.e. when $\ell' = \ell$).

Definition 3. *Let $C : [\ell] \times [\ell] \mapsto [n]$ be a n-coloring for $G_{tri}(\ell, \ell)$. Denote I a subset of $[n]$. Let $\mathcal{P}$ be a path in $G_{tri}(\ell, \ell)$. We say that $\mathcal{P}$ is a I-avoiding path if all its nodes are colored only with colors from $[n] \setminus I$.*

Definition 4 ([5]). *We say that $C : [\ell] \times [\ell] \mapsto [n]$ is a weakly t-reliable n-coloring for $G_{tri}(\ell, \ell)$ (or good (n, t) coloring for convenience), if for each t-color subset $I \subset [n]$:*

- *There exists an I-avoiding path $\mathcal{P}_x$ in $G_{tri}(\ell, \ell)$ from a node on the top row to a node on the bottom row. Such a path is called an I-avoiding top-bottom path.*
- *There exists an I-avoiding path $\mathcal{P}_y$ in $G_{tri}(\ell, \ell)$ from a node on the rightmost column to a node on the leftmost column. Such a path is called an I-avoiding right-left path.*

Remark 1. Note that in the second phase, we need a directed graph, while here we define $G_{tri}(\ell', \ell)$ as undirected. This is allowed since Desmedt et al. showed that for avoiding paths, the direction does not matter.

From the reductions above, Desmedt et al. have demonstrated that it was sufficient to get a weakly t-reliable n-coloring for some $G_{tri}(\ell, \ell)$ in order to construct a t-private protocol for computing the n-product f_G. The cost communication of this protocol is $n - 1$ times the number of edges of $G_{tri}(2\ell - 1, \ell)$ where $G_{tri}(2\ell - 1, \ell)$ is obtained from $G_{tri}(\ell, \ell)$ by a mirror process. Thus, the communication cost of the whole protocol computing f_G is $O(n\,\ell^2)$ group elements.

3 Random Coloring and Counting Method

In this graph coloring problem, two important parameters with respect to the number of parties n are to be taken into account. The first parameter is t, the number of adversaries the protocol must be secure against. Since honest majority is needed to ensure security, we know $t < \lceil \frac{n}{2} \rceil$. If a protocol is secure when $t < \frac{n}{\mu}$, we denote its (largest) collusion resistance as μ. We would like μ to be as close to 2 as possible. The second parameter is the size of the grid side ℓ. Since the number of edges of $G_{tri}(\ell, \ell)$ is a factor of the communication cost of the protocol, we would like to minimize this parameter as much as possible. That is, we want ℓ to be a polynomial in n.

Designing a deterministic coloring method achieving good parameters for t and ℓ at the same time seems quite difficult. In [5], Desmedt et al. turned to analyze the performance of randomly coloring the node of $G_{tri}(\ell, \ell)$ and they developed what we call the *counting method*. In short, they first counted the number of a specific type of random walks. Then, by establishing the equivalence of minimal cutsets and random walks, they plugged the number of random walks into a probabilistic argument which resulted in the existence of good (n, t) colorings when $t < \frac{n}{2.948}$.

Our observation is that, this analysis involves two combinatorial objects: (a specific type of) random walks and minimal cutsets. The central object is the minimal cutset, which has a close relation to good colorings. Then, the equivalence between minimal cutsets and random walks is used to bound the number of such cutsets. In our exposition of the counting method, we emphasize on the importance of minimal cutsets. We use minimal cutsets during the whole proof and only show the equivalence between minimal cutsets and random walks in the last step of the demonstration. Thus, we can adapt the first part of the proof to square lattices without modification to the part involving minimal cutsets as in Sect. 4.

Theorem 1 ([5]). *For any constant $R > 2.948$, if $t \leq \frac{n}{R}$, there exists a black-box t-private protocol for f_G with communication complexity $O(n^3)$ group elements.*

Proof. The algorithm is simple: set $G_{tri}(\ell, \ell)$ with $\ell = O(n)$ (the explicit value of the parameter ℓ will be given later) and we choose a color for each vertex independently and uniformly at random from the set $[n]$. Next, we use the counting method to analyze the effect of this random coloring. The central combinatorial object in this method is *the minimal left-to-right (top-to-bottom) cutset* of $G_{tri}(\ell, \ell)$.

Definition 5 (Cutset/Minimal Cutset). *A set of nodes S in $G_{tri}(\ell, \ell)$ is called a* top-bottom cutset *(resp.* right-left cutset*) if all top-bottom paths (resp. right-left paths) in $G_{tri}(\ell, \ell)$ go through at least one node in S. A cutset S is called* minimal *if removing any node from S destroys the cutset property.*

It is easy to see that every cutset contains a minimal cutset. The relation between minimal cutsets and good (n, t) colorings is established in the following lemma, which will allow us to use this method to a different type of lattices in Sect. 4.

Lemma 1. *Let C be an n-coloring of $G_{tri}(\ell, \ell)$. If every minimal cutset contains more than t colors then C is a good (n, t) coloring for $G_{tri}(\ell, \ell)$.*

Proof. We demonstrate this result by contradiction. Suppose that C is not a good (n, t) coloring for $G_{tri}(\ell, \ell)$. Then, we know that there exists a t-color subset $I \subset [n]$, such that (w.l.o.g) no I-avoiding left-right paths exist in this graph.

We denote the reduced graph of vertices colored in I as H_I, and the reduced graph of vertices colored in $[n] \setminus I$ as $\bar{H}$. We claim that H_I forms a right-left cutset. If it is not the case, then there exists some right-left path in $\bar{H}$ due to planarity and connectivity. This contradicts the hypothesis that no I-avoiding paths exist in $G_{tri}(\ell, \ell)$. So, there is a minimal cutset $S_I \subset H_I$, and the vertices of S_I are only colored with colors in I, forming a contradiction. □

Given this lemma, we can analyze the effect of random coloring as follows. Suppose that we could count the number of minimal cutsets of size k on $G_{tri}(\ell, \ell)$. Then, over the random colorings of $G_{tri}(\ell, \ell)$, we could bound the probability that there exists some minimal cutset that contains no more than t colors. If this probability could be shown to be less than 1 when ℓ is $O(n)$, then we would deduce that there exists some coloring C that is a good (n, t) coloring for $G_{tri}(\ell, \ell)$ according to Lemma 1. Then, using the reduction introduced in Sect. 2 would complete the proof of Theorem 1.

Now, two points remain to be done: first, to bound the number of minimal cutsets; second, to perform the probabilistic analysis. The second point is similar to what Desmedt et al. showed in [5] except that we replace the term *path* employed in [5] with *cutset*. We just include the probabilistic argument here for completeness.

Let $N_P(k, \ell)$ denote the total number of minimal right-left cutsets in $G_{tri}(\ell, \ell)$ of size k. Let $p_x(I)$ ($p_y(I)$) denote the probability that there exists a minimal right-left (top-bottom) cutset P whose node colors are all in the t-subset I representing the set of colluders. We also denote $p(I)$ the probability there exists some minimal cutset that contains only colors in I.

Since node colors are chosen independently and uniformly in $[n]$, each minimal right-left cutset of size k has probability $\left(\frac{t}{n}\right)^k$ to have all its node colors in I. It is clear that $\ell \leq k \leq \ell^2$. So, summing over all possible minimal cutset sizes, we have: $p_x(I) \leq \sum_{k=l}^{\ell^2} N_P(k, \ell) \left(\frac{t}{n}\right)^k$. By symmetry, we have $p_y(I) \leq \sum_{k=l}^{\ell^2} N_P(k, \ell) \left(\frac{t}{n}\right)^k$. So, an upper bound on the probability $p(I)$ is: $p(I) \leq 2 \sum_{k=l}^{\ell^2} N_P(k, \ell) \left(\frac{t}{n}\right)^k$.

Finally, taking a union bound over all $\binom{n}{t}$ possible t-color subsets I, we get an upper bound on the probability p that the random coloring C is not a good (n, t) coloring as

$$p \leq 2 \sum_{k=\ell}^{\ell^2} N_P(k, \ell) \left(\frac{t}{n}\right)^k \binom{n}{t} \qquad (1)$$

Now, we bound the number of minimal cutsets with respect to their respective size k. This is where the counting method is interesting. Instead of directly counting the number of minimal cutsets, we will prove that minimal cutsets, a static structure, are equivalent to some type of random walks, which is a dynamic structure. Then, we will simply bound the number of such walks, which is the subject of investigations in Physics with a rich theory on its own respect.

On an *infinite* planar lattice, a random walk starts from some node and, at each step, it randomly chooses some point from the neighbors of its current vertex as the next step. A *Self-Avoiding Walk* (SAW) is a random walk such that the walker has a memory so that he will avoid any vertex which has been visited previously [15]. It is useful in Physics and Chemistry when people try to model the structure of polymer chain. Here, our focus is on a generalization of SAW: *Neighbor-Avoiding Walk* (NAW). As its name suggests, a NAW is a random walk that avoids the neighbors of this walk. We introduce the following definition for the finite grid $G_{tri}(\ell, \ell)$.

Definition 6 (Restricted NAW). *A restricted right-left (resp. top-bottom) NAW on $G_{tri}(\ell, \ell)$ is a NAW such that:*

- its starting node is on the rightmost column (top row);
- its ending node is on the leftmost column (bottom row);
- and no internal nodes are on the rightmost (top) or leftmost column (bottom row).

The study of NAW is a novelty that we introduce with respect to [5]. The following is an adaptation of Lemma 4.6 from [5]. An illustration is given on Fig. 2 when $\ell = 6$.

Lemma 2. *On $G_{tri}(\ell, \ell)$, a set of nodes is a right-left minimal cutset if and only if it forms a restricted top-bottom NAW.*

There is a rich literature on bounding the number of SAWs on different lattices. Lin and Hsaio showed in [14] that the number N of SAWs or NAWs with respect to number of steps already taken k had the following form:

$$N \approx A \mu^k k^\gamma$$

in which A, μ and γ are constants depending on the type of lattice (triangular, square,...) and walk (SAWs, NAWs,...). Since μ^k constitutes the major fraction of N, μ plays a central role in estimating N. This value μ is called the *connective constant* of the lattice (related to the type of walk). For any walk on any lattice, we define μ as $\mu := \lim_{n \to \infty} (N(k)^{1/k})$. Compared to SAWs, the estimation of μ of NAWs receives far less attention [9]. Desmedt et al. bounded this number on their own as follows.

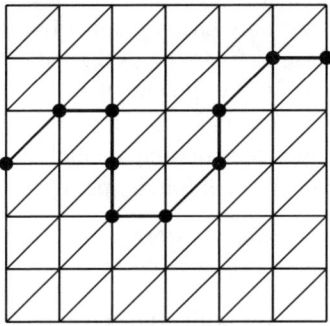

Fig. 2. A NAW on $G_{tri}(6, 6)$ which is a minimal cutset

Lemma 3 ([5]). *The number $M_P(k, \ell)$ of NAWs of length k on infinite triangular lattice is upper bounded as:*
$$M_P(k) \leq c(\mu)\,\mu^k$$
for some constants μ, $c(\mu)$, with $\mu \leq 2.948$. Here, μ is just the connective constant *of NAWs on infinite triangular lattices.*

Remark 2. Note that the set of NAWs on $G_{tri}(\ell, \ell)$ of length k is a subset of NAWs on infinite triangular lattices of length k, so the number of restricted right-left NAWs is upper bounded by $\ell M_P(k) = c(\mu)\,\ell\,\mu^k$ as we have ℓ starting points at the rightmost column.

Remark 3. Note that we bounded the number of NAWs on infinite lattices instead of that of restricted NAWs on $G_{tri}(\ell, \ell)$. Since the set of restricted NAWs on $G_{tri}(\ell, \ell)$ is a subset of NAWs on infinite triangular lattices, finding a specific bound for $G_{tri}(\ell, \ell)$ may lead to some improvements on the value of the connective constant over such graphs.

Given the equivalence between minimal cutsets and restricted NAWs, we get: $N_P(k, \ell) \leq c(\mu)\,\ell\,\mu^k$. So, after substituting $N_P(k, \ell)$ in (1) with $c(\mu)\,\ell\,\mu^k$, we have:

$$p \leq 2\,c(\mu)\,\ell^3 \left(\frac{\mu t}{n}\right)^\ell \binom{n}{t}$$

Thus, if $\frac{n}{t} \geq R > \mu$ on $G_{tri}(\ell, \ell)$, then it is clear that this upper bound on p is less than 1 for sufficiently large ℓ. It is sufficient to have $\ell = O(\log(\binom{n}{t})/\log(n/(\mu t))) = O(n)$, as claimed. This finishes the analysis of the counting approach. □

To summarize what we have done so far, we showed the relation between good coloring and minimal cutset, and use a probabilistic argument to show the existence of such a good coloring. Then, we established the equivalence between minimal cutset and restricted NAW on $G_{tri}(\ell, \ell)$, and bounded the number of restricted NAWs to complete the proof.

One last thing to notice is that the collusion resistance of the protocol is just the connective constant μ. Here, we only have an upper bound for μ in Lemma 3, so one might guess that μ is quite close to 2, giving us a good collusion resistance. However, we now prove that it is not the case by showing that $\mu \geq 1 + \sqrt{2} \approx 2.414$. So, simply improving μ would not give us information about protocols whose collusion resistances are in (2, 2.414). In other words, the counting method on $G_{tri}(\ell, \ell)$ cannot be used to prove the existence of t-private protocol for computing f_G when $\frac{n}{2.414} < t < \frac{n}{2}$.

Theorem 2. *The connective constant μ of NAWs on triangular lattices is at least $1 + \sqrt{2}$.*

Proof. We show a family of NAWs with connective constant $\mu' = 2.414$ by considering a random walker who moves on the infinite triangular lattice following some constraints. Call the node where the walker is currently located the *current* node, and the node before the current node the *last* node.

Consider such a family of random walks formed by the following rule:

1. The walker starts at the origin point. It has three choices: up ($\uparrow$), right ($\rightarrow$) and up-right diagonal($\nearrow$);
2. The possible choices of the walker depend on its last move:

Last Move	Possible Choices
$\uparrow$	$\uparrow, \nearrow$
$\nearrow$	$\uparrow, \rightarrow, \nearrow$
$\rightarrow$	$\rightarrow, \nearrow$

We need to prove that this forms a family of NAWs. First, at every step the walker avoids the neighbors of the last node due to its possible choices. Second, the neighbors of the nodes before the last node lie on the left lower side of the current node, while the walker will only go to the right upper side. So, the set of all such walks forms a family of NAWs.

One can count the number $T(k)$ of NAWs with respect to the number of steps k ($k \geq 1$) already taken as follows. Let f_k be the number of NAWs of length k, when the walker has three choices for the next step (e.g. the last move is $\nearrow$). Let g_k be the number of NAWs of length k, when the walker has two choices for the next move (e.g. the last move is $\uparrow$ or $\rightarrow$). We have the following recursive equations:

$$\begin{cases} f_{k+1} = f_k + g_k \\ f_0 = 1 \end{cases} \qquad \begin{cases} g_{k+1} = 2f_k + g_k \\ g_0 = 0 \end{cases}$$

We get:

$$T(k) = \frac{1}{2}\left(\left(1+\sqrt{2}\right)^{(k+1)} + \left(1-\sqrt{2}\right)^{(k+1)}\right)$$

Recall the definition of connective constant, and we have $\mu' = 1 + \sqrt{2}$. Since this is just a subset of NAWs, we have: $\mu \geq \mu' = 1 + \sqrt{2}$. $\square$

4 The Counting Method on Square Lattices

Let $G_{sqr}(\ell, \ell)$ be the graph after removing the diagonal edges of $G_{tri}(\ell, \ell)$. So, $G_{sqr}(\ell, \ell)$ is just the square grids of side size ℓ. In this section, we adapt the counting method to $G_{sqr}(\ell, \ell)$ and get a protocol that saves about $1/3$ communication complexity compared to the triangular lattices case. However, the collusion resistance of this protocol is not as good as the original one: we show a trivial upper bound 5. Though, we do not get a lower bound, we believe that the collusion resistance is larger than 3 in this case.

Remark 4. We would like to explain why we can color G_{sqr} instead of G_{tri} and still get a protocol for computing f_G. We reason as follows. Remember that in order for an n-coloring C on G_{tri} to be (n, t) good, we require that, for every $I \subset [n]$ of size t, there exist I-avoiding top-bottom and right-left paths. If the diagonal edges in G_{tri} are not used for any I-avoiding paths of $I \subset [n]$, then to consider colorings on $G_{sqr}(\ell, \ell)$ is sufficient.

To apply the counting method to square lattices $G_{sqr}(\ell, \ell)$, we need to examine the proof presented in Sect. 3. It is easy to see that the proof is still valid (by replacing G_{tri} with G_{sqr}) on square lattices up to the point where we need to bound the number of minimal cutsets on square lattices. In the G_{tri} case, we bounded the number of minimal cutsets by showing the equivalence of minimal cutsets and restricted NAWs and bounding the number of the walks instead. It seems difficult to proceed identically over square lattices since it could be shown that a minimal cutset on square lattices may not need to be a *walk*, as shown on Fig. 3.

However, we could show that restricted NAWs on a graph $G_{dia}(\ell, \ell)$ related to $G_{sqr}(\ell, \ell)$ are just minimal cutsets on $G_{dia}(\ell, \ell)$. The graph $G_{dia}(\ell, \ell)$ is simple: you just connect both diagonals of every 1×1 grid in $G_{sqr}(\ell, \ell)$ (see Figure 3). The restricted NAWs on $G_{dia}(\ell, \ell)$ are defined similarly as in Definition 6.

Lemma 4. *A set of nodes S on $G_{sqr}(\ell, \ell)$ is a minimal top-bottom (resp. right-left) cutset if and only if it forms a restricted right-left (resp. top-bottom) NAW on $G_{dia}(\ell, \ell)$.*

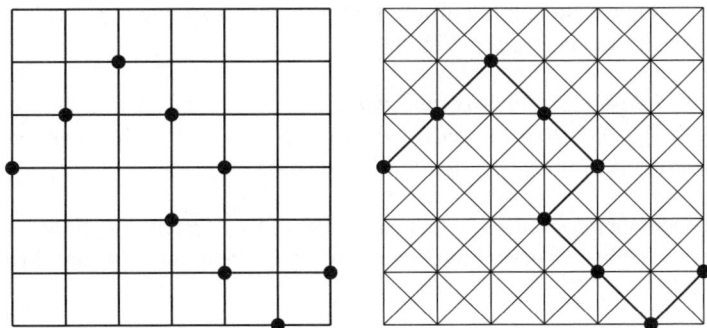

Fig. 3. $G_{sqr}(6, 6)$ and its corresponding $G_{dia}(6, 6)$. The node set presented in the graph is a minimal cutset of $G_{sqr}(6, 6)$. It is not a walk on G_{sqr}, but it is an NAW on G_{dia}.

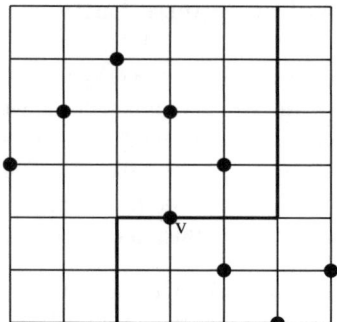

Fig. 4. Unique paths of v

Proof. We first demonstrate the necessary condition: since G_{sqr} is planar, we know S forms a cutset. Then, we claim that it is minimal. First, observe that, on G_{sqr}, we can reach every neighbor of S from the leftmost or the rightmost column. Otherwise, there would be a cycle around the particular neighbor on G_{dia}, which is not allowed for NAWs. Call a neighbor v of S a *left neighbor* if there is a path on G_{sqr} between v and the leftmost column without crossing nodes in S. A *right neighbor* is defined similarly. Thus, a neighbor of S is either a right neighbor or a left neighbor. We have three cases for $u \in S$:

1. u is not on the leftmost or rightmost column: in this case, it could be shown that u must have right and left neighbors at the same time (by enumerating all configurations of NAWs on G_{dia}). So, after removing u from S, we just need to connect its left and right neighbors through u on G_{sqr} to get a right-left path.
2. u is on the leftmost or rightmost column except the four corners: suppose u is on the leftmost column. Then, u must have a right neighbor due to the configurations of NAWs on G_{dia}. So, removing u from S would also give us a right-left path;
3. u is at the four corners of G_{sqr}: since S is restricted, removing u we would immediately get a right-left path (it is the top row or the bottom row).

Now, we look at the sufficient condition. First, we have a simple lemma about minimal cutsets. An illustration is given as Fig. 4.

Lemma 5. *A right-left cutset S is minimal if and only if for all $v \in S$, there is some right-left path P_v, such that the only node from S on P_v is v. For some node v in a minimal cutset S, such a P_v is called the* unique path *of v.*

Proof. The necessary condition: in this case, after removing any $v \in S$, the unique path P_v of v is just a right-left path that does not meet any node in S, destroying the cutset property.

The sufficient condition: suppose there exists $v \in S$ such that for every right-left path P crossing v would cross some other node in S. Then, removing v would not destroy the cutset property, contradicting the assumption about the minimality of S. □

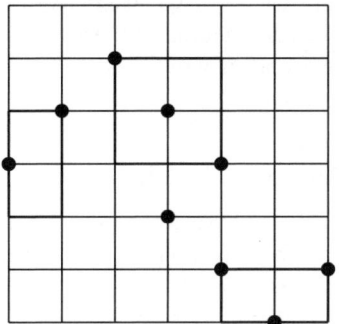

Fig. 5. Different windows of nodes in a minimal cutset of G_{sqr}

Unique paths play an important role in this proof. By using unique paths and the planarity of $G_{sqr}(\ell, \ell)$, we could show the following properties of minimal cutset on G_{sqr} (detailed proofs of those properties are in Appendix A).

Lemma 6. *A minimal right-left cutset contains exactly one node on the top row and one node on the bottom row.*

Lemma 7. *A 1×1 grid contains at most two nodes in a minimal cutset.*

Definition 7. *The* window *of some node v from some node set S that is not on the sides is the 2×2 grid with v at its center. If v is on the leftmost column (or rightmost) column, we call the 2×1 grid with v at the center of its left (or right) column the* half window *of v. If v is on the top row (or bottom) row, we call the 1×2 grid with v at the center of its top row (or bottom row) the* half window *of v.*

Lemma 8. *For minimal right-left cutset, each window contains exactly 3 nodes. For half windows, we have each left/right half window contains exactly 3 nodes, while each top/bottom half window contains exactly 2 nodes.*

We could show that these three properties, plus the minimality property fully characterize restricted top-bottom NAWs on G_{dia}.

Lemma 9. *The minimal right-left cutset S on G_{sqr} is a restricted top-bottom NAW on G_{dia}.*

Proof. The cutset S can be viewed as a walk on G_{dia} under such guidance: the walker starts from the unique node on the top row, and goes to the only node at its half window. While it is not on the bottom row, it always has a unique next step to take according to its current window specified in Lemma 8. Finally, it would reach the bottom row. At that point, it has to stop since he has no choices any longer.

First, notice that such a walk would cross all nodes in S. Otherwise, due to planarity, removing the vertex not on the walk would not destroy S's cutset property. This walk is also restricted due to Lemma 6.

To make this random walk a restricted NAW, we need to show that the walker always avoids the neighbors. First, due to Lemma 7, the next step of the walker avoids the neighbors of the last node. Second, it would also avoids the neighbors of the nodes before the last node due to Lemma 8. Thus, we proved that a minimal cutset on G_{sqr} is also a restricted NAW on G_{dia}. □

This last lemma completes the proof of Lemma 4. □

Having established the equivalence between minimal cutsets on G_{sqr} and restricted NAWs on G_{dia}, we can now apply the counting method to G_{sqr}. Another concern is the connective constant μ_{dia} of restricted NAWs on G_{dia}. By considering 1-step history of NAWs, we could get a trivial upper bound of 5.

Thus, we adapted the counting method to square lattices. Note that the number of edges in G_{sqr} is roughly $2/3$ of the number of edges in G_{tri}. So, we saved the communication complexity of the whole protocol by $1/3$. Table 1 summarizes the comparison of the counting method applied on G_{tri} and G_{sqr}.

Table 1. Statistics of the counting method

	On $G_{tri}(l,\ l)$	On $G_{sqr}(l,\ l)$
Communication Complexity	$c = O(n^3)$	$\frac{2}{3}c$
Collusion Resistance	$2.414 \leq \mu \leq 2.948$	$\mu \leq 5$

5 Conclusion and Open Problems

We showed that the counting method could be applied to square lattices and save communication complexity of the protocol by $1/3$, which is important when implementing the multiparty protocol. We also gave a lower bound of this method for collusion resistance on triangular lattices which shows the limitation of this method on $G_{tri}(\ell, \ell)$.

Note the comparison of applying the counting method to G_{sqr} and G_{tri}. There seems to be a tradeoff between communication complexity and collusion resistance. We think this tradeoff is due to the structure of the lattice and the minimal cutset on this lattice. The interplay between minimal cutset and a specific random walk is important as well. We ask the question of generalizing this method to other types of planar lattices and find which type of random walk corresponds to the minimal cutsets on that lattice.

We emphasize that we bounded the number of walks with respect to number of steps taken on infinite lattices. Due to the reduction of Desmedt et al., we really need to bound the number of random walks on finite lattices and we might hope to obtain security for larger $t = \frac{n}{\mu} > \frac{n}{2.948}$ using particular graphs. So, whether there is difference between those two cases is also an interesting problem.

Acknowledgments

The authors would like to thank Professor Xiaoming Sun for valuable discussions on secret sharing. The authors are also grateful to the anonymous reviewers for their comments to improve the quality of this paper. The two authors' work was sponsored by the

National Natural Science Foundation of China grant 60553001 and the National Basic Research Program of China grants 2007CB807900 and 2007CB807901. Christophe Tartary's research was also financed by the Ministry of Education of Singapore under grant T206B2204.

References

[1] Ben-Or, M., Goldwasser, S., Wigderson, A.: Completeness theorems for non-cryptographic fault-tolerant distributed computation. In: 20th Annual ACM Symposium on Theory of Computing, Chicago, USA, May 1988, pp. 1–10. ACM Press, New York (1988)
[2] Bogetoft, P., Christensen, D.L., Damgård, I.B., Geisler, M., Jakobsen, T., Krøigaard, M., Nielsen, J.D., Nielsen, J.B., Nielsen, K., Pagter, J., Schwartzbach, M., Toft, T.: Multiparty computation goes lives. Cryptology ePrint Archive, Report 2008/068 (January 2008), http://eprint.iacr.org/2008/068.pdf
[3] Cramer, R., Damgård, I.B., Maurer, U.: General secure multi-party computation from any linear secret-sharing scheme. In: Preneel, B. (ed.) EUROCRYPT 2000. LNCS, vol. 1807, pp. 316–334. Springer, Heidelberg (2000)
[4] Damgård, I.B., Ishai, Y.: Scalable secure multiparty computation. In: Dwork, C. (ed.) CRYPTO 2006. LNCS, vol. 4117, pp. 501–520. Springer, Heidelberg (2006)
[5] Desmedt, Y., Pieprzyk, J., Steinfeld, R., Wang, H.: On secure multi-party computation in black-box groups. In: Menezes, A. (ed.) CRYPTO 2007. LNCS, vol. 4622, pp. 591–612. Springer, Heidelberg (2007)
[6] Goldreich, O.: Foundations of Cryptography. Basic Applications, vol. II. Cambridge University Press, Cambridge (2004)
[7] Goldreich, O., Vainish, R.: How to solve any protocol problem - an efficiency improvement. In: Pomerance, C. (ed.) CRYPTO 1987. LNCS, vol. 293, pp. 73–86. Springer, Heidelberg (1988)
[8] Goldwasser, S.: Multi-party computations: Past and present. In: 16th annual ACM symposium on Principles of Distributed Computing, Santa Barbara, USA, August 1997, pp. 1–6. ACM Press, New York (1997)
[9] Guttmann, A.J., Parviainen, R., Rechnitzer, A.: Self-avoiding walks and trails on the 3.12 lattice. Journal of Physics A: Mathematical and General 38, 543–554 (2004)
[10] Hirt, M., Maurer, U.: Robustness for free in unconditional multi-party computation. In: Kilian, J. (ed.) CRYPTO 2001. LNCS, vol. 2139, pp. 101–118. Springer, Heidelberg (2001)
[11] Hirt, M., Maurer, U., Przydatek, B.: Efficient secure multi-party computation. In: Okamoto, T. (ed.) ASIACRYPT 2000. LNCS, vol. 1976, pp. 143–161. Springer, Heidelberg (2000)
[12] Hirt, M., Nielsen, J.B.: Robust multiparty computation with linear communication complexity. In: Dwork, C. (ed.) CRYPTO 2006. LNCS, vol. 4117, pp. 463–482. Springer, Heidelberg (2006)
[13] Lang, S.: Algebra (Revised Third Edition). Springer, Heidelberg (2002)
[14] Lin, K.-Y., Hsaio, Y.C.: Self-avoiding walks and related problems. Chinese Journal of Physics 31(6-I), 695–708 (1993)
[15] Madras, N., Slade, G.: The Self-Avoiding Walk. Probability and Its Applications. Birkhäuser, Basel (1996)
[16] Shor, P.W.: Polynomial-time algorithms for prime factorization and discrete logarithms on a quantum computer. SIAM Journal on Computing 26(5), 1484–1509 (1997)
[17] Yao, A.C.-C.: Protocols for secure computations. In: 23rd Annual IEEE Symposium on Foundations of Computer Science, Chicago, USA, November 1982, pp. 80–91. IEEE Press, Los Alamitos (1982)

A Proofs of Three Properties of Right-Left Minimal Cutsets on $G_{sqr}(\ell, \ell)$

Since the basic ideas of these properties are quite similar, we provide a detailed demonstration for Lemma 10 and we simply show the outline of the proofs for the remaining two properties.

Lemma 10. *A minimal right-left cutset contains exactly one node on the top row and one node on the bottom row.*

Proof. We demonstrate this result by contradiction. Suppose that, for some right-left cutset S, there exist two nodes u and v at the top row and $u, v \in S$. Suppose that u lies on the mth column and v lies on the nth column. Consider the unique paths P_u for u and P_v for v (see Fig 6 for a rough representation of this situation). We can make the assumption that P_u crosses u only once, and P_v crosses v only once.

Now, let the walker A move along P_u from the leftmost column, and walker B move along P_v from the rightmost column. Due to the planarity of the grid, we know that the paths of A and B would meet at some node w that lies on column k, $m \leq k \leq n$ after they cross u and v respectively. Now, if we connect the rest of P_u and the rest of P_v through w we will get a path Q that does not cross any node in S, contradicting with its cutset property. □

Lemma 11. *A 1×1 grid contains at most two nodes in a minimal cutset.*

Proof. We prove this result by contradiction. Assume that, for some minimal top-bottom cutset S, there exists a 1×1 grid in which there are three nodes u, v and $w \in S$. So, we have such a configuration for unique paths P_u, P_v and P_w as shown on Fig. 7.

In this case, if the walker follows P_w from bottom to top, then it is clear that P_w would have no choices but to intersect with P_u or P_v after it crosses w (and after P_u crosses u/P_v crosses v). This would destroy the cutset property of S. □

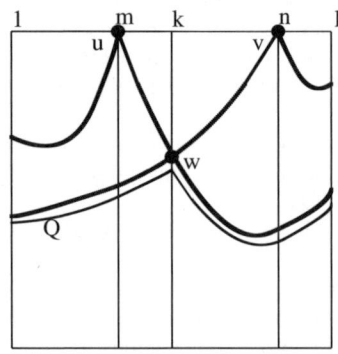

Fig. 6. The path Q does not cross any node in S

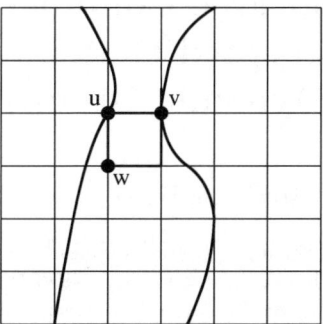

Fig. 7. When some 1×1 grid contains three points from a minimal cutset S

Lemma 12. *For minimal top-bottom cutset, each window contains exactly 3 nodes. For half windows, we have each left/right half window contains exactly 2 nodes, while each top/bottom half window contains exactly 3 nodes.*

Proof. This proof is quite similar to the demonstration of Lemma 11. We just illustrate the configuration of unique paths when the window of v has u, w and t in it. This is a special case, but one can enumerate all cases and find that they are all similar to this one.

From Fig. 8, we can see the unique path of t has to intersect with P_u of P_v after it crosses t (and after P_u crosses u/P_v crosses v), thus destroying the cutset property. □

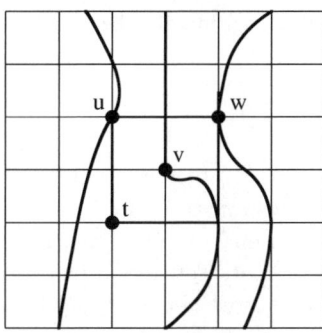

Fig. 8. When some 2×2 grid contains four points from a minimal cutset S

Keyword Field-Free Conjunctive Keyword Searches on Encrypted Data and Extension for Dynamic Groups

Peishun Wang[1], Huaxiong Wang[1,2], and Josef Pieprzyk[1]

[1] Center for Advanced Computing – Algorithms and Cryptography, Department of Computing, Macquarie University, NSW 2109, Australia
{pwang,hwang,josef}@ics.mq.edu.au
[2] Division of Mathematical Sciences, School of Physical and Mathematical Sciences, Nanyang Technological University, Singapore

Abstract. We consider the following problem: a user stores encrypted documents on an untrusted server, and wishes to retrieve all documents containing some keywords without any loss of data confidentiality. Conjunctive keyword searches on encrypted data have been studied by numerous researchers over the past few years, and all existing schemes use keyword fields as compulsory information. This however is impractical for many applications. In this paper, we propose a scheme of keyword field-free conjunctive keyword searches on encrypted data, which affirmatively answers an open problem asked by Golle *et al.* at *ACNS* 2004. Furthermore, the proposed scheme is extended to the dynamic group setting. Security analysis of our constructions is given in the paper.

Keywords: Keyword field, conjunctive keyword search, dynamic group.

1 Introduction

There is a trend that drives owners of their small databases to outsource their IT needs to large professional warehouses. If the server cannot be trusted, sensitive documents should be stored in encrypted forms. In this scenario, the following question arises: how do the clients retrieve an appropriate collection of documents? For example, a client stores her encrypted documents on an untrusted server, and wishes to retrieve all documents containing certain keywords without any loss of data confidentiality. A simple solution would be to download all the documents, decrypt them, and then search the decrypted documents on her local machine. Obviously, this naive solution is inefficient. An ideal solution would be to let the server search the encrypted documents and return only the relevant ones provided the server is not able to obtain any information about the

---

[1] This work was supported by the Australian Research Council under ARC Discovery Projects DP0558773, DP0665035 and DP0663452.
[2] The research of Huaxiong Wang is partially supported by the Ministry of Education of Singapore under grant T206B2204.

keywords and the contents of documents. In the literature, there is a number of research works that address this problem. Keyword (single or conjunctive) search over encrypted data in single-user setting were studied in [2,6,7], and schemes in multi-user setting were proposed in [5,9,13,14,15,16].

For conjunctive key search, we can apply either the schemes based on single keyword search with set intersection operation or meta-keyword techniques. However, Golle et al. [7] argued that both approaches are inefficient. Subsequent works [2,7] were trying to address the efficiency issue. Note that all existing conjunctive keyword search (CKS) schemes were using keyword fields in the index. This setting is useful for some systems, such as email systems. But this requirement is not practical for many other applications. For example, in a database of scientific papers, each paper has its keyword list, and the keywords in each list are arranged in the alphabetical order. So, the same keyword might occur in different positions for different papers. In this situation, using CKS schemes with fixed-position keyword fields is very inefficient. A user must query for a given keyword as many times as there is the number of all possible arrangements of keywords. In this paper, we address this issue and develop a CKS scheme where the keywords can be in an arbitrary order and we call them keyword field-free conjunctive keyword search (KFF-CKS) schemes.

Our Contributions. We propose a keyword field-free scheme for conjunctive keyword search on encrypted data. Our solution is an affirmative answer to the problem asked by Golle et al. at *ACNS* 2004. Security of our construction is based on the l-decisional Diffie-Hellman inversion and discrete logarithm assumptions. To the best of our knowledge, it is the first scheme dealing with conjunctive keyword search without keyword fields in the standard model. Furthermore, we extend our construction for dynamic groups and prove its security under the Weak Diffie-Hellman assumption and LRSW assumption.

Organization. In Section 2, we review the related work. Section 3 provides notation, definitions and cryptographic preliminaries. In Section 4, we construct a KFF-CKS scheme and show the security. In Section 5 we give its extension for the dynamic group setting, prove the security and discuss the efficiency. Finally Section 6 gives conclusions and discusses open problems.

2 Related Work

Golle, Staddon and Waters [7] introduced the notion of conjunctive keyword search over encrypted data and constructed two schemes. Their first scheme compares two hash codes of the keywords to find the desired data, but the transmission overhead of the trapdoors is prohibitive. The second scheme checks two outputs of bilinear pairing constructed from input keywords and tests if the keywords are included in the document. Boneh and Waters [2] proposed a public-key CKS scheme from a generalization of anonymous identity based encryption. Their scheme supports comparison queries (such as greater-than) and general subset queries.

Hwang et al. [9] designed a public key based CKS scheme for a group of users from bilinear pairing. Wang et al. [15] introduced a notion of threshold privacy preserving keyword search, and designed a threshold CKS scheme. Unfortunately, these two works are for static groups and the schemes do not support dynamic groups.

Based on Goh's scheme [6], Park et al. [13] proposed a CKS for dynamic groups, which uses one-way hash chain in reverse order to make session keys, encryption keys and index generation keys. Since all group members use identical secret keys and the keys have to be re-generated for each session, the size of a query grows as the number of sessions increases. Wang et al. [14] addressed the weaknesses of Park et al.'s schemes, and proposed a scheme for dynamic groups. They applied dynamic accumulators, Paillier cryptosystem and blind signatures. Curtmola et al. [5] presented a searchable symmetric encryption for dynamic groups, but their setting is different. In their scheme, the owner of the documents gives a group of users permission to search the documents. Whenever the group changes, the owner has to update the documents and broadcast a new key for the authorized users. Unfortunately, their scheme cannot support a conjunctive keyword search. Very recently Wang et al. [16] presented a new scheme of KFF-CKS for dynamic groups, but the security is proved in the random oracle.

Observe that there is a growing number of papers that consider protocols for private set intersection [10]. Although they address a similar problem to the one we study in this paper, the protocols for private set intersection cannot be applied to our scenario. The reason for that is that the server who needs to know the decryption algorithm, would be able to break the privacy of data.

3 Preliminaries

Notation. Throughout this paper, we use the following notation. Let $a \xleftarrow{R} A$ denote that an element a is chosen uniformly at random from the set A. *PPT* denotes *probabilistic polynomial time*, The symmetric set difference of two sets A and B is denoted by $A \triangle B = (A \setminus B) \cup (B \setminus A)$. For a group G, $|G|$ stands for its cardinality. We assume that the number of keywords associated with a document is fixed to l.

3.1 Definitions

Firstly we recall the known model and formal definition of CKS [2,7], and reintroduce the game of semantic security against chosen-keyword attacks [6,7] for CKS.

In CKS, a client stores encrypted documents on an untrusted server that, however, can be trusted to follow the steps of the protocol correctly. For each encrypted document, the client first generates a secure index with a keyword list associated with the document, and stores both the index and the encrypted document on the server. To retrieve documents containing a particular list of keywords, the client generates a trapdoor for the list and sends it to the server.

Then the server tests each secure index against the trapdoor and returns the matched documents to the client.

Definition 1. *A* **CKS** *consists of the following four algorithms:*

Setup(τ): *The algorithm takes as input a security parameter $\tau \in Z^+$, and outputs the system parameter $PM = \{PK, PR\}$, where PK is the public key and PR is the private key.*

BuildIndex(L, PM): *The algorithm accepts as its input a keyword list L and the system parameter PM, and outputs its secure index I_L.*

Trapdoor(L', PM): *The algorithm takes as its input a keyword list L' and the system parameter PM, and outputs the trapdoor $T_{L'}$ of the list L'.*

Test($T_{L'}, I_L, PK$): *It expects as its input a trapdoor $T_{L'}$, a secure index I_L and the public key PK, and outputs 1 if $L' \subseteq L$, or 0 otherwise.*

Definition 2. *A security game for CKS under adaptive chosen-keyword attacks between an adversary $\mathcal{A}$ and a challenger $\mathcal{B}$ is as follows.*

Setup: $\mathcal{A}$ *adaptively selects a polynomial number of keyword lists from the keyword space, and asks $\mathcal{B}$ for the respective secure indices. For each keyword list L, $\mathcal{B}$ runs the algorithm* **BuildIndex**(L, PM), *obtains the index I_L, and then returns all the indices with respective keyword lists to $\mathcal{A}$.*

Query Phase 1: $\mathcal{A}$ *may query $\mathcal{B}$ for the trapdoor of a keyword list L'. $\mathcal{B}$ runs* **Trapdoor**(L', PM) *to make the trapdoor $T_{L'}$ for $\mathcal{A}$. On receiving $T_{L'}$, $\mathcal{A}$ can invoke* **Test**($T_{L'}, I_L, PK$) *on every index I_L to determine if all keywords in the list L' are contained in L or not.*

Challenge: *After making a polynomial number of queries, $\mathcal{A}$ decides on a challenge by picking two keyword lists L_0 and L_1 such that $\mathcal{A}$ must not have asked for the trapdoor of any word in $L_0 \triangle L_1$, and sends them to $\mathcal{B}$. Then $\mathcal{B}$ chooses $b \xleftarrow{R} \{0, 1\}$, and invokes* **BuildIndex**(L, PM) *to obtain the index I_{L_b} for L_b, then returns I_{L_b} to $\mathcal{A}$.*

Query Phase 2: *After the challenge of determining b is issued, $\mathcal{A}$ is allowed again to query $\mathcal{B}$ a polynomial number of times with the restriction that $\mathcal{A}$ may not ask for the trapdoor of any word in $L_0 \triangle L_1$.*

Response: *Finally $\mathcal{A}$ outputs a bit $b_\mathcal{A}$, and is successful if $b_\mathcal{A} = b$. The advantage of $\mathcal{A}$ in winning this game is defined as $Adv_\mathcal{A} = |Pr[b = b_\mathcal{A}] - 1/2|$, and the adversary is said to have an ϵ-advantage if $Adv_\mathcal{A} > \epsilon$.*

Now we define a general framework for CKS extension in a dynamic group, which were described in [13,14], and review its security requirement as given in [14].

A scheme of CKS extension in a dynamic group includes three parties: a group manager GM, members in the group and a server. GM setups the system, every group member encrypts his data with the group encryption key and stores them together with their corresponding secure indices on the server. When a group member wishes to retrieve the data containing some keywords, she makes a trapdoor for the keywords and sends it the server. For a legitimate member's query, the server checks all secure indices with the trapdoor and sends all matched encrypted data to the member. Finally, the member interacts with GM to decrypt the encrypted data. Any leaving member does not longer access any data in the server, and a joining member not only can store her data on the server, but also is able to retrieve all encrypted data in the server. The formal definition is as follows.

Definition 3. *A scheme of CKS extension in a dynamic group $\mathcal{G}$ consists of the following five components:*

SystemSetup *instantiates the scheme.*
  It has one algorithm **SysSet**(τ) *executed by the group manager GM, which takes as input security parameters (τ), and outputs the system public key PK_s, the group secret key SK_g for all group members and the master key MK for GM.*

AuthCodGen *generates the group membership certificates.*
  It includes the following three algorithms:
  GrpAut$(\mathcal{G}, PK_s, MK)$ *is executed by GM and makes the membership certificate for every member in $\mathcal{G}$. It takes as input the identities $\{ID_i\}_{i=1}^{N}$ of all members $\{M_i\}_{i=1}^{N}$ in $\mathcal{G}$, the system public key PK_s and the master key MK, and outputs membership certificates $\{CT_i\}_{i=1}^{N}$ for all members.*
  MemJon$(\mathcal{G}, \{M_{N+i}\}_{i=1}^{n}, PK_s, MK)$ *is executed by GM interacting with old members when there are new members who wish to join the group. It takes as input the certificates of all members in $\mathcal{G}$, the identities $\{ID_{N+i}\}_{i=1}^{n}$ of all newly joining members $\{M_{N+i}\}_{i=1}^{n}$, the system public key PK_s and the master key MK, and outputs membership certificates $\{CT_{N+i}\}_{i=1}^{n}$ for all new joining members, updated membership certificates for the old members $\{M_i\}_{i=1}^{N}$ and an updated parameter of the system public key PK_s.*
  MemLev$(\mathcal{G}, \{M_{j_i}\}_{i=1}^{n}, PK_s)$ *is executed by GM interacting with the members after some members have left the group. It takes as input the certificates of all members in $\mathcal{G}$, the identities $\{ID_{j_i}\}_{i=1}^{n}$ of all leaving members $\{M_{j_i}\}_{i=1}^{n}$ and the system public key PK_s, and outputs updated membership certificates for the remaining members and an updated parameter of the system public key PK_s.*

DataGen *builds searchable encrypted data that are uploaded to the server.*
  It includes the following two algorithms executed by group members:
  IndGen(R, PK_s, SK_g) *makes a secure index. It takes as input a data R, the system public key PK_s and the group secret key SK_g, and outputs its secure index I_R.*
  DatEnc(R, PK_s, SK_g, I_R) *encrypts the data. It takes as input a data R, the system public key PK_s, the group secret key SK_g and its secure index I_R, and outputs the encrypted data $E(R)$ and uploads $E(R)$ with its I_R to the server.*

DataQuery *retrieves the encrypted data which contains specific keywords.*
  It includes the following three algorithms:
  MakTrp(L', PK_s, SK_g) *is executed by a group member to make a trapdoor of a list of keywords the member wants to search. It takes as input a keyword list L', the system public key PK_s and the group secret key*

SK_g, generates the trapdoor $T_{L'}$ of L', and outputs a query $(T_{L'}, CT_i)$ to the sever.

MemChk(CT_i, PK_s) is executed by the server to check the membership certificate. It takes as input the membership certificate CT_i and the system public key PK_s, and outputs either Yes for access granted or Access Denied to terminate the protocol.

SrhInd$(T_{L'}, I_R, PK_s)$ is executed by the server to scan all secure indices against the trapdoor. It takes as input a trapdoor $T_{L'}$, a secure index I_R and the system public key PK_s, and outputs the encrypted data $E(R)$ for the member when the data includes the searched keywords or No Data Matched for the member when the data does not contain the keywords.

DataDcrypt decrypts the encrypted data.

It includes the following three algorithms:

DatAux$(E(R), CT_i, PK_s)$ is executed by a member to make an auxiliary information associated with the encrypted data to GM. It takes as input the encrypted data $E(R)$, the membership certificate CT_i and the system public key PK_s, and outputs an auxiliary information (U', CT_i) for GM and a one-time secret key ν for the member.

GDcKey$(U', CT_i, PK_s, SK_g, MK)$ is executed by GM to make a decryption key for the member. It takes as input the auxiliary information (U', CT_i), the system public key PK_s, the group secret key SK_g and the master key MK, and outputs the decryption key D or Access Denied for the member.

MemDct$(E(R), D, PK_s, SK_g, \nu)$ is executed by the member to obtain the data. It takes as input the encrypted data $E(R)$, the decryption key D, the system public key PK_s, the group secret key SK_g and the member's one-time secret key ν, and outputs the desired data R.

The scheme should provide data privacy against the server and against a leaving member of the group. This means that server has no information about the data and keywords that are stored. Any member who has left the group should be unable to retrieve any information about the data (except the information he got when he was a member of the group). The scheme should also provide security against impersonation of a legitimate user by anybody (excluding GM) and guarantee that GM knows nothing about the data a member retrieves.

3.2 The Bilinear Pairings

For two cyclic groups G, G_1 with the same large prime order q, a bilinear pairing is defined as a function $e : G \times G \to G_1$ with the following properties:

1. Bilinear: for all $P, Q \in G$ and $a, b \in Z_q$, $e(P^a, Q^b) = e(P, Q)^{ab}$.
2. Non-degenerate: there exist $P, Q \in G$ such that $e(P, Q) \neq 1$, where 1 is the identity of G_1.
3. Computable: for all $P, Q \in G$, $e(P, Q)$ is computable in polynomial time.

A bilinear pairing parameter generator is defined as a polynomial-time algorithm $\mathcal{BG}$, which takes as input a security parameter τ and outputs a uniformly random tuple (e, G, G_1, q) of bilinear pairing parameters, where q is a τ-bit prime.

3.3 Complexity Assumptions

In this section, we briefly review four hardness assumptions, which are the Discrete Logarithm (DL) assumption, l-Decisional Diffie-Hellman Inversion (l-DDHI) assumption [4], Weak Diffie-Hellman (W-DH) assumption [8], and LRSW assumption [12,3].

Assumption 1 (DL Assumption). *Given a finite cyclic group $G = \langle g \rangle$ of prime order q with a generator g. For a given random number $x \in G$, the DL problem is to find an integer t ($0 \leq t < q$) such that $x = g^t$. An algorithm $\mathcal{A}$ is said to have an ϵ-advantage in solving the DL problem if*

$$Pr[\mathcal{A}(g, g^t) = t] > \epsilon.$$

The DL assumption holds in G if no PPT algorithm has at least ϵ-advantage in solving the DL problem in G.

Assumption 2 (l-DDHI Assumption). *Given a tuple $g, g^a, g^{a^2}, \cdots, g^{a^l}$ in a cyclic group G of prime order q and a random element v in G, there is no PPT algorithm that has at least ϵ-advantage in distinguishing between $g^{1/a}$ and v.*

Assumption 3 (W-DH Assumption). *Let G be a cyclic group of some large prime order q. There exists no PPT algorithm such that, given $P, P^v, Q \in G$ without $v \in Z_q$, outputs an element Q^v with at least ϵ-advantage.*

Assumption 4 (LRSW Assumption). *Let $G = \langle g \rangle$ be a cyclic group of some large prime order q. Let $X = g^x$ and $Y = g^y$ be given for two random values $x, y \in Z_q$. Furthermore, let $\mathcal{O}_{X,Y}(\cdot)$ be an oracle such that, given $m \in Z_q$, generates a triple (a, a^y, a^{x+mxy}), where a is a random element of G. There exists no PPT algorithm that has at least ϵ-advantage, given X, Y, g and $\mathcal{O}_{X,Y}(\cdot)$, outputs (m, a, b, c) such that $m \notin \mathcal{Q} \wedge m \in Z_q \wedge m \neq 0 \wedge a \in G \wedge b = a^y \wedge c = a^{x+mxy}$, where $\mathcal{Q}$ is the set of queries made to $\mathcal{O}_{X,Y}(\cdot)$.*

4 KFF-CKS

We construct a KFF-CKS scheme as follows.

Setup(τ): Given a security parameter $\tau \in Z^+$, execute $\mathcal{BG}$ to generate the bilinear pairing parameters (e, G, G_1, q). Choose a random generator g of G, $\alpha \xleftarrow{R} Z_q^* \setminus \{1\}$ and a collision-free one-way hash function $H : \{0,1\}^* \to Z_q$, and then output the public key $PK = \{e, G, G_1, q, g, H\}$ and the private key $PR = \{\alpha\}$.

BuildIndex(L, PK, PR): Given a keyword list $L = \{w_1, \ldots, w_l\}$ of a document, the public key PK and the private key PR, construct a l-degree polynomial

$$f(x) = a_l x^l + a_{l-1} x^{l-1} + \cdots + a_1 x + a_0,$$

such that $\alpha H(w_1), \cdots, \alpha H(w_l)$ are l roots of the equation $f(x) = 0$. Choose $r_s \xleftarrow{R} Z_q^* \setminus \{1\}$, compute $I_i = g^{r_s a_i}$ for $i = 0, 1, \cdots, l$, and send $I_L = \{I_i\}_{i=0}^l$ as the secure index of the document to the server.

Trapdoor(L', PK, PR): Given a keyword list $L' = \{w_{p_1}, \ldots, w_{p_s}\}$ ($s \leq l$), the public key PK and the private key PR, firstly choose $r_u \xleftarrow{R} Z_q^* \setminus \{1\}$. Then, for every keyword w_{p_j} ($j = 1, \cdots, s$), compute $T_{i_j} = g^{r_u(\alpha H(w_{p_j}))^i}$ for $i = 0, 1, \cdots, l$. Finaly compute $T_i = \prod_{j=1}^{s} T_{i_j}$ for $i = 0, 1, \cdots, l$, and send the trapdoor $T_{L'} = \{T_i\}_{i=0}^{l}$ to the server.

Test$(T_{L'}, I_L, PK)$: Given a trapdoor $T_{L'}$, a secure index I_L and the public key PK, compute $V = \prod_{i=0}^{l} e(I_i, T_i)$, and test if $V = 1$. Outputs 1 if so, or 0 otherwise.

Note that, the above KFF-CKS scheme does not require the values of positions of conjunctive keywords in the secure index, which are required as compulsory information in all existing CKS schemes. This means, the positions of keywords in a secure index do not affect the results of searches in a KFF-CKS scheme. Additionally, all existing CKS schemes enable an attacker to know how many keywords in a search keyword list L'. However, in the proposed scheme, an attacker can only know whether the search is done with a single keyword by checking if $e(T_0, T_2) = e(T_1, T_1)$ holds. For a search keyword list containing more than a single keyword, she cannot know the number of keywords.

Theorem 1. *The proposed KFF-CKS scheme is semantically secure against chosen-keyword attacks under the l-DDHI and DL assumptions.*

Proof. Suppose that the scheme is not semantically secure under the security game. Then there exists a PPT adversary $\mathcal{A}$ that wins the security game with an ϵ-advantage. We build an adversary $\mathcal{B}$ that uses $\mathcal{A}$ as a subroutine and breaks the l-DDHI assumption with the $\frac{3}{8}\epsilon$-advantage.

Let $(v, g, g^a, g^{a^2}, \cdots, g^{a^l})$ be $\mathcal{B}$'s l-DDHI challenge. $\mathcal{B}$'s goal is to break the l-DDHI assumption, or in other words to decide whether $v = g^{1/a}$. $\mathcal{B}$ interacts with $\mathcal{A}$ in the security game as follows:

Setup: $\mathcal{A}$ adaptively selects a polynomial number of keyword lists from the keyword space, and ask $\mathcal{B}$ for the respective secure indices. $\mathcal{B}$ replies as follows. Let one of $\mathcal{A}$'s keyword lists be $L_i = (w_{i,1}, \ldots, w_{i,l})$. $\mathcal{B}$ chooses a value $\alpha \xleftarrow{R} Z_q^* \setminus \{1\}$ as the group secret key. For each word $w_{i,j} \in L_i$ ($1 \leq j \leq l$), it picks a value $x_{i,j} \xleftarrow{R} Z_q$ as the hash value $H(w_{i,j})$ of the keyword $w_{i,j}$. As $\mathcal{B}$ has g as a part of l-DDHI challenge, $\mathcal{B}$ can build the secure index I_L in the same way as the algorithm **BuildIndex**(L, PK, PR) does. To be consistent across different queries, $\mathcal{B}$ keeps track of the corresponding pair $(w_{i,j}, x_{i,j})$. Then it return all the indices with respective keyword lists to $\mathcal{A}$.

Query Phase 1: $\mathcal{A}$ may query $\mathcal{B}$ for the trapdoor of a keyword list $L' = \{w'_{p_1}, \ldots, w'_{p_s}\}$ ($1 \leq s \leq l$). For each word $w'_{p_i} \in L'$ ($1 \leq i \leq s$), if w'_{p_i} previously appeared in any one of $\mathcal{A}$'s queries for secure indices or trapdoors, $\mathcal{B}$ takes the previous respective value $x_{i,j}$ as the hash value of w'_{p_i}, otherwise, chooses $x_{p_i} \xleftarrow{R} Z_q$ as its hash value. Also, the corresponding pair (w'_{p_i}, x_{p_i})

has to be kept in memory for future use. Then, with g, $\mathcal{B}$ can make the trapdoor $T_{L'}$ for $\mathcal{A}$ in the same way as the algorithm **Trapdoor**(l', PK, PR) does. Because $\mathcal{B}$ consistently uses the same value for the word w'_{p_i}, $T_{L'}$ is a valid trapdoor for L'. On receiving $T_{L'}$, $\mathcal{A}$ can invoke **Test**$(T_{L'}, I_L, PK)$ on every index I_L to determine if all keywords in the list L' are contained in L or not.

Challenge. After making a polynomial number of queries, $\mathcal{A}$ decides on a challenge by picking two keyword lists L_0 and L_1 such that $\mathcal{A}$ must not have asked for the trapdoor of any word in $L_0 \triangle L_1$, and sends them to $\mathcal{B}$. Then $\mathcal{B}$ chooses $L_b = (w_{b,1}, \ldots, w_{b,l})$, where $b \xleftarrow{R} \{0,1\}$. For every keyword $w_{b,i}$ ($1 \leq i \leq l$), if it previously appeared in any one of $\mathcal{A}$'s queries (including index queries and trapdoor ones), $\mathcal{B}$ takes the previous respective value as its hash value, otherwise, chooses $x_{b,i} \xleftarrow{R} Z_q$ as its hash value. Then $\mathcal{B}$ creates the secure index I_{L_b} in the same way as the algorithm **BuildIndex**(L, PK, PR) does, and returns I_{L_b} to $\mathcal{A}$.

Note that, From the polynomials' algebraical properties, for l numbers $\{x_i\}_{i=1}^l$, there are a polynomial number of l-degree $(l+1)$-coefficient polynomials $f(x)$ such that $f(x_i) = 0$ holds for all $i \in [l]$. That means, in the algorithm **BuildIndex**(L, PK, PR), there are polynomial choices to construct the l-degree polynomial $f(x)$. Additionally, $\mathcal{A}$ does not know the private key α that is chosen independently of any keywords. Therefore, from the view of $\mathcal{A}$, the coefficients of $f(x)$ are distributed uniformly. Under the DL assumption holding in G and G_1, $\mathcal{A}$ cannot compute the coefficients of $f(x)$ or the private key α from the secure indices and trapdoors it queried. That means, at this stage, $\mathcal{A}$ has no way to distinguish the b from 0 or 1.

Query Phase 2: After the challenge of determining b for $\mathcal{A}$ is issued, $\mathcal{A}$ is allowed again to query $\mathcal{B}$ with the restriction that $\mathcal{A}$ may not ask for the trapdoor of any word in $L_0 \triangle L_1$. Let one of $\mathcal{A}$'s queries be $L'_i = (w'_{i,p_1}, \ldots, w'_{i,p_s})$ ($1 \leq s \leq l$). $\mathcal{B}$ chooses $r_u \xleftarrow{R} Z_q^* \setminus \{1\}$ and $r_{t_i} \xleftarrow{R} Z_q$ ($i = 1, \cdots, l$), computes $T_i = g^{r_u r_{t_i} a^{i-1}}$ for $i = 1, \cdots, l$ and $T_0 = v^{r_u}$, and then sends the trapdoor $T_{L'_i} = \{T_i\}_{i=0}^l$ to $\mathcal{A}$. Since $\mathcal{B}$ is given $g, g^a, g^{a^2}, \cdots, g^{a^l}$ as part of l-DDHI challenge, it is able to compute $T_i = (g^{a^{i-1}})^{r_u r_{t_i}}$ ($i = 1, \cdots, l$). On receiving $T_{L'_i}$, $\mathcal{A}$ can invoke **Test**$(T_{L'_i}, I_L, PK)$ on the secure index I_{L_b} to determine if all keywords in the list L'_i are contained in L_b or not.

Observe that, (1) when $L'_i \subseteq L_0 \cap L_1$, if $v = g^{1/a}$ and $r_{t_i} = \frac{\sum_{j=1}^s (\alpha H(w'_{i,p_j}))^i}{a}$ for $i = 1, \cdots, l$, then $T_{L'_i}$ is a correct trapdoor for L'_i, otherwise, not; (2) when $L'_i \not\subseteq L_0 \cap L_1$, if $v = g^{1/a}$, then $T_{L'_i}$ is a correct trapdoor for some other arbitrary keyword list, otherwise, not.

Response. Finally $\mathcal{A}$ outputs a bit $b_{\mathcal{A}}$. If $b_{\mathcal{A}} = b$, $\mathcal{B}$ guesses that $v = g^{1/a}$, otherwise, $\mathcal{B}$ replies $v \neq g^{1/a}$.

Let E-DDHI be the event that $v = g^{1/a}$ in the l-DDHI challenge $(v, g, g^a, g^{a^2}, \cdots, g^{a^l})$, and E-random the event that $r_{t_i} = \frac{\sum_{j=1}^s (\alpha H(w'_{i,p_j}))^i}{a}$ ($i = 1, \cdots, l$). Also let $\text{Succ}_\mathcal{B}$ and $\text{Succ}_\mathcal{A}$ be the events the $\mathcal{B}$ and $\mathcal{A}$ win their respective challenges.

We have

$$Pr(\mathsf{E-DDHI}) = Pr(\overline{\mathsf{E-DDHI}}) = Pr(\mathsf{E-random}) = Pr(\overline{\mathsf{E-random}}) = \frac{1}{2}.$$

When $L'_i \subseteq L_0 \cap L_1$, $T_{L'_i}$ is a correct trapdoor for L'_i if and only if

$$v = g^{1/a} \text{ and } r_t = \frac{\sum_{j=1}^{s} \alpha H(w'_{i,p_j})}{a}.$$

We know that

1. For a correct trapdoor,

$$Pr(\mathsf{Succ}_{\mathcal{B}}|\mathsf{E-DDHI} \wedge \mathsf{E-random}) = Pr(\mathsf{Succ}_{\mathcal{A}}).$$

2. For an incorrect trapdoor, $\mathcal{B}$ returns a random value in reply to the l-DDHI challenge, that is, the answer is independent of b, so

$$Pr(\mathsf{Succ}_{\mathcal{B}}|\overline{\mathsf{E-DDHI} \wedge \mathsf{E-random}}) = \frac{1}{2}.$$

Since

$$Pr(\mathsf{E-DDHI} \wedge \mathsf{E-random}) = 1/4, \ Pr(\overline{\mathsf{E-DDHI} \wedge \mathsf{E-random}}) = 3/4,$$

we have

$$\begin{aligned}Pr(\mathsf{Succ}_{\mathcal{B}}) &= Pr(\mathsf{Succ}_{\mathcal{B}}|\mathsf{E-DDHI} \wedge \mathsf{E-random})Pr(\mathsf{E-DDHI} \wedge \mathsf{E-random}) \\ &+ Pr(\mathsf{Succ}_{\mathcal{B}}|\overline{\mathsf{E-DDHI} \wedge \mathsf{E-random}})Pr(\overline{\mathsf{E-DDHI} \wedge \mathsf{E-random}}) \\ &= \tfrac{1}{4}Pr(\mathsf{Succ}_{\mathcal{A}}) + \tfrac{3}{8}.\end{aligned}$$

When $L'_i \not\subseteq L_0 \cap L_1$, $T_{L'_i}$ is a correct trapdoor for some other arbitrary keyword list if and only if $v = g^{1/a}$. We know that

1. For a correct trapdoor,

$$Pr(\mathsf{Succ}_{\mathcal{B}}|\mathsf{E-DDHI}) = Pr(\mathsf{Succ}_{\mathcal{A}}).$$

2. For an incorrect trapdoor, $\mathcal{B}$ returns a random value in reply to the l-DDHI challenge, that is, the answer is independent of b, so

$$Pr(\mathsf{Succ}_{\mathcal{B}}|\overline{\mathsf{E-DDHI}}) = \frac{1}{2}.$$

So we have

$$\begin{aligned}Pr(\mathsf{Succ}_{\mathcal{B}}) &= Pr(\mathsf{Succ}_{\mathcal{B}}|\mathsf{E-DDHI})Pr(\mathsf{E-DDHI}) \\ &+ Pr(\mathsf{Succ}_{\mathcal{B}}|\overline{\mathsf{E-DDHI}})Pr(\overline{\mathsf{E-DDHI}}) \\ &= \tfrac{1}{2}Pr(\mathsf{Succ}_{\mathcal{A}}) + \tfrac{1}{4}.\end{aligned}$$

Putting them together, we have

$$Pr(\mathsf{Succ}_\mathcal{B}) = \frac{3}{8} Pr(\mathsf{Succ}_\mathcal{A}) + \frac{5}{16}.$$

Finally, the advantage of $\mathcal{B}$ in solving the l-DDHI challenge is

$$\begin{aligned}Pr(\mathsf{Succ}_\mathcal{B}) - \tfrac{1}{2} &= \tfrac{3}{8} Pr(\mathsf{Succ}_\mathcal{A}) + \tfrac{5}{16} - \tfrac{1}{2} \\ &= \tfrac{3}{8}(Pr(\mathsf{succ}_\mathcal{A}) - \tfrac{1}{2}) \\ &> \tfrac{3}{8}\epsilon.\end{aligned}$$

Efficiency discussion. To the best of our knowledge, the proposed KFF-CKS scheme is the first one of CKS without keyword fields. Golle *et al.* [7] worried about the security of keyword fields that may give the server enough information to infer unintended information about the documents. So, they presented an open problem: find schemes for secure search that protects keyword fields. Our construction gives an affirmative answer to their question. Without this constraint, the proposed scheme is more practical for many applications in the real world. Since there is no previous scheme to be compared with, we analyze its efficiency as follows. For building a secure index, the client needs to construct a l-degree polynomial and compute l hash functions, $2l+1$ multiplications and $l+1$ exponentiations; for generating a trapdoor of s keywords, the client needs to compute s hash functions, $3sl - l + s - 1$ multiplications, $2sl$ exponentiations; for testing a secure index, the server needs to compute $l+1$ bilinear pairings and l multiplications. A secure index and a trapdoor have the same size, which is $l+1$ elements of the group G.

5 Extension in the Dynamic Group Setting

5.1 Construction

Now let's extend the proposed KFF-CKS to the dynamic group setting. In the following construction, we use Boneh and Franklin's IBE system [1] to construct a new algorithm for the data decryption.

SystemSetup – *System Instantiation*

SysSet(τ): The GM initializes the system.
  Step 1. Takes a security parameter τ, runs a $\mathcal{BG}$ to generate (e, G, G_1, q). Chooses a random generator g of G, $\alpha, x, y \xleftarrow{R} Z_q^* \setminus \{1\}$, and computes $X = g^x, Y = g^y$.
  Step 2. Chooses two cryptographic hash functions

  $$H : \{0,1\}^* \to Z_q \text{ and } H' : G_1 \to \{0,1\}^{sp},$$

  where $\{0,1\}^{sp}$ is the plaintext space.
  Step 3. Chooses $P, Q \xleftarrow{R} G$, and two values $\lambda, \sigma \xleftarrow{R} Z_q^* \setminus \{1\}$ and computes

  $$P' = P^\lambda, Q' = Q^{(\lambda - \sigma)}.$$

Step 4. Outputs the system public key $PK_s = (e, G, G_1, q, g, X, Y, H, H')$, the group secret key $SK_g = (\alpha, P, P', Q, Q')$, and the master key $MK = (x, y, \lambda, \sigma)$.

AuthCodGen – *Group Authentication*

GrpAut$(\mathcal{G}, PK_s, MK)$: The group $\mathcal{G}$ has N members $\{M_1, \ldots, M_N\}$, and every member M_i $(1 \leq i \leq N)$ has an unique identity ID_i.

Step 1. GM selects $a_i \xleftarrow{R} G$, and computes $b_i = a_i^y, c_i = a_i^{x+H(ID_i)xy}$, then sends M_i the secure codes $\{a_i, b_i, c_i\}$ over a secure channel.

Step 2. The member M_i keeps her membership certificate $CT_i = \{ID_i, a_i, b_i, c_i\}$ secret.

MemJon$(\mathcal{G}, \{M_j\}_{j=N+1,\ldots,N+n}, PK_s, MK)$: Let $A = \{a_i\}_{i=1,\cdots,N}$. New users $\{M_j\}_{j=N+1,\ldots,N+n}$ $(0 < n < q - N)$ with their unique identities $\{ID_j\}_{j=N+1,\ldots,N+n}$, respectively, wish to join the group $\mathcal{G}$.

Step 1. GM chooses $t \xleftarrow{R} Z_q^* \setminus \{1\}$, sends t to the old members over a secure channel, then changes the public key X to be a new one $X' = X^t$.

Step 2. GM selects n random elements $\{a_j\}_{j=N+1,\ldots,N+n}$ from $G \setminus A$, computes $b_j = a_j^y, c_j = a_j^{t(x+H(ID_j)xy)}$, and outputs the secure code $\{a_j, b_j, c_j\}$ for M_j $(j = N+1, \ldots, N+n)$.

Step 3. When the old members $\{M_1, \ldots, M_N\}$ receive t, they update the third part of their secure codes from c_i to be c_i^t $(j = 1, \ldots, N)$.

Step 4 Every member M_i $(i = 1, \ldots, N+n)$ keeps her membership certificate $CT_i = \{ID_i, a_i, b_i, c_i\}$ secret.

MemLev$(\mathcal{G}, \{M_{j_i}\}_{i=1,\ldots,n}, PK_s)$: The members $M_{j_1}, \ldots, M_{j_n}$ $(0 < n < |\mathcal{G}|)$ wish to leave the group $\mathcal{G}$.

Step 1. GM chooses $t \xleftarrow{R} Z_q^* \setminus \{1\}$, sends t to the remaining members, who are still in $\mathcal{G}$ after $\{M_{j_i}\}_{i=1,\ldots,n}$ leave, over secure channels, then changes the public key X to be a new key $X' = X^t$.

Step 2. When the remaining members $\{M_{i'}\}$ (i.e. $\mathcal{G} \setminus \{M_{j_i}\}_{i=1,\ldots,n}$) receive t, they update the third part of their secure codes from $c_{i'}$ to $c_{i'}^t$.

Step 3. Every remaining member $M_{i'}$ keeps her new membership certificate $CT_{i'} = \{ID_{i'}, a_{i'}, b_{i'}, c_{i'}\}$ secret.

DataGen – *Data Building*

IndGen(R, PK_s, SK_g): For a keyword list $L = \{w_1, \ldots, w_k\}$ $(m \geq k \geq 1)$ in a data R, the member runs the algorithm **BuildIndex** of KSS-CKS at Section 4 to create $I_R = I_L$ as the secure index of R.

DatEnc(R, PK_s, SK_g, I_R): The member encrypts her data R as follows: chooses $\gamma \xleftarrow{R} Z_q^* \setminus \{1\}$, computes

$$U = P^\gamma \text{ and } V = R \oplus H'(e(Q, P')^\gamma),$$

let $E(R) = (U, V)$ be the ciphertext of $\mathcal{M}$, and uploads the encrypted data $E(R)$ with its I_R to the server.

DataQuery – *Data Search and Download*

MakTrp(L', PK_s, SK_g): Given a keyword list $L' = \{w_1, \ldots, w_{k'}\}$, the member runs the algorithm **Trapdoor** of KSS-CKS at Section 4 to create the trapdoor $T_{L'}$ of L', and sends the server the query $(T_{L'}, CT_i)$.

MemChk(CT_i, PK_s): The server verifies if the following conditions hold
$$e(a_i, Y) = e(g, b_i) \text{ and } e(X, a_i) \cdot e(X, b_i)^{H(ID_i)} = e(g, c_i).$$
If so, outputs Yes, otherwise, returns the member Access Denied and terminates the protocol.

SrhInd$(T_{L'}, I_R, PK_s)$: If the output of **MemChk**(CT_i, PK_s) is Yes, for a I_R, the server executes the algorithm **Test** of KSS-CKS at Section 4. If the output of **Test** is 1, the server sends the encrypted data $E(R)$ to the member and then checks the next secure index, otherwise, goes to the next secure index. Finally, if there is no data including the specific keywords in the server, the server returns No Data Matched to the member.

DataDcrypt – *Data Decryption*

DatAux$(E(R), CT_i, PK_s)$: For every encrypted data $E(R)$ received, the member chooses a random pair (μ, ν) from Z_q^* such that $\mu\nu = 1 \bmod q$, computes $U' = U^\mu$, then sends the auxiliary information (U', CT_i) to GM and keeps ν as her one-time secret key.

GDcKey$(U', CT_i, PK_s, SK_g, MK)$: When GM receives (U', CT_i), she first checks if the following equations hold
$$e(a_i, Y) = e(g, b_i) \text{ and } e(X, a_i) \cdot e(X, b_i)^{H(ID_i)} = e(g, c_i).$$
If yes, GM computes the decryption key
$$D = e(Q, U')^\sigma,$$
and sends it to the member via a secure channel, otherwise, GM sends the member Access Denied and terminates the protocol.

MemDct$(E(R), D, PK_s, SK_g, \nu)$: On receiving D from GM, the member computes the plaintext
$$R = V \oplus H'(D^\nu \cdot e(Q', U)).$$

5.2 Security

The following Lemma 1 and 2 state the properties of unforgeability and confidentiality of group memberships in the proposed extension of KFF-CKS, and provide user privacy against insiders and data privacy against leaving members, respectively.

Lemma 1. *The group membership authentication process in the proposed extension of KFF-CKS is secure against impersonation attacks of any collusion in the group $\mathcal{G}$ if LRSW assumption holds.*

Proof. First, let's show that it is hard for any collusion in the group $\mathcal{G}$ to forge a valid membership certificate $CT' = \{ID', a', b', c'\}$ for an outsider M' (out of the collusion).

Let's consider that the group $\mathcal{G}$ is static, that is, no member leaves and joins the group $\mathcal{G}$.

Claim. *It is hard for each collusion of up to t ($1 \leq t \leq |\mathcal{G}|$) members in the static group $\mathcal{G}$ to forge an outside user M' (out of the collusion) with a membership certificate $CT' = \{ID', a', b', c'\}$ which can prove that M' is a member of the group $\mathcal{G}$.*

Because every member keeps her membership certificate privately, the t-collusion never knows any other member's certificates. It is clear that the t-collusion acts in the same way as a PPT algorithm $\mathcal{A}$ in the LRSW assumption does, who interacting with the oracle $\mathcal{O}_{X,Y}(\cdot)$ t times cannot computationally output a valid triple (a', b', c') on some value $H(ID')$ that he did not query for. This implies that the t-collusion has negligible success probability to forge a member M' with a valid membership certificate $CT' = \{ID', a', b', c'\}$ under the LRSW assumption.

Furthermore, let's consider that the group $\mathcal{G}$ is dynamic. From the view of the t-collusion as remaining members, after the group $\mathcal{G}$ updates (members joining and leaving) a polynomial times T, besides the t pairs $\{a_i, b_i\}$ unchanged, every member M_u of the t-collusion has a set of pairs $\{t_i, c_u^{\prod_{j=0}^{i} t_j}\}_{i=0,1,\cdots,T}$, where $t_0 = 1$ and $t_1, \cdots, t_T$ are the random values chosen in the algorithms **MemJon** and **MemLev**. In addition, they also obtain a set of updated public keys $\{X^{\prod_{j=0}^{i} t_j}\}_{i=0,1,\cdots,T}$. Although the t-collusion got those extra data from the update of the group $\mathcal{G}$, in fact, the t-collusion can get this type of data as much as he wants by computing easily c_u^v and X^v for some value v. This implies that all those data do not give any more information. According to the **Claim**, we know that the t-collusion in the dynamic group $\mathcal{G}$ either cannot computationally output a valid membership certificate $CT' = \{ID', a', b', c'\}$ for a member M' with identity ID'.

Lemma 2. *The group membership authentication process in the proposed extension of KFF-CKS is secure against impersonation attacks of any leaving member if W-DH and LRSW assumptions hold.*

Proof. From the view of the leaving member $M_{i'}$ with $ID_{i'}$, she has an old invalid membership certificate $CT = \{ID_{i'}, a_{i'}, b_{i'}, c_{i'}\}$, an old public key X and a new public key X^v, where v is unknown random value to her. Suppose that she generates a valid membership certificate $CT' = \{ID'_{i'}, a'_{i'}, b'_{i'}, c'_{i'}\}$ for herself with a non-negligible probability. Then we build an adversary $\mathcal{B}$ that uses $M_{i'}$ as a subroutine to break the W-DH assumption with the same non-negligible probability.

According to the Camenisch and Lysyanskaya's theorem (Theorem 1 in their paper [3], which is under the LRSW assumption), it is intractable for $M_{i'}$ to forge a valid membership certificate with new identity (*i.e.* $ID'_{i'} \neq ID_{i'}$). So, according to the construction, the forged membership certificate should be that $ID'_{i'} = ID_{i'}, a'_{i'} = a_{i'}, b'_{i'} = b_{i'}$ and $c'_{i'} = c^v_{i'}$.

Let $P = g^u, P^v, Q \in \mathcal{G}$ be $\mathcal{B}$'s W-DH challenge, where u is a random number in Z_q and v is unknown. $\mathcal{B}$'s goal is to find Q^v. To describe conveniently, we assume that $M_{i'}$ was in the initial group and than she left firstly. $\mathcal{B}$ simulates GM to interact with $M_{i'}$ as follows:

$\mathcal{B}$ does :	Interaction	$M_{i'}$ does :
$X = P, y \xleftarrow{R} Z_q, Y = g^y$	$\xrightarrow{Setup}$	$\{M_{i'}, ID_{i'}\} \subset \mathcal{G}$
$\vdots$	$\xleftarrow{ID_{i'}}$	Query for her certificate
$w \xleftarrow{R} Z_q, a_{i'} = Q^w, b_{i'} = a^y_{i'},$		
$c_{i'} = a^{u+H(ID_{i'})uy}_{i'}$	$\xrightarrow{a_{i'},b_{i'},c_{i'}}$	$\vdots$
$\vdots$	$\xleftarrow{leaving}$	Left the group $\mathcal{G}$
$X = P^v$		$\vdots$
$\vdots$	$\xleftarrow{c'_{i'}}$	$CT' = \{ID_{i'}, a_{i'}, b_{i'}, c'_{i'}\}$
$A = (c'_{i'})^{((u+H(ID_{i'})uy)\cdot w)^{-1}}$		$\vdots$

Finally, $\mathcal{B}$ gives $Q^v = A$ as the answer to the W-DH challenge.

Let's check the correctness of the answer.

$$\begin{aligned} A &= (c'_{i'})^{((u+H(ID_{i'})uy)w)^{-1}} \\ &= (c_{i'})^{(v(u+H(ID_{i'})uy)w)^{-1}} \\ &= (a_{i'})^{(u+H(ID_{i'})uy)v((u+H(ID_{i'})uy)w)^{-1}} \\ &= (a_{i'})^{v\cdot w^{-1}} \\ &= (Q^w)^{v\cdot w^{-1}} \\ &= Q^v \end{aligned}$$

Therefore, $\mathcal{B}$ breaks the W-DH assumption.

The following Lemma 3 asserts the user privacy against the GM.

Lemma 3. *Data decryption process in the proposed extension of KFF-CKS is secure for user privacy against the group manager.*

Proof. In the process of decryption, GM knows $U' = U^\mu$. Because (μ, ν) is a random pair chosen by the member, ν is the member's one-time secret key, and the discrete logarithm problems in both G and G_1 are hard to solve, it is impossible for GM to compute μ in polynomial time. As μ is a one-time random number, GM cannot distinguish U' from a random number in polynomial time. Therefore, GM is not able to identify the member's desired data in polynomial time.

The security of encryption and decryption algorithms used in our scheme is proved in the Lemma 4.

Lemma 4. *The data cryptosystem in the proposed extension of KFF-CKS is semantically secure.*

Proof. Our encryption algorithm uses Boneh and Franklin's IBE system in a straightforward way. In the process of decryption, the member gets the decryption key $D = e(Q, U')^\sigma$ from GM. Since the discrete logarithm problems in G_1 are hard to solve, it is hard for any PPT adversary to compute the secret key σ, that means, any PPT adversary cannot compute the decryption key D. As the proposed data cryptosystem is a variation of Boneh and Franklin's IBE system, we immediately have that it is semantically secure.

Based on above four lemmas and Theorem 1 at Section 4 that protects the data privacy against the server in the proposed extension of KFF-CKS, we have the following theorem.

Theorem 2. *The the proposed extension of KFF-CKS in the dynamic group setting is secure.*

5.3 Discussion

We now compare the proposed extension of KFF-CKS with Wang *et al*'s scheme [14] in the areas of computation, communication and space complexity. We use the data given in [11] to evaluate the security of the scheme under that the security has to be guaranteed until the year 2020. That means, RSA modulus n is at least 1881 bits, and bilinear pairing systems are over prime fields of at least 188 bits.

5.4 Comparison of Authentication

Since the certificate in our scheme includes 4 points in G, *i.e.*, its size is 752 bits, and the certificate (called PIN number and secure code) in Wang *et al*'s scheme is 2 values in Z_n, *i.e.*, its size is 3762 bits. Our authentication is more efficient than theirs on the communication complexity. The authentication of Wang *et al*'s scheme is based on a dynamic RSA accumulator, and ours is based on bilinear pairing. So, from the view of computation complexity, our authentication is less efficient. However, this overhead benefits our scheme in another way. When the member asks GM to decrypt the encrypted data in Wang *et al*'s scheme, GM does not verify the membership certificate. This means, GM will decrypt the data and return it to the sender. If the server administrator does in same way as the member does, the security of their scheme will be broken down. If the member also sends her membership certificate along with the encrypted data to GM, GM must return the decrypted data to the member who holds the membership certificate instead of the sender; otherwise, the server administrator can use any member's certificate to obtain the data. So, to make their scheme secure, GM must have a directory of email addresses matching with membership certificates. This would increase the burden of GM. Our scheme uses the member's identity as a part of her membership certificate. If all members use their email addresses as their identities, when GM wants to send the member the decryption key, she can use the member's identity to do directly. This property not only protects the data privacy from the server administrator, but also gets rid of the burden of GM.

5.5 Comparison of Encryption and Decryption

Because Wang *et al*'s scheme does not give any detailed construction of encryption and decryption (in fact, no existing scheme constructs the data cryptosystem), we have no way to compare the details between these two schemes. We only analyse in general. In Wang *et al*'s scheme, the data is encrypted twice and decrypted twice. The server sends a whole encrypted data to the member, the member sends a whole encrypted data to GM, and then GM sends a whole encrypted data to the member. So, the communication complexity is 3 times of the encrypted data size. In our scheme, the data is encrypted and decrypted once. The server sends a whole encrypted data to the member and the member sends a half (or less half) of data to GM, and then GM sends a half (or less half) of data (decryption key) to the member, this means, the communication complexity is at most 2 times of the encrypted data size. Hence, our scheme is more efficient than theirs in the computation and communication for the encryption and decryption.

6 Conclusions and Open Problems

We proposed a scheme of KFF-CKS on encrypted data with a standard model, which is the first one for CKS without keyword fields and gives an affirmative answer to the open problem raised in [7]. Besides, we apply it to the dynamic group setting. However, the size of a trapdoor in the proposed KFF-CKS scheme is linear in the number of keywords contained in a secure index, so designing more efficient KFF-CKS schemes with standard models is an open problem, and applying to secure disjunctive keyword search and occurrence queries remains another challenging one.

References

1. Boneh, D., Franklin, M.: Identity-Based encryption from the Weil pairing. In: Kilian, J. (ed.) CRYPTO 2001. LNCS, vol. 2139, pp. 213–229. Springer, Heidelberg (2001)

2. Boneh, D., Waters, B.: Conjunctive, Subset, and Range Queries on Encrypted Data. In: Vadhan, S.P. (ed.) TCC 2007. LNCS, vol. 4392, pp. 535–554. Springer, Heidelberg (2007)
3. Camenisch, J., Lysyanskaya, A.: Signature Schemes and Anonymous Credentials from Bilinear Maps. In: Franklin, M. (ed.) CRYPTO 2004. LNCS, vol. 3152, pp. 56–72. Springer, Heidelberg (2004)
4. Camenisch, J., Hohenberger, S., Lysyanskaya, A.: Compact e-cash. In: Cramer, R. (ed.) EUROCRYPT 2005. LNCS, vol. 3494, pp. 302–321. Springer, Heidelberg (2005)
5. Curtmola, R., Garay, J., Kamara, S., Ostrovsky, R.: Searchable Symmetric Encryption: Improved Definitions and Efficient Constructions. In: ACM CCS 2006, pp. 79–88. ACM Press, New York (2007)
6. Goh, E.-J.: Secure indexes. Cryptology ePrint Archive, Report, 2003/216 (February 25, 2004), http://eprint.iacr.org/2003/216/
7. Golle, P., Staddon, J., Waters, B.: Secure Conjunctive Search over Encrypted Data. In: Jakobsson, M., Yung, M., Zhou, J. (eds.) ACNS 2004. LNCS, vol. 3089, pp. 31–45. Springer, Heidelberg (2004)
8. Hess, F.: Efficient Identity Based Signature Schemes Based on Pairings. In: Nyberg, K., Heys, H.M. (eds.) SAC 2002. LNCS, vol. 2595, pp. 310–324. Springer, Heidelberg (2003)
9. Hwang, Y.H., Lee, P.J.: Public Key Encryption with Conjunctive Keyword Search and Its Extension to a Multi-user System. In: Takagi, T., et al. (eds.) Pairing 2007. LNCS, vol. 4575, pp. 2–22. Springer, Heidelberg (2007)
10. Kissner, L., Song, D.X.: Privacy-Preserving Set Operations. In: Shoup, V. (ed.) CRYPTO 2005. LNCS, vol. 3621, pp. 241–257. Springer, Heidelberg (2005)
11. Lenstra, A.K., Verheul, E.R.: Selecting Cryptographic Key Sizes. In: Imai, H., Zheng, Y. (eds.) PKC 2000. LNCS, vol. 1751, pp. 446–465. Springer, Heidelberg (2000)
12. Lysyanskaya, A., Rivest, R., Sahai, A., Wolf, S.: Pseudonym systems. In: Heys, H.M., Adams, C.M. (eds.) SAC 1999. LNCS, vol. 1758, pp. 184–199. Springer, Heidelberg (2000)
13. Park, H.A., Byun, J.W., Lee, D.H.: Secure Index Search for Groups. In: Katsikas, S.K., López, J., Pernul, G. (eds.) TrustBus 2005. LNCS, vol. 3592, pp. 128–140. Springer, Heidelberg (2005)
14. Wang, P., Wang, H., Pieprzyk, J.: Common Secure Index for Conjunctive Keyword-Based Retrieval over Encrypted Data. In: Jonker, W., Petković, M. (eds.) SDM 2007. LNCS, vol. 4721, pp. 108–123. Springer, Heidelberg (2007)
15. Wang, P., Wang, H., Pieprzyk, J.: Threshold Privacy Preserving Keyword Searches. In: Geffert, V., Karhumäki, J., Bertoni, A., Preneel, B., Návrat, P., Bieliková, M. (eds.) SOFSEM 2008. LNCS, vol. 4910, pp. 646–658. Springer, Heidelberg (2008)
16. Wang, P., Wang, H., Pieprzyk, J.: An Efficient Scheme of Common Secure Indices for Conjunctive Keyword-based Retrieval on Encrypted Data. In: WISA 2008. LNCS. Springer, Heidelberg (to appear, 2008)

Analysis and Design of Multiple Threshold Changeable Secret Sharing Schemes

Tiancheng Lou[1] and Christophe Tartary[1,2]

[1] Institute for Theoretical Computer Science
Tsinghua University
Beijing, 100084
People's Republic of China
[2] Division of Mathematical Sciences
School of Physical and Mathematical Sciences
Nanyang Technological University
Singapore
loutiancheng860214@gmail.com,
ctartary@ntu.edu.sg

Abstract. In a (r, n)-threshold secret sharing scheme, no group of $(r - 1)$ colluding members can recover the secret value s. However, the number of colluders is likely to increase over time. In order to deal with this issue, one may also require to have the ability to increase the threshold value from r to $r'(> r)$, such an increment is likely to happen several times.

In this paper, we study the problem of threshold changeability in a dealer-free environment. First, we compute a theoretical bound on the information and security rate for such a secret sharing. Second, we show how to achieve multiple threshold change for a Chinese Remainder Theorem like scheme. We prove that the parameters of this new scheme asymptotically reach the previous bound.

Keywords: Secret Sharing Scheme, Threshold Changeability, Information Rate, Security Rate, Chinese Remainder Theorem, Dealer Free Update.

1 Introduction

A (r, n)-threshold secret-sharing (TSS) scheme is a cryptographic primitive, allowing a dealer to divide a secret s into n pieces of information called shares (or shadows), distribute them among a group of n participants in such a way that the secret is reconstructible from any r shares while any set of $r - 1$ shadows cannot uniquely determine s. Classical constructions for threshold secret-sharing schemes include the polynomial-based Shamir scheme [12], geometry-based Blakley scheme [3] and the integer-based Chinese Remainder Theorem (CRT) scheme [1].

A common application for TSS schemes is to achieve robustness of distributed security systems. A distributed system is called robust if its security is maintained against an attacker who manages to break into a certain number of components of the system. In many settings, the attacker capabilities are likely to change over time. This threat requires the security level (i.e. the threshold value) to vary as well.

There is a trivial solution to the problem of increasing the threshold parameter of a (r, n)-TSS scheme. The participants simply discard their old shares while the dealer distribute shadows of a (r', n)-TSS scheme to all participants. However, this solution is not very attractive since it requires the dealer to be involved after the setup stage as well as the availability of a secure channel between the dealer and each one of the n group members. Such secure channels may not exist or may be difficult to establish after the initial setup phase.

There already exist TSS schemes allowing the threshold parameters to be changed after the initial setup. Using secret redistribution [6, 11] involves communication amongst the participants in order to redistribute the secret using a new threshold parameter. Although this technique can be applied to standard secret-sharing schemes, its disadvantage is the need of secure channels for communication between participants. Constructions from [5, 2, 9] do not need such secure channels, but they all require the initial secret-sharing scheme to be a non-standard one, i.e. it must specially be designed for threshold increase. Ramp schemes [4, 8] use optimal size of shares but they are not perfect. Other techniques [13, 14] can be applied to existing schemes even if they were set up without consideration to future threshold increases. Unfortunately, those approaches have worse security than the construction presented in [5, 2, 9]. The secret schemes designed in [10, 16] achieve perfect security before and after threshold modification. However, the share size has to be at least twice of the size of secret. Moreover, if we change to threshold c times, the size of the initial shares needs to be at least $(c + 1)$ times as large as the secret's.

In this paper, we first construct an upper-bound on the security rate (ratio between the entropy of a largest unauthorized group and the entropy of the secret) and information rate (ratio between the share size and the secret size) of a changeable-threshold scheme. Second, we propose a new CRT-based secret sharing scheme allowing multiple threshold updates. Our construction allows to choose the security rate of the scheme while having an information rate meeting the previous bound. We will show that our scheme can achieves perfect security, ideal initial scheme and optimal ramp-scheme (the ramp-scheme uses optimal size of shares) easily.

In Sect. 2, we briefly recall some definitions about TSS schemes. In Sect. 3, we discuss the definition of the changeable-threshold secret-sharing scheme as well as the upper-bound on the security rate and information rate for threshold change. In Sect. 4, we present our construction allowing to increase the threshold parameter $c(\geq 1)$ times. After proving its correctness and efficiency, we present two examples: one for standard initial scheme and one for optimal ramp-scheme. The last section concludes the paper.

2 Preliminaries

In this section, we review some basic definitions related to secret sharing.

Definition 1 (TSS Scheme [13]). *Denote* $\mathcal{P} = \{P_1, P_2, \cdots, P_n\}$ *a group of n participants. Let $\mathcal{S}$ be the set of secrets and let the share of P_i come from a set $\mathcal{S}_i$. Denote $\mathcal{R}$ a set of random strings. A (r, n)-Threshold Secret-Sharing (TSS) scheme is a pair of algorithms called the* dealer *and the* combiner *working as follows:*

- For a given secret from $\mathcal{S}$ and some random string from $\mathcal{R}$, the dealer algorithm applies the mapping:

$$\mathcal{D}_{r,n} : \mathcal{S} \times \mathcal{R} \to \mathcal{S}_1 \times \mathcal{S}_2 \times \cdots \times \mathcal{S}_n$$

to assign shares to participants from $\mathcal{P}$.
- The shares of a subset $\mathcal{A} \subseteq \mathcal{P}$ of participants can be input into the combiner algorithm. Denote $\mathcal{S}_\mathcal{A}$ the set of shares of participants from $\mathcal{A}$. The mapping:

$$\mathcal{C}_{r,n} : \mathcal{S}_\mathcal{A} \to \mathcal{S}$$

uniquely determines the secret when $|\mathcal{A}| \geq r$. Otherwise, it fails to uniquely determine the secret value.

The previous definition is rather general and it does not specify what can occur when the secret is not reconstructed. As a consequence, one of the basic problems in the field of secret sharing schemes is to derive bounds on the amount of information revealed by at most $r - 1$ shares.

Definition 2 (Security Rate [15]). *For a (r, n)-TSS scheme with secret s, the* security rate ϕ *is the real number defined as:*

$$\phi = \min \left\{ \frac{H(\mathcal{S}|S_{i_1}, \ldots, S_{i_m})}{H(\mathcal{S})} : \{i_1, \ldots, i_m\} \subseteq \{1, \ldots, n\} \text{ and } m < r \right\}$$

where S_i is the i-th share (for $i \in \{1, \ldots, n\}$).

Definition 3 (Perfect TSS Scheme [15]). *Consider a (r, n)-TSS scheme with the following properties:*

1. *if $|\mathcal{A}| \geq r$ then $H(\mathcal{S}|\mathcal{S}_\mathcal{A}) = 0$*
2. *if $|\mathcal{A}| < r$ then $H(\mathcal{S}|\mathcal{S}_\mathcal{A}) = H(\mathcal{S})$*

where s denote the secret and H is the entropy function. Then, this secret sharing is called perfect.

Note that, for a perfect scheme, we have: $\phi = 1$. A perfect (r, n)-TSS scheme allows the dealer to distribute a secret s amongst a group of n participants in such a way that any r-subgroup of members can reconstruct it while no subsets of less than r participants can gain any information about s.

Another efficiency parameter of secret sharing schemes is the amount of information that the participants must keep secret.

Definition 4 (Information Rate [15]). *For a (r, n)-TSS scheme with secret s, we call* information rate *of the scheme ρ, the value ρ defined as:*

$$\rho = \min \left\{ \frac{H(\mathcal{S})}{H(S_i)} : 1 \leq i \leq n \right\}$$

where S_i is the i-th share (for $i \in \{1, \ldots, n\}$).

Note that, for any perfect secret sharing scheme, we have: $\rho \leq 1$ [15]. The following definition characterize the property that the information rate is in optimal situation.

Definition 5 (Ideal TSS Scheme [15]). *A perfect (r, n)-TSS scheme is called* ideal *if and only if $\rho = 1$.*

In other words, a perfect threshold scheme is ideal when the size of the shares is the same as the secret's. We can easily see that Shamir's scheme is ideal.

An example of non-perfect threshold scheme is given by ramp schemes [4]. Such constructions offer a trade-off between security and share size. We first review the definitions of ramp-schemes as well as optimal ramp-schemes [7].

Definition 6 (Ramp Scheme [4]). *A $(\mathcal{T}, n)$-threshold secret sharing scheme with secret s is said to be a $(\mathcal{C}, \mathcal{T}, n)$-ramp scheme if it satisfies the following properties:*

1. *If $|\mathcal{A}| \geq \mathcal{T}$, then $H(\mathcal{S}|\mathcal{A}) = 0$.*
2. *If $\mathcal{C} < |\mathcal{A}| < \mathcal{T}$, then $0 < H(\mathcal{S}|\mathcal{A}) < H(\mathcal{S})$.*
3. *If $|\mathcal{A}| \leq \mathcal{C}$, then $H(\mathcal{S}|\mathcal{A}) = H(\mathcal{S})$.*

In a ramp scheme, each share size can be smaller than the secret size. However, the smaller the share size gets, the more information about the secret is revealed. We have the following theorem presented in [7].

Theorem 1 ([7]). *For any $(\mathcal{C}, \mathcal{T}, n)$-ramp scheme, we have:*

$$H(\mathcal{S}|S_\mathcal{A}) \geq \frac{\mathcal{T} - \mathcal{R}}{\mathcal{T} - \mathcal{C}} H(\mathcal{S}) \quad \text{and} \quad \forall i \in \{1, \ldots, n\} \; H(S_i) \geq \frac{H(\mathcal{S})}{\mathcal{T} - \mathcal{C}}$$

Definition 7 (Optimal Ramp Scheme [7]). *A $(\mathcal{C}, \mathcal{T}, n)$-ramp scheme is said to be optimal, if it has the property that $H(\mathcal{S}|S_\mathcal{A}) = \frac{\mathcal{T} - \mathcal{R}}{\mathcal{T} - \mathcal{C}} H(\mathcal{S})$ hold for any $\mathcal{A} \subseteq \{1, 2, \ldots, n\}$ such that $|\mathcal{A}| = \mathcal{R}$ and $\mathcal{C} \leq \mathcal{R} \leq \mathcal{T}$ and shares are of minimal size $H(S_i) = \frac{H(\mathcal{S})}{\mathcal{T} - \mathcal{C}}$.*

3 Threshold Changeability for Secret-Sharing Scheme

3.1 Definition and Efficiency Measures

As said in Sect. 1, it sometimes occurs that the security level be changed before the secret is to be reconstructed. Let $\mathcal{P} = \{P_1, \ldots, P_n\}$ be a group of n participants and denote S the set of secrets.

Definition 8 (Threshold Changeability). *A $(r_0 \rightarrow \boldsymbol{r}, n)$-threshold changeable scheme is a threshold scheme where the threshold can be increased $c \, (\geq 1)$ times, $\boldsymbol{r} = (r_1, \ldots, r_c)$ with $r_{i-1} < r_i$ for $i \in \{1, \ldots, c\}$.*

The initial (r_0, n)-threshold scheme is denoted Π_0 and the ith derived (r_i, n)-threshold scheme is denoted Π_i. For any $i \in \{0, \ldots, c\}$ and any $j \in \{1, \ldots, n\}$, we let $\mathcal{S}_{i,j}$ denote the set of j-th shares of Π_i. There exists one dealer algorithm, c combiner (sub-share combiner) algorithms and cn sub-share generation algorithms with the following properties:

- For a given secret from $\mathcal{S}$ and some random string from $\mathcal{R}$, the dealer algorithm applies the mapping:

$$\mathcal{D}_{r_0,n} : \mathcal{S} \times \mathcal{R} \to \mathcal{S}_{0,1} \times \cdots \times \mathcal{S}_{0,n}$$

to assign shares to participants from $\mathcal{P}$.
- For any share from $\mathcal{S}_{i,j}$, there exists a sub-share generation algorithm:

$$\mathcal{E}_{r_0 \to r, i, j} : \mathcal{S}_{i,j} \to \mathcal{S}_{i+1,j}$$

to modify shares for increasing the threshold parameter from r_i to r_{i+1} for any $i \in \{0, \ldots, c-1\}$.
- For any $i \in \{0, \ldots, c\}$, the shares of a subset $\mathcal{A} \subseteq \mathcal{P}$ of participants can be input into the combiner algorithm. Let $\mathcal{S}_{i,\mathcal{A}}$ denote the set of shares of $\mathcal{A}$ in Π_i, if $|\mathcal{A}| \geq r_i$ then the mapping:

$$\mathcal{C}_{r_0 \to r, i} : \mathcal{S}_{i,\mathcal{A}} \to \mathcal{S}$$

reconstructs the secret. And for any $r_i - 1$ participants, it always failed to recover the secret.

In the definitions given above, the sub-share generation algorithms can be probabilistic (dealer free). The third point of Definition 8 involves that, for any r_i-group G, there exists $j_0 \in G$ such that $H(s_{i,j_0}|s_{i+1,j_0}) > 0$. Indeed, in the opposite situation, there would be a r_i-group $\tilde{G}$ such that: $\forall P_j \in \tilde{G} \quad H(s_{i,j}|s_{i+1,j}) = 0$. This would imply that each of the r_i members of $\tilde{G}$ could reconstruct his share related to threshold r_i from his share related to the new value $r_{i+1} (> r_i)$. Thus, we would not have a (r_{i+1}, n)-threshold scheme after threshold update which contradicts the definition of threshold changeability.

Remark. We would like to call the reader's attention to the fact that old shares are assumed to be deleted after performing any threshold update. That is, after updating the threshold value from r_i to r_{r+1}, each of the n participants keeps the share related to the new value r_{i+1} and discards the shadow related to r_i (for $i \in \{0, \ldots, c-1\}$).

The efficiency of a TSS scheme can be measured by its security rate and information rate. We generalize those definitions to the case of a threshold changeable scheme.

Definition 9 (Security and Information Rates). Let $\langle \Pi_0, \ldots, \Pi_c \rangle$ be a $(r_0 \to \mathbf{r}, n)$-threshold changeable scheme where $\mathbf{r} = (r_1, \ldots, r_c)$ with $r_{i-1} < r_i$ for $i \in \{1, \ldots, c\}$. Let ϕ_i denote the security rate of Π_i. The security rate ϕ of the changeable scheme $\langle \Pi_0, \ldots, \Pi_c \rangle$ is defined as $\min_{i \in \{0, \ldots, c\}} \{\phi_i\}$. Let ρ_i denote the information rate of Π_i. The information rate ρ of the changeable scheme $\langle \Pi_0, \ldots, \Pi_c \rangle$ is defined as $\min_{i \in \{0, \ldots, c\}} \{\rho_i\}$.

We will present the definition of deterministic $(r_0 \to \mathbf{r}, n)$-threshold changeable scheme, where $\mathbf{r} = (r_1, r_2 \cdots r_c)$.

Definition 10 (Deterministic Threshold Changeable Scheme). *Let $\langle \Pi_0, \ldots, \Pi_c \rangle$ be a $(r_0 \to r, n)$-threshold changeable scheme. The scheme $\langle \Pi_0, \ldots, \Pi_c \rangle$ is called deterministic, if all the c sub-share generation algorithms are deterministic. In other words, there exist deterministic functions $h_{i,j}$, such that $s_{i+1,j} = h_{i,j}(s_{i,j})$, where $s_{i,j}$ is j-th shadow of Π_i for $i \in \{0, \ldots, c-1\}$ and $j \in \{1, \ldots, n\}$.*

Many existing secret-sharing schemes (like Shamir's construction [12] and the CRT-based secret sharing [1]) are ideal. We have the following result.

Lemma 1. *Let $\langle \Pi_0, \ldots, \Pi_c \rangle$ be a deterministic $(r_0 \to r, n)$-threshold changeable scheme. If the initial (r_0, n)-TSS scheme Π_0 is ideal then the final (r_c, n)-TSS scheme Π_c cannot be ideal.*

Proof. We demonstrate this result by contradiction. Assume the (r_c, n)-TSS scheme Π_c is ideal. We fix $i \in \{1, \ldots, n\}$. We have:

$$I(S_{0,i}; S_{c,i}) = H(S_{0,i}) - H(S_{0,i}|S_{c,i}) = H(S_{c,i}) - H(S_{c,i}|S_{0,i})$$

So, we get:

$$H(S_{0,i}|S_{c,i}) = H(S_{0,i}) - H(S_{c,i}) + H(S_{c,i}|S_{0,i}) = H(S_{c,i}|S_{0,i})$$

Since the algorithm to update the threshold is deterministic, we have: $H(S_{0,i}|S_{c,i}) = H(S_{c,i}|S_{0,i}) = 0$. This means that one can recover $S_{0,i}$ from $S_{c,i}$ for any $i \in \{1, \ldots, n\}$. Thus, the resulting scheme Π_c is also a (r_0, n)-threshold secret-sharing scheme, which is impossible. □

3.2 Upper Bounds on the Security Rate and the Information Rate

Definition 11. *Suppose $\mathcal{T}$ is a (r, n)-TSS scheme with secret s. It is called a (ϕ, ρ) (Semi-Random Dealer and Complete Randomness Recovery Combiner) SRDCRRC-scheme if it has the following properties:*

1. *$\mathcal{T}$ has security rate ϕ. This means that we have $H(\mathcal{S}|S_{i_1}, \ldots, S_{i_m}) \geq \phi H(\mathcal{S})$ for any $\{i_1, \ldots, i_m\} \subseteq \{1, \ldots, n\}$ and $m < r$.*
2. *$\mathcal{T}$ has information rate ρ. This means that we have $H(S_i) \leq \frac{H(\mathcal{S})}{\rho}$ for any $i \in \{1, \ldots, n\}$.*
3. *When the dealer of $\mathcal{T}$ wants to share s, he secretly chooses one random string a and uses the pair $\alpha = (s, a)$ to construct the n shares. The method to output n shares using α is deterministic.*
4. *The combiner of $\mathcal{T}$ can recover the secret s if and only if it can uniquely determine α. In other words, by any r shares, the combiner can reconstruct not only the secret s but also all random bits a.*

Lemma 2. *Suppose $\mathcal{T}$ is a (r, n)-threshold secret-sharing scheme as well as a (ϕ, ρ) SRDCRRC-scheme. Let S_i denote i-th share of $\mathcal{T}$. We have: $H(\alpha) = H(S_1, \ldots, S_r)$.*

Proof. Since the dealer algorithm is deterministic, we have: $H(S_1,\ldots,S_r|\alpha) = 0$. On the other hand, using $S_1,\ldots,S_r$, the combiner can recover the vector α. So, we have: $H(\alpha|S_1,\ldots,S_r) = 0$. As a consequence, we get: $H(\alpha) = H(S_1,\ldots,S_r)$. □

Remark. The previous result is valid for any r shares. We focused on $S_1,\ldots,S_r$ as this will be used to demonstrate the following lemma.

Lemma 3. *Suppose $\mathcal{T}$ is a (r,n)-threshold secret-sharing scheme with secret s as well as a (ϕ,ρ) SRDCRRC-scheme. Then: $H(\alpha) \geq r\phi H(\mathcal{S})$.*

Proof. Let S_i denote the i-th share of $\mathcal{T}$. According to Lemma 2, we have:
$$H(\alpha) = H(S_1,\ldots,S_r) = H(S_1) + H(S_2,\ldots,S_n|S_1)$$
$$= H(S_1) + H(S_2|S_1) + H(S_3,\ldots,S_n|S_1,S_2)$$
$$= \sum_{k=1}^{r} H(S_k|S_1,\ldots,S_{k-1})$$

We get: $H(\alpha) \geq \sum_{k=1}^{r} H(S_k|\{S_1,\ldots,S_r\}\setminus\{S_k\})$.

Let $\mathcal{A}$ be a r-subset and choose any participant i from $\mathcal{A}$, define $\mathcal{B} = \mathcal{A}\setminus\{i\}$ and the size of $\mathcal{B}$ is $r-1$. Let $S_\mathcal{B}$ denote the shares of all participants in $\mathcal{B}$. Since $\mathcal{T}$ has a security rate ϕ, we have $H(\mathcal{S}|S_\mathcal{B}) \geq \phi H(\mathcal{S})$. Using $S_\mathcal{B}$, we get a set of possible secrets $\mathcal{S}'(\subseteq \mathcal{S})$ such that $s \in \mathcal{S}'$ and $H(\mathcal{S}') = \phi H(\mathcal{S})$ where $\mathcal{S}$ is the set of all secrets. Hence, for each $s' \in \mathcal{S}'$, there is a distribution rule[15] $dist(s')$ such that the shares of $\mathcal{B}$ are the same. Since $\mathcal{A}$ is authorized, we must have: $S_i^{dist(s_1)} \neq S_i^{dist(s_2)}$ when $s_1 \neq s_2$ and $s_1, s_2 \in \mathcal{S}'$. Thus: $H(S_i|S_\mathcal{B}) \geq H(\mathcal{S}') \geq \phi H(\mathcal{S})$.

Thus: $\forall k \in \{1,\ldots,r\}$ $H(S_k|\{S_1,\ldots,S_r\}\setminus\{S_k\}) \geq \phi H(\mathcal{S})$. This achieves our proof. □

Theorem 2. *Suppose that there exists a deterministic algorithm for changing a (r,n)-TSS scheme $\mathcal{T}_1$ to (r',n)-TSS scheme $\mathcal{T}_2$. Assume that $\mathcal{T}_1$ is a (ϕ_1,ρ_1) SRDCRRC-scheme and $\mathcal{T}_2$ is a (ϕ_2,ρ_2) SRDCRRC-scheme. We have:*
$$\min(\rho_1,\rho_2) \times \min(\phi_1,\phi_2) \leq \frac{r}{r'}$$

Proof. The dealer algorithm of $\mathcal{T}_2$ is the dealer algorithm of $\mathcal{T}_1$ followed by the deterministic algorithm $\mathcal{A}$ to change the threshold. According to Lemma 3, we have: $H(\alpha) \geq r'\phi_2 H(\mathcal{S})$.

Let $S_{1,i}$ denote the i-th share of $\mathcal{T}_1$. According to Lemma 2, we have:
$$H(S_{1,1},\ldots,S_{1,r}) = H(\alpha) \geq r'\phi_2 H(\mathcal{S})$$

So:
$$\max_{1\leq i\leq n} H(S_{1,i}) \geq \max_{1\leq i\leq r} H(S_{1,i}) \geq \frac{1}{r}\sum_{i=1}^{r} H(S_{1,i}) \geq \frac{1}{r}H(S_{1,1},\ldots,S_{1,r}) \geq \frac{r'\phi_2}{r}H(\mathcal{S})$$

Thus, we get:

$$\rho_1 \leq \frac{H(\mathcal{S})}{\max_{1\leq i \leq n} H(\mathcal{S}_{1,i})} \leq \frac{H(\mathcal{S})}{\frac{r'\phi_2}{r}H(\mathcal{S})} \leq \frac{r}{r'\phi_2}$$

Therefore, we have:

$$\min(\rho_1, \rho_2) \times \min(\phi_1, \phi_2) \leq \rho_1 \phi_2 \leq \frac{r}{r'}$$

$\square$

Remark. Note that if both $\mathcal{T}_1$ and $\mathcal{T}_2$ are perfect secret-sharing schemes, then the information rate of $\langle \mathcal{T}_1, \mathcal{T}_2 \rangle$ is at most $\frac{r}{r'}$. Similarly, if both $\mathcal{T}_1$ and $\mathcal{T}_2$ have shares as large as the secret, then the security rate of $\langle \mathcal{T}_1, \mathcal{T}_2 \rangle$ is at most $\frac{r}{r'}$.

4 Threshold Changeability for CRT Secret-Sharing Schemes

4.1 CRT Secret Sharing Scheme

We now describe the CRT secret sharing scheme presented in [1]. Denote $\mathfrak{S}_i$ the set of all i-subsets of $\{1, \ldots, n\}$. A set of pairwise coprime integers $\{p, m_1, \ldots, m_n\}$ is chosen subject to the following:

$$\exists M : \left(\forall S \in \mathfrak{S}_r \prod_{i \in S} m_i \geq M \right) \text{ and } \left(\forall S \in \mathfrak{S}_{r-1} \prod_{i \in S} m_i \leq \frac{M}{p} \right)$$

The reader may notice that the original definition by [1] is slightly different. However, it can be shown that both definitions are equivalent.

Dealer. Suppose the secret value is s, we can assume that $0 \leq s < p$. Selecting a random integer A in $[0, \frac{M}{p} - 1]$ and set $y = s + Ap$. The set of shadows is $(y_1, \ldots, y_n)$, where $y_i = y \bmod m_i$ for $i \in \{1, \ldots, n\}$.

Combiner. To recover secret s, it clearly suffices to find y. If $y_{i_1}, \ldots, y_{i_r}$ are known, then y is known modulo $\mathcal{N}_1 = \prod_{j=1}^{r} m_{i_j}$ (CRT). As $\mathcal{N}_1 \geq M$, this uniquely determines y and thus s. On the other hand, if only $r - 1$ shadows were known, essentially no information about the key can be recovered. If $y_{i_1}, \ldots, y_{i_{r-1}}$ are known, then we have the value of y modulo $\mathcal{N}_2 = \prod_{j=1}^{r-1} m_{i_j}$. Since $\frac{M}{\mathcal{N}_2} \geq p$ and $\gcd(\mathcal{N}_2, p) = 1$, the collection of numbers n_i with $n_i \equiv y \pmod{\mathcal{N}_2}$ and $n_i \leq M$ cover all congruence classes modulo p, with each class containing at most one more or one less n_i than any other class.

The CRT sharing scheme described above is perfect. However, the construction that we will present in the next section will not as its security rate will not be equal to 1.

4.2 A New CRT-Based Secret Sharing Scheme

In this section, we present our construction which is a modification of the CRT secret sharing scheme. Let n be the number of participants, we choose a set of integers $\{p, q, m_1, \ldots, m_n, w_1, \ldots, w_n\}$ as follows:

1. $\gcd(m_i^{w_i}, m_j^{w_j}) = \gcd(m_i, m_j) = 1$ for $i \neq j$,
2. $\gcd(p, m_i^{w_i}) = \gcd(p, m_i) = 1$ for all i and $q|p$,
3. $\exists M : \left(\forall S \in \mathfrak{S}_r \prod_{i \in S} m_i^{w_i} \geq M \right)$ and $\left(\forall S \in \mathfrak{S}_{r-1} \prod_{i \in S} m_i^{w_i} \leq \frac{M}{q} \right)$.

Share Construction. Suppose the secret value is s, we can assume that $0 \leq s < p$. Selecting a random integer A in $[0, \frac{M}{p} - 1]$, and set $y = s + Ap$. The set of shadows are $(y_1, \ldots, y_n)$, where $y_i = y \bmod m_i^{w_i}$.

Secret Recovery. To recover secret s, it clearly suffices to find y. If $y_{i_1}, \ldots, y_{i_r}$ are known, then y is known modulo $N_1 = \prod_{j=1}^{r} m_{i_j}^{w_{i_j}}$ (CRT). As $N_1 \geq M$, this uniquely determines y and thus s.

On the other hand, if only $r - 1$ shadows were known, we can not uniquely determine the secret s. If $y_{i_1}, \ldots, y_{i_{r-1}}$ are known, then we have the value of y modulo $N_2 = \prod_{j=1}^{r-1} m_{i_j}^{w_{i_j}}$. Since $\frac{M}{N_2} \geq q$ and $\gcd(N_2, p) = 1$, the collection of numbers n_i with $n_i \equiv y \pmod{N_2}$ and $n_i \leq M$ cover all congruence classes modulo q, with each class containing at most one more or one less n_i than any other class. So, the security rate of the scheme:

$$\phi = \frac{H(x|y_{i_1}, y_{i_2}, \ldots, y_{i_{r-1}})}{H(x)} = \frac{\log q}{\log p} = \log_p q$$

The information rate of the scheme is:

$$\rho = \frac{\log p}{\log (\max\{m_i^{w_i} : 1 \leq i \leq n\})} = \frac{\log p}{\max\{w_i \log m_i : 1 \leq i \leq n\}}$$

Remark. If the parameters p and q are equal, we can set $m'_i = m_i^{w_i}$ such that $\{p, m'_1, \ldots, m'_n\}$ became a standard CRT secret sharing scheme defined in Sect. 4.1.

4.3 Construction of a Multiple Threshold Changeable Secret Sharing Scheme

For the threshold increase problem, the basic idea of our method is the following one: to **increase** the threshold parameter from r to $r' > r$, the participants **decrease** values from w_i to $w'_i < w_i$.

For any $\phi \in (0, 1]$, we can get a $(r_0 \rightarrow \mathbf{r}, n)$-threshold changeable scheme, such that the security rate is at least ϕ and the information rate ρ is at least $\frac{r_0}{r_c \phi}$. So, the bound constructed in Theorem 2 is met with equality.

Suppose the secret value is s, we can assume that $0 \leq s < B$. Let $w_{i,j}$ denote the value of w_i after the j-th transitions (the i-th share of scheme Π_j), for $1 \leq i \leq n$ and $0 \leq j \leq c$. Let ϕ be any element of $(0, 1]$. We construct our scheme as follows:

1. GC(s)(Public Parameter Generation)
   (a) Pick any integer $u \geq \left\lceil \frac{r_c^2}{r_0} \right\rceil$, set $k = r_0 \cdot u$ and $d = k \cdot r_c$.
   (b) Pick any integer $\ell \geq r_c + \frac{\phi \cdot \log_2 B}{k} + 2 \log_2 n$, choose $n+1$ distinct primes $m_0 < m_1 < \cdots < m_n$ from the interval $[2^\ell, 2^{\ell+1}]$. Estimates of the density of primes show that one could easily find primes m_i.
   (c) Pick a prime $\hat{m}$ from the interval $[2^{\ell-r_c}, 2^{\ell+1-r_c}]$.
   (d) Set $M = m_0^d$, $q = \hat{m}^k$ and $p = \hat{m}^{\frac{k}{\phi}}$ (we have: $p \geq 2^{(\ell-r_c)\frac{k}{\phi}} \geq 2^{\log_2 B} \geq B$).
   (e) Pick uniformly at random a number A in $[0, \frac{M}{p} - 1]$.
2. D(s,A)(Dealer Setup)
   To share secret s, set $y = s + Ap$. Set $w_{i,0} = \left\lceil \frac{d}{r_0} \right\rceil$, and the i-th initial share is $s_{i,0} = y \bmod m_i^{w_{i,0}}$.
3. E($s_{i,j}$)(Sub-share Generation)
   To generate sub-shares, let $s_{i,j}$ denote the i-th share of Π_j (the scheme after j changes). Set $w_{i,j+1} = \left\lceil \frac{d}{r_{j+1}} \right\rceil$ and the sub-share is: $s_{i,j+1} = s_{i,j} \bmod m_i^{w_{i,j+1}}$.
4. C($s_{i,S,j}$)(Combiner)
   To recover s, it clearly suffices to find y. Suppose $S = \{v_1, \ldots, v_{r_j}\}$, if $s_{v_1, j}, \ldots, s_{v_{r_j}, j}$ are known, by the Chinese remainder theorem, y is known modulo $N = \prod_{k=1}^{r_j} m_{v_k}^{w_{v_k, j}}$. We will prove that $N \geq p$ in the next section.

In this settings, only $p, q, m_1, \ldots, m_n, r_0, r_c$ need to be publicly known when setting up the original scheme. When the participants want to increase the threshold value r_i, they simply need to agree on the new value r_{i+1}. Each of them can compute his new share without any other interaction.

4.4 Scheme Analysis

In this section, we want to proof that our scheme satisfies the following three conditions at any step $j \in \{0, \ldots, c\}$.

C1 : $\forall (i, i') \in \{1, \ldots, n\} \times \{1, \ldots, n\}$ $\gcd(m_i^{w_{i,j}}, m_{i'}^{w_{i',j}}) = 1$ for $i \neq i'$,
C2 : $\forall i \in \{1, \ldots, n\}$ $\gcd(p, m_i^{w_{i,j}}) = 1$ and $q|p$,
C3 : $\left(\forall S \in \mathfrak{S}_{r_j} : \prod_{i \in S} m_i^{w_{i,j}} \geq M \right)$ and $\left(\forall S \in \mathfrak{S}_{r_j - 1} : \prod_{i \in S} m_i^{w_{i,j}} \leq \frac{M}{q} \right)$.

For any $j \in \{0, \ldots, c\}$, conditions C1 and C2 are trivially satisfied due to the choice of $p, q, m_1, \ldots, m_n$ by the dealer. The proofs of the following two lemmas can be found in Appendix A and Appendix B respectively.

Lemma 4. *For any $j \in \{0, \ldots, c\}$, Condition C3 is satisfied if the following two inequalities are satisfied:*

$$\forall S \in \mathfrak{S}_{r_j} \sum_{i \in S} w_{i,j} \geq d \tag{1}$$

$$\forall S \in \mathfrak{S}_{r_j - 1} \sum_{i \in S} w_{i,j} \leq d - k \tag{2}$$

Lemma 5. *For any $j \in \{0, \ldots, c\}$, (1) and (2) hold.*

Combining Lemma 4 and Lemma 5, we can prove that the scheme satisfies the three conditions C1, C2, C3 for any $j \in \{0, \ldots, c\}$.

Our construction is a $(r_0 \to \mathbf{r}, n)$-threshold changeable scheme. The following theorem shows that it has security rate ϕ and the information rate of the scheme ρ asymptotically equals to $\frac{r_0}{r_c \phi}$ for any $0 < \phi \leq 1$.

Theorem 3 (Security and Information Rate). *For any $0 < \phi \leq 1$, the $(r_0 \to \mathbf{r}, n)$-threshold changeable scheme has security rate ϕ. In addition, it asymptotically meets with equality the upper bounds in Theorem 2.*

Proof. For any $0 < \phi \leq 1$, the security rate of the scheme is:

$$\log_p q = \frac{\log q}{\log p} = \frac{\log \hat{m}^k}{\log \hat{m}^{\frac{k}{\phi}}} = \frac{k \log \hat{m}}{\frac{k}{\phi} \log \hat{m}} = \phi$$

The information rate ρ of the scheme is:

$$\rho \geq \min_{1 \leq i \leq n} \left\{ \frac{H(\mathcal{S})}{H(S_i)} \right\} \geq \frac{\log \left(\hat{m}^{\frac{k}{\phi}} \right)}{\max_{1 \leq i \leq n, 0 \leq j \leq c} \{\log (m_i^{w_{i,j}})\}} \geq \frac{(\ell - r_c) \frac{k}{\phi}}{\max_{1 \leq i \leq n, 0 \leq j \leq c} \{(\ell+1)w_{i,j}\}}$$

Therefore, we have:

$$\rho \geq \frac{(\ell - r_c) \frac{k}{\phi}}{(\ell+1) \left\lceil \frac{d}{r_0} \right\rceil} \geq \frac{\ell - r_c}{\ell + 1} \times \frac{r_0 \, k}{r_c \, k + r_0 - 1} \times \frac{1}{\phi} \geq \frac{r_0}{r_c \phi} \times \frac{\ell - r_c}{\ell + 1} \times \frac{k}{k + \frac{(r_0-1)}{r_c}}$$

For any $j \in \{0, \cdots, c\}$, it is easy to see that Π_j is a SRDCRRC-scheme (as defined in Sect.3.2). So, we have:

$$\rho \leq \frac{r_0}{r_c \phi}$$

If ℓ and k are asymptotically large, then we have:

$$\rho = \frac{r_0}{r_c \phi}$$

Note that "ℓ large" means that u is large. So, the upper bound in Theorem 2 is met with equality. □

4.5 Comparison

In this section, we want to compare our construction with previous methods from [10, 16, 13, 14, 7]. It should be remembered that ϕ is to be chosen during the set-up phase. We will see that for different values of ϕ, $\langle \Pi_0, \ldots, \Pi_c \rangle$ can be perfectly secure ($\phi = 1$), an asymptotically optimal ramp-scheme ($\phi = \frac{1}{T-C}$) or it can use a standard initial scheme as Π_0.

The secret sharing schemes designed in [10, 16] achieve perfect security before and after threshold modification. However, the share size has to be at least twice of the size of secret. Moreover, if we change to threshold c times, the information rate is at most $\frac{1}{c+1}$. We have the following result for our construction which is a direct consequence of Theorem 3.

Proposition 1 (Perfect Secure Changeable Scheme). *Let $\langle \Pi_0, \ldots, \Pi_c \rangle$ be a $(r_0 \to \boldsymbol{r}, n)$-threshold changeable scheme (where $\boldsymbol{r} = (r_1, \ldots, r_c)$) as constructed in Sect. 4.3. If we set $\phi = 1$, then $\langle \Pi_0, \ldots, \Pi_c \rangle$ has security rate 1 and information rate ρ such that:*

$$\frac{r_0}{r_c} \times \frac{\ell - r_c}{\ell + 1} \times \frac{k}{k + \frac{(r_0-1)}{r_c}} \leq \rho \leq \frac{r_0}{r_c}$$

This proposition involves that each (r_j, n)-TSS scheme Π_j achieves perfect secrecy (for any $j \in \{1, \ldots, c\}$). This means that the secret s is reconstructible from any r_j shares while no information about s leaks out from any set of $r_i - 1$ shadows.

Techniques in [13, 14] can be applied to existing schemes even if they were set up without consideration of future threshold increases. This is called the *standard initial scheme* approach. Unfortunately, those constructions have worse security. In addition, the secret recovery is only probabilistic. Our construction always guarantees s to be recovered.

We will show how to construct a threshold changeable secret sharing scheme $\langle \Pi_0, \ldots, \Pi_c \rangle$, where Π_0 is a standard CRT scheme (as defined in Sect. 4.1), for any given (r, n) and $\boldsymbol{r} = (r_0, \ldots, r_c)$ with $r_0 = r$. Our idea is to use the construction from Sect. 4.3 which is valid for any $(n, r_0, \ldots, r_c)$. We simply need to choose the construction parameter ϕ of $\langle \Pi_0, \ldots, \Pi_c \rangle$ so that Π_0 is standard scheme. We use the next two lemmas, the proofs of which are in Appendix C and Appendix D respectively.

Lemma 6. *For a $(r_0 \to \boldsymbol{r}, n)$-threshold changeable scheme $\langle \Pi_0, \ldots, \Pi_c \rangle$ where $\boldsymbol{r} = (r_1, \ldots, r_c)$, if we set $\phi = \frac{r_0}{r_c}$, then the initial scheme Π_0 has perfect security.*

Lemma 7. *For a $(r_0 \to \boldsymbol{r}, n)$-threshold changeable scheme $\langle \Pi_0, \ldots, \Pi_c \rangle$ where $\boldsymbol{r} = (r_1, \ldots, r_c)$, if we set $\phi = \frac{r_0}{r_c}$, then the initial scheme Π_0 is a standard CRT scheme.*

When a secret sharing is set-up, the dealer ignores what security level will be required in the future. Thus, the value r_c is a priori unknown. We would like to emphasized that this issue can be overcome easily. Indeed, when setting-up the scheme the dealer simply consider the pair $(r_0, r_{c'})$ where $r_{c'} = n$. He can construct $\langle \Pi_0, \Pi_{c'} \rangle$. When the different threshold updates occur, the participants can recursively construct $\langle \Pi_0, \Pi_1, \Pi_{c'} \rangle$, $\langle \Pi_0, \Pi_1, \Pi_2, \Pi_{c'} \rangle, \ldots, \langle \Pi_0, \Pi_1, \Pi_2, \ldots, \Pi_{c'} \rangle$ without interacting with the dealer. Note that this technique allows to design an (intermediate) SSS for any threshold value from $\{r_0 + 1, \ldots, n\}$.

We can use our method to construct an asymptotically optimal $(\mathcal{C}, \mathcal{T}, n)$-ramp scheme Π. The idea of our construction is the following one. Set $\phi = \frac{1}{\mathcal{T}-\mathcal{C}}$, and use our method from Sect. 4.3 to construct an $((\mathcal{C} - 1) \to \mathcal{T}, n)$-threshold changeable scheme

$\hat{\pi} = \langle \Pi_0, \Pi_1 \rangle$ where $\Pi = \Pi_1$. We have the following result, the proof of which is in Appendix E.

Theorem 4. *The secret sharing scheme Π constructed by the previous method is asymptotically an optimal $(\mathcal{C}, \mathcal{T}, n)$-ramp scheme.*

5 Conclusion

In this paper, we first studied the properties of threshold changeable schemes. We deduced some bounds on the information and security rates for these constructions. Second, we introduce a new CRT-based secret sharing, allowing multiple threshold changes after the original set-up phase without requiring any interactions with the dealer. One benefit of our construction is that the secret is always guaranteed to be recovered after any threshold update contrary to [13, 14] where recovery is only probabilistic. We also demonstrated that a suitable choice of the security rate ϕ led to a perfectly secure construction. As in [13, 14], a point of interest to further investigate is to deal with malicious participants who deviate from the threshold update protocol.

Acknowledgments

The authors would like to thank Professor Xiaoming Sun for valuable discussions on secret sharing. The authors are also grateful to the anonymous reviewers for their comments to improve the quality of this paper. The two authors' work was supported by the National Natural Science Foundation of China grant 60553001 and the National Basic Research Program of China grants 2007CB807900 and 2007CB807901. Christophe Tartary's research was also financed by the Ministry of Education of Singapore under grant T206B2204.

References

[1] Asmuth, C., Bloom, J.: A modular approach to key safeguarding. IEEE Transactions on Information Theory IT-29(2), 208–210 (1983)
[2] Barwick, S.G., Jackson, W.-A., Martin, K.M.: Updating the parameters of a threshold scheme by minimal broadcast. IEEE Transactions on Information Theory 51(2), 620–633 (2005)
[3] Blakley, G.R.: Safeguarding cryptographic keys. In: AFIPS 1979 National Computer Conference, New York, USA, June 1979, pp. 313–317. AFIPS Press (1979)
[4] Blakley, G.R., Meadows, C.: Security of ramp schemes. In: Blakely, G.R., Chaum, D. (eds.) CRYPTO 1984. LNCS, vol. 196, pp. 242–268. Springer, Heidelberg (1985)
[5] Blundo, C., Cresti, A., De Santis, A., Vaccaro, U.: Fully dynamic secret sharing schemes. In: Stinson, D.R. (ed.) CRYPTO 1993. LNCS, vol. 773, pp. 110–125. Springer, Heidelberg (1994)
[6] Desmedt, Y., Jajodia, S.: Redistributing secret shares to new access structures and its applications. Technical Report ISSE TR-97-01, George Mason university (1997)
[7] Jackson, W.-A., Martin, K.M.: A combinatorial interpretation of ramp schemes. Australasian Journal of Combinatorics 14, 51–60 (1996)

[8] Maeda, A., Miyaji, A., Tada, M.: Efficient and unconditionally secure verifiable threshold changeable scheme. In: Varadharajan, V., Mu, Y. (eds.) ACISP 2001. LNCS, vol. 2119, pp. 402–416. Springer, Heidelberg (2001)
[9] Martin, K.: Untrustworthy participants in secret sharing schemes. In: Cryptography and Coding III, vol. 45, pp. 255–264. Oxford University Press, Oxford (1993)
[10] Martin, K.M., Pieprzyk, J., Safavi-Naini, R., Wang, H.: Changing thresholds in the absence of secure channels. Australian Computer Journal 31, 34–43 (1999)
[11] Martin, K.M., Safavi-Naini, R., Wang, H.: Bounds and techniques for efficient redistribution of secret shares to new access structures. The Computer Journal 42(8), 638–649 (1999)
[12] Shamir, A.: How to share a secret. Communications of the ACM 22(11), 612–613 (1979)
[13] Steinfeld, R., Pieprzyk, J., Wang, H.: Lattice-based threshold-changeability for standard CRT secret-sharing schemes. Finite Field and their Applications 12, 653–680 (2006)
[14] Steinfeld, R., Wang, H., Pieprzyk, J.: Lattice-based threshold-changeability for standard Shamir secret-sharing schemes. In: Lee, P.J. (ed.) ASIACRYPT 2004. LNCS, vol. 3329, pp. 170–186. Springer, Heidelberg (2004)
[15] Stinson, D.R.: Cryptography: Theory and Practice. 3rd edn. Chapman & Hall/CRC, Boca Raton (2006)
[16] Tamura, Y., Tada, M., Okamoto, E.: Update of access structure in Shamir's (k, n) threshold scheme. In: The 1999 Symposium on Cryptography and Information Security, Kobe, Japan, January 1999, vol. I, pp. 469–474 (1999)

A   Proof of Lemma 4

Let S be any element of $\mathfrak{S}_{r_j}$. We have: $\forall i \in \{1, \ldots, n\}\, m_i > m_0$. Thus, if we have $\sum_{i \in S} w_{i,j} \geq d$ then we obtain: $\prod_{i \in S} m_i^{w_{i,j}} \geq m_0^d \geq M$.

Let S be any element of $\mathfrak{S}_{r-1}$. Assume that $\sum_{i \in S} w_{i,j} \leq d - k$. We get:

$$\prod_{i \in S} m_i^{w_{i,j}} \leq \prod_{i \in S} (2^{\ell+1})^{w_{i,j}} \leq 2^{(\ell+1)\sum_{i \in S} w_{i,j}} \leq 2^{(\ell+1)(d-k)} \leq \frac{2^{\ell d}}{\left(2^{\ell+1-\frac{d}{k}}\right)^k} \leq \frac{2^{\ell d}}{(2^{\ell+1-r_c})^k}$$

So, we have:

$$\prod_{i \in S} m_i^{w_{i,j}} \leq \frac{M}{q}$$

B   Proof of Lemma 5

We first demonstrate that (1) holds. Let j be any element of $\{0, \ldots, c\}$ and let S be any element of $\mathfrak{S}_{r_j}$. We have:

$$\sum_{i \in S} w_{i,j} \geq r_j \left\lceil \frac{d}{r_j} \right\rceil \geq d$$

Now, we want to demonstrate (2). We consider $j = c$. Let S be any element of $\mathfrak{S}_{r_c}$. We have:
$$\sum_{i \in S} w_{i,j} = (r_c - 1) \left\lceil \frac{d}{r_c} \right\rceil = (r_c - 1) k = d - k$$

Assume that $j \in \{0, \ldots, c-1\}$. We have:
$$k \geq r_0 \left\lceil \frac{r_c^2}{r_0} \right\rceil \geq r_0 \left\lceil \frac{1}{r_0} \times \frac{(r_{c-1} - 1)^2}{r_c - r_{c-1}} \right\rceil \geq \frac{(r_{c-1} - 1)^2}{r_c - r_{c-1}} \geq \frac{(r_j - 1)^2}{r_c - r_j}$$

In addition, we have the following bound:
$$\left\lceil \frac{d}{r_j} \right\rceil \leq \left\lfloor \frac{d + r_j - 1}{r_j} \right\rfloor \leq \frac{d + r_j - 1}{r_j}$$

Let S be any element of $\mathcal{S}_{r_j}$, we have:
$$\sum_{i \in S} w_{i,j} \leq (r_j - 1) \left\lceil \frac{d}{r_j} \right\rceil$$
$$\leq (r_j - 1) \frac{d + r_j - 1}{r_j}$$
$$\leq \frac{(r_j - 1)(k\,r_c + r_j - 1)}{r_j}$$
$$\leq k\,r_c - \frac{k\,r_c - r_j^2 + 2r_j - 1}{r_j}$$
$$\leq d - \frac{k\,r_c - (r_j - 1)^2}{r_j}$$
$$\leq d - k \left(\frac{r_c}{r_j} - \frac{(r_j - 1)^2}{k\,r_j} \right)$$

If $r_j = 1$ then, we have:
$$\sum_{i \in S} w_{i,j} \leq d - k \frac{r_c}{r_j} \leq d - k$$

Otherwise, we have:
$$\sum_{i \in S} w_{i,j} \leq d - k \left(\frac{r_c}{r_j} - \frac{(r_j - 1)^2}{\frac{(r_j-1)^2}{r_c - r_j} r_j} \right) \leq d - k$$

C Proof of Lemma 6

Let S be any element of $\mathfrak{S}_{r_0 - 1}$. Firstly, we want to prove that $\prod_{i \in S} m_i^{w_{i,0}} \leq \frac{M}{p}$. Since $r_0 | k$, we have $r_0 | d$. Therefore:
$$w_{i,0} = \left\lceil \frac{d}{r_0} \right\rceil = \frac{d}{r_0}$$

We get:
$$\sum_{i\in S} w_{i,0} = (r_0-1)\frac{d}{r_0} = d - \frac{d}{r_0} = d - k\frac{r_c}{r_0}$$

We obtain:
$$\prod_{i\in S} m_i^{w_{i,0}} \le \prod_{i\in S}(2^{\ell+1})^{w_{i,0}} \le 2^{(\ell+1)\sum_{i\in S} w_{i,0}} \le 2^{(\ell+1)(d-k\frac{r_c}{r_0})} \le \frac{2^{\ell d}}{\left(2^{\ell+1-\frac{d}{(k\frac{r_c}{r_0})}}\right)^{k\frac{r_c}{r_0}}}$$

Finally, we have:
$$\prod_{i\in S} m_i^{w_{i,0}} \le \frac{2^{\ell d}}{\left(2^{\ell+1-\frac{d}{k}}\right)^{\frac{k}{\phi}}} \le \frac{M}{p}$$

If only $r_0 - 1$ shares $y_{i_1}, \ldots, y_{i_{r_0-1}}$ were known, then have have the value of y modulo $N_3 = \prod_{\lambda=1}^{r_0-1} m_{i_\lambda}^{w_{i_\lambda}}$. Since $N_3 \le \frac{M}{p}$ and $\gcd(N_3, p) = 1$, the collection of numbers n_i with $n_i \equiv y \bmod N_3$ and $n_i \le M$ cover all congruence classes mod p, with each class containing at most one more or one less n_i than any other class. Thus, no useful information(even probabilistic) is available without r shares. Therefore, the initial scheme Π_0 is perfect.

D Proof of Lemma 7

Set $m'_i = m_i^{w_{i,0}}$. Since $\{p, m_1, \ldots, m_n\}$ are pairwise coprime, we always have pairwise coprime integers $\{p, m'_1, \ldots, m'_n\}$. Now, we want to prove that the integers $\{p, m'_1, \ldots, m'_n\}$ satisfy the following conditions:

$$\left(\forall S \in \mathfrak{S}_r \ \prod_{i\in S} m'_i \ge M\right) \text{ and } \left(\forall S \in \mathfrak{S}_{r-1} \ \prod_{i\in S} m'_i \le \frac{M}{p}\right)$$

According to Lemma 4 and Lemma 5, we have:
$$\forall S \in \mathfrak{S}_r \quad \prod_{i\in S} m_i \ge M$$

Using the result in the proof of Lemma 6, we get:
$$\forall S \in \mathfrak{S}_{r-1} \quad \prod_{i\in S} m_i \le \frac{M}{p}$$

Therefore, Π_0 is a standard CRT scheme.

E Proof of Theorem 4

Let S_i denote the i-th share of Π. For $|\mathcal{A}| = \mathcal{R}, \mathcal{C} \leq \mathcal{R} \leq \mathcal{T}$, we have

$$H(\mathcal{S}|\mathcal{S}_\mathcal{A}) = \min\left\{1, \frac{\log\left(\frac{M}{\prod_{i\in A} m_i^k}\right)}{\log \hat{m}^{\frac{k}{\phi}}}\right\} H(\mathcal{S})$$

$$= \min\left\{1, \frac{d\log m_0 - \sum_{i\in A}(k\log m_i)}{\frac{k}{\phi}\log \hat{m}}\right\} H(\mathcal{S})$$

So, we have:

$$H(\mathcal{S}|\mathcal{S}_\mathcal{A}) \geq \min\left\{1, \frac{\ell d - \mathcal{R} k (\ell+1)}{k(\ell-\mathcal{T}+1)(\mathcal{T}-\mathcal{C})}\right\} H(\mathcal{S})$$

$$\geq \min\left\{1, \frac{\ell \mathcal{T} - \mathcal{R}(\ell+1)}{(\ell-\mathcal{T}+1)(\mathcal{T}-\mathcal{C})}\right\} H(\mathcal{S})$$

and:

$$H(\mathcal{S}|\mathcal{S}_\mathcal{A}) \leq \min\left\{1, \frac{(\ell+1)d - \mathcal{R} k \ell}{k(\ell-\mathcal{T})(\mathcal{T}-\mathcal{C})}\right\} H(\mathcal{S})$$

$$\leq \min\left\{1, \frac{(\ell+1)\mathcal{T} - \mathcal{R}\ell}{(\ell-\mathcal{T})(\mathcal{T}-\mathcal{C})}\right\} H(\mathcal{S})$$

If ℓ is asymptotically large, then we have:

$$\frac{H(\mathcal{S}|\mathcal{S}_\mathcal{A})}{H(\mathcal{S})} = \frac{\mathcal{T}-\mathcal{R}}{\mathcal{T}-\mathcal{C}}$$

Therefore, the information rate:

$$\rho = \frac{H(S_i)}{H(\mathcal{S})} = \frac{\log m_i^k}{\log \hat{m}^{\frac{k}{\phi}}} = \frac{k \log m_i}{\frac{k}{\phi}\log \hat{m}}$$

So, we have:

$$\frac{H(S_i)}{H(\mathcal{S})} \geq \frac{\ell}{(\mathcal{T}-\mathcal{C})(\ell-\mathcal{T}+1)}$$

and:
$$\frac{H(S_i)}{H(\mathcal{S})} \leq \frac{\ell+1}{(\mathcal{T}-\mathcal{C})(\ell-\mathcal{T})}$$

Finally, we deduce that, when ℓ is asymptotically large, we have:
$$\frac{H(S_i)}{H(\mathcal{S})} = \frac{1}{\mathcal{T}-\mathcal{C}}$$

Therefore, the scheme Π is an optimal ramp scheme.

Black-Box Constructions for Fully-Simulatable Oblivious Transfer Protocols

Huafei Zhu

C&S Department, I²R, A-STAR, Singapore
huafei@i2r.a-star.edu.sg

Abstract. This paper studies constructions of $\binom{k}{1}$ - oblivious transfer protocols in a black-box way. The security of $\binom{k}{1}$ - oblivious transfer protocols is defined in the real/ideal world simulation paradigm (i.e., the security employs the real/ideal world paradigm for both senders and receivers and thus our construction is fully-simulatable). The idea behind of our constructions is that we first extend the notion of privacy for defensible adversaries in the context of bit-transfer protocols by Ishai, Kushilevitz, Lindell and Petrank at STOC'2006 to the notion of privacy for defensible adversaries in the context of $\binom{k}{1}$-oblivious transfer protocols, and then propose black-box constructions of $\binom{k}{1}$- oblivious transfer protocols secure against defensible adversaries. Finally, we boost the security of our protocols in order to obtain protocols that are secure against malicious adversaries in the fully-simulatable paradigm. We prove that there exist protocols for secure $\binom{k}{1}$ - oblivious transfer without an honest majority and in the presence of static malicious adversaries that rely only on black-box access to a homomorphic encryption scheme. By applying the well-known results of Kilian, we further claim that there exist protocols for secure computation without an honest majority and in the presence of static malicious adversaries that rely only on black-box access to a homomorphic encryption scheme.

Keywords: Black-box constructions, defensible adversary, malicious adversary, oblivious transfer protocols.

1 Introduction

Notions of reducibility in a black-box way between cryptographic primitives are important. Impagliazzo and Rudich [9] observe that most implications in cryptography are proved using a reduction, where the primitive is treated as a black-box and they further show that if the primitive is secure in a black-box way then the construction is also secure. Starting from the seminal paper of Impagliazzo and Rudich, a rich line of works tries to draw the border between possibility and impossibility for black-box reductions in cryptology. For example, Simon [12] shows that no provable construction of a collision-free hash function can exist based solely on a black-box one-way permutation. This result can be viewed as a partial justification for the common practice of treating the collision-free hash function as a cryptographic primitive, rather than attempting to derive it from a weaker primitive. Gertner, Malkin, and Reingold [3] study the efficiency of constructions for pseudo-random generators and universal one-way hash functions based on black-box access to one-way permutations and the relationship between public key encryption and oblivious transfer in [2], [3] and [1]. Horvitz and Katz [7] study black-box constructions of commitments and show that their bounds are tight for the case of perfectly binding schemes in the framework of Impagliazzo and Rudich.

The benefit of black-box constructions is that in cases where previous constructions are non-black-box, the new black-box constructions will yield more efficient protocols that are simpler to describe and to implement. For example, the current non-black-box construction of GMW protocols [5] requires parties to prove in zero-knowledge statements that involve the computation of a trap-door permutation. These zero-knowledge protocols in turn invoke cryptographic primitive for every gate of a circuit computing the trap-door permutation. In contrast, a black-box construction of oblivious transfer from a trap-door permutation would make the number of invocations of the primitive independent of the complexity of implementing the primitive, thus making oblivious transfer more efficient.

Black-construction for secure oblivious transfer protocols is of theoretical interest due to its general importance for constructing general protocols for secure computation [13] and [10]. Very recently, Ishai, Kushilevitz, Lindell and Petrank [8] show a black-box construction of secure bit oblivious transfer protocol that is secure in the ideal/real world model using only black-box access to a family of enhanced trap-door permutations or a to a homomorphic public-key encryption scheme. The idea behind their implementation is that they begin by constructing oblivious transfer protocols that use only black-box access to an enhanced trapdoor permutation or a homomorphic encryption schemes but provide rather weak security guarantees (protocols that are secure in the presence of defensible adversaries) and then boost the security of these protocols in order to obtain protocols that are secure in the presence of malicious adversaries. Their black-construction for secure oblivious transfer protocols uses the $\binom{2}{1}$-oblivious transfer protocol that is implicit in [11]. As a result, the security proof of the protocols presented in [8] relies on the fact that the sender's input are two bits (see Appendix A for more details).

We further remark that this input restriction cannot be removed for the security proof of the schemes presented in [6] as well since the reduction of [6] from the semi-honest bit-oblivious transfer protocol to the defensible bit-oblivious transfer protocols uses the reduction of [8] as a subroutine. A well motivated research problem is thus to study secure oblivious transfer without the limitation of sender's input in a black-box way.

1.1 This Work

This paper studies constructions of $\binom{k}{1}$ - oblivious transfer protocols in a black-box way. The security of $\binom{k}{1}$ - oblivious transfer protocols is defined in the real/ideal world simulation paradigm. We stress that the security of protocols presented in this paper employs the real/ideal world paradigm for both senders and receivers and thus our construction is fully-simulatable. To achieve the goal, we first extend the notion of privacy for defensible adversaries in the context of bit-transfer protocols of [8] to the notion of privacy for defensible adversaries in the context of $\binom{k}{1}$-oblivious transfer protocols and then generalize the result of [8] to construct $\binom{k}{1}$- oblivious transfer that is provably secure in the real/ideal world model ([4], Chapter 7) in a black-box way. We prove the following statement:

Theorem: There exist protocols for secure $\binom{k}{1}$ - oblivious transfer without an honest majority and in the presence of static malicious adversaries that rely only on black-box access to a homomorphic encryption scheme.

Having constructed secure oblivious transfer protocols in a black-box way, it is suffice to apply the well-known results of Kilian [10] that shows that any functionality can be securely computed using black-box access to a secure oblivious transfer. We therefore have the following statement:

Corollary: There exist protocols for secure computation without an honest majority and in the presence of static malicious adversaries that rely only on black-box access to a homomorphic encryption scheme.

1.2 The Technique

To generalize $\binom{2}{1}$-oblivious transfer protocols presented in [8] to $\binom{k}{1}$- oblivious transfer protocols presented in this paper, we will first extend Kushilevitz-Ostrovsky protocol to the general case. That is, we will use linear combination of encryption $E(m_i)^{x_i} E(1)^{y_i}$ for each m_i ($0 \leq i \leq k-1$), where $\{m_i\}_{i=0}^{k-1}$ is the sender's input while (x_i, y_i) is a pair of receiver's random input. The main difference between our protocol and the Kushilevitz and Ostrovsky protocol is that a public/secret key pair (pk, sk) is generated by a sender in our implementation while a public/secret key pair (pk, sk) is generated by a receiver in the Kushilevitz and Ostrovsky protocol. We will argue that such a modification ensures the proposed $\binom{k}{1}$-oblivious transfer protocol secure against defensible adversaries (see Section 3 for more details) in a convenient way.

To boost the security of our protocol in order to obtain protocols that are secure against malicious adversaries in the fully-simulatable paradigm, we make use of the cut-and-choose technique so that if a malicious party is cheated then it will be caught with non-negligible probability. That is, we allow a sender S to choose a pair of keys $(pk, sk) \leftarrow G(1^n)$, and accesses to the encryption algorithm in a black-box way to obtain a cipher-text $e_j = E_{pk}(m_j)$ of the message m_j and then send e_j ($j = 0, \cdots, k-1$) and pk to the receiver R. For each e_j ($j = 0, \cdots, k-1$), the receiver R randomly chooses t strings $\{(x_{1,j}, y_{1,j}), \cdots, (x_{t,j}, y_{t,j})\}$ and computes $c_{i,j} = e_j^{x_{i,j}} E(1)^{y_{i,j}}$. R then randomly reorders all computed $\{c_{i,j}\}$ ($i=1, \cdots, t$ and $j=0, \cdots, k-1$) to generate a random matrix. S and R run a secure two-party coin tossing protocol that accesses a one-way function in a black-box way for generating a string of length tk, where t is a security parameter. The string r will be used to define a set of indices I

$=\{r_{i,j}=0\}$, where $i=1,\cdots,t$, $j=0,\cdots,k-1$. For every $(i,j)\in I$, the receiver R provides a defense $(x_{i,j},y_{i,j})$. At the end of the protocol, the receiver R sends an encryption of linear combination of a message (i.e., $E_{pk}(xm_\sigma+y)$ to S and obtains a decryption from S. Once R has a correct decryption at hand, it can extract m_σ from the received decryption with the help of auxiliary strings (x,y) generated previously by itself.

Road-Map: The rest of this paper is organized as follows: The notion of $\binom{k}{1}$-oblivious transfer protocols secure against defeasible adversaries is introduced and formalized in Section 2. We provide black-box constructions for fully-simulatable $\binom{k}{1}$-oblivious transfer protocols secure against static (yet malicious) adversaries in the real/ideal world paradigm (based on the protocols that are secure against defensible adversaries) in Section 3. We conclude our work in Section 4.

2 Oblivious Transfer Protocols

A $\binom{k}{1}$ - oblivious transfer functionality is formally defined as a function f with two inputs and one output. The first input is a k-tuple message $\overline{m}=(m_0,\cdots,m_{k-1})$, and the second input is an index $\sigma\in\{0,\cdots,k-1\}$. The output is the message m_σ. That is, the sender S, inputs $(m_0,\cdots,m_{k-1})$ and receives no output. In contrast, the receiver R, inputs σ and receives m_σ. By $f(\overline{m},\sigma)$, we denote $(\perp,m_\sigma)$.

2.1 Security in the Presence of Defensible Adversaries

In this section we construct a $\binom{k}{1}$ - oblivious transfer protocol that is secure in the presence of defensible adversaries. The notion of defensible adversary is first introduced and formalized by Ishai, Kushilevitz, Lindell and Petrank [8] in the context of bit-transfer protocols. Informally, a defensible adversary may arbitrarily deviate from the protocol specification. However, at the conclusion of the protocol execution, the adversary must be able to justify or defend by its behavior by presenting an input and a random tape such that the honest party with this input and random tape would behave in the same way as the adversary did. A protocol is private under defensible adversary behavior if it is private in the presence of such adversaries.

We now extend the notion of privacy for defensible adversaries in the context of bit-transfer protocols of [8] to the notion of privacy for defensible adversaries in the context of $\binom{k}{1}$-oblivious transfer protocols. Recall that the standard privacy definition of $\binom{k}{1}$-oblivious transfer protocols requires that the receiver in an oblivious transfer protocol is supposed to obtain one out of the k messages $(m_0,\cdots,m_{k-1})$ in the execution. However the rest values must remain secret. If an adversary's behavior is malicious and cannot provide a good defense[1], then

---
[1] A defense is an explanation of an adversary's behavior during the protocol execution. Such an explanation consists of an input and random tape, and a defense is **good** if an honest party, given that input and random tape, would have sent the same messages as the adversary did during the protocol execution.

no security is guaranteed. When considering defensible adversaries, the requirement is that as long as the adversary can provide a good defense, it can only learn one of k values.

Definition 1. *(good defense for a transcript t): Let t be the transcription of an execution of a protocol $\pi=(S,R)$ between an adversary A and an honest party X (either $X=S$ or $X=R$). Then we say that the pair (x, ρ_x) consists of a good defense by A, if for every l it holds that $\mathtt{sent}_l^A(t) = X(x, \rho_x, \mathtt{received}_{1,\cdots,l-1}^A(t))$.*

Privacy in the Presence of a Defensible Sender. In an oblivious transfer protocol, a sender is not supposed to learn anything about the receiver's input. This means that the sender should not be able to simultaneously present a good defense of its behavior and make a correct guess as to the value of the receiver's input. We define an experiment for a protocol π and an adversary A modelled by a polynomial size family of circuits $\{A_n\}_{n\in N}$.

Experiment $\mathbf{Expt}_\pi^S(A_n)$

1. Choose $\sigma \in \{0, \cdots, k-1\}$ uniformly at random;
2. Let ρ_R be a uniformly distributed random tape for R and let $t=<A_n, R(1^n, \sigma, \rho_R)>$;
3. Let $<(r, \rho_r), \tau>$ be the output of $A_n(t)$. The pair (r, ρ_r) consists of A_n's defense and τ is its guess for σ;
4. Output 1 if and only if (r, ρ_r) is a good defense by A_n for τ in π, and $\tau = \sigma$.

Definition 2. *Let $\pi=(S,R)$ be a $\binom{k}{1}$ - oblivious transfer protocol. We say that π is private in the presence of a defensible sender if for every polynomial size family of circuits $A=\{A_n\}_{n\in N}$ controlling R, for every polynomial $p(\cdot)$ and for all sufficiently large n's*

$$Pr[\mathit{Expt}_\pi^S(A_n) =1] < 1/k + 1/p(n)$$

Privacy in the Presence of a Defensible Receiver. We define an experiment for a protocol π and an adversary A modelled by a polynomial size family of circuits $\{A_n\}_{n\in N}$.

Experiment $\mathbf{Expt}_\pi^R(A_n)$

1. Choose $m_0, \cdots, m_{k-1}$;
2. Let ρ_S be a uniformly distributed random tape for S and let $t = <S(1^n, m_0, \cdots, m_{k-1}, \rho_S), A_n>$;
3. Let $<(r, \rho_r, \sigma), \tau>$ be the output of $A_n(t)$. The pair (r, ρ_r, σ) consists of A_n's defense and τ is its guess for a message m_r such that $r \neq \sigma$;
4. Output 1 if and only if (r, ρ_r, σ) is a good defense by A_n for τ in π, and $\tau = m_r \neq m_\sigma$.

Notice that by A_n's defense, it should have received m_σ. The challenge is therefore to guess the value of m_r ($r \neq \sigma$). If it cannot do this, then the sender's privacy is preserved.

Definition 3. *Let $\pi=(S,R)$ be a $\binom{k}{1}$ - oblivious transfer protocol. We say that π is private in the presence of a defensible receiver if for every polynomial size family of circuits $A=\{A_n\}_{n\in N}$ controlling R, for every polynomial $p(\cdot)$ and for all sufficiently large n's*

$$Pr[Expt^R_\pi(A_n) =1] < 1/k + 1/p(n)$$

Definition 4. *Let $\pi=(S,R)$ be a $\binom{k}{1}$ - oblivious transfer protocol. We say that π is defensible private if it is private in the presence of a defensible sender and a defensible receiver.*

2.2 Black-Box Access to Homomorphic Encryption Algorithm

We assume that the existence of public-key encryption scheme (G, E, D) that is semantically secure which has no decryption error and has the following homomorphic property.

- The plain-text is taken from a finite Abelian group $\mathcal{G}$ determined by the public key. Without loss of generality, throughout the paper, we simply assume that the group $\mathcal{G}$ is an additive group Z_p as that in [8];
- Given any public-key pk generated by the key generation algorithm G, and arbitrary two cipher-texts $c_i = E_{pk}(m_i)$ ($i = 1, 2$), it is possible to efficiently compute a valid encryption of the sum $E_{pk}(m_1 + m_2)$.

A protocol use an encryption in a black-box way means that it refers only to the input/output behavior of the encryption scheme. For any instance of a finite Abelian group $\mathcal{G}$ determined by the public key, we assume that given a triple of group elements (x, y, z) such that $z = mx + y$, it is easy for one to compute the unique group element m. Such an assumption does not rely on the code of the encryption/decryption algorithm.

2.3 Achieving Security against Defensible Adversaries

In this section, we provide a construction of a $\binom{k}{1}$- transfer protocol that is secure in the presence of defensible adversaries.

Our construction: The sender S has k strings $m_0, \cdots, m_{k-1}$; the receiver R has an index $\sigma \in \{0, \cdots, k-1\}$.

The protocol

- The sender S chooses a pair of keys $(pk, sk) \leftarrow G(1^n)$, and accesses to the encryption algorithm in a black-box way to obtain a cipher-text $e_j = E_{pk}(m_j)$ of the message m_j. The sender S sends e_j ($j = 0, \cdots, k-1$) and pk to the receiver R;

- The receiver R, randomly chooses x and y to compute $c = e_\sigma^x E(1)^y$, and sends c to S;
- The sender S sends a decryption λ of c to R;
- The receiver R computes m_σ from the received message λ with the auxiliary input strings (x, y).

Notice that if both S and R are honest, then R receives the correct output λ is of form $(m_\sigma x + y)$ defined over the finite Abelian group $\mathcal{G}$ (say Z_p) which is determined by the public key. We claim that

Theorem 1. *Assume that the encryption scheme (G, E, D) is semantically secure under chosen plain-text attack and has no decryption error, then the above $\binom{k}{1}$- oblivious transfer protocol is secure in the presence of the defensible adversaries.*

Proof. We consider the following two cases:

Case 1: Suppose that S is controlled by a defensible adversary $A = \{A_n\}$, we allow A_n to run a key generation algorithm G. A_n is given an encryption scheme (G, D, E) together with the secret key sk. Suppose now A_n receives a decryption query of a cipher-text c of form $e_\sigma^x E(1)^y$ from the honest receiver R, and A_n is able to guess the correct value m_σ with non-negligible advantage $1/p(n)$, i.e., $\Pr[\text{Expt}_\pi^R(A_n) = 1] < 1/k + 1/p(n)$. Notice that the event $\text{Expt}_\pi^R(A_n) = 1$ that happens with non-negligible advantage $1/p(n)$ means that A_n is able to simultaneously present a good defense of its behavior and make a correct guess as to the value of the receiver's input with non-negligible advantage $1/p(n)$. Notice that the probability that A_n can correctly guess the value σ given $m_\sigma x + y$ with the probability $1/p(n)$. Since the decryption scheme has no decryption error and thus the message m_σ is unconditionally hiding by the random strings x, y (m_σ in essence is a encrypted using a one time encryption scheme by the honest receiver), it follows that $p(n) \leq 1/2^n$.

Case 2: in case that R is controlled by the defensible adversary $A = \{A_n\}$, we allow A_n to run a key generation algorithm G. A_n is given an encryption scheme (G, D, E) but not the secret key sk. Notice that A_n's defense consists of (e_σ, $E(1)$, x, y) as well as m_σ. Since the underlying encryption scheme is semantically secure under chosen plain-text attack, it follows that A_n is able to decrypt one of the given k-tuple cipher-texts with $1/k + 1/p(n)$, where $1/p(n)$ is at most a negligible amount.

3 Black-Box Constructions of Oblivious Transfer Protocols in the Presence Malicious Adversaries

3.1 Adversarial Model

In this paper, we consider malicious adversaries who may arbitrarily deviate from the specified protocol. We however, consider the static corruption model, where one of the parties is adversarial while the other is honest, and this is fixed before the execution begins.

Execution in the Real World Model. In the real world, a malicious party may follow an arbitrary feasible strategy. Let π be a two-party protocol, and let $\overline{M}=(M_1, M_2)$ be a pair of non-uniform probabilistic polynomial time machines. We assume that such a pair is admissible meaning that for at least one $i \in \{1,2\}$ we have M_i is honest. The joint execution of π under $\overline{M}$ in the real model on inputs $\overline{m}=(m_0, \cdots, m_{k-1})$ and $\sigma \in \{0, \cdots, k-1\}$, denoted by $\text{REAL}_{\pi,\overline{M}}(\overline{m}, \sigma)$, is defined as the output of pair of M_1 and M_2 resulting from the protocol interaction.

Execution in the Ideal World Model. An ideal oblivious set transfer proceeds as follows:

- Inputs: The sender S obtains an input pair $\overline{m}=(m_0, \cdots, m_{k-1})$ with $|m_i|=|m_j|$, and the receiver R obtains an input $\sigma \in \{0, \cdots, k-1\}$.
- Send inputs to trusted party: An honest party always sends its inputs to the trust party without any modification. A malicious party may either abort, in which case it sends $\perp$ to the trust party, or sends some other input to the trusted party.
- If the trusted party receives $\perp$ from one of the parties, then it sends $\perp$ to both parties and halts. Otherwise, upon receiving some $(m'_0, \cdots, m'_{k-1})$ from S and σ from R, the trusted party sends m'_σ to R and halts.
- An honest party always outputs the message it has obtained from the trusted party. A malicious party may output an arbitrary function of its initial input and the message obtained from the trusted party.

By f we denote the oblivious transfer functionality and let $\overline{M}=(M_1, M_2)$ be a pair of non-uniform probabilistic expected polynomial-time machines which is admissible. Then the joint execution of f under $\overline{M}$ in the ideal world model, denoted by $\text{IDEAL}_{f,\overline{M}}(\overline{m}, \sigma)$, is defined as the output pair of M_1 and M_2 from the above ideal execution.

Definition 5. *Let f denote the functionality of oblivious transfer protocol and let π be a two-party protocol. Protocol π is said to be a secure oblivious transfer protocol if for every pair of admissible non-uniform probabilistic polynomial-time machines $\overline{A}=(A_1, A_2)$ for the real world model, there exists a pair of admissible non-uniform probabilistic expected polynomial-time time machines $\overline{B}=(B_1, B_2)$ for the ideal world, such that for every k-tuple message $\overline{m}=(m_0, \cdots, m_{k-1})$ of the same length, and for every index $\sigma \in \{0, \cdots, k-1\}$, $\text{IDEAL}_{f,\overline{B}}(\overline{m}, \sigma) \approx \text{REAL}_{\pi,\overline{M}}(\overline{m}, \sigma)$.*

3.2 Achieving Security against Malicious Adversaries

In this section we construct a $\binom{k}{1}$ - oblivious transfer protocol that is secure in the presence of malicious adversaries. The security achieved for malicious sender/receiver is according to the real/ideal world paradigm of security for secure computation. Our construction uses black-box access to a $\binom{k}{1}$- oblivious transfer protocol that is secure against defensible adversaries.

Our Construction. The sender S has k strings $m_0, \cdots, m_{k-1}$; the receiver R has an index $\sigma \in \{0, \cdots, k-1\}$.

1. The sender S chooses a pair of keys $(pk, sk) \leftarrow G(1^n)$, and accesses to the encryption algorithm in a black-box way to obtain a cipher-text $e_j = E_{pk}(m_j)$ of the message m_j. The sender S sends e_j $(j = 0, \cdots, k-1)$ and pk to the receiver R.
2. For each e_j $(j = 0, \cdots, k-1)$, the receiver R randomly chooses t strings $\{(x_{1,j}, y_{1,j}), \cdots, (x_{t,j}, y_{t,j})\}$ and computes $c_{i,j} = e_j^{x_{i,j}} E(1)^{y_{i,j}}$. R randomly reorders all computed $\{c_{i,j}\}$ ($i=1, \cdots, t$ and $j=0, \cdots, k-1$). By $M_{t \times k}$, we denote the randomized matrix of $\{c_{i,j}\}_{t \times k}$.

$$\begin{pmatrix} z_{1,0}, & z_{1,1}, & \cdots & z_{1,k-2}, & z_{1,k-1} \\ z_{2,0}, & z_{2,1}, & \cdots & z_{2,k-2}, & z_{2,k-1} \\ \cdots & \cdots & \cdots & \cdots & \cdots \\ z_{t,0}, & z_{t,1}, & \cdots & z_{t,k-2}, & z_{t,k-1} \end{pmatrix}$$

The receiver R sends the randomized matrix $M_{t \times k}$ to S.
3. S and R run a secure two-party coin tossing protocol that accesses a one-way function in a black-box way for generating a string of length tk: $r = ((r_{1,0}, \cdots, r_{1,k-1}), \cdots, (r_{t,0}, \cdots, r_{t,k-1}))$. The string r is used to define a set of indices $I = \{r_{i,j} = 0\}$, where $i=1, \cdots, t$, $j=0, \cdots, k-1$.
4. For every $(i,j) \in I$, the receiver R provides a defense $(x_{i,j}, y_{i,j})$.
5. S checks that for every $(i,j) \in I$, the received pair $(x_{i,j}, y_{i,j})$ constitutes a good defense by R for $M_{t \times k}$. If not, then S aborts and halts. Otherwise, it continues the next step.
6. R chooses $(i,j) \in I$ such that $z_{i,j} = c_{i^*, \sigma}$, where $c_{i^*, \sigma} = e_\sigma^{x_{i^*, \sigma}} E(1)^{y_{i^*, \sigma}}$, where $i^* \in \{1, \cdots, t\}$ and then sends $z_{i,j}$ to S.
7. S decrypts $z_{i,j}$ to $m_\sigma x_{i^*, \sigma} + y_{i^*, \sigma}$. By $\lambda_{i^*, \sigma}$, we denote $m_\sigma x_{i^*, \sigma} + y_{i^*, \sigma}$. S then sends $\lambda_{i^*, \sigma}$ to R.
8. R retrieves m_σ from the received string $\lambda_{i^*, \sigma}$ using the auxiliary strings $(x_{i^*, \sigma}, y_{i^*, \sigma})$.

Security in the Presence of Malicious Sender. We present a proof that protocol described above is secure in the presence of malicious senders. We present our analysis in the so-called hybrid model, where the honest party uses a trusted party to compute the coin-tossing functionality for them. We now describe the simulator Sim for $A = \{A_n\}$:

- S1) Simulator Sim receives k messages $e_0, e_1, \cdots, e_{k-1}$ from A_n;
- S2) Sim generates a random matrix $M_{t \times k}$ according to Step 2 in the protocol and sends $M_{t \times k}$ to A_n;

- S3) Sim chooses a random string $r \in \{0,1\}^{tk}$ and hands it to A_n, as if it is the output of the coin-tossing functionality, as sent by the trusted party. Let I be the index set derived from r. Sim then sends $(x_{i',j'}, y_{i',j'})$ to A_n such that $z_{i,j} = e_{j'}^{x_{i',j'}} E(1)^{y_{i',j'}}$ for every $(i,j) \in I$.
- S4) The simulator Sim chooses $z_{i,j}$ such that $(i,j) \notin I$ and obtains a message $\lambda_{i',j'}$ such that $E(\lambda_{i',j'}) = z_{i,j} = e_{j'}^{x_{i',j'}} E(1)^{y_{i',j'}}$ from which a decryption of $e_{j'}$ can be derived.
- S5) Sim rewinds A_n to the beginning of the step S3), and then chooses a new random string $\hat{r} \in \{0,1\}^{tk}$ with associated index set $\hat{I}$. We stress that r and $\hat{r}$ are independent random strings. This procedure is performed until Sim obtains every decryption of e_j (i.e., m_j) for $j = 0, \cdots, k-1$.
- S6) Sim sends $\{m_j\}_{j=0}^{k-1}$ to the trusted party and obtains m_σ from the trusted party, where $\sigma \in \{0, \cdots, k-1\}$.

Since the underlying $\binom{k}{1}$-oblivious transfer protocol is secure against defensible sender A_n, it follows that the joint output of Sim and the honest receiver R in the ideal model is computationally indistinguishable from the joint output of A_n and R in the real model.

Security in the Presence of Malicious Receiver. We present a proof that protocol described above is secure in the presence of malicious receivers. The intuition behind this proof is that the cut-of-choose technique forces an adversarial receiver A to be provide a valid request (if cheated, it can be caught with overwhelming probability). We now describe the simulator Sim for $A=\{A_n\}$:

- R1) Simulator Sim runs $G(1^n)$ to generate a pair of keys (pk, sk), and then produces k dummy encryptions $e_0, \cdots, e_{k-1}$;
- R2) Simulator Sim is given a garbled matrix $M_{t \times k}$ as that produced in the real protocol execution;
- R3) Simulator Sim chooses a random string $r \in \{0,1\}^{tk}$ and hands it to A_n, as if it is the output of the coin-tossing functionality, as sent by the trusted party. Let I be the index set derived from r. Upon receiving back pairs $(x_{i',j'}, y_{i',j'})$ for $(i,j) \in I$, simulator Sim checks that they are all valid. That is, simulator Sim checks that $(i,j) \in I$ and there exists a pair (i',j') such that $z_{i,j} = e_{j'}^{x_{i',j'}} E(1)^{y_{i',j'}}$ $(=c_{i',j'})$. If not, then it aborts just like the honest sender.
- R4) Simulator Sim rewinds A_n to the beginning of the previous step R3), and chooses a new random string $\hat{r} \in \{0,1\}^{tk}$ with associated index set $\hat{I}$. We stress that r and $\hat{r}$ are independent random strings. Sim then hands $\hat{r}$ to A_n, and sees if the receiving back pairs $(x_{\hat{i},\hat{j}}, y_{\hat{i},\hat{j}})$ are valid in the sense that $(i,j) \in \hat{I}$ and there exists a pair $(\hat{i},\hat{j})$ such that $z_{i,j} = e_{\hat{j}}^{x_{\hat{i},\hat{j}}} E(1)^{y_{\hat{i},\hat{j}}}$ $(=c_{\hat{i},\hat{j}})$. If not, then it aborts just like the honest sender.
- R5) Upon receiving a decryption request of $z_{i,j}$ such that $(i,j) \in I$, $(i,j) \notin \hat{I}$ from A_n, Sim retrieves σ from the previous opening of $z_{i,j} = e_\sigma^{x_{i',\sigma}} E(1)^{y_{i',\sigma}}$. Let T be the event such that Sim receives the decryption request for $z_{i,j}$ such

that $(i,j) \in I$, $(i,j) \notin \hat{I}$ from A_n. If the event T does not happen, then it repeats R4) until the event T occurs.
- R6) Sim sends σ to the trusted party and outputs what A_n does.

Since there is no output of the honest sender S, it is suffice here to show that the output of Sim in the ideal model is computationally indistinguishable from the output of A_n in the real model. In case that the event T occurs that happens at least with probability $1/4t$, the view of A_n in the simulation with Sim is computationally indistinguishable from its view in a real execution with the honest sender S. Since the underlying $\binom{k}{1}$ - oblivious transfer protocol is secure against defensible sender A_n, it follows that the joint output of Sim and the honest sender S in the ideal model is computationally indistinguishable from the joint output of A_n and S in the real model.

Combing the above results, we have the following claim immediately:

Theorem 2. *There exist protocols for secure $\binom{k}{1}$ - oblivious transfer without an honest majority and in the presence of static malicious adversaries that rely only on black-box access to a homomorphic encryption scheme.*

By applying the well-known results of Kilian [10], we further claim that:

Corollary 1. *There exist protocols for secure computation without an honest majority and in the presence of static malicious adversaries that rely only on black-box access to a homomorphic encryption scheme.*

4 Conclusion

In this paper, black-box constructions for fully-simulatable oblivious transfer protocols have been presented and analyzed. We have shown that our protocols are secure against malicious adversaries in the static adversarial model in the real/ideal world paradigm.

References

1. Choi, S., Dachman-Soled, D., Malkin, T., Wee, H.: Black-Box Construction of a Non-malleable Encryption Scheme from Any Semantically Secure One. In: Canetti, R. (ed.) TCC 2008. LNCS, vol. 4948, pp. 427–444. Springer, Heidelberg (2008)
2. Gertner, Y., Kannan, S., Malkin, T., Reingold, O., Viswanathan, M.: The relationship between public key encryption and oblivious transfer. In: FOCS 2000, pp. 325–335 (2000)
3. Gertner, Y., Malkin, T., Reingold, O.: Lower bounds on the efficiency of generic cryptographic constructions. In: Proceedings of the IEEE Symposium on Foundations of Computer Science, pp. 126–135 (2001)
4. Goldreich, O.: Foundations of Cryptography. Basic Applications, vol. 2. Cambridge University Press, Cambridge (2004)

5. Goldreich, O., Micali, S., Wigderson, A.: How to play any mental game or a completeness theorem for protocols with honest majority. In: STOC, pp. 218–229 (1987)
6. Haitner, I.: Semi-honest to Malicious Oblivious Transfer - The Black-Box Way. In: Canetti, R. (ed.) TCC 2008. LNCS, vol. 4948, pp. 412–426. Springer, Heidelberg (2008)
7. Horvitz, O., Katz, J.: Bounds on the efficiency of black-box commitment schemes. In: Caires, L., Italiano, G.F., Monteiro, L., Palamidessi, C., Yung, M. (eds.) ICALP 2005. LNCS, vol. 3580, pp. 128–139. Springer, Heidelberg (2005)
8. Ishai, Y., Kushilevitz, E., Lindell, Y., Petrank, E.: Black-box constructions for secure computation. In: STOC 2006, pp. 99–108 (2006)
9. Impagliazzo, R., Rudich, S.: Limits on the Provable Consequences of One-Way Permutations. In: STOC 1989, pp. 44–61 (1989)
10. Kilian, J.: Founding Cryptography on Oblivious Transfer. In: STOC 1988, pp. 20–31 (1988)
11. Kushilevitz, E., Ostrovsky, R.: Replication is NOT Needed: SINGLE Database, Computationally-Private Information Retrieval. In: FOCS 1997, pp. 364–373 (1997)
12. Simon, D.R.: Finding Collisions on a One-Way Street: Can Secure Hash Functions Be Based on General Assumptions? In: Nyberg, K. (ed.) EUROCRYPT 1998. LNCS, vol. 1403, pp. 334–345. Springer, Heidelberg (1998)
13. Yao, A.C.-C.: Protocols for Secure Computations. In: FOCS 1982, pp. 160–164 (1982)

Appendix A

The Kushilevitz and Ostrovsky protocol [11]

– Input: the sender S has a pair of bits (s_0, s_1); the receiver R has a bit r;
– The receiver R chooses a pair of keys (pk, sk) by running a key generation algorithm G of a homomorphic encryption E, computes $c = E_{pk}(m)$ and sends c and pk to the sender S;
– The sender uses the homomorphic property and its knowledge of s_0 and s_1 to compute a random encryption $c' = E_{pk}((1-r)s_0 + rs_1)$ and sends c' to the receiver;
– R computes and and outputs $s_r = D_{sk}(c')$.

Claim ([11] and [8]): Assume that the encryption scheme (G, E, D) is indistinguishable under the chosen plain-text attacks and has no decryption errors, The Kushilevitz and Ostrovsky protocol is private in the presence of defensible senders and private for random inputs in the presence of defensible receivers.

Skew Frobenius Map and Efficient Scalar Multiplication for Pairing–Based Cryptography

Yumi Sakemi[1], Yasuyuki Nogami[1], Katsuyuki Okeya[2], Hidehiro Kato[1], and Yoshitaka Morikawa[1]

[1] Okayama University,
3-1-1, Tsushima-naka, Okayama, 700-8530, Japan
{sakemi,nogami,kato,morikawa}@cne.okayama-u.ac.jp
[2] Hitachi, Ltd., Systems Development Laboratory,
292, Yoshida-cho, Tatsuka-ku, Yokohama, 244-0817, Japan
katsuyuki.okeya.ue@hitachi.com

Abstract. This paper considers a new skew Frobenius endomorphism with pairing–friendly elliptic curve $E(\mathbb{F}_p)$ defined over prime field $\mathbb{F}_p$. Then, using the new skew Frobenius map, an efficient scalar multiplication method for pairing–friendly elliptic curve $E(\mathbb{F}_p)$ is shown. According to the simulation result, a scalar multiplication by the proposed method with multi–exponentiation technique is about 40% faster than that by plain binary method.

1 Introduction

Pairing–based cryptographic applications such as ID–based cryptography [2] and group signature authentication [11] have received much attention. In general, pairing is a quite time–consuming operation [3], thus a lot of improvements have been done. For example, twisted Ate pairing [10] and Devegili's work [4] substantially improved Tate and Ate pairings, respectively. When one uses Barreto–Naehrig (BN) *pairing–friendly* elliptic curve whose embedding degree is 12, Ate pairing, for example, is defined as a bilinear map $\mathbb{G}_2 \times \mathbb{G}_1 \to \mathbb{G}_T$, where $\mathbb{G}_2 \subset E(\mathbb{F}_{p^{12}})$, $\mathbb{G}_1 \subset E(\mathbb{F}_p)$, and $\mathbb{G}_T \subset \mathbb{F}_{p^{12}}^*$. p denotes the characteristic. Among scalar multiplications in $\mathbb{G}_1$ and $\mathbb{G}_2$, and an exponentiation in $\mathbb{G}_T$, a scalar multiplication in $\mathbb{G}_1$ is carried out the fastest. Thus, pairing–based cryptographic applications tend to leverage scalar multiplications in $\mathbb{G}_1$. When the elliptic curve is defined over a certain extension field as $\mathbb{G}_2$, Frobenius endomorphism may be efficiently applied for accelerating scalar multiplication by which the number of elliptic curve doublings will be decreased [9]. However, when the definition field is a prime field as $\mathbb{G}_1$, few accelerating techniques have been proposed. Of course, well–known binary, non–adjacent form (NAF), and window methods are available [3]; however, usually they can not much decrease the number of elliptic curve doublings for scalar multiplication. For example, when the key length of elliptic curve cryptography (ECC) is 256–bit, about 256 elliptic curve doublings will be needed. This paper focuses on scalar multiplication on a certain *pairing–friendly* curve define over prime field such as BN curve [1].

Gallant et al. [6] introduced an efficient method for scalar multiplication on elliptic curve defined over prime field, that is denoted by $E(\mathbb{F}_p)$ in this paper. Let P be a rational point in $E(\mathbb{F}_p)$, the method considers a certain integer λ such that $[\lambda]P$ is efficiently computable by some endomorphism. For example, consider an elliptic curve in the form of $y^2 = x^3 + b$, $b \in \mathbb{F}_p$ as BN curve is, where p is the characteristic and satisfies $3 \mid (p-1)$. If there exists an integer λ such that $\lambda^2 + \lambda + 1 \equiv 0 \bmod r$, it is shown that a rational point $P(x_p, y_p) \in E(\mathbb{F}_p)$ satisfies $[\lambda]P = (\epsilon x_p, y_p)$ [6], where ϵ is a primitive third root of unity. In this case, ϵ belongs to $\mathbb{F}_p^*$. If such an *efficiently computable* endomorphism exists, λ–adic representation of scalar s can accelerate scalar multiplication $[s]P$. This paper extends the idea of Gallant et al. method (GLV method) [6] for pairing–friendly elliptic curves such as BN curve because it is shown that BN curve, for example, has such an efficiently computable endomorphism. Then, this paper shows that a more efficient scalar decomposition is given.

As a kind of endomorphisms, *skew* Frobenius endomorphism is known [9]. Conventional skew Frobenius map considers elliptic curve $E/\mathbb{F}_p$ and its quadratic twisted curve $E'/\mathbb{F}_q$ as $y^2 = x^3 + ax + b, a, b \in \mathbb{F}_p$ and $y^2 = x^3 + av^{-2}x + bv^{-3}$ with quadratic non residue $v \in \mathbb{F}_q$, respectively, where q is a power of p. Then, based on the computable isomorphic map between $E'(\mathbb{F}_{q^2})$ and $E(\mathbb{F}_{q^2})$, skew Frobenius map $\hat{\phi}(Q')$ of rational point Q' in $E'(\mathbb{F}_q)$ is given by

$$\hat{\phi}: \begin{cases} E'(\mathbb{F}_q) & \to E'(\mathbb{F}_q), \\ (x,y) & \mapsto (x^p v^{p-1}, y^p v^{3(p-1)/2}). \end{cases} \quad (1)$$

Then, since Q' satisfies $(\hat{\phi}^2 - [t]\hat{\phi} + [p])Q' = \mathcal{O}$, some of scalar multiplications in *subfield–twisted* curve $E'(\mathbb{F}_q)$ will be more efficiently carried out with $\hat{\phi}$–adic expansion of the scalar. Galbraith et al. [5] have shown an efficient scalar multiplication in such a *subfield–twisted* curve with the skew Frobenius endomorphism and GLV method. Note that the conventional skew Frobenius endomorphism is available for a certain twisted elliptic curve. In addition, the above relation is usually efficient when the scalar is larger than the characteristic. The idea shown in this paper considers the isomorphism inversely.

The main proposal of this paper is an efficient scalar multiplication on *pairing–friendly* elliptic curve $E(\mathbb{F}_p)$ defined over prime field $\mathbb{F}_p$ such as BN curve. First, let k and d be embedding degree and twist degree, respectively, this paper considers a new skew Frobenius endomorphism $\tilde{\phi}_{k/d} : E(\mathbb{F}_p) \to E(\mathbb{F}_p)$. Let the order r of $E(\mathbb{F}_p)$ be a prime, it is well–known that a group of the same order r exists in *subfield–twisted* elliptic curve $E'(\mathbb{F}_{p^{k/d}})$ and Devegili et al. [4]

accelerated Ate pairing with BN curve by using the isomorphic map between $E'(\mathbb{F}_{p^2})$ and $E(\mathbb{F}_{p^{12}})$, where the embedding and twist degrees of BN curve are 12 and 6, respectively [1]. On the other hand, the new skew Frobenius endomorphism $\tilde{\phi}_{k/d}$ considers the following procedure: 1) map $P \in E(\mathbb{F}_p)$ to $P' \in E'(\mathbb{F}_{p^k})$, 2) consider its Frobenius map $\phi_{k/d}(P')$ with respect to $\mathbb{F}_{p^{k/d}}$, 3) then inversely map $\phi_{k/d}(P') \in E'(\mathbb{F}_{p^k})$ to the corresponding rational point in $E(\mathbb{F}_p)$.

Next, using the new skew Frobenius map $\tilde{\phi}_{k/d}$, this paper accelerates scalar multiplication in $E(\mathbb{F}_p)$. For example, in the case of BN curve, $k/d = 2$ and it is shown that the following relation holds.

$$[6\chi^2 - 4\chi + 1]P = [(-2\chi + 1)p^2]P = [-2\chi + 1]\tilde{\phi}_2(P), \tag{2}$$

where χ is an integer by which characteristic p of BN curve is given as

$$p = 36\chi^4 - 36\chi^3 + 24\chi^2 - 6\chi + 1. \tag{3}$$

In this paper, it is shown that Eq.(2) gives a more efficient scalar decomposition than using GLV method. After that, this paper shows a simulation result. It shows that the proposed method with the new skew Frobenius endomorphism accelerates scalar multiplication on *pairing–friendly* elliptic curve. In detail, the proposed method achieves about 40% reduction compared to using plain binary method. Thus, it is shown that *pairing–friendly* elliptic curves also have some good potential for scalar multiplications in $E(\mathbb{F}_p)$. Note that well–known window and NAF methods can be additionally applied for the proposed method.

Throughout this paper, p and k denote the characteristic and embedding degree, respectively. $\mathbb{F}_{p^k}$ denotes k-th extension field over $\mathbb{F}_p$ and $\mathbb{F}_{p^k}^*$ denotes the multiplicative group in $\mathbb{F}_{p^k}$. $X \mid Y$ and $X \nmid Y$ mean that X divides and does not divide Y, respectively.

2 Fundamentals

This section briefly reviews elliptic curve, twist technique, skew Frobenius map, Ate pairing, and GLV scalar multiplication.

2.1 Elliptic Curve

Let $\mathbb{F}_p$ be prime field and E be an elliptic curve over $\mathbb{F}_p$ defined as

$$E: y^2 = x^3 + ax + b, \ a, b \in \mathbb{F}_p. \tag{4}$$

$E(\mathbb{F}_p)$ that is the set of rational points on the curve, including the *infinity point* $\mathcal{O}$, forms an additive Abelien group. Let $\#E(\mathbb{F}_p)$ be its order, consider a large prime r that divides $\#E(\mathbb{F}_p)$. The smallest positive integer k such that r divides $p^k - 1$ is especially called *embedding degree*. One can consider pairings such as Tate and Ate pairings by using $E(\mathbb{F}_{p^k})$. In general, $\#E(\mathbb{F}_p)$ is given as

$$\#E(\mathbb{F}_p) = p + 1 - t, \tag{5}$$

where t is the Frobenius trace of $E(\mathbb{F}_p)$.

2.2 Twist Technique

When embedding degree k is equal to $2e$, where e is a positive integer, from Eq.(4) the following quadratic–twisted elliptic curve E' is given.

$$E' : y^2 = x^3 + av^{-2}x + bv^{-3}, \ a, b \in \mathbb{F}_p, \tag{6}$$

where v is a quadratic non residue in $\mathbb{F}_{p^e}$. Then, between $E'(\mathbb{F}_{p^e})$ and $E(\mathbb{F}_{p^{2e}})$, the following isomorphism is given.

$$\psi_2 : \begin{cases} E'(\mathbb{F}_{p^e}) & \to E(\mathbb{F}_{p^{2e}}), \\ (x, y) & \mapsto (xv, yv^{3/2}). \end{cases} \tag{7}$$

In this case, E' is called *quadratic–twisted* curve.

In the same, when embedding degree k satisfies the following conditions, the twisted curves can be respectively considered.

- $k = 3e$ (cubic twist)

$$E : y^2 = x^3 + b, \ b \in \mathbb{F}_p, \tag{8a}$$

$$E' : y^2 = x^3 + bv^{-2}, \tag{8b}$$

where v is a cubic non residue in $\mathbb{F}_{p^e}$ and $3 \mid (p-1)$.

$$\psi_3 : \begin{cases} E'(\mathbb{F}_{p^e}) & \to E(\mathbb{F}_{p^{3e}}), \\ (x, y) & \mapsto (xv^{2/3}, yv). \end{cases} \tag{8c}$$

- $k = 4e$ (quatic twist)

$$E : y^2 = x^3 + ax, \ b \in \mathbb{F}_p, \tag{9a}$$

$$E' : y^2 = x^3 + av^{-1}x, \tag{9b}$$

where v is a quadratic non residue in $\mathbb{F}_{p^e}$ and $4 \mid (p-1)$.

$$\psi_4 : \begin{cases} E'(\mathbb{F}_{p^e}) & \to E(\mathbb{F}_{p^{4e}}), \\ (x, y) & \mapsto (xv^{1/2}, yv^{3/4}). \end{cases} \tag{9c}$$

- $k = 6e$ (sextic twist), Barreto–Naehrig (BN) curve [1] has this form.

$$E : y^2 = x^3 + b, \ b \in \mathbb{F}_p, \tag{10a}$$

$$E' : y^2 = x^3 + bv^{-1}, \tag{10b}$$

where v is a quadratic and cubic non residue in $\mathbb{F}_{p^e}$ and $3 \mid (p-1)$.

$$\psi_6 : \begin{cases} E'(\mathbb{F}_{p^e}) & \to E(\mathbb{F}_{p^{6e}}), \\ (x, y) & \mapsto (xv^{1/3}, yv^{1/2}). \end{cases} \tag{10c}$$

When one uses Barreto–Naehrig curve that is a class of *pairing-friendly* curve, one can apply quadratic/cubic/sextic twist because its embedding degree is 12. Of course, sextic twist is the most efficient for pairing calculation.

Eqs.(7), (8c), (9c), and (10c) are summarized as

$$\psi_d : \begin{cases} E'(\mathbb{F}_{p^e}) & \to E(\mathbb{F}_{p^{de}}), \\ (x, y) & \mapsto (xv^{2/d}, yv^{3/d}). \end{cases} \tag{11}$$

Thus, when twist degree d is even, x–coordinate $xv^{2/d}$ belongs to proper subfield $\mathbb{F}_{p^{k/2}}$ because of $v^{2/d} \in \mathbb{F}_{p^{k/2}}$. In addition, when $d = 2$ or 4, the coefficient of x of the twisted curve E' can be written as $av^{-4/d}$.

2.3 Conventional Skew Frobenius Map [9]

Consider subfield–twisted curve $E'(\mathbb{F}_{p^e})$ as introduced in **Sec.2.2**. The conventional skew Frobenius map $\hat{\phi}$ is defined as follows [9].

$$\hat{\phi} : \begin{cases} E'(\mathbb{F}_{p^e}) & \to E'(\mathbb{F}_{p^e}), \\ (x, y) & \mapsto (x^p v^{2(p-1)/d}, y^p v^{3(p-1)/d}), \end{cases} \tag{12}$$

where x and y are x–coordinate and y–coordinate of rational point, respectively. Let $[s]$ be scalar multiplication for rational point with scalar s as

$$[s]P = \sum_{i=0}^{s-1} P. \tag{13}$$

Then, for rational point $Q' \in E'(\mathbb{F}_{p^e})$, the following relation holds.

$$\left(\hat{\phi}^2 - [t]\hat{\phi} + [p] \right) Q' = \mathcal{O}. \tag{14}$$

This relation is sometimes useful for scalar multiplication in $E'(\mathbb{F}_{p^e})$. Galbraith et al. [5] have shown an efficient scalar multiplication for *subfield–twisted* elliptic curve $E'(\mathbb{F}_{p^e})$ with the conventional skew Frobenius endomorphism $\hat{\phi}$.

2.4 Ate Pairing and Twisted Curve

Let ϕ be Frobenius endomorphism over $\mathbb{F}_p$, i.e.,

$$\phi : \begin{cases} E(\mathbb{F}_{p^k}) & \to E(\mathbb{F}_{p^k}), \\ (x,y) & \mapsto (x^p, y^p). \end{cases} \quad (15)$$

Then, let $\mathbb{G}_1$ and $\mathbb{G}_2$ be

$$\mathbb{G}_1 = E[r] \cap \mathrm{Ker}(\phi - [1]), \quad (16\mathrm{a})$$
$$\mathbb{G}_2 = E[r] \cap \mathrm{Ker}(\phi - [p]), \quad (16\mathrm{b})$$

and let $P \in \mathbb{G}_1$ and $Q \in \mathbb{G}_2$, Ate pairing $\alpha(Q,P)$ is defined as

$$\alpha : \begin{cases} \mathbb{G}_2 \times \mathbb{G}_1 & \to \mathbb{F}_{p^k}^* / (\mathbb{F}_{p^k}^*)^r, \\ (P,Q) & \mapsto \alpha(Q,P), \end{cases} \quad (17)$$

where $E[r]$ denotes a subgroup of rational points of order r in $E(\mathbb{F}_{p^k})$.

As introduced in **Sec.2.2**, we have subfield–twisted curve $E'(\mathbb{F}_{p^e})$, where $k = de$ and d is the twist degree. Devegili et al. improved Ate pairing so as to use rational points $Q' \in E'(\mathbb{F}_{p^e})$ with $Q = \psi_d(Q')$ and $Q' = \psi_d^{-1}(Q)$ [4]. **Fig.1** shows the image of $\mathbb{G}_2$ and $\mathbb{G}_2'$. Corresponding to this relation, this paper proposes a new *skew* Frobenius endomorphism from another viewpoint. It is understood that the following relation holds for $Q' \in \mathbb{G}_2'$ [4].

$$\left(\hat{\phi} - [p]\right) Q' = \mathcal{O} \text{ and thus } \hat{\phi}(Q') = [p]Q'. \quad (18)$$

Because, inversely for $Q \in \mathbb{G}_2$, Ate pairing is explicitly based on

$$(\phi - [p])Q = \mathcal{O} \text{ and thus } \phi(Q) = [p]Q. \quad (19)$$

2.5 GLV Scalar Multiplication [6]

Frobenius and the *skew* Frobenius maps cannot be efficiently applied for a rational point in prime field elliptic curve $E(\mathbb{F}_p)$. For this problem, Gallant et al. [6] have introduced an efficient scalar multiplication method for $E(\mathbb{F}_p)$ *so–called* GLV method. It needs an efficiently computable endomorphism. This section extends the idea for pairing–friendly elliptic curves, especially Barreto–Naehrig (BN) curve in this paper. Consider integer λ such that $\lambda^2 + \lambda + 1 = 0 \bmod r$, where $r = p + 1 - t$. In general, the ratio that $x^2 + x + 1$ is irreducible mod r is $1/2$. However, in the case of BN curve, since the embedding degree of BN curve is 12, it always has two solutions as

$$\lambda = -p^2, \; p^4. \quad (20)$$

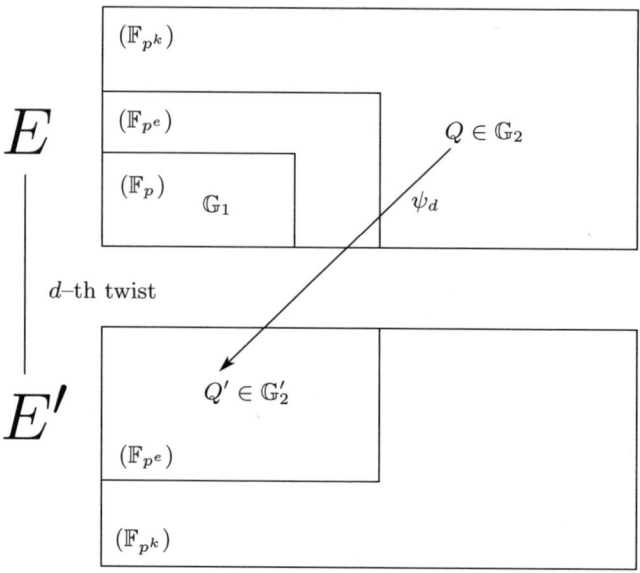

Fig. 1. Relation between $\mathbb{G}_2$ and $\mathbb{G}_2'$

Note that characteristic p and order r of BN curve are respectively given by

$$p(\chi) = 36\chi^4 - 36\chi^3 + 24\chi^2 - 6\chi + 1, \tag{21a}$$
$$r(\chi) = 36\chi^4 - 36\chi^3 + 18\chi^2 - 6\chi + 1, \tag{21b}$$

then $-p^2$ and p^4 are respectively given by

$$-p^2 \equiv -36\chi^3 + 18\chi^2 - 6\chi + 1 \bmod r, \tag{22a}$$
$$p^4 \equiv 36\chi^3 - 18\chi^2 + 6\chi^2 - 2 \bmod r, \tag{22b}$$

where χ is a certain integer. Thus, since λ given above is smaller than p, scalar multiplication $[s]P$, $P \in E(\mathbb{F}_p)$ is reduced to

$$[s]P = ([s_1][\lambda] + [s_2])P, \quad |s_1|, |s_2| < \lambda. \tag{23}$$

In addition, $[\lambda]P$ of $P(x_p, y_p)$ is simply calculated as

$$[\lambda]P = (\epsilon x_p, y_p), \tag{24}$$

where $\epsilon^3 = 1$. Since $6 \mid (p-1)$ for BN curve, $\epsilon \in \mathbb{F}_p^*$. Then, scalar multiplication $[s]P$ will be efficiently calculated with multi–exponentiation technique [3]. Since $\log_2 \lambda \approx (3/4)\log_2 r$ from Eq.(21b) and Eqs.(22), the improvement for the number of elliptic curve doublings is about 25%. The relation Eq.(22a) is also used for twisted Ate pairing [10]. This paper shows a more efficient scalar decomposition with a new skew Frobenius map.

Galbraith et al. have also referred to GLV method [5] in addition to the conventional skew Frobenius map $\hat{\phi}$. Then, it is shown that a scalar multiplication in $E'(\mathbb{F}_{p^e})$ is efficiently calculated. Their proposal is not for the improvement of a scalar multiplication in $E(\mathbb{F}_p)$. It is just the target of this paper.

3 Main Proposal

This section first shows a new *skew* Frobenius endomorphism for elliptic curve defined over prime field $\mathbb{F}_p$. Then, based on it, an efficient scalar multiplication method for pairing–friendly elliptic curve E is proposed. In detail, the proposed method accelerates a scalar multiplication in $E(\mathbb{F}_p)$. In this section, for instance, BN curve is especially dealt with as a pairing–friendly curve.

3.1 Twisted Rational Point

As introduced in **Sec.2.2** and **Sec.2.4**, *subfield–twisted* curve $E'(\mathbb{F}_{p^e})$ is given, where $k = de$ and d is the twist degree. This section considers twisted rational point $P' = \psi_d^{-1}(P), P \in \mathbb{G}_1 \subset E(\mathbb{F}_p)$, where P' belongs to $\mathbb{G}'_1 \subset E'(\mathbb{F}_{p^k})$. **Fig.2** shows a relation between $\mathbb{G}_1$ and $\mathbb{G}'_1$. In what follows, for instance, let the order $r = p + 1 - t$ of $E(\mathbb{F}_p)$ be a prime number. Then, the order of subgroup $\mathbb{G}'_1$ in $E'(\mathbb{F}_{p^k})$ that consists of twisted rational points such as P' is r. This paper considers a new *skew* Frobenius endomorphism from another viewpoint.

3.2 New Skew Frobenius Map

For $P \in E(\mathbb{F}_p) \subset E(\mathbb{F}_{p^k})$, consider $P' = \psi_d^{-1}(P) \in \mathbb{G}'_1 \subset E'(\mathbb{F}_{p^k})$. Note that the coefficients of the defining equation of *subfield–twisted* curve E' are in $\mathbb{F}_{p^e}$ as shown in Eq.(6), in the same of Eq.(18), P' satisfies

$$(\phi_e - [p^e])\, P' = \mathcal{O}, \tag{25}$$

where let P' be $(x_{P'}, y_{P'})$,

$$\phi_e(P') = (x_{P'}^{p^e}, y_{P'}^{p^e}). \tag{26}$$

Therefore, in the same of Eq.(12), for $\forall P(x_P, y_P) \in E(\mathbb{F}_p)$, a new skew Frobenius endomorphism $\tilde{\phi}_e$ is considered as

$$\tilde{\phi}_e : \begin{cases} E(\mathbb{F}_p) & \to E(\mathbb{F}_p), \\ (x, y) & \mapsto (x^p/v^{2(p^e-1)/d}, y^p/v^{3(p^e-1)/d}), \end{cases} \tag{27}$$

Then, the following relation holds.

$$\left(\tilde{\phi}_e - [p^e]\right) P = \mathcal{O} \text{ and thus } \tilde{\phi}_e(P) = [p^e]P. \tag{28}$$

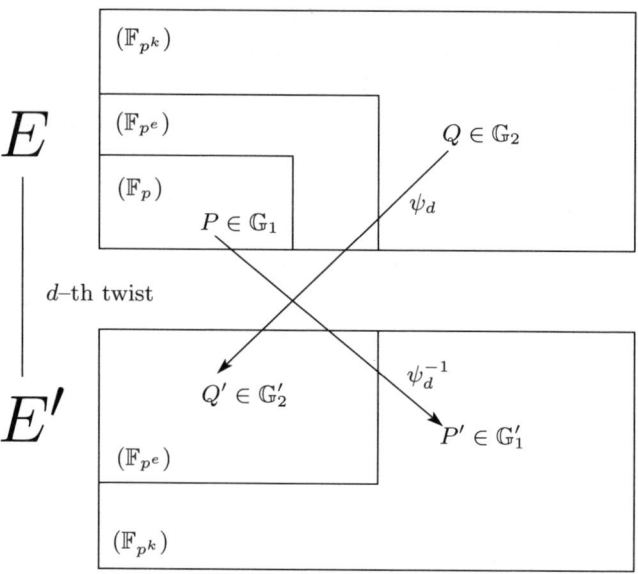

Fig. 2. Twisted rational points in $\mathbb{G}'_1$

When $d = 6$ and $e = 2$ as BN curve, $\tilde{\phi}_2^2(P) = [p^4]P$ and $\tilde{\phi}_2^4(P) = [p^8]P = [-p^2]P$. Thus, Eq.(24) can be also obtained. In other words, Eq.(24) is one of the cases of the new skew Frobenius endomorphism. It is implicitly understood that Eq.(28) is a case of computable endomorphisms discussed in Sect. VI of [8].

3.3 A Relation among χ, p, and $\tilde{\phi}_e$

This section derives a relation among χ, p, and $\tilde{\phi}_e$ that leads to an efficient scalar multiplication in $E(\mathbb{F}_p)$. Note the parameter settings of BN curve given by

$$p(\chi) = 36\chi^4 - 36\chi^3 + 24\chi^2 - 6\chi + 1, \tag{29a}$$

$$r(\chi) = 36\chi^4 - 36\chi^3 + 18\chi^2 - 6\chi + 1 = p(\chi) + 1 - t(\chi), \tag{29b}$$

$$t(\chi) = 6\chi^2 + 1. \tag{29c}$$

$P \in E(\mathbb{F}_p)$ satisfies

$$[r]P = [p + 1 - t]P = \mathcal{O}. \tag{29d}$$

As shown in **App.**A and from Eq.(28), we have

$$[6\chi^2 - 4\chi + 1]P = [(-2\chi + 1)p^2]P = [-2\chi + 1]\tilde{\phi}_2(P). \tag{30}$$

The most important point is that, as shown in Eq.(30), every exponent of powers of p needs to be a multiple of e. Then, it is easily found that Eq.(30) makes scalar multiplications in $E(\mathbb{F}_p)$ efficient. As shown below, Eq.(30) gives a more efficient scalar decomposition than using GLV method.

3.4 Scalar Multiplication in $E(\mathbb{F}_p)$ with $\tilde{\phi}_e$

Consider scalar multiplication $[s]P$, $P \in E(\mathbb{F}_p)$, where scalar s is smaller than r that is given by Eq.(21b). Let ν be $6\chi^2 - 4\chi + 1$, consider ν–adic representation of scalar s in the following form.

$$s = s_1\nu + s_2, \quad s_2 < \nu. \tag{31a}$$

In the case that $r > \nu^2$, s_1 may be larger than ν. For example, when χ is a positive integer, according to Eq.(21b), $r < \nu^2$. Note that ν is not a root of $x^2 + x + 1 \bmod r$. Substituting Eq.(30),

$$s \equiv (-2\chi + 1)s_1 p^2 + s_2 \bmod r. \tag{31b}$$

$(-2\chi + 1)s_1$ is mostly larger than ν, therefore using Eq.(30) once more again,

$$s \equiv (s_3\nu + s_4)\, p^2 + s_2 \equiv s_5 p^4 + s_4 p^2 + s_2 \bmod r, \tag{31c}$$

where s_4 and s_2 are smaller than ν. s_5 may not be smaller than ν but even in such a case it is not so large. In addition, since $p^4 \equiv p^2 - 1 \bmod r$ in this case,

$$s \equiv s_5(p^2 - 1) + s_4 p^2 + s_2 \equiv (s_4 + s_5)p^2 + (s_2 - s_5) \bmod r. \tag{31d}$$

Let $A = s_4 + s_5$ and $B = s_2 - s_5$, $[s]P$ is calculated by

$$[s]P = \left([A]\tilde{\phi}_e + [B]\right) P. \tag{32}$$

Thus, the number of doublings for a scalar multiplication is reduced to about $1/2$ because $\log_2 |A|$ and $\log_2 |B|$ are at most about $(1/2)\log_2 r$. According to Sec.2.5, the proposed method is more efficient than GLV method in this case.

3.5 Other Pairing–Friendly Curves

The proposed method is available not only for BN curve but also for a lot of other pairing–friendly curves. For example, when $k = 18$, characteristic p, order r and Frobenius trace t are given by using an integer variable χ as

$$p(\chi) = (\chi^8 + 5\chi^7 + 7\chi^6 + 37\chi^5 + 188\chi^4 \\ + 259\chi^3 + 343\chi^2 + 1763\chi + 2401)/21, \tag{33a}$$

$$r(\chi) = (\chi^6 + 37\chi^3 + 343)/343, \tag{33b}$$

$$t(\chi) = (\chi^4 + 16\chi + 7)/7. \tag{33c}$$

Then, note that $e = 3$, we have

$$-p^3 \equiv \chi^3 + 18 \bmod r, \quad \text{thus } [\chi^3 + 18]P = -\tilde{\phi}_e(P). \tag{34}$$

In this case, $-p^3$ is one of the solution of $\lambda^2 + \lambda + 1 \equiv 0 \bmod r$. Thus, the improvement by the proposed method is equivalent to that of GLV.

4 Simulation

This section especially considers BN curve with the parameter settings as

$$\chi = 2^{62} + 2^{35} + 2^{24}, \tag{35a}$$
$$E : y^2 = x^3 + 10. \tag{35b}$$

In addition, this simulation used *projective* coordinates for elliptic curve addition and doubling in $E(\mathbb{F}_p)$. The proposed scalar multiplication method was simulated on the computational environment shown in **Table** 1.

Table 1. Computational environment

CPU	Pentium(R)4* 3.0GHz
Cash size	2048KB
OS	Linux(R)† 2.6.21
Language	C
Compiler	gcc 4.2.1
Library	GNU MP 4.2.2 [7]

*Pentium(R) is a registered trademark of Intel Corporation. †Linux(R) is the registered trademark of Linus Torvalds in the U.S. and other countries.

The proposed scalar multiplication method for BN curve, for example, is concluded as **Algorithm 1** in which let smaller scalars A and B be positive numbers for simplicity. Multi–exponentiation technique [3] was applied in this simulation. **Table** 2 shows average timings simulated with a lot of random scalars of 254–bit.

As shown in **Table** 2, the new skew Frobenius map and the proposed scalar multiplication method with multi–exponentiation technique efficiently work. In detail, in the case of BN curve, a scalar multiplication by the proposed method with multi–exponentiation technique is about 40% and 30% faster than those by plain binary and GLV methods, respectively. Note that well–known window and NAF methods can be additionally applied for the proposed method [3].

Table 2. Timing of a scalar multiplication with 254–bit prime order BN curve

	[unit:ms]
plain binary method	3.96
GLV method with multi–exponentiation technique [3]	3.26
proposed method with multi–exponentiation technique [3]	**2.42**

* Average timing with random 254–bit scalars.

Algorithm 1. Proposed scalar multiplication for BN curve

Input : $s \in Z_r$, $P \in E(\mathbb{F}_p)$
Output : $R = [s]P$

Procedure :
    1.   determine scalars A, B such as Eq.(32)
    2. $R \leftarrow \mathcal{O}$, $C \leftarrow \tilde{\phi}_2(P)$, $D \leftarrow \tilde{\phi}_2(P) + P$
    3.   for $\max\left(\lfloor \log_2 A \rfloor, \lfloor \log_2 B \rfloor\right) \geq i \geq 0$,
    4.   if $A_i = 1$ & $B_i = 1$
    5. $R \leftarrow R + D$
    6.   else if $A_i = 1$ & $B_i = 0$
    7. $R \leftarrow R + C$
    8.   else if $A_i = 0$ & $B_i = 1$
    9. $R \leftarrow R + P$
   10. $R \leftarrow R + R$
   11. $i \leftarrow i - 1$
   12.   end for
   13.   output R

Remark: A_i and B_i denote i-th bit of A and B, respectively.

5 Conclusion

This paper has considered a new skew Frobenius endomorphism with pairing–friendly elliptic curve $E(\mathbb{F}_p)$ defined over prime field $\mathbb{F}_p$. Then, using the new skew Frobenius map, an efficient scalar multiplication method for a pairing–friendly elliptic curve $E(\mathbb{F}_p)$ was shown. According to the simulation result, a scalar multiplication by the proposed method with multi–exponentiation technique was about 40% faster than that by the plain binary method.

References

1. Barreto, P.S.L.M., Naehrig, M.: Pairing–Friendly. Elliptic Curves of Prime Order. In: Preneel, B., Tavares, S. (eds.) SAC 2005. LNCS, vol. 3897, pp. 319–331. Springer, Heidelberg (2006)
2. Boneh, D., Lynn, B., Shacham, H.: Short signatures from the Weil pairing. In: Boyd, C. (ed.) ASIACRYPT 2001. LNCS, vol. 2248, pp. 514–532. Springer, Heidelberg (2001)
3. Cohen, H., Frey, G.: Handbook of Elliptic and Hyperelliptic Curve Cryptography. In: Discrete Mathematics and Its Applications. Chapman & Hall CRC, Boca Raton (2005)
4. Devegili, A.J., Scott, M., Dahab, R.: Implementing Cryptographic Pairings over Barreto-Naehrig Curves. In: Takagi, T., Okamoto, T., Okamoto, E., Okamoto, T. (eds.) Pairing 2007. LNCS, vol. 4575, pp. 197–207. Springer, Heidelberg (2007)

5. Galbraith, S.D., Lin, X., Scott, M.: Endomorphisms for faster elliptic curve cryptography on general curves, IACR, ePrint, http://eprint.iacr.org/2008/194.pdf
6. Gallant, R.P., Lambert, R.J., Vanstone, S.A.: Faster Point Multiplication on Elliptic Curves with Efficient Endomorphisms. In: Kilian, J. (ed.) CRYPTO 2001. LNCS, vol. 2139, pp. 190–200. Springer, Heidelberg (2001)
7. GNU MP, http://gmplib.org/
8. Hess, F., Smart, N., Vercauteren, F.: The Eta Pairing Revisited. IEEE Trans. Information Theory, 4595–4602 (2006)
9. Iijima, T., Matsuo, K., Chao, J., Tsuji, S.: Construction of Frobenius maps of twists elliptic curves and its application to elliptic scalar multiplication. In: Proc. of SCIS 2002, IEICE, Japan, pp. 699–702 (2002),
http://lab.iisec.ac.jp/~matsuo_lab/pub/pdf/10b-3_1263.pdf
10. Matsuda, S., Kanayama, N., Hess, F., Okamoto, E.: Optimised Versions of the Ate and Twisted Ate Pairings. In: Galbraith, S. (ed.) Cryptography and Coding 2007. LNCS, vol. 4887, pp. 302–312. Springer, Heidelberg (2007)
11. Nakanishi, T., Funabiki, N.: Verifier-Local Revocation Group Signature Schemes with Backward Unlinkability from Bilinear Maps. In: Roy, B. (ed.) ASIACRYPT 2005. LNCS, vol. 3788, pp. 533–548. Springer, Heidelberg (2005)

A Proof of Eq.(30)

The important point is that, as shown in Eq.(30), every exponent of powers of p needs to be a multiple of e. In order to obtain such a relation, consider the following procedure. First, the following relation holds.

$$36\chi^4 - 36\chi^3 + 18\chi^2 - 6\chi + 1 \equiv 0 \bmod r. \tag{36}$$

From $p \equiv t - 1 \bmod r$,

$$p^2 - 6\chi p + 3p - 6\chi + 1 \equiv 0 \bmod r$$
$$(-6\chi + 3)p \equiv -p^2 + 6\chi - 1 \bmod r. \tag{37}$$

Squaring both sides of Eq.(37) leads to

$$(6\chi - 3)^2 p^2 \equiv (p^2 - 6\chi + 1)^2 \bmod r$$
$$36\chi^2 p^2 - 36\chi p^2 + 9p^2 \equiv p^4 - 12\chi p^2 + 2p^2 + 36\chi^2 - 12\chi + 1 \bmod r. \tag{38}$$

From $p^4 + 1 \equiv p^2 \bmod r$,

$$36\chi^2 p^2 - 36\chi p^2 + 9p^2 \equiv -12\chi p^2 + 3p^2 + 36\chi^2 - 12\chi \bmod r,$$
$$36\chi^2 (p^2 - 1) \equiv (24\chi - 6)p^2 - 12\chi \bmod r,$$
$$6\chi^2 (p^2 - 1) \equiv (4\chi - 1)p^2 - 2\chi \bmod r. \tag{39}$$

Multiplying Eq.(39) by $(p^2 - 1)^{-1}$,

$$6\chi^2 \equiv -(4\chi - 1)p^4 + 2\chi p^2$$
$$\equiv -(4\chi - 1)(p^2 - 1) + 2\chi p^2 \bmod r, \tag{40}$$

where using $p^4 - p^2 + 1 \equiv 0 \mod r$ and based on $\gcd(p^4 - p^2 + 1, p^2 - 1) = 1$, $(p^2 - 1)^{-1}$ is given as

$$p^4 - p^2 + 1 \equiv 0 \mod r,$$
$$-p^2(p^2 - 1) \equiv 1 \mod r,$$
$$(p^2 - 1)^{-1} \equiv -p^2 \mod r. \tag{41}$$

Finally, the following relation is obtained.

$$6\chi^2 - 4\chi + 1 \equiv (-2\chi + 1)p^2 \mod r. \tag{42}$$

Cryptanalysis of MV3 Stream Cipher

Mohammad Ali Orumiehchi[1], S. Fahimeh Mohebbipoor[1],
and Hossein Ghodosi[2]

[1] Zaeim Electronic Ind. R&D Department
No. 21, Nilo St., Brazil St., Vanak Sq., Tehran, Iran
{orumiehchi,mohebbipoor}@zaeim.co.ir
[2] School of Mathematics, Physics, and Information Technology,
James Cook University, Townsville, Qld 4811, Australia
hossein.ghodosi@jcu.edu.au

Abstract. MV3 is a word-based stream cipher, which was presented at the CT-RSA 2007 and SASC 2007 Conferences. Although it supports various key sizes of up to 8192 bits, the security claim of MV3 is that no attack faster than the exhaustive key search can be mounted for keys of length up to 256 bits.

This paper provides a distinguishing attack on the MV3 stream cipher. We will show that the key stream generated in MV3 is distinguishable from random sequences after observing approximately $2^{62.93}$ bits. That is, in the MV3 cipher with keys of length larger than 63 bits, it is possible to design a key search attack faster than the exhaustive search.

Keywords: Stream Ciphers, Cryptanalysis, Distinguishing Attack, MV3 Algorithm.

1 Introduction

Stream ciphers play an important role in practical cryptography; in particular, for encrypting long streams of data. In stream ciphers, the same key stream cannot be used to encrypt two different messages. To overcome this issue, stream ciphers are equipped with a key initialization algorithm that takes an Initial Vector (IV) and a relatively short key string as inputs. The algorithm produces an arbitrarily long key stream. Note that the key string is a long term key and must be kept secure, however, there is no security requirement for the initial vector, and a fresh IV should be chosen when encrypting a new message.

In 2007, Keller *et al.* [3,4] presented a word based stream cipher, called the MV3. Their aim in devising the MV3 cipher was to achieve efficiency by adapting byte-based stream ciphers, such as RC4, into a word based scenario. Although the MV3 cipher supports various key sizes of up to 8192 bits, the security claim is that no attack faster than the exhaustive key search can be mounted for keys of length up to 256 bits.

In this paper, we will show that the MV3 stream cipher is subject to a distinguishing attack that exploits the correlation between the two least significant output bits. In Section 2, we will provide a brief description of the MV3 cipher. In section 3, we will show how our distinguishing attack breaches the security claimed in MV3. We will summarise and conclude in Section 4.

2 A Brief Description of the MV3 Cipher

The main components of MV3 cipher are three vectors A, B, and C of length 32 double words each[1], and a table T that consists of 256 double words. In addition, there are publicly known indices i ($0 \leq i \leq 31$) and u ($0 \leq u \leq 255$), and secret indices j, c, and x, where x, c are double words, and j is an unsigned byte. An overview of the MV3 system is provided below.

2.1 Key Initialization

The key initialization algorithm has two phases. In the first phase, three vectors A, B, C, and table T are initialized with unsigned integer $0xEF$. The algorithm accepts the long term key string K of length *keylength*, which can be any multiple of 32 less than or equal to 8192 (the recommended size is at least 96). This phase, using the key string K, updates the entries of table T. In the second phase of the key initialization algorithm, the initial vector (IV) is used for updating the entries of table T. Since the long term key K is fixed, for every encryption, a fresh IV is chosen, and thus, only the second phase of the key initialization algorithm is performed. A description of the key initialization algorithm is not directly relevant to our analysis, thus it has been omitted.

2.2 Internal State

The internal state of the MV3 cipher is constantly updated via pseudo-random walks. To assure the randomness of the walk, designers of the MV3 cipher have considered the following problems:

Problem 1 – Graph Design: How to design graphs to ensure that their random walks are suitable for stream ciphers that work on arbitrary word sizes.

Problem 2 – Extraction: How to extract bits to output from the nodes visited by the walk.

Problem 3 – Sequencing: How to sequence the nodes visited by the walk so as to diminish any attacks that use relationships between successive outputs.

Solutions to these problems are reflected in the main loop of the MV3 cipher, shown in Figure 1.

Where ($w \ggg n$) denote the 32-bit double word w, is right-rotated by n bits, while $\vee$ and $\oplus$ denote the OR and XOR operations respectively. Also $x \cdot c$ and c^2 are 32-bit modular multiplications and a modular square respectively.

---
[1] A double word is an unsigned 32-bit integer. Note that in a main-frame computer, a 32-bit is a single-word boundary, while a double word consists of 64 bits.

```
1. Input:    length len
2. Output:   stream of length len
3.           repeat len/32 times
4.             for i = 0 to 31
5.               j ← j + (B[i] mod 256)
6.               x ← x + T[j]
7.               C[i] ← (x ≫ 8)
8.               output (x · c) ⊕ A[9i + 5] ⊕ (B[7i + 18] ≫ 16)
9.             end for
10.            u ← u + 1
11.            T[u] ← T[u] + (T[j] ≫ 13)
12.            c ← c + (A[0] ≫ 16)
13.            c ← c ∨ 1
14.            c ← c² (can be replaced by c ← c³)
15.            A ← B,   B ← C
16.          end repeat
```

Fig. 1. The main loop of the MV3 Cipher

2.3 Security Discussion

In [3,4], the authors considered the design rationale of their scheme in order to demonstrate the mechanism that provides the expected level of security. It is worth mentioning that they were aware that statement 13 of their algorithm (i.e. $c \leftarrow c \vee 1$) provides the least significant bit (LSB) of the index c to the attacker, who may use it for a distinguishing attack. Their justification for the necessity of having this operation is that, in the absence of this statement, the attacker (with probability 2^{-16}) can exploit cases where $c = 0$ (due to statement 14, in Figure 1).

3   Cryptanalysis of the MV3 Cipher

Stream ciphers are an example of *computationally secure* cryptosystems. Unlike *provably secure* cryptographic systems (e.g. the ElGamal [2] cryptosystem), in which the security of a cryptosystem is equivalent to solving an intractable problem, there is no precise criteria to measure the security of a stream cipher. Note that the designer of a computationally secure system may provide some evidence (in the form of attacks) in order to support their claim of security, but the fact remains that *they are not aware of any attack that can breach the security of their system*.

We will now show that the MV3 cipher is subject to a distinguishing attack. The attack utilizes statement 13 (i.e. $c \leftarrow c \vee 1$) in the main loop of MV3 algorithm . As has been predicted by the designers of MV3 cipher, this statement provides the least significant bit (LSB) of the index c, and can be used for applying a distinguishing attack.

3.1 Preliminaries

Let $Pr(X = Y)$ denote the probability of having equal values for two variables X and Y, and $[w]_0$ denote the LSB of a double word w. Also let $w_{(i)}$ denote the ith bit of the double word w.

Theorem 1. *In the main loop of the MV3 algorithm, for every 32 steps,*

$$Pr(T[i] = T[j]) = 2^{-8}.$$

where i and j are the random indices between 0 and 255.

Proof. Since table T has only 256 entries, for any random values of indices i and j we have
$$Pr(T[i] = T[j]) = Pr(i = j) = 2^{-8}.$$

Note that for randomly chosen double words w_1 and w_2, from all possible double words, we have $Pr(w_1 = w_2) = 2^{-32}$ (this does not apply to table T with 256 entries). According to the above theorem, the LSB of x is biased. This is because,

$$[x \cdot c]_0 \oplus [(x + T[j] + T[j]) \cdot c]_0 = 0.$$

That is, there exists some linear approximation relations in the output of the main loop.

Theorem 2. *The three vectors A, B, C have the same statistical properties.*

Proof. Obvious, due to statement number 15 of the main loop (see Figure 1).

Theorem 3. *[1] Given n 32-bit variables $x_1, x_2, \ldots, x_n$ and a 32-bit variable k, the following linear approximation*

$$\Gamma_i(x_1 + k) \oplus \Gamma_i(x_2 + k) \oplus \ldots \oplus \Gamma_i(x - n + k) = \Gamma_i(x_1 \oplus x_2 \oplus \ldots \oplus x_n)$$

holds with the probability of $\frac{n+2}{2(n+1)}$ for $i \gg 0$, where Γ_i denotes a linear masking vector over $GF(2)$ which has '1' only on bit positions i and $i+1$. Then $\Gamma_i \cdot x = x_i \oplus x_{i+1}$, where '$\cdot$' denotes the standard inner product.

Proof. See Appendix B.

3.2 A Distinguishing Attack on MV3

Our distinguishing attack explores the correlation between the two least significant bits of x, $A[.]$, and $(B[.] \ggg 16)$ in different times. Our attempt is to find the best bias for relation

$$\text{Output}^i \oplus \text{Output}^{i+1} \oplus \text{Output}^{i_1} \oplus \text{Output}^{i_1+1} = 0 \tag{1}$$

First, we consider $x_t, A[.]$, and $B[.]$ in four different times as the following relations:

$$\text{Output}^i = x^i \cdot c \oplus A[j] \oplus B[k] \quad (2)$$
$$\text{Output}^{i+1} = x^{i+1} \cdot c \oplus A[j'] \oplus B[k']$$
$$\text{Output}^{i_1} = x^{i_1} \cdot c \oplus A[j_1] \oplus B[k_1]$$
$$\text{Output}^{i_1+1} = x^{i_1+1} \cdot c \oplus A[j'_1] \oplus B[k'_1]$$

where $0 \leq i, i_1, j, j_1, j', j'_1, k, k_1, k', k'_1 \leq 31$.

We searched all possible values for i and i_1 in the set of relation (2), such that $|j - j_1|, |k - k_1|, |j' - j'_1|$, and $|k' - k'_1|$ are minimum. Our observation was that the best case is:

$$|j - j_1| = |k - k_1| = |j' - j'_1| = |k' - k'_1| = 2$$

On the other hand, the value x_t is defined as follows:

$$x_t = x_t \quad (3)$$
$$x_{t+1} = (x_t + T[j])$$
$$x_{t+2} = (x_t + T[j] + T[k])$$
$$\text{Const1} = T[j] + T[k]$$

Note that the set of relations in (3) is independent from j and k, since we do not consider any conditions on j and k. Moreover, the value x_τ ($\tau \neq t$) is also considered.

$$x_\tau = x_\tau \quad (4)$$
$$x_{\tau+1} = (x_\tau + T[o])$$
$$x_{\tau+2} = (x_\tau + T[o] + T[p])$$
$$\text{Const2} = T[o] + T[p]$$

However,

$$Pr[\text{Const1} = \text{Const2}] = \frac{2}{\binom{256}{2}} \approx 2^{-13.99}$$

which is far away from 2^{-32} for two 32-bit random sequences. Therefore, a biased relation can be considered as:

$$Pr\left([x_t \cdot c]_0 \oplus [(x_t + \text{Const1}) \cdot c]_0 \oplus [x_\tau \cdot c]_0 \oplus [(x_\tau + \text{Const2}) \cdot c]_0 = 0\right) = \frac{1}{2}(1 + 2^{-13.99}).$$

We can exploit this relation for two least significant bits, using Theorem 3:

$$Pr([x_t \cdot c]_{0,1} \oplus [(x_t + \text{Const1}) \cdot c]_{0,1} \oplus [x_\tau \cdot c]_{0,1} \oplus \quad (5)$$
$$[(x_\tau + \text{Const2}) \cdot c]_{0,1} = 0) \approx \frac{1}{2}(1 + 0.66 \times 2^{-13.99})$$

Table 1. All useful indices of x_t, A[.] and B[.]

Number of Relations	x_t		A[.]		B[.]	
	i	i_1	j	j_1	k	k_1
1	0	14	5	3	18	20
2	0	18	5	7	18	16
3	1	15	14	12	25	27
4	3	21	0	2	7	5
5	4	18	9	7	14	16
6	4	22	9	11	14	12
7	5	19	18	20	21	23
8	5	23	18	20	21	19
9	6	20	27	25	28	30
10	6	24	27	29	28	26
11	7	21	4	2	3	5
12	7	25	4	6	3	1
13	8	22	13	11	10	12
14	8	26	13	15	10	8
15	9	23	22	20	17	19
16	11	29	8	10	31	29
17	12	26	17	15	6	8
18	12	30	17	19	6	4
19	13	27	26	24	13	15
20	14	0	3	5	20	18
21	14	28	3	1	20	22
22	15	1	12	14	27	25
23	15	29	12	10	27	29
24	16	30	21	19	2	4

The relation (5) determines the correlation between $x_t \cdot c$, $(x_t + \text{Const1}) \cdot c$, $x_\tau \cdot c$, and $(x_\tau + \text{Const2}) \cdot c$ as t and τ are times, which are presented in Table 1.

Now, a total biased relation can be written as:

$$([x_i \cdot c] \oplus [(x_i + \text{Const1}) \cdot c] \oplus [x_{i_1} \cdot c] \oplus [(x_{i_1} + \text{Const2}) \cdot c])_{r,r+1} \oplus \quad (6)$$
$$([A_j] \oplus [A_j + \text{AConst1}] \oplus [A_{j_1}] \oplus [A_{j_1} + \text{AConst2}])_{r+7,r+8} \oplus$$
$$([B_k] \oplus [B_k + \text{BConst1}] \oplus [B_{k_1}] \oplus [B_{k_1} + \text{BConst2}])_{r+23,r+24} = 0$$

with probability

$$\frac{1}{2}\left(1 + 2^2 \times (\frac{2}{3})^3 \times 2^{-8} \times (2^{-13.99})^2\right) \approx \frac{1}{2} + 2^{-36.73},$$

where $[A_i]_{j,j+1}$ and $[B_i]_{j,j+1}$ are the jth and $j+1$th bits of the ith element of arrays A and B, respectively. AConst1, AConst2, BConst1, and BConst2 are constant values (as defined in relations 3 and 4). Indices i and i_1 are chosen from rows in Table 1, and $0 \leq r \leq 30$.

Considering the fact that for two independent probability distributions P_0 and P_1, if $|P_0 - P_1| = \frac{1}{d}$, the required number of samples for applying distinguishing attack is $n \approx \frac{1}{2}d^2$; the number of samples for performing the relation (6) is $\frac{1}{2}(2^{36.73})^2 = 2^{72.46}$. However, for each round, there are $31 \times 24 = 2^{9.53}$ relations, such as relation (6), since the number of pairs related in Table 1 is 24, and the number of consecutive 2-bits in a 32-bit word is 31. Therefore, the number of required samples for applying a distinguishing attack in MV3 cipher is given by:

$$n = 2^{-9.53} \times 2^{72.46} = 2^{62.93}.$$

That is, after observing approximately $2^{62.93}$ bits, the key stream generated in the MV3 cipher will be distinguished from a truly random sequence.

3.3 Other Biases

In addition to the above biased relation, some biased relations with different probabilities can be found. However, these biases are less than the above biased relation. We will now explain two other biased relations:

1. This bias uses the correlation between outputs in times t, $t+4$, τ, and $\tau + 4$ as follows:

$$[x_i \cdot c]_{0,1} \oplus [(x_i + \text{Const1}) \cdot c]_{0,1} \oplus [x_{i'} \cdot c]_{0,1} \oplus [(x_{i'} + \text{Const2}) \cdot c]_{0,1} \oplus \quad (7)$$
$$[A_j]_{7,8} \oplus [A_j + \text{AConst1}]_{7,8} \oplus [A_{j'}]_{7,8} \oplus [A_{j'} + \text{AConst2}]_{7,8} \oplus$$
$$[B_k]_{23,24} \oplus [B_k + \text{BConst1}]_{23,24} \oplus [B_{k'}]_{23,24} \oplus [B_{k'} + \text{BConst2}]_{23,24} = 0.$$

with probability

$$\frac{1}{2}\left(1 + 2^2 \times (\frac{2}{3})^3 \times (2^{-22.78})^3\right) \approx \frac{1}{2} + 2^{-69}.$$

For each round, there are $20 + 19 + \ldots + 2 + 1) = 2^{7.7}$ relations, such as relation (7). The number of samples required to perform a distinguishing attack is $2^{129.28}$ (For more details see Appendix A).

1. The other biased relation is achieved by considering outputs in times $t, t+1, t+2, t+3, \tau, \tau+1, \tau+2$, and $\tau+3$. We will have:

$$\text{Output}^t \oplus \text{Output}^{t+1} \oplus \text{Output}^{t+2} \oplus \text{Output}^{t+3} \oplus \quad (8)$$
$$\text{Output}^\tau \oplus \text{Output}^{\tau+1} \oplus \text{Output}^{\tau+2} \oplus \text{Output}^{\tau+3} = 0,$$

with probability $\frac{1}{2} + 2^{-58.31}$. The number of useful relations in each round is equal to $31 \times 50 = 2^{10.6}$. Hence, the required number of samples can be determined by $2^{105.2}$ (similar computations of Appendix A can be done for this case).

Table 2. Theoretical and experimental results related to the length of array T

	Length of array T	theoretical required bits	experimental required bits
1	16	$2^{30.83}$	2^{30}
2	32	$2^{39.2}$	2^{36}
3	48	$2^{44.45}$	2^{41}

3.4 Simulation Results

The presented results are supported by performing a distinguishing attack on a short version of the MV3 Algorithm. The only difference between the original version and the short version is the length of array T which is decreased from 256 to 16, 32, and 48. The simulation results are presented in Table 2. Note that with this arrangement, the length of the internal state is decreased to about 4500, 5000, and 5600 bits for the array lengths of 16, 32, and 48, respectively. As in theoretical results, for the array T with length 16, after observing approximately 2^{30} bits, the output is distinguishable from a random sequence.

4 Conclusions

In [3,4], it is claimed that on their proposed MV3 cipher, no attack faster than the exhaustive key search can be mounted for keys of length up to 256 bits.

We have proposed a distinguishing attack that could distinguish the MV3 output from a truly random sequence, after observing approximately $2^{62.93}$ output bits. This means that the security of MV3 cipher is not higher than 63 bits and theoretically the cipher is insecure for the recommended key size.

References

1. Cho, J., Pieprzyk, J.: Multiple Modular Additions and Crossword Puzzle Attack on NLSv2. In: Garay, J.A., Lenstra, A.K., Mambo, M., Peralta, R. (eds.) ISC 2007. LNCS, vol. 4779, pp. 230–248. Springer, Heidelberg (2007)
2. ElGamal, T.: A Public Key Cryptosystem and a Signature Scheme Based on Discrete Logarithms. IEEE Trans. on Inform. Theory IT-31, 469–472 (1985)
3. Keller, N., Miller, S., Mironov, I., Venkatesan, R.: MV3: A new word based stream cipher using rapid mixing and revolving buffers. In: Abe, M. (ed.) CT-RSA 2007. LNCS, vol. 4377, pp. 1–19. Springer, Heidelberg (2006)
4. Keller, N., Miller, S., Mironov, I., Venkatesan, R.: MV3: A new word based stream cipher using rapid mixing and revolving buffers. In: Third International Workshop on series of The State of the Art of Stream Ciphers (SASC 2007), pp. 275–286 (2007)

Appendix A

We searched all possible values for i and i_1 in the set of relation (8), such that, $|i - i_1|$, $|j - j_1|$, and $|k - k_1|$ are minimum. Our observation was that the best scenario is:
$$|i - i_1| = |j - j_1| = |k - k_1| = 4$$
Therefore, in 5 consecutive turns, the value x_t is as follows:

$$x_t = x_t$$
$$x_{t+1} = (x_t + T[j])$$
$$x_{t+2} = (x_t + T[j] + T[k])$$
$$x_{t+3} = (x_t + T[j] + T[k] + T[\ell])$$
$$x_{t+2} = (x_t + T[j] + T[k] + T[\ell] + T[m])$$
$$\text{Const1} = T[j] + T[k] + T[\ell] + T[m]$$

These sets of relations are independent from j, k, ℓ, and m, since we do not consider any conditions on these indices. Moreover, the value x_τ ($\tau \neq t$) is also considered.

$$x_\tau = x_\tau$$
$$x_{\tau+1} = (x_\tau + T[o])$$
$$x_{\tau+2} = (x_\tau + T[o] + T[p])$$
$$x_{\tau+2} = (x_\tau + T[o] + T[p] + T[q])$$
$$x_{\tau+2} = (x_\tau + T[o] + T[p] + T[q] + T[r])$$
$$\text{Const2} = T[o] + T[p] + T[q] + T[r]$$

However,
$$Pr[\text{Const1} = \text{Const2}] = \frac{4!}{\binom{256}{4}} \approx 2^{-22.78}.$$

Therefore, a biased relation can be considered as:

$$Pr\left([x_t \cdot c]_0 \oplus [(x_t + \text{Const1}) \cdot c]_0 \oplus [x_\tau \cdot c]_0 \oplus [(x_\tau + \text{Const2}) \cdot c]_0 = 0\right) = \frac{1}{2} + 2^{-22.78}.$$

We can utilize this relation for the two least significant bits, using Theorem 3:

$$Pr([x_t \cdot c]_{0,1} \oplus [(x_t + \text{Const1}) \cdot c]_{0,1} \oplus [x_\tau \cdot c]_{0,1} \oplus$$
$$[(x_\tau + \text{Const2}) \cdot c]_{0,1} = 0) \approx \frac{1}{2} + 0.66 \times 2^{-22.78}$$

The above relation determines the correlation between $x_t \cdot c$, $(x_t + \text{Const1}) \cdot c$, $x_\tau \cdot c$, and $(x_\tau + \text{Const2}) \cdot c$ as t and τ are times, which are presented in Table 3.

Table 3. All useful indices of x_t, A[.] and B[.]

nUmber of Relations	x_t		A[.]		B[.]	
	i	i_1	j	j_1	k	k_1
1	0	4	5	9	14	18
2	1	5	14	18	21	25
3	3	7	0	4	3	7
4	4	8	9	13	10	14
5	5	9	18	22	17	21
6	6	10	27	31	24	28
7	8	12	13	17	6	10
8	9	13	22	26	13	17
9	11	15	8	12	27	31
10	12	16	17	21	2	6
11	13	17	26	30	9	13
12	14	18	3	7	16	20
13	15	19	12	16	23	27
14	18	22	7	11	12	16
15	19	23	16	20	19	23
16	20	24	25	29	26	30
17	21	25	2	6	1	5
18	22	26	11	15	18	12
19	23	27	20	24	15	19
20	26	30	15	19	4	8
21	27	31	24	28	11	15

Appendix B

Proof of Theorem 3 – Following [1], we consider two cases: (i) when n is even, and (ii) when n is odd.

Case n is Even

The carry $R(x, y)$ generated in modular addition is defined as follows.

$$R(x,y)_{(0)} = x_{(0)}y_{(0)}$$
$$R(x,y)_{(i)} = x_{(i)}y_{(i)} \oplus \Sigma_{j=0}^{i-1} x_{(i)}y_{(i)} \Pi_{k=j+1}^{i}(x_{(k)} \oplus y_{k})), \quad i = 1, \ldots, 31$$

Let us denote

$$\Phi_{n,(i)} = R(x_1, k)_{(i)} \oplus R(x_2, k)_{(i)} \oplus \ldots \oplus R(x_n, k)_{i)}$$

By definition, $R(x, k)_{(i)} = x_{(i)} k_{(i)} \oplus (x_{(i)} \oplus k_{(i)}) R(x, k)_{(i-1)}$. Then,

$$\Phi_{n,(i)} = k_{(i)}(x_{1,(i)} \oplus x_{2,(i)} \oplus \ldots \oplus x_{n,(i)}) \oplus (x_{1,(i)} \oplus k_{(i)}) R(x_1, k)_{(i-1)} \oplus$$
$$((x_{2,(i)} \oplus k_{(i)}) R(x_2, k)_{(i-1)} \oplus \ldots \oplus (x_n \oplus k_{(i)}) R(x_n, k)_{(i-1)}$$

Thus $\Phi_{n,(i)}$ has the following properties:

- If $\oplus_{t=1}^{n} x_{t,(i)} = 0$, then $(x_{1,(i)}, x_{2,(i)}, \ldots, x_{n,(i)}, k_{(i)})$ and $((1 \oplus x_{1,(i)}), (1 \oplus x_{2,(i)}), \ldots, (1 \oplus x_{n,(i)}), (1 \oplus k_{(i)}))$ produce identical $\Phi_{n,(i)}$.
- If $\oplus_{t=1}^{n} x_{t,(i)} = 1$, then $\Phi_{n,(i)}$ by $(x_{1,(i)}, x_{2,(i)}, \ldots, x_{n,(i)}, k_{(i)})$ is complement to the one by $((1 \oplus x_{1,(i)}), (1 \oplus x_{2,(i)}), \ldots, (1 \oplus x_{n,(i)}), (1 \oplus k_{(i)}))$

Hence, by defining $P_{r,(i)} = Pr[\oplus_{t=1}^{r} R(x_t, k)_{(i-1)} = 0]$, the result is (where $P_0 = 1$):

$$P_{n,(i)} = \frac{1}{2}^{n+1} \left[\Sigma_{r=0}^{\frac{n}{2}} \binom{n}{2r} 2 P_{2r,(i-1)} + \Sigma_{r=0}^{\frac{n}{2}-1} \binom{n}{2r+1} \right]$$

$$= \frac{1}{4} + \frac{1}{2^n} \Sigma_{r=0}^{\frac{n}{2}} \binom{n}{2r} P_{2r,(i-1)}$$

Hence, for $i \gg 0$ we will have:

$$P_{n,(i)} \approx \frac{n+2}{2(n+1)}.$$

By definition, we can write $(x+k)_{(i)} = x_{(i)} \oplus k_{(i)} \oplus R(x, k)_{(i-1)}$. Thus, the result is:

$$\Gamma_i \cdot (x_1 + k) \oplus \Gamma_i \cdot (x_2 + k) \oplus \ldots \oplus \Gamma_i \cdot (x_n + k) \Gamma_i \cdot (x_1 \oplus x_2 \oplus \ldots \oplus x_n)$$
$$= \Gamma_{i-1} \cdot (R(x_1, k) \oplus R(x_2, k) \oplus \ldots R(x_n, k))$$
$$= k_{(i)}(x_{1,(i)} \oplus x_{2,(i)} \oplus \ldots \oplus x_{n,(i)}) \oplus (x_{1,(i)} \oplus k_{(i)} \oplus 1) R(x_1, k)_{(i-1)} \oplus$$
$$(x_{2,(i)} \oplus k_{(i)} \oplus 1) R(x_2, k)_{(i-1)} \oplus \ldots \oplus (x_{n,(i)} \oplus k_{(i)} \oplus 1) R(x_n, k)_{(i-1)}$$

As before, we can establish the following equation:

$$Pr\left[\Phi_{n,(i-1)} \oplus \Phi_{n,(i)} = 0\right] = \frac{1}{4} + \frac{1}{2^n} \Sigma_{r=0}^{\frac{n}{2}} \binom{n}{2r} P_{n-2r,(i-1)}$$

$$= \frac{1}{4} + \frac{1}{2^n} \Sigma_{r=0}^{\frac{n}{2}} \binom{n}{n-2r} P_{n-2r,(i-1)}$$

$$= P_{n,(i)}$$

Therefore, for $i \gg 0$, we have

$$Pr\left[\Phi_{n,(i-1)} \oplus \Phi_{n,(i)} = 0\right] \approx \frac{n+2}{2(n+1)}$$

Case n is Odd

If n is odd, $\Phi_{n,(i)}$ has the following properties.

- If $\oplus_{t=1}^{n} x_{t,(i)} = 0$, then $\Phi_{n,(i)}$ by $(x_{1,(i)}, x_{2,(i)}, \ldots, x_{n,(i)}, 0)$ is complement to the one by $((1 \oplus x_{1,(i)}), (1 \oplus x_{2,(i)}), \ldots, (1 \oplus x_{n,(i)}), 1)$.

- If $\oplus_{t=1}^{n} x_{t,(i)} = 1$, then $\Phi_{n,(i)}$ by $(x_{1,(i)}, x_{2,(i)}, \ldots, x_{n,(i)}, 0)$ is identical to the one by $((1 \oplus x_{1,(i)}), (1 \oplus x_{2,(i)}), \ldots, (1 \oplus x_{n,(i)}), 1)$.

Hence, we can establish the following equation

$$P_{n,(i)} = \frac{1}{2}^{n+1} \left[\Sigma_{r=0}^{\frac{n}{2}} \binom{n}{2r} + \Sigma_{r=0}^{\frac{n}{2}} \binom{n}{2r+1} 2P_{2r+1,(i-1)} \right]$$

$$= \frac{1}{4} + \frac{1}{2^n} \Sigma_{r=0}^{\frac{n}{2}} \binom{n}{2r+1} P_{2r+1,(i-1)}$$

Proceeding as before, we get

$$Pr\left[\Phi_{n,(i-1)} \oplus \Phi_{n,(i)}\right] = \frac{1}{4} + \frac{1}{2^n} \Sigma_{r=0}^{\frac{n}{2}} \binom{n}{2r+1} P_{n-2r-1,(i-1)}$$

$$= \frac{1}{4} + \frac{1}{2^n} \Sigma_{r=0}^{\frac{n}{2}} \binom{n}{n-2r-1} P_{n-2r-1,(i-1)}$$

Therefore, for $i \gg 0$, we have

$$Pr\left[\Phi_{n,(i-1)} \oplus \Phi_{n,(i)}\right] \approx \frac{n+2}{2(n+1)}$$

which completes the proof.

3D: A Three-Dimensional Block Cipher

Jorge Nakahara Jr.

École Polytechnique Fédérale de Lausanne
EPFL, 1015 Lausanne, Switzerland
jorge_nakahara@yahoo.com.br

Abstract. The main contribution of this paper is a new iterated secret-key block cipher called 3D, inspired by the AES cipher. The 3D cipher has an SPN design, operates on 512-bit blocks, uses 512-bit keys, iterates 22 rounds, and employs a 3-dimensional **state**, instead of the 2-dimensional matrix of the AES. The main innovation of 3D includes the multi-dimensional state, generalizing the design of Rijndael, and allowing block sizes beyond the 256-bit boundary. This features motivates the use of 3D as a building block for compression functions in hash functions, MAC and stream cipher constructions requiring large internal states. We explain the design decisions and discuss the security of 3D under several attack settings.

Keywords: block cipher design, 3-dimensional state.

1 Introduction

Secret-key ciphers, such as block and stream ciphers, are designed for fast encryption of large volumes of data. This paper describes a block cipher called 3D, inspired by the design of the AES [16] and with some innovative designs. In the AES, plaintext, ciphertext, subkeys and intermediate data blocks are represented by a 2-dimensional $4\times$ Nb **state matrix** of bytes, where Nb is the number of 32-bit words in a text block. For example, the state matrix of a $4t$-byte text block, $A = (a_0, a_1, a_2, \ldots, a_{4t-1})$, can be represented

$$\text{State matrix} = \begin{pmatrix} a_0 & a_4 & \cdots & a_{4t-4} \\ a_1 & a_5 & \cdots & a_{4t-3} \\ a_2 & a_6 & \cdots & a_{4t-2} \\ a_3 & a_7 & \cdots & a_{4t-1} \end{pmatrix}, \quad (1)$$

with bytes inserted columnwise. This state matrix provides not only a compact representation of the plaintext and ciphertext blocks, but was also motivated by two round transformations in Rijndael: **ShiftRows** and **MixColumns** [16]. The former explicitly operates on the rows of the state, while the latter operates only on the columns of the state.

In Rijndael, the block size is variable and ranges from 128 up to 256 bits in steps of 32 bits [16,26]. In the AES, complete text diffusion is achieved in two rounds, due to a combination of ShiftRows and MixColumns over a 4 × 4 state matrix. Key diffusion, though, takes longer depending on the key size. As the block size increases, it takes more rounds to guarantee fast diffusion for both text and key bits. This may be a reason for the upperbound of 256 bits for the block size in AES. This fact motivates our research, leading to 3D, with a larger block size (512 bits) which makes it attractive as a building block in the Miyaguchi-Preneel, Davies-Meyer or Matyas-Meyer-Oseas construction of compression functions (in this setting, it can be compared to SHA-512 [15]) in hash functions [29, p.340], and for stream modes of operation (OFB, CFB) whose security depends on the size of the internal cipher state, and in pseudorandom number generators [29, p.173].

This paper is organized as follows: Sect. 2 describes the new block cipher 3D; Sect. 3 describes the key schedule algorithm of 3D; Sect. 4 shows a security analyses of 3D; Sect. 5 estimates the software performance of 3D; Sect. 6 concludes the paper.

2 The 3D Block Cipher

The 3D block cipher operates on 512-bit blocks and uses 512-bit keys, both of which are represented as a 4 × 4 × 4 state of bytes (a 3-dimensional cube). The state for a 64-byte data block, $A = (a_0, a_1, \ldots, a_{63})$, is denoted

$$\text{State} = \begin{pmatrix} a_0 & a_4 & a_8 & a_{12} & a_{16} & a_{20} & a_{24} & a_{28} & a_{32} & a_{36} & a_{40} & a_{44} & a_{48} & a_{52} & a_{56} & a_{60} \\ a_1 & a_5 & a_9 & a_{13} & a_{17} & a_{21} & a_{25} & a_{29} & a_{33} & a_{37} & a_{41} & a_{45} & a_{49} & a_{53} & a_{57} & a_{61} \\ a_2 & a_6 & a_{10} & a_{14} & a_{18} & a_{22} & a_{26} & a_{30} & a_{34} & a_{38} & a_{42} & a_{46} & a_{50} & a_{54} & a_{58} & a_{62} \\ a_3 & a_7 & a_{11} & a_{15} & a_{19} & a_{23} & a_{27} & a_{31} & a_{35} & a_{39} & a_{43} & a_{47} & a_{51} & a_{55} & a_{59} & a_{63} \end{pmatrix}, \quad (2)$$

with bytes inserted columnwise. Each square set of 16 bytes is called a slice of the state (Fig. 1). Since all three dimensions of the state are equal, we set an orientation in (2): the set $(a_0, a_1, \ldots, a_{15})$ represents the front slice or first vertical slice; the set $(a_{16}, a_{17}, \ldots, a_{31})$ represents the second vertical slice, and so on. These slices are relevant for operation θ_1, described later. Other vertical slices exist, such as $(a_0, a_1, a_2, a_3, a_{16}, a_{17}, a_{18}, a_{19}, a_{32}, a_{33}, a_{34}, a_{35}, a_{48}, a_{49}, a_{50}, a_{51})$, which is relevant for operation θ_2, described later.

A reason for the 512-bit user key is that key-recovery attacks applied either on top or at the bottom of a given distinguisher will have to recover 512 subkey bits with a complexity of 2^{512}, which is about the exhaustive key search effort, and the same size of the codebook. If the user key was larger, say 1024 bits, shortcut attacks would become less expensive.

The round transformations in 3D are denoted:

- κ_i: a 4 × 4 × 4 state of bytes representing the 512-bit i-th round subkey is exclusive-ored bytewise to the i-th round state; the exclusive-or operation is an involution, and does not seem susceptible to weak keys/subkeys [11];

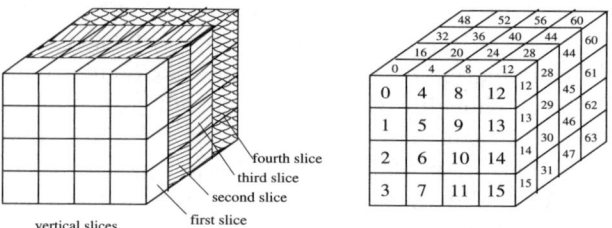

Fig. 1. 3D state with vertical slices and byte numbering

- γ: this nonlinear operation is responsible for the confusion property [35] in 3D, and consists of the bytewise application of the AES S-box to all bytes of the state;
- θ_1, θ_2: these diffusion operations [35] are applied in alternate rounds in 3D. They are identical to ShiftRows in AES, but since the state is 3-dimensional, two different sets of **vertical slices** of the state (Fig. 1) are affected in turn. θ_1 operates on the vertical slices in Fig. 1, and turn (2) into

$$\begin{pmatrix} a_0 & a_4 & a_8 & a_{12} & a_{16} & a_{20} & a_{24} & a_{28} & a_{32} & a_{36} & a_{40} & a_{44} & a_{48} & a_{52} & a_{56} & a_{60} \\ a_5 & a_9 & a_{13} & a_1 & a_{21} & a_{25} & a_{29} & a_{17} & a_{37} & a_{41} & a_{45} & a_{33} & a_{53} & a_{57} & a_{61} & a_{49} \\ a_{10} & a_{14} & a_2 & a_6 & a_{26} & a_{30} & a_{18} & a_{22} & a_{42} & a_{46} & a_{34} & a_{38} & a_{58} & a_{62} & a_{50} & a_{54} \\ a_{15} & a_3 & a_7 & a_{11} & a_{31} & a_{19} & a_{23} & a_{27} & a_{47} & a_{35} & a_{39} & a_{43} & a_{63} & a_{51} & a_{55} & a_{59} \end{pmatrix} ; \quad (3)$$

θ_2 operates similarly, but transforms (2) into

$$\begin{pmatrix} a_0 & a_4 & a_8 & a_{12} & a_{16} & a_{20} & a_{24} & a_{28} & a_{32} & a_{36} & a_{40} & a_{44} & a_{48} & a_{52} & a_{56} & a_{60} \\ a_{17} & a_{21} & a_{25} & a_{29} & a_{33} & a_{37} & a_{41} & a_{45} & a_{49} & a_{53} & a_{57} & a_{61} & a_1 & a_5 & a_9 & a_{13} \\ a_{34} & a_{38} & a_{42} & a_{46} & a_{50} & a_{54} & a_{58} & a_{62} & a_2 & a_6 & a_{10} & a_{14} & a_{18} & a_{22} & a_{26} & a_{30} \\ a_{51} & a_{55} & a_{59} & a_{63} & a_3 & a_7 & a_{11} & a_{15} & a_{19} & a_{23} & a_{27} & a_{31} & a_{35} & a_{39} & a_{43} & a_{47} \end{pmatrix} ; \quad (4)$$

- π: the 4×4 MDS matrix of the Anubis cipher [2] is applied to each column of every vertical slice of the state in (2). The branch number [16] of the Anubis matrix is 5 since it satisfies the MDS (Maximum Distance Separable) property [27]. Since the state is 3-dimensional, complete diffusion is achieved in three rounds, in combination with θ_1 and θ_2. This matrix is an involution, which guarantees the same diffusion power and computational cost for both the encryption and decryption operations. One matrix multiplication by a column of a slice of the state costs 4 xors and 5 xtimes, where xtimes means multiplication by 2 (or the polynomial x) in $GF(2^8)$. Thus, one matrix multiplication by one slice costs 16 xors and 20 xtimes. For one state matrix the cost is 64 xors and 80 xtimes. Let an input slice to π be denoted $(a_0, a_1, \ldots, a_{15})$, and the output slice be $(b_0, b_1, \ldots, b_{15})$. An example of the π transformation for a single slice is

$$\begin{pmatrix} 01_\mathrm{x} & 02_\mathrm{x} & 04_\mathrm{x} & 06_\mathrm{x} \\ 02_\mathrm{x} & 01_\mathrm{x} & 06_\mathrm{x} & 04_\mathrm{x} \\ 04_\mathrm{x} & 06_\mathrm{x} & 01_\mathrm{x} & 02_\mathrm{x} \\ 06_\mathrm{x} & 04_\mathrm{x} & 02_\mathrm{x} & 01_\mathrm{x} \end{pmatrix} \cdot \begin{pmatrix} a_0 & a_4 & a_8 & a_{12} \\ a_1 & a_5 & a_9 & a_{13} \\ a_2 & a_6 & a_{10} & a_{14} \\ a_3 & a_7 & a_{11} & a_{15} \end{pmatrix} = \begin{pmatrix} b_0 & b_4 & b_8 & b_{12} \\ b_1 & b_5 & b_9 & b_{13} \\ b_2 & b_6 & b_{10} & b_{14} \\ b_3 & b_7 & b_{11} & b_{15} \end{pmatrix}, \quad (5)$$

where the subscript $_\mathrm{x}$ denotes hexadecimal notation.

All round transformations in 3D operate bytewise. Bytes are treated as elements over $\mathrm{GF}(2^8) = \mathrm{GF}(2)[\mathrm{x}]/(m(x))$, where $m(x) = x^8 + x^4 + x^3 + x + 1$ is the same irreducible polynomial of AES. A polynomial $p(x) = \sum_{i=0}^{t} a_i \cdot x^i \in \mathrm{GF}(2)[x]$, with $a_i \in \mathrm{GF}(2)$, for $0 \le i \le t$, will be denoted by the numerical value $\sum_{i=0}^{t} a_i \cdot 2^i$, and is shortly represented in hexadecimal notation. For example, $m(x) = \mathtt{11B_x}$.

The i-th full round of 3D, encrypting a text block X, is denoted $\tau_i(X) = \pi \circ \theta_{i \bmod 2 + 1} \circ \gamma \circ \kappa_i(X) = \pi(\theta_{i \bmod 2 + 1}(\gamma(\kappa_i(X))))$, namely function composition, $\circ$, operates in right-to-left order. The last round does not include π, and is denoted $\eta_{r-1}(X) = \theta_{(r-1) \bmod 2+1} \circ \gamma \circ \kappa_{r-1}(X)$. The inverse of a full round is $\tau_i^{-1}(X) = \kappa_i^{-1} \circ \gamma^{-1} \circ \theta_{i \bmod 2+1}^{-1} \circ \pi^{-1}(X)$, and the inverse of the last round is $\eta_{r-1}^{-1}(X) = \kappa_{r-1}^{-1} \circ \gamma^{-1} \circ \theta_{(r-1) \bmod 2+1}^{-1}$. Notice that κ_i is the only key-dependent round operation, whereas γ, θ_1, θ_2 and π are fixed key-independent transformations. Furthermore, there is an output transformation after η_{r-1} consisting of κ_r, the r-th round subkey.

Properties of the round components include:

(a) $\kappa_i = \kappa_i^{-1}$, because the exclusive-or operation is an involution;
(b) $\gamma^{-1} \neq \gamma$ because the AES S-box is not an involution but has order 277182, namely, $\gamma^{277182}[x] = x$, $\forall x \in \mathrm{GF}(2^8)$ (see [34]);
(c) $\theta_i \neq \theta_i^{-1}$, $i \in \{1,2\}$, because the inverse of θ_i requires displacing rows in the opposite direction in each slice; the order of θ_i is 4, that is, $\theta_i^4(X) = X$, for $i = 1, 2$;
(d) $\pi = \pi^{-1}$, because the Anubis matrix is an involution;
(e) $\gamma \circ \theta_i = \theta_i \circ \gamma$, namely, γ and θ_i commute, for $i \in \{1,2\}$, since both operate bytewise; similarly, $\gamma^{-1} \circ \theta_i^{-1} = \theta_i^{-1} \circ \gamma^{-1}$;
(f) $\kappa_i \circ \pi = \pi \circ \kappa_i'$, where $\kappa_i' = \pi^{-1}(\kappa_i)$;
(g) $\kappa_i \circ \theta_{i \bmod 2+1} = \theta_{i \bmod 2+1} \circ \kappa_i^*$, where $\kappa_i^* = \theta_{i \bmod 2+1}^{-1}(\kappa_i)$;
(h) $\kappa_i \circ \gamma \neq \gamma \circ \kappa_i$ because γ is a non-linear operation with respect to exclusive-or;
(i) $\pi \circ \theta_{i \bmod 2+1} \neq \theta_{i \bmod 2+1} \circ \pi$ because π operates on columns of the state while $\theta_{i \bmod 2+1}$ operates on rows of the state.

Using these properties, one can prove that the encryption and decryption frameworks of 3D are similar. Consider the r-round 3D encryption of a plaintext block P, resulting in the ciphertext block

$$C = \kappa_r \circ \eta_{r-1} \circ \bigcirc_{i=0}^{r-2} \tau_i(P) =$$
$$\kappa_r \circ \theta_{(r-1) \bmod 2+1} \circ \gamma \circ \kappa_{r-1} \circ \bigcirc_{i=0}^{r-2} (\pi \circ \theta_{i \bmod 2+1} \circ \gamma \circ \kappa_i)(P). \quad (6)$$

The decryption scheme is

$$P = \bigcirc_{i=r-2}^{0} \tau_i^{-1} \circ \eta_{r-1}^{-1} \circ \kappa_r^{-1}(C), \qquad (7)$$

which can be expressed as $P = \bigcirc_{i=r-2}^{0}(\kappa_i^{-1} \circ \gamma^{-1} \circ \theta_{i \bmod 2+1}^{-1} \circ \pi^{-1}) \circ \eta_{r-1}^{-1} \circ \kappa_r^{-1}(C)$.
From (a) and (d): $P = \bigcirc_{i=r-2}^{0}(\kappa_i \circ \gamma^{-1} \circ \theta_{i \bmod 2+1}^{-1} \circ \pi) \circ \eta_{r-1}^{-1} \circ \kappa_r(C)$. From (e)
and (f): $P = \bigcirc_{i=r-2}^{0}(\kappa_i \circ \theta_{i \bmod 2+1}^{-1} \circ \gamma^{-1} \circ \pi) \circ \kappa_{r-1} \circ \theta_{(r-1) \bmod 2+1}^{-1} \circ \gamma^{-1} \circ \kappa_r(C) = \kappa_0 \circ \theta_1^{-1} \circ \gamma^{-1} \circ \bigcirc_{i=r-1}^{1}(\pi \circ \kappa_i \circ \theta_{i \bmod 2+1}^{-1} \circ \gamma^{-1}) \circ \kappa_r(C) = \kappa_0 \circ \theta_1^{-1} \circ \gamma^{-1} \circ \bigcirc_{i=r-1}^{1}(\kappa_i^* \circ \pi \circ \theta_{i \bmod 2+1}^{-1} \circ \gamma^{-1}) \circ \kappa_r(C) = \kappa_0 \circ \theta_1^{-1} \circ \gamma^{-1} \circ \kappa_1^* \circ \bigcirc_{i=r}^{1}(\pi \circ \theta_{(i-1) \bmod 2+1}^{-1} \circ \gamma^{-1} \circ \kappa_i^*)(C)$,

where $\kappa_r^* = \kappa_r$ and $\kappa_i^* = \pi(\kappa_i)$, for $i < r$. Thus, the encryption (6) and decryption (7) frameworks are similar, except for the order of some round subkeys, and some inverse transformations. Consequently, both schemes have the same cryptographic strength [21].

Properties (h) and (i) show that the round subkeys cannot be moved around or sorted out from the other round transformations because of the non-commutativity property. Thus, it is not possible to arbitrarily remove key-independent cipher operations, such as γ, θ_1, θ_2 and π.

The suggested number of rounds for 3D is 22. This decision is in line with Rijndael, where the block size ranges from 128 up to 256 bits, and roughly one round is added for every additional 32 bits in the block size. Thus, assuming Rijndael with 256-bit block iterates 14 rounds, 3D iterates 22 rounds. This number of rounds is more than enough to counter the attacks described in Sect. 4, and further, there is still a large margin of security. For performance comparison, the AES operates on 128-bit blocks, and iterates (up to) 14 rounds; 3D encrypts four times more texts at a time but iterates $8/14 \approx 57\%$ more rounds.

3 Key Schedule of 3D

For r-round 3D encryption and decryption operations, $(r + 1)$ 512-bit subkeys are needed. The number of rounds is $r = 22$, as explained in Sect. 2.

The key schedule works as follows:

- the 512-bit user key $K = (k_0, k_1, \ldots, k_{63})$ becomes the first round subkey;
- in [36], Wu described an attack on block ciphers with a variable number of rounds. A suggested countermeasure is to combine the number of rounds in the cipher, for instance, in the key schedule, so that cipher instances with different number of rounds are not useful for this attack. This suggestion has been adopted in 3D. Let κ^* represent the exclusive-or of the subkey state with a constant $4 \times 4 \times 4$ matrix depending on the number of rounds, r, and the Anubis matrix:

$$\begin{pmatrix} r & 2r & 4r & 6r & 2r & r & 6r & 4r & 4r & 6r & r & 2r & 6r & 4r & 2r & r \\ 2r & r & 6r & 4r & 4r & 6r & r & 2r & 6r & 4r & 2r & r & r & 2r & 4r & 6r \\ 4r & 6r & r & 2r & 6r & 4r & 2r & r & r & 2r & 4r & 6r & 2r & r & 6r & 4r \\ 6r & 4r & 2r & r & r & 2r & 4r & 6r & 2r & r & 6r & 4r & 4r & 6r & r & 2r \end{pmatrix}, \quad (8)$$

where multiplication is in $GF(2^8)$; these constants are used to avoid patterns in the user key to propagate to round subkeys. Without these constants, a user key with all bytes equal could lead to subkeys with all bytes equal, for instance. It could make 3D susceptible to related-key [4], slide or advanced slide attacks [8], independent of the number of rounds.

- the remaining round subkeys are computed as $K_i = \pi \circ \theta_{i \bmod 2+1} \circ \gamma' \circ \kappa^*(K_{i-1})$, $i \geq 1$, and $K_0 = K$. The transformation γ' consists of the bytewise application of the AES S-box to alternate columns of the state as follows:

$$\begin{pmatrix} S[a_0] & a_4 & a_8 & a_{12} & a_{16} & S[a_{20}] & a_{24} & a_{28} & a_{32} & a_{36} & S[a_{40}] & a_{44} & a_{48} & a_{52} & a_{56} & S[a_{60}] \\ S[a_1] & a_5 & a_9 & a_{13} & a_{17} & S[a_{21}] & a_{25} & a_{29} & a_{33} & a_{37} & S[a_{41}] & a_{45} & a_{49} & a_{53} & a_{57} & S[a_{61}] \\ S[a_2] & a_6 & a_{10} & a_{14} & a_{18} & S[a_{22}] & a_{26} & a_{30} & a_{34} & a_{38} & S[a_{42}] & a_{46} & a_{50} & a_{54} & a_{58} & S[a_{62}] \\ S[a_3] & a_7 & a_{11} & a_{15} & a_{19} & S[a_{23}] & a_{27} & a_{31} & a_{35} & a_{39} & S[a_{43}] & a_{47} & a_{51} & a_{55} & a_{59} & S[a_{63}] \end{pmatrix}.$$
(9)

The encryption subkey generation can be performed on-the-fly. Storing the last round subkey, K_r, instead of K allows on-the-fly decryption subkey generation since all key schedule operations are invertible: $K_i = \kappa^* \circ \gamma'^{-1} \circ \theta_{i \bmod 2+1}^{-1} \circ \pi(K_{i+1})$, $0 \leq i < 22$.

Due to the similarity with the encryption framework, it can be shown that complete key diffusion is achieved after three subkeys are generated, that is, every byte of K_3 already depends on every byte of K_0.

As for performance, notice that the key schedule costs slightly less than a single encryption, although both use similar operations.

4 Security Analyses

In the following, we analyse 3D under several attack settings.

4.1 Plaintext Leakage

Due to the birthday paradox [29], after about $2^{n/2}$ encryptions, either in ECB or CBC modes, an n-bit block cipher starts to leak information about the plaintext [21], in a ciphertext-only (CO) setting. For 3D, this leakage happens after $2^{512/2} = 2^{256}$ block encryptions (or decryptions), which sets an upper-bound on the number of plaintext blocks encrypted before the key has to be changed.

4.2 Related-Key Attack

In [3], Biham developed an attack method on arbitrary n-bit block ciphers, that depends only on the key size. Thus, his attack is also independent of the number of rounds. This attack is supported by the birthday paradox, and has complexity $2^{k/2}$ encryptions, for a k-bit user key. Even though for 3D the key size is equal to the block size, the corresponding attack complexity is $2^{512/2} = 2^{256}$, which matches the attack complexity in Sect. 4.1.

There are many kinds of related-key attacks, such as in Sect. 4.5 and [4,20], and all of them depend on the design of the key schedule algorithm. The key schedule of 3D shares components with its encryption framework (Sect. 3). It implies that (xor) difference propagation works similarly in both schemes, which is relevant for related-key attacks, where the adversary cannot choose the key, but knows or can choose a relationship between keys used for encryption. In particular, it takes three (full) rounds for any single byte difference to spread across the full key state, that is, a single byte difference in the user key(s) will affect the (full) third round subkey and beyond. Consequently, related-key attacks are not expected to be effective against 3D, since any nonzero difference in the key spreads to the entire key state after the third subkey (comparatively, complete diffusion in the key schedule of AES takes six or more rounds depending on the key size).

4.3 Non-surjective and Davies' Attacks

Non-surjective attacks on block ciphers have been suggested by Rijmen et al. in [33], motivated by non-surjective round functions in Feistel ciphers, such as CAST and Khufu [30]. Similarly, Davies' attack [13] exploit the Feistel structure of DES, and subkey bits shared between neighboring S-boxes. The 3D cipher follows an SPN design, and not only its round function, but also its internal components are bijective mappings. Moreover, no subkey bits are duplicated or shared among S-boxes. Therefore, non-surjective attacks do not apply to 3D.

4.4 Interpolation, Higher-Order Differential and χ^2 Attacks

In [17], Jakobsen and Knudsen described attacks on a cipher called PURE and on a variant of the SHARK block cipher [32]. In both cases the attacks were made possible because the ciphers had a compact algebraic (polynomial/rational) expression which could be solved with manageable complexity (up to a certain number of rounds). We have not found any compact (polynomial) representation of round function of 3D (over $GF(2^8)$), or of its round components which leads to an effective attack (to the full 22-round 3D). We do not consider expressions such as in [14], which although compact, did not lead to an effective attack on AES. Analogously, because of the non-linear order of the S-box, we do not expect higher-order differential attacks [23,25] to succeed against 3D. Following a similar reasoning, we do not expect χ^2 attacks [24] nor mod-n attacks [19] to apply to 3D.

4.5 Slide and Advanced-Slide Attacks

In [7,8], the slide and advanced-slide attacks were described against Feistel ciphers whose key schedules had a periodic behavior. Moreover, in these attacks, symmetries in the cipher framework, suggested that this structure could be twisted and slid in order to partially match another copy of itself. Thus, these attacks depend on a self-similarity in the cipher structure, and a degree of periodicity in the key schedule. In 3D, the key schedule was designed to avoid patterns in the user key to propagate to the subkeys, including the periodicity necessary in [7,8]. Moreover, there is a round asymmetry due to θ_1 and θ_2. We conclude that such attacks do not apply to 3D (Sect. 2).

4.6 Truncated Differential Analysis

As a preliminary differential analysis [5], consider **truncated** differentials [23], such as (10), where 'Δ' stands for an arbitrary nonzero exclusive-or byte difference, while '0' stands for a zero byte difference.

$$\begin{pmatrix} \Delta\,0\,0\,0 & 0\,0\,0\,0 & 0\,0\,0\,0 & 0\,0\,0\,0 \\ \Delta\,0\,0\,0 & 0\,0\,0\,0 & 0\,0\,0\,0 & 0\,0\,0\,0 \\ \Delta\,0\,0\,0 & 0\,0\,0\,0 & 0\,0\,0\,0 & 0\,0\,0\,0 \\ \Delta\,0\,0\,0 & 0\,0\,0\,0 & 0\,0\,0\,0 & 0\,0\,0\,0 \end{pmatrix} \xrightarrow{\pi \circ \theta_1 \circ \gamma \circ \kappa_0} \begin{pmatrix} \Delta\,0\,0\,0 & 0\,0\,0\,0 & 0\,0\,0\,0 & 0\,0\,0\,0 \\ 0\,0\,0\,0 & 0\,0\,0\,0 & 0\,0\,0\,0 & 0\,0\,0\,0 \\ 0\,0\,0\,0 & 0\,0\,0\,0 & 0\,0\,0\,0 & 0\,0\,0\,0 \\ 0\,0\,0\,0 & 0\,0\,0\,0 & 0\,0\,0\,0 & 0\,0\,0\,0 \end{pmatrix}$$

$$\xrightarrow{\pi \circ \theta_2 \circ \gamma \circ \kappa_1} \begin{pmatrix} \Delta\,0\,0\,0 & 0\,0\,0\,0 & 0\,0\,0\,0 & 0\,0\,0\,0 \\ \Delta\,0\,0\,0 & 0\,0\,0\,0 & 0\,0\,0\,0 & 0\,0\,0\,0 \\ \Delta\,0\,0\,0 & 0\,0\,0\,0 & 0\,0\,0\,0 & 0\,0\,0\,0 \\ \Delta\,0\,0\,0 & 0\,0\,0\,0 & 0\,0\,0\,0 & 0\,0\,0\,0 \end{pmatrix} \xrightarrow{\theta_1 \circ \gamma \circ \kappa_2}$$

$$\begin{pmatrix} \Delta\,0\,0\,0 & 0\,0\,0\,0 & 0\,0\,0\,0 & 0\,0\,0\,0 \\ 0\,0\,0\,\Delta & 0\,0\,0\,0 & 0\,0\,0\,0 & 0\,0\,0\,0 \\ 0\,0\,\Delta\,0 & 0\,0\,0\,0 & 0\,0\,0\,0 & 0\,0\,0\,0 \\ 0\,\Delta\,0\,0 & 0\,0\,0\,0 & 0\,0\,0\,0 & 0\,0\,0\,0 \end{pmatrix} \xrightarrow{\pi} \begin{pmatrix} \Delta\,\Delta\,\Delta\,\Delta & 0\,0\,0\,0 & 0\,0\,0\,0 & 0\,0\,0\,0 \\ \Delta\,\Delta\,\Delta\,\Delta & 0\,0\,0\,0 & 0\,0\,0\,0 & 0\,0\,0\,0 \\ \Delta\,\Delta\,\Delta\,\Delta & 0\,0\,0\,0 & 0\,0\,0\,0 & 0\,0\,0\,0 \\ \Delta\,\Delta\,\Delta\,\Delta & 0\,0\,0\,0 & 0\,0\,0\,0 & 0\,0\,0\,0 \end{pmatrix}$$

$$\xrightarrow{\theta_2 \circ \gamma \circ \kappa_3} \begin{pmatrix} \Delta\,\Delta\,\Delta\,\Delta & 0\,0\,0\,0 & 0\,0\,0\,0 & 0\,0\,0\,0 \\ 0\,0\,0\,0 & 0\,0\,0\,0 & 0\,0\,0\,0 & \Delta\,\Delta\,\Delta\,\Delta \\ 0\,0\,0\,0 & 0\,0\,0\,0 & \Delta\,\Delta\,\Delta\,\Delta & 0\,0\,0\,0 \\ 0\,0\,0\,0 & \Delta\,\Delta\,\Delta\,\Delta & 0\,0\,0\,0 & 0\,0\,0\,0 \end{pmatrix} \xrightarrow{\pi}$$

$$\begin{pmatrix} \Delta\,\Delta\,\Delta\,\Delta & \Delta\,\Delta\,\Delta\,\Delta & \Delta\,\Delta\,\Delta\,\Delta & \Delta\,\Delta\,\Delta\,\Delta \\ \Delta\,\Delta\,\Delta\,\Delta & \Delta\,\Delta\,\Delta\,\Delta & \Delta\,\Delta\,\Delta\,\Delta & \Delta\,\Delta\,\Delta\,\Delta \\ \Delta\,\Delta\,\Delta\,\Delta & \Delta\,\Delta\,\Delta\,\Delta & \Delta\,\Delta\,\Delta\,\Delta & \Delta\,\Delta\,\Delta\,\Delta \\ \Delta\,\Delta\,\Delta\,\Delta & \Delta\,\Delta\,\Delta\,\Delta & \Delta\,\Delta\,\Delta\,\Delta & \Delta\,\Delta\,\Delta\,\Delta \end{pmatrix} \quad (10)$$

The 4-round truncated differential (10) demonstrates that complete text diffusion in 3D is achieved in exactly three rounds (see the last three rounds). There are 25 active S-boxes [9] in (10), and this fact is independent of the position of the single Δ byte difference after the first round. Analogously, this behaviour is independent of (10) starting with a round using θ_1 or θ_2. Notice that (10) holds with probability $2^8/2^{32} = 2^{-24}$, due to the difference propagation after the first round, where four byte differences turn into a single byte difference. The remaining difference propagation patterns hold with certainty. Comparatively, for 4-round AES there are also at least 25 active S-boxes. These figures show that 3D has the same expected resistance to differential cryptanalysis (DC) as the AES.

An advantage of truncated differentials (compared to conventional differential characteristics) is that the probability of the former is independent of the S-boxes used in the cipher.

Consider the (hypothetical) 2-round iterative truncated differential (11), that holds with probability $(2^8/2^{32})^4 = 2^{-96}$. This probability accounts for the θ_2 transformation in which four nonzero byte differences in the same column become a single output difference after each slice of the state. Each such event has probability $2^8/2^{23} = 2^{-24}$.

$$\begin{pmatrix} \Delta\,0\,0\,0 & \Delta\,0\,0\,0 & \Delta\,0\,0\,0 & \Delta\,0\,0\,0 \\ 0\,0\,0\,0 & 0\,0\,0\,0 & 0\,0\,0\,0 & 0\,0\,0\,0 \\ 0\,0\,0\,0 & 0\,0\,0\,0 & 0\,0\,0\,0 & 0\,0\,0\,0 \\ 0\,0\,0\,0 & 0\,0\,0\,0 & 0\,0\,0\,0 & 0\,0\,0\,0 \end{pmatrix} \xrightarrow{\pi \circ \theta_1 \circ \gamma \circ \kappa_0} \begin{pmatrix} \Delta\,0\,0\,0 & \Delta\,0\,0\,0 & \Delta\,0\,0\,0 & \Delta\,0\,0\,0 \\ \Delta\,0\,0\,0 & \Delta\,0\,0\,0 & \Delta\,0\,0\,0 & \Delta\,0\,0\,0 \\ \Delta\,0\,0\,0 & \Delta\,0\,0\,0 & \Delta\,0\,0\,0 & \Delta\,0\,0\,0 \\ \Delta\,0\,0\,0 & \Delta\,0\,0\,0 & \Delta\,0\,0\,0 & \Delta\,0\,0\,0 \end{pmatrix}$$

$$\xrightarrow{\pi \circ \theta_2 \circ \gamma \circ \kappa_1} \begin{pmatrix} \Delta\,0\,0\,0 & \Delta\,0\,0\,0 & \Delta\,0\,0\,0 & \Delta\,0\,0\,0 \\ 0\,0\,0\,0 & 0\,0\,0\,0 & 0\,0\,0\,0 & 0\,0\,0\,0 \\ 0\,0\,0\,0 & 0\,0\,0\,0 & 0\,0\,0\,0 & 0\,0\,0\,0 \\ 0\,0\,0\,0 & 0\,0\,0\,0 & 0\,0\,0\,0 & 0\,0\,0\,0 \end{pmatrix} \quad (11)$$

For a random permutation the output difference of (11) would appear with probability about $(2^{-8})^{48} = 2^{-384}$ because there are 48 zero byte differences at the output. Thus, (11) is a distinguisher of 3D from a random permutation, for up to six rounds, with probability $(2^{-96})^3 = 2^{-288}$. Repeating (11) four times, namely, for eight rounds, leads to a probability of $(2^{-96})^4 = 2^{-384}$, which is the same as for a random permutation. One can also start the distinguisher with the state after $\pi \circ \theta_1 \circ \gamma \circ \kappa_0$. That means that the iterative truncated differential start in an even round (with θ_2). The results are analogous.

Suppose one makes a pool of 2^{32} chosen plaintexts (CP) in which the bytes in positions (0,16,32,48) of the state (2) range over all possible 32-bit values, while the remaining bytes are arbitrary constants. This pool leads to about 2^{63} text pairs (plaintext and ciphertexts). The output difference contains 60 zero byte differences. Thus, one expects that $2^{63} \cdot (2^{-8})^{60} = 2^{-417} < 1$ pairs satisfy the output difference of (11). This approach does not work.

Suppose one tries to guess the 16 bytes of AK_0, and use pools of 2^{128} plaintexts with difference at bytes in positions (0, 5, 10, 15, 16, 21, 26, 31, 32, 37, 42, 47, 48, 53, 58, 63) of the state. Each such pool can lead to $2^{128}(2^{128}-1)/2 \approx 2^{255}$ text pairs. Still $2^{255} \cdot (2^{-8})^{60} = 2^{-225} < 1$ survives filtering by output difference of (11). Notice that due to the structure of 3D, with θ_1 and θ_2 in every other round, any iterative differential needs to have an even number of rounds, otherwise, it could not be concatenated to itself.

4.7 Linear Analysis

A linear distinguisher [28] for 3D would be similar to (10) except that Δ is replaced by Γ, denoting a nonzero bitmask, while 0 denotes a zero (empty or trivial) bitmask. Thus, such linear distinguisher would reach three rounds with 21 active S-boxes, and according to [16], the associated bias would be $(2^{-4})^{21} = 2^{-84}$. For four rounds, the bias would be $(2^{-4})^{25} = 2^{-100}$. Comparatively, for the AES the number of active S-boxes across four rounds is at least 25. These figures show that 3D has the same expected resistance to linear cryptanalysis as the AES. The questions of linear hulls [31] and multiple linear relations [18] in 3D are left as open problems.

4.8 Multiset Analysis

Consider the first-order multiset [12,6] distinguisher in (12), where 'A' denotes an active byte, 'P' denotes a passive byte, 'B' denotes a balanced byte and '?' denotes an unpredictable byte exclusive-or sum. The distinguisher (12) reaches 4.25 rounds, or more precisely, $\kappa_4 \circ \pi \circ \theta_2 \circ \gamma \circ \kappa_3 \circ \pi \circ \theta_1 \circ \gamma \circ \kappa_2 \circ \pi \circ \theta_2 \circ \gamma \circ \kappa_1 \circ \pi \circ \theta_1 \circ \gamma \circ \kappa_0$.

$$\begin{pmatrix} A\,P\,P\,P & P\,P\,P\,P & P\,P\,P\,P & P\,P\,P\,P \\ P\,P\,P\,P & P\,P\,P\,P & P\,P\,P\,P & P\,P\,P\,P \\ P\,P\,P\,P & P\,P\,P\,P & P\,P\,P\,P & P\,P\,P\,P \\ P\,P\,P\,P & P\,P\,P\,P & P\,P\,P\,P & P\,P\,P\,P \end{pmatrix} \xrightarrow{\pi \circ \theta_1 \circ \gamma \circ \kappa_0}$$

$$\begin{pmatrix} A\,P\,P\,P & P\,P\,P\,P & P\,P\,P\,P & P\,P\,P\,P \\ A\,P\,P\,P & P\,P\,P\,P & P\,P\,P\,P & P\,P\,P\,P \\ A\,P\,P\,P & P\,P\,P\,P & P\,P\,P\,P & P\,P\,P\,P \\ A\,P\,P\,P & P\,P\,P\,P & P\,P\,P\,P & P\,P\,P\,P \end{pmatrix} \xrightarrow{\theta_2 \circ \gamma \circ \kappa_1}$$

$$\begin{pmatrix} A\,P\,P\,P & P\,P\,P\,P & P\,P\,P\,P & P\,P\,P\,P \\ P\,P\,P\,P & P\,P\,P\,P & P\,P\,P\,P & A\,P\,P\,P \\ P\,P\,P\,P & P\,P\,P\,P & A\,P\,P\,P & P\,P\,P\,P \\ P\,P\,P\,P & A\,P\,P\,P & P\,P\,P\,P & P\,P\,P\,P \end{pmatrix} \xrightarrow{\pi}$$

$$\begin{pmatrix} A\,P\,P\,P & A\,P\,P\,P & A\,P\,P\,P & A\,P\,P\,P \\ A\,P\,P\,P & A\,P\,P\,P & A\,P\,P\,P & A\,P\,P\,P \\ A\,P\,P\,P & A\,P\,P\,P & A\,P\,P\,P & A\,P\,P\,P \\ A\,P\,P\,P & A\,P\,P\,P & A\,P\,P\,P & A\,P\,P\,P \end{pmatrix} \xrightarrow{\theta_1 \circ \gamma \circ \kappa_2}$$

$$\begin{pmatrix} A\,P\,P\,P & A\,P\,P\,P & A\,P\,P\,P & A\,P\,P\,P \\ P\,P\,P\,A & P\,P\,P\,A & P\,P\,P\,A & P\,P\,P\,A \\ P\,P\,A\,P & P\,P\,A\,P & P\,P\,A\,P & P\,P\,A\,P \\ P\,A\,P\,P & P\,A\,P\,P & P\,A\,P\,P & P\,A\,P\,P \end{pmatrix} \xrightarrow{\pi}$$

$$\begin{pmatrix} A\,A\,A\,A & A\,A\,A\,A & A\,A\,A\,A & A\,A\,A\,A \\ A\,A\,A\,A & A\,A\,A\,A & A\,A\,A\,A & A\,A\,A\,A \\ A\,A\,A\,A & A\,A\,A\,A & A\,A\,A\,A & A\,A\,A\,A \\ A\,A\,A\,A & A\,A\,A\,A & A\,A\,A\,A & A\,A\,A\,A \end{pmatrix} \xrightarrow{\kappa_4 \circ \pi \circ \theta_2 \circ \gamma \circ \kappa_3} \qquad (12)$$

$$\begin{pmatrix} B\,B\,B\,B & B\,B\,B\,B & B\,B\,B\,B & B\,B\,B\,B \\ B\,B\,B\,B & B\,B\,B\,B & B\,B\,B\,B & B\,B\,B\,B \\ B\,B\,B\,B & B\,B\,B\,B & B\,B\,B\,B & B\,B\,B\,B \\ B\,B\,B\,B & B\,B\,B\,B & B\,B\,B\,B & B\,B\,B\,B \end{pmatrix} \xrightarrow{\gamma} \begin{pmatrix} ?\,?\,?\,? & ?\,?\,?\,? & ?\,?\,?\,? & ?\,?\,?\,? \\ ?\,?\,?\,? & ?\,?\,?\,? & ?\,?\,?\,? & ?\,?\,?\,? \\ ?\,?\,?\,? & ?\,?\,?\,? & ?\,?\,?\,? & ?\,?\,?\,? \\ ?\,?\,?\,? & ?\,?\,?\,? & ?\,?\,?\,? & ?\,?\,?\,? \end{pmatrix}$$

An attack on 4.75-round 3D using (12) would partially decrypt $\kappa_5 \circ \theta_1 \circ \gamma$, and recover κ_5 bytewise. The distinguisher (12) provides an 8-bit condition. After two λ-sets [12], there remains $2^8 \cdot (2^{-8})^2 < 1$ wrong subkey byte candidates. The cost per subkey byte is therefore, $2 \cdot 2^8 = 2^9$ chosen plaintexts (CP), $2^8 \cdot 2^8 + 2^8 \approx 2^{16}$ computations of $\kappa_5 \circ \theta_1 \circ \gamma$. That means $64 \cdot 2^{16} \cdot 0.75/4.25 \approx 2^{19.5}$ 4.75-round computations.

Consider now the higher-order multiset distinguisher (13) that uses λ-sets with 2^{128} texts. A byte belonging to a 128-bit active word is denoted A^* to indicate that although the bytes are scattered across the state, they jointly form a 128-bit active word; similarly, a byte belonging to a 128-bit balanced word is denoted B^*; a byte belonging to a 128-bit passive word is denoted P^*; a byte belonging to a 128-bit even word is denoted E^*; different subscripts indicate different 128-bit words.

$$\begin{pmatrix} A^* & P & P & P & | & P & P & P & P & | & P & P & P & P & | & P & P & P & P \\ P & A^* & P & P & | & P & P & P & P & | & P & P & P & P & | & P & P & P & P \\ P & P & A^* & P & | & P & P & P & P & | & P & P & P & P & | & P & P & P & P \\ P & P & P & A^* & | & P & P & P & P & | & P & P & P & P & | & P & P & P & P \end{pmatrix} \xrightarrow{\theta_1 \circ \gamma \circ \kappa_0}$$

$$\begin{pmatrix} A^* & P & P & P & | & P & P & P & P & | & P & P & P & P & | & P & P & P & P \\ A^* & P & P & P & | & P & P & P & P & | & P & P & P & P & | & P & P & P & P \\ A^* & P & P & P & | & P & P & P & P & | & P & P & P & P & | & P & P & P & P \\ A^* & P & P & P & | & P & P & P & P & | & P & P & P & P & | & P & P & P & P \end{pmatrix} \xrightarrow{\theta_2 \circ \gamma \circ \kappa_1 \circ \pi}$$

$$\begin{pmatrix} A^* & P & P & P & | & P & P & P & P & | & P & P & P & P & | & P & P & P & P \\ P & P & P & P & | & P & P & P & P & | & P & P & P & P & | & A^* & P & P & P \\ P & P & P & P & | & P & P & P & P & | & A^* & P & P & P & | & P & P & P & P \\ P & P & P & P & | & A_* & P & P & P & | & P & P & P & P & | & P & P & P & P \end{pmatrix} \xrightarrow{\pi}$$

$$\begin{pmatrix} E_1^* & P & P & P & | & E_2^* & P & P & P & | & E_3^* & P & P & P & | & E_4^* & P & P & P \\ E_1^* & P & P & P & | & E_2^* & P & P & P & | & E_3^* & P & P & P & | & E_4^* & P & P & P \\ E_1^* & P & P & P & | & E_2^* & P & P & P & | & E_3^* & P & P & P & | & E_4^* & P & P & P \\ E_1^* & P & P & P & | & E_2^* & P & P & P & | & E_3^* & P & P & P & | & E_4^* & P & P & P \end{pmatrix} \xrightarrow{\theta_1 \circ \gamma \circ \kappa_2}$$

$$\begin{pmatrix} E_1^* & P & P & P & | & E_2^* & P & P & P & | & E_3^* & P & P & P & | & E_4^* & P & P & P \\ P & P & P & E_1^* & | & P & P & P & E_2^* & | & P & P & P & E_3^* & | & P & P & P & E_4^* \\ P & P & E_1^* & P & | & P & P & E_2^* & P & | & P & P & E_3^* & P & | & P & P & E_4^* & P \\ P & E_1^* & P & P & | & P & E_2^* & P & P & | & P & E_3^* & P & P & | & P & E_4^* & P & P \end{pmatrix} \xrightarrow{\pi}$$

$$\begin{pmatrix} E_1^* & E_1^* & E_1^* & E_1^* & | & E_2^* & E_2^* & E_2^* & E_2^* & | & E_3^* & E_3^* & E_3^* & E_3^* & | & E_4^* & E_4^* & E_4^* & E_4^* \\ E_1^* & E_1^* & E_1^* & E_1^* & | & E_2^* & E_2^* & E_2^* & E_2^* & | & E_3^* & E_3^* & E_3^* & E_3^* & | & E_4^* & E_4^* & E_4^* & E_4^* \\ E_1^* & E_1^* & E_1^* & E_1^* & | & E_2^* & E_2^* & E_2^* & E_2^* & | & E_3^* & E_3^* & E_3^* & E_3^* & | & E_4^* & E_4^* & E_4^* & E_4^* \\ E_1^* & E_1^* & E_1^* & E_1^* & | & E_2^* & E_2^* & E_2^* & E_2^* & | & E_3^* & E_3^* & E_3^* & E_3^* & | & E_4^* & E_4^* & E_4^* & E_4^* \end{pmatrix} \xrightarrow{\pi \circ \theta_2 \circ \gamma \circ \kappa_3}$$

$$\begin{pmatrix} A_1^* & A_1^* & A_1^* & A_1^* & | & A_2^* & A_2^* & A_2^* & A_2^* & | & A_3^* & A_3^* & A_3^* & A_3^* & | & A_4^* & A_4^* & A_4^* & A_4^* \\ A_1^* & A_1^* & A_1^* & A_1^* & | & A_2^* & A_2^* & A_2^* & A_2^* & | & A_3^* & A_3^* & A_3^* & A_3^* & | & A_4^* & A_4^* & A_4^* & A_4^* \\ A_1^* & A_1^* & A_1^* & A_1^* & | & A_2^* & A_2^* & A_2^* & A_2^* & | & A_3^* & A_3^* & A_3^* & A_3^* & | & A_4^* & A_4^* & A_4^* & A_4^* \\ A_1^* & A_1^* & A_1^* & A_1^* & | & A_2^* & A_2^* & A_2^* & A_2^* & | & A_3^* & A_3^* & A_3^* & A_3^* & | & A_4^* & A_4^* & A_4^* & A_4^* \end{pmatrix} \xrightarrow{\kappa_5 \pi \circ \theta_1 \circ \gamma \circ \kappa_4}$$

$$\begin{pmatrix} B & B & B & B & | & B & B & B & B & | & B & B & B & B & | & B & B & B & B \\ B & B & B & B & | & B & B & B & B & | & B & B & B & B & | & B & B & B & B \\ B & B & B & B & | & B & B & B & B & | & B & B & B & B & | & B & B & B & B \\ B & B & B & B & | & B & B & B & B & | & B & B & B & B & | & B & B & B & B \end{pmatrix} \xrightarrow{\gamma}$$

$$\begin{pmatrix} ? & ? & ? & ? & | & ? & ? & ? & ? & | & ? & ? & ? & ? & | & ? & ? & ? & ? \\ ? & ? & ? & ? & | & ? & ? & ? & ? & | & ? & ? & ? & ? & | & ? & ? & ? & ? \\ ? & ? & ? & ? & | & ? & ? & ? & ? & | & ? & ? & ? & ? & | & ? & ? & ? & ? \\ ? & ? & ? & ? & | & ? & ? & ? & ? & | & ? & ? & ? & ? & | & ? & ? & ? & ? \end{pmatrix} \quad (13)$$

Thus, (13) covers 5.25 rounds. An attack on 5.75-round 3D using (13) would partially decrypt $\kappa_6 \circ \theta_2 \circ \gamma$, and recover κ_6 bytewise, by comparing if each byte position before γ is balanced. The distinguisher (13) provides an 8-bit condition per byte. After two λ-sets [12], there remains $2^8 \cdot (2^{-8})^2 < 1$ wrong subkey byte candidates. The cost per subkey byte is therefore, $2 \cdot 2^{128} = 2^{129}$ chosen plaintexts (CP), $2^8 \cdot 2^{128} = 2^{136}$ computations of $\kappa_6 \circ \theta_2 \circ \gamma$. That means $64 \cdot 2^{136} \cdot 0.75/5.75 \approx 2^{139}$ 5.75-round computations.

4.9 Impossible Differential Analysis

The impossible differential (ID) technique was formerly described in [22]. A 4.75-round impossible differential distinguisher of 3D is depicted in (14), where 'Δ' denotes a nonzero byte difference, '0' denotes a zero byte difference, and '?' denotes an unknown difference (can be zero or not). There are two truncated differentials in (14) that hold with certainty, one in the encryption direction, covering $\pi \circ \theta_2 \circ \gamma \circ \kappa_3 \circ \pi \circ \theta_1 \circ \gamma \circ \kappa_2 \circ \pi \circ \theta_2 \circ \gamma \circ \kappa_1$ and the other in the decryption direction, covering $\kappa_4 \circ \gamma^{-1} \circ \theta_1^{-1} \circ \pi \circ \kappa_5 \circ \gamma^{-1} \circ \theta_2^{-1}$. The contradiction in difference propagation (denoted $\not\to$ and $\not\leftarrow$) happens after the third π layer:

there are four zero byte differences in the decryption direction after π, while all these bytes are nonzero before π. There are similar ID distinguishers that cause contradiction in the other slices of the state.

$$\begin{pmatrix} \Delta\,0\,0\,0 & 0\,0\,0\,0 & 0\,0\,0\,0 & 0\,0\,0\,0 \\ 0\,0\,0\,0 & 0\,0\,0\,0 & 0\,0\,0\,0 & 0\,0\,0\,0 \\ 0\,0\,0\,0 & 0\,0\,0\,0 & 0\,0\,0\,0 & 0\,0\,0\,0 \\ 0\,0\,0\,0 & 0\,0\,0\,0 & 0\,0\,0\,0 & 0\,0\,0\,0 \end{pmatrix} \xrightarrow{\pi \circ \theta_2 \circ \gamma \circ \kappa_1} \begin{pmatrix} \Delta\,0\,0\,0 & 0\,0\,0\,0 & 0\,0\,0\,0 & 0\,0\,0\,0 \\ \Delta\,0\,0\,0 & 0\,0\,0\,0 & 0\,0\,0\,0 & 0\,0\,0\,0 \\ \Delta\,0\,0\,0 & 0\,0\,0\,0 & 0\,0\,0\,0 & 0\,0\,0\,0 \\ \Delta\,0\,0\,0 & 0\,0\,0\,0 & 0\,0\,0\,0 & 0\,0\,0\,0 \end{pmatrix}$$

$$\xrightarrow{\theta_1 \circ \gamma \circ \kappa_2} \begin{pmatrix} \Delta\,0\,0\,0 & 0\,0\,0\,0 & 0\,0\,0\,0 & 0\,0\,0\,0 \\ 0\,0\,0\,\Delta & 0\,0\,0\,0 & 0\,0\,0\,0 & 0\,0\,0\,0 \\ 0\,0\,\Delta\,0 & 0\,0\,0\,0 & 0\,0\,0\,0 & 0\,0\,0\,0 \\ 0\,\Delta\,0\,0 & 0\,0\,0\,0 & 0\,0\,0\,0 & 0\,0\,0\,0 \end{pmatrix} \xrightarrow{\pi}$$

$$\begin{pmatrix} \Delta\,\Delta\,\Delta\,\Delta & 0\,0\,0\,0 & 0\,0\,0\,0 & 0\,0\,0\,0 \\ \Delta\,\Delta\,\Delta\,\Delta & 0\,0\,0\,0 & 0\,0\,0\,0 & 0\,0\,0\,0 \\ \Delta\,\Delta\,\Delta\,\Delta & 0\,0\,0\,0 & 0\,0\,0\,0 & 0\,0\,0\,0 \\ \Delta\,\Delta\,\Delta\,\Delta & 0\,0\,0\,0 & 0\,0\,0\,0 & 0\,0\,0\,0 \end{pmatrix}$$

$$\xrightarrow{\theta_2 \circ \gamma \circ \kappa_3} \begin{pmatrix} \Delta\,\Delta\,\Delta\,\Delta & 0\,0\,0\,0 & 0\,0\,0\,0 & 0\,0\,0\,0 \\ 0\,0\,0\,0 & 0\,0\,0\,0 & 0\,0\,0\,0 & \Delta\,\Delta\,\Delta\,\Delta \\ 0\,0\,0\,0 & 0\,0\,0\,0 & \Delta\,\Delta\,\Delta\,\Delta & 0\,0\,0\,0 \\ 0\,0\,0\,0 & \Delta\,\Delta\,\Delta\,\Delta & 0\,0\,0\,0 & 0\,0\,0\,0 \end{pmatrix} \xrightarrow{\pi}$$

$$\begin{pmatrix} \Delta\,\Delta\,\Delta\,\Delta & \Delta\,\Delta\,\Delta\,\Delta & \Delta\,\Delta\,\Delta\,\Delta & \Delta\,\Delta\,\Delta\,\Delta \\ \Delta\,\Delta\,\Delta\,\Delta & \Delta\,\Delta\,\Delta\,\Delta & \Delta\,\Delta\,\Delta\,\Delta & \Delta\,\Delta\,\Delta\,\Delta \\ \Delta\,\Delta\,\Delta\,\Delta & \Delta\,\Delta\,\Delta\,\Delta & \Delta\,\Delta\,\Delta\,\Delta & \Delta\,\Delta\,\Delta\,\Delta \\ \Delta\,\Delta\,\Delta\,\Delta & \Delta\,\Delta\,\Delta\,\Delta & \Delta\,\Delta\,\Delta\,\Delta & \Delta\,\Delta\,\Delta\,\Delta \end{pmatrix} \xleftarrow{\kappa_4 \circ \gamma^{-1} \circ \theta_1^{-1}}$$

$$\begin{pmatrix} 0\,?\,?\,? & ?\,?\,?\,? & ?\,?\,?\,? & ?\,?\,?\,? \\ 0\,?\,?\,? & ?\,?\,?\,? & ?\,?\,?\,? & ?\,?\,?\,? \\ 0\,?\,?\,? & ?\,?\,?\,? & ?\,?\,?\,? & ?\,?\,?\,? \\ 0\,?\,?\,? & ?\,?\,?\,? & ?\,?\,?\,? & ?\,?\,?\,? \end{pmatrix} \xleftarrow{\pi} \begin{pmatrix} 0\,\Delta\,\Delta\,\Delta & \Delta\,\Delta\,\Delta\,\Delta & \Delta\,\Delta\,\Delta\,\Delta & \Delta\,\Delta\,\Delta\,\Delta \\ 0\,\Delta\,\Delta\,\Delta & \Delta\,\Delta\,\Delta\,\Delta & \Delta\,\Delta\,\Delta\,\Delta & \Delta\,\Delta\,\Delta\,\Delta \\ 0\,\Delta\,\Delta\,\Delta & \Delta\,\Delta\,\Delta\,\Delta & \Delta\,\Delta\,\Delta\,\Delta & \Delta\,\Delta\,\Delta\,\Delta \\ 0\,\Delta\,\Delta\,\Delta & \Delta\,\Delta\,\Delta\,\Delta & \Delta\,\Delta\,\Delta\,\Delta & \Delta\,\Delta\,\Delta\,\Delta \end{pmatrix}$$

$$\xleftarrow{\kappa_5 \circ \gamma^{-1} \circ \theta_2^{-1}} \begin{pmatrix} 0\,\Delta\,\Delta\,\Delta & \Delta\,\Delta\,\Delta\,\Delta & \Delta\,\Delta\,\Delta\,\Delta & \Delta\,\Delta\,\Delta\,\Delta \\ \Delta\,\Delta\,\Delta\,\Delta & \Delta\,\Delta\,\Delta\,\Delta & \Delta\,\Delta\,\Delta\,\Delta & 0\,\Delta\,\Delta\,\Delta \\ \Delta\,\Delta\,\Delta\,\Delta & \Delta\,\Delta\,\Delta\,\Delta & 0\,\Delta\,\Delta\,\Delta & \Delta\,\Delta\,\Delta\,\Delta \\ \Delta\,\Delta\,\Delta\,\Delta & 0\,\Delta\,\Delta\,\Delta & \Delta\,\Delta\,\Delta\,\Delta & \Delta\,\Delta\,\Delta\,\Delta \end{pmatrix} \quad (14)$$

Distinguisher (14) can be used to recover κ_0 in an attack on 5.75-round 3D, by placing (14) in the last 4.75 rounds. The attack would proceed as follows:

(a) choose a pool 2^{32} texts with all possible values in positions 0, 5, 10, 15 of the state, and arbitrary constants in the remaining byte positions. From one pool, one can generate $2^{32}(2^{32}-1)/2 \approx 2^{63}$ pairs with nonzero difference in these four byte positions, and zero difference in the remaining positions;

(b) from (14), about $2^{63} \cdot 2^{-32} = 2^{31}$ pairs satisfy the four zero byte differences at the ciphertext;

(c) guess 32 subkey bits in byte positions 0, 5, 10, 15 of κ_0, and partially decrypt the first round $\pi \circ \theta_1 \circ \gamma \circ \kappa_0$ for the pairs in item (b); filter those pairs that have a single nonzero byte difference in the leftmost column of the first vertical slice of the state after π; this is a 24-bit filtration condition, since it holds with probability 2^{-3*8}; so, $2^{32-24} = 2^8$ wrong key are suggested by (14) per text pair;

(d) due to collisions, the number of wrong subkeys surviving, using one text pool, is $2^{32}(1-2^8/2^{32})^{2^{31}} = 2^{32}(1-2^{-24})^{2^{31}} \approx 2^{32}/e^{128} < 1$, so the correct subkey can be uniquely identified;

The attack complexity is 2^{32} CP, about $2^{32} \cdot 2^{31} = 2^{63}$ one-round computations to recover 32 subkey bits. To recover the full first round subkey requires repeating the attack sixteen times, yielding $16 \cdot 2^{63}/5.75 \approx 2^{65.5}$ 5.75-round computations, and 2^{32} memory.

5 Software Performance

Since 3D and AES/Rijndael share very similar components, it is natural to compare them. Due to the large block size, each 3D encryption roughly equals four AES encryptions, with bytes interleaved due to θ_1 and θ_2. Note that 3D iterates 22 rounds, and the AES has at most 14 rounds (for 256-bit keys). Thus, the latter has a better performance than the former. Although 3D provides more opportunities for parallelism than AES or Rijndael, this feature has not been exploited in performance comparisons.

6 Conclusions

This paper described a new secret-key block cipher called 3D, aimed at secure and fast encryption of large volumes of data. The design of 3D was inspired by the AES, in which text and key blocks are represented by a 2-dimensional state matrix of bytes. The main innovation of 3D is the $4 \times 4 \times 4$ 3-dimensional state of bytes, that led to improvements in design, security and potential applications (hash functions, MACs, stream ciphers, pseudorandom number generators).

Table 1 lists the attack complexities of our security evaluation of 3D.

Table 1. Attack complexities on reduced-round 3D cipher

Attack	Time	Data	Memory	#Rounds	Comments
Multiset	$2^{19.5}$	2^9 CP	2^8	4.75	Sect. 4.8
ID	$2^{65.5}$	2^{36} CP	2^{32}	5.75	Sect. 4.9
Multiset	2^{139}	2^{129} CP	2^{128}	5.75	Sect. 4.8

The block size of 3D can be parameterized. For instance, if the underlying cipher operations were performed over $GF(2^{16})$ instead of over $GF(2^8)$, then the block size would double to $64 \cdot 16 = 1024$ bits, but the storage of a 16×16 S-box becomes prohibitive. We have chosen the field $GF(2^8)$ since it is adequate even for smartcard processing, and because it avoids endianness issues.

Alternatively, keeping the bytewise operations, larger states could also be constructed with dimensions $5 \times 5 \times 5$ or $6 \times 6 \times 6$, for instance, but requiring new and larger MDS matrices. Mini-cipher versions of 3D can use a $3 \times 3 \times 3$ state of bytes, but a new 3×3 MDS matrix is needed. For analysis purposes, mini versions of 3D could use 4-bit words instead of bytes, leading to a 256-bit block cipher.

In [1], Barkan and Biham described the concept of dual ciphers, which means an isomorphism between the original cipher framework and another instance with isomorphic mappings for the plaintext, ciphertext and key. As an example, they described duals of the AES, which also exists for Rijndael and 3D. It is an open problem how to exploit dual ciphers in an effective attacks against AES/Rijndael, 3D and similar ciphers. Analogously, the algebraic attacks described by Courtois and Pieprzyk [10] against the AES (and 3D) still remain as open research problems.

References

1. Barkan, E., Biham, E.: In How Many Ways Can You Write Rijndael. In: Zheng, Y. (ed.) ASIACRYPT 2002. LNCS, vol. 2501, pp. 160–175. Springer, Heidelberg (2002)
2. Barreto, P.S.L.M., Rijmen, V.: The ANUBIS Block Cipher. In: 1st NESSIE Workshop, Heverlee, Belgium (2000)
3. Biham, E.: How to decrypt or even substitute DES-encrypted messages in 2^{28} steps. Information Processing Letters 3(84), 117–124 (2002)
4. Biham, E.: New Types of Cryptanalytic Attacks using Related Keys. In: Helleseth, T. (ed.) EUROCRYPT 1993. LNCS, vol. 765, pp. 398–409. Springer, Heidelberg (1994)
5. Biham, E., Shamir, A.: Differential Cryptanalysis of DES-like Cryptosystems. Journal of Cryptology 1(4), 3–72 (1991)
6. Biryukov, A., Shamir, A.: Structural Cryptanalysis of SASAS. In: Pfitzmann, B. (ed.) EUROCRYPT 2001. LNCS, vol. 2045, pp. 394–405. Springer, Heidelberg (2001)
7. Biryukov, A., Wagner, D.: Advanced Slide Attacks. In: Preneel, B. (ed.) EUROCRYPT 2000. LNCS, vol. 1807, pp. 589–606. Springer, Heidelberg (2000)
8. Biryukov, A., Wagner, D.: Slide Attacks. In: Knudsen, L.R. (ed.) FSE 1999. LNCS, vol. 1636, pp. 245–259. Springer, Heidelberg (1999)
9. Coppersmith, D.: The Data Encryption Algorithm and its Strength Against Attacks. IBM Journal on Research and Development 3(38), 243–250 (1994)
10. Courtois, N.T., Pieprzyk, J.: Cryptanalysis of Block Ciphers with Overdefined Systems of Quadratic Equations. In: Zheng, Y. (ed.) ASIACRYPT 2002. LNCS, vol. 2501, pp. 267–287. Springer, Heidelberg (2002)
11. Daemen, J., Govaerts, R., Vandewalle, J.: Weak Keys for IDEA. In: Stinson, D.R. (ed.) CRYPTO 1993. LNCS, vol. 773, pp. 224–231. Springer, Heidelberg (1994)
12. Daemen, J., Knudsen, L.R., Rijmen, V.: The Block Cipher SQUARE. In: Biham, E. (ed.) FSE 1997. LNCS, vol. 1267, pp. 149–165. Springer, Heidelberg (1997)
13. Davies, D.W., Murphy, S.: Pairs and Triplets of DES S-Boxes. Journal of Cryptology 1(8), 1–25 (1995)
14. Ferguson, N., Schroeppel, R., Whiting, D.: A Simple Algebraic Representation of Rijndael. In: Vaudenay, S., Youssef, A.M. (eds.) SAC 2001. LNCS, vol. 2259, pp. 103–111. Springer, Heidelberg (2001)
15. FIPS 180-2: Secure Hash Standard, SHS (2002), http://csrc.nist.gov/
16. FIPS197: Advanced Encryption Standard (AES), FIPS PUB 197 Federal Information Processing Standard Publication 197, U.S. Department of Commerce (2001)
17. Jakobsen, T., Knudsen, L.R.: The Interpolation Attack on Block Ciphers. In: Biham, E. (ed.) FSE 1997. LNCS, vol. 1267, pp. 28–40. Springer, Heidelberg (1997)
18. Kaliski Jr, B.S., Robshaw, M.J.B.: Linear Cryptanalysis Using Multiple Approximations. In: Desmedt, Y.G. (ed.) CRYPTO 1994. LNCS, vol. 839, pp. 26–39. Springer, Heidelberg (1994)

19. Kelsey, J., Schneier, B., Wagner, D.: Mod n Cryptanalysis, with Applications against RC5P and M6. In: Knudsen, L.R. (ed.) FSE 1999. LNCS, vol. 1636, pp. 139–155. Springer, Heidelberg (1999)
20. Kelsey, J., Schneier, B., Wagner, D.: Related-Key Cryptanalysis of 3-Way, Biham-DES, CAST, DES-X, NewDES, RC2, and TEA. In: Han, Y., Quing, S. (eds.) ICICS 1997. LNCS, vol. 1334, pp. 233–246. Springer, Heidelberg (1997)
21. Knudsen, L.R.: Block Ciphers – A Survey. In: Preneel, B., Rijmen, V. (eds.) State of the Art in Applied Cryptography. LNCS, vol. 1528, pp. 18–48. Springer, Heidelberg (1998)
22. Knudsen, L.R.: DEAL – a 128-bit Block Cipher, Technical Report #151, University of Bergen, Dept. of Informatics, Norway (1998)
23. Knudsen, L.R.: Truncated and Higher Order Differentials. In: Preneel, B. (ed.) FSE 1994. LNCS, vol. 1008, pp. 196–211. Springer, Heidelberg (1995)
24. Knudsen, L.R., Meier, W.: Correlations in RC6 with a Reduced Number of Rounds. In: Schneier, B. (ed.) FSE 2000. LNCS, vol. 1978, pp. 94–108. Springer, Heidelberg (2001)
25. Lai, X.: Higher Order Derivatives and Differential Cryptanalysis. In: Proceedings of Symposium on Communication, Coding and Cryptography, Monte Verita, Switzerland, pp. 227–233 (1994)
26. Lenstra, H.W.: Rijndael for Algebraists (2002), http://math.berkeley.edu/~hwl/papers
27. MacWilliams, F.J., Sloane, N.J.A.: The Theory of Error-Correcting Codes. North-Holland Mathematical Library 16 (1977)
28. Matsui, M.: Linear Cryptanalysis Method for DES Cipher. In: Helleseth, T. (ed.) EUROCRYPT 1993. LNCS, vol. 765, pp. 386–397. Springer, Heidelberg (1994)
29. Menezes, A.J., van Oorschot, P.C., Vanstone, S.A.: Handbook of Applied Cryptography. CRC Press, Boca Raton
30. Merkle, R.C.: A Software Encryption Function, posted to sci.crypt USENET newsgroup (1989)
31. Nyberg, K.: Linear Approximation of Block Ciphers. In: De Santis, A. (ed.) EUROCRYPT 1994. LNCS, vol. 950, pp. 439–444. Springer, Heidelberg (1995)
32. Rijmen, V., Daemen, J., Preneel, B., Bosselaers, A., De Win, E.: The Cipher SHARK. In: Gollmann, D. (ed.) FSE 1996. LNCS, vol. 1039, pp. 99–112. Springer, Heidelberg (1996)
33. Rijmen, V., Preneel, B., De Win, E.: On Weaknesses of Non-Surjective Round Functions. Design, Codes and Cryptography 3(12), 253–266 (1997)
34. Rosenthal, J.: A Polynomial Description of the Rijndael Advanced Encryption Standard. Journal Algebra Appl. 2(2), 223–236 (2003)
35. Shannon, C.E.: Communication Theory of Secrecy Systems. Bell System Technical Journal 28, 656–715 (1949)
36. Wu, H.: Related-Cipher Attacks. In: Deng, R. (ed.) ICICS 2002. LNCS, vol. 2513, pp. 447–455. Springer, Heidelberg (2002)

A Appendix A

A test vector for 3D follows in hexadecimal notation.

- plaintext P_1:

$$\begin{pmatrix} 00_x\ 00_x\ 00_x\ 00_x & 00_x\ 00_x\ 00_x\ 00_x & 00_x\ 00_x\ 00_x\ 00_x & 00_x\ 00_x\ 00_x\ 00_x \\ 00_x\ 00_x\ 00_x\ 00_x & 00_x\ 00_x\ 00_x\ 00_x & 00_x\ 00_x\ 00_x\ 00_x & 00_x\ 00_x\ 00_x\ 00_x \\ 00_x\ 00_x\ 00_x\ 00_x & 00_x\ 00_x\ 00_x\ 00_x & 00_x\ 00_x\ 00_x\ 00_x & 00_x\ 00_x\ 00_x\ 00_x \\ 00_x\ 00_x\ 00_x\ 00_x & 00_x\ 00_x\ 00_x\ 00_x & 00_x\ 00_x\ 00_x\ 00_x & 00_x\ 00_x\ 00_x\ 00_x \end{pmatrix}$$

- key K_1:

$$\begin{pmatrix} 00_x\ 00_x\ 00_x\ 00_x & 00_x\ 00_x\ 00_x\ 00_x & 00_x\ 00_x\ 00_x\ 00_x & 00_x\ 00_x\ 00_x\ 00_x \\ 00_x\ 00_x\ 00_x\ 00_x & 00_x\ 00_x\ 00_x\ 00_x & 00_x\ 00_x\ 00_x\ 00_x & 00_x\ 00_x\ 00_x\ 00_x \\ 00_x\ 00_x\ 00_x\ 00_x & 00_x\ 00_x\ 00_x\ 00_x & 00_x\ 00_x\ 00_x\ 00_x & 00_x\ 00_x\ 00_x\ 00_x \\ 00_x\ 00_x\ 00_x\ 00_x & 00_x\ 00_x\ 00_x\ 00_x & 00_x\ 00_x\ 00_x\ 00_x & 00_x\ 00_x\ 00_x\ 00_x \end{pmatrix}$$

- ciphertext $C_1 = E(K_1, P_1)$:

$$\begin{pmatrix} ef_x\ 93_x\ 49_x\ 10_x & 67_x\ b2_x\ b4_x\ 59_x & ad_x\ 01_x\ 4f_x\ 3a_x & 0c_x\ 97_x\ fe_x\ e7_x \\ f3_x\ ea_x\ f5_x\ 8c_x & 03_x\ 46_x\ 33_x\ ed_x & b6_x\ 22_x\ 7f_x\ 40_x & cd_x\ 02_x\ 52_x\ b3_x \\ d0_x\ ee_x\ f8_x\ 7c_x & eb_x\ 70_x\ 28_x\ da_x & 62_x\ dd_x\ 29_x\ 67_x & 84_x\ 53_x\ 14_x\ 1d_x \\ fe_x\ 58_x\ 54_x\ 33_x & 2b_x\ ab_x\ 40_x\ 34_x & d3_x\ 66_x\ d5_x\ 4c_x & 5f_x\ 63_x\ 0b_x\ 0a_x \end{pmatrix}$$

Construction of Resilient Functions with Multiple Cryptographic Criteria

Chao Li[1,2], Shaojing Fu[1], and Bing Sun[1]

[1] Department of Mathematics and System Science
Science College, National University of Defence Technology
Changsha 410073, China
[2] National Mobile Communications Research Laboratory,
Southeast University, Nanjing 210018, China
lichao_nudt@sina.com

Abstract. Based on a $[u, m, t+1]$-code C, an approach to construct (n, m, t) resilient functions with multiple cryptographic criteria including high nonlinearity, high algebraic degree and nonexistence of nonzero linear structure is described. Particularly, when $u = 2m$, this kind of construction can be made simply.

Keywords: Resilient function, Linear Code, Nonlinearity, Linear structure.

1 Introduction

Resilient functions have wide applications in quantum key distribution, fault-tolerant distributed computing, random sequence for stream ciphers and S-box for block ciphers. It is now well accepted that for an (n, m, t) resilient function in symmetric cipher systems, it must satisfy such properties as high nonlinearity, high algebraic and good propagation character. All of these parameters are important in resisting on different kinds of attacks, so the researches on cryptographic resilient functions are paid more and more attention[1,2,3,4,5]. E.Pasalic, S.Maitra and T.Johamsson constructed many (n, m, t) resilient functions with high nonlinearity by using linear codes in 2002 and 2003 [6,7]. However, we note that the functions with good resiliency and high nonlinearity could imply some cryptographic weakness such as existence of linear structures. For example, [8] demonstrated that the (n, m, t) resilient functions obtained from the paper [4, 6, 7] have nonzero linear structures. In order to get better resilient functions, Y.Z Wei and Y.P.Hu tried to construct (n, m, t) resilient functions with multiple cryptographic criteria including high nonlinearity, high algebraic degree and nonexistence of nonzero linear structure in 2004 [9]. Their construction was based on a $[u, m, t+1]$−code and its dual code. Although they didn't make sure that the two codes are disjoint, but in the proof of lemma 5 of their paper, the properties of disjoint was needed, otherwise, it was impossible to construct a u-basis-set D_c in this lemma.

In this paper, we provide an approach to construct (n, m, t) resilient functions with multiple cryptographic criteria based a $[u, m, t+1]$-code C. Our construction only depends on the linear code C and has nothing to do with its dual code $C^\perp$.

2 Preliminaries

Let F_2 be the binary finite field, the vector space of dimension n over F_2 is denoted by F_2^n and $(F_2^n)^*$ denotes the set of all nonzero vector of F_2^n. By V_n we mean the set of all Boolean functions of n variables, and we interpret a Boolean function $f(x_1, x_2, \cdots, x_n)$ as the output column of its truth table, that is, a binary string of length 2^n having the form:

$$\{f(0,0,\cdots,0),\ f(0,0,\cdots,1),\ \cdots,\ f(1,1,\cdots,1)\}.$$

The weight of f is the number of ones in its output column, and is denoted by $wt(f)$. An n-variable function f is said to be balanced if $wt(f) = 2^{n-1}$.

An n-variable function f can be considered to be a multivariate polynomial over F_2. This polynomial can be express as a sum of products representation of all distinct kth-order$(k < n)$ product terms of the variables. The number of variables in the highest order product term with nonzero coefficient is called the algebraic degree of f (abbr. $deg(f)$).

Functions with degree at most one are called affine functions, affine functions with $f(0) = 0$ are called linear functions. The set of all n-variable affine functions is denoted by A_n, the set of all n-variable affine functions is denoted by L_n. The nonlinearity of an n-variable function f is the distance between f and the set of all n-variable affine functions, this is denoted by $nl(f)$. The walsh transform of an n-variable function f is a real valued function defined as

$$W_f(u) = \sum_{x \in F_2^n} (-1)^{f(x)+x\cdot u}$$

where the dot product of vectors x and u is defined as

$$x \cdot u = x_1 u_1 + x_2 u_2 + \cdots + x_n u_n.$$

An n-variable function f is called t-resilient if and only if $W_f(u) = 0$ for all u with $0 \leq wt(u) \leq t$, and f is said to have a linear structure, say a, if and only if $f(x+a) + f(x)$(abbr. D_f)is a constant function.

Let us consider the vector-valued function $F(x) = (f_1(x), f_2(x), \cdots, f_m(x))$, then the nonlinearity of F is defined as

$$nl(F) = \min\{nl(\sum_{i=1}^{m} \tau_i f_i(x)) | \tau = (\tau_1, \cdots, \tau_m) \in (F_2^m)^*\}.$$

Similarly, the algebraic degree of F is defined as

$$deg(F) = \min\{deg(\sum_{i=1}^{m} \tau_i f_i(x)) | \tau = (\tau_1, \cdots, \tau_m) \in (F_2^m)^*\}.$$

F is said to be an (n,m,t) resilient function if and only if $\sum_{i=1}^{m} \tau_i f_i(x)$ is an t-resilient function for any $\tau = (\tau_1, \tau_2, \cdots, \tau_m) \in (F_2^m)^*$. Moreover, a is said to be a linear structure of F if and only if a is a linear structure of $\sum_{i=1}^{m} \tau_i f_i(x)$ for any $\tau = (\tau_1, \tau_2, \cdots, \tau_m) \in (F_2^m)^*$.

Definition 1. *A set D is called n-basis-set, if it satisfies the following two conditions:*

(1) $D \subset F_2^n$.
(2) *There exists $r_i \in D (i = 1, 2, \cdots, n)$ such that $r_1, r_2, \cdots, r_n$ is a basis of F_2^n, and there exists $i \neq j$ such that $r_i + r_j \in D$, where $1 \leq i, j \leq n$.*

Lemma 1. *[9]If D is an n-basis-set, then the function $f(x) = b \cdot x (x \in D)$ is not a constant function for any $b \in (F_2^n)^*$.*

3 Construction of Resilient Functions with Multiple Cryptographic Criteria

In this section, we will provide a new method to construct (n,m,t) resilient functions with multiple cryptographic criteria. Firstly, we give an example that the $[u,m,t+1]$-code and its dual code are not disjoint, and the construction from [9] is not valid in this case.

Example 1. Consider a [7,3,3]-code C with a basis

$$\{[1,0,0,1,0,1,1], [0,1,0,1,1,1,1], [0,0,1,0,1,0,1]\}.$$

Then the dual code $C^\perp$ of C is a [7,4,2]-code which has a basis

$$\{[1,1,0,0,0,1,0], [0,1,0,0,1,1,1], [0,0,1,0,0,1,1], [0,0,0,1,0,1,0]\}.$$

It is easily seen that $[1,1,1,0,0,0,1] \in C \cap C^\perp$ and there does not exist a matrix T defined in the proof of lemma 5 in [9] which has 2^3 rows and 3 columns such that every 2^3 nonzero codewords obtained in any linear combination of columns (not all zero) is still a 7-basis-set D such that $|D| = 2^3$ and $wt(x) \geq 2$ for any $x \in D$. Hence, the $(7+3,3,1)$ resilient function which does not exist nonzero linear structure can not be constructed by their methods.

Lemma 2. *Let C be a $[u,m,t+1]$-code. Then there exists a u-basis-set D, such that $|D| = 2^q$ and $wt(x) \geq t+1$ for any $x \in D$, where $ln(u+4) \leq q \leq m$.*

Proof. Let $r_1 = (0,1,1,\cdots,1,1,1)$, $r_2 = (1,0,1,\cdots,1,1,1)$, $\cdots$, $r_{u-1} = (1,1,1,\cdots,1,0,1)$, $r_u = (1,1,1,\cdots,1,1,1)$, where $r_1, r_2, \cdots, r_u \in F_2^u$. It is noted that $\{r_1, r_2, \cdots, r_{u-1}, r_u\}$ is a basis of F_2^u. Now we construct a set D of 2^q elements as follows:

(1) $r_1, r_2, \cdots, r_{u-1}, r_u \in D$.
(2) Choose two different $c_1, c_2 \in C$ such that $c_i \neq r_j (i = 1, 2, j = 1, 2, \cdots, u)$ and $c_1 + c_2 \neq r_j (j = 1, 2, \cdots, u)$, let $c_1, c_2, c_1 + c_2 \in D$.
(3) The remaining $2^q - (u + 3)$ elements are chosen arbitrarily from C.

Then D is a u-basis-set such that $|D| = 2^q$ and $wt(x) \geq t + 1$ for any $x \in D$. In fact, since $\{r_1, r_2, \cdots, r_{u-1}, r_u\}$ is a basis of F_2^u, c_1, c_2 can be linearly represented by $\{r_1, r_2, \cdots, r_{u-1}, r_u\}$. Noted that c_1 is independent to c_2, we can find two different vectors from the basis $\{r_1, r_2, \cdots, r_{u-1}, r_u\}$, and substitute the two vectors by c_1, c_2 in this base, these new vectors are still a basis of F_2^u. From definition 1, we obtain that u-basis-set. In addition, since the minimal distance of C is $t + 1$ and $wt(r_j) \geq u - 1$, then for any $x \in D$, $wt(x) \geq t + 1$. □

Theorem 1. Let C be a $[u, m, t + 1]$-code, and let $f(x, y) = \varphi(x) \cdot y + g(x)$, $x \in F_2^q, y \in F_2^u$, where $g(x) = x_1 x_2 \cdots x_q$, and $\varphi(x)$ is a bijection from F_2^q to the u-basis-set D constructed in lemma 2. Then the following results hold:

1) $f(x, y)$ does not exist nonzero linear structure.
2) $f(x, y)$ is an $(n, 1, t)$ resilient function with $n = u + q$.
3) $nl(f) = 2^{n-1} - 2^{u-1}$.
3) $\deg(f) \geq q$.

Proof. 1) For any $(a, b) \in F_2^n$, where $a \in F_2^q$ and $b \in F_2^u$, let

$$D_f = f(x + a, y + b) + f(x, y) = \varphi(x + a) \cdot (y + b) + g(x + a) + \varphi(x) \cdot y + g(x).$$

If $a = 0$, then $D_f = \varphi(x) \cdot b$. From lemma 1, we know that D_f is not a constant function. If $a \neq 0$, then $\varphi(x + a) + \varphi(x) \neq 0$, hence D_f is balanced, it is also not a constant function. According to the definition of linear structure, $f(x, y)$ does not exist nonzero linear structure.

2) Let $a = (a_1, a_2)$, where $a_1 \in F_2^q$ and $a_2 \in F_2^u$ with $0 \leq wt(a) \leq t$. Then

$$W_f(a) = \sum_{x,y}(-1)^{f(x,y)+(a_1,a_2)\cdot(x,y)}$$

$$= \sum_{x,y}(-1)^{\varphi(x)\cdot y + g(x) + a_1 \cdot x + a_2 \cdot y}$$

$$= \sum_x (-1)^{g(x)+a_1 \cdot x} \cdot \sum_y (-1)^{(\varphi(x)+a_2)\cdot y}.$$

From lemma 2, $wt(a_2) \leq t$ and $wt(\varphi(x)) \geq t$, then $\varphi(x) + a_2 \neq 0$ for any $x \in F_2^q$. Hence, $W_f(a) = 0$ for all $a \in F_{2^u}, 0 \leq wt(a) \leq t$.

3) Since

$$W_f(a) = \begin{cases} 0, & \varphi(x) + a_2 \neq 0 \text{ for any } x \in F_2^q, \\ 2^u, & \exists x, \varphi(x) + a_2 = 0. \end{cases}$$

Therefore, $nl(f) = 2^{n-1} - 2^{u-1}$.

4) Since the degree of $g(x)$ is q, then the degree of $\varphi(x) \cdot y + g(x)$ is not less than q. □

Lemma 3. *[6] Let $\{c_0, c_1, \cdots, c_{m-1}\}$ be a basis of a $[u, m, t+1]$-code C, β be a primitive element of F_{2^m} and $\{1, \beta, \cdots, \beta^{m-1}\}$ be a basis of F_{2^m}. Define a bijection $\phi : F_{2^m} \to C$ by*

$$\phi(a_0 + a_1\beta + \cdots + a_{m-1}\beta^{m-1}) = a_0c_0 + a_1c_1 + \cdots + a_{m-1}c_{m-1}$$

Let A and B be two matrices of dimension $(2^m - 1) \times m$ and $m \times m$ respectively as follows:

$$A = \begin{pmatrix} \phi(1) & \phi(\beta) & \cdots & \phi(\beta^{m-1}) \\ \phi(\beta) & \phi(\beta^2) & \cdots & \phi(\beta^m) \\ \vdots & \vdots & \ddots & \vdots \\ \phi(\beta^{2^m-2}) & \phi(1) & \cdots & \phi(\beta^{m-2}) \end{pmatrix}$$

$$B = \begin{pmatrix} \phi(1) & \phi(\beta) & \cdots & \phi(\beta^{m-1}) \\ \phi(\beta) & \phi(\beta^2) & \cdots & \phi(\beta^m) \\ \vdots & \vdots & \ddots & \vdots \\ \phi(\beta^{m-1}) & \phi(\beta^m) & \cdots & \phi(\beta^{2m-2}) \end{pmatrix}$$

Then the following results hold:
(1) For any linear combination of columns (not all zero) of A, each nonzero codeword of C will appear exactly once.
(2) For any linear combination of columns (not all zero) of B, there exist a set of m nonzero codewords such that it is a basis of C.

According to the knowledge of linear algebra and error-corrected codes, the following result is easily verified.

Lemma 4. *Let C be a $[u, m, t+1]$-code, then there exists a $[u, u-m, t^*+1]$-code C^* such that $C \cap C^* = 0$, where $t^* + 1 \geq 1$.*

Based on the above lemmas 3 and 4, we can obtain:

Lemma 5. *Let C be a $[u, m, t+1]$-code and C^* be a $[u, u-m, t^*+1]$-code. Then there exists a matrix T which has 2^q rows and m columns, such that every 2^q nonzero codewords obtained from any linear combination of columns (not all zero) is still a u-basis-set D with $|D| = 2^q$ and $wt(x) \geq d$ for any $x \in D$, where $ln(u+1) \leq q \leq u-m$, $u \geq 2m$, $d = min(t+1, t^*+1)$.*

Proof. Let $\{c_0, c_1, \cdots, c_{m-1}\}$ be a basis of C, β be a primitive element of F_{2^m}, $\{r_0, r_1, \cdots, r_{u-m-1}\}$ be a basis of C^*, β^* be a primitive element of $F_{2^{u-m}}$. Define a bijection $\phi_1: F_{2^m} \to C$ by

$$\phi_1(a_0 + a_1\beta + \cdots + a_{m-1}\beta^{m-1}) = a_0c_0 + a_1c_1 + \cdots + a_{m-1}c_{m-1},$$

and define a bijection $\phi_2: F_{2^{u-m}} \to C^*$ by

$$\phi_2(a_0 + a_1\beta^* + \cdots + a_{m-1}(\beta^*)^{u-m-1}) = a_0r_0 + a_1r_1 + \cdots + a_{u-m-1}r_{u-m-1}.$$

Now we denote four matrices A_1, A_2, B_1, B_2 as follows:

$$A_1 = \begin{pmatrix} \phi_1(1) & \phi_1(\beta) & \cdots & \phi_1(\beta^{m-1}) \\ \phi_1(\beta) & \phi_1(\beta^2) & \cdots & \phi_1(\beta^m) \\ \vdots & \vdots & \ddots & \vdots \\ \phi_1(\beta^{m-1}) & \phi_1(m) & \cdots & \phi_1(\beta^{2m-2}) \end{pmatrix}$$

$$A_2 = \begin{pmatrix} \phi_2(1) & \phi_2(\beta^*) & \cdots & \phi_2((\beta^*)^{m-1}) \\ \phi_2(\beta^*) & \phi_2((\beta^*)^2) & \cdots & \phi_2((\beta^*)^m) \\ \vdots & \vdots & \ddots & \vdots \\ \phi_2((\beta^*)^{u-m-1}) & \phi_2((\beta^*)^{u-m}) & \cdots & \phi_2((\beta^*)^{u-2}) \end{pmatrix}$$

$$B_1 = \begin{pmatrix} \phi_1(\beta^m) & \phi_1(\beta^{m+1}) & \cdots & \phi_1(\beta^{2m-1}) \\ \phi_1(\beta^{m+1}) & \phi_1(\beta^{m+2}) & \cdots & \phi_1(\beta^{2m}) \\ \vdots & \vdots & \ddots & \vdots \\ \phi_1(\beta^{2^m-2}) & \phi_1(1) & \cdots & \phi_1(\beta^{m-2}) \end{pmatrix}$$

$$B_2 = \begin{pmatrix} \phi_2((\beta^*)^{u-m}) & \phi_2((\beta^*)^{u-m+1}) & \cdots & \phi_2((\beta^*)^{u-1}) \\ \phi_2((\beta^*)^{u-m+1}) & \phi_2((\beta^*)^{u-m+2}) & \cdots & \phi_2((\beta^*)^u) \\ \vdots & \vdots & \ddots & \vdots \\ \phi_2((\beta^*)^{2^{u-m}-2}) & \phi_2(1) & \cdots & \phi_2((\beta^*)^{u-m-2}) \end{pmatrix}$$

Let T be the following $2^q \times m$ matrix:

$$T = \begin{pmatrix} A_1 \\ A_2 \\ A_3 \end{pmatrix}$$

where the rows of A_3 are chosen from the rows of B_1 and B_2 arbitrarily. From lemmas 3 and 4, we know that the matrix T has the property that every 2^q nonzero codeword obtained from any linear combination of columns (not all zero) of the matrix T is still a u-basis-set D such that $|D| = 2^q$ and $wt(x) \geq d$ for any $x \in D$. □

Theorem 2. *Let T be the matrix constructed in lemma 5, define*

$$F(x, y) = (f_1(x, y), f_2(x, y), \cdots, f_m(x, y)),$$

where $f_i(x, y) = \varphi_i(x) \cdot y + g_i(x)$ for $x \in F_2^q$ and $y \in F_2^u$, $g_i(x)$ is any Boolean function on F_2^q, and $\varphi_i(x)$ is any bijection from F_2^q to the i-th column of matrix T, $ln(u+1) \leq q \leq u - m$, $u \geq 2m$. Then the following results hold:

(1) $F(x, y)$ does not exist nonzero linear structures.
(2) $F(x, y)$ is (n, m, t) resilient function with $d = min(t, t^*)$ and $n = u + q$.
(3) $F(x, y) = 2^{n-1} - 2^{u-1}$.
(4) The degree of $F(x, y)$ can exceed to $q - 2$.

Proof. Let $\tau = (\tau_1, \tau_2, \cdots, \tau_m) \in (F_2^m)^*$, then

$$\sum_{i=1}^{m} \tau_i f_i(x, y) = \sum_{i=1}^{m} \tau_i \varphi_i(x) \cdot y + \sum_{i=1}^{m} \tau_i g_i(x).$$

From lemma 5 we know that $\sum_{i=1}^{m} \tau_i \varphi_i(x)$ is a bijection from F_2^q to a $u-basis-$ set D, where $|D| = 2^q$ and $wt(x) \geq d$ for any $x \in D$. then we prove (1),(2),(3)as same as the proof of theorem 1.

Next we prove (4). Note that $g_i(x)$ is any Boolean function on F_2^q, we can distinguish two case:

Case 1: $m \leq q \leq u - m$
Let $g_i(x) = x_1 x_2 \cdots x_{i-1} x_{i+1} \cdots x_q$, then $deg(\sum_{i=1}^{m} \tau_i g_i(x)) = q - 1$.

Case 2: $ln(u+1) \leq q \leq m - 1$
Let S be the following set:

$$S = \{x_1 x_2 \cdots x_{k-1} x_{k+1} \cdots \cdots x_{i-1} x_{i+1} \cdots x_q | k \neq i\},$$

and $g_i(x)$ $(1 \leq i \leq m)$ are selected arbitrarily from set S. Hence, $deg(\sum_{i=1}^{m} \tau_i g_i(x)) = q - 2$, we therefore conclude that the degree of $F(x, y)$ can exceed to $q - 2$. □

In the following, we are ready to describe our construction:

Construction Procedure 1
Input: a $[u, m, t+1]$ linear code C^*, Parameter q.
Output: an (n, m, d) resilient function$(n = u + q)$.
Step1 Let $t^* = t + 1$;
Step2 Let $t^* = t^* - 1$;
Step3 Search a $[u, u - m, t^* + 1]-$code C^* such that $C \cap C^* = 0$, if successful go to Step4, otherwise go to Step2;
Step4 Obtain the matrix T defined in Lemma 5;
Step5 Let $f_i(x, y) = \varphi_i(x) \cdot y + g_i(x)$, where $x \in GF(2)^q$ and $y \in GF(2)^u$;
Step6 output $F(x, y) = (f_1(x, y), f_2(x, y), \cdots, f_m(x, y))$.

However, the major difficult in our construction is the fact that our construction is available through computer search (which becomes infeasible for a moderate cardinality of codes). Now we describe an easy way in some special cases.

Let C be a $[2m, m, t+1]-$ code, from lemma 4 we can find a $[2m, m]-$code C^* such that $C \cap C^* = 0$. Let $\{c_0, c_1, \cdots, c_{m-1}\}$ be a basis of C, $\{r_0, r_1, \cdots, r_{m-1}\}$ be a basis of C^*, β be a primitive element in F_{2^m}. Then we define $\phi_1: F_{2^m} \to C$ by

$$\phi_1(a_0 + a_1\beta + \cdots + a_{m-1}\beta^{m-1}) = a_0 c_0 + a_1 c_1 + \cdots + a_{m-1} c_{m-1},$$

and define $\phi_2: F_2^m \to C$ by

$$\phi_2(a_0 + a_1\beta + \cdots + a_{m-1}\beta^{m-1}) = a_0 r_0 + a_1 r_1 + \cdots + a_{m-1} r_{m-1}.$$

Then, it is obvious that $G = [\phi_1(1), \phi_1(\beta), \cdots, \phi_1(\beta^{m-1})]^T$ and $G^* = [\phi_2(1), \phi_2(\beta), \cdots, \phi_2(\beta^{m-1})]^T$ are the generation matrices of C and C^*. Now we define

$$H_0 = [\phi_1(1) + \phi_2(1), \phi_1(\beta) + \phi_2(\beta), \cdots, \phi_1(\beta^{m-1}) + \phi_2(\beta^{m-1})]^T$$
$$H_1 = [\phi_1(1) + \phi_2(\beta), \phi_1(\beta) + \phi_2(\beta^2), \cdots, \phi_1(\beta^{m-1}) + \phi_2(\beta^m)]^T$$
$$\vdots$$
$$H_{2^m-2} = [\phi_1(1) + \phi_2(\beta^{2^m-2}), \phi_1(\beta) + \phi_2(1), \cdots, \phi_1(\beta^{m-1}) + \phi_2(\beta^{m-2})]^T.$$

Theorem 3. *Let $C_0, C_1, \cdots, C_{2^m-2}$ be the linear codes generated by $H_0, H_1, \cdots, H_{2^m-2}$, respectively. Then*
(1) $C \cap C_i = 0$ *for any* $0 \le i \le 2^m - 2$.
(2) $C^* \cap C_i = 0$ *for any* $0 \le i \le 2^m - 2$.
(3) $C_i \cap C_j = 0$ *for any* $0 \le i \ne j \le 2^m - 2$.
(4) $C_0 \cup C_1 \cup \cdots \cup C_{2^m-2} \cup C \cup C^* = F_2^{2m}$.

Proof. (1) For any $(x_0, x_1, \cdots, x_{m-1}) \ne 0$ and $(y_0, y_1, \cdots, y_{m-1}) \ne 0$.

$$\sum_{k=0}^{m-1} x_k \phi_1(\beta^k) + \sum_{k=0}^{m-1} y_k(\phi_1(\beta^k) + \phi_2(\beta^{k+i}))$$
$$= \sum_{k=0}^{m-1} (x_k + y_k)\phi_1(\beta^k) + \sum_{k=0}^{m-1} y_k \phi_2(\beta^{k+i}).$$

Note that $\sum_{k=0}^{m-1}(x_k + y_k)\phi_1(\beta^k) \in C$, $0 \ne \sum_{k=0}^{m-1} y_k\phi_2(\beta^{k+i}) \in C^*$, then $\sum_{k=0}^{m-1}(x_k+y_k)\phi_1(\beta^k) + \sum_{k=0}^{m-1} y_k\phi_2(\beta^{k+i}) \ne 0$. Hence, $C \cap C_i \ne 0$.
(2) For any $(x_0, x_1, \cdots, x_{m-1})$ and $(y_0, y_1, \cdots, y_{m-1})$.

$$\sum_{k=0}^{m-1} x_k \phi_2(\beta^k) + \sum_{k=0}^{m-1} y_k(\phi_1(\beta^k) + \phi_2(\beta^{k+i}))$$
$$= \sum_{k=0}^{m-1} (x_k + y_k)\phi_2(\beta^k) + \sum_{k=0}^{m-1} y_k \phi_1(\beta^{k+i}).$$

Note that $0 \ne \sum_{k=0}^{m-1} y_k\phi_1(\beta^{k+i}) \in C$, $\sum_{k=0}^{m-1}(x_k+y_k)\phi_2(\beta^k) \in C^*$, then $\sum_{k=0}^{m-1}(x_k+y_k)\phi_2(\beta^k) + \sum_{k=0}^{m-1} y_k\phi_1(\beta^{k+i}) \ne 0$. Hence, we also obtain $C^* \cap C_i \ne 0$.
(3) For any $(x_0, x_1, \cdots, x_{m-1})$ and $(y_0, y_1, \cdots, y_{m-1})$.

$$\sum_{k=0}^{m-1} x_k(\phi_1(\beta^k) + \phi_2(\beta^{k+i})) + \sum_{k=0}^{m-1} y_k(\phi_1(\beta^k) + \phi_2(\beta^{k+j}))$$
$$= \sum_{k=0}^{m-1} (x_k + y_k)\phi_1(\beta^k) + \sum_{k=0}^{m-1} (x_k\phi_2(\beta^{k+i}) + y_k\phi_2(\beta^{k+j})).$$

Note that $0 \neq \sum_{k=0}^{m-1}(x_k + y_k)\phi_1(\beta^k) \in C$, $\sum_{k=0}^{m-1}(x_k\phi_2(\beta^{k+i}) + y_k\phi_2(\beta^{k+j})) \in C^*$, then $\sum_{k=0}^{m-1}(x_k + y_k)\phi_1(\beta^k) + \sum_{k=0}^{m-1}(x_k\phi_2(\beta^{k+i}) + y_k\phi_2(\beta^{k+j})) \neq 0$. Hence, we again have $C_i \cap C_j \neq 0$.

(4) Since every linear code has 2^m word, let $|C|$ be the cardinality of C. Then

$$|C_0| + |C_1| + \cdots + |C_{2^m-2}| + |C| + |C^*| = 2^{2m} + 2^m$$
$$\Longrightarrow C_0 \cup C_1 \cup \cdots \cup C_{2^m-2} \cup C \cup C^* = F_2^{2m}. \qquad \Box$$

For special linear codes, we are ready to describe our improved construction.

Construction Procedure 2

Input: a $[2m, m, t+1]$ linear code C, Parameter q.
Output: an (n, m, d) resilient function($n = 2m + q$).
Step1 Obtain a $[2m, m]$−code C^* such that $C \cap C^* = 0$;
Step2 Obtain all the $[2m, m]$−codes $C_0, C_1, \cdots, C_{2^m-2}$ defined in Theorem 2;
Step3 Let $t^* = t + 1$;
Step4 Let $t^* = t^* - 1$;
Step5 Search a $[2m, m, t^*+1]$−code from $C_0, C_1, \cdots, C_{2^m-2}$, if successful go to Step4, otherwise go to Step2;
Step6 Obtain the matrix T defined in Lemma 5;
Step7 Let $f_i(x, y) = \varphi_i(x) \cdot y + g_i(x)$, where $x \in F_2^q$ and $y \in F_2^u$ defined in Theorem 2;
Step8 output $F(x, y) = (f_1(x, y), f_2(x, y), \cdots, f_m(x, y))$.

At last, we compare (n, m, t) resilient functions obtained by our construction with the known constructions.

Table 1. (n, m, t) resilient functions with multiple cryptographic criteria

	Linear Codes needed	Nonlinearity	Degree	Nonzero linear structure
[6]	A $[u, m, t+1]$ code	$2^{n-1} - 2^{u-1}$	$\geq q$	Exist
[7]	Some disjoint $[u, m, t+1]$ codes	$\geq 2^{n-1} - 2^{u-1}$	$\geq m$	Exist
this paper	A $[u, m, t+1]$ code	$2^{n-1} - 2^{u-1}$	$\geq q$	Not exist

4 Conclusion

In this paper, we study the case that the construction in [9] can't work, and describe an improved method for constructing of (n, m, t) resilient functions which satisfy multiple cryptographic criteria. The construction is based on linear codes. Given a $[u, m, t+1]$−code, we describe a method to construct (n, m, t) resilient functions and simplify our construction when $u = 2m$. Our construction provides a new idea in designing cryptographic functions. Besides, it will be of interest to find new methods to get a $[u, u-m, t^*+1]$−code C^* such that C and C^* is disjoint in our future research.

Acknowledgments

The work in this paper is supported by the National Natural Science Foundation of China (No:60573028) and the open research fund of National Mobile Communications Research Laboratory of Southeast University (No:W200805).

References

1. Canteaut, A., Carlet, C.: Propagation characteristics and correlation immunity of highly nonlinear boolean functions. In: Preneel, B. (ed.) EUROCRYPT 2000. LNCS, vol. 1807, pp. 507–522. Springer, Heidelberg (2000)
2. Carlet, C.: On the propagation criterion of degree l and order k. In: Nyberg, K. (ed.) EUROCRYPT 1998. LNCS, vol. 1403, pp. 463–474. Springer, Heidelberg (1998)
3. Pasalic, E.: Degree optimized resilient boolean functions from Maiorana-MCFarland class. In: Paterson, K.G. (ed.) Cryptography and Coding 2003. LNCS, vol. 2898, pp. 93–114. Springer, Heidelberg (2003)
4. Kurosawa, K., Satoh, T.: Design of SAC/PC(l) of order k Boolean functions and three other cryptographic criteria. In: Fumy, W. (ed.) EUROCRYPT 1997. LNCS, vol. 1233, pp. 434–449. Springer, Heidelberg (1997)
5. Zheng, Y., Zhang, X.M.: On plateaued function. IEEE Trans. Inform.Theory 47, 1215–1223 (2001)
6. Pasalic, E., Maitra, S.: Linear code in generalized construction of resilient functions with very high nonlinearity. IEEE Trans. Inform.Theory 48, 2182–2192 (2002)
7. Johansson, T., Pasalic, E.: A construction of resilient functions with high nonliearity. IEEE Trans. Inform.Theory 49, 495–501 (2003)
8. Wei, Y.Z., Hu, Y.P.: Reserch on linear structure of several cryptographic functions. J. of China Institute of Commu. 25, 22–56 (2004)
9. Wei, Y.Z., Hu, Y.P.: A construction of resilient functions with Satisfying Synthetical Cryptographic Criteria. In: IEEE ISOC ITW 2005 on Coding and Complexity, pp. 248–252

Enumeration of Homogeneous Rotation Symmetric Functions over F_p

Shaojing Fu[1], Chao Li[1,2], and Bing Sun[1]

[1] Department of Mathematics and System Science Science College,
National University of Defence Technology,
Changsha 410073, Hunan, China
[2] National Mobile Communications Research Laboratory,
Southeast University, Nanjing 210018, Jiangsu, China
shaojing1984@yahoo.cn

Abstract. Rotation symmetric functions have been used as components of different cryptosystems. Functions in this class are invariant under circular translation of indices. In this paper, we will do some enumeration on homogeneous rotation symmetric functions over F_p. A formula for counting homogeneous rotation symmetric functions over F_p is presented when $\gcd(n,d)$ is a prime power, where n is the number of input variables and d is the algebraic degree of the function, which demonstrates that we solved one of the problems in [7].

Keywords: Rotation symmetry, Algebraic degree, Minimal function, Monic monomial.

1 Introduction

In [1], Pieprzyk and Qu studied some special functions which are used as the components in the rounds of hash algorithm. These functions are called rotation symmetric functions. They are invariant under circular translation of indices, and it is clear that this class of functions are very rich in terms of many cryptographic properties such as nonlinearity and correlation immune. In[2-4], Stanica, Maitra and Clark gave many results on counting the rotation symmetric functions. They also investigated the correlation immune property of these functions. Dalai and Maitra studied rotation symmetric bent functions in [5]. Maximov, Hell and Maitra obtained some interesting results about plateaued rotation symmetric functions in [6]. Yuan Li extended the concept of rotation symmetric functions from F_2 to F_p [7], and he gave a formula to count homogeneous rotation symmetric functions with degree no more than 3. We are here interested in the enumeration of homogeneous rotation symmetric functions over F_p and provide some better results than the previous works.

The paper is organized as follows. Section 2 presents some basic definitions and notations. In Section 3, we do some enumeration on homogeneous rotation symmetric functions over F_p and solve one of the open problems in [7]. Section 4 concludes this paper.

2 Preliminaries

In this paper, p is a prime. Let F_p be the finite field of p elements, and F_p^n be the vector space of dimension n over F_p. An n-variable function $f(x_1, x_2, \cdots, x_n)$ can be regarded as a multivariate polynomial over F_p, that is,

$$f(x_1, x_2, \cdots, x_n) = \sum_{k_1, k_2, \cdots, k_n = 0}^{p-1} a_{k_1, k_2, \cdots, k_n} x_1^{k_1} x_2^{k_2} \cdots x_n^{k_n}$$

where $a_{k_1, k_2, \cdots, k_n} \in F_p$. This representation of f is called the algebraic normal form (ANF) of f. $k_1 + k_2 + \cdots + k_n$ is defined as the degree of term with nonzero coefficient. The greatest degree of all the terms of f is called the algebraic degree of f, denoted by $\deg(f)$. If the degrees of all the terms of f are equal, then we say f is homogeneous. $f(x_1, x_2, \cdots, x_n)$ is called to be affine if $f(x_1, x_2, \cdots, x_n) = a_1 x_1 + a_2 x_2 + \cdots + a_n x_n + a_0$. Particularly, $f(x_1, x_2, \cdots, x_n) = a_1 x_1 + a_2 x_2 + \cdots + a_n x_n$ is called to be linear. We will denote by F_n the set of all functions of n variables and by L_n the set of affine ones. We will call a function nonlinear if it is not in L_n.

For variable $x_i (1 \leq i \leq n)$ and integer $k (0 \leq k \leq n-1)$, we define

$$\rho_n^k(x_i) = \begin{cases} x_{i+k}, & \text{if } i+k \leq n, \\ x_{i+k-n}, & \text{if } i+k > n. \end{cases}$$

Then the definition of ρ_n^k can be extend to tuples and monomials as follows:

$$\rho_n^k(x_1, \cdots, x_n) = \left(\rho_n^k(x_1), \cdots, \rho_n^k(x_n)\right),$$

and

$$\rho_n^k(x_1^{k_1} x_2^{k_2} \cdots x_n^{k_n}) = (\rho_n^k(x_1))^{k_1} \cdots (\rho_n^k(x_n))^{k_n}.$$

Definition 1. *A function $f(x_1, x_2, \cdots, x_n)$ over F_p is called to be rotation symmetric function if for any $x = (x_1, \ldots, x_n) \in F_p^n$ and $0 \leq k \leq n-1$, we have*

$$f\left(\rho_n^k(x_1, x_2, \cdots, x_n)\right) = f(x_1, x_2, \cdots, x_n).$$

3 Enumeration of Homogeneous Rotation Symmetric Functions

In this section, we will enumerate homogeneous rotation symmetric functions over F_p. Let's start with some fundamental definitions.

Definition 2. *A function $f: F_p^n \to F_p$ is called minimal function if*

$$f(x_1, x_2, \cdots, x_n) = \sum_{k=0}^{t^*-1} \rho_n^k(x_1^{k_1} x_2^{k_2} \cdots x_n^{k_n})$$

where $t^* = \min\{t | \rho_n^t(x_1^{k_1} x_2^{k_2} \cdots x_n^{k_n}) = x_1^{k_1} x_2^{k_2} \cdots x_n^{k_n}, \ 0 < t \leq n-1\}$.

Definition 3. *A monic monomial $x_1^{y_1} x_2^{y_2} \cdots x_n^{y_n}$ is analogous to $x_1^{k_1} x_2^{k_2} \cdots x_n^{k_n}$, if there exists a permutation π on n elements such that $(k_1, k_2, \cdots, k_n) = (y_{\pi(1)}, y_{\pi(2)}, \cdots, y_{\pi(n)})$.*

Let $\Omega(d, p, n)$ be the equation system as follow:

$$\Omega(d,p,n) : \begin{cases} y_1 + y_2 + \cdots + y_n = d \\ 0 \leq y_n \leq \cdots \leq y_2 \leq y_1 \leq p-1 \\ y_i \in \mathbb{Z} (1 \leq i \leq n) \end{cases}$$

and $\{(y_1^{(j)}, y_2^{(j)}, \ldots, y_n^{(j)}) | 1 \leq j \leq N_\Omega\}$ be all the solutions of $\Omega(d, p, n)$, where N_Ω is the number of solutions of $\Omega(d, p, n)$.

Now $T(n, d)$ is denoted the number of minimal functions with degree d, and $N(n, d)$ is denoted the number of n-variable homogeneous rotation symmetric functions over F_p with degree d.

Lemma 1. *Let $m_i^{(j)} (0 \leq i \leq p-1, 1 \leq j \leq N_\Omega)$ be the number of times that i appears in $(y_1^{(j)}, y_2^{(j)}, \cdots, y_n^{(j)})(1 \leq j \leq N_\Omega)$, then*

$$N(n,d) = \sum_{j=1}^{N_\Omega} \frac{n!}{m_0^{(j)}! m_1^{(j)}! \cdots m_{p-1}^{(j)}!}.$$

Proof. For a fixed j and the corresponding solution $(y_1^{(j)}, y_2^{(j)}, \cdots, y_n^{(j)})$, the number of monic monomials analogous to $x_1^{y_1^{(j)}} x_2^{y_2^{(j)}} \cdots x_n^{y_n^{(j)}}$ is

$$\binom{n}{m_0^{(j)}} \binom{n - m_0^{(j)}}{m_1^{(j)}} \cdots \binom{n - \sum_{i=1}^{p-2} m_i^{(j)}}{m_{p-1}^{(j)}} = \frac{n!}{m_0^{(j)}! m_1^{(j)}! \cdots m_{(p-1)}^{(j)}!}$$

so $N(n,d) = \sum_{j=1}^{N_\Omega} \frac{n!}{m_0^{(j)}! m_1^{(j)}! \cdots m_{p-1}^{(j)}!}$.

Theorem 1. $N(n,d) \geq p^{\sum_{j=1}^{N_\Omega} \frac{(n-1)!}{m_0^{(j)}! m_1^{(j)}! \cdots m_{p-1}^{(j)}!}} - 1.$

Proof. Note that a homogeneous rotation symmetric function $f(x_1, x_2, \cdots, x_n)$ with degree d is a nonzero combination of minimal functions with degree d. That is

$$f(x_1, x_2, \cdots, x_n) = \sum_{m=1}^{T(n,d)} a_m g_m(x_1, x_2, \cdots, x_n)$$

where $a_m \in F_p$, $g_m(x_1, x_2, \cdots, x_n)$ are minimal functions with degree d.

If a minimal function has the term $x_1^{y_1^{(j)}} x_2^{y_2^{(j)}} \cdots x_n^{y_n^{(j)}}$, then it has all the terms in the set $\{\rho_n^k(x_1^{y_1^{(j)}} x_2^{y_2^{(j)}} \cdots x_n^{y_n^{(j)}}) | 0 \leq k \leq n - 1\}$, It is easy to show that $\#\{\rho_n^k(x_1^{y_1^{(j)}} x_2^{y_2^{(j)}} \cdots x_n^{y_n^{(j)}}) | 0 \leq k \leq n - 1\} \leq n$. From Lemma 1 we know the number of monic monomials with degree d is $\sum_{j=1}^{N_\Omega} \frac{n!}{m_0^{(j)}!m_1^{(j)}!\cdots m_{p-1}^{(j)}!}$. So the number of minimal functions $T(n,d) \geq \sum_{j=1}^{N_\Omega} \frac{(n-1)!}{m_0^{(j)}!m_1^{(j)}!\cdots m_{p-1}^{(j)}!}$. Since $f = 0$ is not counted, we get the result.

Note that if n is a prime and $n \nmid d$, then $\#\{\rho_n^k(x_1^{y_1^{(j)}} x_2^{y_2^{(j)}} \cdots x_n^{y_n^{(j)}}) | 0 \leq k \leq n-1\} = n$ for any $1 \leq j \leq N_\Omega$, so we have the following Corollary.

Corollary 1. *If n is a prime and $n \nmid d$, then:*

$$NU(n,d) = p^{\sum_{j=1}^{N_\Omega} \frac{(n-1)!}{m_0^{(j)}!m_1^{(j)}!\cdots m_{p-1}^{(j)}!}} - 1.$$

In [7], it is an open problem to count n-variable homogeneous rotation symmetric functions with degree d more than 3. In the following theorems, the case $\gcd(n,d) = 1$ and the case $\gcd(n,d) = q^r$ where q is a prime will be solved.

Theorem 2. *If $\gcd(d,n) = 1$, then*

$$T(n,d) = \sum_{j=1}^{N_\Omega} \frac{(n-1)!}{m_0^{(j)}!m_1^{(j)}!\cdots m_{p-1}^{(j)}!}.$$

Proof. Let $m_i^{(j)} (0 \leq i \leq p-1, 1 \leq j \leq N_\Omega)$ as denoted in lemma 1, then $\#\{\rho_n^k(x_1^{y_1^{(j)}} x_2^{y_2^{(j)}} \cdots x_n^{y_n^{(j)}}) | 0 \leq k \leq n-1\} = n$. Otherwise, if $\#\{\rho_n^k(x_1^{y_1^{(j)}} x_2^{y_2^{(j)}} \cdots x_n^{y_n^{(j)}}) | 0 \leq k \leq n-1\} = N < n$, then $N | n$ and $\frac{n}{N} > 1$,

$$\rho_n^N(x_1^{y_1^{(j)}} x_2^{y_2^{(j)}} \cdots x_n^{y_n^{(j)}}) = x_1^{y_1^{(j)}} x_2^{y_2^{(j)}} \cdots x_n^{y_n^{(j)}}$$
$$\Rightarrow x_{N+1}^{y_1^{(j)}} x_{N+2}^{y_2^{(j)}} \cdots x_n^{y_2^{(j)}} x_1^{y_2^{(j)}} \cdots x_N^{y_n^{(j)}} = x_1^{y_1^{(j)}} x_2^{y_2^{(j)}} \cdots x_n^{y_n^{(j)}}$$
$$\Rightarrow \sum_{j=1}^{N} y_1^{(j)} = \sum_{j=N+1}^{2N} y_1^{(j)} = \cdots = \sum_{j=n-N}^{n} y_1^{(j)}$$

It is obviously that $\sum_{j=1}^{N} y_1^{(j)} \neq 1$. Then

$$y_1 + y_2 + \cdots + y_n = d$$
$$\Rightarrow d = \frac{n}{N} \cdot \sum_{j=1}^{N} y_1^{(j)} \Rightarrow \frac{n}{N} | d$$
$$\Rightarrow \gcd(d,n) = \frac{n}{N},$$

which contradicts with the fact that $\gcd(d,n) = 1$. There are $\sum_{j=1}^{N_\Omega} \frac{n!}{m_0^{(j)}!m_1^{(j)}!\cdots m_{p-1}^{(j)}!}$ monic monomials with degree d, so $T(n,d) = \sum_{j=1}^{N_\Omega} \frac{(n-1)!}{m_0^{(j)}!m_1^{(j)}!\cdots m_{p-1}^{(j)}!}$.

Theorem 3. *If* $\gcd(n,d) = q^r$ *for some prime q and integer $r \geq 1$, then*

$$T(n,d) = \sum_{j=1}^{N_\Omega} \frac{(n-1)!}{m_0^{(j)}! m_1^{(j)}! \cdots m_{p-1}^{(j)}!} + \sum_{i=1}^{r} \frac{q^i - 1}{q^i} T\left(\frac{n}{q^i}, \frac{d}{q^i}\right).$$

Proof. First, we make the observation that $T(n,d)$ is the sum between the number of minimal functions which has n terms(abbr. long minimal functions) and the number of minimal functions which has terms less than n(abbr. short minimal functions). Obviously, $f(x_1, x_2, \cdots, x_n) = \sum_{k=0}^{t^*-1} \rho_n^k(x_1^{y_1} x_2^{y_2} \cdots x_n^{y_n})$ has terms less than n, if and only if there exists a minimal block $b = [y_1, y_2, \cdots, y_t]$ such that $(y_1, y_2, \cdots, y_n)$ is covered by concatenating m copies of b. Then it follows that m divides n and m divides d, so $m \mid q^r$. Since b is minimal, then it must be $\#\{\rho_n^k(x_1^{y_1} x_2^{y_2} \cdots x_n^{y_t}) | 0 \leq k \leq n-1\} = n$. Thus

$$\#short\ minimal\ functions = \sum_{i=1}^{r} T\left(\frac{n}{q^i}, \frac{d}{q^i}\right). \tag{1}$$

Let L be the set of monic monomials of all the long minimal functions, S be the set of monic monomials of all the short minimal functions. Recall that the total number of monic monomials with degree d is $\sum_{j=1}^{N_\Omega} \frac{n!}{m_0^{(j)}! m_1^{(j)}! \cdots m_{p-1}^{(j)}!}$. Therefore, $\#L = \sum_{j=1}^{N_\Omega} \frac{n!}{m_0^{(j)}! m_1^{(j)}! \cdots m_{p-1}^{(j)}!} - \#S$. The number of long minimal functions is $\frac{1}{n} \cdot \#L$. Then it follows that

$$\#long\ minimal\ functions = \sum_{j=1}^{N_\Omega} \frac{(n-1)!}{m_0^{(j)}! m_1^{(j)}! \cdots m_{p-1}^{(j)}!} - \frac{1}{n}\sum_{i=1}^{r} \frac{n}{q^i} T\left(\frac{n}{q^i}, \frac{d}{q^i}\right) \tag{2}$$

Putting together (1) and (2), we obtain the number of minimal functions.

The following corollary is the direct result of Theorem 2 and Theorem 3.

Corollary 2. *If $\gcd(d,n) = 1$, then*

$$N(n,d) = p^{\sum_{j=1}^{N_\Omega} \frac{(n-1)!}{m_0^{(j)}! m_1^{(j)}! \cdots m_{p-1}^{(j)}!}} - 1.$$

If $\gcd(n,d) = q^r$ (q prime, $r \geq 1$), then

$$N(n,d) = p^{\sum_{j=1}^{N_\Omega} \frac{(n-1)!}{m_0^{(j)}! m_1^{(j)}! \cdots m_{p-1}^{(j)}!} + \sum_{i=1}^{r} \frac{q^i-1}{q^i} T\left(\frac{n}{q^i}, \frac{d}{q^i}\right)} - 1.$$

Example 1. We count the number of homogeneous rotation symmetric functions with degree 5 over F_p ($p \geq 7, n \geq 5$). It is easily verified that all the solutions of $\Omega(5, p, n)$ are as follows:

$(5, 0, \cdots, 0),\ (4, 1, 0, \cdots, 0),\ (3, 2, 0, \cdots, 0),\ (3, 1, 1, 0, \cdots, 0),$
$(2, 2, 1, 0, \cdots, 0),\ (2, 1, 1, 1, 0, \cdots, 0),\ (1, 1, 1, 1, 1, 0, \cdots, 0).$

Therefore,

(1) if $d \nmid n$, then

$$\sum_{j=1}^{N_\Omega} \frac{(n-1)!}{m_0^{(j)}!m_1^{(j)}!\cdots m_{p-1}^{(j)}!}$$
$$= \frac{(n-1)!}{(n-1)!} + \frac{(n-1)!}{(n-2)!} + \frac{(n-1)!}{(n-2)!} + \frac{(n-1)!}{2!(n-3)!} +$$
$$\frac{(n-1)!}{2!(n-3)!} + \frac{(n-1)!}{3!(n-4)!} + \frac{(n-1)!}{5!(n-5)!}.$$
$$= \frac{(n-1)(n-2)(n-3)(n+16)}{5!} + (n^2 - n + 1)$$

Hence,
$$N(n,5) = p^{\frac{(n-1)(n-2)(n-3)(n+16)}{5!} + (n^2-n+1)} - 1.$$

(2) if $d \mid n$, then

$$\sum_{j=1}^{N_\Omega} \frac{(n-1)!}{m_0^{(j)}!m_1^{(j)}!\cdots m_{p-1}^{(j)}!} + \frac{d-1}{d}T(\frac{n}{d}, 1)$$
$$= \frac{(n-1)(n-2)(n-3)(n+16)}{5!} + (n^2 - n + \frac{9}{5}).$$

Thus,
$$N(n,5) = p^{\frac{(n-1)(n-2)(n-3)(n+16)}{5!} + (n^2-n+\frac{9}{5})} - 1.$$

4 Conclusion

In this paper, we investigated homogeneous rotation symmetric functions over finite field F_p. We get a lower bound on the number of homogeneous rotation symmetric functions by finding solutions of an equation system. And we also give a formula to count homogeneous rotation symmetric functions when the greatest common divisor of the number of input variables and the algebraic degree of the function is a prime power, which partially solve the open problem in [7]. However, for general n, it is still an open problem to count the homogeneous rotation symmetric functions.

Acknowledgments

This work is supported by the National Natural Science Foundation of China (No:60573028) and the open research fund of National Mobile Communications Research Laboratory of Southeast University (No:W200805).

References

1. Pieprzyk, J., Qu, C.X.: Fast Hashing and Rotation-Symmetric Functions. Journal of Universal Computer Science 5(1), 20–31 (1999)
2. Stanica, P., Maitra, S.: Rotation symmetric Boolean functions-count and cryptographic properties. In: Bose, R.C. (ed.) Centenary Symposium on Discrete Mathematics and Applications. Electronic Notes in Discrete Mathematics, vol. 15, pp. 139–145. Elsevier, Amsterdam (2002)

3. Stanica, P., Maitra, S.: A constructive count of rotation symmetric functions. Information Processing Letters 88, 299–304 (2003)
4. Stanica, P., Maitra, S., Clark, J.: Results on rotation symmetric bent and correlation immune Boolean functions. In: Roy, B., Meier, W. (eds.) FSE 2004. LNCS, vol. 3017, pp. 161–177. Springer, Heidelberg (2004)
5. Dalai, D.K., Maitra, S., Sarkar, S.: Results on rotation symmetric bent functions. In: Second International Workshop on Boolean Functions: Cryptography and Applications, BFCA 2006, March 2006, pp. 137–156 (2006)
6. Maximov, A., Hell, M., Maitra, S.: Plateaued Rotation Symmetric Boolean Functions on Odd Number of Variables. In: First Workshop on Boolean Functions: Cryptography and Applications, BFCA 2005, LIFAR, March 7-9, 2005, pp. 83–104. University of Rouen, France (2005)
7. Li, Y.: Results on rotation symmetric polynomials over F_p. Information Sciences Letters 178, 280–286 (2008)

Unconditionally Reliable Message Transmission in Directed Hypergraphs

Kannan Srinathan[2], Arpita Patra[1,*], Ashish Choudhary[1,**], and C. Pandu Rangan[1,***]

[1] Dept of Computer Science and Engineering
IIT Madras, Chennai India 600036
arpita@cse.iitm.ernet.in, ashishc@cse.iitm.ernet.in, rangan@iitm.ernet.in
[2] Center for Security, Theory and Algorithmic Research
International Institute of Information Technology
Hyderabad India 500032
srinathan@iiit.ac.in

Abstract. We study the problem of *unconditionally reliable message transmission* (URMT), where a sender **S** and a receiver **R** are part of a synchronous network modeled as a directed hypergraph, a part of which may be under the influence of an adversary having *unbounded* computing power. **S** intends to transmit a message m to **R**, such that **R** should *correctly* obtain **S**'s message with probability at least $(1 - \delta)$ for arbitrarily small $\delta > 0$. However, unlike most of the literature on this problem, we assume the adversary modeling the faults is **threshold mixed**, and can corrupt different set of nodes in Byzantine, passive and fail-stop fashion simultaneously. The main contribution of this work is the complete characterization of URMT in directed hypergraph tolerating such an adversary, which is done for the first time in the literature.

Keywords: Unbounded Computing Power, Unconditional Reliability.

1 Introduction

Consider a synchronous network, modeled as a directed hypergraph $\mathcal{D} = (\mathcal{P}, \mathcal{E})$ where $\mathcal{P}$ is the set of nodes and $\mathcal{E} \subset \mathcal{P} \times 2^{\mathcal{P}}$ is the set of directed hyperedges. Some of the nodes in the network $\mathcal{D}$ are controlled by an adaptive[1] *threshold mixed* adversary $\mathcal{A}_{(t_b, t_p, t_f)}$ which possesses *unbounded* computing power and

---

[*] Financial Support from Microsoft Research India Acknowledged.
[**] Financial Support from Infosys Technology India Acknowledged.
[***] Work Supported by Project No. CSE/05-06/076/DITX/CPAN on Protocols for Secure Communication and Computation Sponsored by Department of Information Technology, Government of India.
[1] An adaptive adversary corrupts the nodes dynamically during the protocol execution. The nodes to be corrupted may depend upon the information obtained by the adversary so far during the protocol execution.

can corrupt disjoint set of t_b, t_p and t_f nodes in Byzantine, passive and fail-stop fashion respectively. In *Unconditionally Reliable Message Transmission* (URMT) problem over $\mathcal{D}$, a sender $\mathbf{S} \in \mathcal{P}$ wishes to send a message m, chosen from a finite field $\mathbb{F}$ to the receiver $\mathbf{R} \in \mathcal{P}$ (we assume that $\mathbf{S}$ and $\mathbf{R}$ are non-faulty), such that $\mathbf{R}$ recovers m with probability at least $(1-\delta)$, for arbitrarily small $\delta > 0$. If $\delta = 0$, then the problem is called *perfectly reliable message transmission* (PRMT). Directed hypergraph is the most generic network model with the facility of multicasting. In certain scenarios, private one-to-one channels may not exist. Typical examples include Radio transmission and LAN network. Also in many practical scenarios, a base station can broadcast to a set of receivers, but the other way around communication might not be possible. In these cases, directed hypergraph is the only way to model the network.

Intuitively, allowing small probability of error in the transmission should result in improvements in the fault tolerance of PRMT. What exactly is the improvement? We answer this question, considering the most generic network model, namely directed hypergraph. The most natural questions in the context of URMT over directed hypergraphs are: (a) POSSIBILITY: What is the necessary and sufficient condition that a given directed hypergraph $\mathcal{D}$ should satisfy for the possibility of URMT? (b) Does allowing a small probability of error in the reliability of message transmission improves fault tolerance in the network? (c) A directed hyperedge may be visualized as "bunching up" a set of directed (simple) edges. So given a directed hypergraph $\mathcal{D}$, a digraph $\mathcal{G}$ can be obtained from $\mathcal{D}$ by replacing each hyperedge with the corresponding "bunch" of directed edges. Now the natural question is: Does there exists a directed hypergraph $\mathcal{D}$ such that URMT is possible over $\mathcal{D}$ but impossible over $\mathcal{G}$? More precisely, do hyperedges possess some special property/power in the context of URMT? In the sequel, we try to answer these questions.

Existing Work: Considering hypergraph as underlying network model is not quite common in literature. The problem of secure communication against $\mathcal{A}_{t_p}$ in directed hypergraphs has been studied by Franklin et. al. [2]. Later Desmedt et.al. [1] have characterized PRMT over hypergraphs tolerating $\mathcal{A}_{t_b}$.

Hypergraph Network Model and Threshold Mixed Adversary: We follow the hypergraph network model as in [2]. A directed hypergraph is denoted by $\mathcal{D} = (\mathcal{P}, \mathcal{E})$. A typical directed hyperedge e can be written as $e = (v, S)$, where $v \in \mathcal{P}$, $S \subseteq (\mathcal{P} \setminus v)$. We call v as the source node and the nodes in S as the destination nodes of e. The hyperedge e enables node v to send message to the nodes in S, identically. Even if v is corrupted and modifies (stops) the information passing through it, every node in S identically receive the modified information (no information). The hyperedge e is directed since only v can send messages to the nodes in S but the nodes in S cannot communicate among themselves or to v using e. The hyperedge e is secure in the sense that any node outside the set $S \cup \{v\}$ learns nothing about the information sent over e.

We consider an adaptive *threshold mixed adversary* $\mathcal{A}_{(t_b, t_p, t_f)}$, who possesses *unbounded* computing power and controls at most t_b, t_p and t_f nodes in $\mathcal{D}$ in

Byzantine, passive and fail-stop fashion respectively. Once a node is corrupted, it remains so throughout the protocol. If a node P is fail-stop corrupted then the adversary can force P to *crash* at will at any time during the execution of the protocol but can not access its internal data and can not force its behavior to deviate from the protocol. So till P is alive, it honestly follows the protocol. Also once P is crashed, it never becomes alive again. If a node P is passively corrupted then P honestly follows the protocol but the adversary has full access to internal data of P. If a node P is Byzantine corrupted then the adversary has full access to the internal data of P and can force P to deviate from the protocol arbitrarily. We assume that $\mathcal{A}_{(t_b,t_p,t_f)}$ acts in a "centralized" fashion and colludes among different corrupted nodes through "back channels". So, $\mathcal{A}_{(t_b,t_p,t_f)}$ can listen information from at most $(t_b + t_p)$ nodes and can pool all the information observed/obtained at these $t_b + t_p$ nodes in any manner in its local computation.

Why Mixed Adversary ?: In a typical large network, certain nodes may be strongly protected and few others may be moderately/weakly protected. An adversary may fail-stop(/eavesdrop in) a strongly protected node, while he may affect in a Byzantine fashion a weakly protected node. Thus, we may capture the abilities of an adversary in a more realistic manner using t_b, t_p and t_f where t_b, t_p, t_f are the number of nodes under the influence of Byzantine, passive and fail-stop adversary, respectively. Even in practical scenario, when a hacker takes control of a router, it can disrupt the communication in variety of ways. So studying mixed adversary is well motivated.

Our Contribution, Significance and Impact: In this paper, we completely characterize URMT over an arbitrary directed hypergraph $\mathcal{D}$ tolerating $\mathcal{A}_{(t_b,t_p,t_f)}$. Working out a direct characterization of URMT over $\mathcal{D}$, tolerating $\mathcal{A}_{(t_b,t_p,t_f)}$ is highly un-intuitive. Hence, we use the following framework to solve the problem:

Contribution 1. *We propose a method which takes a directed hypergraph $\mathcal{D}$, along with $\mathcal{A}_{(t_b,t_p,t_f)}$ and outputs a corresponding digraph $\mathcal{D}_{under}$, which we call as "underlying digraph" of $\mathcal{D}$, along with a non-threshold mixed adversary $\mathbb{A}_{under}$, such that URMT over $\mathcal{D}$ tolerating $\mathcal{A}_{(t_b,t_p,t_f)}$ is possible iff there exists a "special type of URMT" protocol in $\mathcal{D}_{under}$ tolerating $\mathbb{A}_{under}$.*

Contribution 2. *We then characterize URMT in $\mathcal{D}_{under}$ tolerating $\mathbb{A}_{under}$ and give modifications on it to arrive at the characterization of special type of URMT on $\mathcal{D}_{under}$. This along with Contribution 1 completes the characterization of URMT on $\mathcal{D}$, tolerating $\mathcal{A}_{(t_b,t_p,t_f)}$.*

In the sequel we provide affirmative answers to the following questions by demonstrating examples: (a) Does randomization help in more fault tolerance? (b) Does hyperedges help in the possibility of URMT? (c) Does passive corruption affect reliable communication? Consider the hypergraph $\mathcal{D}$ in Fig. 1 under the influence of $\mathcal{A}_{(1,0,0)}$, where $t_b = 1$ and $t_p = t_f = 0$. We can say the following regarding $\mathcal{D}$ which essentially shows the power of allowing negligible error probability: (a) From [1], PRMT (URMT with $\delta = 0$) over $\mathcal{D}$ tolerating $\mathcal{A}_{(1,0,0)}$ is impossible. (b) URMT over $\mathcal{D}$ tolerating $\mathcal{A}_{(1,0,0)}$ is possible and feasible.

Claim. URMT over $\mathcal{D}$ tolerating $\mathcal{A}_{(1,0,0)}$ is possible and feasible.

PROOF: Consider the following URMT protocol over $\mathcal{D}$. A selects three random values (keys) from finite field $\mathbb{F}$, say K_1, K_2, and K_3. A sends the keys to **S** and **R** through the hyperedge $(A, \{\mathbf{S}, \mathbf{R}\})$. Since $(A, \{\mathbf{S}, \mathbf{R}\})$ is an hyperedge, both **S** and **R** receives the same set of keys or gets nothing. If **S** receives the keys, he authenticates the message m by computing a two tuple $(K_1 + m, K_2(K_1 + m) + K_3)$ and sends it through the path $(\mathbf{S}, B, \mathbf{R})$. **S** also sends the message m over both the paths $(\mathbf{S}, B, \mathbf{R})$ and $(\mathbf{S}, A, \mathbf{R})$. Now if **R** does not receive any key from A, he detects A to be faulty and accepts the message from path $(\mathbf{S}, B, \mathbf{R})$. Otherwise, **R** receives the authenticated tuple say (c, d) over path $(\mathbf{S}, B, \mathbf{R})$ and the keys from A with which **R** checks $d \stackrel{?}{=} K_2 c + K_3$. If the test passes then **R** takes $c - K_1$ as the message, else **R** knows node B is faulty and accepts the message from path $(\mathbf{S}, A, \mathbf{R})$. The proof of correctness of the protocol is similar to the information checking protocol of [3]. It can be shown that except with probability $\delta = \frac{1}{|\mathbb{F}|}$, **R** outputs $m' = m$ [3]. Now by setting $|\mathbb{F}|$ to be arbitrarily large, we can reduce the error probability to an arbitrarily small quantity. □

Next we show that unlike PRMT, *hyperedges do help in the possibility of URMT*. A very straight-forward implication that can be drawn from the characterization of PRMT in directed hypergraph against $\mathcal{A}_{t_b}$, stated in [1], is that, replacing every hyperedge of a hypergraph by a collection of underlying simple directed edges does not affect the possibility of PRMT over the hypergraph. This means there does not exist a hypergraph such that PRMT is possible on it but is impossible in the digraph obtained from the hypergraph. However consider the hypergraph $\mathcal{D}$ in Figure 1 and its corresponding directed graph $\mathcal{G}$, which is obtained from $\mathcal{D}$ by replacing each hyperedge by its underlying simple directed edges. From the previous claim, URMT is possible in $\mathcal{D}$ tolerating $\mathcal{A}_{(1,0,0)}$. However, from [4], URMT is impossible in $\mathcal{G}$ tolerating $\mathcal{A}_{(1,0,0)}$. *Thus we conclude that hyperedges do help in the possibility of URMT but not PRMT.*

One of the long-standing and intuitive belief is that "passive corruption does not affect reliable communication". We contradict the belief by an example for URMT in directed hypergraph. In Figure 1, let $\mathcal{D}$ be under the control of $\mathcal{A}_{(1,1,0)}$,

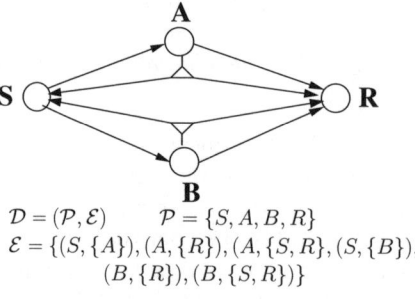
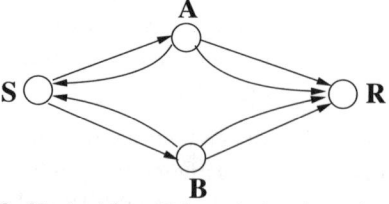

$\mathcal{D} = (\mathcal{P}, \mathcal{E})$ $\mathcal{P} = \{S, A, B, R\}$
$\mathcal{E} = \{(S, \{A\}), (A, \{R\}), (A, \{S, R\}), (S, \{B\}),$
$(B, \{R\}), (B, \{S, R\})\}$

$\mathcal{G}$: Obtained from $\mathcal{D}$ by replacing the six hyperedges by corresponding directed edges.

Fig. 1. Example of network illustrating the power of hyperedges with respect to URMT

where $t_b = t_p = 1$ and $t_f = 0$. Let A be passive corrupted and B be Byzantine corrupted; then the protocol in previous claim will not work. The reason is that adversary always gets the keys which A sends to **S** and **R** (by eavesdropping A). Specifically $\mathcal{A}_{(1,1,0)}$ can use the information he eavesdrop at A, to corrupt the values appropriately at B, in such a way that the tuple along the path $(\mathbf{S}, B, \mathbf{R})$ passes the authentication test. Thus an adversary can *very effectively use the information obtained from the passively corrupted nodes at the nodes which he is controlling in a Byzantine fashion and affect the reliability of the protocol.*

1.1 Digraph Network Model and Non-threshold Adversary

We now give few definitions related to digraph network model and non-threshold adversary, which are used in subsequent sections. A directed network is modeled as a digraph $\mathcal{N} = (\mathbb{P}, \mathbb{E})$ where $\mathbb{P}$ is the set of nodes and $\mathbb{E}$ denotes the set of arcs in the digraph. The network is assumed to be synchronous, that is, any protocol is executed in a sequence of *rounds* wherein in each round, a node can send messages to it's out-neighbors, receive the messages sent in that round by it's in-neighbors and perform some computation on the received messages. A non-threshold adversary structure is an enumeration of all the possible "snapshots" of faults in the network. A single snapshot can be described by an ordered triple (B, E, F), where $B, E, F \subseteq \mathbb{P}$ and B, E and F are pairwise disjoint, and denotes the set of Byzantine, passive and fail-stop corrupted nodes. An adversary structure is a collection of such triples. The adversary structure is *monotone* in the sense that if $(B_1, E_1, F_1) \in \mathbb{A}$, then $\forall (B_2, E_2, F_2)$ such that $B_2 \subseteq B_1$ and $E_2 \subseteq E_1$ and $F_2 \subseteq F_1$, $(B_2, E_2, F_2) \in \mathbb{A}$. During the execution of the protocol, any one set from $\mathbb{A}$ would be active and the nodes from that set will be under the control of adversary throughout the protocol. Any $\mathbb{A}$ can be uniquely represented by listing the elements in its *maximal basis* which we define below:

Definition 1 (Maximal Basis). *For a monotone adversary structure $\mathbb{A}$, its maximal basis $\bar{\mathbb{A}}$ is defined as $\bar{\mathbb{A}} = \{(B, E, F) | (B, E, F) \in \mathbb{A}, \text{ and } \nexists (X, Y, Z) \in \mathbb{A} \text{ such that } (X, Y, Z) \neq (B, E, F) \text{ where } X \supseteq B, Y \supseteq E \text{ and } Z \supseteq F\}.$*

Definition 2 (Strong Path). *A sequence of vertices $(v_1, v_2, v_3, \ldots, v_k)$ is said to be a strong path from v_1 to v_k in digraph $\mathcal{N} = (\mathbb{P}, \mathbb{E})$ if for each $1 \leq i < k$, $(v_i, v_{i+1}) \in \mathbb{E}$. We assume that (v_i, v_i) is a strong path from v_i to itself.*

Definition 3 (Semi-Strong Path). *A sequence of vertices $(v_1, v_2, v_3, \ldots, v_k)$ is said to be a semi-strong path from v_1 to v_k if there exists j, $1 \leq j \leq k$ such that the sequence v_j to v_1 as well as the sequence v_j to v_k are both strong paths. Vertex v_j is called the **head** of the semi-strong path. Any strong path can be viewed as a semi-strong path. For example, the path $(\mathbf{S}, X_{e_5}^{Vir}, \mathbf{R})$ in graph $\mathcal{D}_{under}$ in Fig. 2 is a semi-strong path between $\mathbf{S}$ and $\mathbf{R}$, where $X_{e_5}^{Vir}$ is the head.*

Definition 4 (Authentication Function). *Let $\mathcal{K}_1, \mathcal{K}_2, \mathcal{K}_3 \in \mathbb{F} - \{0\}$ and $m \in \mathbb{F}$. Then $auth(m, \mathcal{K}_1, \mathcal{K}_2, \mathcal{K}_3) = (\mathcal{K}_1 + m, \mathcal{K}_2(\mathcal{K}_1 + m) + \mathcal{K}_3)$.*

Suppose a random triplet $(\mathcal{K}_1, \mathcal{K}_2, \mathcal{K}_3) \in \mathbb{F}^3 - \{(0, 0, 0)\}$ is correctly established between **S** and **R**. For a message m, let **S** computes $auth(m, \mathcal{K}_1, \mathcal{K}_2, \mathcal{K}_3)$ and sends it to **R** through a strong path, over which some of the nodes could be under the control of the adversary. If the adversary does not know $m, \mathcal{K}_1, \mathcal{K}_3$ and $\mathcal{K}_3$ in advance, then $auth$ satisfies the following two important properties: (a) Even if adversary learns $auth(m, \mathcal{K}_1, \mathcal{K}_2, \mathcal{K}_3)$, m will remain unknown to the adversary. (b) If the adversary changes $auth(m, \mathcal{K}_1, \mathcal{K}_2, \mathcal{K}_3)$ to some other value, then except with an error probability of at most $\frac{1}{|\mathbb{F}|}$, **R** will be able to detect it. The proof of both the properties is similar to the proof of information checking protocol of [3] and hence is omitted.

2 Characterization for URMT in Directed Hypergraph

Here we characterize URMT on arbitrary directed hypergraphs tolerating $\mathcal{A}_{(t_b, t_p, t_f)}$.

Definition 5 (Underlying Digraph). *Given a directed hypergraph* $\mathcal{D} = (\mathcal{P}, \mathcal{E})$ *we define the underlying digraph* $\mathcal{D}_{under} = (\mathcal{P}', \mathcal{E}')$ *of $\mathcal{D}$ as follows:* $\mathcal{P}' = (\mathcal{P} \cup \mathcal{V})$ *is the set of nodes (real nodes and virtual nodes). We replace each hyperedge* $e = (v, \{v_{j_1}, v_{j_2}, \ldots, v_{j_\alpha}\}) \in \mathcal{E}$, $\alpha \geq 1$, *with a virtual player* $X_e^{Vir} \in \mathcal{V}$ *and the arcs* (v, X_e^{Vir}), (X_e^{Vir}, v_{j_1}), (X_e^{Vir}, v_{j_2}), \ldots, *and* $(X_e^{Vir}, v_{j_\alpha})$ *in* $\mathcal{E}'$.

A hypergraph, along with its corresponding digraph $\mathcal{D}_{under}$ is given in Fig. 2.

The intuition behind our definition is that for every hypergraph $\mathcal{D}$ influenced by $\mathcal{A}_{(t_b, t_p, t_f)}$, there exists a corresponding digraph $\mathcal{D}_{under}$ and non-threshold mixed adversary $\mathbb{A}_{under}$, such that URMT over $\mathcal{D}$ tolerating $\mathcal{A}_{(t_b, t_p, t_f)}$ is possible iff a "special type of URMT" over $\mathcal{D}_{under}$ tolerating $\mathbb{A}_{under}$ is possible. We begin by defining this "special" kind of URMT protocol called $URMT_{special}$.

Definition 6 ($URMT_{special}$). *A URMT protocol over a digraph* $\mathcal{D}_{under} = (\mathcal{P} \cup \mathcal{V}, \mathcal{E}')$ *is called $URMT_{special}$, if in that protocol, the programs delegated to each of the virtual players (i.e., the players in $\mathcal{V}$) is known to all and is deterministic.*

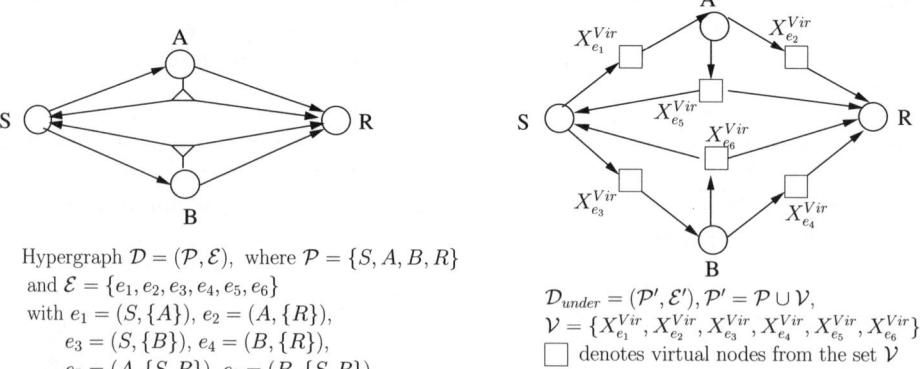

Hypergraph $\mathcal{D} = (\mathcal{P}, \mathcal{E})$, where $\mathcal{P} = \{S, A, B, R\}$
and $\mathcal{E} = \{e_1, e_2, e_3, e_4, e_5, e_6\}$
with $e_1 = (S, \{A\})$, $e_2 = (A, \{R\})$,
$e_3 = (S, \{B\})$, $e_4 = (B, \{R\})$,
$e_5 = (A, \{S, R\})$, $e_6 = (B, \{S, R\})$

$\mathcal{D}_{under} = (\mathcal{P}', \mathcal{E}'), \mathcal{P}' = \mathcal{P} \cup \mathcal{V}$,
$\mathcal{V} = \{X_{e_1}^{Vir}, X_{e_2}^{Vir}, X_{e_3}^{Vir}, X_{e_4}^{Vir}, X_{e_5}^{Vir}, X_{e_6}^{Vir}\}$
☐ denotes virtual nodes from the set $\mathcal{V}$

Fig. 2. A directed hypergraph $\mathcal{D}$ and it's corresponding $\mathcal{D}_{under}$

Definition 7 ($\mathbb{A}_{under}$). *Let $\mathcal{D} = (\mathcal{P}, \mathcal{E})$ be a arbitrary directed hypergraph under the influence of $\mathcal{A}_{(t_b, t_p, t_f)}$. Also let $\mathcal{D}_{under} = (\mathcal{P}', \mathcal{E}')$ be the underlying digraph of $\mathcal{D}$. The non-threshold mixed adversary $\mathbb{A}_{under}$ over $\mathcal{D}_{under}$, corresponding to $\mathcal{A}_{(t_b, t_p, t_f)}$ in $\mathcal{D}$ is defined as:*

$$\mathbb{A}_{under} = \left\{ (B, E, F) \;\middle|\; \begin{array}{l} |B \cap \mathcal{P}| \leq t_b, \; (B \cap \mathcal{V}) = \emptyset, \; |F \cap \mathcal{P}| \leq t_f, \; (F \cap \mathcal{V}) = \emptyset, \\ E = E_{real} \cup E_{vir}, |E_{real} \cap \mathcal{P}| \leq t_p, (E_{vir} \cap \mathcal{P}) = \emptyset, \\ E_{vir} = \left\{ \nu \in \mathcal{V} \;\middle|\; \begin{array}{l} \text{there exists a player } x \in (B \cup E_{real}) \text{ such that} \\ \text{either } (x, \nu) \text{ or } (\nu, x) \text{ is an arc in } \mathcal{D}_{under} \end{array} \right\} \end{array} \right\}$$

To construct an element $(B, E, F) \in \mathbb{A}_{under}$, we first select a *possible* combination of disjoint set of t_b, t_p and t_f nodes from $\mathcal{P}$ (set of physical nodes) and assign them to B, E_{real} and F respectively. Now E_{vir} is constructed by adding the virtual nodes X_e^{Vir} corresponding to hyperedge $e = (v, \{v_{j_1}, v_{j_2}, \ldots, v_{j_\alpha}\})$ such that at least one of the nodes $v, v_{j_1}, v_{j_2}, \ldots, v_{j_\alpha} \in (B \cup E_{real})$. Finally $E = E_{real} \cup E_{vir}$. We now have the following theorem:

Theorem 1. *URMT in a directed hypergraph $\mathcal{D}$ tolerating $\mathcal{A}_{(t_b, t_p, t_f)}$ is possible iff $URMT_{special}$ is possible over $\mathcal{D}_{under}$ tolerating $\mathbb{A}_{under}$.*

PROOF: If part: Let Π' be a $URMT_{special}$ protocol from **S** to **R** over $\mathcal{D}_{under}$ tolerating $\mathbb{A}_{under}$. We now construct a URMT protocol Π in $\mathcal{D}$ tolerating $\mathcal{A}_{(t_b, t_p, t_f)}$, using Π'. In protocol Π', the virtual players run a deterministic program. Thus, if in Π' some message m is sent by $v \in \mathcal{P}$ to $X_e^{Vir} \in \mathcal{V}$ who then forwards the respective outputs to all his out-neighbors, the same may be exactly simulated by v just using m and the code of X_e^{Vir} to compute the outputs of all the out-neighbors of X_e^{Vir}, say $\mu_1, \mu_2, \ldots, \mu_k$ (if there are k out-neighbors of X_e^{Vir}) and respectively sending μ_j to the jth out-neighbor routed through X_e^{Vir} (this kind of simulation is possible since the code run by X_e^{Vir} is deterministic and known to all). This in turn is equivalent to the real player v sending all the respective outputs $\mu_1, \mu_2, \ldots, \mu_k$ to all the out-neighbors via the hyperedge in $\mathcal{D}$ and each out-neighbor picking-up only what is due to him. Note that this step works because of the way in which we have defined the adversary structure $\mathbb{A}_{under}$ — we said that if adversary can read the memory of either the source node or one of the destination nodes of $e = (v, \{v_{j_1}, v_{j_2}, \ldots, v_{j_k}\})$, then the adversary can also read X_e^{Vir}'s memory itself. Consequently, we may assume that all data in X_e^{Vir}'s memory may be safely sent to all his out-neighbors without affecting the correctness of the simulation. It is evident that the view of the adversary as well as the out-neighbors is the same in both the original and the simulated versions.

Only if part: Suppose there exists a URMT protocol Π in the directed hypergraph $\mathcal{D}$. We now show that a $URMT_{special}$ protocol Π' in the digraph $\mathcal{D}_{under}$ exists. This can be seen as follows — we simulate a send of a value m along a hyperedge $e = (v, \{\{v_{j_1}, v_{j_2}, \ldots, v_{j_k}\})$ in the protocol Π over $\mathcal{D}$ by sending the value m first from v to the virtual player corresponding to the hyperedge e, namely, X_e^{Vir}, who then forwards it to the receivers $v_{j_1}, v_{j_2}, \ldots,$ and v_{j_k} in the protocol Π' over the network $\mathcal{D}_{under}$. Hence the theorem holds. □

So according to Theorem 1, our next concern is to characterize $URMT_{special}$ over $\mathcal{D}_{under}$ tolerating $\mathbb{A}_{under}$. For that, in the next section, we first characterize URMT in arbitrary digraphs tolerating non-threshold mixed adversary. This gives the necessary and sufficient condition for the existence of a $URMT$ protocol over $\mathcal{D}_{under}$ tolerating $\mathbb{A}_{under}$. Now, the only reason why a URMT protocol may exist in $\mathcal{D}_{under}$ but a $URMT_{special}$ protocol does not exist is that in $\mathcal{D}_{under}$ there are some virtual players which can not act as a physical node (e.g. can not do random coin toss etc.). The modification required to obtain the characterization of $URMT_{special}$ in arbitrary digraphs ($\mathcal{D}_{under}$) from the characterization of URMT in arbitrary digraphs ($\mathcal{D}_{under}$) is described in section 7.

3 URMT in Digraphs Tolerating Non-threshold Adversary

We now characterize URMT in an arbitrary digraph tolerating an arbitrary non-threshold adversary $\mathbb{A}$. We first prove the following:

Theorem 2. *URMT in a digraph $\mathcal{N}$ tolerating a non-threshold adversary $\mathbb{A}$ is possible iff URMT is possible in $\mathcal{N}$ tolerating any $\mathcal{A} \subseteq \mathbb{A}$ with $|\bar{\mathcal{A}}| = 2$.*

PROOF (SKETCH): Necessity is obvious. For sufficiency, we show that if URMT is possible in $\mathcal{N}$ tolerating any $\mathcal{A} \subseteq \mathbb{A}$ with maximal basis $\bar{\mathcal{A}}$ of size two, then URMT is also possible in $\mathcal{N}$ tolerating any $\mathcal{A} \subseteq \mathbb{A}$ with maximal basis of size three. Then using induction, we show that it is possible to design URMT in $\mathcal{N}$ tolerating entire $\mathbb{A}$. For complete proof, see [5]. □

Theorem 2 shows that in order to get a complete characterization of URMT tolerating entire $\mathbb{A}$, it is enough if we characterize URMT tolerating every $\mathcal{A} \subseteq \mathbb{A}$ with $|\bar{\mathcal{A}}| = 2$. This is our main concern in the rest of the paper.

4 A Sufficient Condition for URMT Tolerating $\mathcal{A} \subseteq \mathbb{A}$ with $|\bar{\mathcal{A}}| = 2$

Theorem 3. *Let $\mathcal{N} = (\mathbb{P}, \mathbb{E})$ be a digraph under the influence of $\mathcal{A}$ with maximal basis $\bar{\mathcal{A}} = \{(B_1, E_1, F_1), (B_2, E_2, F_2)\}$. Suppose $\mathcal{N}$ is such that for each $\alpha \in \{1, 2\}$, there exists a strong path (not necessarily distinct) p_α from $\mathbf{S}$ to $\mathbf{R}$, avoiding nodes from $(B_\alpha \cup F_\alpha)$. Furthermore, there exists a strong path q (not necessarily distinct from p_α's) from $\mathbf{S}$ to $\mathbf{R}$ in $\mathcal{N}$ which avoids nodes from $(B_1 \cup B_2 \cup (F_1 \cap F_2))$. Then there exists an URMT protocol tolerating $\mathcal{A}$.*

PROOF: According to the conditions of the theorem, there exists three strong paths p_1, p_2 and q (not necessarily distinct) from $\mathbf{S}$ to $\mathbf{R}$ in $\mathcal{N}$, such that p_1 avoids nodes from $(B_1 \cup F_1)$, p_2 avoid nodes from $(B_2 \cup F_2)$ and P avoid nodes from $(B_1 \cup B_2 \cup (F_1 \cap F_2))$. To reliably transmit a message m, $\mathbf{S}$ sends m along p_1, p_2 and q. Each intermediate node u along these paths forwards the message that it received to the corresponding neighbor. If nothing is received by the time something should have been received (since the network is synchronous, strict time-out conditions are feasible) then it forwards a new message namely "Null-from-u" to its neighbor. **R** now recovers m as follows: If **R** receives a valid message x along path q then $x = m$ because q is free from both B_1 and B_2. If a "Null-from-u" message is received along q, then if u's predecessor node in q belongs to F_1, then **R** outputs the message that is (guaranteed to be) received along path p_1. Else if u's predecessor node in q belongs to F_2, then **R** outputs the message that is (guaranteed to be) received along path p_2. However, if nothing is received along path q and if the **R**'s predecessor in q belongs to F_1, then **R** outputs the message that is (guaranteed to be) received along path p_1, else **R** outputs the message that is (guaranteed to be) received along path p_2. □

Definition 8. *We call the URMT protocol given in Theorem 3 as protocol Π.*

4.1 Relaxing the Sufficiency Condition of Theorem 3

According to Theorem 3, if the paths p_1, p_2 and q are present in a network $\mathcal{N}$, then URMT is possible over $\mathcal{N}$. Now the question is whether the physical presence of the paths are necessary in $\mathcal{N}$? However, we now show that even in the absence of q, one can design URMT over $\mathcal{N}$ tolerating $\bar{\mathcal{A}}$, provided the effect of q can be simulated over $\mathcal{N}$! This is possible provided $\mathcal{N}$ satisfies certain conditions with respect to $\bar{\mathcal{A}}$.

Example 1: Consider the network in Fig. 3, along with the adversary $\bar{\mathcal{A}}$. In $\mathcal{N}$, path $p_1 = (\mathbf{S}, L, M, \mathbf{R})$ is free from the nodes in $(B_1 \cup F_1)$, and path $p_2 = (\mathbf{S}, H, I, K, \mathbf{R})$ is free from the nodes in $(B_2 \cup F_2)$. However, there does not exist any strong path q which is free from the nodes in $(B_1 \cup B_2 \cup (F_1 \cap F_2))$. So $\mathcal{N}$ does not completely satisfy all the conditions of Theorem 3 with respect to the $\bar{\mathcal{A}}$. However, the effect of q can be simulated in $\mathcal{N}$.

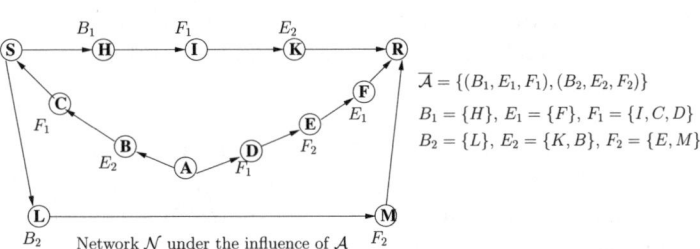

Fig. 3. Network $\mathcal{N}$ updated to $\mathcal{N}_1$

Consider the sub-portion of $\mathcal{N}$ with strong path $(\mathbf{S}, H, I, K, \mathbf{R})$ and semi-strong path $(\mathbf{S}, C, B, A, D, E, F, \mathbf{R})$ (with head A). Now consider the following sub-protocol called Π_1^{sim} executed over this sub-portion to send a value $s \in \mathbb{F}$ from **S** to **R**: First, A sends three random secret keys $K_1, K_2, K_3 \in \mathbb{F}$ to **S** via the strong path $(A, B, C, \mathbf{S})$. If A does not receive all the keys, he uses three random keys of his own choice instead. A then sends $(x, y) = auth(s, K_1, K_2, K_3)$ along strong path $(\mathbf{S}, H, I, K, \mathbf{R})$ to **R**. Now, A sends the same three keys (namely K_1, K_2 and K_3) to **R** along the strong path $(A, D, E, F, \mathbf{R})$. Note that A sends the keys to **R** only after **S** has sent the authenticated message (namely (x_1, y_1))

along the strong path to **R**. This can be done because the system is synchronous and the protocol is executed in rounds.

If **R** does not receive the keys from A, then **R** knows the identity of the set in $\overline{\mathcal{A}}$ that is corrupt because the strong path from A to **R** contains nodes from F_1^* and F_2^*. Similarly, if **R** does not receive any value from **S** along the strong path $(\mathbf{S}, H, I, K, \mathbf{R})$, then **R** can easily conclude that the first set in $\overline{\mathcal{A}}$ is corrupted. However, if **R** receive the keys along $(A, D, E, F, \mathbf{R})$ and tuple (x', y') along $(\mathbf{S}, H, I, K, \mathbf{R})$, then **R** verifies $y' \stackrel{?}{=} x'K_2 + K_3$. If yes, then **R** outputs the message $(x' - K_1)$; else, **R** concludes that first set in $\overline{\mathcal{A}}$ is corrupted.

If the second set (B_2, E_2, F_2) of $\overline{\mathcal{A}}$ is corrupted, then the adversary will know K_1, K_2, K_3 (when A sends them to **S**). But there is no node from B_2 along the strong path from **S** to **R**. So, the authenticated message will reach correctly to **R**. Since there are no nodes from B_2 along the strong path from A to **R**, **R** will either correctly receive the keys or it will not receive any key, depending upon whether the node E crashes or not. If it crashes, then **R** will not receive any key but will know that second set in $\overline{\mathcal{A}}$ is corrupted. On the other hand, if **R** receives the keys from A, then they are correct and so the verification step at **R**'s end will succeed and **R** will correctly output s.

If the first set (B_1, E_1, F_1) of $\overline{\mathcal{A}}$ is corrupted, then adversary will also know the keys by passively listening node F. But in the protocol, A sends the keys to **R**, only after the authenticated message reaches to **R** through the strong path $(\mathbf{S}, H, I, K, \mathbf{R})$. So the node H, which is B_1 type corrupted will not know the keys when the authenticated message passes through H. Hence the delay done by A in sending the keys to **R** plays a very significant role in the subprotocol. In essence, the node from B_1 on path $(\mathbf{S}, H, I, K, \mathbf{R})$ can not change the authenticated message in a consistent manner without being detected by **R** with very high probability. Now similar to information checking protocol of Rabin [3], adversary can forge the authenticated message with probability $\frac{1}{|\mathbb{F}|}$, without knowing K_1, K_2, K_3. Once the authenticated tuple reaches **R**, adversary will also know the keys which A sends to **R**. So now from the authenticated tuple which passed through H and the keys which passed through the node F, adversary can compute m. But now he cannot change it, as **R** already have either recovered m (if the authenticated tuple is received correctly) or knows that the first set in $\overline{\mathcal{A}}$ is corrupted.

Thus, what the above sub protocol achieves is the following: *$\mathbf{R}$'s output which could be either a valid message or a null message with the knowledge of the identity of the set in $\overline{\mathcal{A}}$ which is actually corrupted, is controlled by the adversary who knows the message s. Moreover, if $\mathbf{R}$ receives a valid message, it is indeed the correct message with a very high probability.* This is identical to saying that **S**, with a very high probability, sends a message to **R** through nodes that are in F_1, E_1, F_2 and E_2 respectively. Thus Π_1^{sim} has the effect of simulating a "virtual path" between **S** and **R** with very high probability. So $\mathcal{N}$ in Fig. 3 can be enhanced to network $\mathcal{N}_1$ under the influence of $\overline{\mathcal{A}}_1$ as shown in Fig. 4 where in $\mathcal{N}_1$, there exists a "virtual path" between **S** and **R**, containing intermediate virtual nodes X_1, X_2, X_3 and X_4, where

$X_1 \in F_1, X_2 \in E_1, X_3 \in F_2$ and $X_4 \in E_2$ respectively. Now note that $\mathcal{N}_1$ satisfies the conditions of Theorem 3 with respect to $\bar{\mathcal{A}}_1$, where the virtual path $(\mathbf{S}, X_1, X_2, X_3, X_4, \mathbf{R})$ serves as path q. So the URMT protocol Π (of Theorem 3) can be executed over $\mathcal{N}_1$ tolerating $\bar{\mathcal{A}}$. But we want to design an URMT protocol over $\mathcal{N}$ which is the given physical graph. So we have to simulate the URMT protocol Π executed over $\mathcal{N}_1$ tolerating $\bar{\mathcal{A}}$, into an URMT pro-

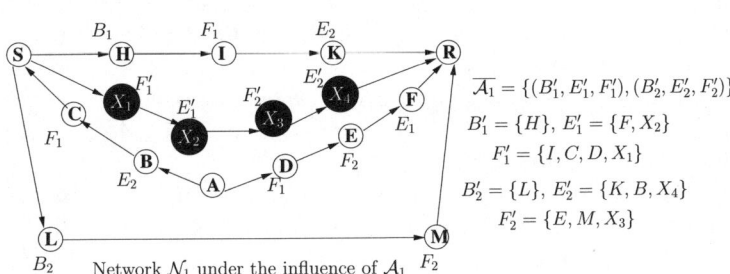

Fig. 4. Network $\mathcal{N}$ updated to $\mathcal{N}_1$

tocol over $\mathcal{N}$ tolerating $\bar{\mathcal{A}}_1$. Our next goal is to demonstrate that simulation. Any value which is sent over p_1 or p_2 in Π over $\mathcal{N}_1$ can be also sent over the same paths in $\mathcal{N}$. Similarly, any value which is sent over the virtual path $(\mathbf{S}, X_1, X_2, X_3, X_4, \mathbf{R})$ in Π over $\mathcal{N}_1$ can be also sent in $\mathcal{N}$ by using the sub-protocol Π_1^{sim}. [2] Thus all the steps of Π over $\mathcal{N}_1$ can be simulated over $\mathcal{N}$ also. If the error probability of sub-protocol Π_1^{sim} is δ' (which is at most $\frac{1}{|\mathbb{F}|}$), then the error probability of the protocol Π simulated over $\mathcal{N}$ is at most $n\delta'$, where n is the number of times sub-protocol Π_1^{sim} is executed. So we can make the error probability of resultant URMT protocol over $\mathcal{N}$ to be at most δ, by appropriately selecting $|\mathbb{F}|$ so that $n\delta' = \delta$.

Summary of the example: In **Example 1**, we demonstrated a graph which contains a "special structure" (which satisfied some "special properties" with respect to $\bar{\mathcal{A}}$). This structure lead to the simulation of a special type of "virtual path" in the original network. Also, though not demonstrated, the "virtual path(s)" could be added *recursively*. Finally, the enhanced graph, with virtual path added, satisfies conditions of Theorem 3 and hence we could simulate Π on enhanced graph. So the idea is that starting from a physical graph, we find the special structures (recursively) and keep on enhancing the graph (step by step through some intermediate graphs) until no more special structure is present on the (enhanced) graph. The final enhanced graph is named as **URMT-BEF-Closure-Digraph** of the original graph (see next section for the formal definition). If **URMT-BEF-Closure-Digraph** satisfies conditions of Theorem 3, then URMT protocol Π exists on the Closure graph. The protocol Π can be run on the physical (original) graph using the sub-protocols that simulate the respective virtual paths present in **URMT-BEF-Closure-Digraph**.

---

[2] Note that each time an independent random triplet of keys are used to execute the sub-protocol Π_1^{sim}.

5   Definition of URMT-BEF-Closure-Digraph

Definition 9 (URMT-BEF-Closure-Digraph). *Let $\mathcal{N} = (\mathbb{P}, \mathbb{E})$ be a digraph influenced by a non-threshold adversary $\mathcal{A}$ with $\overline{\mathcal{A}} = \{(B_1, E_1, F_1), (B_2, E_2, F_2)\}$. We inductively define a sequence of networks $\mathcal{N}_1, \mathcal{N}_2 \ldots$ where the set of vertices, denoted by $\mathbb{P}_i$, of the network $\mathcal{N}_i$ is defined as $\mathbb{P}_i = \mathbb{P} \cup \mathbb{V}_i$ with $\mathbb{V}_1 = \emptyset$ and the set of edges, say $\mathbb{E}_i$, of the network $\mathcal{N}_i$ is defined as $\mathbb{E}_i = \mathbb{E} \cup A_i$ with $A_1 = \emptyset$. The set V_i denotes the set of virtual nodes in $\mathcal{N}_i$, while A_i denotes the set of virtual edges in $\mathcal{N}_i$. We also define a corresponding sequence of adversary structures with maximal basis of two elements each, viz., $\mathcal{A}_1, \mathcal{A}_2, \ldots$, where $\mathcal{A}_1 = \mathcal{A}$. The details are as follows:*

The network $\mathcal{N}_i, i \geq 2$ can be constructed from the network $\mathcal{N}_{i-1}$ in four different ways by applying one of the constructions from Table 1. In the table, a typical entry like

$$\#n \left| \begin{array}{l} A \to X_1 \to \\ X_2 \to X_3 \to \\ X_4 \quad \to \quad B \\ \text{where} \\ X_1 \quad \in \\ F_1, X_2 \in F_2, \\ X_3 \quad \in \quad E_1, \\ X_4 \in E_2 \end{array} \right| \begin{array}{l} \bullet \text{ Head} \to A \text{: avoids nodes from } ((B_1 \cup B_2 \cup \\ F_2 \cup E_1) \setminus \{A, B\}) \text{ with condition } \mathcal{Q}_1 \\ \bullet \text{ Head} \to B \text{ avoids nodes from } ((B_1 \cup B_2 \cup \\ (F_1 \cap F_2)) \setminus \{A, B\}) \\ \bullet A \to B \text{ avoids nodes from } ((B_2 \cup (F_1 \cap F_2)) \setminus \\ \{A, B\}) \text{ with condition } \mathcal{Q}_2 \end{array} \right| \begin{array}{c} \text{[diagram]} \end{array}$$

means the following:

"In the nth way of construction, we could potentially add a virtual path with four new virtual nodes X_1, X_2, X_3 and X_4 and five new virtual edges to $\mathcal{N}_{i-1}$ to obtain $\mathcal{N}_i$. Specifically, we add directed edges $(A, X_1), (X_1, X_2), (X_2, X_3), (X_3, X_4)$ and (X_4, B) if and only if the digraph $\mathcal{N}_{i-1} = (\mathbb{P}_{i-1}, \mathbb{E}_{i-1})$ is such that there exists two physical nodes A, B in $\mathcal{N}_{i-1}$, such that for the two elements (B_1, E_1, F_1) and (B_2, E_2, F_2) in $\overline{\mathcal{A}}_{i-1}$, both the following (1 and 2) arc true:

1. *there does not exist four nodes $w_1 \in (\mathbb{V}_{i-1} \cap F_1), w_2 \in (\mathbb{V}_{i-1} \cap F_2), w_3 \in (\mathbb{V}_{i-1} \cap E_1)$ and $w_4 \in (\mathbb{V}_{i-1} \cap E_2)$ such that the edges $(A, w_1), (w_1, w_2), (w_2, w_3),$*

   (w_3, w_4) and (w_4, B) belong to $\mathbb{E}_{i-1}$. This means n^{th} construction has not been already used for nodes A and B. This is interpreted by the second column of the entry.

2. *Both the following (a and b) hold:*

   (a) *there exists a semi-strong path, say q with head y from A to B in $\mathcal{N}_{i-1}$, such that the strong path from y to A avoids nodes from $((B_1 \cup B_2 \cup F_2 \cup E_1) \setminus \{A, B\})$ and satisfies condition $\mathcal{Q}_1$ (possibly null). Similarly, the strong path from y to B avoids nodes from $((B_1 \cup B_2 \cup (F_1 \cap F_2)) \setminus \{A, B\})$. This is interpreted by the first two bulleted items in the third column.*

   (b) *there exists a strong path, say p from A to B in $\mathcal{N}_{i-1}$, such that p avoids nodes from $((B_2 \cup (F_1 \cap F_2)) \setminus \{A, B\})$. The path p satisfies the condition $\mathcal{Q}_2$ (possibly null). This is the interpretation of the third bulleted item in the third column. Further in addition to $\mathcal{Q}_2$, the following condition*

must always be satisfied by p: for each $i \in \{1,2\}$, every occurrence of a node from $(B_i \cup F_i) \setminus \{A, B\}$ (if any) in p is after the last occurrence of a node from $B_{\bar{i}} \setminus \{A, B\}$ (if any), where if $i = 1$ ($i = 2$), then $\bar{i} = 2$ ($\bar{i} = 1$). Though not stated in the entry, the last condition should be always satisfied by the strong path(s) from A to B in all the constructions.

If one of the above two conditions (1 and 2) fails, we continue to work with $\mathcal{N}_{i-1}$ influenced by $\mathcal{A}_{i-1}$. However, if both of them are true, then we let $\mathbb{V}_i = \mathbb{V}_{i-1} \cup \{X_1, X_2, X_3, X_4\}$ which implies that $\mathbb{P}_i = \mathbb{P}_{i-1} \cup \{X_1, X_2, X_3, X_4\}$; and we let $\mathbb{A}_i = \mathbb{A}_{i-1} \cup \{(A, X_1), (X_1, X_2), (X_2, X_3), (X_3, X_4), (X_4, B)\}$ which implies $\mathbb{E}_i = \mathbb{E}_{i-1} \cup \{(A, X_1), (X_1, X_2), (X_2, X_3), (X_3, X_4), (X_4, B)\}$; finally we let the new nodes X_1, X_2, X_3 and X_4 to be added to F_1, F_2, E_1 and E_2 respectively. That is, if $\overline{\mathcal{A}}_{i-1} = \{(B_1, E_1, F_1), (B_2, E_2, F_2)\}$, then we let $\overline{\mathcal{A}}_i = \{(B_1, E_1 \cup \{X_3\}, F_1 \cup \{X_1\}), (B_2, E_2 \cup \{X_4\}, F_2 \cup \{X_2\})\}$." The figure in the fourth column of the entry denotes the complementary view of the conditions specified in the third column of the entry. The labels along the edges of the figure denote the the set of allowable adversarial nodes along the semi-strong path and strong path(s) between A and B. For example, in the figure, we have put sets E_2 and F_1^* along the edge $y \to A$ which means that the nodes along the strong path from y to A can be completely honest (denoted by **H**) or may contain nodes from sets E_2 and F_1^*, where $F_i^* = F_i \setminus (F_1 \cap F_2)$, $i \in \{1, 2\}$.

Remark 1. A pair of vertices (A, B) may permit at most twenty-four augmentations, corresponding to one of the constructions from Table 1. When no augmentation is possible, we stop the process. Thus, starting from $\mathcal{N}_1$, if we build a sequence of distinct networks $\mathcal{N}_1, \mathcal{N}_2, \cdots, \mathcal{N}_\nu$ through the augmenting process, we observe that $\nu \leq 24\binom{n}{2}$, where $n = |\mathbb{P}|$ denotes the set of nodes in $\mathcal{N}$. Also, we may consider the pairs of vertices in any order and augmentation may also be done in any order for a given pair of vertices. The URMT-BEF-closure-digraph of $\mathcal{N}$, denoted by $\mathcal{N}^*_{URMT_{BEF}}$ is defined as $\mathcal{N}^*_{URMT_{BEF}} = \mathcal{N}_\nu$. The corresponding adversary structure is $\mathcal{A}^* = \mathcal{A}_\nu$, where $|\bar{\mathcal{A}}^*| = 2$.

An illustration of constructing URMT-BEF-Closure-Digraph is given in [5]. We now informally mention few properties of the constructions.

Property 1 (Principle Behind the Constructions). In general, if $\mathcal{N}_{i-1}$ is augmented to $\mathcal{N}_i$ by applying some construction to A, B in $\mathcal{N}_{i-1}$ and if some value s is sent over the resultant virtual path from A to B in $\mathcal{N}_i$, then there always exist a sub-protocol Π^{sim} (as demonstrated in **Example 1**), which when executed over $\mathcal{N}_{i-1}$ has one of the following outcomes: (a) Π^{sim} correctly sends s from A to B over $\mathcal{N}_{i-1}$ with negligible error probability, as demonstrated in **Example 1**; (b) Π^{sim} may fail to send s, in which case it facilitates B to correctly know the exact identity of the corrupted set, as demonstrated in **Example 1**. The basic format of the sub-protocol $\Pi^{simulate}$ will be more or less same for all the constructions (as shown in **Example 1**). We do not provide the Π^{sim} protocol for every construction given in Table 1 due to space constraint.

Lemma 1. $\mathcal{N}^*_{URMT_{BEF}}$ *is finite and is unique (up to isomorphism).*

PROOF: Finiteness follows from Remark 1. The proof of uniqueness property is similar to the proof of Lemma 2 in [6] [3]. □

Property 2 (Property of $\mathcal{A}^*$). If $\bar{\mathcal{A}} = \bar{\mathcal{A}}_1 = \{(B_1, E_1, F_1), (B_2, E_2, F_2)\}$ and $\bar{\mathcal{A}}^* = \{(B'_1, E'_1, F'_1), (B'_2, E'_2, F'_2)\}$, then we have $B'_1 = B_1, B'_2 = B_2$, $(F'_1 \cap F'_2) = (F_1 \cap F_2)$ and $(E'_1 \cap E'_2) = (E_1 \cap E_2)$. This is because the B_i's are never changed and no new virtual node is simultaneously added to both the fail-stop sets or both the passive sets at any stage in any of the constructions.

6 Characterization of URMT Tolerating $\mathcal{A}$ with $|\bar{\mathcal{A}}| = 2$

We now give first ever true characterization of URMT in an arbitrary digraph $\mathcal{N}$ tolerating an adversary structure $\mathcal{A}$ with $|\bar{\mathcal{A}}| = 2$, in terms of $\mathcal{N}^*_{URMT_{BEF}}$.

Theorem 4. *Let $\mathcal{N} = (\mathbb{P}, \mathbb{E})$ be a digraph. Let $\mathcal{N}$ be under the influence of a non-threshold adversary $\mathcal{A}$ with $\bar{\mathcal{A}} = \{(B_1, E_1, F_1), (B_2, E_2, F_2)\}$. Furthermore, let $\mathcal{N}^*_{URMT_{BEF}} = (\mathbb{P}^*, \mathbb{E}^*)$ denotes the URMT-BEF-closure-digraph of network $\mathcal{N}$ with respect to $\mathcal{A}$. Moreover, let $\mathcal{N}^*_{URMT_{BEF}}$ be under the control of $\mathcal{A}^*$ where $\mathcal{A}^*$ is the adversary closure of $\mathcal{A}$ with $\bar{\mathcal{A}}^* = \{(B'_1, E'_1, F'_1), (B'_2, E'_2, F'_2)\}$. Then URMT between $\mathbf{S}$ and $\mathbf{R}$ is possible in $\mathcal{N}$ tolerating $\mathcal{A}$ iff (a) for each $\alpha \in \{1,2\}$, there exists a strong path (not necessarily distinct) p_α from $\mathbf{S}$ to $\mathbf{R}$ in $\mathcal{N}$ avoiding nodes from $(B_\alpha \cup F_\alpha)$ and (b) there exists a strong path P (not necessarily distinct from p_α's) from $\mathbf{S}$ to $\mathbf{R}$ in $\mathcal{N}^*_{URMT_{BEF}}$, avoiding nodes from $(B'_1 \cup B'_2 \cup (F'_1 \cap F'_2))$.*

PROOF: **Sufficiency**: In order to prove the sufficiency of the Theorem 4, we begin with a definition.

Definition 10 ($URMT_{forward}$). *An URMT protocol over digraph $\mathcal{N}_i = (\mathbb{P} \cup \mathbb{V}_i, \mathbb{E} \cup \mathbb{A}_i)$ is called an $URMT_{forward}$ protocol, if in the protocol, the virtual nodes (nodes in $\mathbb{V}_i$) are capable of only receiving and forwarding messages and do no other computation; i.e., they do not use any internal random coins.*

In order to prove the sufficiency of the Theorem 4, we first show that if the conditions of Theorem 4 are satisfied, then we can design an $URMT_{forward}$ protocol over $\mathcal{N}^*_{URMT_{BEF}}$ tolerating $\bar{\mathcal{A}}^*$ (Lemma 2). We then show that if there exists an $URMT_{forward}$ protocol over $\mathcal{N}_i$ for $i > 1$ tolerating $\bar{\mathcal{A}}_i$, then there exists an $URMT_{forward}$ protocol over $\mathcal{N}_{i-1}$ tolerating $\bar{\mathcal{A}}_{i-1}$ (Lemma 3). Now any $URMT_{forward}$ protocol over the original graph $\mathcal{N} = \mathcal{N}_1$ is actually an URMT protocol over $\mathcal{N}$. Since $\mathcal{N}^*_{URMT_{BEF}}$ is finite and unique (see Lemma 1), sufficiency of Theorem 4 follows from Lemma 2 and Lemma 3.

Lemma 2. *If the conditions of Theorem 4 are satisfied, then there exists an $URMT_{forward}$ protocol in $\mathcal{N}^*_{URMT_{BEF}}$ tolerating $\bar{\mathcal{A}}^*$.*

Lemma 3. *For any $i > 1$, there exists an $URMT_{forward}$ protocol in $\mathcal{N}_i$ tolerating $\bar{\mathcal{A}}_i$ iff there exists an $URMT_{forward}$ protocol in $\mathcal{N}_{i-1}$ tolerating $\bar{\mathcal{A}}_{i-1}$.*

---

[3] In [6], the authors have given the construction of closure graph by considering only Byzantine adversary. The constructions given here can be viewed as non-trivial generalization of the constructions given in [6].

Please see the full version of the paper [5] for the proofs of above two lemmas. Now the proof of sufficiency of the Theorem 4 follows from the Lemma 1, 2 and 3. We now proceed to prove the necessity part of the Theorem 4.

Necessity (sketch): The necessity of path p_α in $\mathcal{N}$ is obvious. The necessity of path P in $\mathcal{N}^*_{URMT_{BEF}}$ is proved by contradiction. Suppose there exists an URMT protocol Π^* in $\mathcal{N}^*_{URMT_{BEF}}$ (and hence in $\mathcal{N}$) tolerating $\bar{\mathcal{A}}^*$ even in the absence of path P in $\mathcal{N}^*_{URMT_{BEF}}$. Since P does not exist, it implies that each of the strong paths from **S** to **R** in $\mathcal{N}^*_{URMT_{BEF}}$ contain nodes from $(B'_1 \cup B'_2 \cup (F'_1 \cap F'_2))$. We now divide the set of nodes (virtual + physical) in $\mathcal{N}^*_{URMT_{BEF}}$ as follows: let Y_1 be the set of all nodes that have a strong path to **R** in $\mathcal{N}^*_{PPSMT_{BEF}}$ that does not use any vertex from $(B'_1 \cup B'_2 \cup (F'_1 \cap F'_2))$. Furthermore, let $X_1 = \mathbb{P}^* \setminus (B'_1 \cup B'_2 \cup (F'_1 \cap F'_2) \cup Y_1)$. Clearly, $\mathbf{R} \in Y_1$ and $\mathbf{S} \in X_1$. Moreover, it is evident from the definition of Y_1 that there are no edges from any node in X_1 to any node in Y_1. The necessity of P is now proved in two parts:

1. We first show that if there are no reverse path(s) from the node(s) in Y_1 to the node(s) in X_1, then in the absence of P, there always exists an adversary strategy using which $\bar{\mathcal{A}}^*$ can violate the reliability property of Π^*.
2. We next show that even if there is some reverse path, say p, from Y_1 to X_1, then also presence of p does not help in the possibility of URMT (in the absence of P), thereby maintaining the impossibility of URMT in $\mathcal{N}^*_{URMT_{BEF}}$ as projected above. This is tricky to prove. In order to prove this, we consider all possible allowable behavior of path p. We then show that corresponding to each different status of p, the strong path(s) from X_1 to Y_1 should definitely satisfy certain properties. If not, then we could augment $\mathcal{N}^*_{URMT_{BEF}}$ by applying at least one of the constructions, thus contradicting the fact that $\mathcal{N}^*_{URMT_{BEF}}$ is **URMT-BEF-Closure-Digraph**. Now once it is shown that corresponding to each status of p, the strong path(s) from X_1 to Y_1 exhibit certain properties, we prove that there always exists an adversary strategy which disallows p to help in the possibility of URMT.

So existence of P is necessary for possibility of Π^* on $\mathcal{N}^*_{URMT_{BEF}}$. This in turn implies the necessity of P in $\mathcal{N}^*_{URMT_{BEF}}$ for the possibility of URMT in $\mathcal{N}$. The complete proof is given in [5]. □

Theorem 4 is demonstrated with an example in [5]. We have thus characterized URMT in an arbitrary directed graph tolerating a non-threshold mixed adversary. As stated earlier this also provides the characterization for the possibility of URMT on $\mathcal{D}_{under}$ tolerating $\mathbb{A}_{under}$.

7 Characterization of $URMT_{special}$ on $\mathcal{D}_{under}$

We now characterize $URMT_{special}$ (see Definition 6) in the "underlying digraph" $\mathcal{D}_{under}$ (Definition 5) tolerating $\mathbb{A}$. Now the only reason why a $URMT$ protocol may exist in $\mathcal{D}_{under}$ tolerating $\mathcal{A}$ but an $URMT_{special}$ does not exist in $\mathcal{D}_{under}$ (tolerating $\mathcal{A}$) is that in $URMT_{special}$ protocol, the nodes in $\mathcal{V}$ in $\mathcal{D}_{under}$ are forced to toss coins (which according to Definition 6, they cannot do). Now from the proof of sufficiency of Theorem 4, the problem comes when in the protocol, a node y from $\mathcal{V}$ in $\mathcal{D}_{under}$ is acting as the head of semistrong path between two nodes A and B (in one of the constructions in Table 1) and is forced to send some random secret keys $K_1, K_2, K_3 \in \mathbb{F}$ to A and B (as done in the sub-protocol in **Example 1**). Since the virtual nodes from $\mathcal{V}$ cannot do any random computation in $URMT_{special}$ protocol, we have to modify the definition of URMT-BEF-Closure-Digraph to obtain $URMT_{special}$-BEF-Closure-Digraph of $\mathcal{D}_{under}$ under the influence of $\mathcal{A}$. We highlight only the modifications.

Definition 11 ($URMT_{special}$**-BEF-Closure-Digraph**). *Let $\mathcal{N} = \mathcal{D}_{under} = (\mathcal{P}', \mathcal{E}')$ be the "underlying digraph" of a directed hypergraph $\mathcal{D} = (\mathcal{P}, \mathcal{E})$, where $\mathcal{P}' = (\mathcal{P} \cup \mathcal{V})$. Let $\mathcal{D}_{under}$ be under the influence of $\mathcal{A}$ with $\overline{\mathcal{A}} = \{(B_1, E_1, F_1), (B_2, E_2, F_2)\}$. We inductively define a sequence of directed networks $\mathcal{N}_1, \mathcal{N}_2 \ldots$ with $\mathcal{N}_1 = \mathcal{N}$, where the set of vertices, denoted by $\mathcal{P}'_i$, of the network $\mathcal{N}_i$ is $\mathcal{P}'_i = \mathcal{P}' \cup \mathbb{V}_i$ with $\mathbb{V}_1 = \emptyset$ and the set of edges, say $\mathcal{E}'_i$, of $\mathcal{N}_i$ is $\mathcal{E}'_i = \mathcal{E}' \cup A_i$ with $A_1 = \emptyset$. We also define a corresponding sequence of adversary structures with two elements each, viz., $\mathcal{A}_1, \mathcal{A}_2, \ldots$, where $\mathcal{A}_1 = \mathcal{A}$.*

The network $\mathcal{N}_i$ is augmented from $\mathcal{N}_{i-1}$ by applying different constructions from Table 1 (as done in Definition 9), with certain additional restrictions imposed. We mention these restrictions. Let A, B be two nodes in $\mathcal{N}_{i-1}$, where both $A, B \in \mathcal{P}$. Thus A, B are physical nodes in $\mathcal{D}_{under}$. Let p be a strong path between A, B and q be a semi-strong path between A, B with head y. Now suppose that paths p and q satisfy the condition of one of the constructions in Table 1, say $\mathcal{C}$. Let according to $\mathcal{C}$, S_A and S_B denotes the set of adversarial nodes which should be absent along the strong path from y to A and B respectively. Now we can augment $\mathcal{N}_{i-1}$ by applying $\mathcal{C}$ to A and B, if one of the following (extra) conditions are satisfied:

*1. **The head y of q is such that $y \in \mathcal{P}$ (y is a Physical node in $\mathcal{N}_{i-1}$)**: In this case, $\mathcal{C}$ is directly applied to A and B (as done in Definition 9).*

*2. **The head y of q is such that $y \in \mathcal{V}$ (y is a Virtual node in $\mathcal{N}_{i-1}$)**: In this case we put some additional constraints as follows: Let $z \in \mathcal{P}$ be the immediate out-neighbor of y on the path from y to B and $x \in \mathcal{P}$ be the unique in-neighbor of y. Note that according to the definition of $\mathcal{D}_{under}$ (see Definition 5), if $y \in \mathcal{V}$, then it implies that the out-neighbor of y on the path from y to B (z) and the in-neighbor of y (x) are physical nodes in $\mathcal{D}_{under}$. Hence both x and z are physical nodes in $\mathcal{N}_{i-1}$. Since $y \in \mathcal{V}$ and is not allowed to toss random coins, it cannot perform any synchronization; i.e., in any protocol, we cannot ask y to send some "secret" information to A first and send the same "secret" information to B, only after A has send some "authenticated" message to B (this principle is used in the sub-protocol in **Example 1**). With these properties of y, z and x, we now mention the additional constraints on z and x:*

1. Restriction on z: $z \notin (S_A \cap (E_1 \cup E_2)) \cup S_B$.

   Remark: *Informally, the above restriction says that z can not be under the influence of a passive adversary set which is not allowed over the path from*

y to A in $\mathcal{C}$. This is so because in any protocol, y being a virtual node ($\in \mathcal{V}$), sends every information received from its in-neighbor $\boldsymbol{x}$, simultaneously to both z and the first node from y to A. So if $\mathcal{C}$ requires the path from y to A should not contain nodes from certain type of passive adversary set, then the same type of passive adversary set should not influence z too. With this restriction on z, if any synchronization is needed from y in the protocol (we have used such synchronization from y when y is a physical node in the subprotocol in **Example 1**), can be taken care by z. We will explain this more elaborately in the proof of Theorem 5.

2. Restriction on $\boldsymbol{x}$: (a) $\boldsymbol{x} \notin (F_1 \cap F_2)$ and (b) If $E_i \in S_A$, then $\boldsymbol{x} \notin E_i \cup B_i$, for $i \in \{1, 2\}$

Remark: When the head y of path q is virtual node, all the computations supposed to be done by y in the protocol, is actually done by $\boldsymbol{x}$. The above restriction says that if path from y to A should devoid of E_i, then $\boldsymbol{x}$ can not belong to $E_i \cup B_i$. In addition, $\boldsymbol{x} \notin F_1 \cap F_2$. We prove the necessity and sufficiency of the restriction in sequel.

If z and $\boldsymbol{x}$ follows the above restrictions, then we can augment $\mathcal{N}_{i-1}$ by applying $\mathcal{C}$ to A and B. Otherwise, $\mathcal{C}$ cannot be applied to A and B. Since $\mathcal{C}$ can be any of the 24 constructions from Table 1, we get 24 corresponding additional constructions when $y \in \mathcal{V}$. We do not provide these additional constructions here due to space constraint. The interested reader can see [5].

Now the characterization of $URMT_{special}$ in $\mathcal{D}_{under}$ is given by the following theorem:

Theorem 5. Let $\mathcal{N} = \mathcal{D}_{under} = (\mathcal{P}', \mathcal{E}')$ be the "underlying digraph" of a directed hypergraph $\mathcal{D} = (\mathcal{P}, \mathcal{E})$, where $\mathcal{P}' = \mathcal{P} \cup \mathcal{V}$ and $\mathcal{V}$ is the set of virtual nodes. Then $URMT_{special}$ is possible in $\mathcal{N}$ tolerating a non-threshold adversary $\mathbb{A}$ iff for every $\mathcal{A} \subseteq \mathbb{A}$ with $\overline{\mathcal{A}} = \{(B_1, E_1, F_1), (B_2, E_2, F_2)\}$ both the following hold:

1. The network $\mathcal{N}$ is such that for each $\alpha \in \{1, 2\}$ the deletion of nodes in $((B_\alpha \cup F_\alpha) \setminus \{\mathbf{S}, \mathbf{R}\})$ does not eliminate all the strong paths from $\mathbf{S}$ to $\mathbf{R}$.
2. The $URMT_{special}$-BEF-Closure-Digraph of network $\mathcal{N}$ with respect to the adversary structure $\mathcal{A}$, viz., $\mathcal{N}^*_{URMTspl_{BEF}} = (\mathbb{P}^*, \mathbb{E}^*)$ is such that, there exists a strong path from $\mathbf{S}$ to $\mathbf{R}$ in $\mathcal{N}^*_{URMTspl_{BEF}}$, induced by the set of vertices $(\mathbb{P}^* \setminus (B'_1 \cup B'_2 \cup (F'_1 \cap F'_2))) \cup \{\mathbf{S}, \mathbf{R}\}$ where the adversary structure closure $\mathcal{A}^*_{spl} = \{(B'_1, E'_1, F'_1), (B'_2, E'_2, F'_2)\}$.

For the proof, see the full version of the paper [5]. Now Theorem 5, along with Theorem 1, completely characterize URMT over directed hypergraph $\mathcal{D}$, tolerating $\mathcal{A}_{(t_b, t_f, t_p)}$. In the full version of the paper [5], we demonstrate Theorem 5 + Theorem 1 on hypergraph $\mathcal{D}$ shown in Fig. 2, tolerating $\mathcal{A}_{(1,0,0)}$ and $\mathcal{A}_{(1,1,0)}$. We show that URMT is possible tolerating $\mathcal{A}_{(1,0,0)}$ but impossible tolerating $\mathcal{A}_{(1,1,0)}$ (as claimed in section 1).

Table 1. The various constructions (#1 to #4) to augment $\mathcal{N}_{i-1}$ to $\mathcal{N}_i$. In the figures, y denotes the head of semi-strong path between A and B and the labels along the edges, represents the permissible category of adversary sets in permitted order for the construction. $F_i^* = F_i \setminus (F_1 \cap F_2)$ for $i \in \{1, 2\}$.

No.	Temporary Link	Conditions & Figure	
#1	$A \to X_1 \to X_2 \to X_3 \to X_4 \to B$, $X_1 \in F_1$, $X_2 \in E_1$, $X_3 \in F_2$, $X_4 \in E_2$	1. $y \to A$: $((B_1 \cup B_2 \cup F_2 \cup E_1) \setminus \{A, B\})$ 2. $y \to B$: $((B_1 \cup B_2 \cup (F_1 \cap F_2)) \setminus \{A, B\})$ 3. $A \to B$: Path p: $((B_2 \cup (F_1 \cap F_2)) \setminus \{A, B\})$ **with the last node from F_1^* before the first node from E_1 and the last node from F_2^* before the first node from E_2.**	
		1. $y \to A$: $((B_1 \cup B_2 \cup F_1 \cup E_2) \setminus \{A, B\})$ 2. $y \to B$: $((B_1 \cup B_2 \cup (F_1 \cap F_2)) \setminus \{A, B\})$ 3. $A \to B$: Path p: $((B_1 \cup (F_1 \cap F_2)) \setminus \{A, B\})$ **with the last node from F_1^* before the first node from E_1 and the last node from F_2^* before the first node from E_2.**	
		1. $y \to A$: $((B_1 \cup B_2 \cup F_1 \cup E_1) \setminus \{A, B\})$ **with the last node from F_2^* before the first node from E_2.** 2. $y \to B$: $((B_1 \cup B_2 \cup (F_1 \cap F_2)) \setminus \{A, B\})$ 3. $A \to B$: for each $i \in \{1, 2\}$, Path p_i: $((B_i \cup (F_1 \cap F_2)) \setminus \{A, B\})$ **with the last node from F_1^* before the first node from E_1 and the last node from F_2^* before the first node from E_2.**	
		1. $y \to A$: $((B_1 \cup B_2 \cup F_2 \cup E_2) \setminus \{A, B\})$ **with the last node from F_1^* before the first node from E_1.** 2. $y \to B$: $((B_1 \cup B_2 \cup (F_1 \cap F_2)) \setminus \{A, B\})$ 3. $A \to B$: for each $i \in \{1, 2\}$, Path p_i: $((B_i \cup (F_1 \cap F_2)) \setminus \{A, B\})$ **with the last node from F_1^* before the first node from E_1 and the last node from F_2^* before the first node from E_2.**	
		1. $y \to A$: $((B_1 \cup B_2 \cup (F_1 \cap F_2) \cup E_1) \setminus \{A, B\})$ 2. $y \to B$: $((B_1 \cup B_2 \cup (F_1 \cap F_2)) \setminus \{A, B\})$ 3. $A \to B$, Path p: $(B_2 \cup (F_1 \cap F_2)) \setminus \{A, B\})$ **with the last node from F_1^* before the first node from E_1 and the last node from F_2^* before the first node from E_2.** 4. $A \to B$, Path Q: $(B_1 \cup B_2 \cup (F_1 \cap F_2))$	
		1. $y \to A$: $((B_1 \cup B_2 \cup (F_1 \cap F_2) \cup E_2) \setminus \{A, B\})$ 2. $y \to B$: $((B_1 \cup B_2 \cup (F_1 \cap F_2)) \setminus \{A, B\})$ 3. $A \to B$, Path p: $(B_1 \cup (F_1 \cap F_2)) \setminus \{A, B\})$ **with the last node from F_1^* before the first node from E_1 and the last node from F_2^* before the first node from E_2.** 4. $A \to B$, Path Q: $(B_1 \cup B_2 \cup (F_1 \cap F_2))$	
#2	$A \to X_1 \to X_2 \to X_3 \to X_4 \to B$, $X_1 \in E_1$, $X_2 \in F_1$, $X_3 \in F_2$, $X_4 \in E_2$	Similar to the construction #1 except that the condition "with the last node from F_1^* before the first node from E_1" is removed from the strong path(s) from A to B in all the six cases	Similar to #1 except that first restriction on the ordering of vertices in the strong path(s) from A to B is relaxed
#3	$A \to X_1 \to X_2 \to X_3 \to X_4 \to B$, $X_1 \in F_1$, $X_2 \in E_1$, $X_3 \in E_2$, $X_4 \in F_2$	Similar to the construction #1 except that the condition "with the last node from F_2^* before the first node from E_2" is removed from the strong path(s) from A to B in all the six cases	Similar to #1 except that second restriction on the ordering of vertices in the strong path(s) from A to B is relaxed
#4	$A \to X_1 \to X_2 \to X_3 \to X_4 \to B$, $X_1 \in F_1$, $X_2 \in F_2$, $X_3 \in E_1$, $X_4 \in E_2$	Similar to the construction #1 except that both the conditions "with the last node from F_1^* before the first node from E_1" and "with the last node from F_2^* before the first node from E_2" are removed from the strong path(s) from A to B in all the six cases	Similar to #1 except that both restrictions on the ordering of vertices in the strong path(s) from A to B are relaxed

References

1. Desmedt, Y., Wang, Y.: Perfectly secure message transmission revisited. In: Knudsen, L.R. (ed.) EUROCRYPT 2002. LNCS, vol. 2332, pp. 502–517. Springer, Heidelberg (2002)
2. Franklin, M., Yung, M.: Secure hypergraphs: Privacy from partial broadcast. In: Proc. of 27th Ann. Symposium on Theory of Computing, pp. 36–44 (1995)
3. Rabin, T., Ben-Or, M.: Verifiable secret sharing and multiparty protocols with honest majority. In: Proc. of 21st ACM STOC, pp. 73–85 (1989)
4. Shankar, B., Gopal, P., Srinathan, K., Pandu Rangan, C.: Unconditional reliable message transmision in directed networks. In: Proc. of SODA 2008 (2008)
5. Srinathan, K., Patra, A., Choudhary, A., Pandu Rangan, C.: Unconditionally reliable message transmission in directed hypergraphs. Cryptology Eprint Archive Report 2008/371
6. Srinathan, K., Pandu Rangan, C.: Possibility and complexity of probabilistic reliable communication in directed networks. In: Proc. of 25th PODC, pp. 265–274. ACM Press, New York (2006)

An Open Framework for Remote Electronic Elections

Yu Zhang

Macau University of Science and Technology, Macau SAR China
Laboratory of Computer Science,
Institute of Software, Chinese Academy of Science, Beijing, China
yu.zhang@ens-cachan.org

Abstract. We propose a framework for remote electronic elections with an independent, trustworthy authorization proxy. Unlike existing voting systems, voter authorization is separated from particular elections in our scheme, and is done through reusable credentials granted by the proxy. Moreover, different types of elections can fit in the framework, with different sets of legitimate voters and even different designs of voting and tabulation. We also define a cryptographic protocol for the credential generation and the election registration.

1 Introduction

Designing a secure e-voting system has been a research issue for more than 20 years, mainly in the field of cryptography. While there are still many researchers working on it, some real voting systems have been put in practice in recent years, though few of them succeed [22]. Most work on electronic voting systems focus on the cryptographic design that meets some special requirements of e-voting systems, like receipt-freeness or coercion-resistance, and many interesting protocols have been proposed [15, 27, 16, 3, 21, 10].

It is expected that in the future, electronic election schemes will be much more widely and frequently used than today. A typical case would be that an individual participates in multiple elections, and very likely, different elections may have different sets of legitimate voters, e.g., the democrats for an intraparty election. Then how can he vote via remote e-voting systems? In most existing systems, he must first identify himself as a valid voter for the election, then the system will generate a distinguished credential which allows him to cast valid ballots. Authorization is probably not an issue of the computer part in those *on-the-spot* voting schemes like Prêt-à-Voter [8, 28] or Punchscan [17], where voters are implicitly required to be present at the voting spot and authorization will be done in person. But it is an issue in remote voting systems, as it can be very expensive for voters to do on-the-spot authorization in every election.

Some recent proposals of remote voting schemes introduce anonymous credentials for proving the eligibility of voters [21, 11]. While these schemes do introduce interesting mechanisms to prevent coercion, they all assume that there must exist untappable channels during the registration so that coercers cannot simulate the complete procedure of a voter. In particular, credentials will be granted via these untappable channels.

We notice that such untappable channels can be very expensive for every election when an individual participates in multiple elections. Can we just register *once for all*? It motivates us to propose an open voting framework, where we introduce an independent *authorization proxy* and voting credentials are generated and granted by the proxy. What distinguishes our scheme from other credential-based voting systems is the re-usability of credentials, which allow voters to participate in multiple elections without doing authorization every time. By doing so, we avoid implementing the expensive untappable channels for every election, and voter eligibility is achieved by credentials, with the proxy providing necessary aid to election authorities.

Meanwhile, anonymous credentials has been well studied in cryptography and there are many credential systems which provide much more functionality than what we need here [7, 12, 9, 24, 4], so instead of giving yet another cryptographic implementation of e-voting, we are actually proposing an architectural approach of designing e-voting systems. We argue that careful integrating existing credential systems and voting systems should be more reliable and offer more flexibility than designing everything from scratch, hence our framework is *open* in the sense that different systems can be plugged into it, with necessary adaption. We see this as our main contribution though we also propose a cryptographic protocol for registration and credential generation to illustrate the usability of the scheme.

Outline. The next section explains the architecture of the voting framework and how component systems interact. Section 3 gives an informal analysis of what should be met by each component, then in Section 4 we propose a cryptographic protocol for credential generation and election registration. Section 5 concludes and discusses on the implementation and security analysis of the scheme.

2 The Open Voting Framework

Figure 1 shows the global architecture of the voting framework with two independent election cases, where we may have different election authorities, ballot designs, vote collection and tabulation methods. Notice that eligible voters in the two elections can be different, but they all come from the same large set of individuals, e.g., citizens of the nation or students in the campus. This point distinguishes our scheme with other existing voting schemes.

The authorization of voters is done with the aid of an *authorization proxy*, independent of both elections: an eligible voter can go to the proxy, prove his identity, and ask for a *credential*, which will be used to prove his eligibility in the voting procedure. If he participates in both elections, use the same credential, or he can request for a new credential as he wishes. The acquisition of credentials is totally separated from particular elections and can be done at any time, provided that the voter will not miss his election. When an election is going on, the proxy offers necessary information to the election authorities and helps them to check the eligibility of voters, without revealing their identities.

The authorization proxy is assumed to be trustworthy, robust, and independent of any election. Meanwhile, we do not specify who should be the authorities of a particular election, neither the design of voting and tabulation phases — we regard them as external parts of the framework. This is to keep the framework open, so that organizers of particular elections can take a voting scheme that best meets their requirements,

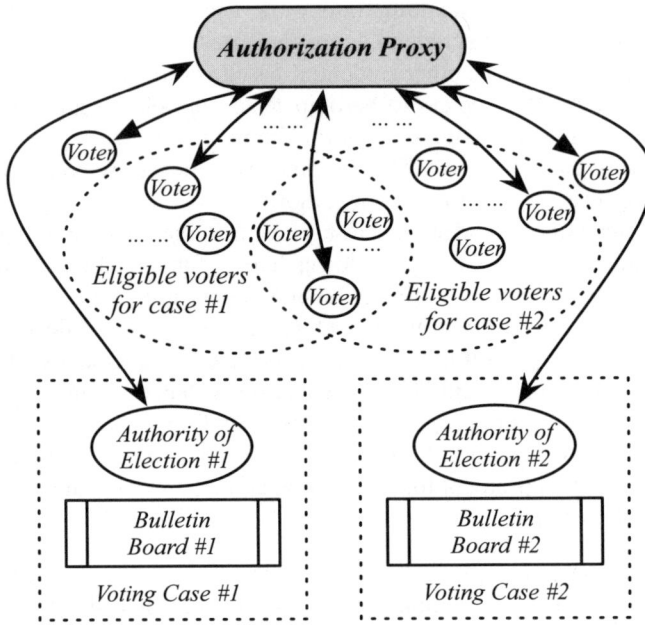

Fig. 1. The architecture of the voting framework with two voting cases

or even design the voting system on their own. But more importantly, such a scheme prevents the election authorities from direct identification of voters, minimizing the interaction between the two.

Indeed, the open framework offers more flexibility (and more democracy in some sense) — if voters complain about the voting scheme in use, it is always possible to replace it with relatively lower cost. However, the security of the whole system then heavily depends on the external voting schemes. We shall discuss on that in Section 3.

2.1 Agents

There are three kinds of agents in our voting scheme: voters, the authorization proxy, and election authorities. The first two kinds of agents are election-independent and can be involved in multiple cases, while each election authority is specific to a particular election.

– *Voters* in our scheme are just individuals that will potentially participate in some elections. Each individual is uniquely identified at the authorization proxy and holds an anonymous credential which will authorize him to vote in elections.
– The *authorization proxy* is a trusted, independent authority whose essential responsibility is the management of credentials, including delivering private credentials to individuals and generating public credentials of eligible voters in response to the request of election authorities. He also deals with individuals' requests for renewing credentials, and sends notifications when credentials are expired.

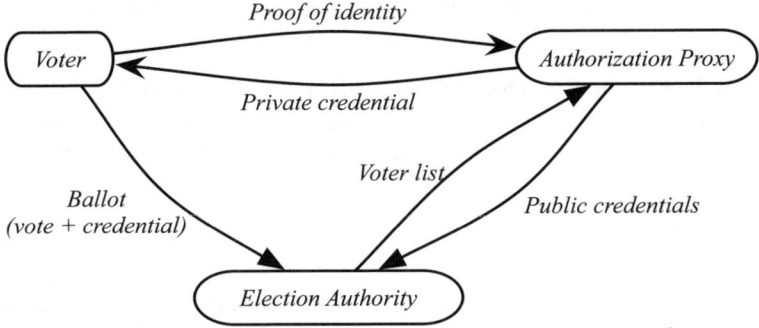

Fig. 2. Interactions between agents in a single voting case

- *Election authorities* are responsible for particular elections. They collect ballots, check their validity, tally and announce the final result. These are standard functionalities of authorities in most voting systems.

Assumption 1 (Universally trustworthy proxy). *Authorization proxies are universally trustworthy. They never cooperate with adversaries, coerced voters and corrupted election authorities.*

Figure 2 shows the interactions between the three types of agents in a single election.

2.2 Credentials

The credential delivering in the framework is a phase independent of any particular election. Basically, a potential voter can request for a credential at any time provided that he will not miss his election. For achieving a valid credential, he must first prove his identity to the proxy. The proxy then generates a distinguished credential and sends it to the requester, and keeps a record in his secret storage. In general, the record contains the requester's unique ID (e.g., the citizen ID or the student number), the credential, expiring date (credentials should be renewed periodically for better security), and other information like the requester's contact, etc.

Note that the credentials mentioned above are private credentials and it is assumed that the proxy will never reveal any credential to anybody other than the owner. For election authorities being able to check the voter eligibility, the proxy need to produce a public correspondence for each legitimate credential. These public credentials are either published on the proxy's bulletin board if there is one, or secretly transmitted to election authorities, and the proxy must ensure the integrity of the information, usually supplying a digital signature. The proxy also provides a mechanism for election authorities to check, when they receive a private credential, whether it belongs to a legitimate voter without knowing the identity of the owner.

It has been noticed in [11] that for the sake of coercion-resistance, there must be some phase during an election where adversaries cannot simulate a voter and the registration is a good time for this. They in addition assume that there is at least one honest register authority whose channel to voters is *untappable*, and in practice, this can be an *off-line* authority. While it is expensive to have this assumption for every election, we can assume, at lower cost in our framework, that the channel between the proxy and voters is untappable.

Assumption 2 (Untappable channel for delivering credentials). *The channel between each individual voter and the authorization proxy is untappable. The delivering of private credentials is physically separated from any agent other than the proxy and the involved voter.*

2.3 Registration

Registration phase is the only interface between the authorization proxy and external voting systems. When preparing an election, the election authorities (usually the registrars) first submit to the proxy a list containing all IDs of eligible voters, via some secure channel. The proxy then generates the corresponding public credential for each ID, performs a secret shuffling, then sends the resulted list back to election authorities or publishes it on the bulletin board.

Since voters can request for new credentials, it is important for the proxy to publish non-obsolete public credentials. A simple solution is to announce a *registration deadline* when an election starts: if a voter's credential is going to expire before the deadline, he must renew it; and the proxy will not publish the list of public credentials until the deadline. Meanwhile, voting can take place immediately when the election starts because authorities does not have to check the eligibility of voters before the voting starts — they can postpone it till the tabulation phase. The scheme can easily endure multiple casting while tallying only one of them if the external voting system has a proper tabulation policy on dealing with duplicate ballots.

2.4 Voting and Tabulation

Our voting framework itself does not define the exact protocols of voting and tabulation. However, external voting systems must be credential based in order that they can make use of the authorization functionality of the proxy. When a voter casts his ballot, he usually needs to attach his credential with the vote to prove eligibility. Several existing voting schemes already introduce credentials [21, 11] and can be adapted and fit in our framework. We give a concrete example in Section 4.

3 Security Requirements

It is very likely that elections in different circumstances will have different security goals. It is also what motivates us to define an *open* framework to offer more flexibility to election organizers. While security analysis of the whole voting system depends on the design of external election schemes, the framework itself needs to provide enough security support so that when the design of the external election scheme is secure enough, the whole system can meet even the strongest security requirements.

In fact, it has been widely accepted that the analysis of complex security systems should be performed based on precise and formal models. Indeed, many formal models for information security, especially for cryptographic protocols, have been proposed in the past decade. Some automated tools for verifying security protocols are also developed and successfully used in practice (see [26] for a recent survey). In this paper, instead of doing a formal analysis, we only informally describe the security requirements that the voting system should meet. But a complete and general formal modelling of e-voting systems (not just the one presented here) is certainly interesting and will be our future work.

3.1 Security of e-Voting

This section summarizes the security properties that an e-voting system should satisfy in general and we point out which properties are internal of our framework and which depend on the design of external voting and tabulation.

Vote privacy: the fact that a voter voted in a particular way is not revealed to any other agent. In other words, vote privacy means that no adversary can link a particular vote with the voter who casted it.

Since the communication channels can reveal the identities of senders, in most e-voting systems. it is assumed that the voting channels are anonymous. We also have this assumption in our scheme:

Assumption 3 (Anonymous voting channel). *The channels through which voters cast their ballots are anonymous.*

In practice, anonymous channels can be implemented using Chaum's mix [5] or the onion routing system [29].

Given the above assumption, vote privacy then depends on the information that a voter will transmit over the network. Essentially, these are ballots casted by voters, whose format or design is from external voting systems. But in voting systems based on anonymous credentials, ballots generally include credentials, so it is important that credentials themselves do not reveal the owners' identities. Later we define more precisely the privacy of credentials in our framework.

Voter eligibility. Only legitimate voters can vote, or more precisely, only ballots of legitimate voters will be tallied. In many modern voting systems, casting a ballot is actually posting it on a public bulletin board which is usually appendable by anybody. It is of course possible that election authorities grant the writing privilege to eligible voters only, but that again requires authorization and increases the risk of violating privacy.

In our scheme, voter eligibility, or preferably vote eligibility, is partially ensured by the trusted authorization proxy in the registration protocol: if all voters agree on the list of legitimate identities submitted by election authorities, then the list returned by the proxy contains one and only one public credential for each legitimate voter. In addition, external voting systems must be able to remove ballots with invalid credentials, i.e., whose public correspondences are not in the list provided by the proxy.

Voter verifiability. Individual voter can verify whether his vote is effectively counted. It depends on the protocol of vote collection and tabulation. In our scheme, voters must first be able to verify that their public credentials appear in the list produced by the proxy. Note that this is not trivial since the proxy does not necessarily publish the list, but simply sends it to election authorities, so corrupted authorities can remove credentials from the list or entirely replace it with another one, hence it is necessary for voters to check the integrity of the list.

Universal verifiability. Voters can verify whether all votes are correctly tallied in the final result. If the voters accept the collection of votes before tallying, universal verifiability is then a property of the tabulation protocol, which is defined by the external voting system.

Receipt-freeness. No voter can prove that he voted in a particular way. Receipt-freeness is in particular needed for preventing vote-buying. While this heavily depends on the ballot format, a poorly-designed credential alone can be a receipt, hence violating the receipt-freeness of the whole system.

Coercion-resistance. Coercers cannot force a voter to vote in a particular way. This is an even stronger property than receipt-freeness. A common solution in recent coercion-resistant schemes [21,11] is to allow voters to generate fake credentials so that they can send with them the ballots that a coercer forced them to. It is also assumed that election authorities can detect fake credentials and eliminate attached ballots.

Security of Credentials. Managing credentials is the essential functionality of the authorisation proxy. Though many security properties mentioned above depend on external voting schemes, without combined with particular ballots, credentials themselves should satisfy some security requirements.

Non-forgeability. No agent other than the proxy can generate a valid credential. In the computational model, it means that the probability of forging a credential should be negligible.

Privacy. If a voter submit his private credential to the election authorities, via an anonymous channel, no adversary or corrupted authority can link the credential with the identity of its owner.

Verifiability. The proxy can prove secretly to the voter, usually through a *designated verifier proof* [19], that his credential is correctly encoded in the list of public credentials if he is a legitimate voter. This property is optional when the Assumption 1 holds.

Coercion-resistance. An adversary or a coercer cannot force a voter to reveal his private credential. We assume that the coercer and the coerced voter does not trust each other, so even if the voter is willing to reveal his credential, he is not able to prove that the revealed credential is a real one. This actually implies that the credentials are receipt-free.

4 Cryptographic Protocols

In this section we give a cryptographic protocol for generating credentials and registering elections. Note that the paper is not trying to design yet another complete, ready-for-use election scheme, so we do not define these protocols as internal of the framework, but rather an example to illustrate the usability.

4.1 Setup

We write $\mathcal{I}$ for the large set of identities of individuals, containing all potential voters. For the moment, we assume that there is only one authorization proxy and we write AP for the proxy.

$\mathcal{G}$ is a very large group of bitstrings for generating credentials. In particular, we assume that credentials are simply elements of $\mathcal{G}$ and the size of the group $\mathcal{G}$ should be large enough to prevent forgeability.

Assumption 4 (Large credential group). *There exists a group $\mathcal{G}$ whose size is sufficiently larger than $|\mathcal{I}|$ so that adversaries cannot forge a true credential or detect fake credentials with non-negligible probability.*

We also assume that the encryption over the group $\mathcal{G}$ is asymmetric and probabilistic. For every $\theta \in \mathcal{G}$, we write $\mathsf{E}(\theta, k)$ for the space of the ciphertexts of encrypting θ with key k.

Assumption 5 (Plaintext-equivalence-test). *There exists a plaintext-equivalence-test protocol PET for the probabilistic encryption over $\mathcal{G}$, such that for every two encrypted credentials s_1, s_2, $\mathsf{PET}(s_1, s_2)$ equals 1 if $s_1, s_2 \in \mathsf{E}(\theta, k)$ for some $\theta \in \mathcal{G}$ and some key k, and a random number otherwise.*

cred is a function that transforms a private credential to its public representation. In particular, $\mathbf{cred}(\theta, k) \in \mathsf{E}(\theta, k)$. If ℓ is a list of identities, we also write $\mathbf{PubList}(\ell, k)$ for the *shuffled* list of corresponding public credentials. The shuffling is a random permutation performed by the proxy and kept secret.

4.2 Credential Generation

Anonymous credentials was first introduced by Chaum in 1980s [6] to protect the privacy of individuals when offering the accessibility to resources. Many systems and protocols have been proposed ever since [7, 12, 9, 24, 4] and we believe most of them can be integrated in our framework with various of external voting schemes. But instead of using those complex systems which are usually designed for much more sophisticated circumstances, we propose here a simpler protocol for generating credentials that provides enough security for electronic elections. Our proposed protocol is based on the one used in the JCJ-scheme [21].

Upon sufficient proof of the identity of an individual $i \in \mathcal{I}$, the authorization proxy generates a set of pair-wise distinguished random strings

$$\Theta_i = \{\theta_i, \delta_i^1, \ldots, \delta_i^{n_i} \mid \theta_i \in_U \mathcal{G}, \delta_i^k \in_U \mathcal{G}, k = 1, \ldots, n_i\},$$

where $\mathcal{G}$ is the large El-Gamal group. The proxy then sends these strings to the individual i via an untappable channel (Assumption 2). Assumption 4 ensures the non-forgeability of true credentials.

Intuitively, the string θ_i is the true credential for i and $\delta_i^1, \ldots, \delta_i^{n_i}$ are fake credentials. We write Δ for the universal set of fake credentials, i.e., $\Delta = \bigcup_{i \in Id}(\Theta_i / \{\theta_i\})$. The following two conditions must hold for credentials:

(CRED-1) $\forall i \in \mathcal{I}, \theta_i \notin \Delta$.
(CRED-2) $\forall i, j \in \mathcal{I}$ s.t. $i \neq j$, $\theta_i \neq \theta_j$.

The two conditions guarantee that real credentials never mix up with each other or with fake credentials, i.e., the proxy offers a unique credential for each individual. (Note that (CRED-1) does not stand automatically from the above definition of Δ.) Meanwhile, it does not matter whether a fake credential has been granted to two or more individuals. They are given to voters to cheat coercers: when coerced, voters submit their coerced votes with the fake credentials, which is assumed to be eliminated in the tabulation phase. This is similar to that in the JCJ-scheme, where a coerced voter choose by himself a random group member of $\mathcal{G}$ as the fake credential. Their approach is dangerous when the size of $\mathcal{G}$ is not large enough because the fake credential will likely be a true credential of another voter.

Note that n_i – the number of fake credentials granted to the individual i – varies for different individuals and is kept secret by the proxy, so that when coerced, a voter can always hide his true credential. He is not able to prove his true credential without additional information because he cannot convince the coercer that all of his credentials has been revealed.

Public credentials are generated when an election E starts: when the AP receives the list of legitimate identities of the election, he first generates a pair of asymmetric keys $(\mathsf{PK}_E, \mathsf{SK}_E)$ for the election, then he produces a public credential $\vartheta_i = \mathbf{cred}(\theta_i, \mathsf{PK}_E)$ for every identity i in the voter list (θ_i is the corresponding private credential).

Compared with the credential generation protocol used in the JCJ-scheme, the novelty of ours is that we allow voters to *reuse* their credentials in multiple elections. While this is also possible in the JCJ-scheme, it has to be ensured that different election cases must have the *same* set of legitimate voters, which is certainly too restrictive in our framework.

4.3 Registration Protocol

The registration protocol specifies how the election authorities achieve from the authorization proxy the list of public credentials of legitimate voters. When starting an election E, the election authorities send to the proxy ℓ_E, the list of legitimate identities in the election. The proxy then responds by the shuffled list $\mathbf{PubList}(\ell_E, \mathsf{PK}_E)$ of corresponding public credentials. By assumption 1, if the ℓ_E is not modified during the transmission, the returned list contains all and only public credentials of individuals in ℓ_E. If the proxy has his own private bulletin board which everybody can read but nobody other than the proxy can write to, then he can simply publish the list on his bulletin board. If there is no such board and the list has to be transmitted via a normal communication channel, then the registration protocol must first mutually authenticate the election authority and the proxy, and offer them a secure transition.

Essentially, the authentication between the two parties can be done through the well-known Needham-Schroeder-Lowe public key protocol [23]. The messages after the handshake phase of the NSL protocol provide data integrity and can be:

$$EA \rightarrow AP : \mathsf{enc}(\{n_E, \ell_E\}, k) \tag{1}$$

$$AP \rightarrow EA : \mathsf{sig}(\{n_E, \ell_E, \mathsf{PK}_E, \mathbf{PubList}(\ell_E, \mathsf{PK}_E)\}, \mathsf{SK}_{AP}) \tag{2}$$

where n_E is the unique election ID, PK_E is the public key generated by the proxy for the election only, k is the session key established during the handshake phase, enc is standard symmetric encryption and sig is a signature scheme. n_E and ℓ_E is necessary to be included in the second message for identifying the right election. If the AP has a private bulletin board, the second message is also what he publishes there.

4.4 An Example of Voting and Tabulation

For building a concrete voting system, it remains to define the protocols of voting and tabulation. We briefly describes how other voting schemes can be adapted and fit in, based on the voting protocol proposed by Juels et al. [21], but we skip most cryptographic details.

Voting. The candidates in the JCJ-scheme are encoded as elements of the group where voter credentials are generated. In our framework, it can be done by the AP to avoid collision, using the group $\mathcal{G}$. The candidate slate is put in the message (2) in the registration protocol.

When the election starts and the AP publishes the candidate slate, the voter i can cast a ballot for the candidate c comprising two El-Gamal ciphertexts (E_1, E_2), respectively for the candidate choice c and his credential θ_i. He also includes proofs showing that the candidate choice c is valid and he knows θ_i and c simultaneously. The voter then sends the ballot to the bulletin board of the election, via an anonymous channel (Assumption 3).

Tabulation. To tally the ballots posted on the bulletin board, the election authorities first verify the correctness of every ballot and eliminates those invalid. Then they separate the vote and the credential in each of the remained ballot and get two lists — a list of encrypted votes and a list of encrypted credentials. Now perform the *plaintext equivalence test* [18, 25] on the latter list to remove duplicate credentials, as well as their corresponding votes in the other list. Perform PET again on each credential, with the public credential list produced by the AP, and remove the illegitimate credentials (and the corresponding votes). In the end, the tabulation authority decrypts the remained votes, tallies and publishes the result.

5 Conclusion and Discussion

We propose in this paper a novel framework for remote electronic elections. Not like existing e-voting systems, our scheme has a universally independent authorization proxy and separates the voter authorization from particular elections. More importantly, voters can participate in multiple elections without doing authorization each time, by using reusable credentials. In particular, we do not require that elections in the framework must have the same set of voters, while it is a restriction in other voting schemes e.g. [21]. Some other voting schemes completely remove the registration phase, assuming the existence of a public key infrastructure and using the identity-based ring signature [10]. But their scheme achieves only receipt-freeness, and it will be interesting to see whether it can be extended to achieve coercion-resistance.

We recall that our motivation is not to propose yet another secure e-voting system that focuses on the cryptographic design to meet non-standard security properties. The open framework in this paper is rather an architectural design of remote e-voting systems that separates the authorization and registration phase, which should be carefully designed in remote elections, from the design of real voting systems, so that system designers do not have to start from scratch and can concentrate on the integration of external voting schemes with the credential system.

5.1 The Authorization Proxy

Assumption 1 makes the authorization proxy the central point of attacks, hence its robustness is very critical in our framework. One way to improve the robustness of the proxy is to introduce multiple proxies and election authorities will choose one of them for the election, or if voters complain about some proxy, the election can change to another one, but that will require voters to register at all proxies.

It is also possible to use distributed scheme of credential generation as in [11], where credentials are generated by multiple proxies, each only having one share of a credential, and revealing a particular credential needs to corrupt all or a majority of proxies. But in that case, we need to redefine the registration protocol, especially the generation of the list of public credentials, as the link between voter identities and their public credentials must not be derivable from the two lists in the registration protocol.

The idea of having universally independent authorization proxies can be extended to the tabulation phase, by introducing a tabulation proxy who is also independent of particular elections and can perform the tabulation for multiple elections. However, since the tabulation depends highly on the design of ballot, it will probably demand a uniform ballot format and introduce new problems of implementation and security.

5.2 Formal Analysis

We point out in Section 3 that security analysis of complex e-voting systems should be performed based on formal models and techniques. While there are many formal models for verifying traditional cryptographic protocols [26], very little work is known to be done for electronic voting systems. What should be mentioned here is the work by Delaune et al. [14]. They did probably the first, complete formal analysis for several e-voting protocols, based on the *applied Pi-calculus* [1], which is a formal language for reasoning about communicating processes with cryptographic primitives in the Dolev-Yao model. They give a formal definition of some special security properties like receipt-freeness and coercion-resistance based on the notion of *observational equivalence*, and use the technique called *bisimulation* to prove those properties. Jules et al. have also defined a formal model for verifying e-voting system when they propose their own coercion-resistant scheme [21]. Their model is essentially a computational model, hence more realistic but also harder to automate compared to that of Delaune et al., which is still a Dolev-Yao model (cryptography is assumed to be perfect and adversaries do not perform any cryptanalysis). There are some other formal models based on the epistemic logic [20, 2].

It will be interesting to see how these models can be applied to our framework. Because it is an open scheme and can be instantiated with different credential systems and voting protocols, the challenge of doing formal analysis would be verifying desired security properties that are preserved by the integration of component systems. As noticed in [13] that security properties usually do not compose, even if the component systems have already been proved secure, the final system might not be.

References

1. Abadi, M., Fournet, C.: Mobile values, new names, and secure communication. In: ACM SIGPLAN-SIGACT Symposium on Principles of Programming Languages (POPL), pp. 104–115 (2001)
2. Baskar, A., Ramanujam, R., Suresh, S.P.: Knowledge-based modelling of voting protocols. In: Proceedings of the 11th conference Theoretical Aspects of Rationality and Knowledge (TARK), pp. 62–71. ACM, New York (2007)
3. Baudron, O., Fouque, P.-A., Pointcheval, D., Stern, J., Poupard, G.: Practical multi-candidate election system. In: ACM Symposium on Principles of Distributed Computing (PODC), pp. 274–283. ACM, New York (2001)
4. Camenisch, J., Lysyanskaya, A.: An efficient system for non-transferable anonymous credentials with optional anonymity revocation. In: Pfitzmann, B. (ed.) EUROCRYPT 2001. LNCS, vol. 2045, pp. 93–118. Springer, Heidelberg (2001)
5. Chaum, D.: Untraceable electronic mail, return addresses, and digital pseudonyms. Communications of the ACM 24(2), 84–88 (1981)
6. Chaum, D.: Security without identification: Transaction systems to make big brother obsolete. Communications of the ACM 28(10), 1030–1044 (1985)
7. Chaum, D., Evertse, J.-H.: A secure and privacy-protecting protocol for transmitting personal information between organizations. In: Odlyzko, A.M. (ed.) CRYPTO 1986. LNCS, vol. 263, pp. 118–167. Springer, Heidelberg (1987)
8. Chaum, D., Ryan, P.Y.A., Schneider, S.A.: A practical voter-verifiable election scheme. In: di Vimercati, S.d.C., Syverson, P.F., Gollmann, D. (eds.) ESORICS 2005. LNCS, vol. 3679, pp. 118–139. Springer, Heidelberg (2005)
9. Chen, L.: Access with pseudonyms. In: Dawson, E.P., Golić, J.D. (eds.) Cryptography: Policy and Algorithms 1995. LNCS, vol. 1029, pp. 232–243. Springer, Heidelberg (1996)
10. Chow, S.S., Liu, J.K., Wong, D.S.: Robust receipt-free election system with ballot secrecy and verifiability. In: Network and Distributed System Security Symposium, pp. 81–94 (2008)
11. Clarkson, M.R., Chong, S., Myers, A.C.: Civitas: Toward a secure voting system. In: IEEE Symposium on Security and Privacy 2008, pp. 354–368. IEEE Computer Society, Los Alamitos (2008)
12. Damgård, I.: Payment systems and credential mechanisms with provable security against abuse by individuals. In: Goldwasser, S. (ed.) CRYPTO 1988. LNCS, vol. 403, pp. 328–335. Springer, Heidelberg (1990)
13. Datta, A., Derek, A., Mitchell, J.C., Roy, A.: Protocol composition logic (pcl). Electronic Notes in Theoretical Computer Science 172, 311–358 (2007)

14. Delaune, S., Kremer, S., Ryan, M.: Coercion-resistance and receipt-freeness in electronic voting. In: IEEE Computer Security Foundations Workshop (CSFW-19), pp. 28–42. IEEE Computer Society, Los Alamitos (2006)
15. Fujioka, A., Okamoto, T., Ohta, K.: A practical secret voting scheme for large scale elections. In: ASIACRYPT 1992. LNCS, vol. 718, pp. 244–251. Springer, Heidelberg (1992)
16. Hirt, M., Sako, K.: Efficient receipt-free voting based on homomorphic encryption. In: Preneel, B. (ed.) EUROCRYPT 2000. LNCS, vol. 1807, pp. 539–556. Springer, Heidelberg (2000)
17. Hosp, B., Popoveniuc, S.: An introduction to punchscan. Technical report (2006), http://www.punchscan.org/papers/popoveniuc_hosp_punchscan_introduction.pdf
18. Jakobsson, M., Juels, A.: Mix and match: Secure function evaluation via ciphertexts. In: Okamoto, T. (ed.) ASIACRYPT 2000. LNCS, vol. 1976, pp. 162–177. Springer, Heidelberg (2000)
19. Jakobsson, M., Sako, K., Impagliazzoand, R.: Designated verifier proofs and their applications. In: Maurer, U.M. (ed.) EUROCRYPT 1996. LNCS, vol. 1070, pp. 143–154. Springer, Heidelberg (1996)
20. Jonker, H., Pieters, W.: Receipt-freeness as a special case of anonymity in epistemic logic. In: IAVoSS Workshop On Trustworthy Elections, WOTE 2006 (2006)
21. Juels, A., Catalano, D., Jakobsson, M.: Coercion-resistant electronic elections. In: Proceedings of the 2005 ACM Workshop on Privacy in the Electronic Society, pp. 61–70. ACM, New York (2005)
22. Kohno, T., Stubblefield, A., Rubin, A.D., Wallach, D.S.: Analysis of an electronic voting system. In: IEEE Symposium on Security and Privacy, pp. 27–40. IEEE Computer Society, Los Alamitos (2004)
23. Lowe, G.: An attack on the needham-schroeder public-key authentication protocol. Information Processing Letters 56(3), 131–133 (1995)
24. Lysyanskaya, A., Rivest, R.L., Sahai, A., Wolf, S.: Pseudonym systems. In: Heys, H.M., Adams, C.M. (eds.) SAC 1999. LNCS, vol. 1758, pp. 184–199. Springer, Heidelberg (2000)
25. MacKenzie, P.D., Shrimpton, T., Jakobsson, M.: Threshold password-authenticated key exchange. In: Okamoto, T. (ed.) ASIACRYPT 2000. LNCS, vol. 1976, pp. 385–400. Springer, Heidelberg (2000)
26. Meadows, C.: Ordering from satan's menu: a survey of requirements specification for formal analysis of cryptographic protocols. Science of Computer Programming 50(1-3), 3–22 (2004)
27. Okamoto, T.: Receipt-free electronic voting schemes for large scale elections. In: Christianson, B., Lomas, M. (eds.) Security Protocols 1997. LNCS, vol. 1361, pp. 25–35. Springer, Heidelberg (1998)
28. Ryan, P.Y.A., Schneider, S.A.: Prêt á voter with re-encryption mixes. In: Gollmann, D., Meier, J., Sabelfeld, A. (eds.) ESORICS 2006. LNCS, vol. 4189, pp. 313–326. Springer, Heidelberg (2006)
29. Syverson, P.F., Goldschlag, D.M., Reed, M.G.: Anonymous connections and onion routing. In: IEEE Symposium on Security and Privacy 1997, pp. 44–54. IEEE Computer Society, Los Alamitos (1997)

Conditional Payments for Computing Markets

Bogdan Carbunar and Mahesh Tripunitara

Motorola Inc., Applied Research and Technology Center
1301 E. Algonquin Rd., Schaumburg, IL 60196, USA
{carbunar,tripunit}@motorola.com

Abstract. The problem of outsourcing computations in distributed environments has several security challenges. These challenges stem from the lack of trust between the outsourcer and a worker. Previous work has extensively considered one side of the trust problem - the efficient verification of the completion of the outsourced computation. We believe this to be the first work that simultaneously addresses the other side of trust - ensuring valid remuneration for the work. We propose a solution in which the outsourcer embeds a verifiable payment token into the computation to be performed. With high probability, the worker can verify that if it completes the computation it will retrieve the payment, and the outsourcer is convinced that if the worker retrieves the payment then it has completed the computation. We also discuss the robustness of our scheme against two possible attacks that target the desired security properties, and possible extensions to our scheme.

1 Introduction

The ability of computer owners to donate computing resources and to harness available compute cycles on remote hosts has motivated the recent development of large distributed volunteer computing projects. Ranging from searches for prime numbers (GIMPS, PrimeGrid) to searches for extraterrestrial intelligence (SETI@home), climate forecast (Climateprediction.net), and protein folding (FOLDING@home) such projects have created unprecedented computing settings, comparable in performance to the most powerful supercomputers. For instance, SETI@home encompasses more than 1.3 million registered computers, totaling over 265 TeraFLOPS; between 1999 and 2007 the project has consumed more than 2.7 million years of computation time.

A majority of such distributed computations deploy a master-workers paradigm, supported by a centralized server infrastructure and multiple volunteer workers. A server (outsourcer) decomposes the problem into smaller jobs, each of which can be completed in a few hours on a typical personal computer. Workers obtain jobs from and report results back to the outsourcer.

In this paper we focus on an abstract setting of this environment, where an *outsourcer*, O, needs to compute a function $f : D \longrightarrow R$ for all values in D where D is large set. The outsourcer does this by partitioning D into subsets $D_1, \ldots, D_n$ and assigning the task of computing f over each D_i to a different *worker* W. Several realistic settings can be mapped to this rather abstract setting. Examples include searching for large prime numbers, solving large 0-1 integer linear programming problems or solving RSA's key-finding challenge.

This setting has two basic security issues. One issue is O's lack of trust in the workers. O does not necessarily trust that W will do its assigned job, that is, compute f over every $d_{i,j} \in D_i$. The other security issue is the workers' lack of trust in O. Since W is usually incentivized to work for O, for instance, through the use of money, W must be able to trust that it will be paid by O if it does its job.

The issue of O's trust in W has been considered extensively in the literature [5, 6, 10, 11]. An effective solution is to use *ringers* [5]. With ringers, O does not have to perform the entire computation itself (that would defeat the purpose of outsourcing), but is able to ensure with overwhelming probability that W did indeed compute f over all $d_{i,j} \in D_i$. We present a more detailed overview of ringers in Section 2.1.

The issue of W's trust in O, however, has not received much attention. In particular, we point out that the work on ringers [5] suggests at the outset that there are settings in which O may not be trustworthy. However, the solution itself assumes that O is trusted. There are at least two situations in which O may not be deemed to be trustworthy. One is if O is not an established entity, such as a working group or a large corporation. Such entities may have more to lose (e.g., by way of reputation) than to gain by cheating some W in the context of a particular outsourced job. However, if O is relatively unknown, then W may consider it to be untrustworthy. The other situation is similar, and is when O chooses to remain anonymous. O may want to remain anonymous because, for example, a revelation about the nature of the job and its association with O may alert O's business competitors.

The problem can be solved easily if we assume the existence of an online trusted third party that mediates between O and W. That is, the mediator keeps O's money in escrow and verifies the completeness of the job performed by W. In case of a successful job completion, the mediator transfers the money to W, otherwise, it transfers them back to O. This is not a realistic solution as (i) the mediator needs to know extensive details about the job and the parties involved and (ii) the mediator needs to consume resources (CPU cycles) for each job verification performed.

Contributions. The focus of this paper is on the *simultaneity problem*; O cannot pay W without assurance that W has completed or will complete the job and W does not want to work unless it has been paid or has assurance that it will be paid. Similar to [5], our work also assumes only rational "lazy-but-honest" workers. A lazy-but-honest worker will try to minimize the amount of work it needs to perform in order to retrieve the payment, however, it will provide O with the results of that work.

In Section 3, we introduce a framework for embedding payments into outsourced jobs. We propose several security properties, to be satisfied by any solution to this problem, requiring that (i) given the job and the embedded payment, W can verify the validity of the payment, that is, verify that if it completes the job it will be able to retrieve the payment and (ii) O can be certain that W cannot retrieve the embedded payment unless it completes a high percentage of the job.

Within the proposed framework, we propose a solution for the simultaneity problem where the outsourcer uses a threshold sharing scheme to split the payment into multiple shares and obfuscates a randomly chosen subset of the shares with solutions to parts of the job. As the payment shares are generated using a threshold sharing scheme, the worker needs to retrieve only a subset of the shares in order to reconstruct the payment. Moreover, the workers use random challenges to verify the correctness of the obfuscated payment. Note that even though our solution uses a trusted bank to generate and transfer payments, the bank is offline and is not involved in the interaction between the outsourcer and worker.

2 The Setting

We have, as entities, (i) an outsourcer, O, and, (ii) a worker, W. In addition, we have (iii) a bank, B. We need B as we assume that W is incentivized by money. That is, W (or anyone else) recognizes a payment token as valid based on its strong binding with B (e.g., with a digital signature).

B is offline in that O and W independently transact with it outside of any exchanges they have as part of the outsourcing. Furthermore, B's role is purely as a financial "holding company". B has no interest or participation in the nature of the outsourcing between O and W. O and W trust B to play this role of a bank.

An *outsourcing instance* is associated with an outsourcer O and a worker W, and is a tuple, $\langle F_i, P_i, S_i \rangle$ that comprises the following. We keep our terminology consistent with prior work [5].

- A *job*, which is a triple $F_i = \langle f, D_i, M_i \rangle$, where $f \colon D \longrightarrow E$ is a function on the finite domain D, $D_i \subseteq D$ and M_i is a set of values of interest for O. W needs to compute $f(x)$ for all $x \in D_i$ and return those x values for which $f(x) \in M_i$.
- A *payment scheme*, P_i that is *issued* by B. We leave P_i opaque for now; it can be thought of as an e-cash payment token from one of several e-cash schemes (for example, [1, 2]). We require that P_i have particular properties for our schemes to work; we discuss these in Section 3.
- A *screener*, $S_i(x, f(x), P_i) \longrightarrow \{0,1\}^*$. S_i is typically implemented as a program that takes as input an entry from the domain D_i of f, its corresponding image from the range E and the payment scheme P_i. The output of S_i is a string. The intent behind S is to identify "valuable" outputs of f, either for O (solutions for the job F_i) or for W (values that aid W in retrieving the payment associated with the job).

There are the following three stages in our model of outsourced distributed computation.

Initialization. O prepares the outsourcing instance F_i and payment P_i and sends them to W.

Verification. W validates P_i to gain assurance that it will be paid once it completes the job.

Computation and Payment. W performs computation. For each input $x \in D_i$, it computes $f(x)$ and uses the screener S to find $\langle x, f(x) \rangle$ pairs of interest and communicates these back to O. In using S, it is able to derive its payment.

2.1 Ringers - An Overview

We now discuss ringers and how they are used to solve the problem of the trust in W - O needs to be able to establish that W does indeed perform all the computations that were outsourced to him. Golle and Mironov [5] present the following "bogus ringers" solution.

Initialization. O chooses an integer $2m$, the number of ringers; a ringer is a kind of sample. It picks a random integer $t \in [m+1, \ldots, 2m]$ to be the number of true ringers, and $2m - t$ to be the number of bogus ringers. The distribution of t in $[m+1, \ldots, 2m]$ is $d(t) = 2^{2m-t-1}$. A true ringer x^t is a randomly chosen member of D_i (recall that D_i is the domain of the function f to be computed by W). A bogus ringer x^b is such that $x^b \notin D_i$. O computes $f(x)$ for every true and bogus ringer x. These post-images are included in the screener S_i that is sent to W. (We clarify how S_i works below.)

Verification. There is no verification phase in the original ringers scheme as O is assumed to be trusted. The lack of trust in O is what we address in this paper.

Computation and Payment. The screener S_i is such that it takes as input a pair $\langle x, f(x) \rangle$ and tests whether $f(x) \in \{y, y_1, \ldots, y_{2m}\}$ where y is the post-image for whose pre-image O is searching, and each y_j is the post-image of a true or bogus ringer. If $f(x)$ is indeed in that set, then S_i outputs x; otherwise it outputs the empty string. W computes f for each element in D_i, processes each through S_i, collects all the outputs of S_i and sends them to O to receive its payment.

We point out that if W honestly does its work, then what it sends O at the end is the set of true ringers, and possibly the special pre-image for which O is looking. The ringers ensure that W does its entire work. The bogus ringers make it more difficult to stop prematurely and still make O believe that it did its entire work. We emphasize that whenever we use words such as "ensure," "difficult" or "impossible" in this paper, we mean probabilistically. Specifically, given that the *coverage constant* denotes the fraction of the job completed by the worker, we reproduce here Theorem 2 from [5].

The bogus ringers scheme ensures a coverage constant of $1 - \frac{1}{n2^{n+1}} - (\frac{4}{n})^n$.

From the standpoint of performance, there is a trade-off between the minimum number of true ringers, n, and the security of the scheme. The probability that cheating by W will go undetected falls exponentially as n increases. We anticipate that n is much smaller than $|D_i|$ and therefore the extra work on O is minimal. The extra work on W is also minimal because all S_i does is lookups for membership in a set.

3 Our Overall Approach

As we mention in the previous section, the original ringers scheme does not address the scenario that O is untrustworthy from the standpoint of paying W once it does the work. We address the two sub-problems of trust simultaneously. In this section, we introduce the properties that need to be satisfied by a solution and present a framework for solutions. We propose a specific solution within this framework in Section 4. Figure 1 illustrates our framework.

In our framework, in the initialization stage, O embeds the payment in the ringers it generates, before sending it to the worker. The payment embedding needs to satisfy the following properties.

Definition 1. *(Outsourcer Assurance) Given the initial payment and job instance, the worker is able to redeem the payment only if with high probability it correctly completes the entire computation.*

We adopt the following schemes so our solution can have this property.

Payment splitting. There is a *payment splitting* scheme and corresponding *payment reconstruction* scheme. The payment splitting scheme can be run by O, takes as input the payment P_i and outputs a set $\{p_i^1, \ldots, p_i^{2m}\}$ such that some subset of the set can be put through the reconstruction scheme to retrieve the payment. We call each p_i^a a *payment piece*.

Embedding. There exists an *embedding scheme* which takes as input some piece p_i^a and some (true or bogus) ringer r and outputs r_i^a that can also act as a ringer (that is, it is indistinguishable from a ringer). There is a corresponding *retrieval scheme* that can be used to retrieve the ringer and the payment piece from r_i^a.

After receiving the payment and the job, but before starting to perform the computation, the worker should be able to verify the payment's validity. For this, we need the payment to satisfy the following property.

Definition 2. *(Payment Verifiability) The worker can verify that the payment received from the outsourcer is valid, that is, that after correctly completing the job, it will be able to redeem the payment with high probability.*

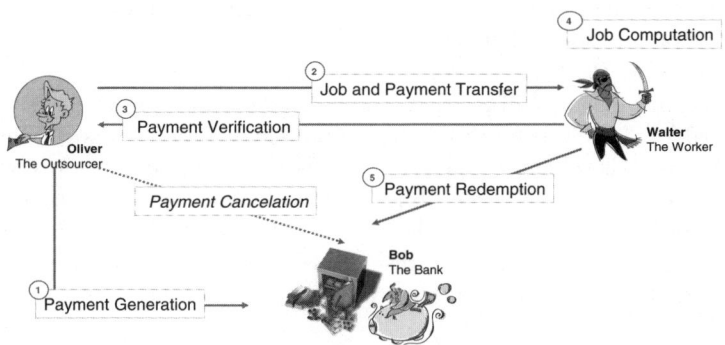

Fig. 1. Solution Framework

To achieve this property, we need the following solution components.

Identification. There exists a *payment piece identification scheme*, with which it is possible to: (i) identify that some ringer r_i^a indeed embeds a payment piece, and, (ii) identify whether two ringers, r_i^a and r_i^b, are embedding pieces from the same payment scheme.

Verification. There exists a *verification scheme* in which W queries O for some $q < 2m$ payment pieces where $2m$ is the total number of pieces. W is able to identify that the pieces are all part of the same payment scheme.

In the computation and payment stage, W needs to be able to redeem the extracted payment token with B. O imposes a time limit on W so that if W does not finish the job within a certain time-frame (negotiated by O and W), then O can cancel the payment. Consequently, we need the following property.

Definition 3. *(***Guaranteed Rollback***) If W is unable to finish the job in time, the outsourcer is guaranteed to receive its money back from the bank.*

We point out that both O and W trust B to operate like a bank. O trusts B to jointly create a payment scheme and maintain a *holding account* for it until cancellation or redemption. W trusts that provided it is able to produce sufficient evidence of having the payment token, B will redeem it for him. To achieve the above property, the bank needs to provide the following functionality.

Redemption. B provides a *redemption scheme* via which W is able to redeem a payment token that it retrieves by completing its job.

Cancellation. B provides O with a *cancellation scheme* via which O can cancel the holding account and retrieve its money if it is not redeemed in time.

In our specific solution discussed in Section 4, we specify each of the above schemes. We make the observation that B does not need to be online at the time when W finishes a job, in order for W to be able to redeem the retrieved payment token. Instead, a time stamping authority T can be employed by W in order to authenticate the timely execution of the job. Then, W has a longer, predefined time interval for contacting the bank, providing the payment and proving its job completion timeliness, before O can cancel the payment. However, for simplicity of presentation, in the following, the redemption and canceling steps do not include the use of T.

The solution presented in Section 4 was designed initially to use a variant of Chaum et al.'s [2] offline e-cash scheme as payment. Moreover, we envision that other offline e-cash schemes (such as Brands' [1]) can be used in conjunction with our solution. The use of e-cash has the additional benefit of preserving the privacy of the outsourcer and of the workers. However, due to the complexity added by such e-cash schemes, we present our solution in the context of a simple e-cash scheme that does not preserve the anonymity of its users.

Notations. In the following we use the notation $x \hookrightarrow_R D$ to denote the fact that the value x is randomly chosen from the domain D. We also use $x; y$ to denote the concatenation of strings x and y. $E_K(M)$ denotes the symmetric encryption of message M with key K. For a given symmetric key algorithm, let s denote the key's bit size. Let H be a one-way (hash) function. Let $H(M)$ be the hash of message M and let h be $H(M)$'s bit size. Using RSA's [7] notations, let $\langle e_X, N_X \rangle$ and $\langle d_X, p_X, q_X \rangle$ denote the public and the private key of participant X, where $N_X = p_X q_X$ is the public modulus and e_X and d_X are X's public and private exponent. Then $E_X(M)$ denotes the encryption of message M with X's public exponent and $S_B(M)$ denotes the signature of message M using X's private exponent. Let N be the bit size of the public modulus used for the encryption and signature scheme.

While not explicitly shown, for clarity of presentation, all the messages sent in the following solution are signed with the private key of the source and encrypted with the private key of the receiver (or a symmetric session key), in order to provide confidentiality and authentication. Moreover, in order to prevent participants from signing arbitrary messages, we assume signatures are provided over the desired message concatenated with a fresh random number, chosen by the signer. We however omit such details for clarity purposes.

4 Payment Splitting Based on Secret Splitting

Our solution works as follows. The outsourcer splits a payment into $2m + p$ shares such that any $2m$ shares reconstruct the payment. It then uses ringers to obfuscate a subset of the $2m+p$ shares, asks the bank to sign the shares and sends the obfuscated shares together with the remaining non-obfuscated shares to the worker. The worker does not know neither which nor how many of the $2m + p$ values received were obfuscated. The worker can challenge the outsourcer to reveal q (a parameter) randomly chosen shares, on which the outsourcer reveals the corresponding ringers (for obfuscated shares) and the bank's signature. If the verification is successful, the worker performs the job. Specifically, it treats each point from the job's input domain as a potential ringer in order to discover and reveal the obfuscated shares. After completing the job (before the deadline) the worker uses the discovered shares and the remaining, cleartext ones in order to reconstruct the payment. The use of the payment's threshold splitting step is to ensure that even if the outsourcer corrupts up to p shares and is not caught during the verification step, the worker is still able to reconstruct the payment. The details of the solution follow.

Initialization. Let $F_i = \langle f, D_i \rangle$ be the job to be outsourced by O to W. Let p and q be two security parameters, $c\sqrt{m} < p, q < m$, for a constant c. O performs the following step.

- Pick a symmetric key $K \hookrightarrow_R \{0,1\}^s$ and generate the tuple $\langle Id(O), Id(W), SN, v, T \rangle$. Send the tuple and K to B. SN is a fresh serial number, v is the currency value of this token and T is the job deadline.

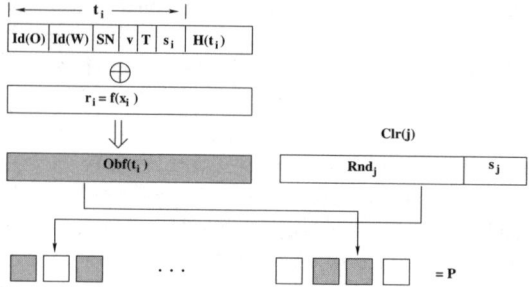

Fig. 2. Generation of Obf and Clr shares. The Obf and Clr values are randomly permuted (lower side in the figure) to generate the payment structure to be sent to W.

When B receives such a message, it computes the payment token $t = E_K(S_B(\langle Id(O), Id(W), SN, v, T \rangle))$ and stores the tuple $\langle SN, v, T, t, K \rangle$ in local storage. It then sends to O the payment token t and the verification value $t_V = S_B(H(\langle Id(O), Id(W), SN, v, T \rangle))$. O then performs the following steps.

- **Payment Splitting:** Use a $(2m, 2m+p)$ secret sharing scheme, like Shamir's scheme [9] to generate $2m+p$ shares $s_1, .., s_{2m+p}$ of t, such that any but not less than $2m$ shares are required to compute t. Let $\mathcal{SS}$ be the reconstruction function, that given any $2m$ of the inputs $s_1, .., s_{2m+p}$ outputs t. The convention is that whoever knows t is able to cash the underlying payment.
- Pick an integer $k \hookrightarrow_R \{m+p+1, .., 2m-q\}$ with distribution $d(k) = 2^{m-p-q-k-1}$ just like in [5] and keep it secret. k denotes the number of ringers.
- Use the shares $s_1, .., s_{2m+p}$ to generate $2m+p$ payment tokens $t_i = \langle Id(O), Id(W), SN, v, T, s_i \rangle$, $i = 1..2m+p$. That is, each payment token is a wrapper for one of the shares s_i. Send the payment tokens t_i to B along with t, k, m, p and q.

When B receives this message, it first verifies that $m+p+1 < k < 2m-q$, then compares t against the value previously stored for O and uses $\mathcal{SS}$ to verify that all the shares s_i contained in the token shares t_i are unique and that any $2m$ of them indeed reconstruct t. This verification step could be probabilistic. If any verification fails B aborts and penalizes O's account. Otherwise, B uses the value k and the payment tokens t_i to generate the set $FV = \{H(t_{k+1}), ..., H(t_{2m+p})\}$ and stores it along with the tuple initially stored for O, $\langle SN, v, T, t, K, FV \rangle$. Then, B generates and sends to O, $2m+p$ values of the form $S_B(H(t_i))$, $i = 1..2m+p$. When O receives these values it performs the following steps.

- Choose k values $x_1, .., x_k \hookrightarrow_R D_i$ and compute their images, $r_i = f(x_i)$, $i = 1..k$. The r_i's are called *ringers*.
- **Embedding:** Use each ringer r_i to obfuscate one payment token t_i, by computing the value $Obf_i = r_i \oplus (t_i; H(t_i))$. Let $sz = |Obf_i|$. Since $k < 2m+p$, not all the shares are obfuscated. For each of the remaining $2m+p-k$ shares,

$t_l = \langle Id(O), SN, v, s_l \rangle$, $l = k+1..2m+p$, compute the value $Clr_l = (Rnd_l; s_l)$, where $Rnd_l \hookrightarrow_R \{0,1\}^{sz-|s_l|}$ (see Figure 4 for an illustration). Note that the previously defined set FV, stored by B, is a verification set for the cleartext shares. Its use will become clear later, in the redemption step.

- Let $O_i = \{Obf_1,..,Obf_k, Clr_{k+1},..,Clr_{2m+p}\}$. The set O_i contains both the obfuscated and the non-obfuscated values. Let $V_i = \{S_B(H(t_1)),..,S_B(H(t_k))\} \cup \{R_{k+1},..,R_{2m+p}\}$, where $R_{k+1},..,R_{2m} \hookrightarrow_R \{0,1\}^N$. N is the size of the public modulus (of B). Thus, V_i consists of B's signatures on the k obfuscated payment tokens, along with $2m+p-k$ indistinguishable random values (replacing B's signatures on the cleartext values from set FV).
- Let π_1 and π_2 denote different random permutations. Then, the payment scheme is $P_i = \langle P, Ver_i, t_V, 2m+p \rangle$, where the set $P = \pi_1(O_i)$ (see Figure 4), Ver_i is the verification structure, $Ver_i = \pi_2(V_i)$ and as previously defined, $t_V = S_B(H(\langle Id(O), Id(W), SN, v, T\rangle))$.
- Outsource the job F_i to W by sending the tuple $\langle F_i, P_i, SN, v, T \rangle$.

We make the observation that the set Ver_i does not contain B's signatures on the non-obfuscated payment tokens, $Clr_{k+1},..,Clr_{2m+p}$. Also, the $Clr_{k+1},..,Clr_{2m+p}$ shares cannot be distinguished from the $Obf_1,..,Obf_k$ shares. This prevents W, when receiving P and Ver_i, from revealing the $Clr_{k+1},..,Clr_{2m+p}$ values from P by searching the set Ver_i.

Verification. After receiving the job, W proceeds to verify the correctness of the payment P_i in the following manner.

- Verify the correctness of the job payment, using the value $t_V = S_B(H(\langle Id(O), Id(W), SN, v, T\rangle))$. That is, W verifies that the payment was generated by O for W, has the serial number SN, is for currency amount v, is valid for redemption before time T and is authenticated by B.
- Let Shr be the set of payment token shares known to W. Initially, $Shr = \emptyset$.
- Select indexes $c_1,..,c_q \hookrightarrow_R \{1,..,2m+p\}$, $q < m$ and send them to O. O processes each index c_j separately in the following manner.
- **Identification-1:** If the c_jth element of the payment set P, denoted by $P(c_j)$, corresponds to an obfuscated payment token share, t_o, O answers with the pre-image x of the ringer used for the obfuscation of this value. W then computes $P(c_j) \oplus f(x)$. If the $P(c_j)$ value is valid, the result of this operation should be of the form $(t_o; H(t_o))$. W first verifies that the value t_o has the format $t_o = \langle Id(O), Id(W), SN, v, T, s_o\rangle$. W then verifies whether the set Ver_i contains B's signature on the $H(t_o)$ value. If any of these checks fails, W aborts the protocol. Otherwise, $Shr = Shr \cup s_o$, $P = P - P(c_j)$ and $Ver_i = Ver_i - S_B(H(t_o))$.
- **Identification-2:** If $P(c_j)$ is a non-obfuscated payment token of format $(Rnd_n; s_n)$, O provides W with the $S_B(H(t_n))$ value received from B during the initialization phase, but which it has not sent to W during the initial job transfer. W checks that $H(Id(O), Id(W), SN, v, T, s_n) = V_B(S_B(H(t_n))$. If

this verification does not check, W aborts the protocol. Otherwise, $Shr = Shr \cup s_n$.

Note that since $q < m < k$, O will not be forced to reveal all its k ringers.

Computation. W performs the job $F_i = \langle f, D_i, M_i \rangle$, by evaluating f on each $x \in D_i$. Let Sol denote the set of elements from the domain D_i that satisfy the condition desired by O. Initially $Sol = \emptyset$. For each $f(x)$ computed, W calls the screener S_i, defined as follows.

- If $f(x) \in M_i$, then $Sol = Sol \cup x$.
- For $i = 1..2m + p$, compute $f(x) \oplus P(i)$, where $P(i)$ is the ith element of the payment set P. If the result is of the form $(t; H(t))$, with t of the form $\langle Id(O), Id(W), SN, v, T, s \rangle$ and $S_B(H(t)) \in Ver_i$, then do $Shr = Shr \cup s$, $P = P - P(i)$, $Ver_i = Ver_i - S_B(H(t))$. That is, an obfuscated share has been revealed.

At the end of the computation, W sends to O the solution set Sol.

Redemption. If W finishes the job before the deadline T, it sends the share set Shr to B, along with the tuple $\langle SN, v, T \rangle$. B retrieves from its local storage the tuple $\langle SN, v, T, t, K, FV \rangle$ that has the same SN, v and T values and where $FV = \{H(t_{k+1}), ..., H(t_{2m+p})\}$. B verifies that the request comes from the worker W whose id is contained in the token $t = E_K(S_B(\langle Id(O), Id(W), SN, v, T \rangle))$. B only accepts this redemption request once and if the current time is less than T. B sends to W the set FV. Let $CShr$ be the set of non-obfuscated shares that W needs to identify. Initially, $CShr = \emptyset$. W performs the following actions.

- For each value in P (there should be $2m+p-k$ elements left), treat the value as if being of format $(Rnd_n; s_n)$, where Rnd_n is a random number and s_n is a payment share. Compute $t_n = \langle Id(O), Id(W), SN, v, T, s_n \rangle$ and look for the hash of this value in the set FV. If a match is found, $CShr = CShr \cup s_n$.
- Send the $CShr$ set to B.

B verifies the correctness of the shares in $CShr$, by also looking them up in FV. B then uses all the shares from the set Shr, plus $2m - |Shr|$ shares from $CShr$ to reconstruct t. If it succeeds, it transfers the payment to W's account.

Cancellation. If the current time exceeds T, W cannot redeem the payment. O however, can cancel the payment, by giving t to B. If W has not redeemed the payment before time T, B reimburses O.

4.1 Computation Overhead

For the bank, the most expensive part of the protocol is computing a signature on $2m + p$ payment shares. Considering a slightly outdated computer (Intel Pentium(R) 4 CPU 3.20GHz) and the values of m and p investigated above, our OpenSSL implementation performed this operation in 100ms. The overhead imposed by our solution on a worker consists of $2m + p$ xor and cryptographic hash operations for each value from the job's input domain. On the computing platform previously mentioned, more than one million MD5 operations can be performed per second on 64 byte blocks, making this overhead negligible.

4.2 Analysis

We now consider two attacks on our scheme. The goal of an attack is to undermine one of the properties that we discuss in Section 3. We also discuss the extent to which our scheme is susceptible to these attacks.

Invalid payment shares. In this attack, the outsourcer O attempts to include invalid payment shares in place of legitimate shares in what is embedded in the job. The objective is to undermine the payment verifiability property and get an honest W to accept the job, but not get paid when he completes it.

Claim 1. *The probability that an invalid payment shares attack is detected is lower bounded by $1 - e^{-c^2/2}$.*

Proof. We first observe that for the attack to succeed at all O must replace at least $p + 1$ legitimate payment shares with bit strings that cannot be used to reconstruct the original payment. We recall that the bank does not verify the well-formedness of the payment shares when it signs them, but instead leaves this process to W, in the verification step. The verification step consists of the random revelation of q out of the $2m+p$ payment token shares. The probability that any of W's challenges chooses an invalid payment share is

$$1 - \frac{(2m-1)...(2m-q)}{(2m+p)...(2m+p-q+1)} > 1 - (\frac{2m-q}{2m+p-q+1})^q =$$

$$1 - (1 - \frac{p+1}{2m+p-q+1})^q > 1 - e^{-(p+1)q/(2m+p-q+1)} > 1 - e^{-c^2/2}$$

As O generates more invalid shares, this probability increases quickly. ∎

Empirical Evaluation. Figure 3 depicts W's chance of detecting a malicious outsourcer that sends $p + 1$ "bad" shares, when $m = 100$. We note that as the values of p and q increase, the probability quickly becomes close to 1. For instance, even when $p=20$, for 30 challenges (out of the 220 total shares), the probability of capturing a malicious O that cheats as much as to prevent W from recovering the payment, is larger than 96%. For $p=30$, the probability becomes larger than 99%.

The consequence of Claim 1 is that our scheme is quite robust against the invalid payment shares attack. The worker W is able to detect the attack in the query phase with high probability.

Premature payment reconstruction. In this attack, the worker W attempts to reconstruct a legitimate payment-token based on his knowledge of the redundancy that is built into the payment-splitting scheme. The objective of this attack is to undermine the oursourcer assurance property.

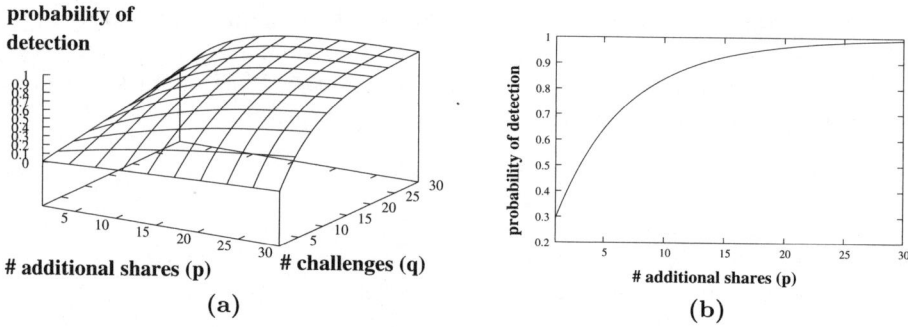

Fig. 3. (a) Probability of detection of malicious outsourcers as a function of the number of additional shares p and of the number of challenges q, for $m = 100$. (b) Probability of detection as a function of the number of additional shares p, for $q = 30$. For a $p = 30$ and $q = 30$, the probability of detecting an outsourcer that corrupts $p + 1$ shares is larger than 99%. Note that in this case $p = q = 3\sqrt{m}$.

The attack is carried out as follows. After recovering a certain number of payment shares that are embedded in the true ringers, W attempts to verify that the remaining ringers are bogus while simultaneously trying to extract the payment. Assume that he has $k - x$ payment pieces that he has extracted legitimately from true ringers (there are a total of k true ringers).

He premises that the remainder are bogus ringers and chooses sets of $2m - k + x$ from which he extracts what he believes are payment pieces. He then reconstructs each set of $2m$ pieces and checks for duplicates among the reconstructions. If there are any duplicates, then that is the reconstructed payment he seeks. We observe that there are at most $r = \binom{2m + p - k + x}{2m - k + x}$ reconstructions he needs to perform, and $r \geq \left(\frac{2m - k + x + 1}{p}\right)^p$. For prudent choices of m, k and p that satisfy the preconditions we discuss in Section 4, this upper bound on the number of reconstructions that W must perform for each x is exponential in p.

However, we recognize that this upper bound is loose, particularly if we consider the probability with which W is able reconstruct the legitimate payment from two different combinations of payment pieces. A detailed analysis of this probability, and how many trials it is likely to take W to verify that he has succeeded with a probability, say 50%, is beyond the scope of this paper. We conjecture that the number of trials is polynomial in our parameters, m, p, k and x. Consequently, it is possible that the premature payment reconstruction attack is a legitimate attack on our scheme, and we discuss possible countermeasures for it below.

We point out that what we call the premature payment reconstruction attack is related closely to Golle and Mironov [5]'s notion of the coverage constant (see Section 2.1). The coverage constant is the fraction of the domain D_i over which the worker W computes the function f before his investment in continuing to compute f over the remainder of the domain is higher than his risk of being found out as not having completed the job.

The notion of a coverage constant does not make sense in our scheme as the worker no longer depends on verification by the outsourcer before he is paid. He has all the data he needs to reconstruct the payment; however, it is embedded in the job.

Extensions

We briefly outline two extensions to our solution, that address the premature payment reconstruction attack. In the first extension, instead of sending clear-text shares along with the ringer obfuscated ones, the outsourcer encrypts each clear-text share before sending it to the worker. During the verification step, the outsourcer presents to the worker the bank's signature on each encrypted share challenged by the worker. The key K_{enc} used to encrypt the clear-text shares is essentially a puzzle, consisting not only of all the ringers that the worker needs to reveal during the computation but also of a random number, whose value the worker needs to "guess". That is, the key $K_{enc} = \Pi_{i=1}^{k} x_i * R \bmod s$, for a large prime s. The x_i values are the pre-images of the ringers. Let b be the bit size of ringer pre-images, where b is a system wide parameter. Its value can be achieved with both smaller and larger ringer pre-images, by hashing the ringer pre-images and then computing the residue modulo a publicly known b-bit prime.

The value R has a pre-defined bit size b', for instance $b' \in [20, 50]$ and its purpose is to prevent the worker from stopping the job prematurely. This is achieved by requiring the worker, after finishing the job, to multiply all the discovered ringer pre-images and then exhaustively search the space $2^{b'}$ for the value R that enables it to correctly decrypt the shares that where not revealed during the computation. This solution makes it harder for the worker to perform the premature payment reconstruction attack. That is, if the worker stops the computation early and has not retrieved all the ringer pre-images, it will have to also search all the spaces of size 2^b for the missing values, whose exact number is also unknown.

In the second extension, the outsourcer also encrypts the clear-text shares before sending them to the worker. However, instead of using a symmetric key algorithm, the outsourcer uses a public key algorithm. Each clear-text share is encrypted with the public key from a public/private key pair, whose private key is stored at the bank under the corresponding transaction. During the verification step, the outsourcer reveals the clear-text share corresponding to the encrypted share challenged by the worker. Knowledge of the public key enables the worker to verify the share's validity. At the end of the job, the worker sends to the bank not only the shares recovered during the computation but also the ones that are still encrypted. The bank uses the private key associated with this transaction to decrypt the remaining encrypted shares and reconstruct the payment. Note that in this extension, a lazy worker needs to guess the $k - x$ value. If $k - x < k - p$, then the bank will be unable to recover the payment and the worker will lose all credit for the completed percentage of the job.

5 Related Work

A framework for securely distributing computations in a commercial environment is proposed in [5] and [6]. A trusted supervisor is assumed to distribute the computations, verify their correctness and give due payments. Golle and Stubblebine [6] use computation duplication to provide result verification. In the same setting, Szajda et al. [11] propose a strategy for distributing redundant computations, that increases resistance to collusion and decreases associated computation costs. Instead of redundantly distributing computations.

Golle and Mironov [5] introduce the ringer concept to elegantly solve the problem of verifying computation completion for the "inversion of one-way function" class of computations. Du et al. [3] solve this problem by requiring the workers to commit to the computed values using Merkle trees. The outsourcer verifies the job completeness by querying the values computed for several sample inputs. The Merkle tree commitment prevents the workers from changing the outputs of their computations. Szajda et al. [10] and Sarmenta [8] propose probabilistic verification mechanisms for increasing the chance of detecting cheaters. In particular, Szajda et al. [10] propose a solution that works for optimization functions and Monte Carlo simulations.

Gentry et al. [4] introduce the concept of secure distributed human computations. While computers are still employed to solve large, difficult problems, humans can be used to provide candidate solutions for problems that are hard for computers (e.g., image analysis or speech recognition). This work proposes the use of payouts not only as a reward for solving problems, but also in the reverse manner. That is, humans could be asked to solve simple problems (image labeling, CAPTCHA solution gathering, proofreading short texts, etc) as payment for small Internet services.

Our work extends the ringer concept of Golle and Mironov [5] to solve the outsourcer trust problem, that is, when the computation outsourcer is not trusted to provide the payment after the computation is performed. None of the research of which we are aware attempts to solve this problem. Essentially, our solution forces the outsourcer to embed verifiable correct payment shares into the outsourced computation. Thus, the worker receives the payment up front, but is able to retrieve all the payment shares only if it performs a high fraction of the work.

6 Conclusions

In this paper we study the simultaneity problem in distributed computing markets. We provide a solution that embeds payments into the jobs outsourced to workers. Our solution allows a worker to verify the validity of the embedded payment, before starting the job, but does not allow it to retrieve the payment before finishing the job. We provide the outsourcer with the guarantee that a worker will only be able to retrieve a payment if it completes the assigned job, and the worker with the guarantee that it will retrieve the payment when it finishes the job.

References

1. Brands, S.: Untraceable off-line cash in wallets with observers (extended abstract). In: Stinson, D.R. (ed.) CRYPTO 1993. LNCS, vol. 773, pp. 302–318. Springer, Heidelberg (1994)
2. Chaum, D., Fiat, A., Naor, M.: Untraceable electronic cash. In: Goldwasser, S. (ed.) CRYPTO 1988. LNCS, vol. 403, pp. 319–327. Springer, Heidelberg (1990)
3. Du, W., Jia, J., Mangal, M., Murugesan, M.: Uncheatable grid computing. In: Proceedings of the 24th International Conference on Distributed Computing Systems (ICDCS) (2004)
4. Gentry, C., Ramzan, Z., Stubblebine, S.G.: Secure distributed human computation. In: ACM Conference on Electronic Commerce (2005)
5. Golle, P., Mironov, I.: Uncheatable distributed computations. In: Proceedings of RSA Conference 2001, Cryptographer's track. LNCS, pp. 425–440. Springer, Heidelberg (2001)
6. Golle, P., Stubblebine, S.G.: Secure distributed computing in a commercial environment. In: Syverson, P.F. (ed.) FC 2001. LNCS, vol. 2339, pp. 279–304. Springer, Heidelberg (2002)
7. Rivest, R., Shamir, A., Adleman, L.: A method for obtaining digital signatures and public-key cryptosystems. Communications of the ACM 21(2) (1978)
8. Sarmenta, L.F.G.: Sabotage-tolerance mechanisms for volunteer computing systems. In: Future Generation Computer Systems: Special Issue on Cluster Computing and the Grid, March 18 (2002)
9. Shamir, A.: How to share a secret. Communications of the ACM 22(11), 612–613 (1979)
10. Szajda, D., Lawson, B., Owen, J.: Hardening functions for large-scale distributed computations. In: Proceedings of IEEE Symposium on Security and Privacy, pp. 216–224 (2003)
11. Szajda, D., Lawson, B., Owen, J.: Toward an optimal redundancy strategy for distributed computations. In: Proceedings of the 2005 IEEE International Conference on Cluster Computing (Cluster) (2005)

High-Speed Search System for PGP Passphrases

Koichi Shimizu, Daisuke Suzuki, and Toyohiro Tsurumaru

Information Technology R&D Center, Mitsubishi Electric Corporation,
5-1-1 Ofuna, Kamakura, Kanagawa 247-8501, Japan
{Shimizu.Koichi@ea,Suzuki.Daisuke@bx,
Tsurumaru.Toyohiro@da}.MitsubishiElectric.co.jp

Abstract. We propose a high-speed passphrase-search system for PGP using FPGA for the purpose of evaluating PGP's passphrase-based security. In order to implement a high-speed search circuit on a single FPGA, we manage to surmount three major hurdles in PGP. The first one, multiprecision arithmetics which arises a problem of speed, is cleared by reducing the number of arithmetics needed. The second one, heavy iteration of hashing which also lowers the search speed, is settled by pipelining the hash function. The last one, candidate passphrase generation which cannot be implemented on hardware, is treated by combining a PC with the FPGA. We thereby achieve a throughput of 56 Gbps per FPGA that amounts to 1.1×10^5 passphrases per second. Compared with a fully software-based search, it shows 38 times faster the speed. We also propose to use an embedded FPGA system and to have part of software such as passphrase generation, to be run on a CPU inside the FPGA. We expect the search system to be more self-contained in an FPGA and thus to have a lower risk of data bus bottleneck between PCs and FPGAs especially in a massive parallel system where many FPGAs are connected to one PC.

1 Introduction

Since the DES cracker [1], hardware-based cryptanalysis has attracted much attention because of its superior speed. Many cryptanalytic machines have been proposed so far and had big impacts on security issues, both theoretical and realistic. For example, [2] proposes a device for integer factorization using the number field sieve, which, if actually built, would be able to factor a 1024-bit number in a year, at a cost of ten million dollars. [3,4], a series of works by the same authors, also presents a sieving machine. In [4], the machine with three Virtex-4 FPGAs and one FPGA-like processor called DAPDNA-2 can factor a 768-bit integer in 270 years. [5] targets E-Passport and realizes a practical attack on its Basic Access Control keys, using COPACOBANA. COPACOBANA [6] is a cryptanalytic machine with 120 Xilinx Spartan-3 FPGAs suitable for parallel computation. According to the authors, it is now possible to search for DES keys exhaustively within a week with COPACOBANA. Hardware-based cryptanalysis has its important role today especially when FPGAs are available at fairly low rates.

While many of the machines are based on random or exhaustive search, there are more sophisticated ways to attack specific kinds of cryptographic systems. For example, dictionary attacks can be employed against systems which uses passphrase-based authentication since users usually choose meaningful passphrases, such as simple dictionary words or pronouceable ASCII strings, instead of random byte sequences. Such cryptanalytic methods, however, often involve operations hard to realize in hardware like creations of variable length data, database references and pattern-matching, and thus have seldom been implemented on FPGAs.

In view of all that, we focus on PGP, which is a widely used cryptographic system and employs a passphrase-based key management scheme. We target the scheme and propose a search system for passphrases which consists of PCs and FPGAs, typically one PC and many FPGAs connected to it. We choose Virtex-4 FX series by Xilinx as a target FPGA, which embeds a PowerPC or two inside it, anticipating that we will use it as an embedded platform and thus realize the sophisticated attacks which need software processing. Our goal with the search system is to evaluate the security of passphrases by giving a concrete amount of time and resources required for recovering them.

PGP is a hybrid system which combines symmetric and asymmetric ciphers, and hash functions to ensure a high level of security and there seem to be three major hurdles to surmount so as to perform a realistic attack against PGP.

- First, our attack target is a user's asymmetric private key, which means that we have to perform multiprecision arithmetics to verify the correctness of each candidate key in the final stage.
- Second, PGP includes a large number of times of hashing to convert a passphrase into a symmetric key with which to encrypt the private key.
- Lastly, but not the least, we need to generate candidate passphrases. As mentioned above, such a procedure cannot be handled by hardware.

Later in the paper, we give detailed explanations of how we manage to resolve the problems. Here is a brief summary.

The first one raises a problem of speed. Multiprecision arithmetic is fundamentally slower to some orders of magnitude than other cryptographic arithmetic, and requires fairly large resources. [7] is an example of a high-speed and compact implementation for modular exponentiation, which, with the use of Virtex-4 DSP hard macros, can perform a 512-bit modular exponentiation in 0.261 ms and requires only 3937 SLICEs. That is extremely fast for multiprecision arithmetic but is still too slow to match the speed of symmetric arithmetic. Our strategy is to reduce the number of multiprecision arithmetics needed for the final verification and thereby to assign the task to software for less area consumption (Section 3). As to the second one, the problem is the iteration of a specific procedure, hashing here. In general, this kind of iteration structure can efficiently implemented on hardware using a pipeline architecture. We thus employ it to implement the iteration of hashing. However, it is not to implement a pipelined hash function that is the very crucial point but to feed data to the pipelined hash with enough speeds (Section 4). For the last one, we combine PCs with FPGAs.

The difficulty in this case lies in data transmission rates of the bus between the PCs and FPGAs. It is probable that the low rate bus becomes a bottleneck for high speed cryptanalysis so we need to minimize the data transmission.

Careful investigations of PGP as above allows us to implement a circuit on a single FPGA to perform a fast search for passphrases. The circuit can search for 1.1×10^5 passphrases per second.

2 Overview of the Search System

OpenPGP [8] is a program designed mainly for encryption and signature generation of email, which has a long history and is now widespread. As its name implies, there was the original PGP (Pretty Good Privacy), and OpenPGP is the standadized version of the PGP. There are now 2 major implementations of OpenPGP, that is, PGP [9] and GnuPG [10] but in this paper we prefer to use the simple and well-known term PGP to mean OpenPGP because we do not discuss anything specific to each implementation.

2.1 Short Description of FPGA

Efficient implementation of algorithms is always a subject of great importance and interest in the field of cryptograpy, and FPGAs have now become increasingly popular as a device to boost it.

An FPGA (Field-Programmable Gate Array) is a kind of semiconductor device whose logic blocks are programmable in a sense that users can redesign or reimplement new logic circuits on it repeatedly. The logic blocks consist of roughly two basic elements, LUTs (Lookup Tables) and FFs (Flip-Flops). LUTs are used to implement combinational logic functions, and FFs are to store data. The programmable nature makes it easy to develop applications and hence it is now a popular choice to use FPGAs when planning to exploit hardware acceleration for some processes.

There is another popular device called an ASIC (Application-Specific Integrated Circuit). As the name implies, ASICs are developed and optimized for each specific application, and cannot be reprogrammed once manufactured. They are generally faster than FPGAs and the prices are cheaper. On the other hand, the total development cost is higher since it is necessary to set up factories to produce each particular ASIC, so ASICs tend to be used when the production volume is high.

FPGAs are usually on extension boards or peripherals, and connected to PCs via PCI or USB buses, or other communication ports.

2.2 Passphrase-Based Security of PGP

PGP employs a passphrase-based encryption algorithm to store users' private keys securely on PCs. The algorithm proceeds as follows. It first lets a user to choose their passphrase, and then formats the passphrase in some way and hash it. Second it encrypts the user's asymmetric private key using the hash value as a symmetric key, and last records the encrypted key in a file called a *secret keyring*. For example, under the default settings of GnuPG 1.4.5, a passphrase is first concatenated with an 8-byte nonce or *salt* and then processed by the SHA-256 [11] compression function 1025 times repeatedly. Then its outcome is used as a key for AES [12] to encrypt a private key of DSA [13] or Diffie-Hellman key exchange scheme (see Fig. 1). Here the salt is intended to prevent use of precomputation by attackers.

This scheme helps users manage their private keys with ease at the cost of some security, say, makes possible search for passphrases, which usually is more efficient than for symmetric keys themselves. We assume that the searcher can access the secret keyring, which actually is possible in such cases as follows. One case is that in an office while an owner of a keyring goes off on a coffee break, one of their co-workers can just copy it. Another case is that a law enforcement confiscates a criminal's PC that contains email encrypted using PGP.

2.3 Search System for PGP Passphrases

From here we think of a search system that consists of one PC and one FPGA. The PC generates candidate passphrases by software, and the FPGA converts them into symmetric keys using a fully pipelined hash function, decrypts the DSA private key with the converted keys and filters out incorrect passphrases. It should be noted here that this system is probably one of the few applications where fully pipelined hash architecture works effectively. The reason is that in most cryptographic applications, block ciphers and multiprecision integer arithmetics are more heavily used and thus are more critical to the speed of the system as a whole than hash functions.

Our system achieves a throughput of 56 Gbps, which indicates that a system of reasonable size, *e.g.* 100 PCs with 600 FPGAs connected to them, can search for about 2^{51} passphrases per year. In other words, almost any type of passphrases that are used in practice can be recovered (discussed in Section 5.2). Compared with a fully software-based search, our system is 38 times faster.

In actually designing the architecture we find that logics other than the pipelined hash function also consume a large amount of resources. We hence have to shrink the circuit to fit in a single FPGA, since if a large circuit is divide into multiple FPGAs, that usually causes a bottleneck in communication. Details about our optimization techniques are given in Sections 3 and 4. Here is a brief description of the key points.

– *Passphrase filtering algorithm* (Section 3).
  In order to select likely correct passphrases out of candidates, the format of private key packets is checked. By doing this, we can reduce the number of candidates, and as a result the number of multiprecision arithmetics, to one out of 2^{160}. The rate is so low that it suffices to perform multiprecision arithmetics with software by a PC instead of with hardware by an FPGA. It contributes to minimize the size of the architecture and also helps to cut down the amount of data transmitted from the FPGA to the PC.

– *Efficient pipelined architecture* (Section 4).
  On top of the hash architecture being fully pipelined, the passphrase-padding architecture, which feeds data to the hash circuit, also needs pipelining efficiently so that the feeding speed can catch up with that of the hash. It is even more difficult to implement it than the hash itself because if we employ a straightforward implementation, we get too large a circuit to place in a single FPGA. By making a full use of Distributed Memory (dual port RAM using LUT), we succeed in squeezing this to 1/4, placing it to a single FPGA and also making it faster.
– *Balance between software operations in PC and hardware operations in FPGA*
  It is not related to the circuit size but crucial to the high speed search so worth mentioning here. As already mentioned, the total throughput of the system can be spoiled by the bus bottleneck. The data bus used is reasonably supposed to be 32-bit 33MHz PCI or PCI Express x1 as of 2008. There is much chance that the fairly low throughput, 1056Mbps in the former case or 2.5Gbps in the latter, spoils the potential of high-speed FPGAs. So we carefully assign each of the PGP operations to a PC or an FPGA to minimize the necessary data transmission between the PC and the FPGA (Fig. 1).

We would like to point out that the system proposed here can be used for almost any combination of cryptographic algorithms supported in PGP (*e.g.*, CAST-128, SHA-1, RIPEMD besides SHA-256 and AES implemented here), by simply rewriting the configurations inside FPGAs. It is because the passphrase hashing algorithms of PGP are the same regardless of the choices, and pipelined

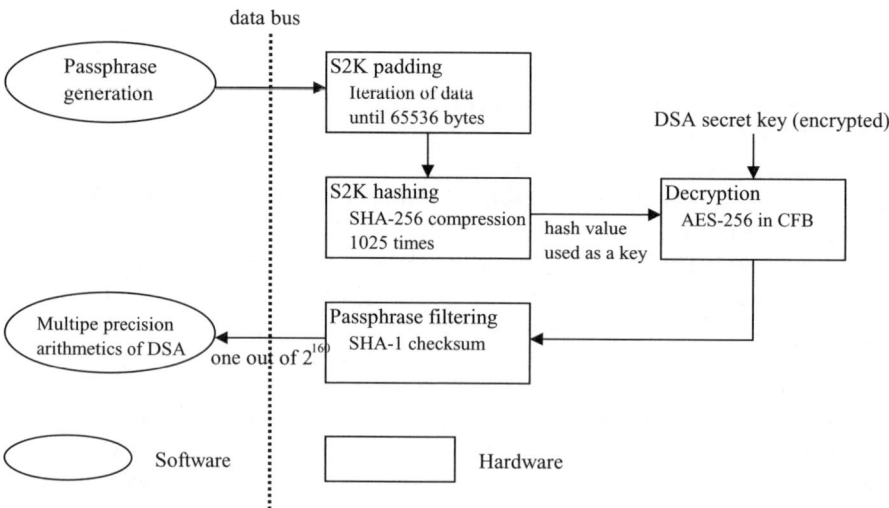

Fig. 1. The procedure to encrypt the secret keyring, under the default settings of GnuPG version 1.4.5.

structures can be implemented for any hash functions within the similar order of resources of FPGAs.

3 PGP Algorithms in Detail

In this section we describe in detail the encryption methods of PGP. That will, as a result, explain the decryption methods of our search. We also present an algorithm that filters out incorrect candidate passphrases before performing multiprecision integer (MPI) arithmetics on them. It can reduce the number of candidates by 2^{-160} and thereby the number of MPI arithmetics needed. In this paper, we will call it the *passphrase filtering algorithm*.

In the rest of this paper, we basically assume the default settings of GnuPG version 1.4.5. Under the settings, DSA and Diffie-Hellman are used for digital signatures and for key exchanges, respectively. While the private keys of the two are encrypted with the same passphrase, we decide to attack the DSA one since it is shorter in length. Although CAST-128 and SHA-1 are the defaults as a symmetric cipher and a hash function, we use AES and SHA-256 instead considering the individual security. It should be noted here that the generality is not lost here since essentially the same attack applies to other choices of algorithms.

3.1 Passphrase Hashing

In PGP, passphrases are converted to keys of a block cipher by methods called *string-to-key* (S2K). There are three types of S2K : simple S2K, salted S2K and iterated and salted S2K. In our settings, iterated and salted S2K is used.

In this algorithm, a passphrase is first concatenated with a 'salt', a nonce of 8 bytes. The salted passphrase (salt||passphrase) is then concatenated with itself repeatedly to form a string of 65536 bytes (See Fig. 3). This procedure is called *iteration* (OpenPGP[8]). The salted and iterated passphrase is subsequently input to SHA-256 to produce a key K of AES. Since the message block size of SHA-256 is 64 bytes, calculations of the SHA-256 compression function is performed 1025 times.

We here denote the concatenation of strings $S_1, S_2, \cdots, S_n$ as $(S_1||S_2||\cdots||S_n)$. We will also use the notation $(B_1, B_2, \cdots, B_m)$ to mean the concatenation of bytes $B_1, B_2, \cdots, B_m$.

3.2 Encryption Using a Block Cipher

Next using the obtained key K, PGP encrypts a private key of DSA. The private key is bundled as a packet $P = (LM||M||S)$, each block of which means as follows.

- LM
  The bit length of M. $LM = (LM_1, LM_2)$ (2 bytes)
- M
  The DSA private key. $M = (M_1, M_2, \ldots, M_l)$ (l bytes) where $l \leq 20$ due to the specification[13].

– S

A checksum of $(LM||M)$. The actual content and size varies according to the PGP settings. In one case, it is a simple additive sum of all bytes of LM and M mod 65536, and the size is 2 bytes. In the other case, it is a SHA-1 hash value of $(LM||M)$ and the size is 20 bytes.

Here all the numbers are encoded in big-endian order. The total length of P is 42 bytes or less, which amounts to three blocks of AES. We will call P a *private key packet* in what follows. The secret keyring contains the initial vector IV of AES, the ciphertext $C = E_{\mathrm{AES}}(IV, P)$, and the salt. Here E_{AES} denotes AES encryption in CFB mode.

3.3 Passphrase Filtering Algorithm

In order to find the correct passphrase, the ciphertext C is decrypted with keys made from trial passphrases and then the plaintext counterparts are tested through public-key MPI arithmetics. As shown later our search circuit fits in a single FPGA yet is huge so we choose to exclude an MPI circuit from the FPGA and to include a software one in the PC. That is made possible by the fact that a large number of passphrases can be filtered out checking the validity of them before performing MPI in the final stage. Actually only one set of MPI arithmetics per 2^{160} passphrases is needed. Doing such a small portion with software in the PC does not at all affect the overall performance.

Let us suppose that we decrypt the ciphertext C and obtain the plaintext $P(ph)$ that corresponds to a passphrase ph. To check the validity of ph, we focus on the format of $P(ph)$ as a private key packet. As mentioned in Section 3.2, a private key packet includes a checksum in 2 ways, that is, a 2 byte additive sum or 20 byte SHA-1 hash value of the first 22 byte part of the key. We explain the algorithm to filter out incorrect passphrases for each case.

Case 1: Additive sum. In this case, there are three criteria for passphrase filtering as given below and those enable us to reduce the number of candidate passphrases to one out of 2^{32}.

1. LM: Due to the property of the CFB mode, the byte lengths of P and the ciphertext $C = E_{\mathrm{AES}}(IV, P)$ are equal (*cf.* Fig. 2). Thus

$$\lfloor (LM + 7)/8 \rfloor = |M| = |C| - 4 , \qquad (1)$$

   where $|A|$ means the byte length of A.

2. First byte of M : Since the integer M is given in big-endian order, the bit pattern of its first byte M_1 is specified by LM. For $m = LM \bmod 8$, M_1 must be of the following form.

$$M_1 = (0^{8-m \bmod 8} 1* \cdots *)_2 . \qquad (2)$$

3. Checksum S: This must also be consistent.

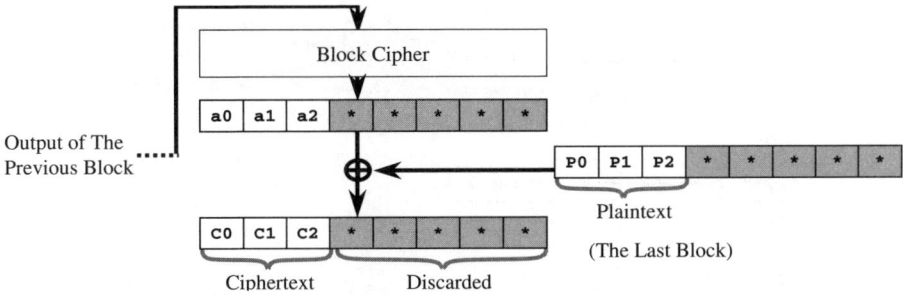

Fig. 2. CFB mode. An example where the last block of the plaintext is 3 bytes. The bytes indicated by '*' are not necessary in recovering the plaintext and thus may be discarded. Consequently, the ciphertext has the same byte length as its plaintext.

The above three are examined one by one and once an inconsistency is detected, the FPGA moves on to the next candidate. The conditions 1 and 2 reduces the number of candidates to 2^{-16}, as can be seen as follows. For each value of $m = LM \bmod 8$, $\lfloor (LM + 7)/8 \rfloor$ takes 2^{13} values; $0, 1, \cdots, 2^{13} - 1$ when $m = 0$ and $1, 2, \cdots 2^{13}$ when $m \neq 0$, with the equal probability 2^{-13}. Eqn(1) is therefore satisfied with probability 2^{-13}. For Eqn(2), the probability is $(1/2^{8-m \bmod 8}) \cdot (1/2)$, and thus the overall probability Pr is given by

$$Pr = \frac{1}{8} \cdot \sum_{m=0}^{7} \left(\frac{1}{2^{13}} \cdot \frac{1}{2^{8-m \bmod 8}} \cdot \frac{1}{2} \right) = 2^{-16}(1 - 2^{-8}) < 2^{-16}.$$

Together with the checksum, these conditions reduce the number of candidate passphrases to one out of 2^{32}.

Case 2 : SHA-1 hash value. This is the default under GnuPG 1.4.5. It is very simple yet highly effective for passphrase filtering. The probability for a random 160-bit string to be equal to the SHA-1 hash value of some given input, $(LM||M)$ in this case, is 2^{-160}, which directly means that we can reduce the number of candidate passphrases to one out of 2^{160}. Taking into account Eqns (1), (2) we can reduce the figure further to 2^{-176}, although we think 2^{-160} is satisfactory for the purpose and thereby did not include the 2^{-16} logic in the circuit.

4 Implementation Architecture

As mentioned in Section 1, we use a pipelined hash architecture for passphrase hashing. The optimization techniques of the hash logic will be discussed in Section 4.2.

Before that, we describe the *passphrase padding logic* in Section 4.1, which feeds the salted and iterated passphrases (*c.f.*. Section 3.1) into the hash function. In actually designing the architecture inside the FPGA, we find that logics other than the pipelined hash function consume a large amount of resources and the largest of them is the padding circuit.

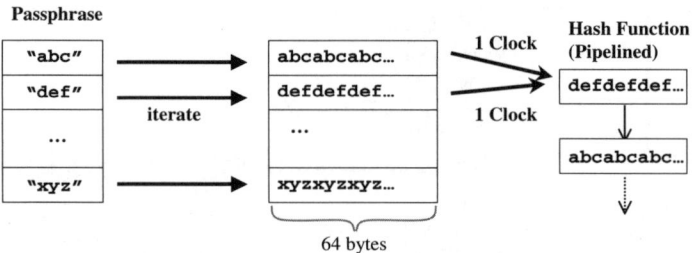

Fig. 3. The image of the 'iteration' of passphrases. Each passphrase is concatenated with itself repeatedly and made into a string of 65536 bytes plus padding of SHA-256, *i.e.*, 1025 blocks of SHA-256 compression function. Each block is then input to the hash function. The salt is omitted here for the sake of simplicity. In designing the passphrase padding logic, iterating a passphrase is allowed to take multiple clocks, while each buffered string must be fed into the hash pipeline within one clock.

4.1 Passphrase Padding Logic

This logic feeds the salted and iterated passphrases into the pipelined hash function. It concatenates the salted passphrase, which is received from the PC, with itself repeatedly to make blocks of 64 bytes to be processed in the hash function (see Fig. 3). Hereafter, we will call this logic the *passphrase padding logic*.

The difficulty in designing this is: it must generate a 64 byte block in every clock cycle to catch up with the pipelined hash function and at the same time be small enough to fit in a single FPGA. To meet both of these requirements, we introduce a new serial-parallel converter which consists of dual port memory using LUT (hereafter, *Distributed Memory*).

The most straightforward construction for such padding circuit would be a serial-parallel logic using flip-flops (FFs) for storing candidate passphrases, followed by shift registers with selectors that feeds the iterated passphrases into the hash function. However, this type of architecture is in fact even larger than the pipelined hash function and thus the whole circuit will most likely not fit into a single FPGA. The numbers of FFs and LUTs needed to implement the shift registers and selectors are at least 32,768 and 16,384 respectively.

So we adopt here a structure that makes use of Distributed Memory, which enables us to implement the padding circuit with approximately 6,000 FFs and 10,000 LUTs. The main idea is as follows. We first divide the structure into two main blocks: that is (see Fig. 4):

- *passphrase iterator* (PIT): The salted passphrases, as originally received from the PC, are stored in Block SelectRAMs [17]. This logic iterates the salted passphrases by controlling the read addresses of the Block SelectRAMs. Note that only one byte from each passphrase is output to the IPB per clock.
- *iterated passphrase buffer* (IPB) : This circuit stores the iterated passphrases and then outputs them to the hash circuit. It is allowed to take multiple clocks in receiving a passphrase from the PIT, but it must output a *block of 64 bytes* to the hash circuit in every clock.

Next we change the flow of bytes of each passphrase (look at the bottom of Fig. 4). Namely, the passphrases change their alignment in the IPB depending on the packet. For instance, the bytes from each passphrases are aligned diagonally in the IPB for the first packet, and vertically for the second and so forth. Under this construction, PIT only needs to output one byte from each passphrase within each clock, thus it can be formed by Distributed Memory.

Note that the number of LUTs necessary for the PIT is only 1/8 of the number of FFs required by the straightforward one. On top of this, by introducing the PIT, the $64-1$ selector is replaced by two rotation shifters which have a smaller area and can easily be pipelined. In general, $n-1$ selector requires the area of $O(n)$ whereas rotation shifter needs only $O(\log n)$.

We used 64 sets of Distributed Memory for the IPB, since the input to SHA-256 is 64 bytes. Thus for efficient implementation, SHA-256's pipeline stage needs to be a multiple of 64. Hence we designed SHA-256 with 128 pipeline stages (see next subsection).

4.2 Pipelined Hash Function

Since this part is critical to the performance of the whole system, our goal is to maximize the throughput as much as possible. Efficient implementations of SHA-256 on FPGAs have already been given using a loop architecture [14,15,16]. We here adopt a pipeline architecture since it establishes much greater throughputs. As mentioned in the previous subsection, our pipeline architecture consists of

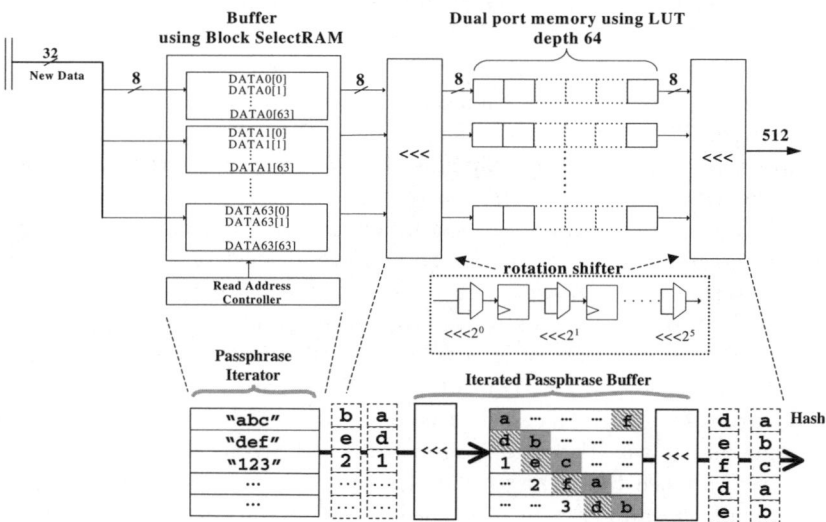

Fig. 4. The passphrases changes its alignment in the IPB depending on the packet. In this example, they are located diagonally in the IPB. As soon as the 64 bytes of an iterated passphrase is buffered, it is transferred to the hash function, one block per every clock.

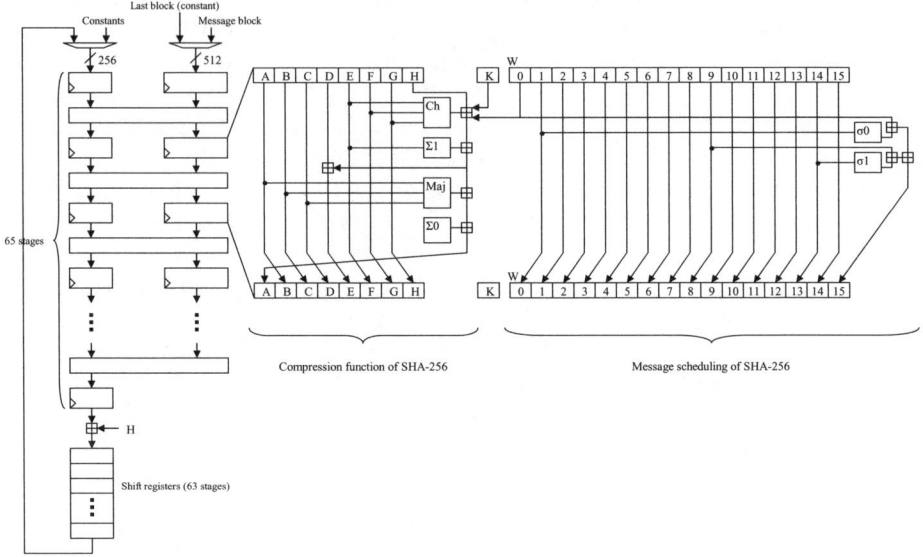

Fig. 5. Pipelined SHA-256 architecture

128 stages to make the passphrase padding efficient. Out of the 128 stages, 66 are actually doing the hash calculation and the rest are shift registers using SRL16 [17], which is a shift-register LUT. One LUT functions as a 16-bit shift register.

The block diagram is given in Fig.5. In general, maximum speeds in pipeline architectures are achieved when each stage has an equally balanced delay and bus widths between stages are narrow. In the case of SHA-256, simply implementing the compression function as one pipeline stage is good, in particular considering the area consumption.

Another problem with a design of a pipelined architecture is in reducing the number of registers. Obviously, we need to have at least one 256-bit register to store the internal state and one 512-bit register to store the message schedule in each stage of SHA-256. This means that when pipeline stages are placed for each step function, registers of at least $64 \times (256 + 512) = 50,688$ is necessary, which amounts to 60% of FFs contained in the target device.

On the other hand, LUTs can be used as a shift register without the reference of the value on the way (hereafter, they are called SRLs (Shift register LUTs)). That is, we can use SRLs instead of FFs if the purpose is just to generate latencies, while it cannot form a serial-to-parallel conversion. Only part of the registers are referred to for the message scheduling in each clock cycle. To be exact, only one word (a four-byte block) is read from step 0 to step 15 and four words are after step 16. Therefore, we can reduce the number of FFs by instead using SRLs for those sectors that are not referred to for a few stages in a row.

4.3 Other Logics

We have no challenging requirements for other logics so do not consider any particular optimization for them. Below are the brief summary of their implementation.

AES decryption: The AES circuit uses the SHA-256 outputs as decryption keys. The pipelined SHA-256 outputs 128 hash values in every 128×1025 clock cycles, one value in 1025 cycles on average. On the other hand the size of the asymmetric private key to be decrypted is 42 bytes, which amounts to three blocks of AES. The AES is hence allowed 1025 cycles to decrypt three blocks with each key. The requirement is very easy and we hence adopt a loop architecture where there is one AES core with a quarter round implemented in order to minimize the area consumption.

Passphrase filtering: As we describe in Section 3.3, we use SHA-1 hash values to filter passphrases. The data to be hashed is 22 bytes and that amounts to one block as an input to SHA-1. In the same way as the AES decryption, we have 1025 cycles to hash one block and to compare values. That is still easy and we implement the circuit in a straightforward manner.

5 Evaluation

5.1 Performance of the Circuit

Our target device is Virtex-4 FX100-10 and we use Synplify Pro 8.6.2 for synthesis, and Xilinx ISE 9.2.04i for place and route. The results of the evaluation are given in Table 1. We must make comments on the figures of area. The upper part of the table shows the evaluation results by parts and the lower part as a whole. Due to the boundary optimizations by the development tools, the area consumption as a whole becomes less than the sum of each part.

The pipelined SHA-256 operates at 118 MHz, processing 512 bits of input in every cycle and one passphrase in 1025 cycles. That means it achieves the throughput of 56 Gbps and can test 1.1×10^5 passphrases per second. This figure shows that our circuit is at least 38 times faster than a PC with a Pentium 4

Table 1. Performance of the circuit

Algorithm	Area			Frequency (MHz)
	LUTs	FFs	RAMs	
Passphrase Padding	8,665	5,210	16	145†
SHA-256	44,989	25,384	0	118
the Others	2,006	1,077	11	133†
Total* (out of)	51,573 (84,352)	32,690 (84,352)	27 (376)	118

† To be faster than 118MHz is enough.

Table 2. Search speed by software and by hardware

Implementation	passphrases/sec
Software	3,001
Hardware	115,121

3.8GHz running the fastest SHA-256 implementation up to now [19]. We say 'at least' because we only take into account the SHA-256 to assess the performance of the software search. Iteration of SHA-256 is the heaviest part of the PGP passphrase scheme and hence decides the speed of the search system, but other parts such as a block cipher certainly count. While they can run in parallel with SHA-256 in FPGAs they cannot in PCs and so the speed difference becomes larger than 38 times.

In Section 5.2, we give a concrete example of an actual passphrase search.

5.2 Concrete Example Figures of the Search System

Now we give a concrete and realistic example of our search system and evaluate the security strength of PGP passphrases. First we show in Table 2 how many passphrases per second can be tested by software and by hardware. The hardware refers to our circuit and the software is the one mentioned in ther previous section.

To give an illustration of the actual speed, let us consider how many devices are needed to find correct passphrases in a year under 3 possible conditions. One condition is that we search for passphrases of 3 dictionary words from the vocabulary of about 20,000 that adult native speakers of English actively use on average [20], another is 7 random ASCII characters, and the other is 3 dictionary words from COD (Concise Oxford English Dictionary), which has 240,000 entries in its eleventh edition. In short we give three cases each of which has a total of $20000^3 = 8 \times 10^{12}$ passphrases, $94^7 \fallingdotseq 6.5 \times 10^{13}$ ones, and $240000^3 \fallingdotseq 1.4 \times 10^{16}$ ones. The evaluation result is shown in Table 3. The table tells us that passphrases of 3 words from our daily vocabulary and of 7 random ASCIIs are easily broken by a highly realistic FPGA-based system using our circuit. They also are fairly probable to be broken by software. In case of 3 dictionary words from COD, even an FPGA-based system seems unrealistic but still not necessarily impracticable while a software-based system is totally impossible.

Table 3. The numbers of devices needed to find correct passphrases in a year

Condition (search for what)	FPGAs needed	PCs needed
3 dictionary words (from 20,000)	2	84
7 random ASCII characters	17	685
3 dictionary words (from 240,000)	3,807	146,070

We take up 'Diceware' [21] as another interesting example. It is a passphrase generation software and has a list of 7,776 words to choose words from, in the hope that it makes passphrases which are easy to memorize and strong at the same time. If picking 4 words out of the list, there are 7776^4 possible passphrases, which can be searched for within a year with 1,007 FPGAs. The amount seems highly realistic so in order to secure an email, at least 5 words from the list must be chosen to form a passphrase. An example passphrase of this kind is

```
cleft cam synod lacy yr ,
```

which is not always easy for most people to memorize.

5.3 Hints to Improve the PGP Security

PGP has heavy iteration of hashing as a countermeasure to exhaustive search. It sure is effective against sotware-based search but does not do as good as expected against hardware-based search as seen thus far. As a result, although the S2K circuit is overwhelming in its size, we manage to implement a whole search circuit on a single FPGA, achieving a high throughput at the same time.

But a small bit of tricks does do good to improve security. Instead of using the simple iteration structure, making the S2K algorithms more complex is effective while it does not necessarily sacrifice the performance as a cryptosystem. For example, using multiple hash algorithms or more complicated padding rules makes the implementation size dramatically larger to be beyond the limit of one FPGA. We mention here again dividing a large architecture into multiple FPGAs greatly reduces the throughput.

6 Using Embedded FPGA Systems for Cryptanalysis

As mentioned earlier, when a cryptanalytic method includes procedures not suitable for hardware, PCs are generally used to do them through software (Fig. 6 (a)). In that case, the data bus between the PC and the FPGA may arise as a bottleneck since if implementing a cryptographic function on FPGAs with pipeline architicure, a throughput of more than some Gbps can easily be gained, which throughput exceeds the bus transmission limit, as can be seen in our search circuit where pipelined SHA-256 achieves the throughput of 56 Gbps.

In case of PGP, such a bottleneck does not actually appear because of the heavy S2K iteration. One passphrase is transmitted through the bus, and then concatenated with itself and expanded to 1024 times the original size inside the FPGA, which situation balances the unevenness between the low-speed bus and the high-speed FPGA. We can hence realize a high-speed search system with all the software run on the PC. But the bottleneck problem still remains when parallelizing the FPGA operation. Due to the narrow data bus, it is difficult to connect many FPGAs to one host PC. If one PC can host only one FPGA, for example, 1,000 PCs are needed for 1,000 FPGAs (Fig. 6 (α)), which is unrealizable with respect to space and cost.

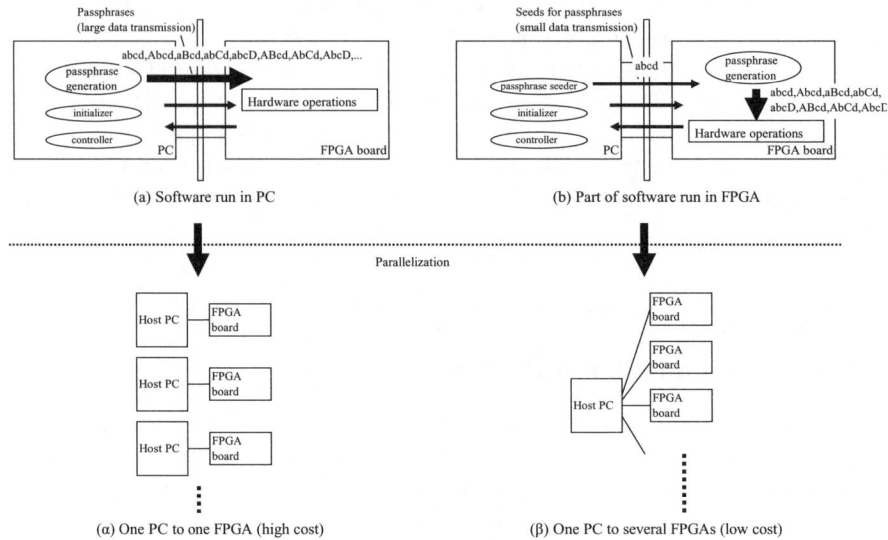

Fig. 6. Combination system of PCs and FPGAs

If using the simple S2K method where there is no heavy iteration of passphrases, the bottleneck immediately appears whether or not parallelizing the operation. Such situations can easily happen in many cryptographic systems other than PGP, such as the familiar passphrase-based scheme Microsoft Office employs, in which each passphrase is hashed only once.

That is the reason we put an eye on Virtex-4 FX's which embed a PowerPC 405 CPU (or two). Utilizing the CPU enables a structure called an embedded FPGA system (Fig. 6 (b)), where part of software is operated by an FPGA and thus the communication between a PC and an FPGA becomes small, since it is only necessary for initialization and for controlling the FPGA. That settles the bottleneck problem and enables us to develop more flexible cryptanalytic devices which enjoys the high-speed operations of the FPGAs and to parallelize the operation easily (Fig. 6 (β)).

7 Conclusion

In this paper, we propose a passphrase-search system for PGP using pipelined hash architecture with the throughput of 56 Gbps. A system with one Virtex-4 can search for 1.1×10^5 passphrases per second, which means that if we build a system of reasonable size, for example, with 1,000 FPGAs, we can search for more than 2^{51} passphrases per year. It means that almost any type of passphrases used in practice can be recovered. We can deal with almost any sort of passphrases simply by rewriting generator software since candidate passphrases are generated by PCs. For example, simple dictionary words, dictionary words with additional

ASCII characters, or gramatically correct sentences up to a certain number of words are among such passphrases as can be well treated.

When attacking other passphrase-based cryptosystems such as the one Microsoft Office employs, a problem arises. The data bus between PCs and FPGAs is probable to be a bottleneck since most of the cryptosystems do not have an iteration structure that PGP has. Hashing only one block is extremely light and can be implemented to have a high throughput that exceeds the bus transmission limit. So we propose to use an embedded FPGA system for cryptanalysis. Assigning part of software to CPUs inside the FPGAs, we can reduce the data transmission and thus clear the bottleneck.

References

1. The Electric Frontier Foundation, Cracking DES: Secrets of Encryption Research, Wiretap Politics, and Chip Design. O'Reilly & Associates, Inc., Sebastopol (1998)
2. Shamir, A., Tromer, E.: Factoring Large Numbers with the TWIRL Devices. In: Boneh, D. (ed.) CRYPTO 2003. LNCS, vol. 2729, pp. 1–26. Springer, Heidelberg (2003)
3. Izu, T., Kogure, J., Shimoyama, S.: CAIRN 2: An FPGA Implementation of the Sieving Step in the Number Field Sieve Method. In: Paillier, P., Verbauwhede, I. (eds.) CHES 2007. LNCS, vol. 4727, pp. 364–377. Springer, Heidelberg (2007)
4. Izu, T., Kogure, J., Shimoyama, S.: CAIRN 3: An FPGA Implementation of the Sieving Step with the Lattice Sieving. In: Proc. of the 2007 Special-purpose Hardware for Attacking Cryptographic Systems (SHARCS 2007), pp. 33–39 (2007)
5. Liu, Y., Kasper, T., Lemke-Rust, K., Paar, C.: E-Passport: Cracking Basic Access Control Keys. In: Meersman, R., Tari, Z. (eds.) OTM 2007, Part II. LNCS, vol. 4804, pp. 1531–1547. Springer, Heidelberg (2007)
6. Kumar, S., Paar, C., Pelzl, J., Pfeiffer, G., Schimmler, M.: Breaking Ciphers with COPACOBANA - A Cost-Optimized Parallel Code Breaker. In: Goubin, L., Matsui, M. (eds.) CHES 2006. LNCS, vol. 4249, pp. 101–118. Springer, Heidelberg (2006)
7. Suzuki, D.: How to Maximize the Potential of FPGA Resources for Modular Exponentiation. In: Paillier, P., Verbauwhede, I. (eds.) CHES 2007. LNCS, vol. 4727, pp. 272–288. Springer, Heidelberg (2007)
8. Network Working Group, OpenPGP Message Format, RFC 4880 (2007), http://tools.ietf.org/pdf/rfc4880.pdf
9. PGP Corporation Home Page, http://www.pgp.com/
10. The GNU Privacy Guard, http://www.gnupg.org/
11. NIST, Secure Hash Standard (SHS), FIPS-PUB 180-2 (2002), http://csrc.nist.gov/publications/fips/fips180-2/fips180-2.pdf
12. NIST, Advanced Encryption Standard (AES), FIPS-PUB 197 (2001), http://csrc.nist.gov/publications/fips/fips197/fips197.pdf
13. NIST, Digital Signature Standard (DSS), FIPS-PUB 186-2 (2000), http://csrc.nist.gov/publications/fips/fips186-2/fips186-2-change1.pdf
14. Chaves, R., Kuzmanov, G., Sousa, L., Vassiliadis, S.: Improving SHA-2 Hardware Implementations. In: Goubin, L., Matsui, M. (eds.) CHES 2006. LNCS, vol. 4249, pp. 298–310. Springer, Heidelberg (2006)

15. McEvoy, R.P., Crowe, F.M., Murphy, C.C., Marnane, W.P.: Optimisation of the SHA-2 family of hash functions on FPGAs. In: Proc. of the 2006 IEEE Computer Society Annual Symposium on Emerging VLSI Technologies and. Architectures (ISVLSI 2006), pp. 317–322 (2006)
16. Helion Technology, http://www.heliontech.com/
17. Xilinx, Inc., Virtex-4 User Guide (2007),
 http://www.xilinx.com/support/documentation/user_guides/ug070.pdf
18. Xilinx, Inc., Virtex-4 Family Overview (2007),
 http://www.xilinx.com/support/documentation/data_sheets/ds112.pdf
19. Matsui, M.: How Far Can We Go on the x64 Processors? In: Robshaw, M.J.B. (ed.) FSE 2006. LNCS, vol. 4047, pp. 341–358. Springer, Heidelberg (2006)
20. Goulden, R., Nation, P., Read, J.: How large can a receptive vocabulary be? Applied Linguistics 11(4), 341–363 (1990)
21. Reinhold, A.G.: The Diceware Passphrase Home Page (2003),
 http://world.std.com/~reinhold/diceware.html

Workload Characterization of a Lightweight SSL Implementation Resistant to Side-Channel Attacks

Manuel Koschuch[1], Johann Großschädl[2], Udo Payer[3], Matthias Hudler[1], and Michael Krüger[1]

[1] FH Campus Wien – University of Applied Sciences,
Daumegasse 3, A–1100 Vienna, Austria
{manuel.koschuch,matthias.hudler,michael.krueger}@fh-campuswien.ac.at
[2] University of Bristol, Department of Computer Science,
Merchant Venturers Building, Woodland Road, Bristol, BS8 1UB, United Kingdom
johann.groszschaedl@cs.bris.ac.uk
[3] Institute for Applied Information Processing and Communications (IAIK),
Graz University of Technology, Inffeldgasse 16a, A–8010 Graz, Austria
udo.payer@iaik.tugraz.at

Abstract. Ever-growing mobility and ubiquitous wireless Internet access raise the need for secure communication with devices that may be severely constrained in terms of processing power, memory capacity and network speed. In this paper we describe a lightweight implementation of the Secure Sockets Layer (SSL) protocol with a focus on small code size and low memory usage. We integrated a generic public-key crypto library into this SSL stack to support elliptic curve cryptography over arbitrary prime and binary fields. Furthermore, we aimed to secure the SSL handshake against side-channel attacks (in particular simple power analysis) by eliminating all data-dependent or key-dependent branches and memory accesses from the arithmetic operations and compare the resulting performance with an unprotected implementation. Our lightweight SSL stack has only 6% of the code size and RAM requirements of OpenSSL, but outperforms it in point multiplication over prime fields when no appropriate countermeasures against side-channel attacks are implemented. With such countermeasures, however, the execution time of a typical SSL handshake increases by roughly 50%, but still completes in less than 160 msec on a 200 MHz iPAQ PDA when using an elliptic curve over a 192-bit prime field.

Keywords: Network Security, Efficient Implementation, Elliptic Curve Cryptography, Side-Channel Analysis, Performance Evaluation.

1 Introduction

Traditional research in network security has assumed the endpoints of a communication channel to be secure and only considered an adversary trying to attack the communication itself. Possible attacks include eavesdropping on the channel and the forging, injection, modification, and replay of messages [18]. With the paradigm shift to more and more mobile devices being used to access networks like the Internet, this adversary model must be adapted to incorporate attacks on the communication endpoints themselves too, since most mobile devices are not tamper-resistant. For example, an adversary could try to obtain the secret key used to encrypt the communication by analyzing side-channel information (e.g. timing or power) leaking from a device [25]. Therefore, secure networking does not only require secure protocols, but also a secure implementation of these protocols and the involved cryptographic algorithms.

The current "de-facto" standard for secure communication over an insecure, open medium like the Internet is the Secure Sockets Layer (SSL) protocol [12] and its successor, the Transport Layer Security (TLS) protocol [11]. Both use a combination of public-key and secret-key cryptographic techniques to ensure the confidentiality, integrity, and authenticity of communication between a client and a server. Traditionally, the SSL protocol has employed RSA or Diffie-Hellman (DH) for key establishment, and RSA or DSA for authentication. However, all these cryptosystems are highly computation-intensive, which can result in an unacceptably long delay when establishing an SSL connection on a mobile device with restricted processing capabilities and memory resources [37]. Elliptic curve cryptography (ECC) [4] is a viable alternative to traditional public-key schemes like RSA or DH because of its higher level of security per bit: a properly chosen 160-bit ECC system is claimed to be as secure as a 1024-bit RSA system [16]. In 2006, the TLS protocol was revised to include ECC for public-key services, and since then, cipher suites using ECDH for key exchange and ECDSA for authentication can be negotiated during the handshake phase [6].

Any security protocol is only as secure as its underlying cryptographic algorithms. From a mathematical point of view, the security of both ECDSA and ECDH relies on the Elliptic Curve Discrete Logarithm Problem (ECDLP), which is supposed to be intractable when a suitable elliptic curve group of sufficiently large order is used [4]. However, cryptanalytic attacks are, in general, not the biggest threat to the security of SSL, in particular if an attacker has access to the device on which the protocol is executed so that he can monitor side-channel information like running time or power consumption. The information leaked through these side channels can be used to mount different kinds of attacks such as timing analysis, Simple Power Analysis (SPA), or Differential Power Analysis (DPA) [20,21]. In fact, the "weakest link" of SSL is often the implementation of the cryptographic algorithms, which has been demonstrated by several successful side-channel attacks on unprotected (or insufficiently protected) versions of OpenSSL [1,3,7,8].

The ECC algorithms executed during the handshake phase of the SSL/TLS protocol are potentially vulnerable to timing analysis, SPA, and DPA, whereby the concrete feasibility of each of these attacks depends on the cipher suite and whether the client or the server is targeted. For example, the ECC cipher suites from [6] use either ephemeral or static ECDH keys; in the former case it suffices to protect the ECDH implementation against SPA attacks, while in the latter case also countermeasures against timing analysis and DPA attacks need to be effective. Fortunately, there exists a rich literature dealing with the protection of elliptic curve cryptosystems against timing analysis, SPA, and DPA attacks [2,5,16]. Each of the proposed countermeasures has its specific advantages and disadvantages with respect to execution time, memory requirements, and code size. While the performance of the different countermeasures has been analyzed in detail (at least theoretically by counting the number of field operations), their impact on memory footprint and code size is still relatively unexplored.

Contributions. In the present paper we analyze the workload characteristics of a "lightweight" SSL implementation optimized for small code size and low memory footprint. In addition, we provide a detailed breakdown of the individual phases of an SSL handshake to determine how much influence the cryptographic operations actually have on the overall running time. We furthermore evaluate the impact of side-channel countermeasures on the performance, code size, and memory footprint of our SSL implementation. In the past, the cost of timing and SPA resistance for ECC has only been studied on basis of a single scalar multiplication. However, in practice, a cryptosystem is typically not an application *per se*, but part of an application like SSL, TLS, S-MIME, etc. Thus, the important question is how a certain countermeasure impacts the characteristics of the whole application (e.g. its performance or memory consumption) because this allows one to draw conclusions about the quality and/or suitability of the applied countermeasure. For example, what does it mean if a countermeasure increases the execution time of ECDH by a factor of two? Will the delay of the SSL handshake increase by the same factor? Or will the delay just increase by a factor of 1.5? Or will there be no additional delay at all? How do side-channel countermeasures impact the code size and memory footprint of the SSL stack? Is it possible to achieve side-channel resistivity without sacrificing code size and memory footprint? All these questions have not been addressed in the past; with the present paper we intend to fill this gap.

The work described in this paper is based on MatrixSSL [31], a lightweight SSL implementation written in ANSI C whose source code is available under the GNU General Public License (GPL). MatrixSSL in its original form features only RSA as public-key primitive, but not ECC. Therefore, we implemented a generic public-key crypto library which supports traditional cryptosystems like RSA, DH, as well as ECC over arbitrary prime and binary extension fields. We integrated this crypto library together with the ECC cipher suites defined in [6] into MatrixSSL. Actually, we implemented two version of the crypto library: a conventional version without countermeasures and a side-channel resistant version where we eliminated all key-dependent branches and memory accesses from the arithmetic operations. *Our main goal was to keep the code size (i.e. the size of the binary executable) and the memory footprint (i.e. the consumed run-time memory) of the SSL implementation at an absolute minimum, even at the price of an increase in execution time.* The test platform on which we collected the timings is an iPAQ PDA equipped with a 200 MHz StrongARM processor.

Outline. The remainder of this paper is structured as follows: Section 2 gives an overview of the SSL protocol with a special focus on the initial handshake and describes where and how ECC can be incorporated into this handshake. Section 3 elaborates on side-channel attacks and how they can be mounted against elliptic curve cryptosystems. Section 4 then discusses our implementation and the measures we took to reduce the side-channel leakage. In Section 5 we present the results we achieved and give a detailed breakdown of the single phases of an SSL handshake. Section 6 finally summarizes our results and findings.

2 Secure Sockets Layer Protocol

The Secure Sockets Layer (SSL) protocol and its successor, the Transport Layer Security (TLS) protocol [11], are standardized protocol suites enabling secure communication between a client and a server over an insecure network. The main focus in the design of these protocols lay in modularity, extensibility, and transparency. Applications that want to benefit from encrypted, authenticated communication only have to use the read/write calls provided by the appropriate API, and the protocol itself takes care of key exchange, message encryption and decryption, authentication, and integrity.

SSL uses a combination of symmetric (i.e. secret-key) and asymmetric (i.e. public-key) techniques, whereby the actual algorithms to be used are negotiated by the communicating parties. After the parties have been authenticated and keying material has been exchanged using public-key cryptography in the initial handshake process, all messages are encrypted and their integrity is checked on basis of symmetric algorithms.

The next subsection describes the handshake protocol in detail, followed by two subsections which explain where and what type of ECC primitives can be incorporated into this process.

2.1 SSL Handshake

Table 1 gives an overview of all messages that may be exchanged during the handshake process, whereby time advances from top to bottom. A connection is established by the client sending the *ClientHello* message, basically containing a list with all the cipher suites supported by the client. This list consists of a combination of identifiers for the different cryptographic algorithms used in the handshake phase and for the data transfer thereafter. For example, the identifier DHE-RSA-AES256-SHA means ephemeral Diffie-Hellman for key agreement, RSA for authentication purposes, AES-256 as symmetric cipher when the connection is established, and SHA-1 to compute the message authentication codes.

The server's *ServerHello* message contains the identifier of the cipher suites chosen for the connection (the handshake is aborted here if client and server do not share a cipher suite). Usually, the server also sends its certificate and, if the certificate does not contain enough information to establish a shared secret, also a *ServerKeyExchange* message. The *CertificateRequest* message is rarely sent in open environments, since it is assumed that very few clients are in possession

Table 1. SSL handshake, optional messages printed *italic*

Client	Server
ClientHello	
	ServerHello
	Certificate
	ServerKeyExchange
	CertificateRequest
	ServerHelloDone
Certificate	
ClientKeyExchange	
CertificateVerify	
ChangeCipherSpec	
Finished	
	ChangeCipherSpec
	Finished

of a valid certificate. In closed surroundings (e.g. a corporate network), this requirement can obviously be strengthened such that mutual authentication can be enforced. The client then checks the validity of the server's certificate, sends (if requested) its own certificate and, to proof that it is actually in possession of the private key connected with this certificate, a *CertificateVerify* message containing the signed concatenation of all messages exchanged until now. In the *ClientKeyExchange* message it provides the server with all data necessary to establish a shared pre-master secret; the actual content of this message depends on the chosen cipher suite. The *ChangeCipherSpec* message is, strictly speaking, not part of the handshake protocol anymore; it just signals both parties that all messages from this moment on have to be encrypted using the symmetric cipher initially agreed upon and the key derived from the shared pre-master secret. So the *Finished* message is the first encrypted message, containing all the messages exchanged during the handshake. If both parties can successfully decrypt this message and verify its content, they can start to transfer application data.

Elliptic curve cryptography can be employed at two places in the handshake process: for the signature generation/verification and for the establishment of a pre-master secret [6,14]. When initiating an ECC-based handshake, not only the cryptographic algorithms have to be agreed upon, but also the so-called domain parameters, which specify (among other things) the elliptic curve E to be used, the underlying finite field $GF(q)$, and a base point $P \in E$ that generates a large subgroup of prime order n [4,5,16]. In ECC, a private key is simply a random number $k < n$, and the corresponding public key is the point $Q = k \cdot P$.

2.2 Elliptic Curve Diffie-Hellman (ECDH)

The elliptic curve equivalent of the "traditional" Diffie-Hellman key exchange relies on the intractability of the (computational) Elliptic Curve Diffie-Hellman Problem (ECDHP); that is, given an elliptic curve E over a finite field $GF(q)$, a base point P on curve E, and two points $Q_A = k_A \cdot P$ and $Q_B = k_B \cdot P$, find the point $S = k_A \cdot k_B \cdot P$ without knowledge of k_A, k_B. It is clear that the ECDHP is no harder than the Elliptic Curve Discrete Logarithm Problem (ECDLP) as solving the latter would solve the former as well. A detailed description of the ECDH protocol and the hard mathematical problem its security is based upon can be found in [5,16]. Similar to the conventional Diffie-Hellman protocol, the ECDH protocol allows two entities to establish a shared secret over an insecure communication channel. An attacker can intercept the two public keys Q_A and Q_B, but knowledge of P, Q_A, Q_B does not enable him to calculate the shared secret S, nor does it enable him to deduce the private keys k_A and k_B.

The ECC cipher suites defined in RFC 4492 allow for static and ephemeral ECDH keys [6]. Cipher suites with static ECDH require the server's certificate to contain an ECDH-capable public key. This public key is nothing else than a point on the elliptic curve, calculated by scalar multiplication of the server's secret key and the base point [5]. The server does not need to send a *ServerKey-Exchange* message since the *Certificate* message already includes all the keying information required by the client. Upon receipt of the *Certificate* message, the client generates its own ECDH key pair consisting of a private key (i.e. a random number) and a public key (i.e. the scalar product of the random number and the base point), and sends the latter back to the server in the *ClientKeyExchange* message. Now both the client and the server can calculate a shared secret by scalar multiplication of their own private key and the public key obtained from the other party. So, in summary, a total of two scalar multiplications are to be performed by the client, and one scalar multiplication by the server.

2.3 Elliptic Curve Digital Signature Algorithm (ECDSA)

The Elliptic Curve Digital Signature Algorithm (ECDSA) is the elliptic curve implementation of the Digital Signature Algorithm (DSA). Besides an elliptic curve key pair, a secure hash function is needed for the generation/verification of an ECDSA signature. Algorithm 4.29 in [16] shows the signature generation process in detail. The main operation is a scalar multiplication $k \cdot P$, which, in turn, is performed through arithmetic operations in the underlying finite field $GF(q)$. Furthermore, a few arithmetic operations (including inversion) modulo the order n of the base point P are to be carried out; these operations have, in general, only little impact on the overall execution time.

RFC 4492 [6] specifies the use of ECDSA-based certificates in TLS 1.1 as an alternative to RSA and DSA (resp. DSS) certificates. When using a cipher suite with ephemeral ECDH, the server's certificate must contain an ECDSA-capable public key, and the server must sign the ephemeral ECDH key it embeds in the *ServerKeyExchange* message with the private key corresponding to the public key in the certificate. On the other hand, when using static ECDH, the server does not need to sign the ECDH key since the signature is already contained in the certificate. However, cipher suites with static ECDH have the disadvantage that they do not provide forward secrecy (see [6] for further details).

Algorithm 4.30 in [16] describes the verification of an ECDSA signature that has to be performed by the client during the SSL handshake in order to check the server's certificate. Two scalar multiplications and one point addition are performed in step 5 of Algorithm 4.30, but they can be combined by using an approach know as "Shamir's trick" [16].

3 Side-Channel Attacks

In contrast to "ordinary" cryptanalytic attacks, Side Channel Attacks (SCAs) do not attack the hard mathematical problem upon which the security of a system is based, but rather its actual implementation [25]. Using secondary channels like the time taken to perform a computation, power needed for a calculation, or even electromagnetic radiation emitted by a device during operation, it is often possible to deduce accurate information about the data being currently processed. With some additional knowledge about the implementation, it may even be possible to reveal the secret key or to extract information leading to the discovery of the secret key. In the past, almost every cryptographic algorithm has been successfully attacked using side channel cryptanalysis, whether it was RSA (e.g. [20,34]), ECC (e.g. [13,29]), or AES (e.g. [30,3]). Depending on the approach used, from a single up to several millions of measurements have to be taken in order to extract the desired information.

Several successful side channel attacks against OpenSSL have been reported in the literature [1,7,8]. In addition to that, stand-alone ECC implementations have been successfully attacked exploiting information leaked from either the group arithmetic (e.g. scalar multiplication) or the field arithmetic (e.g. final subtractions in modular multiplication [33,35]).

3.1 SCA on ECC-Based SSL Handshake

In this paper we consider three types of side-channel attacks: Timing Analysis (TA), Simple Power Analysis (SPA), and Differential Power Analysis (DPA). The reader is referred to [25] for a detailed description of how these attacks can be carried out in practice. We assume an attacker with physical access to both the SSL/TLS server and the client, which enables him not only to collect accurate timing information, but also allows him to measure the power traces needed to conduct an SPA or DPA attack.

The ECDSA private-key operations executed on the server need appropriate protection against SCA since knowledge of the server's private key would allow an attacker to impersonate the server, i.e. to create false servers with the same identity. As already mentioned, ECC-based cipher suites with ephemeral ECDH keys require the server to sign these keys using ECDSA. Fortunately, ECDSA signature generation is "by design" not vulnerable to timing and DPA attacks as the scalar multiplication is performed with a random number[1]. However, an SPA attack on the scalar multiplication is possible, and, if successful, provides the attacker with the random number, which eventually enables him to deduce

---

[1] A DPA attack is theoretically possible on the modular multiplication carried out in step 5 of Algorithm 4.29 in [16] since this operation involves the private key.

the private key. Therefore, the scalar multiplication in the signature generation operation requires countermeasures against SPA attacks. The ECDSA verification is not susceptible to side-channel attacks.

When using ephemeral ECDH, the scalar multiplications on both the server and the client are carried out with random numbers. Consequently, ephemeral ECDH is not vulnerable to timing and DPA attacks, but an SPA attack can be mounted (either on the client side or on the server side) to retrieve the random value with which the scalar multiplication is performed. This would allow the attacker to calculate the pre-master secret, which he can then use to decrypt the communication between client and server. Therefore, ephemeral ECDH key exchange requires an SPA-resistant implementation of the scalar multiplication on both the client and the server. The situation becomes more complicated if the server uses a static ECDH key. A compromise of this key would be disastrous because it enables an attacker to decrypt all SSL sessions conducted with static ECDH, including past ones of which he captured the network traffic. Another point to consider is that a TLS/SSL handshake with static ECDH is vulnerable not only to SPA, but also to TA and DPA attacks. As mentioned in Subsection 2.2, the server's final step of the key exchange is the scalar multiplication of its own private key and the public key it received from the client in the *ClientKey-Exchange* message. However, as this scalar multiplication is performed with the same private key in every run of the protocol (and different, but known, public keys), it must be implemented to withstand TA, SPA, and DPA attacks.

3.2 Protecting ECC against SCA

In the context of ECC, the goal of an SPA attack is, roughly speaking, to deduce the sequence of group operations (i.e. point additions, point doublings) from a power trace acquired during the execution of a scalar multiplication [16]. The more point addition and point doubling differ in their power profile, the easier it is to recover (bits of) the secret scalar. So, in order to foil SPA attacks, the scalar multiplication should be implemented in such a way that always the same operations are executed, independent of the operands. Proposed techniques to achieve this range from the integration of dummy operations at the field and/or group level (e.g. double-and-add-always method [10], Montgomery ladder [17]) over unified or indistinguishable formulae for point addition and doubling [9] to algorithms for scalar multiplication with a fixed sequence of group operations [26]. Yet another option is to use an alternative parameterization or curve representation with more regularity in the scalar multiplication, e.g. Montgomery form, Hessian form, Jacobi form [16]. Of course, all these approaches require an SPA-resistant implementation of the field arithmetic as well. It was shown in [33] and [35] that irregularities in the implementation of modular addition and modular multiplication (e.g. conditional final subtractions) lead to differences in execution time and power consumption, which can be exploited in TA and SPA attacks. Therefore, the arithmetic algorithms should be implemented without data-dependent conditional statements (e.g. if-then-else constructs) so that the control flow becomes independent of the operands being processed.

To mount a DPA attack, an adversary must first collect a (sufficiently large) set of power traces, each trace acquired as the device executes a scalar multiplication with a different base point. Then, the adversary uses statistical analysis techniques to find a correlation between an intermediate state predicted by guessing bits of the secret scalar and the device's instantaneous power consumption [2]. The goal of DPA countermeasures is to break such correlation; in the context of ECC this can be achieved through the randomization of both inputs of the scalar multiplication: the base point P and the scalar k [5,10].

Applying the SPA countermeasures described before results in an implementation with constant execution time, which essentially prevents TA attacks. The randomization of the secret scalar also helps to thwart timing attacks [2].

4 Implementation

As basis for our work we used the MatrixSSL library [31], an open-source implementation of the SSL/TLS protocol written in ANSI C. MatrixSSL is targeted for use in resource-constrained embedded systems and provides both server and client functionality. However, in its original form, MatrixSSL only supports the traditional cipher suites based on DH, RSA, and DSA, but not the ECC cipher suites specified in [6]. Therefore, we replaced the entire public-key part of the library with our own implementation and integrated ECDH key exchange and ECDSA signing/verification on arbitrary elliptic curves over prime and binary extension fields. Our focus was on a small and memory-saving implementation; thus, we abstained from using optimized reduction techniques for standardized primes (such as the NIST primes [28]) and irreducible polynomials. Instead, we realized the field arithmetic with "generic" algorithms for modular reduction, in particular Montgomery's algorithm [27]. To assess the impact of SCA countermeasures on performance and memory requirements, we implemented both a straightforward (i.e. unsecured) version of the public-key library and a version with all data-dependent branches and memory accesses removed from the field and group arithmetic.

Table 2 shows a rough comparison between the size of our library (with and without SCA countermeasures), the original MatrixSSL implementation, and the OpenSSL library we used for reference purposes. The memory footprint is given for a single SSL connection using an elliptic curve over a 192-bit prime field in all cases except for the original MatrixSSL stack, where 1024-bit RSA was used

Table 2. Comparison of code size and memory footprint of SSL libraries

Implementation	Number of source files	Lines of code	Size of executable	Memory footprint
Orig. MatrixSSL	30	∼9,500	114 kB	15.18 kB
Our SSL w/o CM	50	∼10,800	140 kB	9.57 kB
Our SSL with CM	50	∼10,900	141 kB	9.64 kB
OpenSSL 0.9.8	1,100	∼250,000	2,400 kB	182.34 kB

due to the lack of ECC support. A quick look at the number of source code files and the lines of code reflects the different design philosophies of MatrixSSL and OpenSSL. The latter is a full-featured SSL/TLS implementation with a number of performance enhancements, including special modular reduction algorithms for standardized fields [28], hand-written assembly code for performance-critical tasks, and code-size increasing optimizations like loop unrolling. MatrixSSL, on the other hand, is optimized for use in embedded systems and comprises only a fraction of the code size and memory requirements of OpenSSL. The integration of our public-key crypto library with ECC support increases the code size by 26 kB in relation to the original MatrixSSL version. However, using ECC instead of RSA/DH reduces the memory footprint by roughly one third from 15 kB to less than 10 kB.

The results in Table 2 show that our approach of making the SSL handshake side-channel resistant (which will be described in detail in Subsection 4.2) entails only a minimal increase in memory footprint and has almost no impact on the code size. In addition to that, our protected implementation has just 6% of the size of OpenSSL[2]. The memory footprint of our protected SSL implementation is by a factor of 18 smaller than that of OpenSSL.

4.1 Straightforward ECC Implementation

The unprotected version of our crypto library is realized in a fairly straightforward way. We used Algorithm 2.9 in [16] to implement the multiple-precision multiplication and Montgomery's well-known algorithm for modular reduction [27]. In order to keep the code size of our library at a minimum, we did not include optimized reduction functions for special primes like the NIST primes. Also the curve arithmetic over $GF(p)$ is based on well-known algorithms. We represent the elliptic curve points using the mixed Jacobian-affine coordinates described in [16, Sect. 3.2.2]. The scalar multiplication over $GF(p)$ is performed according to the double-and-add technique with non-adjacent-form (NAF) representation of the scalar to save some point additions. For ECDSA verification, Shamir's trick [16] in combination with a joint-sparse-from (JSF) representation of the scalars is used to interleave the two scalar multiplications [32]. We decided to not implement a window method for scalar multiplication because we aimed to keep the memory footprint at a minimum.

Also the algorithms for arithmetic in $GF(2^m)$ are well documented and fairly straightforward to implement. We used the so-called left-to-right comb method with windows of width 4 for the multiplication of binary polynomials [24]. Furthermore, we implemented a generic reduction function for irreducible trinomials and pentanomials. The term generic in this context means that the reduction function accepts arbitrary trinomials and pentanomials as input. In addition, we also included the Montgomery reduction for binary polynomials in our library to support irreducible polynomials which are not trinomials or pentanomials

---

[2] Although there have been attempts of stripping OpenSSL down, the resulting library was still about 580 kB in size (see [22] for details).

[19]. The scalar multiplication over $GF(2^m)$ is performed according to the well-known algorithm of Lopez and Dahab [23].

4.2 SCA-Resistant ECC Implementation

In order to protect the arithmetic in $GF(p)$, all conditional operations such as conditional subtractions of the prime p have to be replaced by unconditional subtractions where the subtrahend is either p or 0. Conditional operations do not only occur in the field addition and field subtraction operations, but also in the Montgomery multiplication and the Montgomery squaring. In order to get unconditional code, we extended the array holding the prime p with a second array holding only zeros (this happens exactly once, so the additional storage overhead of this zero-array can be neglected). Then, all conditional branches are replaced by index calculations into this extended array to either subtract the actual prime p, or only zero. This removes any runtime dependency on the data being processed and allows one to realize field arithmetic operations with constant execution time, regardless of the operands being processed[3].

Another problem one has to deal with in the field addition is the comparison of the sum with the prime p. An exact comparison is a costly operation and should be avoided. Instead, we just check whether the addition produced a carry (which means that the bitlength of the sum exceeds the bitlength of p) and we use this carry to calculate the index into the extended array from which the subtrahend for the unconditional subtraction is loaded. If the addition produced a carry[4], then the subtrahend is p, otherwise it is 0. Note that a "secure" field addition actually requires to perform two unconditional subtractions, and even after these two subtractions the result may not be fully reduced. Fortunately, the Montgomery multiplication can be adapted to cope with incompletely reduced operands (see [36] for more details). For the secure implementation of the scalar multiplication over $GF(p)$, we used the the Montgomery ladder [17, Algorithm 1] as it is very modest in terms of code size and memory requirements.

The arithmetic in $GF(2^m)$ is easy to protect against SPA attacks. In fact, the only function that needed a "tweak" was the reduction modulo the irreducible polynomial. Also here we tolerate incompletely reduced intermediate results to get rid of data-dependent branches [15].

In order to thwart DPA attacks, we randomize the scalar and also apply the point randomization technique described in [16]. Since the scalar multiplication over $GF(p)$ is carried out in projective Jacobian coordinates, but the points are

---

[3] Note that the approach of unconditional subtraction of either p or 0 protects against timing attacks, but may be vulnerable to an SPA attack. For example, when the subtrahend is the zero-array, the register into which the words of the subtrahend are loaded does not change its content, and hence it may consume less power than when the subtrahend is the prime p. A simple solution to this problem is to (partially) unroll the loop of the subtraction function and interchange the registers into which the individual words of the minuend and subtrahend are loaded.

[4] For sake of simplicity, we assume that the bitlength is a multiple of the processor's word size, which is always the case with the NIST primes on a 32-bit processor.

transmitted in affine coordinates to save bandwidth, it is possible to compute the scalar multiplication with any point represented by $(\lambda^2 x, \lambda^3 y, \lambda)$ with (x, y) being the original (i.e. affine) point. The overhead for this operation in an entire scalar multiplication is negligible. A similar blinding technique can be used to make the scalar multiplication over $GF(2^m)$ DPA-resistant.

5 Experimental Results

All results reported in this paper were obtained by executing the SSL software on a Compaq iPAQ h3600 with a StrongARM SA-1100 clocked at 200 MHz and running Familiar Linux v0.8.2. The iPAQ was connected to a PC using the USB port of its cradle and initiated SSL sessions with the server running there. The timings were collected using the `gettimeofday` method due the to the lack of a dedicated cycle counter. We measured the execution time of a sufficiently large number of iterations to ensure the accuracy of the results.

Table 3. Execution time (in msec) of a scalar multiplication

Implementation	$GF(p_{192})$	$GF(p_{224})$	$GF(p_{256})$	$GF(2^{163})$	$GF(2^{191})$	$GF(2^{233})$
Our SSL w/o CM	23.4	33.4	47.3	38.5	44.1	94.2
Our SSL with CM	50.0	72.7	102.5	38.5	44.1	94.2
OpenSSL 0.9.8	36.5	48.4	54.3	31.3	33.7	64.7

Table 3 summarizes the timings for a scalar multiplication on standardized elliptic curves over 192, 224, and 256-bit prime fields, as well as 163, 191, and 233-bit binary fields. Our unsecured implementation outperforms OpenSSL on elliptic curves over prime fields, which is a remarkable result when considering that OpenSSL contains many performance-increasing optimizations (e.g. special modular reduction techniques for standardized primes, hand-written assembly code for frequently executed operations, advanced window methods for scalar multiplication), while our implementation uses the Montgomery algorithm for modular reduction, the double-and-add method for scalar multiplication, and is written entirely in ANSI C. The side-channel countermeasures roughly double the execution time, mainly due to the use of the Montgomery ladder[5]. In the $GF(2^m)$ case, there are no differences between the secured and the unsecured implementation because the Lopez-Dahab method for scalar multiplication does not necessitate special SPA countermeasures, and the countermeasures against DPA have virtually no impact on the overall execution time.

Table 4 shows the timings for an ECDSA signature verification. The benefit of Shamir's trick for multiple point multiplication over prime fields is obvious since a naive implementation of a computation of the form $k \cdot P + l \cdot Q$ would

---

[5] The Montgomery ladder not only increases the number of point additions, but also requires a more costly implementation of the point addition with the ability to add two points given in projective coordinates.

Table 4. Execution time (in msec) of ECDSA signature verification

Implementation	$GF(p_{192})$	$GF(p_{224})$	$GF(p_{256})$	$GF(2^{163})$	$GF(2^{191})$	$GF(2^{233})$
Our SSL w/o CM	30.1	44.0	61.3	78.1	91.8	189.9
Our SSL with CM	33.0	49.1	67.9	78.1	91.8	189.9
OpenSSL 0.9.8	38.4	48.6	66.3	66.3	72.5	133.7

take more than twice the time of an ordinary scalar multiplication. Even though ECDSA verification does not leak any confidential information, we realized it on basis of the SPA-resistant implementation of the $GF(p)$-arithmetic to reduce the overall code size. The results in Table 4 also indicate that eliminating all data-dependent branches and memory accesses from the field arithmetic increases the execution time by a mere 10%. When using a binary field as underlying algebraic structure, the ECDSA verification is significantly slower than an ordinary scalar multiplication because Shamir's trick can not be used in combination with the Lopez-Dahab method.

Finally, Table 5 shows the timings for an entire SSL handshake from the first *ClientHello* message to the *Finished* message. These timings were measured on the iPAQ PDA, which acts as SSL client initiating a handshake using a cipher suite with static ECDH. Hence, the timings mainly contain the execution time of the ECDH key exchange (i.e. two scalar multiplications on the client) and the signature verification. The remaining time is spent for protocol processing and for administrative purposes. We eliminated deviations due to unsteady network conditions by using a direct connection between the iPAQ and the PC on which the SSL server is running. In summary, the implemented countermeasures for protecting ECC over $GF(p)$ increase the latency of the entire SSL handshake by roughly 50% compared to an unprotected implementation, but still allow for more than acceptable performance (on the 200 MHz PDA, an entire handshake based on 192-bit ECC can be completed in less than 160 msec).

Figure 1 depicts a breakdown of an entire SSL handshake using ECC over a 192-bit prime field. The ECDH key exchange and the ECDSA signature verification constitute the main portion of the handshake on the client side, taking a total of roughly 90% of the entire handshake time. This justifies attempts for speeding up public-key operations for the transmission of small messages. The larger the transmitted messages become, the lower the fraction of the handshake time and, as a direct consequence, the lower the impact of public-key operations gets in relation to the secret-key operations (i.e. bulk encryption).

Table 5. Execution time (in msec) of an entire SSL handshake

Implementation	$GF(p_{192})$	$GF(p_{224})$	$GF(p_{256})$	$GF(2^{163})$	$GF(2^{191})$	$GF(2^{233})$
Our SSL w/o CM	95.0	128.0	175.0	177.0	195.5	408.5
Our SSL with CM	154.0	220.8	307.5	177.0	195.5	408.5
OpenSSL 0.9.8	106.0	136.0	186.0	110.0	160.0	287.0

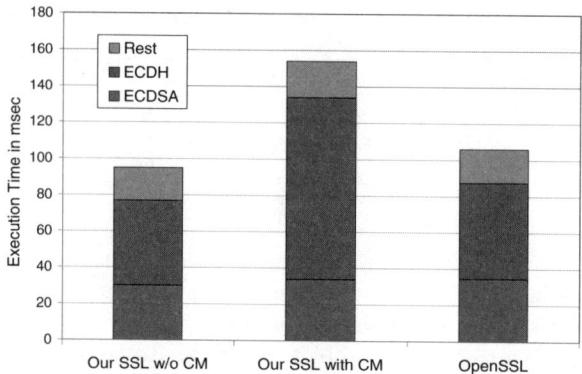

Fig. 1. Breakdown of the handshake using ECC over a 192-bit prime field

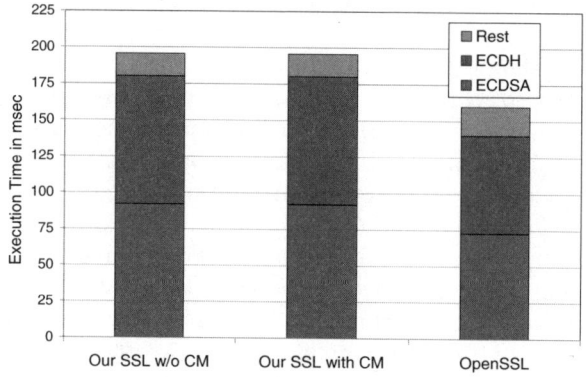

Fig. 2. Breakdown of the handshake using ECC over a 191-bit binary field

Figure 2 shows the same breakdown as Figure 1, but for ECC over a 191-bit binary field. There are mainly two things that can be observed: First, there is almost no difference in running time between the secured and unsecured implementation (due to the features of the Lopez-Dahab method) and second, because Shamir's trick can not be used together with the Lopez-Dahab method, the time for an ECDSA signature verification is now almost the same as the time for an ECDH protocol run, both mainly dominated by two scalar multiplications. The fraction of the protocol-related overhead remains the same as for the handshake using ECC with SCA-resistant prime field arithmetic, namely about 10%.

6 Conclusions

In this paper we analyzed the workload characteristics of a lightweight SSL implementation into which we integrated a generic ECC library with support for arbitrary prime and binary extensions fields. Our focus was on small code size and low memory footprint rather than on pure performance. In order to assess the impact of SCA countermeasures, we implemented two versions of the library: a straightforward one that does not consider side-channel leakage, and a secure one featuring countermeasures against TA, SPA, and DPA attacks. Our results show that the execution time of a scalar multiplication over GF(p) increases by a factor of two when using the Montgomery ladder instead of the conventional double-and-add method with NAF representation of the scalar. However, the overall latency of the SSL handshake increases by about 50% compared to the unsecured implementation, but is still perfectly acceptable for many embedded applications. In summary, our lightweight SSL implementation is a little slower than OpenSSL, but has only a fraction of its code size (141 kB instead of 2400 kB) and memory footprint (9.64 kB instead of 182 kB). On the other hand, the situation is quite different for binary extensions fields. A straightforward implementation using the Lopez-Dahab method for scalar multiplication provides good protection against timing and SPA attacks, and therefore the performance penalty due to the integration of SCA countermeasures is very small. Putting it all together, our work demonstrates that an SSL implementation can be made side-channel resistant without sacrificing memory footprint and code size. The penalty is a moderate performance degradation for ECC over GF(p), while the performance of ECC over GF(2^m) is almost unaffected.

Acknowledgements

The work described in this paper has been supported by the EPSRC under grant EP/E001556/1 and, in part, by the European Commission through the IST Programme under contract IST-2002-507932 ECRYPT. The information in this document reflects only the authors' views, is provided as is and no guarantee or warranty is given that the information is fit for any particular purpose. The user thereof uses the information at its sole risk and liability.

References

1. Acıiçmez, O., Schindler, W., Koç, Ç.K.: Improving Brumley and Boneh timing attack on unprotected SSL implementations. In: Proceedings of the 12th ACM Conference on Computer and Communications Security (CCS 2005), pp. 139–146. ACM Press, New York (2005)
2. Avanzi, R.M.: Side channel attacks on implementations of curve-based cryptographic primitives. Cryptology ePrint Archive, Report 2005/017 (2005), http://eprint.iacr.org
3. Bernstein, D.J.: Cache-timing attacks on AES (preprint, 2005), http://cr.yp.to/mac.html#cachetiming
4. Blake, I.F., Seroussi, G., Smart, N.P.: Elliptic Curves in Cryptography. Cambridge University Press, Cambridge (1999)
5. Blake, I.F., Seroussi, G., Smart, N.P.: Advances in Elliptic Curve Cryptography. Cambridge University Press, Cambridge (2005)

6. Blake-Wilson, S., Bolyard, N., Gupta, V., Hawk, C., Möller, B.: Elliptic Curve Cryptography (ECC) Cipher Suites for Transport Layer Security (TLS). Internet Engineering Task Force, Network Working Group, RFC 4492 (2006)
7. Brumley, D., Boneh, D.: Remote timing attacks are practical. In: Proceedings of 12th USENIX Security Symposium (SECURITY 2003), pp. 1–14. USENIX (2003)
8. Canvel, B., Hiltgen, A.P., Vaudenay, S., Vuagnoux, M.: Password interception in an SSL/TLS channel. In: Boneh, D. (ed.) CRYPTO 2003. LNCS, vol. 2729, pp. 583–599. Springer, Heidelberg (2003)
9. Chevallier-Mames, B., Ciet, M., Joye, M.: Low-cost solutions for preventing simple side-channel analysis: Side-channel atomicity. IEEE Transactions on Computers 53(6), 760–768 (2004)
10. Coron, J.-S.: Resistance against differential power analysis for elliptic curve cryptosystems. In: Koç, Ç.K., Paar, C. (eds.) CHES 1999. LNCS, vol. 1717, pp. 292–302. Springer, Heidelberg (1999)
11. Dierks, T., Rescorla, E.K.: The Transport Layer Security (TLS) Protocol Version 1.1. Internet Engineering Task Force, Network Working Group, RFC 4346 (2006)
12. Freier, A.O., Karlton, P., Kocher, P.C.: The SSL Protocol Version 3.0. Internet Draft (1996), http://wp.netscape.com/eng/ssl3/draft302.txt
13. Goubin, L.: A refined power-analysis attack on elliptic curve cryptosystems. In: Desmedt, Y.G. (ed.) PKC 2003. LNCS, vol. 2567, pp. 199–210. Springer, Heidelberg (2002)
14. Gupta, V., Gupta, S., Chang Shantz, S., Stebila, D.: Performance analysis of elliptic curve cryptography for SSL. In: Proceedings of the 3rd ACM Workshop on Wireless Security (WiSe 2002), pp. 87–94. ACM Press, New York (2002)
15. Gura, N., Eberle, H., Chang Shantz, S.: Generic implementations of elliptic curve cryptography using partial reduction. In: Proceedings of the 9th ACM Conference on Computer and Communications Security (CCS 2002), pp. 108–116. ACM Press, New York (2002)
16. Hankerson, D.R., Menezes, A.J., Vanstone, S.A.: Guide to Elliptic Curve Cryptography. Springer, Heidelberg (2004)
17. Joye, M.: Highly regular right-to-left algorithms for scalar multiplication. In: Paillier, P., Verbauwhede, I. (eds.) CHES 2007. LNCS, vol. 4727, pp. 135–147. Springer, Heidelberg (2007)
18. Kaufman, C., Perlman, R., Speciner, M.: Network Security: Private Communication in a Public World. Prentice Hall, Englewood Cliffs (2002)
19. Koç, Ç.K., Acar, T.: Montgomery multiplication in $GF(2^k)$. Designs, Codes and Cryptography 14(1), 57–69 (1998)
20. Kocher, P.C.: Timing attacks on implementations of Diffie-Hellman, RSA, DSS, and other systems. In: Koblitz, N. (ed.) CRYPTO 1996. LNCS, vol. 1109, pp. 104–113. Springer, Heidelberg (1996)
21. Kocher, P.C., Jaffe, J., Jun, B.: Differential power analysis. In: Wiener, M. (ed.) CRYPTO 1999. LNCS, vol. 1666, pp. 388–397. Springer, Heidelberg (1999)
22. Lenzlinger, B., Zingg, A.: Mini Web Server supporting SSL. M.Sc. Thesis, Zurich University of Applied Sciences Winterthur (2000)
23. López, J., Dahab, R.: Fast multiplication on elliptic curves over $GF(2^m)$ without precomputation. In: Koç, Ç.K., Paar, C. (eds.) CHES 1999. LNCS, vol. 1717, pp. 316–327. Springer, Heidelberg (1999)
24. López, J., Dahab, R.: High-speed software multiplication in $\mathbb{F}_{2^m}$. In: Roy, B., Okamoto, E. (eds.) INDOCRYPT 2000. LNCS, vol. 1977, pp. 203–212. Springer, Heidelberg (2000)

25. Mangard, S., Oswald, E., Popp, T.: Power Analysis Attacks: Revealing the Secrets of Smart Cards. Springer, Heidelberg (2007)
26. Möller, B.: Securing elliptic curve point multiplication against side-channel attacks. In: Davida, G.I., Frankel, Y. (eds.) ISC 2001. LNCS, vol. 2200, pp. 324–334. Springer, Heidelberg (2001)
27. Montgomery, P.L.: Modular multiplication without trial division. Mathematics of Computation 44(170), 519–521 (1985)
28. National Institute of Standards and Technology (NIST). Recommend Elliptic Curves for Federal Government use. Technical report (1999), http://csrc.nist.gov/CryptoToolkit
29. Okeya, K., Sakurai, K.: A second-order DPA attack breaks a window-method based countermeasure against side channel attacks. In: Chan, A.H., Gligor, V.D. (eds.) ISC 2002. LNCS, vol. 2433, pp. 389–401. Springer, Heidelberg (2002)
30. Osvik, D.A., Shamir, A., Tromer, E.: Cache attacks and countermeasures: The case of AES. In: Pointcheval, D. (ed.) CT-RSA 2006. LNCS, vol. 3860, pp. 1–20. Springer, Heidelberg (2006)
31. PeerSec Networks, Inc. MatrixSSL 1.7.1 (September 2005), http://www.matrixssl.org
32. Solinas, J.A.: Low-Weight Binary Representations for Pairs of Integers. Technical report CORR 2001-41, University of Waterloo, Waterloo, Canada (2001)
33. Stebila, D., Thériault, N.: Unified point addition formulæ and side-channel attacks. In: Goubin, L., Matsui, M. (eds.) CHES 2006. LNCS, vol. 4249, pp. 354–368. Springer, Heidelberg (2006)
34. Walter, C.D., Thompson, S.: Distinguishing exponent digits by observing modular subtractions. In: Naccache, D. (ed.) CT-RSA 2001. LNCS, vol. 2020, pp. 192–207. Springer, Heidelberg (2001)
35. Walter, C.D.: Simple power analysis of unified code for ECC double and add. In: Joye, M., Quisquater, J.-J. (eds.) CHES 2004. LNCS, vol. 3156, pp. 191–204. Springer, Heidelberg (2004)
36. Yanık, T., Savaş, E., Koç, Ç.K.: Incomplete reduction in modular arithmetic. IEE Proceedings – Computers and Digital Techniques 149(2), 46–52 (2002)
37. Zhao, L., Iyer, R., Makineni, S., Bhuyan, L.: Anatomy and performance of SSL processing. In: Proceedings of the 5th International Symposium on Performance Analysis of Systems and Software (ISPASS 2005), pp. 197–206. IEEE Computer Society Press, Los Alamitos (2005)

Authenticated Directed Diffusion

Eric K. Wang, Lucas C.K. Hui, and S.M. Yiu

The University of Hong Kong, Pokfulam, Hong Kong

Abstract. Directed Diffusion(DD) is a method of data dissemination especially suitable in distributed sensing scenarios. It has been known well in the application of wireless sensor network routing. Although it is very popular as a data-centric routing protocol for wireless sensor network(WSN), it faces several types of serious attacks. We proposes a new protocol ("Authenticated Directed Diffusion" (ADD)) which extends the directed diffusion protocol. According to the resource constraint of WSN, we adopt a real time one-way key chain and authenticated blacklist diffusion to achieve the authenticity and integrity in the routing process for directed diffusion with relative low overhead. Authenticated Directed Diffusion mainly tackle three problems(DoS attack,sinkhole attack and bogus routing attack) which Directed Diffusion can not handle. The simulation result shows that the performance of Authenticated Directed Diffusion is acceptable.

Keywords: Directed Diffusion, Authentication, Wireless Sensor Networks.

1 Introduction

Directed Diffusion(DD)[4] is a data-centric routing protocol in that all communication is for named data. It provide a mechanism for a limited flood of a query toward an event, and then set up reverse gradients to send data back along the best route.

Directed diffusion consists of several elements: interests, data messages, gradients, and reinforcements. An interest message is a query or an interrogation which specifies what a user wants. Each interest contains a description of a sensing task that is supported by a sensor network for acquiring data. Typically, data in sensor networks is the collected or processed information of a physical phenomenon. Such data can be an event which is a short description of the sensed phenomenon. In directed diffusion, data is named using attribute-value pairs. A sensing task is disseminated throughout the sensor network as an interest for named data. This dissemination sets up gradients within the network designed to "draw" events (i.e.,data matching the interest). Specifically, a gradient is direction state created in each node that receives an interest. The gradient direction is set toward the neighboring node from which the interest is received. Events start flowing towards the originators of interests along multiple gradient paths. The sensor network reinforces one, or a small number of these paths.

Here we give a brief introduction of the DD protocol phases. For more details, please refer to [4].

This protocol includes four phases.

1. interest propagation phase
2. routing setup phase
3. reinforcement phase
4. data propagation phase

1.1 Interest Propagation Phase

The first step is interest propagation phase. the sink broadcasts an interest message periodically to all the neighbors. Every node maintains an interest cache. At receiving an interest, a node checks whether the interest is already in it's cache. If there is no such an interest entry inside it's cache, the node generate an interest entry and related fields such as gradient field. The entry has a single gradient towards the neighbor from which the interest was received. The gradient specifies both a data rate and a direction in which to send events.

1.2 Routing Setup Phase

The second step is low-rate data propagation and routing setup phase. The source node identify whether it has the same interest cache matched. If it is, the node sends low-rate data to those who has a gradient. Nodes receive a data message from their neighbors try to confirm whether there is a matching interest entry in their cache. If the answer is yes, the nodes cache the received message and forward it to their neighbors.

1.3 Reinforcement Phase

Next, it is the reinforcement phase. When the above low-rate data reaches the sink along multiple paths, the sink then selects and reinforces one particular path in order to draw down higher quality events. To reinforce the path, the sink re-sends the original interest message with a smaller interval.

1.4 Data Propagation Phase

The last phase is the data propagation phase. The source node computes the highest requested event rate among all its outgoing gradients and sends them to its neighbors. The message receiver checks the matching interest entry's gradient list. If there is a lower data rate than the received data rate, it may down convert the data to the appropriate gradient. And it also does some in-network data aggregation before re-sending the message in order to make the data aggregation more efficient. Finally, data is propagated along the path.

2 Security Concern of Directed Diffusion

Although DD has several nice features such as (1)data-centric dissemination, (2)reinforcement based adaptation to the best path and (3)in-network aggregation and caching, it has not been designed for security purpose. It is threatened by multiple attack models (bogus routing information, selective forwarding, sink holes, sybil wormholes and Dos attacks). Our contribution is mainly to tackle three of them, DOS attacks, sink hole attacks and bogus routing information.

2.1 DoS Attack

Due to the sensors' inherent limitations, directed-diffusion based wireless sensor network is easily attacked by DoS attack [8]. An effective form of DoS attack against directed diffusion is to overwhelm nodes that are many hops away by flooding interests packets, which will quickly exhaust the limited energy, communication bandwidth, memory, and CPU of resource-limited sensor nodes. Another effective form of DoS attack against directed diffusion is to flood data packets, which also exhaust the resources of nodes.

2.2 Bogus Routing Information

Another kind of attacks against DD is to target the gradient information between nodes. By spoofing, altering, or replaying gradient information, adversaries may be able to create routing loops, attract network traffic, extend or shorten source routes, generate false error messages, partition the network, increase end-to-end latency, etc.

2.3 Sinkholes Attack

In a sinkhole attack for DD, the adversary's goal is to lure nearly all the traffic from a particular area through a compromised node, creating a metaphorical sinkhole with the adversary at the center. Because nodes on, or near, the path that packets follow have many opportunities to tamper with application data, sinkhole attacks can enable many other attacks (selective forwarding, for example). Sinkhole attacks typically work by making a compromised node look especially attractive to surrounding nodes.

2.4 Other Attacks

Besides the above three attacks, there are still some other attacks such as selective forwarding, sybil attacks and wormholes attacks [2]. In a selective forwarding attack, malicious nodes may refuse to forward certain messages such as Interests messages from base station and simply drop them, ensuring that they are not propagated any further. Sybil attacks is that single node presents multiple identities to other nodes and significantly affect fault-tolerance schemes like distributed storage, multi-path routing, topology maintenance. Wormhole attack is that an adversary tunnels messages received in one part of the network over a low-latency link and replays them in a different part. The simplest instance of this attack is a single node situated between two other nodes forwarding messages between the two of them.

3 Related Works

Perrig et al. (2002) proposed Security Protocols for Sensor Networks, SPINS, a suite of security protocols optimised for sensor networks [1]. It consists of two secure building blocks SNEP and μTESLA, which runs on top of TinyOS, a small, event driven operating system for sensor node. Secure Network Encryption Protocol, SNEP, is used to provide confidentiality through encryption and authentication, in addition to integrity, using a message authentication code (MAC). It adds 8 bytes per message and maintains a counter at both end points. It can prevent eavesdroppers from inferring the message content from the encrypted message and provides data authentication. However, for each data transmission, each node needs to calculate and store four keys, which is very costly. Also each communication pair shares a master key. Thus, SNEP is not good for sensor to sensor communications.

μTESLA protocol uses an one way hash chain number as the key to generate a message authentication code (MAC) of a broadcast message. A different one way hash number is allocated for each time slot, and this number is used to generate MACs for the packets sent in that time slot. To tolerate packet losses, it has been extended by introducing multi-level one-way hash chain. A higher-level one way hash number is used to bootstrap low-level one-way hash numbers. But they both have some limitations. μTESLA requires that the base station and the nodes be loosely time synchronized while time synchronization is costly and vulnerable to attacks. And the node who receives a packet can not authenticated it immediately, Usually it needs the latency to finish authentication of packets. Moreover, adversary can forge the packet during the key disclosure interval among different sensor nodes to cheat those nodes which has not received the disclosed key because of packet delay. Actually, μTESLA protocol is mainly designed for broadcasting for the scenario that one sender faces multiple receivers. It is able to provide security for base station broadcasting at some degree. But it is not feasible to apply μTESLA protocol to route through the whole sensor network.

Wang et al.(2005) [3] is the only one previous work for secure directed diffusion, it employs the TESLA to do the authentication and symmetric encryption to protect the nonce in the message packets in order to prevent replay attacks. Unfortunately, it does not support the in-network aggregation process. And it needs loosely time synchronization and extra communication overhead to convey the keys and . It costs too much and is vulnerable to attacks.

4 Authenticated Directed Diffusion Protocol

Our protocol include two parts, one is real-time one way hash chain authentication, the other is the authenticated blacklist diffusion with the interests diffusion.

A one-way hash chain is employed as an efficient and simple solution on resource-constrained sensor nodes for mitigating DoS and replay attacks along paths. A one-way hash chain[5] is a sequence of numbers generated by a one-way function F, that has the property that for a given x it is easy to compute y = F(x). However, given F and y, it is computationally infeasible to determine x, such that $x = F^{-1}(y)$. A one-way hash key chain is a sequence of numbers s_i, $s_{i-1}, \ldots, s_0$, such that : $0 < i < n$ and $s_i = F(s_{i+1})$. To generate a key, we first select a random number s_t as the seed, and successively apply function F on st to generate other numbers in the sequence.

The protocol includes a pre-load setup and the same phases as DD.

1. pre-load setup
2. interest propagation phase
3. routing setup phase
4. reinforcement phase
5. data propagation phase

4.1 Pre-load Setup

Base station randomly chooses a seed (k_t), and it generates a key chain until k_0 by $F(k_t)$, $F(k_{t-1})$, $F(k_{t-2})$, $F(k_1)$, where $k_0 = F(k_1)$. Then each node in the network is pre-loaded by an initial verifier $v_0 = k_0$. We can refer to figure 1. Moreover, each node also maintains its own one way hash key chain. Suppose a node Ni, it maintains HNi_0, HNi_1,.. HNi_m where $HNi_{m-1} = F(HNi_m)$. Node i shares a symmetric key Sn_i with base station.

4.2 Step1- Interest Propagation

Since the interest should be cached by all the sensor nodes, it should not be allowed to be modified during diffusion. When the sink sends out the first interest, it floods a packet in the form of {INTEREST1|Blacklist1|MAC_{k1}(INTEREST1| Blacklist1)|k1}. When a node Ni in the network receives the packet, it verifies if $F(k1) = v_0$, if so, then it verifies if MAC_{k1}(INTEREST1|Blacklist1)= MAC'_{k1}(INTEREST1|Blacklist1). At the same time, it checks if the source who sent out the packet is not in the blacklist. If so, the packet is validated and be forwarded to next node until the interest is flooded to the whole network. Then v_0 is updated and set to be k_1. Moreover, in order to tolerate packet latency or loss, we adopt ($\triangle$ times verification test) to check if $F_{ki} = v_0$. If the packet is not validated after the verification process has been performed $\triangle$ times or the

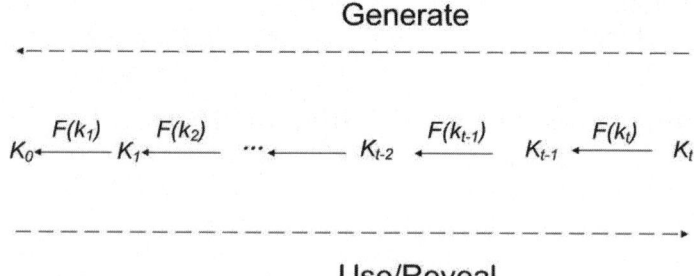

Fig. 1. One-way key chain

source node sent out the packet is in the blacklist, Ni simply drops the packet. The default value of $\triangle$ is 3.

The pseudocode of the step is as follows:
For any node who receives interest:
If (sender is in the blacklist) then {discard the message };
Else
 If ($F(k_i)=v_0$) and
 ($MAC_{k1}(INTEREST1|Blacklist1) = MAC'_{k1}(INTEREST1|Blacklist1)$),
 then { check the cache to store the interest and broadcast it to next hops;
 $v_0=ki$; };
 Else {discard the message}

4.3 Gradients Establishment

Each node M maintains a unique one-way hash chain HM:$<HM_i,HM_{i-1},....HM_1,HM_0>$. When M sends data to the base station, it includes an value number from HM in the packet:

The pseudocode of the step is as follows:
For any node who receives interest:
If (sender is in the blacklist) then {discard the message };
Else
 If (DATA.type=initial.type) , then {broadcast it to next hops; };
Else {discard the message}

Here we give one scenario example as figure 2 . Suppose node Nf is the right source node which matches the INTEREST task.

Path	Routing Data
1	{*DATA1*|*MAC $_{HMi1}$ (DATA1)*|*[HMi0]$_Snf$* |*{IDnf}*}}
2	{*DATA1*|*MAC $_{HMi1}$ (DATA1)*|*[HMi0]$_Snf$* |*{IDnf}*}}
3	{*DATA1*|*MAC $_{HMi1}$ (DATA1)*|*[HMi0]$_Snf$* |*{IDnf}*}}
4	{DATA1|MAC $_{HMi1}$ (DATA1)|[HMi0]$_Snf$ |{IDnf, IDnd}}
5	{DATA1|MAC $_{HMi1}$ (DATA1)|[HMi0]$_Snf$ |{IDnf, IDne }}
6	{DATA1|MAC $_{HMi1}$ (DATA1)|[HMi0]$_Snf$ |{IDnf, IDnd}}
7	{DATA1|MAC $_{HMi1}$ (DATA1)|[HMi0]$_Snf$ |{IDnf, IDne}}
8	{DATA1|MAC $_{HMi1}$ (DATA1)|[HMi0]$_Snf$ |{IDnf, IDnd , IDna}}
9	{DATA1|MAC $_{HMi1}$ (DATA1)|[HMi0]Snf |{IDnf, IDnc}}
10	{DATA1|MAC $_{HMi1}$ (DATA1)|[HMi0]Snf |{IDnf, IDnc}}
11	{DATA1|MAC $_{HMi1}$ (DATA1)|[HMi0]$_Snf$|{IDnf, IDnd , IDna}}
12	{DATA1|MAC $_{HMi1}$ (DATA1)|[HMi0]$_Snf$|{IDnf, IDne , IDnb}}

Where {*IDnf*} is the node list of the path. DATA1 is the data that node F collects by the description of the INTEREST1.

For node D:
- Receive the packet from node F
- Send {DATA1\|MAC $_{HMi1}$ (DATA1)\|[HMi0]$_Snf$ \|{IDnf, IDnd }} to node A and node C.

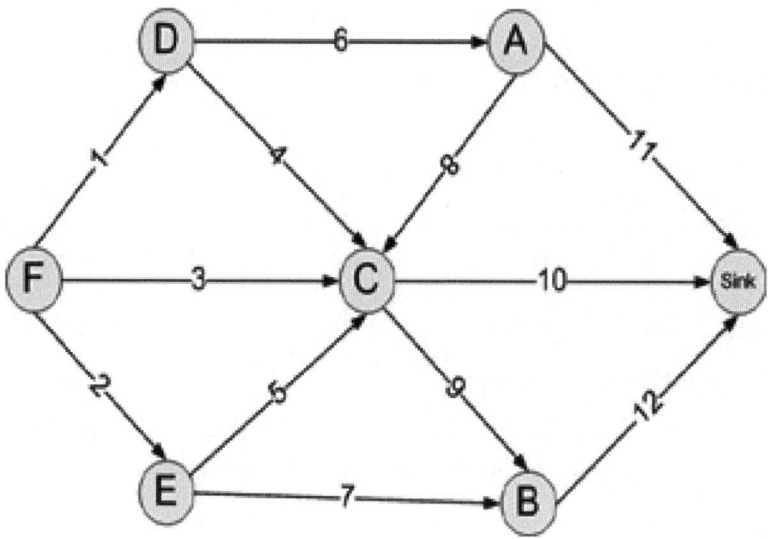

Fig. 2. Gradient Step2

For node F:

- Randomly generates a nonce(*nonce1*)
- broadcast $\{DATA1|MAC\ _{HMi1}\ (DATA1)|[HMi0]_{Snf}\ |\{IDnf\}\}$
- Send $\{DATA1|MAC\ _{HMi1}\ (DATA1)|[HMi0]_{Snf}\ |\{IDnf\}\}$ to D,C and E

For node C:

- Receive the packet from node F
- Send {DATA1|MAC $_{HMi1}$ (DATA1)|[HMi0]Snf |{IDnf, IDnc }}to Node B and sink.

For node E:

- Receive the packet from node F
- Send {DATA1|MAC $_{HMi1}$ (DATA1)|[HMi0]$_{Snf}$ |{IDnf, IDne }}to node B and C.

For node A:

- Receive the packet from node D
- Send {DATA1|MAC $_{HMi1}$ (DATA1)|[HMi0]$_{Snf}$ |{IDnf, IDnd , IDna }} to node C and sink.

For node B:

- Receive the packet from node E
- Send {DATA1|MAC $_{HMi1}$ (DATA1)|HMi1|[HMi0]$_{Snf}$ |{IDnf, IDne , IDnb }} to sink.

For the sink
- Receive three packets from different neighbours node A,B,C
- Receive {DATA1|MAC $_{HMi1}$ (DATA1)|HMi1|[HMi0]$_{Snf}$ |{IDnf, IDnd, IDna }} from node A
- Receive {DATA1|MAC $_{HMi1}$ (DATA1)|[Ni0]Snf |{IDnf, IDne, IDnb }} from node B
- Receive {DATA1|MAC $_{HMi1}$ (DATA1)|HMi1|[HMi0]Snf |{IDnf, IDnc }} from node C
- Check if node F is in the blacklist, if not
- decrypt [HMi0]$_{Snf}$ by the share key Snf and gets the first key of Node F's one-way chain HMi0
- Check if HMi1 is the right derived key from node F.
- Checks if the DATA1 is from node F and has not been modified.
- Check if nonce1 could be decrypted by using the intermediate nodes' shared key in turn.
- If all of the three packets in the above pass the verification, the sink now has three paths $\{F, E, B\},\{F, D, A\}$ and $\{F, C\}$.

4.4 Path Reinforcement

After sink receives data from different neighbors, it should choose one path to reinforce it. Usually,the sink chooses a path based on lower delay or shorter hop. But because wormhole attacker or a laptop-class attacker can be easy to supply a higher quality route than normal nodes, in order to defend malicious attacks, the sink could choose a path probabilistically. And the detailed probability distribution depends on the different designer. One of the simplest probability distributions can be set to be a random distribution.

We suppose that the sink chooses path {F, C} ,path{3,4} to reinforce. In order to propagate a reinforcement the sink firstly sends a packet in the form of {*REINFORCEMENT1*|{*F,C*}|*Blacklist2*| {*IDnf, HMi0*}} *MAC* $_{k2}$ {*REINFORCEMENT1*|{*F,C*}| *Blacklist2*|{*IDnf, HMi0*}}|*k2* }. The node, which receives the packet, checks if the packet is from the sink by verifying if $k2$ is validate and if REINFORCEMENT1, Blacklist2 or $\{ID_{nf}, HM_{i0}\}$ has been modified in the diffusion. If either check fails, the node discards the two packets. Otherwise the node checks if it is an intermediate node on the path. If the node is on the path that is being reinforced, it records the reinforcement information in its cache. And it sets its own verifier of Node F as HM_{i0}. Otherwise it does nothing. We can refer to figure 3.

4.5 Data Routing Back

After the reinforcement, node F sends out {DATA2|MAC $_{HMi2}$(DATA2 |{Dnf}} to on the established path by the appropriate gradient.

A node that receives the above packet from its neighbor firstly checks if the DATA2 are from node F and have not been modified in the diffusion. Then the node attempts to find a matching interest entry and corresponding appropriate gradients in its cache. At last the node re-sends the packet to the appropriate neighbors.

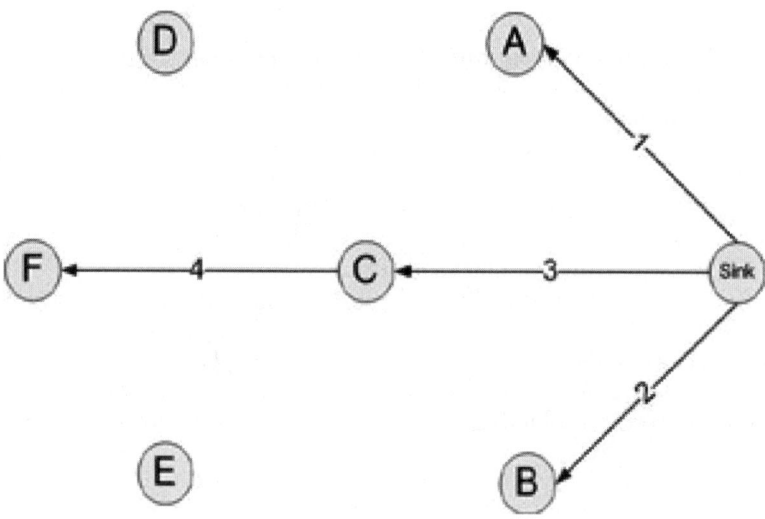

Fig. 3. Reinforcment

5 Security Analysis

The protocol can effectively guarantee the integrity of Data transferred in the network. Once the data is modified, the receiver can detect it.

And it can effectively defend bogus routing attack and sinkhole attack by data authentication and blacklist. We adopt intrusion detection method [10] to generate blacklist which is able to show the nodes who are malicious around them. Broadcasting blacklist has two ways, one is that blacklist can be broadcasted periodically by sink, one is to broadcast blacklist with interests data sent out by sink. According to the protocol situation, we adopt the latter one, thus the protocol "Authenticated Directed Diffusion" has the same communication rounds with the original Directed Diffusion protocol.

Attack	GR	CB	RR	DD	ADD
Bogus Routing	✓	×	✓	✓	×
DoS	×	✓		✓	×
Sinkholes	×	×	✓	✓	×

GR:Geographic Routing
CB:Cluster Based
RR: Rumor Routing
DD: Directed Diffusion
ADD: Authenticated Directed Diffusion

Because we adopt blacklist broadcasting, each node who receives the blacklist can judge whether the nodes around it is in the blacklist. According to the timely blacklist, nodes can effectively detect malicious nodes, who are able to be against sinkholes attacks and bogus routing attacks.

5.1 Remain Security Issue

One possible attack on ADD is that a malicious node can listen to and block all packets sent from the source node, and in addition, collect all the keys included in these packets. These accumulated keys can be used to generate a flash flood against subsequent intermediate nodes by sending a burst of spurious packets in a very short period of time. Since the subsequent intermediate nodes have not seen these keys, they will validate the corresponding packets and forward them. However, such an attack is limited in two respects. First, the adversary will have to wait for a relatively long period of time to collect a large number of valid key numbers that it is blocking. Second, the adversary can send only as many packets as the number of key numbers it has collected, i.e. such an attack can be sustained for only a short period of time.

6 Performance Analysis

6.1 Comparison

Protocol	DD	ADD
Communication rounds	4	4
Overhead	34bytes+Data size	Data size
Node Computation	1 hmac	0 hmac

We have simulated ADD on NS2 version 2.28, a network simulator. We adopted a regular n × n grid with n^2 sensor nodes as our basic simulation network topology. The communication radius is set to $\sqrt{2}$ which allows the nearest eight neighbors to be reached. The base station is placed at the left bottom, and the source node is at the right top. The following table shows our basic configurations of this simulation.

Parameter	Value
Total Area	10m × 10m ∼ 100m × 100m
Number of nodes	10 ∼ 150
Initial Energy	5 Joule/Node
Data rate	300 kbps
Transmission Range	30m
Packet size	64 bytes
Data Sources	1∼ 5
Offered load	4 ∼ 6 pkts. per sec

We set up multiple test configurations, such as simulation time is set to 5 second, 10 second, 20 second and 50 second to make the simulation running in different configurations.

6.2 Communication Overhead

Because the steps of ADD has totally complied with the communication steps of original Directed Diffusion, ADD has the same communication rounds with DD.

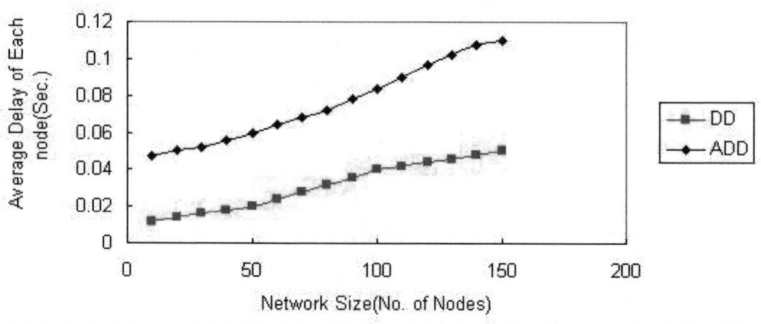

Fig. 4. Average delay of each node

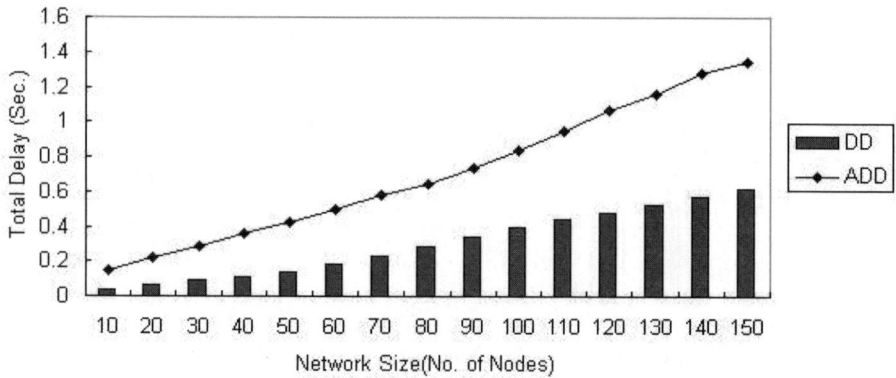

Fig. 5. Total delay of all nodes

The only extra overhead is that the size of transmitted data of ADD is bigger than DD and the computation of HMACs.

In the process of generating one-way hash key chain, we adopt One-way sequence number generation introduced in [6]. We use 30 bytes data as original interest test data because the default packet size is 30 bytes. A complete authenticated DD packet includes Interest(or Data), Blacklist, HMAC output and Key. We adopt SHA-1 as HMAC function and key length is 32 bits(4 bytes). The output size of HMAC of SHA-1 is 20 bytes. The blacklist is 10 bytes default. So the complete packet size is 64 bytes, and this is the communication overhead. Figure 4 is the result of average delay of packets transmission and figure 5 is the result of total transmission delay. From the results, we can see that the cost increase only 0.3 second when the network size is 50 ,and it increases about 1 second when the network size is 150. Then we know that the time delay of the ADD message is acceptable for most applications.

7 Conclusion

The original directed diffusion protocol for wireless sensor network has not involved security issues. We propose an extended directed diffusion protocol for wireless sensor network with authenticity and integrity capability without increasing communication rounds. It can effectively avoid DoS attack. It can effectively defend sinkhole attack and bogus routing information attack. Although it's overall computation overhead is higher than the original DD protocol, it is still worthy for its security performance.

7.1 Future Work

In the coming future, we are going to simulate various attacks on Authenticated Directed Diffusion protocol to validate its security properties.

References

1. Perrig, A., Szewczyk, R., Wen, V., Culler, D., Tygar, J.D.: SPINS: Security Protocols for Sensor Networks. Mobile Computing and Networking, Rome, Italy (2001)
2. Hu, Y.-C., Perrig, A., Johnson, D.B.: Packet leashes: a defense against wormhole attacks in wireless networks. In: IEEE Infocom (2003)
3. Wang, X., Yang, L., Chen, K.: SDD: Secure Directed Diffusion Protocol for Sensor Networks. In: Castelluccia, C., Hartenstein, H., Paar, C., Westhoff, D. (eds.) ESAS 2004. LNCS, vol. 3313, pp. 205–214. Springer, Heidelberg (2005)
4. Intanagonwiwat, C., Govindan, R., Estrin, D., Heidemann, J., Silva, F.: Directed Diffusion for Wireless Sensor Networking. ACM/IEEE Transactions on Networking 11(1), 2–16 (2002)
5. Lamport, L.: Constructing digital signatures from one-way function. Technical report SRI-CSL-98, SRI International (October 1979)
6. Deng, J., Han, R., Mishra, S.: The performance evaluation of intrusion-tolerant routing in wireless sensor networks. In: Zhao, F., Guibas, L.J. (eds.) IPSN 2003. LNCS, vol. 2634. Springer, Heidelberg (2003)
7. Karlof, C., Wagner, D.: Secure Routing in Wireless Sensor Networks: Attacks and Countermeasures, Sensor Network Protocols and Applications (SNPA 2003) (May 2003)
8. Wood, A., Stankovic, J.: Denial of service in sensor networks. IEEE Computer 35(10), 54–62 (2002)
9. Di Pietro, R., Mancini, L.V., Law, Y.W., Etalle, S., Havinga, P.: LKHW: a directed diffusion-based secure multicast scheme for wireless sensor networks. In: Parallel Processing Workshops, 2003. Proceedings 2003 International Conference, October 6-9, 2003, pp. 397–406 (2003)
10. Dousse, O., Tavoularis, C., Thiran, P.: Delay of Intrusion Detection in Wireless Sensor Networks. In: MobiHoc 2006, Florence, Italy, May 22–25 (2006)

A New Message Recognition Protocol for Ad Hoc Pervasive Networks

Atefeh Mashatan and Douglas R. Stinson[*]

Cryptography, Security, and Privacy Research Group
David R. Cheriton School of Computer Science
University of Waterloo
Waterloo, Ontario, Canada N2L 3G1
{amashata,dstinson}@math.uwaterloo.ca
http://crysp.uwaterloo.ca/

Abstract. We propose a message recognition protocol which is suitable for ad hoc pervasive networks without the use of hash chains. Hence, we no longer require the devices to save values of a hash chain in their memories. This relaxes the memory requirements. Moreover, we do not need to fix the total number of times the protocol can be executed which implies a desired flexibility in this regard. Furthermore, our protocol is secure without having to consider families of assumptions that depend on the number of sessions the protocol is executed. Hence, the security does not weaken as the protocol is executed over time. Last but not least, we provide a practical procedure for resynchronization in case of any adversarial disruption or communication failure.

Keywords: Cryptographic Protocols, Authentication, Recognition, Pervasive Networks, Ad Hoc Networks.

1 Introduction

In this paper, we examine the notion of *message recognition* which is a weaker notion compared to message authentication. It refers to the process where two parties initially meet in an authenticated setting, and later, one party is assured that the received message over the insecure channel is sent from the same second party. In other words, message recognition provides data integrity with respect to the source of the message. Standard approaches of public-key and secret-key cryptography provide many solutions for message authentication or recognition, digital signature schemes for instance. However, these techniques either require enough computational power to handle public-key operations, or they assume the existence of a shared secret. These assumptions may not be reasonable for some constraint scenarios such as ad hoc pervasive networks. Moreover, assuming a trusted third party in ad hoc networks settings is often undesirable.

This setting has been motivated in [5] by the following example. Consider Alice and Bob, two strangers who meet in a party for the first time. They make

---
[*] Douglas R. Stinson's research is supported by NSERC discovery grant 203114-06.

a bet before they leave the party. Later, the outcome turns out to be in favour of Alice, and a few days later, Bob receives a message claiming to be sent from Alice. The message includes a bank account number and asks Bob to deposit Alice's prize to that bank account. How can Bob be assured that this message was indeed sent from the entity who introduced herself as "Alice" in the party? That is, Bob wants to *recognize* "Alice", whoever she was, or a message that was sent from her. This problem has a solution if Alice and Bob exchange some information, which is not necessarily secret, at the party.

As another example, suppose we let Alice and Bob be small devices. They once meet in an authenticated setting. Then, they are placed in a hostile environment. Later, Alice sends messages to Bob and she wants Bob to recognize the messages that are sent from her. The adversary, Eve, is present all the time and would like to make Bob accept a message sent from Eve as a message from Alice. Eve has the ability to choose messages and make Alice send them to Bob. Note that Eve wins if Bob accepts a message that Alice has never sent to be a message from Alice.

The common approach to these problems in the literature is to assume the availability of two channels: an authenticated narrow-band channel for the initialization step and the usual insecure broadband channel. The authenticated channel is denoted by $\Rightarrow$ and the insecure channel by $\rightarrow$. The adversary is assumed to have full control over the messages sent over the insecure channel. She can listen to these messages, modify them or stops any flow over this channel. She can also insert a new message of her choice over this channel. On the other hand, she can only read the messages sent over the authenticated channel, but cannot modify them or stall them from delivery.

Recently, there has been a lot of activity in this area of research to design message recognition protocols. Assuming availability of a time-stamping service or the use of signatures, [1] proposes a message recognition protocol. Assuming a rather heavy amount of computation and communication, [8] proposes a recognition protocol called "Remote User Authentication Protocol". Using a hash chaining technique, [5] and [9] proposed an interactive recognition protocol where the number n is fixed to be the maximum number of messages to be authenticated. Each pair of users willing to communicate must have a separate pair of hash chains, which puts a relatively heavy memory requirement on the small devices. Furthermore, the security assumptions for this protocol depend on the number of sessions the protocol has been executed which gives birth to the notion of "depth-i security". We briefly summarize the existing results and discuss why they need to be improved.

We further propose a new design for message recognition in ad hoc pervasive networks and explain the advantages of using this new design compared to previous alternatives. Our proposed recognition protocol does not make use of hash chains. As a result, we no longer require the small devices to save values of a hash chain in their memories. This relaxes the memory requirements. Moreover, the passwords are set to be chosen at random in each session. Hence, they are independent of one another and are refreshed in each session. This can be done for an arbitrary number of times, so we do not need to fix the total number of times the protocol can be executed.

As the passwords corresponding to each session are chosen at random and are independent of one another, we do not need to consider assumptions that depend on the number of sessions the protocol is executed. Consequently, the security does not weaken as the protocol is executed over time. We *commit* to a password by sending its hash value, so that Eve cannot change it. Further, we need to *bind* two consecutive passwords, in order to detect adversarial intrusions and to be able to resynchronize in such a case. Last but not least, we provide a practical procedure for resynchronization in case of any possible adversarial disruption or communication failure.

Section 2 summarizes the existing results on message recognition protocols. In Sect. 3, we propose a new message recognition protocol and its resynchronization technique followed by a discussion about the advantages of using this protocol. Section 5 is devoted to the proof of the security of this protocol based on the assumptions listed in Sect. 4.

2 Literature Review on Message Recognition Protocols

Here, we briefly examine the existing recognition protocols and discuss their performance and practicality in ad hoc pervasive settings where communication bandwidth, computational power, and memory capacity are rather low.

Anderson et al. proposed the Guy Fawkes protocol in [1]. The first variant of this protocol assumes that a time-stamping service is available for every session. The second variant avoids this assumption by using a signature in the initialization step. Moreover, it requires that users commit to messages one session a head of time. That is, users are supposed to perform two sessions to authenticate a single message.

The "Remote User Authentication Protocol" was proposed in [8]. It uses a message authentication code (MAC) and requires that users compute a lot of MAC values. The MAC values are sent over the authenticated channel. This is a concern in our setting since the authenticated channels usually have low bandwidth. Moreover, the amount of computations and communication assumed in this protocol may not be desirable in a pervasive network of devices with low computational power.

The "Zero Common-Knowledge (ZCK)" protocol was proposed in [9]. They use the values of a hash chain as keys for a MAC. This protocol was implemented in [4] as a proof-of-concept. The observations from this implementation ensured that this protocol is suitable for devices with low computational power, low code space, low communication bandwidth and low energy resources. It also raised a couple of areas of concern, mainly denial-of-service and memory complexity.

Note that [4] explored the practicality of the ZCK protocol and not its security proof. Later, [5] found a problem in the security proof of this protocol and proposed a variant to fix the problem. Similar to the original ZCK protocol, they form a hash chain by fixing the number n to be the maximum number of messages to be authenticated. Alice and Bob randomly choose a_0 and b_0, respectively. Then, they respectively form hash chains $a_i = h(a_{i-1})$ and $b_i = h(b_{i-1})$, $i = 1, \ldots, n$. Note that for each pair of users wishing to communicate, there must be a separate pair of hash chains. This means that if a device wants to communicate with m users, it has to deal with m different hash chains of length n. This is of concern when dealing with small devices in a pervasive network with memory constraints, also noted by [4].

Furthermore, [5] has to consider security assumptions that depend on the number of sessions the protocol has been executed in order to prove the security of their protocol in the standard model. In particular, they have to treat the first session separately and then deal with the security of session i inductively. In other words, they prove "depth-i security" of their protocol based on assumptions such as "depth-i non-invertability", "depth-i Second Pre-image Resistance", "depth-i unforgeability", and "depth-i combined security". In other words, these are families of assumptions, that should hold for each i, $1 \leq i \leq n$. As they note in their paper, one could argue that, as the number of times the protocol is executed, its security weakens.

It is of interest to design a message recognition protocol that avoids assumptions that depend on the number of sessions the protocol has been executed and do not require the devices to have a high enough memory capacity to save several hash chains. Next, we describe a new message recognition protocol with such properties.

3 A New Message Recognition Protocol without the Use of Hash Chains

In this section, we describe the details of our proposed protocol. The initialization phase, execution of the protocol, and the resynchronization process are separately described. The section is concluded by examining the advantages of using this protocol in comparison to previous designs.

We begin by describing the internal states of Alice and Bob. Internal state of Alice includes:

- x_0 and x_1: the *passwords* for this session and the next session, respectively.
- $X_0 = H(x_0)$ and $X_1 = H(x_1)$: the *committing hash values* of the passwords.
- $\mathcal{X}_0 = H(x_0, X_1) = H(x_0, H(x_1))$: the *binding hash value* of the passwords.
- y^*_{-1}, Y^*_0, $\mathcal{Y}^*_0$: Bob's most recent password, committing hash value, and binding hash value accepted by Alice.

Similarly, internal state of Bob includes:

- y_0 and y_1: the *passwords* for this session and the next session, respectively.
- $Y_0 = H(y_0)$ and $Y_1 = H(y_1)$: the *committing hash values* of the passwords.
- $\mathcal{Y}_0 = H(y_0, Y_1) = H(y_0, H(y_1))$: the *binding hash value* of the passwords.
- x^*_{-1}, X^*_0, $\mathcal{X}^*_0$: Alice's most recent password, committing hash value, and binding hash value accepted by Bob.

```
              Alice                                    Bob
       Choose random x₀ and x₁ and          Choose random y₀ and y₁ and form
       form X₀ := H(x₀), X₁ := H(x₁),       Y₀ := H(y₀), Y₁ := H(y₁),
                                    X₀, 𝒳₀
       and 𝒳₀ := H(x₀, X₁)          ─────→  and 𝒴₀ := H(y₀, Y₁)
                                    Y₀, 𝒴₀
                                    ←─────
       Let y*₋₁ :=⊥, Y*₀ = Y₀, 𝒴*₀ = 𝒴₀.    Let x*₋₁ :=⊥, X*₀ = X₀, 𝒳*₀ = 𝒳₀.
```

Fig. 1. Initialization Phase of the New Message Recognition Protocol

In this protocol, x_0 and y_0 are considered to be passwords of the current session. Similarly, x_1 and y_1 are the passwords of the next session. We *commit* to a password by sending its hash value, so that Eve cannot change it. Further, we *bind* two consecutive passwords, in order to detect adversarial intrusions and to be able to resynchronize in such a case.

Alice performs the initialization phase as follows:

– Choose random x_0 and x_1.
– Compute $X_0 := H(x_0)$, $X_1 := H(x_1)$, and $\mathcal{X}_0 := H(x_0, X_1)$.
– Send $X_0, \mathcal{X}_0$ to Bob over the authenticated channel.
– Receive $Y_0, \mathcal{Y}_0$ from Bob over the authenticated channel.
– Let $y^*_{-1} :=\perp, Y^*_0 - Y_0$, and $\mathcal{Y}^*_0 - \mathcal{Y}_0$.

Similarly, Bob executes the initialization phase according to the following steps:

– Choose random y_0 and y_1.
– Compute $Y_0 := H(y_0), Y_1 := H(y_1)$, and $\mathcal{Y}_0 := H(y_0, Y_1)$.
– Receive $X_0, \mathcal{X}_0$ from Alice over the authenticated channel.
– Send $Y_0, \mathcal{Y}_0$ to Alice over the authenticated channel.
– Let $x^*_{-1} :=\perp, X^*_0 = X_0$, and $\mathcal{X}^*_0 = \mathcal{X}_0$.

The initialization phase of the protocol is depicted in Fig. 1. Next, we move on to the description of the proposed message recognition protocol illustrated in Fig. 2.

On input (m, Bob), Alice's execution can be described as follows:

– Choose a random x_2.
– Compute $X_2 := H(x_2), \mathcal{X}_1 := H(X_1, X_2)$, and $h = H[m, x_0]$.
– Send m, h to Bob and wait to receive $y'_0, Y'_1, \mathcal{Y}'_1$ from Bob. Resend m, h if Bob did not respond.
– If $H(y'_0) = Y^*_0$ and $H(y'_0, Y'_1) = \mathcal{Y}^*_0$, then send $(x_0, X_1, \mathcal{X}_1)$ to Bob and update internal state: $y^*_{-1} := y'_0$, $Y^*_0 := Y'_1$, $\mathcal{Y}^*_0 := \mathcal{Y}'_1$, $x_0 := x_1$, $x_1 := x_2$, $X_0 := X_1$, $X_1 := X_2$, and $\mathcal{X}_0 := \mathcal{X}_1$. Otherwise, initiate resynchronization with Bob.

```
┌─────────────────────────────────────────────────────────────────────────────┐
│ Internal-state of Alice:                    Internal-state of Bob:          │
│ $x_0, x_1, X_0, X_1, \mathcal{X}_0, y^*_{-1}, Y^*_0, \mathcal{Y}^*_0$.      $y_0, y_1, Y_0, Y_1, \mathcal{Y}_0, x^*_{-1}, X^*_0, \mathcal{X}^*_0$. │
│                                                                             │
│         Alice                                       Bob                     │
│                                                                             │
│ Receive input $(m, \text{Bob})$                                             │
│ Choose a random $x_2$ and form                                              │
│ $X_2 := H(x_2), \mathcal{X}_1 := H(x_1, X_2)$.                              │
│ Compute $h = H[m, x_0]$.      $\xrightarrow{m, h}$  Receive $m', h'$.       │
│                                                                             │
│                                             Choose a random $y_2$ and form  │
│                                             $Y_2 := H(y_2), \mathcal{Y}_1 := H(y_1, Y_2)$. │
│ Receive $y'_0, Y'_1, \mathcal{Y}'_1$.  $\xleftarrow{y_0, Y_1, \mathcal{Y}_1}$ │
│                                                                             │
│ If $H(y'_0) = Y^*_0$ and $H(y'_0, Y'_1) = \mathcal{Y}^*_0$,                 │
│ then send $(x_0, X_1, \mathcal{X}_1)$ and                                   │
│ update your internal state:                                                 │
│   $y^*_{-1} := y'_0, Y^*_0 := Y'_1, \mathcal{Y}^*_0 := \mathcal{Y}'_1$,     │
│   $x_0 := x_1, x_1 := x_2$,                                                 │
│   $X_0 := X_1, X_1 := X_2, \mathcal{X}_0 := \mathcal{X}_1$.                 │
│ else initiate resynchronization.                                            │
│                                 $\xrightarrow{x_0, X_1, \mathcal{X}_1}$  Receive $x'_0, X'_1, \mathcal{X}'_1$. │
│                                             If $H(x'_0) = X^*_0, H(x'_0, X'_1) = \mathcal{X}^*_0$, │
│                                                 and $h' = H[m', x'_0]$,    │
│                                             then update your internal state: │
│                                                 $x^*_{-1} := x'_0, X^*_0 := X'_1, \mathcal{X}^*_0 := \mathcal{X}'_1$, │
│                                                 $y_0 := y_1, y_1 := y_2$,  │
│                                                 $Y_0 := Y_1, Y_1 := Y_2, \mathcal{Y}_0 := \mathcal{Y}_1$, │
│                                                 and output $(\text{Alice}, m')$. │
│                                             else initiate resynchronization. │
└─────────────────────────────────────────────────────────────────────────────┘
```

Fig. 2. New Message Recognition Protocol

Bob, on the other hand executes the protocol in the following manner:

- After receiving m', h', choose a random y_2.
- Compute $Y_2 := H(y_2)$ and $\mathcal{Y}_1 := H(y_1, Y_2)$.
- Send $y_0, Y_1, \mathcal{Y}_1$ to Alice and wait to receive $x'_0, X'_1, \mathcal{X}'_1$. Resend $y_0, Y_1, \mathcal{Y}_1$ to Alice if Alice did not respond.
- If $H(x'_0) = X^*_0$ and $H(x'_0, X'_1) = \mathcal{X}^*_0$, and $h' = H[m', x'_0]$, then update internal state: $x^*_{-1} := x'_0$, $X^*_0 := X'_1$, $\mathcal{X}^*_0 := \mathcal{X}'_1$, $y_0 := y_1$, $y_1 := y_2$, $Y_0 := Y_1$, $Y_1 := Y_2$, and $\mathcal{Y}_0 := \mathcal{Y}_1$, and output (Alice, m'). Otherwise, initiate resynchronization with Alice.

In case of no adversarial intrusion or communication failure, all the conditions verify and Alice and Bob will not initiate a resynchronization process. When they realize that one of the conditions does not hold, they suspect a communication failure or a possible adversarial intrusion. Hence, they need to resynchronize in order to make sure they have the correct commitment and binding hash values. The synchronization process is illustrated in Fig. 3. Bob sends $y_0, Y_1, \mathcal{Y}_1$ to Alice and Alice sends $x_0, X_1, \mathcal{X}_1$ to Bob. Note that Alice should already have y_0, Y_1 and she is verifying if they match with what she has. Similarly, Bob is verifying

```
┌─────────────────────────────────────────────────────────────────────┐
│ Internal-state of Alice:                  Internal-state of Bob:    │
│ $x_0, x_1, X_0, X_1, \mathcal{X}_0, y_{-1}^*, Y_0^*, \mathcal{Y}_0^*$. │  $y_0, y_1, Y_0, Y_1, \mathcal{Y}, x_{-1}^*, X_0^*, \mathcal{X}_0^*$. │
│                                                                     │
│         Alice                                      Bob              │
│                                                                     │
│ Choose a random $x_2$ and form            Choose a random $y_2$ and form │
│ $X_2 := H(x_2), \mathcal{X}_1 := H(x_1, X_2)$.    $Y_2 := H(y_2), \mathcal{Y}_1 := H(y_1, Y_2)$. │
│ Receive $y_0', Y_1', \mathcal{Y}_1'$.                                │
│                     $\xleftarrow{y_0, Y_1, \mathcal{Y}_1}$           │
│                                                                     │
│                     $\xrightarrow{x_0, X_1, \mathcal{X}_1}$ Receive $x_0', X_1', \mathcal{X}_1'$. │
│                                                                     │
│ If $y_{-1}^* = y_0'$ and $Y_0^* = Y_1'$,    If $x_{-1}^* = x_0'$ and $X_0^* = X_1'$, │
│ then $\mathcal{Y}_0^* := \mathcal{Y}_1'$,    then $\mathcal{X}_0^* := \mathcal{X}_1'$, │
│ else initiate resynchronization.         else if $H(x_0') = X_0^*$ and $H(x_0', X_1') = \mathcal{X}_0^*$, │
│                                            then $x_{-1}^* := x_0', X_0^* := X_1', \mathcal{X}_0^* := \mathcal{X}_1'$. │
│                                          else initiate resynchronization. │
└─────────────────────────────────────────────────────────────────────┘
```

Fig. 3. The Resynchronization Process

if x_0, X_1 match with what he has. However, the values of $\mathcal{X}_1$ and $\mathcal{Y}_1$ are new. It is possible for the adversary to make either Alice or Bob compute a binding hash value in a bogus session. In that case, the binding hash value is refreshed. Note that the resynchronization process is not symmetrical. This is due to the fact that Bob may detect an intrusion after Alice has updated her state. In this case, the values $x_0, X_1, \mathcal{X}_1$ that Alice sends during the resynchronization process need to be verified differently.

Since we are not using a hash chain, the memory requirement on the devices is relaxed. The octuple $(x_0, x_1, X_0, X_1, \mathcal{X}_0, y_{-1}^*, Y_0^*, \mathcal{Y}_0^*)$ is all Alice needs to communicate with Bob and she will need another octuple for each different user. In the previous protocols, the devices had to deal with a hash chain for every single device they wanted to communicate with. Storing all the values of a hash chain, for example $a_0, a_1, \ldots, a_n$ is too demanding for low-end devices. On the other hand, storing only the root value of the hash chain, for instance a_0, requires too many computations at each session. The alternative is to employ a time-storage trade-off and store some of the hash values, see for example [2]. Still, there are some storage and computational requirements associated with this implementation. Our proposal for not having to deal with a hash chaining technique avoids any memory or computational requirement of this nature for every session.

Moreover, the passwords are set to be chosen at random in each session. Hence, they are independent of one another and are refreshed in each session. As a result, we do not need to consider assumptions that depend on the number of sessions the protocol is executed. Consequently, the security does not weaken as the protocol is executed over time.

Furthermore, the devices can run this protocol as many times as they want and the total number of sessions is not fixed. This provides extra flexibility compared to the protocols based on the hash chain technique. Next, we look at the security assumptions relevant for this new protocol.

4 Security Assumptions

In this section, we define new notions of hash function security, mainly **Paired Pre-image Resistance, (PPR)**, **Paired Second-Pre-image Resistance, (PSPR)**, **Paired Collision Resistance, (PCR)**, **Binding Pre-image Resistance, (BPR)** . Each notion is presented as a game between a player Oscar and a Challenger. Note that these assumptions are independent of the number of sessions the protocol has been executed. In other words, in contrast to the approach taken in [5], where they have to assume "depth-i non-invertability", "depth-i Second Pre-image Resistance", "depth-i unforgeability", and "depth-i combined security" for every i, $1 \leq i \leq n$, we only require four assumptions.

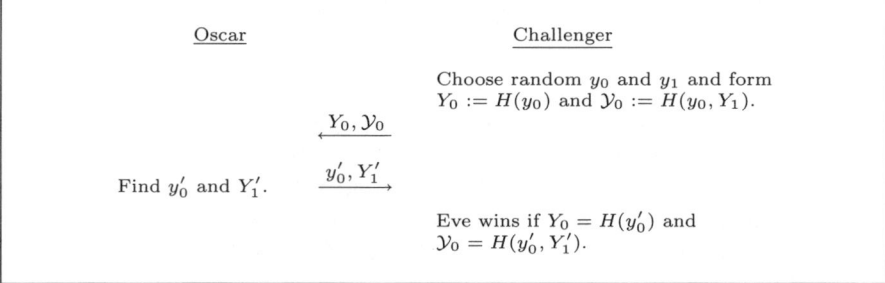

Fig. 4. Paired Pre-image Resistance

Depicted in Fig. 4 is the PPR notion. We note that the PPR property is analogous to the notion of "depth-2 non-invertability" defined in [5]. Furthermore, this one assumption is replacing a whole family of assumptions; termed "depth-i non-invertability", for $1 \leq i \leq n$.

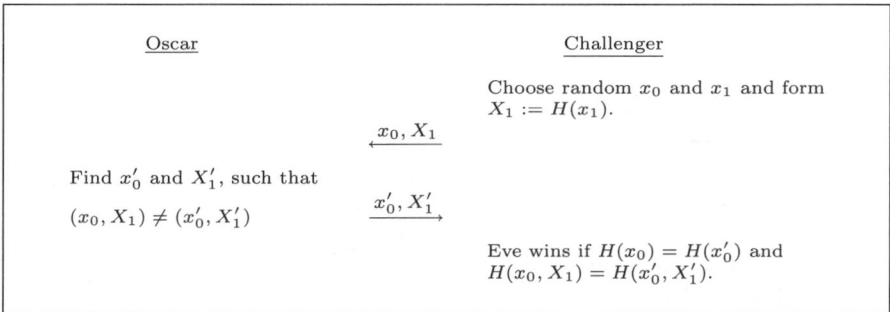

Fig. 5. Paired Second-pre-image Resistance

Figure 5 illustrates the PSPR notion. This notion is analogous to "depth-2 Second pre-image Resistance" defined in [5]. It is replacing the family of assumptions termed "depth-i Second pre-image Resistance", for i, $1 \leq i \leq n$.

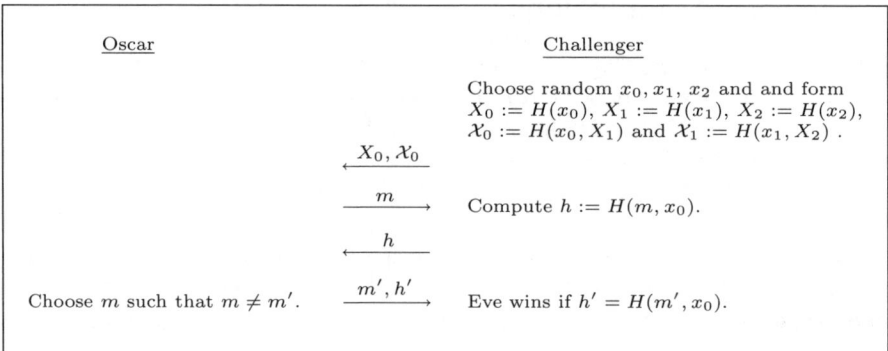

Fig. 6. Paired Collision Resistance

The notion of PCR is depicted in Fig. 6. Analogous to this notion, [5] defines "depth-2 unforgeability". Note that the PCR notion is replacing a family of assumptions termed "depth-i unforgeability", for i, $1 \leq i \leq n$.

In Sect. 5, we will see that the PCR, PPR, and PSPR notions prevent attacks that start and finish during one session. Moreover, attack scenarios spanning over two sessions are also analyzed and the BPR notion illustrated in Fig. 7 is associated to these attacks.

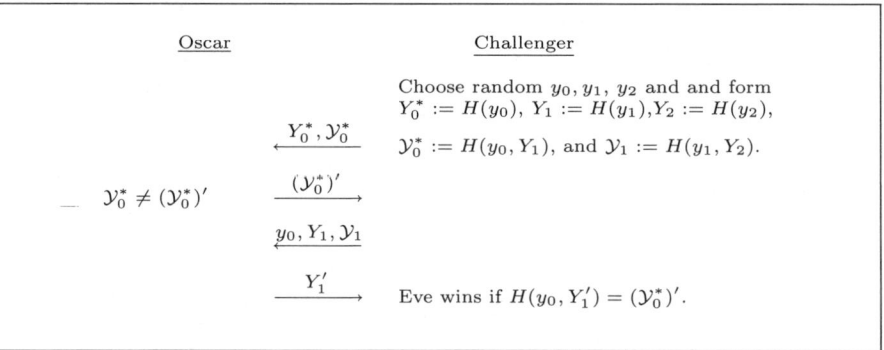

Fig. 7. Binding pre-image Resistance

Next, we prove the security of our protocol, based on the assumption that PPR, PSPR, PCR, and BPR games are hard to win.

5 Security of the Proposed Recognition Protocol

Recall that the goal of the adversary is to make Bob accept a message m' that was never sent from Alice. A successful attack is where that Bob is deceived and he outputs (Alice, m').

Let $(x_0, x_1, X_0, X_1, \mathcal{X}_0, y_{-1}^*, Y_0^*, \mathcal{Y}_0^*)$ and $(y_0, y_1, Y_0, Y_1, \mathcal{Y}_0, x_{-1}^*, X_0^*, \mathcal{X}_0^*)$ be the internal states of Alice and Bob, respectively. Now, assume that Eve, having been passive all along, mounts a successful attack for the first time and Bob actually outputs (Alice, m'), where $m \neq m'$. Since, Eve had been passive before this attack, we can assume that $y_{-1}^* = y_0, Y_0^* = H(y_0) = Y_0, \mathcal{Y}_0^* = \mathcal{Y}_0 = H(y_0, H(y_1))$, $x_{-1}^* = x_0, X_0^* = X_0 = H(x_0)$, and $\mathcal{X}_0^* = \mathcal{X}_0 = H(x_0, H(x_1))$. Eve may complete her attack in one session, or she may mount an attack that spans more than one session. First, we examine one-round attacks.

5.1 One-Session Attacks

In order to exhaustively list all possible one-round attacks against our protocol, we adapt the notation of [3] in labelling different orderings of the flows. This notation labels each flow sent by the adversary by either **A**, if the recipient is Alice, or by **B**, when the recipient is Bob. For example, an ordering of ABAB corresponds to the following attack scenario:

- **A**: Eve sends m to Alice and she responds with m, h.
- **B**: Eve sends m', h' to Bob and he replies with $y_0, Y_1, \mathcal{Y}_1$.
- **A**: Eve sends $y_0', Y_1', \mathcal{Y}_1'$ to Alice and receives $x_0, X_1, \mathcal{X}_1$ from her.
- **B**: Eve sends $x_0', X_1', \mathcal{X}'_1$.

It is proved in [3] that the number of different possible attacks against a three round protocol is $\binom{4}{2} = 6$. These attacks are described, using the above mentioned labelling, to be AABB, ABBA, BABA, ABAB, BBAA, and BAAB. Next, we will analyze each of these attack scenarios.

We prove that the BABA attack scenario can be reduced to the ABBA attack. In other words, if the adversary can mount a successful attack of type BABA, then she also succeeds in the ABBA attack scenario. Similarly, one can show that the BAAB and ABBA attack scenarios can be reduced to the ABAB case. Hence, it remains to investigate the AABB, BBAA, and ABAB attack scenarios. We prove that the AABB, BBAA, and ABAB attacks are not possible by reducing them to the PPR, PSPR, or PCR games. Then, we show the aforementioned reductions.

Attack of Type AABB

Illustrated in Fig. 8 is the attack of type AABB. In this attack scenario, Eve finishes her interactions with with Alice before she starts her interactions with Bob. In other words, Eve has to first deceive Alice in order to get her to reveal the information she needs to then deceive Bob.

If Eve successfully deceives Alice, then she receives $(x_0, X_1, \mathcal{X}_1)$. Now, Eve computes $h' = H(m', x_0)$, for m' of her choice. She then sends m', h' to Bob. Finally, she completes her attack with setting $(x_0', X_1', \mathcal{X}_1') = (x_0, X_1, \mathcal{X}_1)$ and sending it to Bob.

In order to deceive Alice, Eve has to find y_0' and Y_1' such that $Y_0 = H(y_0')$ and $\mathcal{Y}_0 = H(y_0', Y_1')$, where Y_0 and $\mathcal{Y}_0$ were transmitted in the session immediately before the attack. Note that Eve, not having seen (y_0, Y_1), has sent (y_0', Y_1'), which has been accepted by Alice. This is exactly the problem of PPR, depicted in Fig. 4.

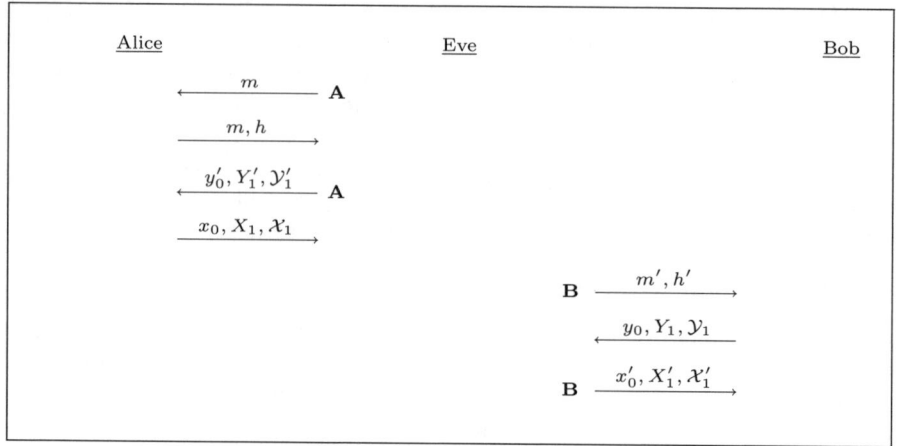

Fig. 8. Attack of Type AABB

Attack of Type BBAA

The attack of type BBAA is illustrated in Fig. 9. In this scenario, Eve interacts with Alice after she has finished interacting with Bob. That is, she receives $(y_0, Y_1, \mathcal{Y}_1)$ from Bob before she has to choose $(y'_0, Y'_1, \mathcal{Y}'_1)$. If she chooses $(y'_0, Y'_1, \mathcal{Y}'_1)$ such that $(y_0, Y_1) \neq (y'_0, Y'_1)$ and remains undetected by Alice, then, Eve can be reduced to a successful player against the PSPR game of Fig. 5. We deal with the case where $(y_0, Y_1) = (y'_0, Y'_1)$ and $\mathcal{Y}_1 \neq \mathcal{Y}'_1$ in Sect. 5.2. The only remaining case is that, having received $(y_0, Y_1, \mathcal{Y}_1)$ from Bob, Eve lets $(y'_0, Y'_1, \mathcal{Y}'_1) = (y_0, Y_1, \mathcal{Y}_1)$ to avoid being detected by Alice.

A successful attack of this type implies that Bob has accepted m'. That is, not having seen (x_0, X_1), Eve has found x'_0, X'_1. Once Eve finds the appropriate

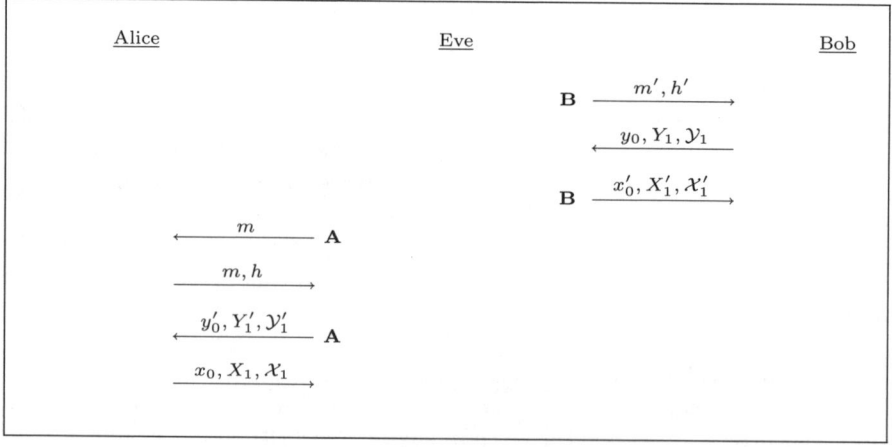

Fig. 9. Attack of Type BBAA

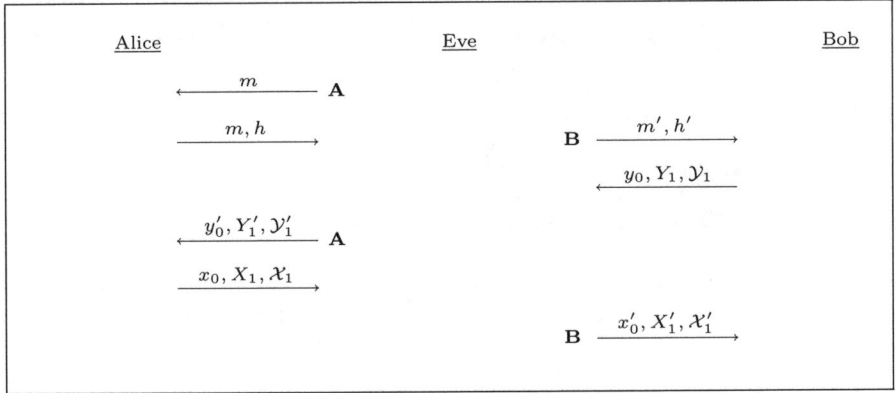

Fig. 10. Attack of Type ABAB

x'_0 and X'_1, she can compute $h' = H(m', x'_0)$, for an m' of her choice. Note that Eve has received X_0 and $\mathcal{X}_0$ from the previous session. Now, she has to find x'_0, X'_1 such that $X_0 = H(x'_0)$ and $\mathcal{X}_0 = H(x'_0, X'_1)$. This translates to the notion of PPR if we replaces each x value by its corresponding y value.

Attack of Type ABAB

Figure 10 illustrates the attack of type ABAB. In this attack, Eve receives the correct $(y_0, Y_1, \mathcal{Y}_1)$ from Bob before she has to send $(y'_0, Y'_1, \mathcal{Y}'_1)$ to Alice. As it was discussed in the case of the BBAA attack, Eve will be detected by Alice unless she sets $(y'_0, Y'_1, \mathcal{Y}'_1) = (y_0, Y_1, \mathcal{Y}_1)$. This way Alice will not detect Eve and she will reveal $(x_0, X_1, \mathcal{X}_1)$. The adversary has two choices now. She either sets $(x'_0, X'_1) = (x_0, X_1)$ and send it to Bob, or she sends (x'_0, X'_1) to Bob where $(x'_0, X'_1) \neq (x_0, X_1)$. We will analyze each of these two cases separately.

Let us first consider the case where $(x'_0, X'_1) = (x_0, X_1)$. In this case, the adversary has collected $(X_0, \mathcal{X}_0)$ from previous session. She then sends m to Alice and Alice replies with (m, h). She will then send (m', h') to Bob. At this point the rest of the flows are determined to be the following: She receives $(y_0, Y_1, \mathcal{Y}_1)$ from Bob, sets $(y'_0, Y'_1, \mathcal{Y}'_1) = (y_0, Y_1, \mathcal{Y}_1)$, and sends it to Alice. Further, she receives $(x_0, X_1, \mathcal{X}_1)$ from Alice, lets $(x'_0, X'_1, \mathcal{X}'_1) = (x_0, X_1, \mathcal{X}_1)$, and sends it Bob. Hence, this case is exactly the notion of PCR depicted in Fig. 6.

The second case is when $(x'_0, X'_1) \neq (x_0, X_1)$. Assume that Eve can mount a successful attack of type ABAB with $(x'_0, X'_1) \neq (x_0, X_1)$. That is, she has collected $X_0, \mathcal{X}_0$ from previous session. She chooses m and receives h such that $h = H(m, x_0)$. Then, she submits m', h'. Finally, she receives x_0, X_1 and she is supposed to send x'_0, X'_1 such that $(x'_0, X'_1) \neq (x_0, X_1)$, $H(x_0) = H(x'_0)$, $H(x_0, X_1) = H(x'_0, X'_1)$, and $h' = H(m', X'_0)$. We reduce Eve to a successful player against the Challenger of PSPR game, depicted in Fig. 5. The reduction is illustrated in Fig. 11.

Note that, Oscar is playing against the Challenger of PSPR and at the same time he is playing the role of both Alice and Bob against Eve.

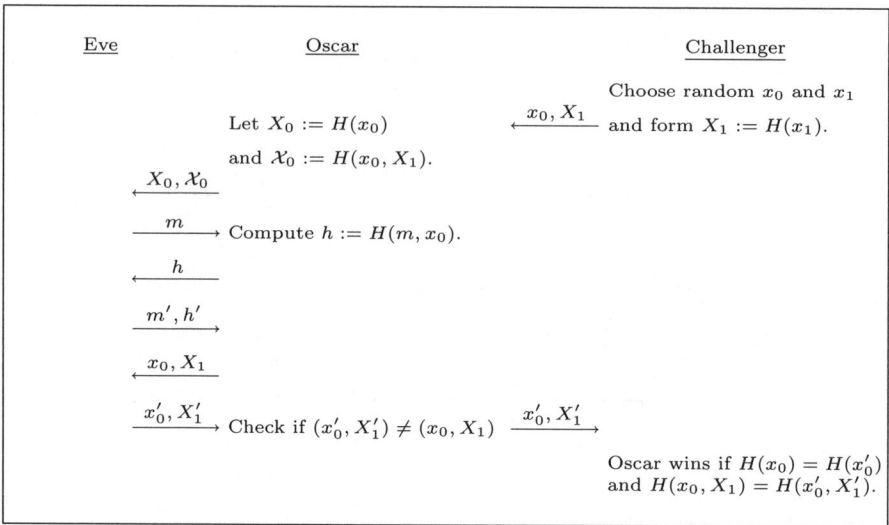

Fig. 11. Reducing Eve to a Player Against the Challenger of PSPR

We begin by reducing the BABA attack to the ABBA attack. Further, we reduce the ABBA attack to the ABAB attack that was analyzed in Sect. 5. Finally, the only remaining attack scenario, BAAB, is also reduced to the ABAB attack. This concludes the analysis of the six different attack scenarios.

Reducing BABA attack to ABBA Attack
Attack of type ABBA is depicted in Fig. 12 and Fig. 13 illustrates the attack of Type BABA.

These two attacks differ only in the order of the first two steps. The ABBA attack is as follows:

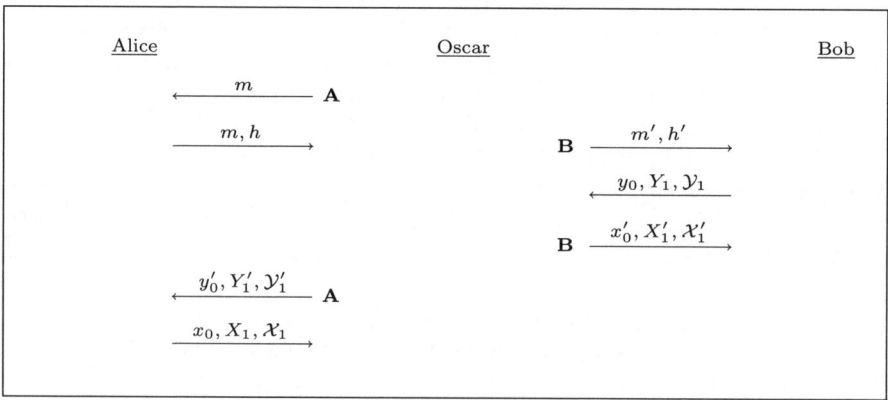

Fig. 12. Attack of Type ABBA

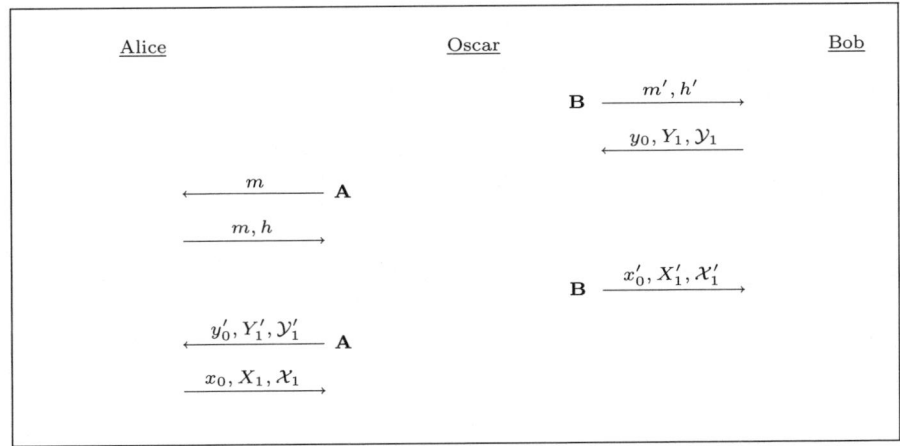

Fig. 13. Attack of Type BABA

- **A**: Oscar sends m to Alice and she responds with m, h.
- **B**: Oscar sends m', h' to Bob and he replies with $y_0, Y_1, \mathcal{Y}_1$.
- **B**: Oscar sends $x'_0, X'_1, \mathcal{X}'_1$.
- **A**: Oscar sends $y'_0, Y'_1, \mathcal{Y}'_1$ to Alice and receives $x_0, X_1, \mathcal{X}_1$ from her.

The BABA attack has the following order:

- **B**: Oscar sends m', h' to Bob and he replies with $y_0, Y_1, \mathcal{Y}_1$.
- **A**: Oscar sends m to Alice and she responds with m, h.
- **B**: Oscar sends $x'_0, X'_1, \mathcal{X}'_1$.
- **A**: Oscar sends $y'_0, Y'_1, \mathcal{Y}'_1$ to Alice and receives $x_0, X_1, \mathcal{X}_1$ from her.

Note that in the BABA attack scenario, the choice of m is independent of what the values of y_0, Y_1 and $\mathcal{Y}_1$ are. That is, knowing $y_0, Y_1, \mathcal{Y}_1$ before choosing m is not going to help Oscar. On the other hand, he is committing himself to m', h' before receiving any values, such as h, that could possibly help him. If Oscar wins by first choosing m', h' and then receiving h in the BABA attack scenario, then he can also win the ABBA attack by using the same values m, m', and h'.

Reducing ABBA Attack to ABAB

Recall the ABAB attack described in Sect. 5:

- **A**: Eve sends m to Alice and she responds with m, h.
- **B**: Eve sends m', h' to Bob and he replies with $y_0, Y_1, \mathcal{Y}_1$.
- **A**: Eve sends $y'_0, Y'_1, \mathcal{Y}'_1$ to Alice and receives $x_0, X_1, \mathcal{X}_1$ from her.
- **B**: Eve sends $x'_0, X'_1, \mathcal{X}'_1$.

This attack differes from the ABBA attack in the order of the last two steps. In the ABAB attack, Eve first receives $x_0, X_1, \mathcal{X}_1$ from Alice, then she has to send $x'_0, X'_1, \mathcal{X}'_1$ to Bob. Whereas in the case of the ABBA attack, Oscar has to send $x'_0, X'_1, \mathcal{X}'_1$ to Bob before he receives $x_0, X_1, \mathcal{X}_1$ from Alice. If Oscar has a winning strategy in the ABBA attack, the Eve can use him in her ABAB attack by sending the same values of $x'_0, X'_1, \mathcal{X}'_1$ that Oscar sends to Bob.

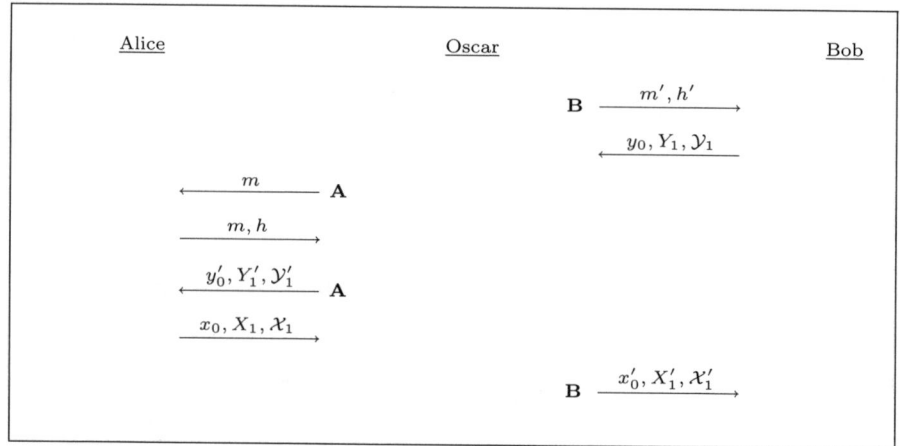

Fig. 14. Attack of Type BAAB

Reducing BAAB Attack to ABAB

Depicted in Fig. 14 is the attack Type of BAAB.

Recall that knowing $y_0, Y_1, \mathcal{Y}_1$ before choosing m is not going to help Oscar. Moreover, in the BAAB attack, Oscar is first committing himself to m', h'. If Oscar wins the BAAB attack by first choosing m', h' and then receiving h, then so will Eve in the ABAB attack, by just using the same values m, m', and h'.

5.2 Two-Session Attacks

Now consider attack scenarios which span two or more sessions. The adversary is active but remains undetected in all sessions of the attack. She then submits her message in the last session of the attack. If she tampers with y_0, Y_1, x_0, or X_1 and remains undetected, then we go back to the cases described above. Hence, it remains to examine the cases when she changes the binding hash values. We look at the case where Eve changes the value of $\mathcal{Y}_1$ to $\mathcal{Y}_1'$. The case where Eve alters $\mathcal{X}_1$ to $\mathcal{X}_1'$ is analogous due to the symmetry of the protocol structure.

Assume that Eve changes $\mathcal{Y}_1$ to $\mathcal{Y}_1'$ and does not touch y_0 or Y_1. She goes undetected in this session because Alice verifies y_0 and Y_1, but only records $\mathcal{Y}_1'$ without verification. She then updates her state as follows $y_{-1}^* := y_0$, $Y_0^* := Y_1$, $(\mathcal{Y}_0^*)' := \mathcal{Y}_1'$.

In the next session, Alice sends $(y_0, Y_1, \mathcal{Y}_1)$ and Eve has to change it to an appropriate $(y_0', Y_1', \mathcal{Y}_1')$ to remain undetected. Otherwise, Alice will call for resynchronization. Alice checks to see if $H(y_0') = Y_0^*$ and $H(y_0', Y_1') = (\mathcal{Y}_0^*)'$. We treat the two cases $y_0 = y_0'$ and $y_0 \neq y_0'$ separately.

If $H(y_0') = Y_0^*$ and $y_0 \neq y_0'$, then Eve, having seen y_0, has found y_0' such that $H(y_0') = H(y_0)$. This means that Eve has found a second pre-image of y_0.

On the other hand, when $y_0 = y_0'$, the condition $H(y_0') = Y_0^*$ holds. Then, Alice verifies to see if $H(y_0, Y_1') = (\mathcal{Y}_0^*)'$. If it holds, then Eve is a successful player in the BPR game of Fig. 7.

If the adversary were to mount an attack that spans over more than two rounds, she would have to successfully pass the second round. However, the above discussion shows that the adversary can only pass the second session without being detected if she can win the BPR game or SPR game.

5.3 The Security Theorem

We investigated all possible attacks against the message recognition protocol of Fig. 2 by considering two different cases, namely if the attack is taking place over one session, or if it spans more than one session. We examined these two cases separately.

In the first case, there are six possible attack scenarios: BABA, BAAB, ABBA, AABB, BBAA, and ABAB. Attacks of type BABA, BAAB, and ABBA can be reduced to the ABAB case. Further, we showed that a successful adversary (Eve) in attacks of type AABB, BBAA, and ABAB attacks can be reduced to a successful player (Oscar) in the PPR, PSPR, or PCR games.

In the case of attacks that occur over more than one session, we showed that the successful adversary can be reduced to a successful player against the BPR or SPR games.

This concludes the analysis of different attack scenarios and proves the following theorem

Theorem 1. *A successful adversary who can efficiently deceive Bob in outputting (Alice, m'), where Alice never sent m', implies an efficient algorithm in winning PPR, PSPR, PCR, or BPR hash function games.*

This theorem precisely identifies the required properties for a hash function to be used in the message recognition protocol of Fig. 2. There is no concrete construction of such a hash function. However, no one knows how to prove that a concrete construction of a hash function has any non-trivial property. It is a standard approach taken in the literature to assume some properties for an idealized hash function and to prove security of a given protocol assuming these assumptions. Note that the same approach was taken in [5]. One can analyze these games in the random oracle model and compare their hardness to more standard hash function security notions, see for example [7] and [6].

6 Conclusion and Final Remarks

We proposed a new design for message recognition protocols suitable for ad hoc pervasive networks. This proposal does not make use of hash chains. Hash chaining techniques have been used in recent designs of message recognition protocols. In this approach, the small devices are required to save values of a hash chain in their memories for every single user they want to communicate with. Since we do not use this technique, we no longer require the small devices to save values of a hash chain in their memories. This relaxes the memory requirements.

Moreover, the passwords are chosen at random in each session. Hence, they are independent of one another and are being refreshed in each session. This can be done for any arbitrary number of times, so we do not need to fix the total number of times the protocol can be executed which implies a desired flexibility in this regard.

As the passwords are independent of one another, we do not need to consider assumptions that depend on the number of sessions the protocol is executed. Whereas recent designs based on the hash chaining technique had to assume families of assumptions based on the number of sessions the protocol is executed. This implies that their security weakens as the number of sessions increases. Since we are not using hash chains, the security of our protocol is independent of the number of times the protocol is executed.

Finally, a practical procedure for resynchronization is provided. This implies that in case of any possible adversarial disruption or communication failure, the protocol can be recovered.

References

1. Anderson, R., Bergadano, F., Crispo, B., Lee, J.-H., Manifavas, C., Needham, R.: A new family of authentication protocols. In: ACMOSR: ACM Operating Systems Review, vol. 32, pp. 9–20 (1998)
2. Coppersmith, D., Jakobsson, M.: Almost optimal hash sequence traversal. Financial Cryptography, 102–119 (2002)
3. Gehrmann, C.: Multiround unconditionally secure authentication. Designs, Codes, and Cryptography 15(1), 67–86 (1998)
4. Hammell, J., Weimerskirch, A., Girao, J., Westhoff, D.: Recognition in a low-power environment. In: ICDCSW 2005: Proceedings of the Second International Workshop on Wireless Ad Hoc Networking (WWAN) ICDCSW 2005), Washington, DC, USA, pp. 933–938. IEEE Computer Society, Los Alamitos (2005)
5. Lucks, S., Zenner, E., Weimerskirch, A., Westhoff, D.: Entity recognition for sensor network motes. GI Jahrestagung (2), 145–149 (2005)
6. Mashatan, A., Stinson, D.R.: Noninteractive two-channel message authentication based on hybrid-collision resistant hash functions. IET Information Security 1(3), 111–118 (2007)
7. Mashatan, A., Stinson, D.R.: Interactive two-channel message authentication based on interactive-collision resistant hash functions. International Journal of Information Security (to appear, 2008)
8. Mitchell, C.J.: Remote user authentication using public information. In: Paterson, K.G. (ed.) Cryptography and Coding 2003. LNCS, vol. 2898, pp. 360–369. Springer, Heidelberg (2003)
9. Weimerskirch, A., Westhoff, D.: Zero common-knowledge authentication for pervasive networks. In: Matsui, M., Zuccherato, R.J. (eds.) SAC 2003. LNCS, vol. 3006, pp. 73–87. Springer, Heidelberg (2004)

Author Index

Abdalla, Michel   133
Asano, Tomoyuki   31

Bringer, Julien   149

Carbunar, Bogdan   317
Chabanne, Hervé   149
Chen, Kefei   1
Choudhary, Ashish   285

Deng, Robert H.   1
Desmedt, Yvo   18

Fu, Shaojing   268, 278

Galindo, David   120
Ghodosi, Hossein   240
Großschädl, Johann   349
Guo, Jian   49

Hiwatari, Harunaga   31
Huang, Xinyi   64
Hudler, Matthias   349
Hui, Lucas C.K.   366

Icart, Thomas   149
Izabachène, Malika   133

Joye, Marc   98

Kato, Hidehiro   226
Koschuch, Manuel   349
Krüger, Michael   349
Kusakawa, Masafumi   31

Li, Chao   268, 278
Li, Fagen   108
Lipmaa, Helger   18
Liu, Joseph K.   80
Liu, Shengli   1
Lopez, Javier   120
Lou, Tiancheng   196

Mashatan, Atefeh   378
Matsuda, Seiichi   31
Mohebbipoor, S. Fahimeh   240
Morikawa, Yoshitaka   226
Mu, Yi   80

Nakahara Jr., Jorge   252
Nogami, Yasuyuki   226

Okeya, Katsuyuki   226
Orumiehchi, Mohammad Ali   240

Patra, Arpita   285
Payer, Udo   349
Phan, Duong Hieu   18
Pieprzyk, Josef   178
Pointcheval, David   133

Qiao, Youming   162

Rangan, C. Pandu   285
Roman, Rodrigo   120

Sakemi, Yumi   226
Shimizu, Koichi   332
Shirase, Masaaki   108
Srinathan, Kannan   285
Steinfeld, Ron   49
Stinson, Douglas R.   378
Sun, Bing   268, 278
Sun, Hung-Min   49
Susilo, Willy   80
Suzuki, Daisuke   332

Takagi, Tsuyoshi   108
Tartary, Christophe   162, 196
Tripunitara, Mahesh   317
Tso, Raylin   64
Tsurumaru, Toyohiro   332

Wang, Eric K.   366
Wang, Huaxiong   49, 178
Wang, Peishun   178
Weng, Jian   1
Wu, Mu-En   49

Yi, Xun   64
Yiu, S.M.   366
Yuen, Tsz Hon   80

Zhang, Yu   304
Zhu, Huafei   214

Printing: Mercedes-Druck, Berlin
Binding: Stein+Lehmann, Berlin